The Gentrification Debates

Uniquely well suited for teaching, this innovative text-reader strengthens students' critical thinking skills, sparks classroom discussion, and also provides a comprehensive and accessible understanding of gentrification.

Japonica Brown-Saracino is assistant professor of sociology at Loyola University Chicago where she specializes in urban and community sociology, cultural sociology, and the study of race, ethnicity, and sexuality. Her work on gentrification, which draws on her ethnographic data, has appeared in *City and Community and Theory and Society,* as well as in a book, *A Neighborhood That Never Changes: Gentrification, Social Preservation, and the Search for Authenticity.*

METROPOLIS AND MODERN LIFE

A Routledge Series

Edited by **Anthony Orum and Zachary Neal,** University of Illinois, Chicago

This Series brings original perspectives on key topics in urban research to today's students in a series of short accessible texts, guided readers, and practical handbooks. Each volume examines how long-standing urban phenomena continue to be relevant in an increasingly urban and global world, and in doing so, connects the best new scholarship with the wider concerns of students seeking to understand life in the twenty-first century metropolis.

Books in the Series:
Common Ground: Readings, Reflections, and New Frontiers edited by Anthony Orum and
    Zachary Neal

Forthcoming
The Urban Instinct by Nan Ellin

Also of Interest from Routledge
Gentrification by Loretta Lees, Tom Slater, and Elvin Wyly
The Gentrification Reader edited by Loretta Lees, Tom Slater, and Elvin Wyly
City Life from Jakarta to Dakar: Movements at the Crossroads by AbdouMaliq Simone
Foodies: Democracy and Distinction in the Gourmet Foodscape by Josée Johnston and
    Shyon Baumann
Branding New York: How a City in Crisis Was Sold to the World by Miriam Greenberg
The Global Architect by Donald McNeill
Housing Policy in the United States, Second Edition by Alex F. Schwartz

The Gentrification Debates

Edited by Japonica Brown-Saracino
Loyola University Chicago

Routledge
Taylor & Francis Group

NEW YORK AND LONDON

First published 2010
by Routledge
711 Third Avenue, New York, NY 10017, USA

Simultaneously published in the UK
by Routledge
2 Park Square, Milton Park, Abingdon, Oxon OX14 4RN

Routledge is an imprint of the Taylor & Francis Group, an informa business

Typeset in Utopia by Swales & Willis Ltd, Exeter, Devon

Library of Congress Cataloging in Publication Data
  The gentrification debates / [edited by] Japonica Brown-Saracino.
  p. cm. —(Metropolis and modern life)
  Includes bibliographical references and index.
  ISBN-13: 978–0–415–80164–5 (hardback : alk. paper)
  ISBN-10: 0–415–80164–8 (hbk)
  ISBN-13: 978–0–415–80165–2 (pbk. : alk. paper)
  ISBN-10: 0–415–80165–6 (pbk)
  1. Gentrification. I. Brown-Saracino, Japonica.
  HT170.G454 2010
  307.3'416—dc22
  2009044477

ISBN10: 0–415–80164–8 (hbk)
ISBN10: 0–415–80165–6 (pbk)

ISBN13: 978–0–415–80164–5 (hbk)
ISBN13: 978–0–415–80165–2 (pbk)

BRIEF CONTENTS

TABLE OF CONTENTS

PART I: WHAT IS GENTRIFICATION? DEFINITIONS AND KEY CONCEPTS
JAPONICA BROWN-SARACINO

   This 1964 essay by Ruth Glass first introduced the term "gentrification" and in so doing inagurated the inquiries and traditions that this book documents. Glass' essay describes her impression of London's gentrification and explores some of its origins, while also offering predictions about gentrification's future in London and other cities.

   This selection from the second chapter of geographer Neil Smith's book, The New Urban Frontier, *provides a short overview of a number of historical urban changes and processes that the author suggests are closely related to what many of us would term "gentrification" today. In so doing, the selection reveals Smith's perspective on gentrification's central characteristics.*

   Drawing from the sociologist Sharon Zukin's chapter, "Gentrification and Cuisine,"

PART IV: WHAT ARE THE OUTCOMES AND CONSEQUENCES OF GENTRIFICATION?

JAPONICA BROWN-SARACINO

In this selection from Derek Hyra's The New Urban Renewal: The Economic Transformation of Harlem and Bronzeville, *the author draws on data collected in New York's Harlem and Chicago's Bronzeville—two predominately African-American neighborhoods experiencing gentrification—to present an argument about the factors that influence gentrification's outcomes. Hyra suggests that municipal level factors, such as the structure and tenor of city government, shape gentrification and help to determine place-specific consequences for longtime residents.*

Drawing on data collected through fieldwork in a gentrifying Chicago neighborhood, Gina Perez demonstrates gentrification's costs for poor and working class Latino residents. She demonstrates how neighborhood youth and community organizations negotiate gentrification's daily challenges, from harassment by store clerks and police officers to the loss of housing.

Mary Pattillo's "Avenging Violence with Violence," from her book, Black on the Block, *reveals intra-racial class conflict that characterizes daily life in a predominately African-American neighborhood experiencing an influx of affluent, African-American newcomers. Pattillo's rich data demonstrate the daily tensions and conflicts that characterize the neighborhood, as well as the work that local institutions perform to ensure that the neighborhood meets gentrifiers' needs and tastes.*

Relying on data gathered in New York City, this selection from Lance Freeman's There Goes the 'Hood: Views of Gentrification from the Ground Up, *examines gentrification's costs and benefits for longtime residents. Freeman argues that gentrification may benefit some longtime residents, primarily as a result of middle class gentrifiers' social networks and successful advocacy for the improvement of local institutions and services.*

This selection from Richard Florida's influential book, The Rise of the Creative Class, *suggests that cities and towns can take steps to encourage the in-movement of creative professionals who value, among other place attributes, diversity, cultural attractions, and outdoor recreational amenities. The presence of this class, Florida suggests, can, in turn, help to ensure a municipality's economic revitalization, benefiting the local tax base and strengthening local institutions.*

SERIES FOREWORD

The Gentrification Debates, edited by Japonica Brown-Saracino

This series brings original perspectives on key topics in urban research to today's students in a series of short accessible texts, guided readers, and practical handbooks. Each volume examines how long-standing urban phenomena continue to be relevant in an increasingly urban and global world, and in doing so, connects the best new scholarship with the wider concerns of students to understand life in the twenty-first century metropolis.

In this addition to the series, Japonica Brown-Saracino addresses one of the most fundamental changes modern cities have experienced: Gentrification. Gentrification typically refers to the influx of economic capital into previously poor or working class neighborhoods that is driven by commercial investors and new, affluent residents. The influx of capital, new residents and businesses drives and reflects a broader series of changes in the physical, political, social and cultural terrain of the neighborhood, resulting in longtime residents' displacement. But do the new residents actually help to improve the overall life of a place, by bringing in more wealth, or do they simply undermine it, by driving out the older, poorer residents? This is one of several important debates that motivate the new scholarship on the changing character of cities and towns today. In this timely and singular book, Japonica Brown-Saracino introduces readers to the key debates about gentrification and does so in a way that illuminates different points of view while also prompting new questions for both students and scholars. Though much of the work on gentrification has been filtered through the lens of political economy, this book attends to this perspective while also introducing a new and powerful voice to the literature that reveals the consequences of the meanings people assign to themselves and to the places in which they live.

Anthony Orurn
Zachary Neal
Series Editors

ACKNOWLEDGEMENTS

I extend sincere thanks to my series editors, Anthony Orum and Zachary Neal, as well as to my Routledge editor, Steve Rutter. I thank Tony and Zak first and foremost for encouraging me to write this book, which, as they predicted, proved to be a challenging and rewarding endeavor. I also thank my editors for their practical and intellectual support throughout the writing and editing process. Thanks are also due to Leah Babb-Rosenfeld for her editorial assistance.

This book has benefited from feedback from a variety of sources, including from my series editors, several reviewers, Brooke Brown-Saracino, Lida Maxwell, and Jon Norman. I thank my editors for securing helpful reviews, and the reviewers for their time and thoughtful suggestions. Special appreciation is reserved for Jon Norman who offered tremendously productive and insightful suggestions during the revision process.

I owe a debt of gratitude to Corey Fields for suggesting that I form a gentrification reading group while I was writing section introductions. I offer many thanks to the graduate students from Loyola University Chicago and Northwestern University who composed the group. Together we read many of the selections included in this book, and the group's insights about the gentrification literature and anecdotes from their own field sites helped shape not only this book's content, but my thinking about gentrification.

Of course, this book would not have been feasible without the intellectual support and encouragement I received from my teachers and mentors when I first learned about and studied gentrification. There are too many individuals to thank here, but I owe special appreciation to those who have guided my study of gentrification, including, but not limited to, Mary Pattillo, Albert Hunter, Henry Binford, Wendy Griswold, and Rick Fantasia.

During the course of writing and research, I benefited from the support of Loyola University Chicago's Department of Sociology, as well as from the assistance of several graduate students: David Orta, Cesraea Rumpf, Dara Lewis, and Todd Fuist. Todd deserves special thanks for his tireless effort to track down the rights holders for the excerpts included in the book.

Last but far from least, I reserve special thanks and appreciation for my partner, Lida Maxwell, who patiently endured my alternating bouts of writer's block and furious work, and, as always, readily offered her suggestions and insights.

Overview: The Gentrification Debates

Japonica Brown-Saracino

I cannot recall the first time that I heard the term "gentrification." However, I do remember when someone first defined the concept for me. I was a college sophomore, enrolled in an urban sociology course. Many of the ideas, processes, and histories we studied fascinated me, but the professor's description of gentrification particularly intrigued me.

As he explained it—or, more accurately, as I recall him explaining it a dozen or so years ago—gentrification is characterized by the movement of creative professionals, such as artists and writers, and, later, of other members of the middle class, such as educators and bankers, to central city neighborhoods in search of affordable housing in close proximity to museums, music venues, and other cultural attractions that they value. They move into low-rent areas populated by working class individuals who are often members of white ethnic or racial minority groups. Sometimes these in-movers purchase homes that they renovate or restore to satisfy their needs and tastes. In other instances they rent.

Whether they buy or rent, a variety of factors draw them to certain central city neighborhoods. In some instances, my professor suggested, individual or corporate real estate investors encourage the in-movement of the gentry by refurbishing buildings and marketing them to the middle class (Hackworth 2002). In other instances local government encourages the gentrification of economically depressed neighborhoods through a variety of methods including, but not limited to, tax incentives, policing strategies aimed at creating a hospitable environment for newcomers, and the sale of city-owned property (Mele 2000, Badyina & Golubchikov 2005, Hyra 2008). In addition, in some periods, the federal government provided tax breaks for the restoration of historic homes in certain designated areas (e.g., Gale 1980). In still other cases, it is newspaper articles (Brown-Saracino & Rumpf 2008), word of mouth, or the establishment of businesses catering to the gentry that attract the middle class to an area (Zukin 1990, Ley 1996, Deener 2007, Zukin et al. 2009). As an illustration of the latter influence, in the Munjoy Hill neighborhood of Portland, Maine where I am currently conducting fieldwork, many lesbian and bisexual women report that the presence of a queer-friendly coffee shop encouraged their relocation to the neighborhood, which had previously been home to white working class individuals, as well as Sudanese and Somali immigrants (on Portland's gentrification see Lees 2003, 2006).

Regardless of whether they purchase or rent, the gentry's in-movement, combined with the boosterism of city officials and private investors, is of tremendous consequence. Local businesses increasingly cater to the gentry's tastes (Deener 2007, Zukin et al. 2009). For

instance, a bar begins selling Belgian beer and the corner grocery adds organic milk to
its inventory. Chains, such as Starbucks or the Gap, may also move to the neighborhood
and, in turn, serve as a symbol of neighborhood change that encourages the further in-
movement of the gentry. Property owners recognize that gentrifiers are able to pay higher
rents and home prices than most of the neighborhood's longtime residents can afford, and
as a result rent and property values increase. Local property taxes rise concomitantly. As a
result of mounting housing costs, many longtime residents must leave in search of affordable housing—thus disrupting social and familial traditions and networks. Displacement
is a particular threat for members of social groups that, in the aggregate, tend to have
fewer economic resources, such as African-Americans and Latinos, single parents, and
the elderly (Henig 1984, Bondi 1991, Perez 2006).

However, physical displacement is not the only challenge that longtime residents face.
Cultural, social and political changes surface in gentrification's early stages (see Clay 1979,
Kerstein 1990). For instance, in an effort to stay in business the corner store must either
cater to newcomers' tastes (hence the organic milk) or lose its lease. In the event that it
closes, another business—perhaps a yoga studio or an upscale bistro—will take its place.
Such changes may alienate or out-price longtime patrons, and, even more pressingly,
longtime residents who worked in the corner store lose their jobs and part of their social
support network when it closes. Local politicians, observing such economic and demographic changes, often cater to the needs and interests of new affluent residents who have
financial resources to support their campaigns and who will, should gentrification continue, compose their constituency (Shaw 2005, Wyly & Hammel 2005). As a result, many
long-timers feel that their needs are ignored or even subverted and local political forums
and some street interactions become acrimonious (Zukin 1987).

As longtime residents leave the neighborhood in search of affordable housing and
work opportunities, new, more affluent residents—lawyers, doctors, investment bankers, etc.—take their place. Eventually, some of the artists and writers who often compose
gentrification's first wave face their own displacement (Clay 1979, Kerstein 1990) and as
gentrification advances neighborhood institutions, including schools, churches, and
libraries, adjust to accommodate new, more affluent residents. These institutions also
receive an influx of resources that newcomers provide or demand. In many cases, in a
decade or less, the neighborhood will appear to be completely transformed. Not only do
new people populate it, but a combination of infrastructural improvements, new businesses and refurbished homes transform its appearance. High-end cars take the place of
older models on neighborhood streets, new store awnings appear in the commercial district, and homes receive updated porches, windows, and coats of paint. The local library
branch may expand its selection and the city may clear streets of snow more frequently
than they did in the past. Newcomers and city officials frequently report that the neighborhood is safer and cleaner than it has been in decades.

When my professor offered the above description, he was likely thinking of the gentrifying places that many scholars and journalists write about, such as New York's Greenwich
Village or Paris' Marais. However, I found myself thinking of the small town in western
Massachusetts where I spent much of my childhood. At the time, most scholars regarded
gentrification as an urban process and did not think of rural areas as being susceptible to
the economic, demographic, and aesthetic transformations that characterize gentrification.[1] Yet, to me, the change process that I had witnessed in my rural hometown seemed to
parallel that of the central city neighborhoods my professor described.

As I have written elsewhere (Brown-Saracino 2009), in the early 1980s my parents were among a wave of young professionals who, attracted by inexpensive housing costs, a rural landscape, and burgeoning professional and economic opportunities in regional population centers, relocated to hill towns in western Massachusetts. As a child, my neighbors included dairy and cattle farmers, factory workers, truck drivers, and mechanics born and raised in town. However, other neighbors were more like my parents. These included newcomers who commuted south to professional posts in Northampton or, to the north, in Brattleboro, Vermont, and college educated back-to-the-landers who relied on their acreage or creative skills to support themselves through ventures such as organic farming, weaving, storytelling, writing, or woodworking. My parents often returned from the annual Town Meeting, held in the small town hall on the Town Common, with tales of conflict between new and longtime residents that paralleled the acrimony my professor described between urban gentrifiers and long-timers. In my hometown, conflict frequently centered on newcomers' interest in land conservation, for they worried that without conservation developers would replace dairy farms with high-end condominium units, destroying natural landscapes and the town's rural character. For their part, many longtime residents resented newcomers' increasing political power and feared that they would lose control of their land through zoning restrictions and other policy changes for which newcomers advocated. Over time, property values and taxes rose, and some longtime residents were displaced. Others sold acreage to pay their mortgage or taxes, thus losing land on which they depended for their livelihood, and new, expensive homes appeared in what had once been pasture or woodlot, transforming the landscape.

As a college student, in my mind the transformation of my rural hometown seemed parallel to my professor's description of urban gentrification. Was it possible, I wondered, for gentrification to occur in a rural area? Was it appropriate to use the term "gentrification" to describe the economic upscaling and displacement that I had witnessed in my small hometown? Might changes in a small Massachusetts town parallel the transformation of rural Illinois (Salamon 2005), Wisconsin (Macgregor 2005), or West Yorkshire (Smith & Phillips 2002)? Do some small town political officials encourage gentrification, as many argue to be the case in urban neighborhoods (Shaw 2005, Wyly & Hammel 2005)? Does gentrification transform village commercial centers in the same manner as those in the central city (Zukin et al. 2009)?

After some thought, I worked up the courage to pose these questions to my professor. Was gentrification a purely urban process, I asked? My professor said that most define gentrification as an urban process. However, he also said that he supposed that it could occur outside of the central city. To his knowledge, few had written about this and he encouraged me to pursue the question of whether gentrification occurs in rural areas by studying my hometown.

The question that first emerged in my undergraduate class informed a broader set of questions about gentrification that I continue to pursue. After writing a senior thesis based on a study of my hometown, I conducted a comparative ethnography of four communities experiencing an influx of highly educated, residentially mobile, and relatively affluent newcomers: two central city Chicago neighborhoods, a small, coastal tourist town in Massachusetts, and a rural farming community in Maine (Brown-Saracino 1999, 2004, 2006, 2007, 2009). In the end, I regard gentrification as a community change process that occurs most frequently in the central city, but that is not specific to that context. Many scholars agree (see Parsons 1980, Phillips 2004, Smith & Holt 2005, Smith & Phillips 2001), but others call for a narrower definition. In short, without meaning to, my inaugural socio-logical research forced me to directly consider one of the debates that color the gentrifica-tion literature: namely, how to define gentrification and specify its geographic parameters. In other words, it pushed me to consider the question of whether gentrification is a strictly urban process.

This book is not about the differences between urban and small town gentrification, but it *is* about the sort of disagreement I outline above: exactly how broad should our defi-nition of gentrification be? What are gentrification's basic characteristics? What are the stakes of broadening our image of gentrification to include the transformation of non-urban areas, or of including additional cases that depart in other ways from the descrip-tion my professor offered? For instance, what are the implications for our understanding of the "gentrifier" of acknowledging that some neighborhoods are not first gentrified by the white artists and writers central to many images of gentrification (Taylor 2002, Pattillo 2007, Hyra 2008)?

Another student in my undergraduate urban sociology class may have been less intrigued by the question of whether gentrification is a strictly urban process, and more interested in documenting the frequency with which it occurs in African-American or Latino working class neighborhoods. Some might have visited the professor's office to ask if the displacement of longtime residents is inevitable. Still others might have wanted to know if the gentrifiers who engage in gentrification are responsible for the process, or if it is supported by city or national policies (e.g., Hackworth 2002, Hyra 2008). In short, cumu-latively my fellow students might have interrogated and debated many of the facets of the description our professor offered.

Students are not the only individuals to pose such questions. Since Ruth Glass first coined the term "gentrification" in 1964, scholars in a variety of disciplines have studied and written about the process. For instance, they have debated whether a return of people or of capital to the central city drives gentrification, the sincerity of some gentrifiers' taste for "diversity," and whether the economic revitalization that gentrification typically pro-duces outweighs the human cost of longtime residents' displacement.

Indeed, scholarship on gentrification is expansive and much of it is defined by debate and deliberation about its many facets. However, perhaps as a reaction to the breadth and diversity of gentrification scholarship, too often a single book or article proffers a narrow perspective on the process, generally by taking one side or another in the gentrification debates. Specifically, when authors devote attention to debate over gentrification, they typically attend to a single area of disagreement: the question of whether gentrification's benefits for the middle class and for urban economies outweigh its costs for longtime resi-dents (e.g., see Smith & Williams 1986, Lees et al. 2008). In Roland Atkinson's terms, a vari-ety of individuals and groups have "sparred" over whether gentrification is a "savior" or "destroyer of central city vitality" (2003: 2343).

For instance, in their 1986 gentrification anthology, Neil Smith and Peter Williams draw the reader's attention to the debate between those who regard gentrification as a har-binger of a desirable urban renaissance and those who view it as an instrument of urban restructuring that has negative consequences for poor and working class residents (1986: 12). This is an enormously important debate, but at this date it is an oversimplification to suggest that it is the only issue worthy of attention, for, as this book argues, scholars' per-spectives on this debate are informed by a broader set of conversations and disagreements about several facets of gentrification.[2]

In this sense, this book is different than those that have come before. Most centrally, it encourages us to consider a number of debates about gentrification and in so doing draws our attention to a variety of ways of thinking about the process and of approaching the study of gentrifying places. Furthermore, it challenges the dominant inclination among gentrification scholars to attend narrowly to debates surrounding the relationship between political-economy and gentrification, specifically to how elites' interests are prioritized over and above those with less economic or political capital and how this inequality, in turn, is reproduced in and marks urban lives and landscapes.[3] While the political-economic approach raises a set of undeniably pertinent questions to which this book devotes a great deal of attention, particularly about gentrification's relation to broader conflict between those who possess economic resources and those who do not, singular devotion to this approach runs the risk of focusing our attention on a limited number of gentrification's facets. Specifically, it attends to the role of coalitions of elites (Logan & Molotch 1987) and the broad economic and political shifts that help enable gentrification at the cost of attention to numerous other facets of gentrification that are central to the lives of social actors involved in the process and to the idiosyncratic ways in which gentrification unfolds in distinct places. For instance, singular attention to how gentrification reproduces and extends economic inequalities distracts us from a series of debates about how longtime residents respond to gentrification (Martin 2007, Pattillo 2007, Brown-Saracino 2009), gentrifiers' understanding of their role in the process (Caulfield 1998, Taylor 2002, Pattillo 2007, Brown-Saracino 2009), and the everyday, local decision-making processes that contribute to the economic, political, social, and cultural characteristics of gentrifying places (e.g., Betancur 2002, Martin 2007).

Furthermore, to suggest that there is a single gentrification debate—that the only question or debate worthy of attention is between those who regard the process as a harbinger of renaissance and those who view it as a destructive extension of broader economic and political shifts (Smith 1986, Slater 2006, Lees et al. 2008)—is to deny many gray areas within the literature and the overlap between these two dominant positions. Most pressingly, it runs the risk of positioning arguments that do not neatly adhere to a political-economy perspective as straw men, typically by presenting them as falling in the gentrification-as-renaissance camp. *The Gentrification Debates* explores a broad variety of perspectives on gentrification and documents how a plethora of perspectives—from the political-economy framework to an emphasis on the import of the cultural tastes of the "new middle class" (Caulfield 1994, Ley 1996, 2003, Butler 1997)—emerged from a series of conversations between scholars with opposing viewpoints.

Why attend to multiple debates about gentrification rather than the single and undeniably important question of gentrification's costs and benefits that others attend to? First, more than one area of disagreement characterizes the literature and, for this reason, attending to the full range of gentrification debates provides a more comprehensive overview of how the process and scholarship on it have developed over four and a half decades. In this sense, this book provides a more complete overview of the genealogy of the gentrification literature and encourages the reader to develop an understanding of how several areas of debate inform one another, as well as the broad aforementioned debate about gentrification's costs and benefits. Second, scholars do not just debate gentrification when they challenge one another about how to define the process, explain gentrification's origins and limits, or explicate its outcomes. They also invoke and debate a series of terms and concepts that scholars in a variety of disciplines rely on. For instance, when we discuss how we should define the "gentrifier" we are not just debating the role and characteristics of a set of actors involved in gentrification, but also what we mean when we refer to someone as "middle class" and how to understand the relationship between traits such as race, income, and gender, and ideology and behavior. In short, debates about gentrification evoke a plethora of broad questions that are worthy of our attention and that, in turn, inform the way we think about gentrification, as well as about a number of other dimensions of our social world. Thus, by introducing readers to a number of intellectual traditions to which the gentrification debates relate, this book provides tools of inquiry that can be applied not only to gentrification but to a host of other social phenomena as well. Finally, by outlining a variety of perspectives on gentrification and mapping their relationships to one another I anticipate that this book will encourage further inquiries into the process: that it will answer questions about gentrification while also inviting debate and new lines of study. In short, following a long tradition in the social sciences, this book traces how scholars have questioned dominant gentrification research paradigms in hopes of opening up new lines of debate and inquiry. It is my goal that, as a result, it will encourage readers to add their own voices to the conversations that inform our understanding of gentrification and a number of related concepts and processes.

As this book's title, which borrows from a phrase that the geographer Neil Smith used in a 1986 essay, suggests, *The Gentrification Debates* is centered on four key areas of disagreement in the gentrification literature.[4] These include debates about 1) how to define and recognize gentrification, 2) how, where, and when gentrification occurs, 3) gentrifiers' characteristics and motivations for engaging in the process, and 4) gentrification's outcomes and consequences.

Each of the book's four sections includes excerpts from articles and book chapters that provide varying perspectives on these debates. Cumulatively, they provide a comprehensive—if not exhaustive—overview of more than four decades of gentrification scholarship and orient us toward ongoing debates.[5] On the one hand, in keeping with the political economy perspective, the book's selections document the influence of the market and state and of the gentry's economic interests in gentrification. However, on the other hand, it also attends to the meanings residents assign to gentrifying places and interactional dynamics of a variety of actors engaged in the process. It is my hope that the book will spark further debate and discussion, both in the classroom and beyond. Such debate is productive in the sense that it strengthens scholarship on gentrification, as well as our reading of the literature by challenging assumptions and continually renewing our view of the process and related concepts. More generally, debate is valuable because it calls for us to engage with a set of key questions about a process that has become fundamental to many cities across the globe. Whether gentrification displaced you from your childhood home, or, conversely, ensured that your family profited from rising home values, or whether coverage of the process simply fills the pages of your local paper, it is likely that gentrification has influenced either your life or the lives of many around you. Thus, comprehensive knowledge of gentrification is paramount not only for an understanding of contemporary cities, but also if we wish to be informed and engaged members of a world in which gentrification is increasingly pervasive—at least, as the second section of this book considers, in certain contexts (Smith 2002, Atkinson & Bridge 2005). The next paragraphs provide a brief overview of the concepts and questions central to the book's readings, as well as to the debates of which they are a part.

What is Gentrification? The first section of the book presents several influential essays on how gentrification should be defined and how we can recognize it when we see it. It includes seminal readings, such as Ruth Glass' 1964 essay introducing the term and identifying the process. It also includes readings that pose questions such as whether gentrification can occur outside of urban areas, whether it should be identified by the characteristics of in-movers or of longtime residents, and whether we should categorize it by a set of outcomes, such as rising property values or displacement, or by a set of causes, such as some gentrifiers' appreciation for social diversity or desire to live near their place of work, or government policies designed to encourage developers' investment in gentrifying neighborhoods. The introduction to the first section poses a set of questions about gentrification's central defining characteristics, as well as about how gentrification is different than other forms of redevelopment. The readings also provide guideposts for recognizing gentrification by outlining the changes one can expect to observe in a place undergoing gentrification.

How, Where and When Does Gentrification Occur? The book's second section presents readings offering contrasting perspectives on the factors that produce gentrification. Readings include those that argue that gentrification is a product of market conditions, that suggest that national, state, and local government policies facilitate gentrification, and, finally, arguments about how gentrifiers' tastes and needs help to produce gentrification.

Together the readings represent two sides of a central debate in the gentrification literature about the relative import of *production* and *consumption factors* for producing gentrification (see Smith & Williams 1986, Zukin 1987). In so doing, it reviews an underlying debate about culture's role in gentrification, namely about whether gentrifiers' tastes and beliefs drive gentrification or whether, once gentrification is underway, cultural objects are manipulated to appeal to gentrifiers (Griswold 1986). It also presents diverse responses to questions about why some places gentrify while others do not, as well as about why some gentrify before others.

This section therefore pushes the reader to consider arguments about the economic and political factors that facilitate gentrification, such as housing markets and city policies, as well as arguments about the cultural tastes and meanings that encourage the gentry's participation in the process and that help to determine where they move. For instance, the essays provide at least two explanations—either competing or complimentary, depending on your perspective—for why people like my parents moved back-to-the-land in the 1970s and 1980s. Production explanations suggest that the decline of industry and the rise of the professional-managerial class enabled college educated individuals to move away from cities that once were manufacturing and employment centers (Ehrenreich & Ehrenreich 1979). In addition, they might contend that rising housing costs in Northeastern metropolises and the concomitant failure of the New England family farm encouraged young couples' movement to the country, where land and homes were relatively inexpensive. In contrast, supply side explanations suggest that the above shifts cannot alone account for why some young professionals moved to rural hill towns, while many others preferred central city neighborhoods. They would urge us to take my parents' leftist politics, particularly their environmentalism and appreciation for rural landscape, into account.

Who Are Gentrifiers and Why Do They Engage in Gentrification? The third section includes seminal readings that portray gentrifiers as white, middle class "pioneers" who take pleasure in taming the urban frontier (Spain 1993, Smith 1996). However, it departs from most summaries of the gentrification literature by presenting readings that complicate our dominant image of gentrifiers. Specifically, it highlights gentrifiers' demographic diversity, as well as the variety of attitudes toward gentrification that they articulate. Readings also present diverse explanations for gentrifiers' motivations for participating in the process, from a desire for economic gain and to "save" the central city from blight, to appreciation for diversity and a distaste for suburbia. In sum, this section provides readers with an understanding of gentrifiers' demographic and ideological diversity, as well as with a set of guiding questions with which to consider the relationship between gentrifiers' personal traits and their approaches to gentrification.

In short, the third section asks the reader to consider how he or she would respond to a central set of questions about how to define and identify the gentrifier. Specifically, it asks: are gentrifiers marked by a set of shared demographic traits, a common ideological orientation to place and gentrification, or by the intentions behind their participation in gentrification?

What are the Outcomes and Consequences of Gentrification? The final section provides an overview of the outcomes and consequences of gentrification, from readings that document the physical displacement of poor and working class longtime residents and first-wave gentrifiers, to those that point to their "social displacement" (Chernoff 1984). It includes recent scholarship that argues that gentrification is less detrimental to longtime residents than previous work suggested (e.g., Freeman & Braconi 2002, 2004), as well as criticisms of such scholarship (e.g., Newman & Wyly 2006, Slater 2006).

The diversity of topics, perspectives, and cases included in this book are one indication of the sheer volume of gentrification scholarship. Academics in a variety of fields—including, but not limited to, sociology, anthropology, political science, planning, urban studies, geography, performance studies, and African-American studies—have written on the topic, as have many journalists (see Brown-Saracino & Rumpf 2008). The breadth and diversity of the literature presented a challenge when it came to selecting voices and perspectives for inclusion in the book, for no single reader can include all exemplary scholarship, nor represent every facet of gentrification research.

In the end, I chose to include excerpts from articles and chapters that marked key turning points in gentrification scholarship, stimulated debate, or spurred new lines of inquiry and disagreement. The work of a few key thinkers, specifically Sharon Zukin and Neil Smith, whose scholarship has had disproportionate influence on key lines of debate, appear more than once in the reader. However, while the book contains essays by leading gentrification scholars, it also includes excerpts from publications that emerged from doctoral dissertations and master's theses. In short, excerpts were selected because they influenced debate and/or represent key perspectives on a variety of issues of import for gentrification scholars. References to additional micro-debates and resources appear throughout the book, in my introductions to the sections, as well as in the selections that compose each section, and I encourage readers to continue their reading and discussion, as well as to undertake their own studies of gentrification.

It is my hope that *The Gentrification Debates* will provide readers with the combination of resources that spurred my initial interest in gentrification. Specifically, the book is designed to partner a clear set of terms and concepts central to gentrification with exposure to the debates that helped form them. I expect that together these two elements will encourage the reader to trace the development of the gentrification literature, as well as to interrogate and even challenge central terms and concepts. After all, the book reminds us that gentrification scholarship, like any other line of inquiry, has room for new voices, perspectives, and lines of debate.

NOTES

1. On rural gentrification see, among others, Parsons 1980, Phillips 2004, Smith & Holt 2005, Smith & Phillips 2001, Macgregor 2005.
2. Smith and Williams attend to several facets of this debate, such as questions about whether production or consumption factors produce gentrification, but they frame such questions as subsets of the broader, single debate outlined above. In contrast, this book suggests that numerous debates color and structure the literature, four of which this text highlights.
3. As this book documents, while the political economy perspective is of great value and is indisputably the prevailing framework for thinking about gentrification, it is not the only available framework.
4. To be specific, Smith refers to "*the* gentrification debate" (1986: 3, *emphasis added*) as does Atkinson in a 2003 essay. See discussion above on the limits of attending to a single debate about gentrification.
5. For a comprehensive overview of the gentrification literature see Lees et al. (2008 & forthcoming).

PART I

*W*hat is Gentrification?
Definitions and Key Concepts

INTRODUCTION: WHAT IS GENTRIFICATION?
DEFINITIONS AND KEY CONCEPTS

A few years ago an undergraduate in my Race and Place seminar raised his hand after our first classroom discussion of gentrification. "I think that my hometown is gentrifying," he said, providing a brief description of the small Midwestern city in which he grew up. "Before today I didn't know what to call it, but I'm pretty sure that it is gentrifying." A few months later he wrote a paper documenting how the in-movement of affluent newcomers, encouraged by the gentrification of neighboring cities, local land use policies, and readily available mortgages, contributed to the transformation of the social, economic, and physical characteristics of his city.

As this anecdote suggests, many have an image, however vague, of gentrification. One may not know the word for gentrification or have devoted thought to its definition, but many nonetheless possess an intuitive sense of what gentrification *is* (Becker 1998). Why is this the case? It may be the result of the ubiquity of media coverage on gentrification, or the sheer number of those who, like my student, have firsthand experience with the process (see Lees et al. 2008).

Indeed, you and your classmates may already have different understandings of gentrification. As a result, when you stop to think about how you would define gentrification and discuss this with others, you may find that your classmates' definitions are quite distinct from your own. For instance, in a class you may have viewed the documentary *Flag Wars*, which profiles the movement, buoyed by realtors, of white, middle class gay men into a predominately working class, African-American neighborhood in Columbus, Ohio. As a result, at the center of your image of gentrification are dilapidated Victorian houses restored to opulence by gentrifiers armed with financial capital, their own labor, and taste for historical authenticity. You might "unpack" this image to realize that, in your mind, gentrification entails the displacement of lifelong residents by gentrifiers who do not share long-timers' racial or class identity. You might also recognize that you regard the restoration of older homes as a defining characteristic of gentrification and that you believe that gentrification is fueled not only by individual renovators, but also by government officials, such as those who pass and enforce ordinances that require homeowners to meet the costly standards of official historic districts and who threaten to close long-timers' institutions for failing to meet new zoning standards.

However, if you were to ask another what her image of gentrification is she might mention Sharon Zukin's pioneering book on the process, *Loft Living*, which centers on middle class artists and professionals who purchased space in New York industrial buildings in the 1970s and transformed them into studios and homes, and, as a result, helped spur local economic, social, and cultural transformation. Comparing your images, you realize that Zukin's case does not include the Victorians or immediate displacement of longtime residents so central to your notion of gentrification. Instead, it emphasizes the displacement, facilitated in part by changes that city officials made to zoning laws, of light industry, neighborhood shops, and squatters.

Someone else might volunteer that the term "gentrification" makes him think of the small New England fishing village where his grandparents live. You find yourself arguing about whether the restoration of nineteenth-century village homes by middle class newcomers and the displacement of fishermen and their families constitutes gentrification. Soon your questions expand: Can gentrification occur outside of the city? Must it include the displacement of longtime residents? If displacement is a defining characteristic of gentrification, should we term a revitalization process "gentrification" if the displaced are light manufacturing concerns, store owners, and squatters, rather than renters or homeowners?

In short, despite the fact that, upon reflection, you may realize that you have been exposed to gentrification through firsthand experience, the media, or in school, you may be uncertain about how to define the process, as well as about how to reconcile the concepts central to your image of gentrification with those of your classmates.

It may either calm or concern you to know that despite their general agreement about gentrification's defining traits, experts engage in similar debates about how to define the process. In one period debate about how to define gentrification was so heightened that Damaris Rose called for scholars to embrace "definitional chaos" (1984; see also Atkinson 2003, Criekengen & Doly 2003), arguing that this "chaos" most accurately captures the complexities of an evolving and somewhat idiosyncratic process. In response, others lobbied for retreat from this "chaos"—calling for agreement about gentrification's central traits (Zukin 1987, Smith 1996).

Perhaps as a result of such calls, after decades of scholarship researchers have come to some agreement about gentrification's central characteristics. As the readings in this section demonstrate, while scholars acknowledge that gentrification varies by time, place, and stage of gentrification (Clay 1979, Kerstein 1990), for the most part they concur that among gentrification's defining traits are an influx of capital and resultant displacement, and the transformation of local "social character" (Glass 1964: xx), culture, amenities, and physical infrastructure (Warde 1991, Atkinson 2003). Most also agree that government policies and broad economic and demographic shifts—such as banks' liberal lending practices in the late twentieth and early twenty-first centuries, the transformation of many North American and western European industrial cities into service-economy hubs, and the maturation of the baby-boom generation in the 1970s and 1980s—facilitate gentrification.

Like many other scholars, the anthropologist Gina Perez offers a straightforward definition of gentrification, describing it as:

> an economic and social process whereby private capital (real estate firms, developers) and individual homeowners and renters reinvest in fiscally neglected neighborhoods through housing rehabilitation, loft conversions, and the construction of new housing stock. Unlike urban renewal,

gentrification is a gradual process, occurring one building or block at a time, slowly reconfiguring the neighborhood landscape of consumption and residence by displacing poor and working-class residents unable to afford to live in 'revitalized' neighborhoods with rising rents, property taxes, and new businesses catering to an upscale clientele.

(2004: 139)

This definition captures many of the characteristics that scholars agree define gentrification: an influx of capital and resultant social, economic, cultural, and physical transformation and displacement (see Atkinson 2003).

If there is general agreement among scholars about these defining traits, what is there left to debate about? To varying degrees the authors in this section provide definitions and descriptions of gentrification that overlap with Perez's. However, each author emphasizes distinct elements of Perez's definition. For instance, some stress the displacement of poor and working-class residents, while others devote greater attention to the transformation of housing stock. Underlying debate about how to define gentrification are a few pressing questions. As this section details, first and foremost is the question of whether to define gentrification by its causes, outcomes, or everyday character. A second related question is about *which* of gentrification's causes, outcomes, or dimensions typify the process. A third question involves *where* gentrification takes place. In the process of posing and answering these questions scholars argue about *which* cases of revitalization should be deemed "gentrification," while simultaneously pushing each other to construct definitions that acknowledge gentrification's variability—i.e. the fact that its precise characteristics and dynamics vary, to an extent, by time, place, and stage of gentrification (Clay 1979, Kerstein 1990).

In the following pages, I first outline a key disagreement related to gentrification's definition and parameters: the question discussed above of whether we should define gentrification by its causes, outcomes, or the character of the process. Second, I outline how debates about when gentrification began, where it occurs, and what its outer limits are reveal underlying disagreement about this same definitional problem, specifically about whether to define gentrification by its causes, outcomes, or the daily interactions and choices that characterize the process.

Generally speaking, most scholars' definitions of gentrification center on gentrification's outcomes or consequences, rather than on its causes or on the character of the process—its everyday manifestations and progress (see Brown-Saracino 2009). Specifically, as an essay in this section by Neil Smith suggests, scholars and others emphasize economic revitalization, transformation of the built environment, and displacement as key signifiers of the process. Why do many definitions hinge on gentrification's outcomes? As this book's fourth section reveals, scholars debate facets of gentrification's outcomes and consequences, such as displacement rates. However, there is greater collective agreement about gentrification's outcomes than about its causes and I believe that this is why many definitions emphasize economic revitalization, aesthetic change, and displacement.

Most of the readings in this section question this general consensus on the centrality of outcomes to our definition of gentrification by focusing instead on gentrification's causes. Specifically, in the readings that follow you will find that every author either implicitly or explicitly attends to gentrification's *causes* and many regard these as central to the definition of gentrification that they propose. The authors' attention to causation is neither representative of the broader literature nor happenstance. Rather, it is a product of the fact that within the literature there is much debate about gentrification's sources, and because this book is organized around areas of contention, essays debating gentrification's causes are thus disproportionately central to *The Gentrification Debates.*

That said, while many of the authors of the essays in this section emphasize causal factors in their definitions, they disagree about *which* causal factors are foundational to gentrification. For instance, in the essay in which she coined the term "gentrification" Ruth Glass explicitly links gentrification to the restoration of historic homes. Like Sharon Zukin, whose essay, "Gentrification as Market and Place" offers its own definition of gentrification, Glass suggests that shifting ideological orientations to the city encouraged middle class individuals to invest in central city properties that a previous generation had devalued. According to this argument, if the city had remained undesirable in the eyes of the middle class, homeowners would not have taken advantage of political and economic shifts that opened the central city to them. Thus, scholars like Zukin and Glass hold gentrifiers' cultural valuation of the central city as an important component of our concept of gentrification.

In contrast, others cite demographic trends, such as the rising number of married women in the workforce in the second half of the twentieth century as contributing factors (see Marukusen 1981, Bondi 1991, Warde 1991). Three of this section's authors, Neil Smith, Sharon Zukin and Ruth Glass, turn to deindustrialization as well as social policies that stripped cities of economic and infrastructural resources in the middle of the twentieth century as enabling conditions for gentrification. In their view, such change and policies reduced central city property values and, in turn, invited the speculation and investment that characterizes gentrification. In turn, Neil Smith regards what he terms a "revanchist" approach to urban policy, which punishes or seeks to take revenge on the city's poor residents (1996: 43–44), as a key contributing factor, and conceives of this revanchism as part of an effort to restructure the city to benefit the elite. Likewise, Sharon Zukin writes that "gentrification persists as a collective effort to appropriate the center for elements of a new urban middle class" (1991: 187).

The next section of the book will attend more closely to such causal arguments. For now, suffice it to say that many scholars include causal factors, of one kind or another, in their descriptions and analyses of gentrification. However, because there is significant disagreement about gentrification's causes, as well as a dearth of attention to the processes or everyday characteristics of gentrification (Brown-Saracino 2009), when it comes to defining gentrification many scholars emphasize the *outcomes* of the process. That is, many more scholars agree about gentrification's outcomes than about its causes, and, for this reason, common definitions tend to hinge on that which gentrification produces, such as displacement and the related transformation of a place's economic, social, and physical character.

As a side note, as you read this section you may realize that with few exceptions the authors do not explicitly attend to the everyday process of gentrification. For the most part, their conceptualizations do not hinge on daily evidence of gentrification's progress: the sound of hammers and saws as workmen refurbish houses, the individuals seated at a new coffee shop or bistro, campaign posters for a pro-gentrification mayoral candidate that color shop windows, or terse words between neighbors who come from distinct economic backgrounds. Which of these elements, you might ask yourself, might one reasonably expect to find in most gentrifying places and how central should they be to our conceptualization of the process?

The disagreement I have outlined thus far—about whether gentrification is characterized by its outcomes, causes, or the character of the process—directly addresses the question of how to define the process. However, many other scholars approach this question less directly. For instance, tension about how to define gentrification is apparent in essays in this section that consider when gentrification began, where it occurs, and how to recognize its outer limits.

Nearly all of the essays in this section consider the question of when gentrification began. What does the question of when gentrification began have to do with defining the term? In short, scholars tell origin stories about gentrification as a way of arguing that certain characteristics of the process—those present in its earliest history—should be considered its *defining* characteristics. In addition, they reveal varying opinions about the centrality of gentrification's causes and outcomes to the definition.

Many trace gentrification to the period just before 1964 when Ruth Glass coined the term in the introduction to a book on London. However, others, like geographer Neil Smith, in an essay in this section, suggest that we can trace its roots to the century before Glass first wrote of gentrification (see also Clark 2005). Specifically, in his "Short History of Gentrification," Smith suggests that "something more akin to contemporary gentrification made an appearance in the middle of the nineteenth century" (1996: 35–36), then known as "embourgeoisement" (Smith 1996; see also Gaillard 1977, Harvey 1985, Engels 1975: 71).

In her essay describing London's gentrification Ruth Glass identifies an ideology that embraced urban living for the middle class—in her terms, "a switch from suburban to urban aspirations" (1964: xxxi)—as a defining characteristic. As a result, she argues that urban renewal projects—government funded slum clearance and infrastructural transformations such as the construction of interstate highways through working class neighborhoods—enabled gentrification (1964: xvii), but, like Gina Perez (2004), she regards urban renewal as a *precursor* to gentrification, *not* as gentrification itself. Thus, authors such as Glass and Perez disagree with Smith. They do not believe that "gentrification" is responsible for the transformation of *all* of the neighborhoods from which poor and working class residents have been displaced to suit the needs and tastes of the middle class. Why do they disagree? On my reading, Glass worried that if we collapsed all such transformations under the umbrella of gentrification, this would negate how gentrifiers' ideological appreciation for city life enabled gentrification. In other words, she regards changes in the middle class' view of the city as an essential precursor to gentrification, and therefore as fundamental to a definition of the process.

In contrast, others offer descriptions of gentrification's history that imply that we can identify the process by its outcomes, rather than its causes. As Neil Smith notes (1996: 36), Friedrich Engels, writing of the mid-nineteenth century appropriation of poor and working class quarters for the middle class wrote, "No matter how different the reasons may be, the result is everywhere the same" (1975: 71). In other words, if mid-nineteenth century planning movements (ibid.) or mid-twentieth century urban renewal projects destroyed poor and working class enclaves for the benefit of the middle class, as well as the economic and political elites, why exclude them from our conceptualization of "gentrification"?

This powerfully suggests that a view of gentrification as a historically enduring process closely relates to presumptions about how we should definite it—about what gentrification *is*. Some suggest that we should identify gentrification by its consequences, such as economic upscaling and longtime residents' displacement, *rather than by its causes*, such as the rise of a neoliberal state (Harvey 1989, Smith 1996, Peck 2006, Lees et al. 2008), the middle class' increasing appreciation for features of urban life (Glass 1964, Caulfield 1994, Ley 1996), the decline of rent control, or a free market approach to urban planning (Glass 1964: xx).

Questions about when a process began are often paired with questions about its outer (temporal and spatial) limits. Three of the selections in this section, most centrally Loretta Lees' article on the super-gentrification of a Brooklyn neighborhood, encourage speculation about how much gentrification can evolve and still be "gentrification" (see also Bondi 1991). In short, they invite the question: *what are gentrification's limits?*

When Ruth Glass coined the term she did not anticipate that we would use it today, nor did she predict that we would apply it to places like New York and Chicago, let alone the many global cities that Rowland Atkinson and Gary Bridge argue are gentrifying (2004). In fact, Glass thought that gentrification was specific to London and to the period in which she was writing. She speculated that, "London, always a 'unique city', may acquire a rare complaint. While the cores of other large cities in the world, especially of those in the United States, are decaying . . . London may soon be faced with an *embarras de richesse* in her central area" (xx). This notion seems almost quaint after more than forty years of gentrification scholarship and in a context in which scholars suggest that gentrification is endemic to many of the world's financial capitals and when it also occurs in less affluent cities (Atkinson and Bridge 2004), as well as in some suburban and rural areas (Smith & Defillipis 1999, Hackworth & Smith 2001, Smith 2002: 442). On one thing scholars are in uniform agreement: gentrification did not stop in London, nor was it limited to the last third of the twentieth century.

Yet recognition of gentrification as an expanding process raises pertinent questions about the malleability of our definition. To what extent is the gentrification that Loretta Lees highlights in her essay, "Super-Gentrification," which displaces property-rich, high earning Brooklyn professionals, the same process that displaced working class small business owners in Glass' London? After all, most definitions of gentrification presume that the process takes root in places that are "disinvested and devalued" (Lees 2003: 2487), and the Brooklyn neighborhood Lees describes is anything but disinvested. Likewise, do the same defining traits characterize the gentrification of Mumbai and Los Angeles, as Atkinson and Bridge might argue (2004)?

Most would probably agree that it is safe to assume that the gentrification process is not identical across time and space. Indeed, many refer to stages of gentrification, noting how the process changes and evolves over time in a single neighborhood or town, typically as the place becomes increasingly upscale (e.g., Clay 1979, Pattison 1983, Kerstein 1990). This, in turn, raises a question about the stakes of applying an older term to a continually evolving process. As Lees asks of her own argument that "super-gentrification" occurs in some high-end neighborhoods, by broadening our conception of gentrification to include such cases do we risk "making the meaning of the term so expansive as to lose any conceptual sharpness and specificity" (2003: 2491)? Likewise, Roland Atkinson asks, "is the term gentrification really up to the job after 40 years or is it to be more subtly defined and discerned in different contexts?" (2003: 2443).

This is not cause for despair, for even those who challenge us to recognize gentrification in unexpected places and forms identify the process by the set of traits introduced earlier in this essay: an influx of capital, social, economic, cultural, and physical transformation, and displacement (see Warde 1991). They sometimes disagree about *who* is displaced or *how much* capital was present before a new influx, but they nonetheless concur on the import of these traits.

Why is there disagreement about how to define gentrification? Primarily, it results from a combination of the breadth of gentrification and of our attention to it. Scholars in a variety of fields have studied a diversity of cases of gentrification that vary across both time and space, and this invites awareness of departures from any neat, single definition. Furthermore, many definitions come with attendant intellectual stakes. For instance, those who study political economy are likely to emphasize the role of government policies and the market in their definitions, while those who are especially attentive to culture may proffer definitions that place greater emphasis on gentrifiers' ideology and cultural tastes (e.g., Ley 1986, Caulfield 1994).

Having called our attention to a few defining traits of gentrification about which there is fairly widespread agreement, I invite readers to use the readings to come to their own conclusions about how to define the process. In so doing, I encourage the reader to consider what gentrification *is* and what it is *not*. What are the stakes of developing a definition broad enough to encompass the full range—or something close to it—of cases that scholars, journalists, and others label "gentrification"? On the other hand, what are the consequences of adopting a narrower definition and suggesting that some such cases are not, in fact, "gentrification"?

I believe that such questions are worthy of our attention, for how we define gentrification is of practical and intellectual import. For instance, definitions may influence the areas of a city in which a nonprofit organization builds affordable housing, the places scholars study and that journalists document, as well as what we measure when we study "gentrification" (see Ley 1986). Finally, as the opening vignette suggests, it may also, to a degree, influence how we think about the places where we live as well as about our relationship to the people with whom we share a changing neighborhood or town.

DISCUSSION QUESTIONS

1. Is gentrification a strictly urban process? What are the consequences of broadening our definition of gentrification to include revitalization processes in nonurban locales?
2. Should we define gentrification by a common set of outcomes, causes, or dimensions of daily life?
3. Based on the arguments presented in the readings, when do you think gentrification began? What are the stakes of your answer to the question?
4. Which revitalization processes do you regard as distinct from gentrification?
5. How central are gentrifiers and longtime residents' demographic characteristics, such as their racial, ethnic, class, gender, or sexual identity, to your definition of gentrification?

ACTIVITIES

1. View the documentary *Flag Wars*. If your knowledge of gentrification were limited to the film, what definition of the process would you generate?
2. View the documentary *7th Street* about the gentrification of New York's Alphabet City. If your knowledge of gentrification were limited to the film, what definition of the process would you generate?

a. If you've viewed both of the above documentaries, consider how each influences your definition of gentrification. Can the same definition be applied to each case? Why or why not?

b. If you could film your own documentary about gentrification based on your personal definition of the process, which people, places, policies, and interactions would it document?

3. Read a novel set in a gentrifying neighborhood, such as Denis Lehane's *Mystic River* (2001) or Jonathan Lethem's *Fortress of Solitude* (2003). What language and imagery does the author use to describe gentrification? How do you think the author would define gentrification?

4. How do you define gentrification? Draft a definition and compare it to your classmates' definitions, as well as to the definitions presented in the readings. Why are your definitions different?

RESOURCES

Atkinson, R. 2003. "Introduction: Misunderstood Saviour or Vengeful Wrecker? The Many Meanings and Problems of Gentrification" *Urban Studies* 40 2343–2350.

Lees, L. 2007. "Progress in Gentrification Research?'" *Environment and Planning A* 39 228–234.

Slater, T., Curran, W., & Lees, L. 2004. "Gentrification Research: New Directions and Critical Scholarship" *Environment and Planning A* 36 1141–1150.

CHAPTER 1

Aspects of Change

Ruth Glass

I

London can never be taken for granted. The city is too vast, too complex, too contrary and too moody to become entirely familiar. And there are moments when well-known features of her townscape stand out surprisingly, as they might to a foreign tourist or to the expatriate who at last comes home.

From Kensington to King's Cross early on a June morning the sights and sounds of London just awakening have a novel clarity. The roads of Georgian and Victorian houses converted into flats are still packed with parked cars; the Espresso bars are still locked up; the new under-pass (or rather bottleneck) at Hyde Park Corner is still empty; the tall Hilton Hotel at Park Lane, recently finished, stands out clumsily; Marble Arch and Grosvenor Square, now deserted, where the American eagle is so conspicuous, are a reminder of days of international crisis, of protest demonstrations, of bewilderment and fear. In this region of 'high rise' office blocks, apartment houses, genteel shop windows and an occasional supermarket, prosperity is freshly painted on: there is an air of expectancy. But all that is left far behind already ten minutes later in the peeling plaster zone of Euston, where the monotony of narrow back streets, grimy and dreary, is only rarely interrupted by a once-Italian café or a more recent Indian restaurant; and then again by glimpses of a remarkable 'vertical feature'—the Post Office tower off Tottenham Court Road. Nor has King's Cross acquired a look very different from that it had twenty or thirty years ago. And yet it works differently. The armies of commuters who arrive every morning to work in Central London have grown steadily. And nowadays most of the porters are black or brown men from the West Indies.

At any hour, London in 1963 shows the juxtaposition of new and old, both in the fabric and in the structure of society. The innovations, just because they are unequally distributed and often apparently incongruous, are more visible than the old patches. Even so, they might well be deceptive. And for those of us whose own personal history is entangled with London's post-war history, it may be rather difficult to recognize all the signs of ageing, as well as of rejuvenation, in the face of the city. But some of these changes are unmistakable.

There is a gleam of affluence in most of Central London and in many of the suburbs—of a much more widespread affluence than has ever been there before. At least so it seems at first sight. It shows itself in an abundance of goods and gadgets, of cars and new buildings—in an apparently mounting flow of consumption. There are far more soft and hard drinking and eating places than there used to be (and they are open for longer hours). The shops are crammed with personal and household paraphernalia which had previously been neither in mass production nor for mass use. The wrapping and labelling of commodities—small or large, practical or ornamental, frozen or fresh, dehydrated or puffed up—have a new gloss. The luxuries of yesterday, or the imitations of yesterday's luxuries, have become the necessities of today for large sections of the population.

Together with—or rather because of—this new diversity of consumption, there is also, apparently, a new uniformity. Superficially, class distinctions in looks, clothes and in domestic equipment have narrowed considerably: differences in many of these respects are now more noticeably determined by age than by social status. Conventional terms of social categorization, such as 'black-coated worker' or 'white-collar worker', no longer have a straightforward descriptive value.

It is often said—by anyone who sees contemporary London after a considerable absence—that the city is in the process of being 'Americanized'. Indeed, judging from general impressions of the city's looks and standards of living, the contrast between Central London and mid-town Manhattan, for example, is no longer as striking as it used to be before, and immediately after, World War II. London is now decidedly a representative of the affluent Western world, with fewer individual characteristics than she had in a previous period. But in being just that, London is also experiencing, increasingly, the hardships inherent in that affluent world. And—typical again—it seems that she is not making a good job of coping with them.

As a place in which to settle, to work, to move about in, London has become acutely harassing and highly inefficient. This is largely the result of a long history of trial and error in urban development. The various notions or measures which have been adopted at different stages to make London smaller, and which in some respects have succeeded in doing so, have also made London larger. Just because the population size of the County has steadily declined—both through a voluntary and a planned dispersal—the size of the metropolitan area has been steadily expanded. People have been sent, or have wanted to go, farther and farther outwards, though many of them are still dependent, directly or indirectly, upon the employment and services located in Central London. All sorts of factors have contributed to this process of suburbanization—the increasing mobility of labour resulting from improvements in employment conditions and in transport; the general rise in standards of living; social aspirations (in particular, the frequent association of the idea of suburbia with that of 'respectability'); as well as general policies and schemes. But the total effect upon London has hardly been a satisfactory one. The problems of 'bigness' have not been solved; they have been shifted and changed.

Even now, the County is still losing population, while the number of jobs in Central London is still growing; and thus also the number of commuters who work in the centre. Their daily journeys are still becoming longer, more awkward, and more expensive in terms of individual and social costs. And these long journeys every morning and evening—whether of people or goods, by rail or road—impede short-distance traffic in the central area. In fact, though communications have become faster, more convenient and more varied, they have also become slower and more cumbersome. All day long, Central London is a zone of bottlenecks, of stand-stills, of almost frozen traffic. Any of the special occasions, special and yet part of the metropolitan routine—a Buckingham Palace garden party, a fall of snow, a State visit, the Chelsea flower show—can produce utter chaos. There is no room for manoeuvre.

But the traffic problem—the Number One problem at first sight—is only the most overt symptom of new incongruities in the habitat and society of London. Socially and ideologically, too, communications are strained: they have been both speeded up and obstructed. People travel about more; they see and hear more of events at home and abroad. And yet, driving in their cars, sitting in front of their television screens, they are more on their own than they used to be. While knowledge of science and technology is expanding rapidly, though at an unequal rate in different fields, it does so within the framework of a society which is remarkably slow in developing its capacities for self-recognition and rational organization. The acquisition of knowledge, moreover, in advancing as in stationary disciplines, is arranged so as to put a premium on departmentalization. Already, before his career has started, the sixth-form schoolboy or the student finds it difficult to leave his cell. On balance, have our horizons been widened or narrowed?

Social distances have become simultaneously both shorter and longer. There is a good deal of movement—pedestrian, vehicular, occupational. With the advance of technology, with the increase in the division of labour and of consumer expenditure, new occupations have developed, especially middle-class occupations. (Look at the advertisements in the 'quality' newspapers. Wanted: project engineer, production executive, system analyst, computer shift leader, sales promotion specialist, attitude tester, beauty operator, public relations manager, window-dresser, and many more of many different kinds.) Some of the old menial occupations are becoming extinct, or are likely to disappear. There has been some re-shuffling of social groups,

mainly again among the middle classes. New minority groups have appeared. But none of this movement is matched by an increase in genuine social mobility. The old class alignments are being maintained—or copied. And they may even at times be more noticeable, and be less taken for granted, than before, just because some of the conventional status distinctions have become blurred. Altogether, is there more or less social claustrophobia than there was in a previous period?

II

Although such questions have become commonplace, they cannot be avoided. We meet them wherever we go, certainly in London. All around us, we see so many contradictory tendencies; and the same phenomena are subject to contradictory interpretations. Perhaps this was always so, and it is the sharpened awareness of history in the making—on a scale, with a speed and complexity visibly greater than ever before—which directs the attention of some contemporary 'participant-observers' so strongly to the equivocal aspects of the current situation. But, be that as it may, if one does look at society as one finds it, here and now, as closely and widely as possible, one cannot help being preoccupied with the ambiguities in its conditions and prospects.

It could be said, for example, that Britain, in general—or London, in particular—has more social homogeneity than in the inter-war and immediate post-war periods. Millions of people from different social classes and localities consume the same diet of radio and television programmes, advertisements and films; they are subject to a national network of retail outlets, newspapers, public services, institutions and organizations; they uphold the same national symbols. Differences between modes of life in city, suburb and village have become fainter. There are not only daily, but also weekly and seasonal journeys to and fro—as a result of the increasing use of private transport and of holidays with pay. There is also more sameness in the physical environment both between and within areas of the country than there used to be. Urban diffusion—in ecnomic and cultural terms—was preceded, and is still accompanied, by the vast spread of suburbia, some of whose characteristics have been introduced in or near urban centers, as well as in the countryside. It had been the dream of nineteenth century British reformers—a dream revived and translated into concrete plans during the inter-war and immediate post-war years—to re-make cities in the image of idealized rustic settlements, and to introduce urban amenities into rural areas. This dream has not been an idle one. Urban, suburban and rural areas have thus been encouraged to merge into one another; and they have lost some of their differentiating features.

Similar effects have, moreover, been brought about by a combination of deliberate and incidental developments. The large programme of urban reconstruction and re-building since World War II has had the result of reducing the contrasts between rich and poor districts within the boundary of the present County. Indeed, some of the conventional distinctions have been reversed; the new homes of working class and lower middle class people, who are municipal tenants, are frequently superior in design and appearance to the older 'luxury flats' and expensive houses of private tenants or owner-occupiers. Local authority housing and ancillary schemes have so much improved the looks and amenities of several districts—in sections of Paddington, Kensington, Westminster and elsewhere—that private developers have been prompted to renovate adjacent streets. The days when the building of a municipal estate in a 'respectable' area was

bitterly resented, and when such an estate was ostracized by its better-off neighbours, are now past—at least in and around Central London.

When the *New Survey of London Life and Labour* was carried out in the late twenties, it was found in its review of 'forty years of change'—the forty years which had gone by since Charles Booth's voluminous first survey was begun—that the reduction of poverty had been greater in the western than in the eastern area.[1] In general, the distinction between east and west had been accentuated. But since then, this process has, apparently, not continued. Large areas of the East End have been transformed—in a manner which contributes a good deal to the prestige of municipal architecture, even if it is not invariably of a high standard. And while planning and public enterprise have played a positive part in diminishing the outward differences between London's residential districts, *laissez faire* has played a part also, though in the long run a negative one.

One by one, many of the working class quarters of London have been invaded by the middle classes—upper and lower. Shabby, modest mews and cottages—two rooms up and two down—have been taken over, when their leases have expired, and have become elegant, expensive residences. Larger Victorian houses, downgraded in an earlier or recent period—which were used as lodging houses or were otherwise in multiple occupation—have been upgraded once again. Nowadays, many of these houses are being sub-divided into costly flats or 'houselets' (in terms of the new real estate snob jargon). The current social status and value of such dwellings are frequently in inverse relation to their size, and in any case enormously inflated by comparison with previous levels in their neighbourhoods. Once this process of 'gentrification' starts in a district, it goes on rapidly until all or most of the original working class occupiers are displaced, and the whole social character of the district is changed. There is very little left of the poorer enclaves of Hampstead and Chelsea: in those boroughs, the upper-middle class take-over was consolidated some time ago. The invasion has since spread to Islington, Paddington, North Kensington—even to the 'shady' parts of Notting Hill—to Battersea, and to several other districts, north and south of the river. (The East End has so far been exempt.) And this is an inevitable development, in view of the demographic, economic and political pressures to which London, and especially Central London, has been subjected.

Competition for space has become more and more intense in London. Various factors combine to sharpen this competition—the 'natural increase' of commerce and related economic activities; the emergence of new occupations and pursuits; the demands for travelling and parking space made by the rapidly growing motorcar population;[2] the improvements and consequent spatial expansion of social, educational and ancillary services. The upward swing in standards of living, moreover, not only contributes to all the other space requirements, but also increases those of individual households, and helps to create more households. As real incomes and aspirations rise, as people get married earlier and live longer, existing households split up, and there is a higher ratio of households to population, with a consequent increased demand for separate dwellings.[3] Last but not least, the competition for space thus produced is bound to get out of hand, and lead to a spiral of land values, if it is neither anticipated nor controlled. And this is precisely what has happened.

The *Greater London Plan* of 1944[4] was prepared in a restrictionist mood—on premises inherited from a period of economic depression, when there were fears of, and also neo-malthusian hopes for, a population decline; and when it was thought that the metropolitan area could be rigidly contained. The plan did not take either the demographic or economic facts of life into account: it was based on the assumption that there would be a stationary population, economy and culture. It has hardly been a suitable framework for the guidance of development in a period of expansion. And while it has been (and is still) used as such, with various qualifications, its cardinal positive concept—that of genuine 'planning' in the public interest—has been increasingly abandoned. Since the fifties, town and country planning legislation has, in essence, been anti-planning legislation: the 1947 Act has been drastically amended; development rights have been de-nationalized; development values have been unfrozen; real estate speculation has thus been 'liberated'. These measures, together with the relaxation of rent control, have given the green light to the continuing inflation of property prices with which London, even more than other large cities, is afflicted.[5] In such circumstances, any district in or near London, however dingy or unfashionable before, is likely to become expensive; and London may quite soon be a city which illustrates the principle of the survival of the fittest—the financially fittest, who can still afford to work and live there.[6] (Not long ago, the then Housing Minister advised those who cannot pay the price to move out.) Thus London, always a 'unique city', may acquire a rare complaint. While the cores of other large cities in the world, especially of those in the United States, are decaying, and are becoming ghettoes of the 'underprivileged', London may soon be faced with an *embarras de richesse* in her central area—and this will prove to be a problem, too.

But whatever the consequences of such a surfeit of honey, the fact remains that the social geography of London shows some signs of a drawing together—the broad divisions are less striking than they were twenty or even ten years ago. And yet there are also contrary signs of a moving apart—of a new kind of diversification, which may well be equally, if not more, significant.

As standards of living rise and land values even more so, as old working class districts are reconstructed, and others are increasingly hemmed in, the remaining pockets of blight become denser. Some of these quarters, off the beaten track—which are low on the list of municipal development and not 'ripe' for private investment—are left to decay. They have been neglected for so long that they are taken for granted. Others, nearer the main routes, adjacent to expanding middle class areas, become lodging-house districts, where all sorts of people who have to keep, or who want to obtain, a foothold in Central London are crammed together—and frequently have to pay exorbitant rents for the privilege. Such districts cannot be so easily by-passed: they are quite often in the news; they figure in crime statistics; they are the places where the most notorious shark landlords operate; their mobile population, and especially the owners of their 'widowers' houses', have connexions with social groups at all levels, from the top to the bottom of the social scale. Not all the inhabitants of these 'zones of transition' are in fact poor. Here are people who must stay near their work in the centre, or who cannot afford to move to the suburbs. Here are families who are at the tail end of the municipal housing queue; and also those who are not eligible for such housing, or who cannot pay local authority rents. Here are immigrants from other parts of Britain or overseas who nowadays can find hardly any open doors—especially if their skin is coloured—and who have to take the left-overs of accommodation, however dingy, however expensive. They go to houses which are already crowded; several of them share a room to meet the cost. It is a motley collection of people who are pushed into these 'twilight' zones—long established

Londoners and newcomers; Europeans and Asians; the Irish, the West Indians, the Poles; families of 'respectable' manual and clerical workers; students; delinquents and prostitutes. All of them have one thing in common: their housing needs are being exploited; and the very frictions which their crowded, insecure situation creates tend to be exploited, too. It is in such districts that the many sub-cultures of London come together and yet remain estranged.

But the anachronistic slums and the tense zones of transition are not the only places in which the pluralism of London society is visible. Wherever we go, we can get glimpses of the many unfamiliar worlds in this one metropolitan constellation. We can see them in the mean streets, in luxury flats, along the roads of suburban ribbon development; in places like Eel Pie Island, where various cliques of teenagers congregate; in jazz clubs, coffee bars, Soho joints, and expense account restaurants; in the withdrawing rooms of earnest religious or political sects; at Speakers' Corner in Hyde Park or the Earls Court Road; at meetings in Trafalgar Square; in public libraries, senior common rooms, and at soirées of the Royal Society. We get an inkling of the existence of other remote and yet nearby worlds through migration statistics; through fascist news-sheets and 'nigger-baiting' scrawls on the walls of back alleys; through unsavoury court cases or complaints before rent tribunals; in reading Press items about witch rites, ghost hunts, visits from Martians, and take-over bids. And then again, we may hear of the 'hidden' societies through reports of hospital almoners, N.S.P.C.C. inspectors, or social workers who bring 'meals on wheels' to lonely old people. It is an amazing, still largely obscured, panorama that thus begins to be visible—a conglomeration of groups who move, so to speak, on separate tracks, even if they do meet occasionally at a station. And in this assembly, it is not only the marginal men who appear to be segregated—the atavistic, the cranky, the lunatic fringes, the various 'security risks', the backroom boys of business tycoons—but also the many inbred intellectual and artistic circles; the fraternities of the young; and large sections of the population whose mode of life is unknown because they live, anonymously, in secluded domesticity. They are not represented in the popular or highbrow serials.

> '*There are those who are in darkness*
> *And there are others in the light*
> *And sure one sees those in brightness*
> *Those in darkness are out of sight.*'[7]

What is this new pattern, and is it in fact new? There is some interlocking of social groups. Even so, the impression remains—and often it is the dominant one—that there is increasing segmentation. It seems that what is happening is neither an obliteration nor an accentuation of long established class cleavages, but the superimposition of a criss-cross web of social divisions, which has as yet been hardly recognized.

Indeed, it is difficult to trace this pattern just because it is so ambiguous and incoherent, neither tied together nor sharply divided. It is the pattern of a society which lacks both deliberate concord and straightforward conflict: it seems to consist of a tangle of sub-groups and sub-cultures which, however dissimilar, manage to co-exist, without much mutual awareness, in fairly self-contained compartments. Apparently, they can do so, at least at present, because they are lodged in a setting which is by and large sufficiently spacious to accommodate disparate elements, with partitions solid enough to muffle dissonant noises; which is sufficiently well provided with standardized supplies—of commodities, newsprint and verbiage—to camouflage differences among the consumers; and which is believed to be sufficiently hygienic to prevent epidemics of physical or social

pathology. Such are the comforts of society in an 'advanced' industrial economy, as seen nowadays in the largest city of the Commonwealth.

This society has been characterized by various adjectives—affluent, open, irresponsible. There is inertia and complacency; there is also a good deal of talk about social malaise, decline of morals, lack of purpose, disintegration of 'community'. Dichotomous terms are fashionable once again—the 'two nations' (used nowadays in referring to the South and North of Britain); the 'two cultures'. Even the alien word *Angst* has been introduced into the vocabulary of editorials. No doubt, it is a confused society, or rather a series of societies—both anxious and self-satisfied; and the various epithets applied to it do not make confusion less confounded. They have quickly gained currency as clichés and even as *idées fixes*, which can be dismissed, or which can be accepted as substitutes for more thorough, perhaps more unpalatable, analyses. Anyhow, the need for such analyses is only intermittently evident: in general, confusion is more real than is apparent. It tends to be concealed by the whole apparatus of communications that gives the impression of clarity, candour and close-ups. The apparent mobility of passengers, goods and news; the weighty comments and tactful gossip in some sections of the Press; the intimate 'revelations' in others; the presence of faces and places from near and far at the domestic fireside—all this has promoted illusions of 'togetherness'; of 'mingling with the mighty' (without having to go to Madame Tussaud's); of watching a full display of the social scene.[8] And as the image of the frank and free society is so assiduously promoted, there is bound to be severe disappointment whenever it is manifestly fictitious. But it is only on rare critical occasions that more than a few even begin to know what they do not know.

The major influences to which we are nowadays subjected can have, and do have, both integrating and divisive effects. And it seems that it is the latter, however disguised, which are predominant. [. . .]

All these tendencies, and their manifold ramifications, are reflected in London—more plainly and thus also more confusingly here than elsewhere in Britain. London's physical structure has been influenced by the ups and downs of post-war history—by the earlier spurts of planning in the public interest, and by the later phases of *laissez-faire*, profitable for particular private interests. Large-scale municipal development remains as the testimony of the late forties and early fifties, and is here and there still being rounded off. The growing array of commercial and residential showpieces—of imitation 'towers' which are generally more imposing in price than in height or design—represents the latter period. And so do the forgotten slums, the 'half-way houses' for homeless people, and the sordid 'zones of transition' which are wedged in between the expanding well-to-do districts.

Change and stagnation exist side by side. Despite war-time destruction and the shifts in post-war direction, the general land-use map of the County and its fringes has been a remarkably persistent one. The residential quarters and open spaces, the various kinds of offices, retail trade, entertainment, of professional and social services—all these have largely remained, or have been re-established, in the same locations in which they were long ago. It is the manufacturing industries which have moved; their expansion has taken place in the outer areas; the small workshops have tended to disappear. There has thus been some sorting-out of land use in areas where homes, commercial and industrial establishments were crowded together. And the more detailed maps show other revisions as well—changes within each of the broad 'land-use classes', as well as changes in the occupancy and appearance of the buildings which represent the various categories of land use. Independent retailers have given way to chain stores; the sites of small food shops have been taken by supermarkets, and those of shabby Italian restaurants by Espresso bars. The social status of many residential areas is being uplifted. Offices are increasingly housed in 'prestige' buildings; and there is a tendency to reserve the scarce costly space available for people in 'prestige' occupations, while the more menial clerical workers are replaced by machines, or are 'decentralized'. (This tendency, characteristic of central areas of high land values, is already far more advanced in American cities, especially in Manhattan.) In general, moreover, the process of differentiation in land use has continued. The districts of Harley Street, Fleet Street and Bloomsbury, for example, have become even more specialized: they are now definite enclaves of the particular functions with which their names have long been synonymous. (Similarly, antique dealers have taken over most of the shops in streets, as in parts of Kensington, in which there were a few well known antique shops before.) Altogether there has thus been a great deal of displacement. All those who cannot hold their own in the sharp competition for space—the small enterprises, the lower ranks of people, the odd men out—are being pushed away. And although the squeeze is becoming tighter still, only sporadic efforts have been made so far to counteract it. Not much has been done to utilize the existing space more economically, and to provide more space—to dig down (for car parks and tunnels); to build upwards; to reconstruct whole districts and roads, like layer cakes, on several levels. [. . .]

Despite the considerable shifts of population, of fortunes and policies, the socio-geographical pattern of Greater London has, therefore, been a rather stubborn one.

It still presents the divisions inherent in a society with an acknowledged class structure—and in a society, moreover, whose inherent conflicts have been averted or softened because upper class modes of living were regarded less with enmity than with curiosity; they were taken as models to be imitated, and handed down from the middle to the lower groups of the social hierarchy. London's suburban sprawl is indicative of such imitations. Already, during the nineteenth century, the main status symbol of the aspiring middle classes was some version of the aristocratic country house (or better still the acquisition of the genuine article); later on, white-collar and manual workers in steady employment asserted their position in a suburban villa—or, like Mr Pooter, in a substitute for a suburban villa. It was mainly the poorer sections of the metropolitan working class—especially the people of the East End and of the southern riverside boroughs—who wanted to stay behind in 'good old London', and who have throughout retained their loyalties to their own districts. But even they have had to participate increasingly in the suburban exodus.

So London has grown in a conservative fashion, by a process of aggregation, producing more of the same. In the course of expansion, the old social boundaries have been perpetuated and extended. Indeed— as described by W. Ashworth in the case of suburban development in Essex—in general, both the scale and nature of London's expansion have had the effect of inhibiting, rather than of encouraging, radical changes in socio-geographical alignments.

Recently, however, there have been signs of new tendencies, and thus of new combinations and of new splits in the established pattern. Upper class standards are seen to be more ambiguous, and are no longer so widely accepted as models as they were before. There are, moreover, shifts in the orientation of the upper and middle classes themselves: their anti-urban bias, in particular, has been substantially modified. Similarly, the higher ranks of the working class, whose ambitions were previously focused upon suburbia, have begun to change their minds. The alterations in the domestic economy of all these groups; the earlier establishment of households as a result of younger marriages; the growing proportion of married women in employment; the difficulties and rising cost of journeys to work—all these factors contribute to a switch from suburban to urban aspirations.[9] Especially among the vast contingent of commuters who arrive every morning in Central London, there are many who would now much prefer to live nearer to the core of the London labour market. Thus although the drift to the suburbs is continuing, it has become to a considerable extent an involuntary one—dictated by the increasingly acute shortage of reasonably priced accommodation in or around the County of London.[10] In current circumstances this new demand for homes near the metropolitan centre is bound to remain largely unsatisfied. For it has arisen, and it is growing, at a time when the de-control of property values and rents has made private enterprise predominant in urban development;[11] and when the resulting new spurt in real estate speculation has greatly intensified the competition for, and the pressure on, space. [. . .]

NOTES

1. Hubert Llewellyn Smith, ed., *The New Survey of London Life and Labour*, 9 vols., 1930–35. See Vol. VI, *Survey of Social Conditions, the Western area*, pp. 1–28.
2. During the past twelve years, the number of motor car licences issued by the London County Council has more than trebled: from 128,575 licences (one per 8.7 households) in 1950 to 408,830 (one per 2.7 households in the L.C.C. area) in 1962.
3. From 1931 to 1961, average household size declined from 3.69 to 2.89 persons per household

in the County of London, and similarly in Greater London (the Conurbation). Thus while there was a decrease of 27 per cent in the total population of the County during that period, there was only a decrease of 7 per cent in the number of actual separate households—quite apart from that of 'concealed' households who could not establish themselves as separate units because they could not find separate dwellings of their own. (If most of the latter had in fact split off, the total number of households in the County would have remained stable, or would even have slightly increased.) During that period of thirty years, the population of the London Conurbation has remained almost stationary (there was a drop of one per cent only); but the number of actual separate households (excluding 'concealed' households) has increased by 25 per cent.

4. Patrick Abercrombie, *Greater London Plan, 1944.*

5. The Town and Country Planning Act, 1947, nationalized both development rights and post-1947 development values; through various devices, it stabilized land values at the 1947 level; it stipulated that a 'development charge' had to be paid into the public purse for the 'betterment' of land values accruing from post-1947 'development' in the statutory sense. These measures helped to create a coherent planning system: they were essential counterparts of the provisions for development control laid down in the Act. Without them, such control is bound to defeat its purpose: in particular, the permissions for 'development' (given by local planning authorities) would be bound to lead to land speculation; to a rise in the value of any land whose development has been sanctioned, and can be profitably carried out; and thus also, of course, to the build-up of considerable pressures to modify the operations of development control so that they yield, generally, the maximum private profits in the use of land. Subsequent legislation amending the 1947 Act has had the very effect, first, of inviting such pressures; and then of giving way to them. Following a White Paper issued by the first post-war Conservative Government (in November 1952), the Town and Country Planning Act of 1953 abolished the development charge (and also certain compensation provisions of the 1947 Act). The amending Act of 1954 provided (with a number of exceptions) that compensation would be payable for the prevention or severe restriction of development imposed through planning control. This legislation was the first step in the de-nationalization of development rights and values; and in the restoration of a free market in land. The Town and Country Planning Act,

1959, completed the process. While previously the principle of stabilizing land values at the 1947 level was still maintained—though with significant modifications—the 1959 Act abolished the principle. In essence, the Act stipulated that land bought by public authorities through compulsory acquisition—or by agreement instead of compulsory acquisition—should be paid for on the basis of the full current market value of the land, including its full development value at the time of acquisition. This was not (as it seemed to many people at the time) a highly technical, rather innocuous measure. It has had, predictably, far-reaching consequences. Since then, the free market in land has been generally restored. Similarly, a free market in rents has been largely restored, mainly through the Rent Act, 1957. The weakening of public control in all matters of urban development (in the broadest sense) brought about by this legislation has been accelerated, moreover, by a variety of other statutory and administrative measures—such as reductions in the real value of Exchequer contributions to housing subsidies (for municipal housing); by the increasing stringency in local authority finance; and by the growing tendency to delegate various functions, including planning fuctions, to the smaller local authorities. (The Town and Country Planning Acts here mentioned, together with other relevent statutes or sections of statutes, have been consolidated in the Town and Country Planning Act, 1962. The provisions concerning compulsory acquisition are also consolidated in the Land Compensation Act, 1961.)

6. This kind of trend has cumulative effects. As land values rise, the scarce expensive commercial space has to be allocated increasingly to the higher levels of managerial and executive staffs. Thus already in 1951, Central London had a disproportionate share of jobs for men in occupations classified in the Census as belonging to social classes I and II. These were the people who at that time still lived predominantly in the suburbs, and had to travel daily to their places of work in the centre. Consequently, the proportion of these 'upper' social classes was then considerably higher among the daytime male occupied population of the central, East End and South Bank employment zones than among the nighttime resident male population of these areas. But as journeys to work become more harassing, it is such upper and middle class people, especially, who think of acquiring—and who indeed need and can afford to acquire—some sort of a home, if only a *pied à terre*, near their places

of work. Hence there is a mounting spiral: the competition for both commercial and residential space is bound to grow; and land values and rents are bound to rise still further—so long as they remain decontrolled.

7. Bertold Brecht's *Threepenny Opera*, the final verse of the Moritat.

8. In some circles—well beyond Fleet Street, Soho, Bloomsbury and Hampstead—the revival of political satire, a by-product of the current period of transition as it has been of similar periods elsewhere, also contributes to such illusions. Satire, though by no means the same as political critique, can so easily be regarded as evidence of uninhibited critique—by and for 'insiders'.

9. This change from suburban to urban aspirations is, moreover, both reflected and accentuated by a corresponding (though not unanimous) trend in the attitudes of architects and town planners. (This latter trend gained strength mainly through the Festival of Britain in 1951—through its exhibitions at the South Bank and in Lansbury, . . .) And the varied examples of genuinely 'urban design', which have accordingly been provided by architects—especially by those working for public authorities—have in turn encouraged pro-urban orientations among groups of potential 'clients'.

10. The steady decline in the population of the County of London has continued in the decade 1951 to 1961; and it is apparently still continuing. During this last decade, the out-county rings of the Conurbation (and the Conurbation as a whole) have also begun to show a population decline—for the first time in this century. The Conurbation itself has become an 'inner' area. The frontiers of the still-expanding 'Greater London' are being pushed even further outwards.

11. Private enterprise is certainly predominant in non-residential development, and increasingly also, once again, in the provision of housing. In 1951, 12 per cent of all new permanent dwellings built during that year were provided by private enterprise; in 1961, the comparable figure had risen to 64 per cent. (Thus conversely, the share of public authorities in the provision of new housing had dropped from 88 per cent to 36 per cent.) So far, the increase in the share of private enterprise housing has not been quite so steep in the London Conurbation as in the country as a whole; nor has it been equally distributed throughout the Conurbation.

CHAPTER 2

A Short History of Gentrification

Neil Smith

[. . .] Although the emergence of gentrification proper can be traced to the post-war cities of the advanced capitalist world, there are significant precursors. In his well-known poem, "The Eyes of the Poor," Charles Baudelaire wraps a proto-gentrification narrative into a poem of love and estrangement. Set in the late 1850s and early 1860s, amid Baron Haussmann's destruction of working-class Paris and its monumental rebuilding (see Pinkney 1972), the poem's narrator tries to explain to his lover why he feels so estranged from her. He recalls a recent incident when they sat outside a "dazzling" cafe, brightly lit outside by gaslight, making its debut. The interior was less alluring, decorated with the ostentatious kitsch of the day; hounds and falcons, "nymphs and goddesses bearing piles of fruits, pâtés and game on their heads," an extravagance of "all history and all mythology pandering to gluttony." The cafe stood at the corner of a new boulevard which was still strewn with rubble, and as the lovers swoon in each other's eyes, a bedraggled poor family—father, son and baby—stops in front of them and stares large-eyed at the spectacle of consumption. "How beautiful it is!" the son seems to be saying, although no words were uttered: "But it is a house where only people who are not like us can go." The narrator feels "a little ashamed of our glasses and decanters, too big for our thirst," and for a moment connects in empathy with "the eyes of the poor." Then he turns back to his lover's eyes, "dear love, to read *my* thoughts there." But instead he sees only disgust in her eyes. She bursts out: "Those people with their great saucer eyes are unbearable! Can't you go tell the manager to get them away from here?" (Baudelaire 1947 edn. no. 26).

Marshall Berman (1982: 148–150) uses this poem to introduce his discussion of "modernism in the streets," equating this early *embourgeoisement* of Paris (Gaillard 1977; see also Harvey 1985a) with the rise of bourgeois modernity. Much the same connection was made at the time, albeit across the English Channel. Eighty years before Robert Park and E. Burgess (Park *et al.* 1925) developed their influential "concentric ring" model for the urban structure of Chicago, Friedrich Engels made a similar generalization concerning Manchester:

> Manchester contains, at its heart, a rather extended commercial district, perhaps half a mile long and about as broad, and consisting almost completely of offices and warehouses. Nearly the whole district is abandoned by dwellers. . . . This district is cut through by certain main thoroughfares upon which the vast traffic concentrates, and in which the ground level is lined with brilliant shops.

. . . With the exception of this commercial district, all Manchester proper [comprises] unmixed working-people's quarters, stretching like a girdle, averaging a mile and a half in breadth, around the commercial district. Outside, beyond this girdle, lives the upper and middle bourgeoisie.

(Engels 1975 edn.: 84–85)

Engels had a keen sense of the social effects of this urban geography, especially the efficient concealment of "grime and misery" from "the eyes of the wealthy men and women" residing in the outer ring. But he also witnessed the so-called "Improvements" of mid-nineteenth-century Britain, a process for which he chose the term "Haussmann." "By the term 'Haussmann,'" he explained, "I do not mean merely the specifically Bonapartist manner of the Parisian Haussmann"—the Prefect of Paris, who was building boulevards through the "closely built workers' quarters and lining them on both sides with big luxurious buildings," for the strategic purpose of "making barricade fighting more difficult," and for turning "the city into a luxury city pure and simple" (Engels 1975 edn.: 71). Rather, he suggested, this was a more general process:

By "Haussmann" I mean the practice, which has now become general, of making breaches in the working-class quarters of our big cities, particularly in those which are centrally situated, irrespective of whether this practice is occasioned by considerations of public health and beautification or by demand for big, centrally located business premises or by traffic requirements. . . . No matter how different the reasons may be, the result is everywhere the same: the most scandalous alleys and lanes disappear to the accompaniment of lavish self-glorification by the bourgeoisie on account of this tremendous success.

(Engels 1975 edn.: 71)

Earlier examples of gentrification have been cited. Roman Cybriwsky, for example, provides a nineteenth-century print depict-ing a family's displacement from a tenement in Nantes in 1685. He reports that the Edict of Nantes, signed by Henry IV in 1598, guaranteed poor Huguenots certain rights including access to housing, but when the edict was revoked nearly a century later by Louis XIV, wholesale displacement took place at the hands of landlords, merchants and wealthier citizens (Cybriwsky 1980). Be that as it may, something more akin to contemporary gentrification made an appearance in the middle of the nineteenth century, whether known by the name "embourgeoisement," "Haussmann" or the "Improvements." It was hardly "general," to use Engels' word, but sporadic, and it was surely restricted to Europe since few cities in North America, Australia or elsewhere had the extent of urban history to provide whole neighborhoods of disinvested stock. Chicago was barely ten years old when Engels made his first observations of Manchester; and as late as 1870, there was little urban development in Australia. The closest parallel in North America might be the process whereby one generation of wooden buildings was quickly torn down to be replaced by brick structures and these in turn—at least in the older east-coast cities—were demolished to make room for larger tenements or single-family houses. It would be misleading to consider this gentrification, however, insofar as such redevelopment was an integral part of the outward geographical expansion of the city and not, as with gentrification, a spatial reconcentration.

Even as late as the 1930s and 1940s, gentrification remained a sporadic occurrence, but by this time precursor experiences of gentrification were also turning up in the United States. The flavor remained resolutely European and aristocratic, however, laced through with liberal guilt. The spirit of the enterprise is well captured in a recent retrospective by Maureen Dowd, recalling the Georgetown scene in Washington, DC's most gentrified neighborhood through the eyes of patrician hostess turned historian Susan Mary Alsop:

> They gentrified Georgetown, an unfashionable working-class neighborhood with a large black contingent. As Mrs. Alsop told *Town and Country* magazine: "The blacks kept their houses so well. All of us had terrible guilt in the 30's and 40's for buying places so cheaply and moving them out.
>
> The gentry and the hostesses faded through the 1970s.
>
> (Dowd 1993: 46)

Similar scenes were being lived out in Boston's Beacon Hill (Firey 1945), albeit with a different local flavor, or for that matter in London, although of course genteel society had in no way relinquished its claim to many London neighborhoods in quite the same fashion.

So what makes all of these experiences "precursors" to a gentrification process that began in earnest in the postwar period? The answer lies in both the extent and the systemic nature of central and inner-city rebuilding and rehabilitation beginning in the 1950s. The nineteenth-century experiences in London and Paris were unique, resulting from the confluence of a class politics aimed at the threatening working classes and designed to consolidate bourgeois control of the city, and a cyclical economic opportunity to profit from rebuilding. The "Improvements" were certainly replicated in different ways and at a lesser scale in some other cities—Edinburgh, Berlin, Madrid, for example—but, as in London and Paris, they were historically discrete events. There are no systematic "improvements" in London in the first decades of the twentieth century, or a continued *embourgeoisement* of Paris in the same period systematically altering the urban landscape. As regards the incidences of gentrification in the mid-twentieth century, these were so sporadic that the process was unknown in the majority of large cities. It was very much an exception to larger urban geographic processes. Its agents, as in the case of Georgetown or Beacon Hill, were generally from such a limited social stratum and in many cases so wealthy that they could afford to thumb their patrician noses at the mere dictates of the urban land market— or at least mold the local market to their wonts.

This all begins to change in the postwar period, and it is no accident that the word "gentrification" is coined in the early 1960s. In Greenwich Village in New York, where gentrification was associated with a nascent counterculture; in Glebe in Sydney, where sustained disinvestment, rental deregulation, an influx of southern European immigrants, and the emergence of a middle-class resident action group all conspired toward gentrification (B. Engels 1989); in Islington in London where the process was relatively decentralized; and in dozens of other large cities in North America, Europe and Australia, gentrification began to occur. And nor was this process long confined simply to the largest cities. By 1976, one study concluded that nearly half of the 260 US cities with a population of more than 50,000 were experiencing gentrification (Urban Land Institute 1976). Barely twelve years after Ruth Glass had coined the term, it was no longer just New York, London and Paris that were being gentrified, but Brisbane and Dundee, Bremen and Lancaster, PA.

Gentrification today is ubiquitous in the central and inner cities of the advanced capitalist world. As unlikely a city as Glasgow, simultaneously a symbol and stronghold of working-class grit and politics, was sufficiently gentrified by 1990, in a process fueled by an aggressive local state, to be adopted as "European City of Culture" (Jack 1984; Boyle 1992). Pittsburgh and Hoboken are perhaps US equivalents. In Tokyo, the central ward of Shinjuku, once a meeting place for artists and intellectuals, has become a "classic battleground" of gentrification amid a rampaging real estate market (Ranard 1991). Likewise Montparnasse in Paris, Prague's response to an unleashed real estate market since 1989 has been torrid gentrification, almost on the scale of Budapest's (Sýkora 1993), while in Madrid it was the end of Franco's fascism and a comparative democratization of urban government that cleared the way for reinvestment (Vázquez 1992). In the Christianhavn area around the experimental "free city" of Christiania on Copenhagen's waterfront (Nitten 1992), and in the back streets of Granada adjacent to the Alhambra, gentrification proceeds in tense affinity with tourism. Even outside the most developed continents—North America, Europe and Australasia—the process has begun to take place. In Johannesburg, the gentrification of the 1980s (Steinberg *et al.* 1992) has been significantly attenuated by a new kind of "white flight" since the election of the ANC in April 1994 (Murray 1994: 44–48), but the process has also affected smaller cities such as Stellenbosch (Swart 1987). In São Paulo a very different pattern of disinvestment in land has taken place (Castillo 1993), but a modest renovation and reinvestment in the Tatuapé district accommodates small business owners and professionals who work in the central business district but who can no longer afford the rapidly inflating prices of the most prestigious central enclaves such as Jardin. Much of this redevelopment involves "verticalization" (Aparecida 1994) as land served by basic services is scarce. More generally, the "middle zones" around São Paulo and Rio de Janeiro are experiencing development and redevelopment for the middle class (Queiroz and Correa 1995: 377–379).

Not only has gentrification become a widespread experience since the 1960s, then, but it is also systematically integrated into wider urban and global processes, and this too differentiates it from earlier, more discrete experiences of "spot rehabilitation." If the process that Ruth Glass observed in London at the beginning of the 1960s, or even the planned remake of Philadelphia's Society Hill during the same period, represented somewhat isolated developments in the land and housing markets, they did not remain so. By the 1970s gentrification was clearly becoming an integral residential thread in a much larger urban restructuring. As many urban economies in the advanced capitalist world experienced the dramatic loss of manufacturing jobs and a parallel increase in producer services, professional employment and the expansion of so-called "FIRE" employment (Finance, Insurance, Real Estate), their whole urban geography underwent a concomitant restructuring. Condominium and cooperative conversions in the US, tenure conversions in London and international capital investments in central-city luxury accommodations were increasingly the residential component of a larger set of shifts that brought an office boom to London's Canary Wharf (A. Smith 1989) and New York's Battery Park City (Fainstein 1994) and the construction of new recreational and retail landscapes from Sydney's Darling Harbour to Oslo's AckerBrygge. These economic shifts were often accompanied by political shifts as cities found themselves competing in the global market, shorn of much of the traditional protection of national state institutions and regulations: deregulation, privatization of housing and urban services, the dismantling of welfare services—in short, the remarketization of public functions—quickly followed, even in bastions of social democracy such as Sweden. In this context, gentrification became a hallmark of the emerging "global city" (Sassen 1991), but was equally a presence in national and regional centers that were themselves experiencing an economic, political and geographical restructuring (M. P. Smith 1984; Castells 1985; Beauregard 1989).

In this regard, what we think of as gentrification has itself undergone a vital transition. If in the early 1960s it made sense to think of gentrification very much in the quaint and specialized language of residential rehabilitation that Ruth Glass employed, this is no longer so today. In my own research I began by making a strict distinction between gentrification (which involved rehabilitation of existing stock) and redevelopment that involved wholly new construction (N. Smith 1979a), and at a time when gentrification was distinguishing itself from large-scale urban renewal this made some sense. But I no longer feel that it is such a useful distinction. Indeed 1979 was already a bit late for this distinction. How, in the larger context of changing social geographies, are we to distinguish adequately between the rehabilitation of nineteenth-century housing, the construction of new condominium towers, the opening of festival markets to attract local and not so local tourists, the proliferation of wine bars—and boutiques for everything—and the construction of modern and postmodern office buildings employing thousands of professionals, all looking for a place to live (see, for example, A. Smith, 1989)? This after all describes the new landscapes of downtown Baltimore or central Edinburgh, waterfront Sydney or riverside Minneapolis. Gentrification is no longer about a narrow and quixotic oddity in the housing market but has become the leading residential edge of a much larger endeavor: the class remake of the central urban landscape. It would be anachronistic now to exclude redevelopment from the rubric of gentrification, to assume that the gentrification of the city was restricted to the recovery of an elegant history in the quaint mews and alleys of old cities, rather than bound up with a larger restructuring (Smith and Williams 1986).

Having stressed the ubiquity of gentrification at the end of the twentieth century, and its direct connection to fundamental processes of urban economic, political and geographical restructuring, I think it is important to temper this vista with a sense of context. It would be foolish to think that the partial geographical reversal in the focus of urban reinvestment implies the converse, the end of the suburbs. Suburbanization and gentrification are certainly interconnected. The dramatic suburbanization of the urban landscape in the last century or more provided an alternative geographical locus for capital accumulation and thereby encouraged a comparative disinvestment at the center—most intensely so in the US. But there is really no sign that the rise of gentrification has diminished contemporary suburbanization. Quite the opposite. The same forces of urban restructuring that have ushered new landscapes of gentrification to the central city have also transformed the suburbs. The recentralization of office, retail, recreation and hotel functions has been accompanied by a parallel decentralization which has led to much more functionally integrated suburbs with their own more or less urban centres—edge cities as they have been called (Garreau 1991). If suburban development has in most places been more volatile since the 1970s in response to the cycles of economic expansion and contraction, suburbanization still represents a more powerful force than gentrification in the geographical fashioning of the metropolis.

From the 1960s to the 1990s, however, as academic and political critiques of suburbanization were mounting, gentrification for many came to express an extraordinary optimism, warranted or otherwise, concerning the future of the city. The urban uprisings and social movements of the 1960s notwithstanding, gentrification represented a wholly unpredicted novelty in the urban landscape, a new set of urban processes that took on immediate symbolic importance. The contest over gentrification represented a struggle not just for new and old urban spaces but for the symbolic political power to determine the urban future. The contest was as intense in the newspapers as it was in the streets, and for every defense of gentrification such as that by the Real Estate Board of New York there was an assault against gentrification-induced displacement, rent increases and neighborhood change (see, for example, Barry and Derevlany 1987). But the contest over gentrification was also played out in the usually more bromidic pages of academic journals and books. [...]

REFERENCES

Aparecida de Souza, M. A. (1994) *A Identidade da Metrópole*, São Paulo: Editora da Universidade de São Paulo.

Barry, J. and Derevlany, J. (1987) *Yuppies Invade My House at Dinnertime*, Hoboken: River Publishing.

Baudelaire, C. (1947) *Paris Spleen*, New York: New Directions.

Beauregard, R. (1989) *Economic Restructuring and Political Response*, Urban Affairs Annual Reviews 34, Newbury Park, Calif.: Sage Publications.

Berman, M. (1982) *All That Is Solid Melts into Air: The Experience of Modernity*, New York: Simon and Schuster.

Boyle, M. (1992) "The cultural politics of Glasgow, European City of Culture: making sense of the role of the local state in urban regeneration," unpublished Ph.D. dissertation, Edinburgh University.

Castillo, R. (1993) "A fragmentato da terra. Propriedade fundisria absoluta e espaco mercadoria no municipio de São Paulo," unpublished Ph.D. dissertation, Universidade de São Paulo.

Cybriwsky, R. (1980) "Historical evidence of gentrification," unpublished MS, Department Geography, Temple University.

Dowd, M. (1993) "The WASP descendancy," *New York Times Magazine* October 31: 46–48.

Engels, B. (1989) "The gentrification of Glebe: the residential restructuring of an inner Sydney suburb, 1960 to 1986," unpublished Ph.D. dissertation, University of Sydney.

Engels, F. (1975 edn.) *The Housing Question*, Moscow: Progress Publishers.

Fainstein, S. (1994) *The City Builders: Property, Politics and Planning in London and New York*, Oxford: Basil Blackwell.

Firey, W. (1945) "Sentiment and symbolism as ecological variables," *American Sociological Review* 10: 140–148.

Gaillard, J. (1977) *Paris: La Ville*, Paris: H. Champion.

Garreau, J. (1991) *Edge City: Life on the Frontier*, New York: Doubleday.

Harvey, D. (1985) *Consciousness and the Urban Experience: Studies in the History and Theory of Capitalist Urbanization*, Oxford: Basil Blackwell.

Jack, I. (1984) "The repackaging of Glasgow," *Sunday Times Magazine*, December 2.

Murray, M. J. (1994) *The Revolution Deferred: The Painful Birth of Post-apartheid South Africa*, London: Verso.

Nitten. (1992) *Christiania Tourist Guide*, Nitten: Copenhagen.

Park, R. E., Burgess, E. W. and McKenzie, R. (1925) *The City*, Chicago: University of Chicago Press.

Pinkney, D. H. (1972) *Napoleon III and the Rebuilding of Paris*. Princeton, N.J.: Princeton University Press.

Queiroz Ribeiro, L. C. and Correa do Lago, L. (1995) "Restructuring in large Brazilian cities: the center/periphery model," *International Journal of Urban and Regional Research* 19: 369–382.

Ranard, A. (1991) "An artists' oasis in Tokyo gives way to gentrification," *International Herald Tribune* January 4.

Sassen, S. (1991) *The Global City*, Princeton, N.J.: Princeton University Press.

Smith, A. (1989) "Gentrification and the spatial contribution of the state: the restructuring of London's Docklands," *Antipode* 21, 3: 232–260.

Smith, M. P. (ed.) (1984) *Cities in Transformation: Class, Capital and the State*, Urban Affairs Annual Reviews 26. Newbury Park. Calif.: Sage Publication.

Smith, N. (1979) "Toward a theory of gentrification: a back to the city movement by capital not people," *Journal of the American Planning Association* 45: 538–548.

Steinberg, J., van Zyl, P. and Bond, P. (1992) "Contradictions in the transition from urban apartheid: barriers to gentrification in Johannesberg," in D. M. Smith (ed.) *The Apartheid City and Beyond: Urbanization and Social Change in South Africa*, London: Routledge.

Swart. P. (1987) "Gentrification as an urban phenomenon in Stellenbosch, South Africa," *Geo-Stell* 11: 13–18.

Sýkora, L. (1993) "City in transition: the role of rent gaps in Prague's revitalization," *Tijdschrift voor Economische en Sociale Geografie* 84: 281–293.

Urban Land Institute. (1976) *New Opportunities for Residential Development in Central Cities*, Report No. 25, Washington, D.C.: The Institute.

Vazquez, C. (1992) "Urban policies and gentrification trends in Madrid's inner city," *Netherlands Journal of Housing and Environmental Research* 7, 4: 357–376.

CHAPTER 3

Gentrification as Market and Place

Sharon Zukin

[…] Gentrification refers to a profound spatial restructuring in several senses. It refers, first, to an expansion of the *downtown*'s physical area, often at the expense of the *inner city*. More subtly, it suggests a diffusion outward from the geographical center of downtown's *cultural* power. Ultimately, gentrification—a process that seems to reassert a purely *local* identity—represents downtown's social transformation in terms of an *international* market culture.

Gentrification is commonly understood in a much narrower sense. Not only does it generally refer to housing, especially the housing choice of some members of a professional and managerial middle class, it usually describes this choice in individualistic terms. Yet the small events and individual decisions that make up a specific spatial process of gentrification feed upon a larger social transformation. Each neighborhood's experience of gentrification has its own story—yet every downtown has its "revitalized" South End (in Boston), Quality Hill (in Kansas City), or Goose Island (in Chicago). Regardless of topography, building stock, and even existing populations, gentrification persists as a collective effort to appropriate the center for elements of a new urban middle class.*

The notion of gentrifiers as "urban pioneers" is properly viewed as an ideological justification of middle-class appropriation. Just as white settlers in the nineteenth century forced Native Americans from their traditional grounds, so gentrifiers, developers, and new commercial uses have cleared the downtown "frontier" of existing populations.[1] This appropriation is coordinated, logically enough, with a local expansion of jobs and facilities in business services. While some of these jobs have decentralized to the suburbs, the city's economy as a whole has shifted toward finance, entertainment, tourism, communications, and their business suppliers. Yet neither corporate expansion nor gentrification has altered a general trend of urban economic decline, decreasing median household income, and income inequality. Instead, gentrification makes inequality more visible by fostering a new juxtaposition of landscape and vernacular, creating "islands of renewal in seas of decay."[2]

Reinvestment in housing in the center relies on capital disinvestment since 1945 (or, more accurately, since 1929) that made a supply of "gentrifiable" building stock available. But it also reflects a demand for such building stock that was shaped by a cultural shift. This in turn represents a "reflexive" consumption that is based on higher education and a related expansion of consumers of both high culture and trendy style: these are potential gentrifiers.[3]

The private-market investments of gentrification effectively took over the role of clearing out the center just at the point when public programs of urban renewal ran out of federal funding and alienated supporters from every racial group and social class. Gentrifiers, moreover, often used noninstitutional sources of capital, including inheritance, family loans, personal savings, and the sweat equity of their own renovation work. Gentrification thus constituted a transition in both the mode of downtown development—from the public to the private sector, from large to small-scale projects, from new construction to rehabilitation—and the source of investment capital.

At the same time, the entire political economy of the center city was changing, the result of a long structural process of deindustrialization and cyclical decline in property values. Large manufacturers had moved out of the center since the 1880s, arguing that the multistory arrangement of the buildings and congested streets was functionally obsolete. Dependent on horizontal layout of production processes, truck deliveries, and automobile commuting, manufacturers preferred new green-field plants in suburban locations. Suburban land prices, taxes, and wages also exerted an appeal. But the small manufacturers who remained in the center, often concentrated in late-nineteenth-century loft buildings downtown, paid rents so low they seemed anachronistic. Although they had been hit severely during the 1960s by competition from overseas production and import penetration, such centrally located activities as apparel manufacturing and printing continued to thrive in low-rent clusters near customers, competitors, and suppliers. In New York, they also benefited from mass transit lines that connected downtown and midtown Manhattan to more distant working-class areas where low-wage, often immigrant and minority workers lived.

Despite their economic viability and historic association with downtown areas, these manufacturers lived under the gun. They were perceived as interlopers by the growth machine of landed elites, elected officials, and real estate developers. Their socially obsolete vernacular posed a barrier to expanding the downtown landscape of economic power. During the 1960s, simultaneously with urban renewal programs on the one hand and new office construction in the suburbs on the other, many city administrations turned to reforming mayors who formed a new coalition with corporate business and banking interests. Mayor John Lindsay in New York, for example, shed City Hall's New Deal alliances with small business and labor unions for a more favorable orientation toward the financial sector, including real estate developers. From Lindsay on, New York's mayors backed a growth machine that explicitly focused on service-sector expansion throughout downtown Manhattan.[4]

Provided businesses had a need or desire to be located downtown, the price of property there was by this point relatively low. While a "rent gap" reflected the cyclical loss of economic value at the center, some private-sector institutions—mainly banks and insurance companies, the offices of foreign-owned corporations, and financial services—remained committed to a downtown location for its symbolic value.[5] Yet downtown had never completely excluded "upscale" use. A small number of patrician households had always remained in Boston's Back Bay and Beacon Hill, and Philadelphia's Society Hill and Rittenhouse Square.[6] Small areas such as these, which never lost economic and cultural value, served as springboards of "revitalization" in the center.

With one eye on redevelopment contracts and the other on property values, the patricians who owned downtown land were in an ideal position to direct a new mode of development that increased economic value. They also controlled the sources of investment capital, city government authorizations, and cultural legitimacy that are needed for a massive shift in land use, because they shaped the policies of banks, city planning commissions, and local historical societies. New York may have been an exception, for the patricians with property in downtown Manhattan—who now lived uptown or in the suburbs—pressed only for new building and highway construction until 1973.

In Philadelphia, however, the upper-class residents of Society Hill and their associates in banking and city government started a fairly concerted effort at preservation-based revitalization in the late 1950s. From house tours of Elfreth's Alley, they proceeded to government subsidies for slum clearance of nearby neighborhoods and new commercial construction. Twenty years later, just in time for the bicentennial celebration of the Declaration of Independence, their residential enclave downtown near the Delaware waterfront was surrounded by a large area devoted to historic preservation, tourism, new offices for insurance and financial corporations, and not coincidentally, gentrification in nearby Queen Village. The displaced were small businesses, including manufacturers, and working-class, especially Italian and Puerto Rican, residents.[7]

In downtown Manhattan, by contrast, the displacement of low-rent and "socially obsolete" uses from around 1970 was part of the politics of culture. Specifically, the landscape of downtown Manhattan was shaped by an unexpected triumph on the part of an artists' and historic preservationists' coalition. Formed to defend living and working quarters that cultural producers had established in low-rent manufacturing lofts, artists' organizations protested the demolition of these areas by the growth coalition. They also claimed the legal right to live and work in buildings zoned for manufacturing use alone, on the basis of their contribution to New York City's economy. Since the 1960s, nontraditional forms of art and performance had indeed attracted a larger, paying public. Their gradual concentration in downtown lofts connected these spaces with a downtown arts economy.

In a competition over downtown space between the arts producers, manufacturers, and real estate developers, which lasted until 1973, the artists emerged as victors. Yet they could not have won the right to live in their lofts without powerful allies. Their political strategy relied not only on the growing visibility of artists' clusters, but also on the patronage of some landed and political elite members who otherwise would have supported the growth coalition. Saved by the cultural values of historic preservation and the rising market values of an arts economy, the lofts of downtown Manhattan were transformed from a light manufacturing into a cultural zone. This process ran parallel, we see with hindsight, to gentrification.[8] The legitimation of "loft living" in downtown Manhattan marked a symbolic as well as a material change in the landscape. Cleared of "obsolete" uses like manufacturing by an investment flow apparently unleashed "from below," downtown space demanded a visual, sensual, and even conceptual reorientation. Just as the new mode of development downtown reflected a new organization of production, so many of the gentrifiers' cultural practices related to a new organization of consumption.

At the outset, gentrifiers' fondness for restoring and preserving a historical style reflected real dismay at more than a decade of publicly sponsored urban renewal and private commercial redevelopment, which together had destroyed a large part of many cities' architectural heritage. The photographic exhibit (1963) and book on *Lost New York* (1967), for example, documented the handsome stone, masonry, and cast-iron structures that had dominated downtown Manhattan from the Gilded Age to World War II. Most of these buildings were torn down in successive periods of redevelopment as downtown commerce moved farther north. For a long time, demolition signified improvement. But the destruction in the early 1960s of Pennsylvania Station, a railroad terminal of the grand era whose soaring glass dome was replaced by a mundane office building, dramatized the loss of a collective sense of time that many people felt.[9]

The photographic exhibitions that were mounted for *Lost Boston, Lost Chicago*, and *Lost London* showed a nearly universal dissatisfaction with slash-and-burn strategies of urban redevelopment. Criticism ranged from aesthetics to sociology. The journalist Jane Jacobs, whose family had moved into a mixed residential and industrial area in the oldest part of Greenwich Village, argued for the preservation of old buildings because they fostered social diversity. She connected small, old buildings and cheap rents with neighborhood street life, specialized, low-price shops, and new, interesting economic activities: in other words, downtown's social values. Studies by the sociologists Herbert Gans and Marc Fried suggested, moreover, that for its residents, even a physically run-down inner-city community had redeeming social value.[10]

The rising expense and decreasing availability of new housing in the center worked in tandem with these developing sensitivities. Meanwhile, new patterns of gender equality and household independence diminished the old demand for housing near good schools, supermarkets, and neighborhood stores, at least for those families without children or with adequate funds for private schools. While they couldn't afford Park Avenue, or wouldn't be caught dead on the Upper East Side, highly educated upper-middle-class residents viewed the center in light of its social and aesthetic qualities. Equally well educated lower-income residents—notably, those who had chosen cultural careers and those who lived alone, including significant numbers of women and gays—viewed the center in terms of its clustering qualities. Relatively inexpensive building stock in "obsolete" areas downtown provided both groups of men and women with opportunities for new cultural consumption.[11]

New middle-class residents tended to buy houses downtown that were built in the nineteenth century. They painstakingly restored architectural detail covered over by layers of paint, obscured by repeated repairs and re-partitions, and generally lost in the course of countless renovations. The British sociologist Ruth Glass first noted their presence in the early 1960s as an influx of "gentry" into inner-city London neighborhoods. While the new residents did not have upper-class incomes, they were clearly more affluent and more educated than their working-class neighbors. The neighbors rarely understood what drew them to old houses in run-down areas near the center of town. Since that time, however, gentrifiers have become so pervasive in all older cities of the highly industrialized world that their cultural preferences have been incorporated into official norms of neighborhood renewal and city planning.[12]

With its respect for historic structures and the integrity of smaller scale, gentrification appeared as a rediscovery, an attempt to recapture the value of place. Appreciating the aesthetics and social history of old buildings in the center showed a cultural sensibility and refinement that transcended the postwar suburban ethos of conformity and kitsch. Moreover, moving downtown in search of social diversity made a statement about liberal tolerance that seemed to contradict "white flight" and disinvestment from the inner city. By constructing a social space or *habitus* on the basis of cultural rather than economic capital, gentrification apparently reconciled two sets of contradictions: between landscape and vernacular, and market and place. On the one hand, gentrifiers viewed the dilapidated built environment of the urban vernacular from the same perspective of aesthetics and history that was traditionally used for viewing landscape. On the other hand, their demand to preserve old buildings—with regard to cultural rather than economic value—helped constitute a market for the special characteristics of place.[13]

Yet as the nature of downtown changed, so did gentrification. The concern for old buildings that was its hallmark has been joined, since the early 1980s, by a great deal of new construction. Combined commercial and residential projects near the financial district—like Docklands in London or Battery Park City in New York—exploit the taste for old buildings and downtown diversity that gentrifiers "pioneered." By virtue of its success, however, we no longer know whether gentrification is primarily a social, an aesthetic, or a spatial phenomenon.

Small-scale real estate developers slowly awakened to the opportunity of offering a product based on place. "You find a prestigious structure that is highly visible and built well, preferably something prewar," says a housing developer who converted a neo-Gothic Catholic seminary in a racially mixed neighborhood near downtown Brooklyn to luxurious apartments. "You find it in a neighborhood that still has problems but is close to a park, a college, good transportation—something that will bring in the middle class. And almost by the time you are through, other buildings around it will have started to be fixed up."[14]

Downtown loft areas formed a more specialized real estate market because they had a special quality. Their association with artists directly invested living lofts with an aura of authentic cultural consumption. If the artist was "a full-time leisure specialist, an aesthetic technician picturing and prodding the sensual expectations of other, part-time consumers," then the artist's loft and the surrounding quarter were a perfect site for a new, reflexive consumption.[15]

Markets are not the only arbiters of a contest for downtown space between landscape and vernacular.[16] The key element is that the social values of existing users—for example, working-class residents and small manufacturers—exert a weaker claim to the center than the cultural values of potential gentrifiers. Gentrification joins the economic claim to space with a cultural claim that gives priority to the demands of historic preservationists and arts producers. In this view, "historic" buildings can only be appreciated to their maximum value if they are explained, analyzed, and understood as part of an aesthetic discourse, such as the history of architecture and art. Such buildings rightfully "belong" to people who have the resources to search for the original building plans and study their house in the context of the architect's career. They belong to residents who restore mahogany paneling and buy copies of nineteenth-century faucets instead of those who prefer aluminum siding.

Gentrifiers' capacity for attaching themselves to history gives them license to "reclaim" the downtown for their own uses. Most of them anyway tend not to mourn the transformation of local working-class taprooms into "ye olde" bars and "French" bistros. By means of the building stock, they identify with an earlier group of builders rather than with the existing lower-class population, with the "Ladies' Mile" of early-twentieth-century department stores instead of the discount stores that have replaced them.

Mainly by virtue of their hard work at restoration and education, the urban

vernacular of ethnic ghettos and working-class neighborhoods that were due to
be demolished is re-viewed as Georgian,
Victorian, or early industrial landscape—
and judged worthy of preservation. "In
this new perspective [a gentrified neigh-
borhood] is not so much a literal place as
a cultural oscillation between the prosaic
reality of the contemporary inner city and
an imaginative reconstruction of the area's
past."[17]

The cultural claim to urban space poses
a new standard of legitimacy against the
claim to affordability put forward by a low-
status population. Significantly, cultural
value is now related to economic value.
From demand for living lofts and gentrification, large property-owners, developers, and elected local officials realized
that they could enhance the economic
value of the center by supplying cultural
consumption.**

In numerous cases, state intervention
has reinforced the cultural claims behind
gentrification's "market forces." New zoning
laws banish manufacturers, who are forced
to relocate outside the center. Since 1981,
moreover, the U.S. tax code has offered
tax credits for the rehabilitation of historic
structures. Although the maximum credit
was lowered, and eligibility rules tightened,
in 1986, the Tax Reform Act retained benefits for historic preservation. Every city
now has procedures for certifying "landmark" structures and districts, which tend
to restrict their use to those who can afford
to maintain them in a historic style. But
when landmarking outlives its usefulness
as a strategy of restoring economic value at
the center—as it apparently did in New York
City by the mid 1980s—local government is
capable of shifting gears and attacking the
very notion of historic preservation.[18]

Gentrification received its greatest boost
not from a specific subsidy, but from the
state's substantive and symbolic legitimation of the cultural claim to urban space.

This recognition marked cultural producers as a symbol of urban growth. While
storefront art galleries and "French" restaurants became outposts and mediators
of gentrification in specific neighborhoods,
cities with the highest percentage of artists
in the labor force also had the highest rates
of downtown gentrification and condominium conversion.[19]

Yet the aesthetic appeal of gentrification is both selective and pliable. It can
be abstracted into objects of cultural consumption that bear only a distant relation
to the downtown areas where they were
once produced. "Before Fior di Latte," reads
an advertisement for a new brand of "fresh"
cheese mass marketed by Pollio Dairy
Products Corporation, "you had to go to *latticini* [dairy] stores in Italian neighborhoods
to buy fresh mozzarella. Store owners made
the delicious white cheese daily and kept
it fresh in barrels of lightly salted water."
The point is that it is no longer necessary
to go the ethnic neighborhoods downtown
to consume their heritage; international
trade and mass distribution can reproduce
a historically "authentic" product. "To capture this fragile, handmade essence of fresh
mozzarella," the ad continues, "Polly-O
uses methods and equipment imported
from Italy. We even pack each individual
serving of Fior di Latte in water to keep it
moist and fresh up to 25 days." No need for
latticini when fresh mozzarella is sold in
supermarkets.

The organization of consumption thus
has a paradoxical effect on downtown
space. Initially treated as unique, the cultural value of place is finally abstracted into
market culture. [...]

NOTES

* Race poses the most serious barrier to all new
private-sector capital investment, including gentrification. During the 1970s, as housing prices
continued to climb and the housing supply failed
to keep pace with demand, white gentrifiers

became "bolder" about moving into nonwhite neighborhoods, or more tolerant of the costs in security and services such residence imposed. Only when gentrification risks displacing people of color—notably, in Harlem—is there even a chance of mobilizing against it. Even then, as in industrial displacement, the victims are either bought out or permitted to buy into the new structure—in this case, the improved housing stock.

** However, when investment in new projects is viable, economic claims to the center take precedence over cultural claims. The absolute failure of a historic preservation movement in Hong Kong is the exception that proves the rule. "'In New York, London, Paris or Rome, none of this [demolition] would ever have been allowed to happen,' said David Russell, an architect and the founder of the colony's Heritage Society, which disbanded five years ago after losing three major preservation fights in a row" (*New York Times*, March 31, 1988).

1. Neil Smith, "Gentrification, the Frontier, and the Restructuring of Urban Space," in *Gentrification of the City*, ed. Neil Smith and Peter Williams (Boston: Allen & Unwin, 1986), pp. 15–20. While it may fool the middle class, this ideological smokescreen is transparent to the "indigenous." As a Hispanic attorney for a municipal agency in New York City describes the co-op conversion of the apartment house where she is living, "Gentrification is contemporary manifest destiny used to move out minorities, and that's why I'm staying. They're so used to Puerto Ricans who can't afford to buy that I'm going to buy" (*New York Times*, March 27, 1988).

2. See Peter D. Sahlins, "The Limits of Gentrification," *New York Affairs* 5, no. 4 (1979): 3–12; Brian J. L. Berry, "Islands of Renewal in Seas of Decay," in *The New Urban Reality*, ed. Peter E. Peterson (Washington, D.C.: Brookings Institution, 1985), pp. 35–55; J. I. Nelson and J. Lorence, "Employment in Service Activities and Inequality in Metropolitan Areas," *Urban Affairs Quarterly* 21, no. 1 (1985): 106–25; Smith, *Uneven Development* and "Of Yuppies and Housing: Gentrification, Social Restructuring, and the Urban Dream," *Society and Space* 5 (1987): 151–72.

3. For a detailed review of economic and cultural approaches to gentrification, see Sharon Zukin, "Gentrification: Culture and Capital in the Urban Core," *Annual Review of Sociology* 13 (1987): 129–47.

4. For general political background, see Jack Newfield and Paul DuBrul, *The Abuses of Power* (New York: Viking, 1977), and Martin Shefter,

Political Crisis/Fiscal Crisis (New York: Basic Books, 1987).

5. On the rent gap, see Neil Smith, "Toward a Theory of Gentrification: A Back to the City Movement by Capital Not People" *Journal of the American Planners Association* 45 (1979): 538–48; for criticism of the concept, noting that redevelopment by gentrification is only one possible option, see Robert A. Beauregard, "The Chaos and Complexity of Gentrification," in *Gentrification of the City*, ed. Smith and Williams, pp. 35–55; and for defense of the rent gap explanation in terms of opportunity, see Smith, "Of Yuppies and Housing."

6. For an early acknowledgment of these "exceptions" to the ecological model, see Walter Firey, "Sentiment and Symbolism as Ecological Variables," *American Sociological Review* 10, no. 2 (1945): 140–48.

7. See Neil Smith, "Gentrification and Capital: Theory, Practice and Ideology in Society Hill," *Antipode* 11, no. 3 (1979): 24–35; Paul R. Levy and Roman A. Cybriwsky, "The Hidden Dimensions of Culture and Class: Philadelphia," in *Back to the City*, ed. Shirley Bradway Laska and Daphne Spain (New York: Pergamon, 1980), pp. 138–55; Roman A. Cybriwsky, David Ley, and John Western, "The Political and Social Construction of Revitalized Neighborhoods: Society Hill, Philadelphia, and False Creek, Vancouver," in *Gentrification of the City* ed. Smith and Williams, pp. 92–120; and Conrad Weiler, "The Neighborhood's Role in Optimizing Reinvestment: Philadelphia," in *Back to the City*, ed. Laska and Spain, pp. 220–38.

8. See Sharon Zukin, *Loft Living: Culture and Capital in Urban Change*, 2d ed. (New Brunswick, N.J.: Rutgers University Press, 1989).

9. Nathan Silver, *Lost New York* (New York: Schocken, 1967).

10. Jane Jacobs, *The Death and Life of Great American Cities* (New York: Vintage Books, 1961); Herbert Gans, *The Urban Villagers* (New York: Free Press, 1962); Marc Fried and Peggy Gleicher, "Some Sources of Satisfaction in the Residential Slum," *Journal of the American institute of Planners* 72, no. 4 (1961): 305–15. Also see Special Committee on Historic Preservation, U.S. Conference of Mayors, *With Heritage So Rich* (New York: Random House, 1966; repr. 1983).

11. On the low cost of living downtown for single women, see Damaris Rose, "Rethinking Gentrification: Beyond the Uneven Development of Marxist Theory," *Society and Space* 1 (1984): 47–74, and on the spatial formation of the gay community in San Francisco, see Manuel Castells, *The City and the Grassroots* (Berkeley and Los Angeles: University of California Press, 1983), ch. 14.

12. For the initial description, see Ruth Glass's introduction to *London: Aspects of Change*, ed. Centre for Urban Studies (London: MacGibbon & Kee, 1964), pp. xiii–xlii. For glowing support of the widespread diffusion of the mode of development that combines gentrification, historic preservation, and downtown reinvestment in the United States, see "Spiffing Up the Urban Heritage" (cover story), *Time*, November 13, 1987, pp. 72ff.

13. The work of Pierre Bourdieu seems basic to this analysis, especially his emphasis on the tastes of people with more cultural than economic capital. See Bourdieu, *Distinction: A Social Critique of the Judgement of Taste*, trans. Richard Nice (Cambridge, Mass.: Harvard University Press, 1984). My argument nonetheless suggests a more complex and historically contingent account of, first, the rising social acceptance of cultural capital, and, second, its association with the current transformation of the urban center, which is as observable in the IVième, Vième, or XVième arrondissements of Paris as in New York.

14. Andree Brooks, "About Real Estate: Brooklyn School Converted to Housing," *New York Times*, March 25, 1988. Of course, the developer exaggerates both the rapidity and feasibility of gentrification in this area.

15. Quotation on the artist from Meyer Schapiro, quoted in Diana Crane, *The Transformation of the Avant-Garde: The New York Art World, 1940–1985* (Chicago: University of Chicago Press, 1987), p. 83. For the rise of the real estate market in living lofts, and their transformation from artists' to luxury housing, see Zukin, *Loft Living*.

16. John Logan and Harvey Molotch make a start toward recognizing the complexity of the gentrification process by incorporating the Marxist conflict between use values and exchange values: "Whether among rich or poor neighborhoods, in the central city or urban fringe, neighborhood futures are determined by the ways in which entrepreneurial pressures from outside intersect with internal material stakes and sentimental attachments" (*Urban Fortunes*, p. 123).

17. Quotation from Patrick Wright, "The Ghosting of the Inner City," in *On Living in an Old Country: The National Past in Contemporary Britain* (London: Verso, 1985), pp. 228–29. On the contested claims for space around Union Square in downtown Manhattan between discount stores that cater to an immigrant, working-class, and outer-borough clientele, and the cultural values of the early-twentieth-century loft buildings that make up the Ladies' Mile, see Martin Kroneuer, "Urban 'Revitalization' and Community Participation" (Ph.D. diss., Free University of Berlin, 1987); cf. Rosalyn Deutsche, "Krzysztof Wodiszko's *Homeless Projection* and the Site of Urban 'Revitalization,'" *October* 38 (Fall 1986): 63–98.

18. Other cities, however, may have stronger proneighborhood, antidevelopment orientations. In Chicago, for example, the administration of Mayor Harold Washington countered developers' plans to convert the manufacturing zone of Goose Island while gentrification and new construction expanded the downtown elsewhere.

19. National Endowment for the Arts study of artists and gentrification cited in Dennis E. Gale, *Neighborhood Revitalization and the Postindustrial City: A Multinational Perspective* (Lexington, Mass.: Lexington Boooks, 1984), p. 155.

CHAPTER 4

Super-gentrification: The Case of Brooklyn Heights, New York City

Loretta Lees

Summary. This paper is an empirical examination of the process of 'super-gentrification' in the Brooklyn Heights neighbourhood of New York City. This intensified regentrification is happening in a few select areas of global cities like London and New York that have become the focus of intense investment and conspicuous consumption by a new generation of super-rich 'financifiers' fed by fortunes from the global finance and corporate service industries. This latest resurgence of gentrification can be distinguished from previous rounds of revitalisation and poses important questions about the historical continuity of current manifestations of gentrification with previous generations of neighbourhood change.

1. INTRODUCTION

Gentrification research has traditionally focused on the economic and cultural appreciation of formerly disinvested and devalued inner-city areas by an affluent middle class. In this paper, I want to examine a somewhat different phenomenon: 'super-gentrification'. By super-gentrification, I mean the transformation of already gentrified, prosperous and solidly upper-middle-class neighbourhoods into much more exclusive and expensive enclaves. This intensified regentrification is happening in a few select areas of global cities like London and New York that have become the focus of intense investment and conspicuous consumption by a new generation of super-rich 'financifiers' fed by fortunes from the global finance and corporate service industries. We can begin to understand some of what super-gentrification involves by considering the story of a fairly ordinary four-storey brownstone house in Brooklyn Heights, New York City, which I will tell by drawing on interviews with the householder (D) who first gentrified the house and his next-door-neighbour (S). I want to use the biography of this building to reflect critically on some familiar ways of explaining gentrification and the challenges posed to them by what I am calling super-gentrification. After a brief discussion of my data and methods, I then document the history and gentrification of Brooklyn Heights, and the extent and impact of super-gentrification on the pre-existing community. Finally, the paper concludes with a discussion of what is new and what is historically and geographically specific about this latest form of gentrification.

2. THE BIOGRAPHY OF A BROWNSTONE

In 1962, as gentrification began to take off in Brooklyn Heights, a young lawyer working in Lower Manhattan paid $28 000 for a small four-storey Brownstone. . . . He and his wife had rented an apartment in Brooklyn Heights for the previous four years and liked the neighbourhood. As D explained to me:

> At the time we had very limited resources so we had to find something that was reasonably inexpensive and at the time we felt we had to buy something north of Joralemon Street because of the nature of below Joralemon Street which was very heavily rental units to Hispanics, mostly Puerto Rican rooming houses. But because price was a big factor for us we ended up buying south of Joralemon Street anyway, and the property was quite small
> (interview with D, August 2002).

At the time, the property was divided into three apartments: the basement level and parlour floor were the owners' apartment, while the second and top floors contained small, rent-controlled apartments occupied by working-class Irish families.

> We owned the whole building subject to two rent control leases. It was a rather big speculation on our behalf. We didn't know how, or whether, we'd get rid of them at all
> (interview with D, August 2002).

The family living on the top floor left voluntarily after eight months when the husband of the family had a heart attack and was advised by his doctor that he should no longer climb the stairs to his top-floor, walk-up apartment. D took over their apartment. D and his wife now lived in a house in which they had use of the top and bottom floors but not the middle floor that still contained a rent-controlled apartment. Seven years after he moved in, D finally evicted this tenant:

> The other tenant left because we evicted them. We filed a petition to have them evicted on the grounds (permissible under the rent control law) which if a landlord had an immediate and compelling need for the space for his own use he can evict the tenant. I investigated the law. We already had one child and were about to have a second child and needed the space
> (interview with D, August 2002).

D invested sweat equity in his brownstone. He estimates that he spent approximately $40 000 on improvements, mostly in the early years:

> It was electrical, heating, painting, etc . . . relatively minor. A lot of it was cosmetic. The goal was to retain period features. I even bought, for a nominal sum, two fireplaces that had been ripped out of other houses and put them in my children's bedrooms
> (interview with D, August 2002).

Thus far, the story is a fairly familiar one of middle-class upgrading and working-class displacement. Indeed, it is almost a textbook case of gentrification as first described by Ruth Glass (1964). What has happened to the house since 1995, however, illustrates in microcosm a new process I am calling super-gentrification (compare with Dangschat's (1991) typology of the ultra-gentrifier).

When his family circumstances changed in the mid 1990s, D put the house in which he had raised his family on the market. His broker valued the house at $640 000—or nearly 23 times more than what he had paid for it some 30 years before. Within a week, an English woman employed on Wall Street as a broker specialising in Japanese bonds and securities, had agreed a purchase price of $595 000 and written a personal cheque for the full amount! Previous generations of gentrifiers needed mortgages and so were subject to banking loan officers' ideas about who, what and where in the city was suitable for gentrification. By contrast, in New York, there is now a new generation flush with the exorbitant rewards of the global finance and corporate service industries (see Warf, 2000). They are able to marshal previously unheard of sums to finance their domestic reproduction. It is not only the volume and source of the assets they mobilise that mark out these 'financifiers' from previous generations of gentrifiers, but also, I would suggest, their lifestyles and values as well.

The story of our house after its sale is taken up by the next door neighbour, S:

> She didn't move in straight away because it took her nine months to renovate the house. Meanwhile she rented an apartment for an astronomical fee elsewhere in the Heights . . . She was English, he was Australian—he used to wear orange shell suits and gold chains . . . .
>
> The renovations cost her way more than the house: a minimum of three-quarters of a million. She gutted the place . . . took out weight-bearing walls, knocked out ceilings and floors, everything. They completely changed the floor plan. My house was covered in dust from the demolition for months . . . They installed central air conditioning, walk in closets, and wall to wall cables. In [one of D's children] old room on the top floor they even put in a marblized bathroom with a Jacuzzi. Then they didn't like it, so they pulled it all out and redid it again!

S. goes on to refer rather scathingly to the quite different lifestyles and values of the incomers:

> The garden said it all. When D lived there, there was a mature urban garden, with grape vine, ivy, clematis, crab apple tree, etc. They were control freaks . . . they couldn't deal with stuff growing! They pulled it all up and turfed over the whole garden . . . They suburbanised it—green lawn and BBQ and nothing else! They brought Scottsdale, Arizona, to Brooklyn Heights . . .
>
> One day on my way home from work I noticed what looked like an outhouse in their front area . . . It was so big. It was a shed they got built for their garbage cans. I was going to

say something but the historic preservation people got there first . . .

> She got pregnant 4–5 months after moving in and had twins. They had only lived there a year when they upped and moved to Scottsdale, Arizona. Then a couple from Cobble Hill bought it for over $1.75 million!!—computer folk with two kids who loved the state of the art wiring
>
> (interview with S, August 2002).

3. THIRD-WAVE GENTRIFICATION

The emergence of super-gentrification is just one example of how gentrification shifted into top gear during the long economic boom of the 1990s. This latest resurgence of gentrification, which Jason Hackworth and Neil Smith (2001) have dubbed 'third-wave' gentrification to distinguish it from previous rounds of revitalisation, poses important questions about the historical continuity of current manifestations of gentrification with previous generations of neighbourhood change.[1]

One important issue is about the location and scale—or the 'distanciation' (see Giddens, 1981, 1984)—of gentrification: the ways in which both the underlying processes of gentrification and the material changes they produce are stretched and sustained over time and space. According to Neil Smith (2002, p. 427) gentrification is now a global urban strategy that has displaced the liberal urban policy of old with a new revanchist urbanism, "densely connected into the circuits of global capital and cultural circulation" and concerned with capitalist production rather than social reproduction. As Smith notes (p. 439) gentrification is now evident well beyond the familiar core of Anglo-American cities commonly studied by urban geographers. It is being documented across the globe from Mexico (Jones and Varley, 1999) to Israel (Gonen, 2002). Moreover, academics no longer restrict the term 'gentrification' to processes located in the city centre.

Increasingly, they also use it to describe similar changes in the suburbs (see N. Smith, 2002, p. 442; Hackworth and Smith, 2001; Smith and Defilippis, 1999) and even rural areas (see Smith and Philips, 2001, on 'greentrified rurality' and D. Smith, 2002).

Not only does 'third-wave' gentrification now occur in a variety of sites, but it also takes a myriad of forms. It can be of the *traditional* or *classic* form—that is, by individual gentrifiers renovating old housing through sweat equity or by hiring builders and interior designers and so leading to the embourgeoisement of a neighbourhood and the displacement of less wealthy residents. It is now also increasingly *state-led* with national and local governmental policy tied up in supporting gentrification initiatives (see Lees, 2003; Atkinson, 2002; N. Smith, 2002; Hackworth and Smith, 2001; Wyly and Hammel, 1999). In a departure from the traditional concern with renovating old housing stock, some now argue that gentrification can also be *new build* (see Morrison and McMurray, 1999). Nor is it always residential—it can also be *commercial* (see Kloosterman and van der Leun, 1999). This proliferation of gentrification at different scales, at different sites and in different forms suggests that gentrification has truly become the 'plague of locusts' that N. Smith (1984, p. 152) once described it as.

Adding 'super-gentrification' to this long list of gentrification forms, I realise that I am running the considerable risk of making the meaning of the term so expansive as to lose any conceptual sharpness and specificity. A number of scholars have argued that gentrification is a 'chaotic' concept describing the contingent and geographically specific results of different processes operating in different ways in different contexts (see Rose, 1984; Beauregard, 1986). This is nowhere more true than with the process of super-gentrification. Indeed, I maintain that there are several reasons why

we should consider the case of super-gentrification in more detail.

First, it provides a concrete manifestation of sometimes rather abstract claims made about the relationships between global economic and urban-scale processes. For instance, Neil Smith (2002, p. 441) argues that the "hallmark of [this] latest phase of gentrification" is the "reach of global capital down to the local neighbourhood scale". The relationships among global economic processes, local places and communities are nowhere more obvious than in the super-gentrification of Brooklyn Heights. Closely tied, through the labour market, to global financial markets, super-gentrifying neighbourhoods like Brooklyn Heights are peculiarly positioned global spaces/places. While it is important to recognise the specificity of its location within the global space economy, there is no reason to assume that the processes of super-gentrification at play in Brooklyn Heights are totally unique to it. Indeed, Butler and Robson (2001a, pp. 5 and 10–12) have suggested that Barnsbury in London is also "witnessing second generation (re)gentrification", driven largely by finance and financial-sector workers employed in the City of London. And there is anecdotal evidence that Park Slope, located in Brooklyn not far from Brooklyn Heights, is experiencing super-gentrification too (see Lees, 2000; Slater, 2003).

Secondly, by highlighting new processes *intensifying the economic valorisation of*—and consequent social and cultural changes in—already gentrified neighbourhoods, the concept of super-gentrification presents something of a challenge to traditional explanatory models of gentrification, which presume an end-point to the process. Stage models of gentrification were developed in the 1970s and 1980s both to explain the process and to predict the future course of gentrification (see Kerstein, 1990, for a review). For example, Clay

(1979, pp. 57–60) outlined a schema from stage one (pioneer gentrification) through to stage four (maturing gentrification). Similarly Dangschat's (1991) gentrification typology presumed that pioneer gentrifiers would be succeeded in a final phase of gentrification by 'ultragentrifiers', who were distinguished from pioneers on the basis of age and aggregate income. Like the now-discredited climax ecology models of vegetation invasion and succession on which they were predicated (see Hagen, 1992), such gentrification stage models assume that the process of gentrification will eventually reach a stable and self-perpetuating final climax stage of 'mature gentrification'. The example of super-gentrification demonstrates the folly of this assumption about the stability both of the underlying processes and of the resulting patterns of gentrification.[2] As Chris Hamnett argued some time ago now:

> It should be clear that gentrification is merely another stage in a continuing historically contingent sequence of residential-area evolution. There are no universally and temporally stable residential patterns
> (Hamnett, 1984, p. 314).

Drawing on neo-Marxist rent-gap models, Hackworth and Smith (2001) have recently produced a schematic history of gentrification in New York City, which they divide into three distinct waves separated by two transitional periods of recession-induced restructuring of the institutional context and mechanisms through which gentrification occurred. Their very useful heuristic model of gentrification was not designed with the predictive intention of early stage models and so does not commit the fallacy of constant conjunction (Sayer, 1992). But its emphasis on the dialectic of disinvestment and reinvestment and the attractions of "reinvesting in disinvested inner-urban areas so alluring for investors" leads Hackworth and Smith (2001, p. 468,

469) to discount the possibility of intensified investment in first wave neighbourhoods, like Brooklyn Heights, that "have already been fully invested". That oversight seems somewhat surprising, given their emphasis on the dynamism of restless capital as a driving-force behind the new manifestations of the process they so helpfully document. [. . .]

NOTES

1. Hackworth and Smith (2001, p. 467) date the onset of post-recession or third-wave gentrification to approximately 1993–94.
2. I do not want to discredit stage models of gentrification *per se*, for they are very useful explanatory tools, rather I want to discredit the specific assumption of an end-stage in these models.

REFERENCES

Atkinson, R. (2002) *Does gentrification help or harm urban neighbourhoods? An assessment of the evidence-base in the context of the New Urban Agenda.* CNR Paper 5 (www.neighbourhoodcentre.org.uk).

Beauregard, R. (1986) The chaos and complexity of gentrification, in: N. Smith and P. Williams (Eds) *Gentrification of the City*, pp. 35–55. Boston, MA: Allen and Unwin.

Butler, T. and Robson, G. (2001) *Negotiating the new urban economy: work, home and school: negotiating middle class life in London.* Paper presented at the Annual RGS-IBG Conference, Plymouth.

Clay, P. (1979) *Neighborhood Renewal: Middleclass Resettlement and Incumbent Upgrading in American Neighborhoods.* Massachusetts and Toronto: Lexington Books.

Dangschat, J. (1991) Gentrification in Hamburg, in: J. van Weesep and S. Musterd (Eds) *Urban Housing for the Better-Off: Gentrification in Europe*, pp. 63–88. Utrecht: Stedelijke Netwerken.

Giddens, A. (1981) *A Contemporary Critique of Historical Materialism: Volume 1: Power, Property and the State.* London: Macmillan.

Giddens, A. (1984) *The Constitution of Society.* Cambridge: Polity Press.

Glass, R. (1964) Aspects of change, in: Centre for Urban Studies (Ed.) *London: Aspects of Change*, pp. xiii–xlii. London: McGibbon and Kee.

Gonen, A. (2002) Widespread and diverse neighborhood gentrification in Jerusalem, *Political Geography,* 21, pp. 727–737.

Hackworth, J. and Smith, N. (2001) The changing state of gentrification, *Tijdschrift voor Economische en Sociale Geografie*, 92, pp. 464–477.

Hagen, J. (1992) *An Entangled Bank: The Origins of Ecosystem Ecology.* New Brunswick: Rutgers University Press.

Hamnett, C. (1984) Gentrification and residential location theory: a review and assessment, in: D. T. Herbert and R. J. Johnston (Eds) *Geography and the Urban Environment: Progress in Research and Application, Vol. 6*, pp. 283–319. London: John Wiley.

Jones, G. and Varley, A. (1999) The reconquest of the historic centre: urban conservation and gentrification in Puebla, Mexico, *Environment and Planning A*, 31, pp. 1547–1566.

Kerstein, R. (1990) Stage models for gentrification: an examination, *Urban Affairs Quarterly*, 25, pp. 620–639.

Kloosterman, R. and Leun, J. van der (1999) Just for starters: commercial gentrification by immigrant entrepreneurs in Amsterdam and Rotterdam neighborhoods, *Housing Studies*, 14, pp. 659–677.

Lees, L. (2000) A re-appraisal of gentrification: towards a 'geography of gentrification', *Progress in Human Geography*, 24, pp. 389–408.

Lees, L. (2003) Visions of 'Urban Renaissance': the Urban Task Force Report and the Urban White Paper, in: R. Imrie and M. Raco (Eds) *Urban Renaissance? New Labour, Community and Urban Policy*, pp. 61–82. Bristol: The Policy Press.

Morrison, P. and McMurray, S. (1999) The inner city apartment versus the suburb: housing sub-markets in a New Zealand city, *Urban Studies*, 35, pp. 377–397.

Rose, D. (1984) Rethinking gentrification: beyond the uneven development of Marxist urban theory, *Environment and Planning D*, 1, pp. 47–74.

Sayer, A. (1992) *Method in Social Science: A Realist Approach*, 2nd edn. London: Routledge.

Slater, T. (2003) *The geography of the gentrifying 'North American' neighbourhood: a comparison of South Parkdale, Toronto, Canada, and Lower Park Slope, New York City, USA.* Unpublished PhD thesis, King's College London.

Smith, D. (2002) Extending the temporal and spatial limits of gentrification: a research agenda for population geographers, *International Journal of Population Geography*, 8, pp. 385–394.

Smith, D. and Philips, D. (2001) Socio-cultural representations of greentrified Pennine rurality, *Journal of Rural Studies*, 17, pp. 457–469.

Smith, N. (1984) *Uneven Development: Nature, Capital and the Production of Space.* Oxford: Basil Blackwell.

Smith, N. (2002) New globalism, new urbanism: gentrification as global urban strategy, *Antipode*, 34, pp. 427–450.

Smith, N. and Defilippis, J. (1999) The reassertion of economics: 1990s gentrification in the Lower East Side, *International Journal of Urban and Regional Research*, 23, pp. 638–653.

Warf, B. (2000) New York: the Big Apple in the 1990s, *Geoforum*, 31, pp. 487–499.

Wyly, E. and Hammel, D. (1999) Islands of decay in seas of renewal: housing policy and the resurgence of gentrification, *Housing Policy Debate*, 10, pp. 711–798.

CHAPTER 5

Globalisation and the New Urban Colonialism

Rowland Atkinson and Gary Bridge

Gentrification is now global. It is no longer confined to western cities. Processes of neighbourhood change and colonisation represented by an increasing concentration of the new middle classes can be found in Shanghai as well as Sydney, or Seattle. Nor is it now limited to the 'global' cities, the focus of much of the gentrification debate to date. It can now be found in new regional centres such as Leeds (United Kingdom) and Barcelona (Spain) as well as capital cities previously not associated with the process such as Moscow, Brussels and Berlin. All of this is to say nothing of the now rampant and almost exhaustive process of gentrification in cities like San Francisco, London, New York, and Melbourne. For some gentrification is now no longer even confined to cities, with examples of growing rural gentrification in the UK (Philips 1993; D. Smith 2003), or upstate New York.

The geographical spread of gentrification or 'gentrification generalised' as Neil Smith has recently called it (Smith 2002) raises questions about how much gentrification is a part of globalisation, involving, in this case, the growth of an international professional managerial class and the new or rehabilitated residential enclaves which they choose to colonise. To what extent is gentrification an important component for city governments of wider 'regeneration'

strategies involving commercial or prestigious flagship arts of sporting facilities—what Monje and Vicario in this book call 'the Guggenheim effect' in the wake of Frank Gehry's museum in Bilbao? Alternatively how does the fact that gentrification has moved into very different urban contexts—rapidly urbanising, post-colonial, post communist, or communo/capitalist all overlaid by a diversity of cultural and religious forms—inflect, or indeed generate, a very different process? Is global gentrification hallmarked by its cultural, national or regional specificities?

A further set of questions is raised by these contextual details when pitched at the global scale. To what extent is gentrification a global phenomenon, with diverse causes and characteristics, or a phenomenon of globalisation, conceived as a process of capital expansion, uneven urban development and neighbourhood changes in 'new' cities? At the very least these questions raise a much wider research agenda than has often been presupposed by numerous local case studies at the neighbourhood and city scales in past years.

The current nature and extent of gentrification raises questions not just about its interrelations with globalisation but also its manifestation as a form of new urban colonialism. The geographical spread of gentrification over the last twenty years has been reminiscent of earlier waves of colonial and mercantile expansion, itself predicated on gaps in economic development at the national scale. It has moved into new countries and cities of the global 'south' but has also now cascaded down the urban hierarchies of regions within the urban north where it has been established for much longer. In short, gentrification appears to have migrated centrifugally from the metropoles of North America, Western Europe and Australasia. This has happened at the same time as market reform, greater market permeability and population migration have promoted internal changes in the economies of countries not previously associated with gentrification.

Contemporary gentrification has elements of colonialism as a cultural force in its privileging of whiteness, as well as the more class-based identities and preferences in urban living. In fact not only are the new middle-class gentrifiers predominantly white but the aesthetic and cultural aspects of the process assert a white Anglo appropriation of urban space and urban history.

The colonial aspects of gentrification are also evident through the universalising of certain forms of (de)regulation. There is the obvious spread of market discipline, such as the privatisation of housing markets in ex-communist countries for example. The neighbourhood transitions that result are accompanied, or indeed sometimes led by, an expansionist neoliberalism in public policy that often accentuates the social divisions between gentrifiers and the displaced. As Hammel and Wyly argue in this book, these policies have resulted in a kind of neo-colonialism in the US context.

Gentrification in a global context also has the aspect of colonialism as the universalisation of forms of public administration. There is a trend towards urban governments

around the world, of whatever particular political complexion, adopting gentrification as a form of urban regeneration policy broadly connected with an entrepreneurial style of urban governance (Harvey 1989) and a focus on the middle classes as the new saviour of the city. As Neil Smith has argued, gentrification as urban policy has been tied to a whole range of 'revanchist' public policy measures (such as zero tolerance for the homeless in New York) that represents the elite re-taking the urban core (Smith 1996).

At the neighbourhood level itself poor and vulnerable residents often experience gentrification as a process of colonisation by the more privileged classes. Stories of personal housing dislocation and loss, distended social networks, 'improved' local services out of sync with local needs and displacement have always been the darker underbelly of a process which, for city boosters, has represented something of a saviour for post-industrial cities (Atkinson 2003b). Again Neil Smith (1996) has long argued that the symbolic and practical implications of the movement of the gentrification 'frontier' are profound and have had enormous implications for the fate and status of the colonised.

Those who come to occupy prestigious central city locations frequently have the characteristics of a colonial elite. They often live in exclusive residential enclaves and are supported by a domestic and local service class. Gentrifiers are employed in what Gouldner (1979) called 'new class' occupations, and are marked out by their cosmopolitanism. Indeed in many locations, especially in ex-communist European and east Asian countries, they often are western ex-patriots employed by transnational corporations to open up the markets of the newly emerging economies.

We suggest that debates emerging in gentrification research also capture the degree to which the 'colonial rule' of gentrification can be sustained in some of its outposts and at its margins. Twenty years ago Damaris Rose coined the term 'marginal gentrifier' to capture some of the variability of profiles and motives of those in the gentrification process (in her case poorer female lone parents) (Rose 1984). Now the sheer extent of gentrification raises questions about the gentrifier and neighbourhood types involved, especially away from the core cities and locations, calling for an expanded imagination and nuanced reading of the profile and contextual unravelling of the process. This has led to discussions about the emerging differences of provincial forms of gentrification and instances where the gentrification aesthetic has a weaker link to class identity (Dutton in this volume and Bridge 2003). In other words, the wider social, economic, political and cultural benchmarks within which gentrification has been interpreted have themselves shifted dramatically in a quarter of a century. [. . .]

FORTY YEARS OF GENTRIFICATION RESEARCH

It is exactly forty years since the term 'gentrification' was coined by Ruth Glass in 1964. It is worth returning to Glass's original definition as a way of judging just what has happened to gentrification and gentrification research in the subsequent four decades:

> One by one, many of the working class quarters of London have been invaded by the middle classes, upper and lower. Shabby, modest mews and cottages—two rooms up and two down—have been taken over, when their leases have expired, and have become elegant, expensive residences. Large Victorian houses, downgraded in an earlier or recent period—which were used as lodging houses or were otherwise in multiple occupation—have been upgraded once again. Nowadays, many of these houses are being subdivided into costly flats or 'houselets' (in terms of the new real estate snob jargon). The current social status and value of such dwellings are frequently in inverse relation to their size, and in any case enormously inflated by comparison with previous levels in their neighbourhoods. Once this process of 'gentrification' starts in a district, it goes on rapidly until all or most of the original working class occupiers are displaced, and the whole social character of the district is changed.
>
> (Glass 1964: xviii–xix)

Since the time of Glass's article more than a thousand research papers, monographs, book chapters, government evaluations and reports have been written on the subject. Early developments were concerned essentially with an empirical mapping of the extent of the process in the larger western cities. Early definitions, like that of Glass, tended to focus on the residential housing market and the rehabilitation of existing properties. In the introduction to their landmark collection Smith and Williams defined gentrification as 'the rehabilitation of working-class and derelict housing and the consequent transformation of an area into a middle-class neighbourhood' (Smith and Williams 1986: 1). Since then the definition has been widened by some to include vacant land (usually in prior industrial use) and newly built designer neighbourhoods, as well as neighbourhoods of working-class housing suggesting a portability to the concept which has grown over time.

Where Glass's definition focused on 'sweat equity' gentrification, with the middle-class householder rehabilitating, or hiring a small builder to gentrify their dwelling, more recent discussions have included off-the-peg new-build developments, often beside water or in other landmark locations in the city. And most recently Smith has argued that gentrification has widened yet again to become a new form of neo-liberal urban policy (Smith 2002). Certainly the impacts of gentrification have been hotly disputed politically, with certain municipal governments, hungry for tax dollars, in the US and elsewhere, welcoming middle-class resettlement of the inner city. Alternatively a diversity of grassroots neighbourhood groups have opposed gentrification because of its effects in displacing the poor and the vulnerable (Marcuse 1989; Atkinson 2001a, 2001b; Slater 2002). Table 5.1 summarises some of the main neighbourhood impacts of gentrification.

As the significance of this social/physical neighbourhood change was noted, the conceptual meaning of gentrification, its origins and characteristics became the subject of dispute. Early interpretations saw it as a 'back to the city' movement of middle-class suburbanites wanting better

Table 5.1 Summary of neighbourhood impacts of gentrification

Positive	Negative
	Displacement through rent/price increases
	Secondary psychological costs of displacement
Stabilisation of declining areas	Community resentment and conflict
Increased property values	Loss of affordable housing
	Unsustainable speculative property
Reduced vacancy rates	Price increases homelessness
Increased local fiscal revenues	Greater take of local spending through lobbying/articulacy
Encouragement and increased viability of further development	Commercial/industrial displacement
Reduction of suburban sprawl	Increased cost and changes to local services
	Displacement and housing demand pressures on surrounding poor areas
Increased social mix	Loss of social diversity (from socially disparate to rich ghettos)
Rehabilitation of property both with and without state sponsorship	Under-occupancy and population loss to gentrified areas

proximity to jobs and the kind of cultural and recreational infrastructure that were hard to find on city peripheries (Laska and Spain 1980). From a Marxist perspective Smith countered this with the assertion that gentrification was a 'movement of capital, not people'. For Smith gentrification was explained by the 'rent gap' which was the difference between the potential value of inner urban land (low—because of abandonment due to de-industrialisation and suburbanisation) and its potential value (if put to a higher and 'better' use). When the gap between actual and potential values was wide enough investors would discount the riskiness of inner urban land because of the greater opportunity for profit by re-investing on devalorised land and closing the rent gap. Gentrification was one way of closing the rent gap.

While the rent gap theory was set in a Marxist critique of global capitalism it focused on the relativities of land values between a city and its suburbs. At its widest, the explanation looks to an urban system within the nation-state. Equally, it is hard to imagine Ley's 'following the hippies' explanation of the urban liberal neighbourhood movements in waterside Vancouver accounting for the massive expansion of gentrification in 1980s London, which although involving an enlargement of the professional managerial class, was associated strongly with financial deregulation of the City of London (Big Bang). In earlier explanations of gentrification both 'capital' and 'culture' were very firmly located in a national context.

The early distinction between a back-to-the-city movement of capital or a back-to-the-city movement of people has persisted in the literature on gentrification in various guises (production/consumption, capital/culture, supply/demand, production of gentrifiable housing/production of gentrifiers, Marxist or liberal explanations). David Ley (1986, 1996) in his work on Canada has suggested how the bohemianism of a student generation following the hippy era fed the pro-urbanism of this generation as they entered new middle-class occupations. This lifestyle aesthetic informed their activism in neighbourhood preservation and the politics of a liveable city (Ley 1996). At the same time in the USA Neil Smith has argued that middle-class pro-urbanism has now been replaced by a desire for revenge on the poor and the socially marginal. This 'revanchism' has taken the form of middle classes re-occupying, forcibly in some cases, and re-appropriating the central core of the city through the operation of the property market, gentrification, and by other means, for example the use of the police and legal agencies.

Some authors have sought to encompass the insights of both capital and cultural explanations for gentrification. Sharon Zukin's (1982, 1995) work suggests how cultural innovation, particularly around the activities of artists, can at first attract and then in fact be displaced by commercial forms of gentrification—capital captures culture. Chris Hamnett (1994b) has argued that neither culture nor capital arguments are particularly germane and points to the expansion of professional occupational sectors in key cities, of which gentrification is a residential manifestation. Loretta Lees (2000) suggests that the complex geography of gentrification means that both culture and capital explanations have a part to play. More recently there have been some attempts to reconcile culture and capital arguments by using the work of Pierre Bourdieu to look at gentrification as a manifestation of cultural capital (Butler 2003; Butler and Robson 2001; Bridge 2001a, 2001b).

At the same time as we might chart this move from description to explanation there have been numerous case studies which have looked at particular neighbourhood or city examples of the process. However, on the whole there has been more theory and less observation in recent times with perhaps not enough work to connect the two and engage with pragmatic policy responses to gentrification. This is highlighted by the use of urban pioneer terminology in the UK urban renaissance documentation which sought to promote a new life for Britain's cities (Lees 2003c). Economic and local state institutions often seem strongly motivated by re-capturing the middle class in the central city as both a symbol of, and mechanism for, success. All of this only serves to maintain and sustain moves towards a gentrifying imperative in many cities.

THE GENTRIFIED NEIGHBOURHOOD IN A GLOBAL CONTEXT

Whatever the emphasis given to capital or culture we argue that gentrification today must be seen in the context of globalisation. Globalisation has become a complex term expressing conflicting conceptualisations of growing economic, political and cultural interchanges at the ultimate geographical scale. For Cable (1999) 'globalization has become a portmanteau term—of description, approval or abuse' (p. 2) while, for theorists like Giddens, globalisation represented a decoupling of space and time with knowledge and culture being shared around the globe in very short timespans (1990). For other writers globalisation has been expressed as a kind of re-articulation of state power (Brenner 1998) at supra and sub-state levels which have become increasingly significant.

The literature on globalisation has not been geared towards the level of the neighbourhood. However, in the context of neighbourhood changes like gentrification it would seem increasingly important to acknowledge that neighbourhood scales may be an important locus of concentrations of professionals and managerial groups in networks of dialogue and co-ordination of state and sub-state governance structures. In short, the neighbourhood has been under-recognised as the site of the reproduction of a wider set of power relations and contacts which operate at local, urban, regional, and international levels.

On the political left globalisation has been seen as an ideology of and for that of the political right, a justification for unilat-eral trading partnerships, persistent and widening inequalities and a pro-growth movement that has extended largely west-ern economic hegemony at the expense of the global 'south'. The contested nature of the debate on globalisation should not be understated. Key questions remain over the role of the state, global economic actors and corporations and the relative impact on and involvement of the world's poor. However, our focus in this book here is less on the globalisation debate itself, but, rather, on the connections between processes of global social and economic change and upward changes at the neighbourhood scale.

Literature on the effects of globalisation has often focused on its impacts on poorer social groups generally and burgeoning international trade specifically. Processes of global migration by social elites and population displacement of the poor have largely operated in separate social spheres with the former generally being unregu-lated and embraced while the latter has been seen as a distinctive and unwelcome fallout of regional conflicts. Even in the 'advanced' industrial west competition for foreign investment, financial services and the groups servicing these developments, have led away from welfare and social jus-tice agendas in an attempt to remain com-petitive. The market has been portrayed as a natural reality. The effect in many cities has become increasingly apparent with labour market deregulation, neighbourhood revi-talisation and welfare retrenchment leading to progressively ghettoised poverty isolated from work opportunities (Cross and Moore 2002; Friedrichs 2002).

At the crest of this wave of urban rede-velopment and colonisation ride the gen-trifiers who appear as both the emissaries of global capital flows as well as new-found victims of employment restructuring instigated some years back (Sennett 1998; Butler 2003). For Butler a key message is that gentrification itself may be understood as a response to the insecurities of rapid flows of global finance and identity. Sense of place has become a basis for the onto-logical security of professionals seeking the habitus of neighbourhood living with like-minded people.

The explanation offered by Smith's rent gap formulation (1979, 1996) now seems to underpin an expanded cognitive map of search and re-location activities of elite social fractions, be they political, cultural or economic. In a sense the decision to locate in Seattle is no longer a world apart from London in its amenity or ambience, even less its distance by jet. At another level in the professional and urban hierarchy this might be a choice between Athens and Auckland, Madrid and Mumbai. International services, ICT linkages, increasing urban homogeneity of services and 'feel', as well as rapid travel, mean that many more 'new' neighbourhoods exist insulated from local poverty, wider systemic inequalities and public squalor (Graham and Marvin 2001).

Gentrification appears as a facet of the global forces acting on rapidly urba-nising cities in the south and on post-communist cities where the impacts are particularly complex. In cities of the south massive in-migration from the countryside in search of work and strong in situ fertility combines with restrictions in the supply of land, because of private ownership, which has resulted in unprece-dented levels of unemployment, inadequate shelter and homelessness. At the same time the communications and financial services sectors have expanded in many of these cities, resulting in a larger professional managerial class. In residential terms this has resulted in a reinforcement and expansion of colonial patterns of neighbourhood segregation with many elites retreating into gated communities, or leaving the city for luxury residential developments in ex-urban locations.

Foreign Direct Investment has been moving away from the west for the last decade. This measure of relative expansion of transnational corporations and globalisation has been growing particularly quickly in Eastern Europe and developing countries since 1992, though the asset base of these companies often remains largely in the West and other developed economies. In Eastern Europe and post-communist cities social divisions have increased in a housing market that is at once commodifying property relations and subject to the repatriation of property to pre-communist owners. The particular configuration of these forces led to city by city and neighbourhood differences in the extent and impact of gentrification, as Ludk Sýkora points out in this volume.

A further element of gentrification, as an aspect of globalising tendencies, has been neighbourhood-to-neighbourhood connections between geographically dispersed locations. This has already been suggested in the connections between the residential destinations of the cosmopolitan professional managerial class but there is the other side of the global city represented by social networks of recruitment and migration of low-paid personal service workers who, for instance, clean the offices and apartments of the professional elite (Sassen 2000b). The transnational migration and sustained identities of unskilled service workers tie disparate neighbourhoods together in ways

explored by Jerry Krase in his chapter in this volume.

Nevertheless we should be both receptive and critical to the idea that gentrifiers float somehow weightlessly in their residential choices. The economic forces that drive residential mobility are often tempered by the gravitational forces of social networks, kin and friendship ties, as well as national background and heritage. However, networks of elites and cosmopolitan professional managerial classes present challenges in terms of understanding their culture, lifestyle and social cohesion. This cosmopolitan class has skills that now transfer anywhere and can be argued to possess 'decontextualised cultural capital' (Hannerz 1996: 108) that allow portable social resources to be deployed in new contexts. This ability to transfer professional skills has created a super-mobile fraction that consider their identities in a global context (Rofe 2003) while professional and managerial groups more embedded in national and neighbourhood contexts perhaps aspire to these kinds of networked and boundless identities.

Cosmopolitan elites in exclusive residential enclaves may have stronger ties to similar neighbourhoods in other global cities than to the city that surrounds them (Sassen 2000a, 2000b, 1998; Rofe 2003). They live in the neighbourhood equivalent of a city-state. Increasing rapidity of information flows, financial transactions, population migration and travel have all helped to connect people, institutions and states in ways that have had profound consequences not just for societies but also the cities and neighbourhoods of cities. In short, there is an increasing sense that what is happening at a global scale is being articulated in small urban areas, transmitted by key social groups who have selectively grown as a result of a shift towards personal, financial and information services and boosted by both free and selective trading at the global scale. In this sense, it is no coincidence that cities like New York, Tokyo and London were at the vanguard of gentrification activity linked to a space of flows of information and finance (Graham and Marvin 2001; Hamnett 2003; Castells 1996). Like Merton's foot-loose 'cosmopolitans' (1957) gentrifiers form a residential class who share an identity shaped by locational preferences, stage in the lifecycle, occupation and a social network that crosses national boundaries.

As well as the gap in land values between city and suburb there are now relativities that inform investment decisions on specific neighbourhoods at a global scale. Whether it be Battery Park City, New York, or Chelsea Harbour and Islington, London, or Darling Harbour, Sydney or the smaller scale versions in numerous other cities, investment opportunities are now driven by super-profits on highly valued locations, rather than by comparisons with devalorised land: a kind of global 'rent gap'. These investments in luxury residential developments are made by transnational corporations and involve architects with international reputations. Neil Smith's point is that this model of urban reinvestment is driving much more modest projects sponsored by national urban policy in the form of versions of 'urban renaissance'.

Figure 5.1 considers the critical processes underpinning the transformations we have been discussing at significant spatial scales.

These processes may be conceived as drivers of local neighbourhood change with diverse outcomes as well as intrinsic processes of globalisation.

The global forces consist of communications technology that creates a 'space of flows' (Castells 1996) between certain key locations in a global context. It consists of a transnational set of elite gentrifiers both following and being created by the expansion of financial services in certain key cities and the real estate investment that exploits these changes in the labour market. These changes have been particularly concentrated in the major global cities (such as London, New York, San Francisco and Tokyo) and the newly emerging global cities, such as Shanghai, but they also impact on many large cities in regional settings. The effects of these changes are also felt lower down the urban hierarchy as suitable neighbourhoods have been 'filled up' in leading cities so that gentrification has been pushed to other areas hitherto not considered. In addition to this cascade effect (Hamnett 2003) a much wider range of city types and locations are feeling the impact of international trade.

As we pass to the national level interest rate levels impact on the amount of activity in the residential market but also the degree of overseas investment in that market. The degree to which nations are placing themselves (or are able to place themselves) as tertiary or quarternary specialists in a global

Figure 5.1 Spatial scales of global transformation and forces shaping neighbourhood change

Global		National		City		Neighbourhood
• Migration of the rich and educated • Global governance and trade policy rules • Financial markets • Communications and travel (ICT and transport infrastructure)	⇨	• Policies on inward investment • Migration of the poor • Welfare infrastructure • Property rights and legislation • Relative scale of middle class	⇨	• City administration: – Receptiveness/ subsidy of investment – Labour regulations – Fiscal autonomy • Local infrastructure- amenity environment quality of life	⇨	• Gentrification • Ghettoized poverty

marketplace impacts on the size and prominence of the professional managerial class *vis-à-vis* the working class and other economic groups. National legal frameworks for property ownership are also important. This has taken a particular prominence in post-communist cities where ownership is being transferred or is subject to dispute. It is also significant in many cites of the global south where the high levels of private land ownership severely restrict the ability of municipal governments to obtain land for social or affordable housing development.

At the city level the overall labour market mix will determine the degree to which gentrification is manifest in the urban form. Even with continued suburbanisation pockets of gentrification are visible even where the total number of professional managerial workers is quite modest. The reasons for this may vary widely, from utilitarian consideration of accessibility to city centre jobs to aesthetic and lifestyle choices. In cities where there has been a significant historical shift from manufacturing to service sector employment (of both high and low skills) the impacts of gentrification in terms of displacement of working-class and poorer residents are likely to be greatest. In some rapidly growing cities of the south, such as São Paulo or Beijing, both service sector and manufacturing employment are growing apace with the bifurcated effects in terms of social residential divides of wealth and poverty. The existing tenure structure of a country also has an impact. In countries where renting has been the norm (such as the Netherlands or Eastern European countries), the impacts of gentrification have hitherto been more restricted but now provide a weaker set of property relations through which gentrification has easily cut a swathe.

Related to levels of de-industrialisation (or absence of industrialisation) and the size of the city is the overall quality of life in different cities. Access to open space, to leisure and cultural facilities and the general liveability and manageability of the particular urban environment has been significant in attracting gentrifiers, as Ley (1996) and others noted some years ago. The quality of life in the city is now seen by many city governments as a key element to sell the city to prospective middle-class residents, to lure them back from the suburbs. This last point is related to the idea of urban government as entrepreneur, rather than manager, a change noted by David Harvey fifteen years ago (Harvey 1989).

The place marketing of cities (Kearns and Philo 1993) and other forms of civic boosterism and growth coalitions (Logan and Molotch 1987) has become more evident as cities increasingly compete with each other for inward-investment. With Florida's (2003) popular argument that city competitiveness is essentially linked to where bohemian, gay and professionals wish to locate, gentrification has been reconfirmed to city fathers as the route to economic success. The particular parts of the city that investors or gentrifiers head for are determined by their architectural desirability or symbolic value as a landmark location. Clearly neighbourhood distinctions in tenure mix are vital as well as the degree of disinvestments in the local housing stock, although the latter tend to be more important in the early stages of gentrification. [. . .]

REFERENCES

Atkinson, R. (ed.) (2003) 'Gentrification in a new century: misunderstood saviour or vengeful wrecker? What really is the problem with gentrification?', *Urban Studies*, (special issue), 40(12): 2343–50.

Brenner, N. (1998) 'Global cities, global states: global city formation and state territorial restructuring in contemporary Europe', *Review of International Political Economy*, 5(1): 1–37.

Bridge, G. (2001a) 'Bourdieu, rational action and the time-space strategy of gentrification', *Transactions of the Institute of British Geographers*, 26(2): 205–16.

Bridge, G. (2001b) 'Estate agents as intermediaries between economic and cultural capital: the "gentrification premium" in the Sydney housing market', *International Journal of Urban and Regional Research*, 25(1) March: 87–101.

Bridge, G. (2003) 'Time–Space trajectories in provincial gentrification', *Urban Studies*, 40: 2545–56.

Butler, T. and Robson, G. (2001a) 'Social capital, gentrification and neighbourhood change in London: a comparison of three South London neighbourhoods', *Urban Studies*, 38: 2145–62.

Butler, T. and Robson, T. (2001b) 'Coming to terms with London: middle-class communities in a global city', *International Journal of Urban and Regional Research*, 25: 70–86.

Cable, V. (1999) *Globalization and Global Governance*, London: Royal Institute of International Affairs.

Castells, M. (1996) *The Rise of the Network Society*, Oxford: Blackwell.

Cross, M. and Moore, R. (2002) *Globalization and the New City: Migrants, Minorities and Urban Transformations in Comparative Perspective*, London: Palgrave.

Florida, R. (2003) *The Rise of the Creative Class: and How It's Transforming Work, Leisure, Community and Everyday Life*, New York: Basic Books.

Friedrichs, J. (2002) 'Globalization, urban restructuring and employment prospects', in M. Cross and R. Moore (eds) *Globalization and the New City: Migrants, Minorities and Urban Transformations in Comparative Perspective*, London: Palgrave, pp. 119–32.

Giddens, A. (1990) *The Consequences of Modernity*, Cambridge: Polity Press.

Glass, R. (1964) 'Introduction: aspects of change', in Centre for Urban Studies (ed.) *London: Aspects of Change*, London: MacGibbon and Kee.

Gouldner, A. (1979) *The Future of Intellectuals and the Rise of the New Class*, London: Macmillan.

Graham, S. and Marvin, S. (2001) *Splintering Urbanism: Networked Infrastructures, Technological Mobilities and the Urban Condition*, London: Routledge.

Hamnett, C. (1994) 'Socio-economic change in London: professionalisation or polarisation', *Built Environment*, 20: 192–204.

Hamnett, C. (2003) 'Gentrification and the middle-class remaking of Inner London, 1961–2001', *Urban Studies*, 40(12): 2401–26.

Hannerz, U. (1996) *Transnational Connections: Culture, People, Places*, London: Comedia.

Harvey, D. (1989) 'From managerialism to entrepreneurialism: the transformation of urban governance in late capitalism', *Geografiska Annaler*, 71B(1): 3–17.

Kearns, G. and Philo, C. (eds) (1993) *Selling Places: The City as Cultural Capital, Past and Present*, Oxford: Pergamon Press.

Laska, S. and Spain, D. (eds) (1980) *Back to the City: Issues in Neighbourhood Renovation*, Oxford: Pergamon Press.

Lees, L. (2000) 'A reappraisal of gentrification: towards a "geography of gentrification"', *Progress in Human Geography*, 24(3): 389–408.

Lees, L. (2003) 'Visions of "urban renaissance": the urban task force report and the urban white paper', in R. Imrie and M. Raco (eds) *Urban Renaissance? New Labour, Community and Urban Policy*, Bristol: Policy Press, pp. 66–82.

Ley, D. (1986) 'Alternative explanations for inner-city gentrification', *Annals of the Association of American Geographers*, 76: 521–35.

Ley, D. (1996) *The New Middle Class and the Remaking of the Central City*, London: Oxford University Press.

Logan, J. and Molotch, H. (1987) *Urban Fortunes: The Political Economy of Place*, Berkeley and Los Angeles, CA: University of California Press.

Marcuse, P. (1989) 'Gentrification, homelessness and the work process: housing market and labour markets in the quartered city', *Housing Studies*, 4(3): 211–20.

Merton, R. K. (1957) *Social Theory and Social Structure*, Glencoe: Free Press.

Phillips, M. (1993) 'Rural gentrification and the processes of class colonisation', *Journal of Rural Studies*, 9(2): 123–40.

Rofe, M. (2003) '"I want to be global": theorising the gentrifying class as an emerges elite global community', *Urban Studies*, 40(12): 2511–27.

Rose, D. (1984) 'Rethinking gentrification: beyond the uneven development of Marxist urban theory', *Environment and Planning D: Society and Space*, 1: 47–74.

Sassen, S. (1998) *Globalisation and its Discontents*, New York: New Press.

Sassen, S. (2000a) *The Global City: New York, London, Tokyo*, 2nd edn, Princeton, NJ: Princeton University Press.

Sassen, S. (2000b) *Cities in a World Economy*, 2nd edn, Thousand Oaks, CA: Pine Forge Press.

Sennett, R. (1998) *The Corrosion of Character: The Personal Consequences of Work in the New Capitalism*, London: W.W. Norton.

Slater, T. (2002) 'Looking at the "North American City" through the lens of gentrification discourse', *Urban Geography*, 23(1): 131–53.

Smith, D. (2003) 'Extending the temporal and spatial limits of gentrification: a research agenda for population geographers,' *International Journal of Population Geography*, 8(6): 385–394.

Smith, N. (1979) 'Toward a theory of gentrification: a back to the city movement capital, not people', *Journal of the American Planning Association*, 45(4): 583–48.

Smith, N. (1996) *The New Urban Frontier: Gentrification and the Revanchist City*. New York: Routledge.

Smith, N. (2002) 'New globalism, new urbanism: gentrification as global urban strategy, *Antipode*, 34(3): 428–50.

Zukin, S. (1982) *Loft Living: Culture and Capital in Urban Change*, Baltimore: Johns Hopkins University Press.

Zukin, S. (1995) *The Cultures of Cities*, Cambridge, MA: Blackwell.

PART II

*H*ow, Where and When Does Gentrification Occur?

INTRODUCTION

The readings in this section of the book address two related areas of debate within the gentrification literature. The first is about the centrality of several general conditions to the rise of gentrification in many cities across the globe. As the first section of the book began to reveal, students of gentrification debate about the relative import for gentrification of political, economic, physical (e.g., characteristics of local housing stock and of the landscape), demographic, and cultural conditions. In short, scholars offer multiple and sometimes competing explanations for why gentrification occurs and, more specifically, for its endemic quality over the last forty years. The second debate is, in simplest terms, about explanations for why some places gentrify, while others do not. Relatedly, they also deliberate over why some cities and neighborhoods experience gentrification years or even decades *before* other cities and neighborhoods. For instance, they might offer competing explanations for why artists gentrified Chicago's Wicker Park, a historically Polish neighborhood with a large working class Latino population (Lloyd 2005), before professionals began refurbishing homes in Chicago's predominately African-American North Kenwood-Oakland neighborhood (Pattillo 2008).

While at first glance these areas of debate may seem trivial, the questions that inspire them are of consequence. Imagine that you are interning for a city planning office that has funds to construct affordable housing units. Data demonstrate that in recent decades gentrification has displaced many low income and working class residents of central city neighborhoods, many of whom are Latino or African-American. For this reason, you believe that the city should, at the very least, offset displacement by building affordable units in a neighborhood that is likely to experience gentrification in the coming decade. You review the literature to identify indicators that suggest that a place is ripe for gentrification and develop a report for your employers. This section's readings will outline many of the indicators that you might look for.

Those involved with planning are not the only individuals who undertake such calculations. Imagine the developer who wishes to determine which city or neighborhood to invest in or the city councilwoman who seeks to predict who her constituency will be when she runs for re-election. Many individual gentrifiers and business owners make similar calculations. For instance, when conducting research for my book, *A Neighborhood That*

Never Changes, a gentrifier explained how he decided to purchase a home in Chicago's Argyle neighborhood:

> "It was incredibly bad on the street where I bought. [But] the deal I got on a condo was unbelievable. I just couldn't pass it up . . . It was a renovated building. It was really spacious. I got a five-bedroom place. My mortgage right now, I couldn't even rent a studio apartment for what I pay for the mortgage . . . *and I had known that progress kept coming north up the lake*" (Brown-Saracino 2009: 72, *my emphasis*).

By visiting neighborhoods and talking with friends this homebuyer believed that he could trace gentrification's trajectory through Chicago—"progress kept coming north up the lake"—and, indeed, Argyle has experienced substantial gentrification in the decade since he purchased. As he was searching for a soon-to-gentrify-neighborhood, social service agencies a few blocks from the condominium he purchased also suspected that gentrification was coming to Argyle and for this reason they began preparing to meet the needs of longtime residents whom they predicted would soon face displacement and the disruption of longstanding social support networks.

How did the homeowner and social workers accurately predict that Argyle would gentrify? What is the precise calculus that such individuals rely on? While this section's readings do not offer straightforward predictions of which places will gentrify next, they do offer a review of competing explanations for how gentrification occurs and why certain places experience gentrification while others do not. For instance, sociologist Christopher Mele outlines how city policy makers, developers, small business owners, and even artists and punks contributed to the gentrification of New York's East Village.

Cumulatively, the readings offer a long list of the actors and processes central to explaining the where, when, how, and why of gentrification. These range from developers to individual gentrifiers and from cycles of property devaluation to neoliberal economic policy. While this section will familiarize you with the actors and processes that the literature attends to, it will also introduce you to a set of debates about those actors and processes, specifically about the relative weight of individual actors and trends, as well as about the influence of *classes* of people and processes that create and shape gentrification.

Gentrification scholars often break such actors and processes into two classes or categories of factors. *Production* or *supply side factors* include cycles of disinvestment and reinvestment in central city neighborhoods, neoliberal state policies that help facilitate and sustain free market capitalism (Harvey 1989, Peck 2006), deindustrialization and the rise of a global service economy, and liberal mortgage lending policies. As an example, in the literature's first decades scholars debated the hypothesis that gentrification occurs when there is a shortage of middle class housing outside of the central city, thus pushing members of the middle class into inner-city neighborhoods (Gale 1979, Berry 1980), and many continue to advocate for Neil Smith's rent-gap hypothesis, which suggests that gentrifiers and investors take advantage of a gap between current and potential ground rent values. In short, supply side explanations suggest that economic and political conditions enable gentrification and that in some places and times conditions align to produce the buildings, funding, and state policies required for the gentrification of a particular neighborhood.

In contrast, *consumption* or *demand side explanations*, proposed by scholars like David Ley (1986, 1996; see also Caulfield 1994), counter that a market cannot exist without complimentary consumer demand and preferences. That is, they suggest that housing stock, economics, and state policies influence gentrification, but that gentrification would not occur without gentrifiers who wish to participate in the process (e.g., Gale 1979, Ley 1986). Indeed, some who advocate for demand side explanations suggest that markets and states respond to consumer demand for gentrification, rather than vice versa. Behind this class of explanations is belief in the central role of the gentrifier in driving gentrification, as well as the belief that culture—typically in the form of gentrifiers' tastes—helps fuel gentrification. Scholars who advocate for this position suggest that an ideological shift—what Ruth Glass refers to as "a switch from suburban to urban aspirations" (1964: xxxi)—enabled gentrification. They propose that without a set of cultural changes, such as increasing interest in diversity (Ley 1996, Butler & Robson 2001, Rose 2004, Berrey 2005, Lloyd 2005) and taste for historic properties (Zukin 1987, Beauregard 1990, Smith 2002), gentrifiers would not participate in the process.

According to David Ley's influential argument, which is at the center of many consumption explanations, gentrification is closely related to the tastes of the expanding "new middle class." In an article published in 1986 he rejects Neil Smith's rent-gap hypothesis, arguing that evidence for it is "entirely lacking" in Canada (531). He also suggests that for many gentrifiers residence in the central city is not a matter of economic necessity, for they could afford to live in more expensive locales, such as certain suburbs (ibid.: 524). Thus, as his essay in this section suggests, he concludes that a cultural and political sensibility closely attached to the new middle class—the white collar workers associated with a post-industrial, service-oriented economy (Bell 1973, Caulfield 1994, Ley 1996)—drives gentrification. Ley argues that members of the new middle class relocate in search of certain place attributes, such as diversity, a sense of history, and landscape amenities (1986, 1996).

For many years the divide between production and consumption camps was fairly rigid, but not all gentrification scholars fell neatly on either side of the debate and the line between the two camps is increasingly blurry. In fact, many argue that production and consumption factors play mutually supportive roles in gentrification (e.g., Beauregard 1986, Hamnett 1991, Ley 2003). However, there is less agreement about which set of factors *drives or spurs* gentrification. Indeed, scholars provide competing answers to a central question in the literature: *What creates a market for gentrification, production or consumption factors?*

Some of the essays in this section answer this question in absolute terms. For instance in the 1979 article described above, geographer Neil Smith overtly rejects individual preference or consumption explanations for gentrification. This rejection is abundantly clear in the subtitle to his article, "A Back to the City Movement by Capital, not People." The argument Smith puts forth in the article—that disinvestment in properties in certain central city neighborhoods produced a gap between current and potential land rents and therefore enabled investors, from individual gentrifiers to investment firms, to profit by investing in or speculating on such properties—is arguably among the most influential pieces of gentrification scholarship to date.

Others demonstrate how supply and demand factors conspire to create markets. For instance, in a selection from his book on the gentrification of New York's East Village Christopher Mele suggests that city government and investors built on first-wave gentrifiers' art scene to increase demand for residence in the gentrifying neighborhood. He writes, "Municipal agencies sought to promote their own interests and those of developers through manipulation of certain symbols representative of the East Village art scene and not others" (2000: 239).

The question of whether supply or demand factors drive gentrification is not the only issue that researchers debate. Even among production-side theorists there is disagreement about the relative weight of specific supply side factors. For instance, scholars ask: *What is the relative influence of market conditions versus government policies and practices?* Neil Smith argues that gentrification is "an expected product of the relatively unhampered operation of the land and housing markets" (1979: 538). This acknowledges government's import, but nonetheless emphasizes the role of economic processes. In the section's final reading, Kevin Fox Gotham builds on this by suggesting that in some instances, such as in the gentrification of New Orleans' French Quarter that he details, large corporations play a central role in gentrification (2005). In contrast, several of the readings in this section suggest that *coalitions* of politicians, policy makers, media, developers, and financial institutions work together to ensure the gentrification of certain neighborhoods. In a selection from their highly acclaimed book, *Urban Fortunes*, John Logan and Harvey Molotch refer to these as "growth machine coalitions" (1986).

Cumulatively, the readings in this section of the book encourage us to ask: *What role does culture play in gentrification?* Scholars answer this question in a number of different ways. For instance, Gary Bridge suggests that Sydney estate agents interpret and market to the tastes of longtime residents and potential gentrifiers (2001), and Sharon Zukin demonstrates how cities use an "arts infrastructure" (1982: 131) to lure capital to the central city. Christopher Mele, on the other hand, suggests that gentrifiers and investors are drawn to the East Village, in part, by appreciation for the "glamour of poverty" (2000: 236) and that local amenities, such as galleries and restaurants, reflect and market to this set of tastes.

As the above examples demonstrate, while such authors believe that culture plays a role in gentrification they do not all concur about what that role is. For instance, they debate about whether markets *respond to* or *produce* cultural motivations for participation in gentrification (Brown-Saracino 2009; see also Borer 2006). Put in different terms, some also ask whether culture encourages gentrification or is used to justify it after the fact. For instance, Neil Smith writes of a frontier myth that glamorizes the role of gentrifiers who imagine that they are helping to "settle" the "dangerous" central city. He suggests that this myth helps "to socialize a wholly new and therefore challenging set of processes into safe ideological focus. As such, the frontier ideology justifies monstrous incivility in the heart of the city" (1996: 18).

The central debate from which these questions about culture arise—about the relative primacy of production and consumption explanations for gentrification—is apparent in efforts to answer two additional questions about gentrification: first, in work that seeks to explain why gentrification occurs in some places, and second, in related work on the relationship between globalization and gentrification. The following paragraphs explore each of these micro-debates and their relationship to broader conversations about consumption and production.

Where does gentrification occur? Some research, such as Neil Smith's rent-gap hypothesis, turns to production-side explanations to answer this question. Smith suggests that gentrification occurs where the gap between existing and potential ground rents is greatest (1979). Also borrowing from production-side arguments, many suggest that gentrification occurs in neighborhoods or cities that are in close proximity to other affluent areas (e.g., Ley 1986). This contagion-explanation is apparent in my aforementioned informant's explanation for his decision to purchase in Argyle: "gentrification kept coming north up the lake." Furthermore, a host of scholars suggest that gentrification flourishes where politicians and planners promote revitalization, such as by creating employment opportunities for "high-wage white-collar workers" (Wyly et al. 1998; see also Berry 1985), using the police to enforce middle class norms of social behavior (Mele 2000, Taylor 2002, Pattillo 2007), or by donating or selling land or buildings for redevelopment on the private market (Logan & Molotch 1987).

In contrast, consumption-side explanations suggest that places gentrify largely because they possess amenities that appeal to the gentrifying class. These amenities include, but are not limited to, social diversity (Ley 1986, Berrey 2005), landscape amenities, such as water views, close proximity to downtown jobs, bike trails (Ley 1986, Florida 2002), or historic properties (Ley 1986). Research on the gentrification of suburban and rural areas suggests that technological changes, such as those that permit telecommuting, allow individuals to relocate from employment centers in search of place amenities, such as historical "authenticity" or proximity to outdoor leisure activities (Macgregor 2005, Brown-Saracino 2009).

Indeed, many scholars agree that gentrification is expanding—not only within the urban centers in which it first emerged and into rural areas, but also across the globe. Roland Atkinson writes that, "The map of gentrification appears to be extending steadily. It would certainly appear that public policy designs as well as the systemic facilitation of gentrification are taking place at a much wider scale than was the case even a few years ago" (2003: 2343). However, there is debate about why gentrification is expanding. As Atkinson alludes to, some regard this as primarily a result of "public policy designs" (2003: 2343; see also Smith 1989, Bailey and Robertson 1997), while others point to the expansion of the "new middle class" (Ley 1996), or, more generally, to globalization.

Explanations for this expansion—particularly for its global quality—mirror the divide between production and consumption explanations. For instance, Neil Smith's allegiance to production-side explanations is apparent in his argument that gentrification "is densely connected into the circuits of global capital and cultural circulation" (2002: 427). Smith regards gentrification as a method or strategy of global expansion of capital (ibid.: 446–447) that neoliberal state policies largely drive. For Smith, neoliberalism rests on the belief "that the free and democratic exercise of individual self-interest led to the optimal collective social good; and that the market knows best" (ibid.: 429). Thus, in his view, states, both individually and in cooperation with one another, give the market the freedom to accumulate capital as it sees fit, with relatively little concern for the welfare of those harmed by accumulation strategies, such as gentrification.

Others suggest that the relationship between globalization and gentrification rests on an increasingly global competition for resources between cities (Lees et al. 2008: 167, Harvey 1989, Mitchell 2003). They suggest that gentrification is one strategy that cities use to accumulate capital and to mark themselves as distinct, attractive, or cutting edge. For instance, in early 2009 when the International Olympic Committee toured Chicago to evaluate its bid to host the 2016 Olympics, their guides ushered them not only to athletic fields and tennis facilities, but also through the city's most upscale sections. Likewise, cities worry about their global city rankings (Hersch 2009). Such rankings matter not only because they might help secure the Olympics or encourage companies to relocate to a given city, but also because they attract tourists and gentrifiers who are members of a global elite (Rofe

2003). Many cities are convinced of the import of such rankings. For instance, in March of 2009 *Forbes Magazine* named Portland, Maine "America's Most Livable City." When I arrived two months later to conduct fieldwork the city had placed a banner listing the honor across a central avenue.

For the most part, scholars have suggested that gentrification flourishes in cities at the top of the global economy (Sassen 1998). However, the essay by Atkinson and Bridge in the book's first section suggests that gentrification is not limited to such cities (see also Smith 2002). Indeed, as they note, gentrification has been observed in cities across the globe, including in post-communist nations and industrialized places. Why has this expansion occurred? Borrowing from consumption-side explanations, Atkinson and Bridge allude to the increasing concentration of the new middle class or "international professional managerial class" as a key contributing factor (2005; see also Ley 1996). However, this is not the only explanation they provide for the gentrification of a range of cities within and beyond North America, Europe, and Australia. Specifically, they suggest that market reforms of the kind that Smith (2002) details also play a role, but they place greater emphasis than Smith on the choices and movement of those who compose the gentrifying class, arguing that in the context of gentrification this new middle class mirrors their colonial predecessors (Atkinson & Bridge 2005: 3). How does this class decide where to live? According to Atkinson and Bridge the location of the transnational corporations at which many work are of significant influence.

Thus, Atkinson and Bridge speak to the debate between consumption and production explanations for gentrification—adopting a hybrid approach—while also proposing answers to questions about why gentrification is expanding and where it takes place. On the one hand they borrow from consumption-side explanations to suggest that the tastes of the global new middle class who seek, among other amenities, "access to open space, to leisure and cultural facilities" (2005: 11; see also Ley 1996, Florida 2002) guides gentrification. On the other hand, relying on production-side logic, they suggest that the choices of the global companies for which some members of the new middle class work—choices influenced by many of the conditions that Neil Smith specifies (2002)—also determine which locales gentrify.

Thus, when scholars seek to answer questions about how, where, why, and when gentrification occurs they repeatedly consider the relationship between production and consumption explanations. As you read the selections in this portion of the book, I encourage you to think about how you would answer the questions that color the literature. Given the evidence that the authors present, do you believe that supply or demand factors drive gentrification? Depending on how you answer that question, which supply and which demand factors do you think are paramount? Finally, what role do the readings, individually and cumulatively, suggest that culture plays in gentrification?

You might also think about how you would tackle the planning intern's task of predicting which neighborhoods will gentrify next. Assuming that the task were your own, would you look for evidence of a rent gap, or seek to identify the neighborhoods in which the city has recently funded beautification efforts or improved streets and sidewalks? Alternately, would you tour neighborhoods to determine where young artists rent studio space or ask realtors about the neighborhoods in which they are listing new properties? In turn, you might consider what your answers suggest about your response to the broader questions that underline them about how, why, when, and where gentrification occurs and where you fall in the debate between consumption and production explanations.

As you consider these questions I encourage you to return to the line of inquiry that frames the book's first section, for the way that we define gentrification influences how we answer questions about where, when, how, and why gentrification occurs. For instance, if the movement of the middle class into previously disinvested areas is central to your definition of gentrification, you may be more likely than those who emphasize the import of the new middle class' appreciation for urbanity to identify gentrification in suburban and rural areas (Atkinson 2003: 2344). Likewise, if the displacement of longstanding residents and related demographic shifts are central to your definition, then perhaps you do not consider the development of previously uninhabited lots to be part and parcel of gentrification's expansion (for criticisms of this view see Bourne 1993; see also Wyly et al. 1998). In other words, I encourage you to return to the definition of gentrification that you settled on when reading the previous section and to consider the production and consumption debates when you think anew about the stakes of the qualities of person, place, and process your definition emphasizes.

DISCUSSION QUESTIONS

1) Which are of greater influence for gentrification, production or consumption factors?

   a. What evidence do you believe is required to support either argument?

2) Which production or consumption factors do you believe are of greatest import for gentrification?

   a. How or why might this vary by context, such as by city, nation, or decade?

3) What role do you believe culture plays in gentrification?

   a. If you believe that culture plays a central role, is it because it is consciously manipulated to spur gentrification or because it unconsciously draws gentrifiers to specific locales?

4) What are gentrification's consequences for longtime residents' cultures?

5) In recent years several scholars have published books on the gentrification of predominately African-American neighborhoods by African-American gentrifiers (e.g., Taylor 2002, Pattillo 2007, Boyd 2008, Hyra 2008). Do you believe that this reflects changes in gentrification or changes in gentrification scholarship? Be sure to support your argument with evidence from the readings.

ACTIVITIES

1. Interview several residents of a gentrifying neighborhood who vary in terms of their length of residence, economic position, and other demographic characteristics, such as race, ethnicity, age, gender, or sexual identity. What explanations do they provide for their neighborhood's gentrification? How do their explanations vary based on their economic traits, demographic characteristics, or length of residence?

2. Interview several city officials or planners in a city experiencing gentrification. What explanations do they provide for why certain neighborhoods have gentrified?

   a. If you conducted the first and second activities consider the similarities and differences between the answers that residents, officials, and planners provided. If you conducted only one activity, speak with a classmate who conducted the alternate activity about the differences between your findings.

3. Review the two documentaries and two novels referenced in the previous section—*Flag Wars, 7th Street, Mystic River* (2001) and *Fortress of Solitude* (2003). What does each imply about gentrification's origins?

4. Select and read five journalistic accounts of gentrification. What explanation, if any, do they provide for when, why, how, and where gentrification occurs?

RESOURCES

Heidkamp, C.P., & Lucas, S., 2006. "Finding the Gentrification Frontier Using Census Data: The Case of Portland, Maine," *Urban Geography*, Vol. 27, 101–125.

Lees L., 2000. "A Reappraisal of Gentrification Towards a 'Geography of Gentrification'," *Progress in Human Geography* 24, 389–408.

Ley, D., 1986. "Alternative Explanations of Inner-city Gentrification: A Canadian Assessment," *Annals of the Association of American Geographers*, Vol. 76, 521–535.

Ley, D., 1993. "Gentrification in Recession: Social Change in Six Canadian Inner Cities, 1981–1986," *Urban Geography*, Vol. 13, 230–256.

Wyly, E.K., & Hammel, D.J., 2000. "Capital's Metropolis: Chicago and the Transformation of American Housing Policy," *Geografiska Annaler. Series B, Human Geography*, 82, 181–206.

CHAPTER 6

Toward a Theory of Gentrification:
A Back to the City Movement by Capital, not People

Neil Smith

Consumer sovereignty hypotheses dominate explanations of gentrification but data on the number of suburbanites returning to the city casts doubt on this hypothesis. In fact, gentrification is an expected product of the relatively unhampered operation of the land and housing markets. The economic depreciation of capital invested in nineteenth century inner-city neighborhoods and the simultaneous rise in potential ground rent levels produces the possibility of profitable redevelopment. Although the very apparent social characteristics of deteriorated neighborhoods would discourage redevelopment, the hidden economic characteristics may well be favorable. Whether gentrification is a fundamental restructuring of urban space depends not on where new inhabitants come from but on how much productive capital returns to the area from the suburbs.

Following a period of sustained deterioration, many American cities are experiencing the gentrification of select central city neighborhoods. Initial signs of revival during the 1950s intensified in the 1960s, and by the 1970s these had grown into a widespread gentrification movement affecting the majority of the country's older cities.[1] A recent survey by the Urban Land Institute (1976) suggests that close to half the 260 cities with over 50,000 population are experiencing rehabilitation in the inner city areas. Although nationally, gentrification accounts for only a small fraction of new housing starts compared with new construction, the process is very important in (but not restricted to) older northeastern cities.

As the process of gentrification burgeoned so did the literature about it. Most of this literature concerns the contemporary processes or its effects: the socio-economic and cultural characteristics of immigrants, displacement, the federal role in redevelopment, benefits to the city, and creation and destruction of community. Little attempt has been made to construct historical explanations of the process, to study causes rather than effects. Instead, explanations are very much taken for granted and fall into two categories: cultural and economic.

Cultural. Popular among revitalization theorists is the notion that young, usually professional, middle-class people have changed their lifestyle. According to Gregory Lipton, these changes have been significant enough to "decrease the relative desirability of single-family, suburban homes" (1977, p. 146). Thus, with a trend toward fewer children, postponed marriages, and a fast rising divorce rate, younger homebuyers and renters are trading in the tarnished dream of their parents for a new dream defined in urban rather than suburban terms. Other researchers emphasize the search for socially distinctive communities as sympathetic environments for individual self-expression (Winters 1978), while still others extend this into a more general argument. In contemporary "post-industrial cities," according to D. Ley, white-collar service occupations supersede blue-collar productive occupations, and this brings with it an emphasis on consumption and amenity not work. Patterns of consumption come to dictate patterns of production; "the values of consumption rather than production guide central city land use decisions" (Ley 1978, p. 11). Inner-city resurgence is an example of this new emphasis on consumption.

Economic. As the cost of newly constructed housing continues to rise and its distance from the city center to increase, the rehabilitation of inner- and central-city structures is seen to be more viable ecnomically. Old but structurally sound properties can be purchased and rehabilitated for less than the cost of a comparable new house. In addition, many researchers stress the high economic cost of commuting—the higher cost of gasoline for private cars and rising fares on public transportation—and the economic benefits of proximity to work.

These conventional hypotheses are by no means mutually exclusive. They are often invoked jointly and share in one vital respect a common perspective—an emphasis on *consumer preference* and the constraints within which these preferences are implemented. This they share with the broader body of neoclassical residential land use theory (Alonso 1964; Muth 1969; Mills 1972). According to the neoclassical theory, suburbanization reflects the preference for space and the increased ability to pay for it due to the reduction of transportational and other constraints. Similarly, gentrification is explained as the result of an alteration of preferences and/or a change

in the constraints determining which preferences will or can be implemented. Thus in the media and the research literature alike, the process is viewed as a "back to the city movement." This applies as much to the earlier gentrification projects, such as Philadelphia's Society Hill (accomplished with substantial state assistance under urban renewal legislation), as it does to the later schemes, such as Baltimore's Federal Hill or Washington's Capitol Hill (mainly private market phenomena of the 1970s). All have become symbolic of a supposed middle- and upper-class pilgrimage back from the suburbs.[2] But as yet it remains an untested if pervasive assumption that the gentrifiers are disillusioned suburbanites. As early as 1966, Herbert Gans declared: "I have seen no study of how many suburbanites were actually brought back by urban-renewal projects" (1968, p. 287). Though this statement was made in evidence before the Ribicoff Committee on the Crisis of the Cities, Gans's challenge seems to have fallen on deaf ears. Only in the late 1970s have such studies begun to be carried out. This paper presents data from Society Hill and other revitalized neighborhoods, examines the significance of these results in terms of the consumer sovereignty theory, and attempts to deepen our theoretical understanding of the causes of gentrification.

A RETURN FROM THE SUBURBS?

Once the location of William Penn's "holy experiment," Society Hill housed Philadelphia's gentry well into the nineteenth century. With industrialization and urban growth, however, its popularity declined, and the gentry together with the rising middle class, moved west to Rittenhouse Square and to the new suburbs in the northwest and across the Schuylkill River. Society Hill deteriorated rapidly, remaining in slum condition until 1959. In that year, an urban renewal plan was implemented.

Within ten years Society Hill was transformed and—"the most historic square mile in the nation" according to Bicentennial advertising—it again housed the city's middle and upper classes. Few authentically restored houses now change hands for less than $125,000. Noting the enthusiasm with which rehabilitation was done, the novelist Nathanial Burt observed that "Remodeling old houses is, after all, one of Old Philadelphia's favorite indoor sports, and to be able to remodel and consciously serve the cause of civic revival all at once has gone to the heads of the upper classes like champagne" (1963, pp. 556–57). As this indoor sport caught on, therefore, it became Philadelphia folklore that "there was an upper class return to center city in Society Hill" (Wolf 1975, p. 325). As Burt eloquently explains:

> The renaissance of Society Hill . . . is just one piece in a gigantic jigsaw puzzle which has stirred Philadelphia from its hundred-year sleep, and promises to transform the city completely. This movement, of which the return to Society Hill is a significant part, is generally known as the Philadelphia Renaissance (1963, p. 539).

By June 1962 less than a third of the families purchasing property for rehabilitation were from the suburbs[3] (Greenfield & Co. 1964, p. 192). But since the first people to rehabilitate houses began work in 1960, it was generally expected that the proportion of suburbanites would rise sharply as the area became better publicized and a Society Hill address became a coveted possession. After 1962, however, no data were officially collected. The following table presents data sampled from case files held by The Redevelopment Authority of Philadelphia; the data is for the period up to 1975 (by which time the project was essentially complete) and represents a 17 percent sample of all rehabilitated residences. (Table 6.1.)

It would appear from these results that only a small proportion of gentrifiers did in fact return from the suburbs; 14 percent in the case of Society Hill, compared with 72 percent who moved from elsewhere within the city boundaries. A statistical breakdown of this latter group suggests that of previous city dwellers, 37 percent came from Society Hill itself, and 19 percent came from the Rittenhouse Square district. The remainder came from several middle- and upper-class suburbs annexed by the city in the last century—Chestnut Hill, Mt. Airy, Spruce Hill. This suggests a consolidation of upper- and middle-class white residences in the city, not a return from the present day suburbs.[4] Additional data from Baltimore and Washington D.C. on the percentage of returning suburbanites support the Society Hill data (Table 6.2).

In Philadelphia and elsewhere an urban renaissance may well be taking place but it

Table 6.1 The origin of rehabilitators in Society Hill, 1964–1975

Year	Same address	Elsewhere in the city	Suburbs	Outside SMSA	Unidentified	Total
1964	5	9	0	0	0	14
1965	3	17	7	0	0	27
1966	1	25	4	0	2	32
1969	1	9	2	0	0	12
1972	1	12	1	2	0	16
1975	0	1	0	0	0	1
Total	11	73	14	2	2	102
Percentage by origin	11	72	14	2	2	100

is not a significant return from the suburbs as such. This does not disprove the consumer sovereignty hypothesis but suggests some limitations and refinements. Clearly, it is possible—even likely—that younger people who moved to the city for an education and professional training have decided against moving back to the suburbs. There is a problem, however, if this is to be taken as a definitive explanation, for gentrification is not simply a North American phenomenon but is also happening in numerous cities throughout Europe (see, for example, Pitt 1977) where the extent of prior middle-class suburbanization is much less and the relation between suburb and inner city is substantially different.[5] Only Ley's (1978) more general societal hypothesis about post-industrial cities is broad enough to account for the process internationally, but the implications of accepting this view are somewhat drastic. If cultural choice and consumer preference really explain gentrification, this amounts either to the hypothesis that individual preferences change in unison not only nationally but internationally—a bleak view of human nature and cultural individuality—or that the overriding constraints are strong enough to obliterate the individuality implied in consumer preference. If the latter is the case, the concept of consumer preference is at best contradictory: a process first conceived in terms of individual consumption preference has now to be explained as resulting from cultural uni-dimensionality. The concept can be rescued as theoretically viable only if it is used to refer to collective social preference, not individual preference.

This refutation of the neoclassical approach to gentrification is only a summary critique and far from exhaustive. What it suggests, however, is a broader conceptualization of the process, for the gentrifier as consumer is only one of many actors participating in the process. To explain

gentrification according to the gentrifier's actions alone, while ignoring the role of builders, developers, landlords, mortgage lenders, government agencies, real estate agents, and tenants, is excessively narrow. A broader theory of gentrification must take the role of producers as well as consumers into account, and when this is done, it appears that the needs of production—in particular the need to earn profit—are a more decisive initiative behind gentrification than consumer preference. This is not to say in some naive way that consumption is the automatic consequence of production, or that consumer preference is a totally passive effect caused by production. Such would be a producer's sovereignty theory, almost as one-sided as its neoclassical counterpart. Rather, the relationship between production and consumption is symbiotic, but it is a symbiosis in which production dominates. Consumer preference and demand for gentrified housing can be created after all, and this is precisely what happened in Society Hill.[6] Although it is of secondary importance in initiating the actual process, and therefore in explaining why gentrification occurred in the first place, consumer preference and demand are of primary importance in determining the final form and character of revitalized areas—the difference between Society Hill, say, and New York's SoHo.

Table 6.2 The origin of rehabilitators in three cities

City	Percent city dwellers	Percent suburbanites
Philadelphia		
Society Hill	72	14
Baltimore		
Homestead Properties	65.2	27
Washington D.C.		
Mount Pleasant	67	18
Capitol Hill	72	15

Source: Baltimore City Department of Housing and Community Development (1977), Gale (1976, 1977).

The so-called urban renaissance has been stimulated more by economic than cultural forces. In the decision to rehabilitate an inner city structure, one consumer preference tends to stand out above the others—the preference for profit, or, more accurately, a sound financial investment. Whether or not gentrifiers articulate this preference, it is fundamental, for few would even consider rehabilitation if a financial loss were to be expected. A theory of gentrification must therefore explain why some neighborhoods are profitable to redevelop while others are not. What are the conditions of profitability? Consumer sovereignty explanations took for granted the availability of areas ripe for gentrification when this was precisely what had to be explained.

Before proceeding to a more detailed explanation of the process, it will be useful to step back and examine gentrification in the broader historical and structural context of capital investment and urban development. In particular, the general characteristics of investment in the built environment must be examined.

INVESTMENT IN THE BUILT ENVIRONMENT

In a capitalist economy, land and the improvements built onto it become commodities. As such they boast certain idiosyncracies of which three are particularly important for this discussion. First, private property rights confer on the owner near-monopoly control over land and improvements, monopoly control over the uses to which a certain space is put.[7] From this condition we can derive the function of ground rent. Second, land and improvements are fixed in space but their value is anything but fixed. Improvements on the land are subject to all the normal influences on their value but with one vital difference. On the one hand, the value of built improvements on a piece of land, as well as on surrounding land, influences the ground rent that landlords can demand; on the other hand, since land and buildings on it are inseparable, the price at which buildings change hands reflects the ground rent level. Meanwhile land, unlike the improvements built on it, "does not require upkeep in order to continue its potential for use" (Harvey 1973, pp. 158–59) and thereby retains its potential value. Third, while land is permanent, the improvements built on it are not, but generally have a very long turnover period in physical as well as value terms. Physical decay is unlikely to claim the life of a building for at least twenty-five years, usually a lot longer, and it may take as long in economic (as opposed to accounting) terms for it to pay back its value. From this we can derive several things: in a well-developed capitalist economy, large initial outlays will be necessary for built environment investments; financial institutions will therefore play an important role in the urban land market (Harvey 1973, p. 159); and patterns of capital depreciation will be an important variable in determining whether and to what extent a building's sale price reflects the ground rent level. These points will be of central importance in the next section.

In a capitalist economy, profit is the gauge of success, and competition is the mechanism by which success or failure is translated into growth or collapse. All individual enterprises must strive for higher and higher profits to facilitate the accumulation of greater and greater quantities of capital in profitable pursuits. Otherwise they find themselves unable to afford more advanced production methods and therefore fall behind their competitors. Ultimately, this leads either to bankruptcy or a merger into a larger enterprise. This search for increased profits translates, at the scale of the whole economy, into the long-run economic growth; general economic stability is therefore synonymous with overall economic growth. Particularly when economic growth is hindered elsewhere in the industrial sector, the built environment becomes a target for much profitable investment, as is particularly apparent with this century's suburbanization experience. In this case, spatial expansion rather than expansion *in situ* was the response to the continual need for capital accumulation. But suburbanization illustrates well the two-sided nature of investment in the built environment, for as well as being a vehicle for capital accumulation, it can also become a barrier to further accumulation. It becomes so by dint of the characteristics noted above: near-monopoly control of space, the fixity of investments, the long turnover period. Near-monopoly control of space by landowners may prevent the sale of land for development; the fixity of investments forces new development to take place at other, often less advantageous, locations, and prevents redevelopment from occurring until invested capital has lived out its economic life; the long turnover period of capital invested in the built environment can discourage investment as long as other sectors of the economy with shorter turnover periods remain profitable. The early industrial city presented just such a barrier by the later part of the nineteenth century, eventually prompting suburban development rather than development *in situ*.

During the nineteenth century in most eastern cities, land values displayed the classical conical form—a peak at the urban center, with a declining gradient on all sides toward the periphery. This was the pattern Hoyt (1933) found in Chicago. With continued urban development the land value gradient is displaced outward and upward; land at the center grows in value while the base of the cone broadens. Land values tend to change in unison with long cycles in the economy; they increase most rapidly during periods of particularly rapid capital accumulation and decline temporarily during slumps. Since suburbanization

relied on considerable capital investments in land, construction, transportation, etc., it too tended to follow this cyclical trend. Faced with the need to expand the scale of their productive activities, and unable or unwilling for a variety of reasons to expand any further where they were, industries jumped out beyond the city to the base of the land value cone where extensive spatial expansion was both possible and relatively cheap. The alternative—substantial renewal and redevelopment of the already built up area—would have been too costly for private capital to undertake, and so industrial capital was increasingly sent to the suburbs. This movement of industrial capital began in force after the severe depression of 1893–97, and was followed by a substantial migration of capital for residential construction. In the already well-established cities, the only significant exception to this migration of construction capital was in the central business district (CBD) where substantial skyscraper office development occurred in the 1920s. As will be shown, the inner city was adversely affected by this movement of capital to the suburbs where higher returns were available. A combination of neglect and concerted disinvestment by investors, due to high risk and low rates of return, initiated a long period of deterioration and a lack of new capital investment in the inner city.

Land values in the inner city fell relative to the CBD and the suburbs, and by the late 1920s Hoyt could identify for Chicago a newly formed "valley in the land-value curve between the Loop and outer residential areas". This valley "indicates the location of these sections where the buildings are mostly over forty years old and where the residents rank lowest in rent-paying ability" (Hoyt 1933, pp. 356–8). Throughout the decades of most sustained suburbanization, from the 1940s to the 1960s, this valley in the land value curve deepened and broadened due to a continued lack of productive capital investment. By the late 1960s the valley may have been as much as six miles wide in Chicago (McDonald and Bowman 1979). Evidence from other cities suggests that this capital depreciation and consequent broadening of the land value valley occurred throughout the country's older cities (Davis 1965; Edel and Sclar 1975), producing the slums and ghettos that were suddenly discovered as "problems" in the 1960s by the long gone suburban middle class.

A theory of gentrification will need to explain the detailed historical mechanisms of capital depreciation in the inner city and the precise way in which this depreciation produces the possibility of profitable reinvestment. The crucial nexus here is the relationship between land value and property value. As they stand, however, these concepts are insufficiently refined. Land value for Hoyt, was a composite category referring to the price of undeveloped plots and the expected future income from their use; the type of future use was simply assumed. Property value, on the other hand, is generally taken to mean the price at which a building is sold, including the value of the land. To elaborate the relationship between land value and the value of buildings in fuller detail, then, it will be necessary to disaggregate these two measures of value into four separate but related categories. These four categories (house value, sale price, capitalized ground rent, potential ground rent) remain fully or partially obscure and indistinguishable under the umbrella concepts land value and property value.

House value. Consistent with its emphasis on consumer preference, neoclassical economic theory explains prices as the result of supply and demand conditions. But if, as suggested above, the search for a high return on productive investments is the primary initiative behind gentrification, then the specific costs of production (not just the quantity of end-product—supply) will be central in the determination of prices. In opposition to neoclassical theory, therefore, it will be necessary to separate the value of a house from its price. Following the classical political economists (Smith, Ricardo), and after them Marx, this paper takes as axiomatic a labor theory of value: the value of a commodity is measured by the quantity of socially necessary labor power required to produce it. Only in the market place is value translated into price. And although the price of a house reflects its value, the two cannot mechanically be equated since price is also affected by supply and demand conditions. Thus, value considerations (the amount of socially necessary labor power) set the level about which the price fluctuates. With housing, the situation is more complex because individual houses return periodically to the market for resale. The house's value will also depend, therefore, on its rate of depreciation through use, versus its rate of appreciation through the addition of more value. The latter occurs when further labor is performed for maintenance, replacement, extensions, etc.

Sale price. A further complication with housing is that the sale price represents not only the value of the house, but an additional component for rent since the land is generally sold along with the structures it accommodates. Here it is preferable to talk of ground rent rather than land value, since the price of land does not reflect a quantity of labor power applied to it, as with the value of commodities proper.

Ground rent and capitalized ground rent. Ground rent is a claim made by landowners on users of their land; it represents a reduction from the surplus value created over and above cost-price by producers on the site. Capitalized ground rent is the actual quantity of ground rent that is appropriated by the landowner, given the present land use. In the case of rental housing where the landlord produces a service on land he or she owns, the production and ownership functions are combined and ground rent becomes even more of an intangible category though nevertheless a real presence; the landlord's capitalized ground rent returns mainly in the form of house rent paid by the tenants. In the case of owner occupancy, ground rent is capitalized when the building is sold and therefore appears as part of the sale price. Thus, sale price = house value + capitalized ground rent.

Potential ground rent. Under its present land use, a site or neighborhood is able to capitalize a certain quantity of ground rent. For reasons of location, usually, such an area may be able to capitalize higher quantities of ground rent under a different land use. Potential ground rent is the amount that could be capitalized under the land's "highest and best use." This concept is particularly important in explaining gentrification.

Using these concepts, the historical process that has made certain neighborhoods ripe for gentrification can be outlined.

Capital depreciation in the inner city. The physical deterioration and economic depreciation of inner-city neighborhoods is a strictly logical, "rational" outcome of the operation of the land and housing market. This is not to suggest it is at all natural, however, for the market itself is a social product. Far from being inevitable, neighborhood decline is

> the result of identifiable private and public investment decisions. . . . While there is no Napoleon who sits in a position of control over the fate of a neighborhood, there is enough control by, and integration of, the investment and development actors of the real estate industry that their decisions go beyond a response and actually shape the market
> (Bradford and Rubinowitz 1975, p. 79).

What follows is a rather schematic attempt to explain the historical decline of inner-city neighborhoods in terms of the institutions, actors, and economic forces involved. It requires the identification of a few salient processes that characterize the different stages of decline, but is not meant as a definitive description of what every neighborhood experiences. The day-to-day dynamics of decline are complex and, as regards the relationship between landlords and tenants in particular, have been examined in considerable detail elsewhere (Stegman 1972). This schema is, however, meant to provide a general explanatory framework within which each neighborhood's concrete experience can be understood. It is assumed from the start that the neighborhoods concerned are relatively homogeneous as regards the age and quality of housing, and, indeed, this tends to be the case with areas experiencing redevelopment.

1. New construction and the first cycle of use. When a neighborhood is newly built the price of housing reflects the value of the structure and improvements put in place plus the enhanced ground rent captured by the previous landowner. During the first cycle of use, the ground rent is likely to increase as urban development continues outward, and the house value will only very slowly begin to decline if at all. The sale price therefore rises. But eventually sustained depreciation of the house value occurs and this has three sources: advances in the productiveness of labor, style obsolescence, and physical wear and tear. Advances in the productiveness of labor are chiefly due to technological innovation and changes in the organization of the work process. These advances allow a similar structure to be produced at a lower value than would otherwise have been possible. Truss frame construction and the factory fabrication of parts in general, rather than on-site construction, are only the most recent examples of such advances. Style obsolescence is secondary as a stimulus for sustained depreciation in the housing market and may occasionally induce an appreciation of value, many old styles being more sought after than the new. Physical wear and tear also affects the value of housing, but it is necessary here to distinguish between minor repairs which must be performed regularly if a house is to retain its value (e.g., painting doors and window frames, interior decorating), major repairs which are performed less regularly but require greater outlays (e.g., replacing the plumbing or electrical systems), and structural repairs without which the structure becomes unsound (e.g., replacing a roof, replacing floor boards that have dry rot). Depreciation of a property's value after one cycle of use reflects the imminent need not only for regular, minor repairs but also for a succession of more major repairs involving a substantial investment. Depreciation will induce a price decrease relative to new housing but the extent of this decrease will depend on how much the ground rent has also changed in the meantime.

2. Landlordism and homeownership. Clearly the inhabitants in many neighborhoods succeed in making major repairs and maintaining or even enhancing the value of the area's housing. These areas remain stable. Equally clearly, there are areas of owner-occupied housing which experience initial depreciation. Homeowners, aware of imminent decline unless repairs are made, are likely to sell out and seek newer homes where their investment will be safer. At this point, after a first or subsequent cycle of use, there is a tendency for the neighborhood to convert to rental tenancy unless repairs are made. And since landlords use buildings for different purposes than owner occupiers, a different pattern of maintenance will ensue. Owner occupiers in the housing market are simultaneously both consumers and investors; as investors, their primary return comes as the increment of sale price over purchase price. The landlord, on the other

hand, receives his return mainly in the form of house rent, and under certain conditions may have a lesser incentive for carrying out repairs so long as he can still command rent. This is not to say that landlords typically undermaintain properties they possess; newer apartment complexes and even older accomodations for which demand is high may be very well maintained. But as Ira Lowry has indicated, "undermaintenance is an eminently reasonable response of a landlord to a declining market" (1960, p. 367), and since the transition from owner occupancy to tenancy is generally associated with a declining market, some degree of undermaintenance can be expected.

Undermaintenance will yield surplus capital to be invested elsewhere. It may be invested in other city properties, it may follow developers' capital out to the suburbs, or it may be invested in some other sector of the economy. With sustained undermaintenance in a neighborhood, however, it may become difficult for landlords to sell their properties, particularly since the larger financial institutions will now be less forthcoming with mortgage funds; sales become fewer and more expensive to the landlord. Thus, there is even less incentive to invest in the area beyond what is necessary to retain the present revenue flow. This pattern of decline is likely to be reversed only if a shortage of higher quality accommodations occurs, allowing rents to be raised and making improved maintenance worthwhile. Otherwise, the area is likely to experience a net outflow of capital, which will be small at first since landlords still have substantial investments to protect. Under these conditions it becomes very difficult for the individual landlord or owner to struggle against this decline. House values are falling and the levels of capitalized ground rent for the area are dropping below the potential ground rent. The individual who did not undermaintain his property would be forced to charge higher than average rent for the area with little hope of attracting tenants earning higher than average income which would capitalize the full ground rent. This is the celebrated "neighborhood effect" and operates through the rent structure.

3. Blockbusting and blow out. Some neighborhoods may not transfer to rental tenancy and they will experience relative stability or a gentler continuation of decline. If the latter occurs, it is the owner occupants who undermaintain, though usually out of financial constraints rather than market strategy. With blockbusting, this decline is intensified. Real estate agents exploit racist sentiments in white neighborhoods that are experiencing declining sale prices; they buy houses relatively cheaply, and then resell at a considerable markup to black families, many of whom are desperate to own their first home. As Laurenti's research suggests, property values are usually declining before blockbusting takes place and do not begin declining simply as a result of racial changes in ownership (Laurenti 1960). Once blockbusting has taken place, however, further decline in house values is likely due to the inflated prices at which houses were sold and the consequent lack of resources for maintenance and mortgage payments suffered by incoming families. Blow out, a similar process, operates without the helping hand of real estate agents. Describing the process as it operated in the Baltimore housing market during the 1960s, Harvey et al. (1972; see also Harvey 1973, p. 173) point to the outward spread of slums from the inner city (the broadening of the land value valley) and the consequent squeezing of still healthy outer neighborhoods against secure upper middle-class residential enclaves lying further out. Thus squeezed, owner occupants in an entire neighborhood are likely to sell out, often to landlords, and flee to the suburbs.

3. Redlining. Undermaintenance gives way to more active disinvestment as capital depreciates further and the landlord's stake diminishes; house value and capitalized ground rent fall, producing further decreases in sale price. Disinvestment by landlords is accompanied by an equally "rational" disinvestment by financial institutions which cease supplying mortgage money to the area. Larger institutions offering low downpayment, low interest rate loans find they can make higher returns in the suburbs with a lower chance of foreclosure and less risk of declining property values. Their role in the inner city is taken over initially by smaller, often local organizations specializing in higher risk financing. Redlined by larger institutions, the area may also receive loans insured by the FHA. Though meant to prevent decline, FHA loans have often been ineffectual and have even contributed to decline in places (Bradford and Rubinowitz 1975, p. 82). The loans allow properties to change hands but do little to encourage reinvestment in maintenance so the process of decline is simply lubricated. Ultimately, medium and small-scale investors also refuse to work the area, as do mortgage insurers.

Vandalism further accelerates depreciation and becomes a problem especially when properties are temporarily vacant between tenants (Stegman 1972, p. 60). Even when occupied, however, it may be a problem, especially if a building is being undermaintained or systematically "milked." Subdivision of structures to yield more rental units is common at this stage. By subdividing, the landlord hopes to intensify the building's use (and profitability) in its last few years. But eventually landlords will disinvest totally, refusing to make repairs and paying only the necessary costs—and then often only sporadically—for the building to yield rent.

5. Abandonment. When landlords can no longer collect enough house rent to cover the necessary costs (utilities and taxes), buildings are abandoned. This is a neighborhood phenomenon, not something that strikes isolated properties in otherwise stable areas. Much abandoned housing is structurally sound and this seems paradoxical. But then buildings are abandoned not because they are unuseable, but because they cannot be used *profitably*. The final act of abandonment may be triggered (but not caused) by a variety of events, including the strict enforcement of the building code by the city housing department. Also at this stage of decline, there is a certain incentive for landlords to destroy their own property through arson and collect the substantial insurance payment.

GENTRIFICATION—THE RENT GAP

The previous section presented a summary explanation of the process commonly but misleadingly referred to as filtering. It is a common process in the housing market and affects many neighborhoods but is by no means universal. It is included here precisely because gentrification is almost always preceded by filtering, although the process need not occur fully for gentrification to ensue. Nor should this decline be thought of as inevitable. As Lowry quite correctly insists, filtering is not due simply "to the relentless passage of time" but to "human agency" (1960, p. 370). The previous section has suggested who some of these agents are, and the market forces they both react to and help create. That section also suggests that the objective mechanism underlying filtering is the depreciation and devaluation of capital invested in residential inner-city neighborhoods. This depreciation produces the objective economic conditions that make capital *revaluation* (gentrification) a rational market response. Of fundamental importance here is what I call the rent gap.

The rent gap is the disparity between the potential ground rent level and the actual ground rent capitalized under the present land use. In the case of filtering, the rent gap is produced primarily by capital depreciation (which diminishes the proportion of the ground rent able to be capitalized) and also by continued urban development and expansion (which has historically raised the potential ground rent level in the inner city). The valley which Hoyt detected in his 1928 observation of land values can now be understood in large part as the rent gap. Only when this gap emerges can redevelopment be expected since if the present use succeeded in capitalizing all or most of the ground rent, little economic benefit could be derived from redevelopment. As filtering and neighborhood decline proceed, the rent gap widens. Gentrification occurs when the gap is wide enough that developers can purchase shells cheaply, can pay the builders' costs and profit for rehabilitation, can pay interest on mortgage and construction loans, and can then sell the end product for sale price that leaves a satisfactory return to the developer. The entire ground rent, or a large portion of it, is now capitalized; the neighborhood has been "recycled" and begins a new cycle of use.

Once the rent gap is wide enough, gentrification may be initiated in a given neighborhood by several different actors in the land and housing market. And here we come back to the relationship between production and consumption, for the empirical evidence suggests strongly that the process is initiated not by the exercise of those individual consumer preferences much beloved of neoclassical economists, but by some form of collective social action[8] at the neighborhood level. The state, for example, initiated most if not all of the early schemes, and though it plays a lesser role today, is still important. More commonly today, with private market gentrification, one or more financial institutions will reverse a long standing redlining policy and actively target a neighborhood as a potential market for construction loans and mortgages. All the consumer preference in the world will amount to nought unless this long absent source of funding reappears; mortgage capital is a prerequisite. Of course, this mortgage capital must be borrowed by willing consumers exercising some preference or another. But these preferences are not prerequisites since they can be socially created, as was seen above. Along with financial institutions, professional developers have acted as the collective initiative behind gentrification. A developer will purchase a substantial proportion of the properties in a neighborhood, rehabilitate them, then sell them for profit. The only significant exception to this predominance of collective action occurs in neighborhoods adjacent to already gentrified areas. There indeed, individual gentrifiers may be very important in initiating rehabilitation. Their decision to rehabilitate followed the results from the previous neighborhood, however, which implies that a sound financial investment was uppermost in their minds. And they still require mortgage capital from willing institutions.

Three kinds of developers typically operate in recycling neighborhoods: (a) professional developers who purchase property, redevelop it, and resell for profit; (b) occupier developers who buy and redevelop property and inhabit it after completion; (c) landlord developers who rent it to tenants after rehabilitation.[9] The developer's return on investment comes as part of the completed property's sale price; for the landlord developer it also comes in the form of house rent. Two separate gains comprise the return achieved through sale: capitalization of enhanced ground rent, and profit (quite distinct from builder's profit) on the investment of productive capital (see Smith 1979). Professional and landlord developers are important—contrary to the public image, they were by far the majority in

Society Hill—but occupier developers are more active in rehabilitation than they are in any other sector of housing construction. Perhaps the main reason for this can be traced to the very nature of gentrification and the characteristics of investment in the built environment discussed above. Urban renewal, like rehabilitation, occurs where a rent gap has been opened up, but in the case of renewal either the dilapidated stock is unsound structurally, or the remaining structures are unsuitable for new uses. While the technical and spatial requirements for industrial and commercial buildings have altered substantially in the last hundred years, those for residences have not, and structurally sound town houses are quite useable given the right economic conditions. But since the land has already been developed and an intricate pattern of property rights laid down, it is difficult for the professional developer to assemble sufficient land and properties to make involvement worthwhile. Even landlord developers tended to be rehabilitating several properties simultaneously or in sequence. The fragmented structure of property ownership has made the occupier developer, who is generally an inefficient operator in the construction industry, into an appropriate vehicle for recycling devalued neighborhoods.

Viewed in this way, gentrification is not a chance occurrence or an inexplicable reversal of some inevitable filtering process. On the contrary, it is to be expected. The depreciation of capital in nineteenth century inner-city neighborhoods, together with continued urban growth during the first half of the twentieth century, have combined to produce conditions in which profitable reinvestment is possible. If this rent gap theory of gentrification is correct, it would be expected that rehabilitation began where the gap was greatest and the highest returns available, i.e., in neighborhoods particularly close to the city center and in neighborhoods where the sequence of declining values had pretty much run its course. Empirically, this seems to have been the case. The theory also suggests that as these first areas are recycled, other areas offering lower but still substantial returns would be sought out by developers. This would involve areas further from the city center and areas where decline was less advanced. Thus in Philadelphia, Fairmount and Queen Village are the new "hot spots" (Cybriwsky 1978; Levy 1978), and the city's triage policy for allocating block grant funds makes part of North Philadelphia a likely candidate for future redevelopment.

The state's role in earlier rehabilitation schemes is worthy of note. By assembling properties at fair market value and returning them to developers at the lower assessed price the state accomplished and bore the costs of the last stages of capital devaluation, thereby ensuring that developers could reap the high returns without which redevelopment would not occur. Today, with the state less involved in this process, developers are clearly able to absorb the costs of devaluing capital that has not yet fully depreciated. That is, they can pay a relatively high price for properties to be rehabilitated, and still make a reasonable return. It seems then, that the state has been successful in providing the conditions that would stimulate private market revitalization.

To summarise the theory, gentrification is a structural product of the land and housing markets. Capital flows where the rate of return is highest, and the movement of capital to the suburbs along with the continual depreciation of inner-city capital, eventually produces the rent gap. When this gap grows sufficiently large, rehabilitation (or for that matter, renewal) can begin to challenge the rates of return available elsewhere, and capital flows back.

CONCLUSION

Gentrification has demonstrated that contrary to the conventional wisdom, middle- and upper-class housing is capable of intensive land use. Just how intensive is not clear, however. There is significant evidence that the once steep rent gradient is flattening out (Yeates 1965, Edel and Sclar 1975); and if this is the case, potential ground rent in inner-city neighborhoods may actually have decreased, presumably due to efficient transportation links to the suburbs and excessive crowding downtown. What this might mean for gentrification or for the commercial and recreational redevelopment that is also happening in some cities ought to be a topic for further research. Another topic for empirical investigation is the extent to which capital depreciation must occur in an area before gentrification can occur. This all assumes the filtering process to be the fundamental source of the rent gap, and while this is certainly so in the U.S. it may not be elsewhere. Although capital depreciation and filtering prepared the way for gentrification in Islington (Pitt 1977), in general, one would not expect it to be so prevalent in the U.K. housing market where much working class housing is produced by local government action, not the private market. In this case, rising ground rent levels due to urban expansion and development may be more important in accounting for the rent gap.

Gentrification is a back to the city movement all right, but of capital rather than people. The people taking advantage of this returning capital are still, as yet, from the city. If the city continues to attract productive capital (whether for residential or other construction) we may witness a fundamental restructuring of urban space comparable with suburbanization. Then, indeed, it would become a back to the city movement by people too—middle- and upper-class people, that is—while the working class and the poor would inherit the old declining suburbs in a cruelly ironic continuation of the filtering process. They would then be trapped in the suburbs, not the inner city. As was emphasized in the discussion of suburbanization, investment in the built environment is a major vehicle for capital accumulation. This process is cyclical and, because of the long life and fixity of such investments, new cycles of investment are often associated with crises and switches of the location of accumulation (Harvey 1978). Seen in this context, gentrification and other kinds of urban renaissance could be the leading edge (but in no way the cause) of a larger restructuring of space. According to one scenario this restructuring would be accomplished according to the needs of capital; a restructuring of middle-class culture may well accompany and influence it, but would be secondary. According to a second scenario, the needs of capital would be systematically dismantled, to be displaced by the social, economic, and cultural needs of people as the principle according to which the restructuring of space occurs.

NOTES

1. Gentrification is the process of converting working-class areas into middle-class neighborhoods through the rehabilitation of the neighborhood's housing stock.
2. That the earlier projects required substantial state initiative and subsidy did not exclude them from being explained in terms of consumer preference. In Philadelphia, for example, the Greater Philadelphia Movement (GPM) was responsible for getting the state to implement Society Hill's renewal plan, and it consistently claimed that the demand to revitalize was ever-present but the cost constraints and risk were too great for private capital and individuals. It was the responsibility of the state, they argued, to use the available federal legislation to subsidize the project, thereby removing the constraints and serving a broader civic cause. On GPM's role in Society Hill, see Adde (1969, pp. 33–6). For the purposes of this paper, I am distinguishing between gentrification and urban renewal not according to whether the process is privately or publicly funded, but

according to whether it is a rehabilitation process or purely new construction. As should become clear from the main argument of the paper, the distinction between public and private funding simply represents (in this context) two different mechanisms for carrying out the one essential process.
3. By suburbs I mean here the area outside the present city boundary but inside the SMSA. The older suburbs that now appear inside the city due to consequent annexations are therefore counted as sections of the city. This definition is justified here since one of the main selling points of gentrification is that it will bring additional tax revenues to the city. Clearly, annexed suburbs already pay their taxes to the city.
4. This kind of consolidation may be experienced by other cities. Several of the cities examined by Lipton (1977) display a similar consolidation.
5. For further discussion of the cross-Atlantic comparison, see Smith (1979).
6. Advertising is a primary means of creating demand. In Society Hill, the Old Philadelphia Development Corporation employed a Madison Avenue professional to sell the project (Old Philadelphia Development Corporation 1970).
7. Certainly zoning, eminent domain, and other state regulations put significant limits on the landowner's control of land, but in North America and Western Europe, these limitations are little more than cosmetic. Within these limitations, the property market continues to operate quite freely.
8. By "collective social action" I mean simply activity that is carried on jointly and simultaneously by people, not by individuals acting alone.
9. I omit speculators here for the obvious reason that they invest no productive capital. They simply buy property in the hope of selling it at a higher price to developers. Speculators do not produce any transformation in the urban structure.

REFERENCES

Adde, L. (1969) *Nine Cities: Anatomy of Downtown Renewal,* Washington D.C.: Urban Land Institute.

Alonso, W. (1964) *Location and Land Use,* Cambridge Mass.: Harvard University Press.

Baltimore City Department of Housing and Community Development. (1977) *Homesteading—The Third Year, 1976,* Baltimore: the Department.

Bradford, C. and Rubinowitz, L. (1975) "The urban–suburban investment–disinvestment process: consequences for older neighborhoods," *Annals of the American Academy of Political and Social Science* 422: 77–86.

Burt, N. (1963) *The Perennial Philadelphians*, London: Dent and Son.

Cybriwsky, R. (1978) "Social aspects of neighborhood change," *Annals of Association of American Geographers* 68: 17–33.

Davis, J. T. (1965) "Middle class housing in the central city," *Economic Geography* 41: 238–251.

Edel, M. and Sclar, E. (1975) "The distribution of real estate value changes: metropolitan Bostan, 1870–1970," *Journal of Urban Economics* 2: 366–387.

Gale, D.E. (1976) "The back-to-the-city movement ... or is it?" Occasional Paper, Department of Urban and Regional Planning, The George Washington University.

Gale, D.E. (1977) "The back-to-the-city movement revisited," Occasional Paper, Department of Urban and Regional Planning, The George Washington University.

Gans, H. (1968) *People and Plans*, New York: Basic Books.

Greenfield, A. M. and Co. Inc. (1964) "New town houses for Washington Square East: a technical report on neighborhood conservation," prepared for the Redevelopment Authority of Philadelphia.

Harvey, D. (1973) *Social Justice and the City*, Baltimore: Johns Hopkins University Press.

—— (1978) "The urban process under capitalism: a framework for analysis," *International Journal of Urban and Regional Research* 2, 1: 100–131.

Harvey, D., Chaterjee, L., Wolman, M. and Newman, J. (1972) *The Housing Market and Code Enforcement in Baltimore*, Baltimore: City Planning Department.

Hoyt, H. (1933) *One Hundred Years of Land Values in Chicago*, Chicago: University of Chicago Press.

Laurenti, L. (1960) *Property Values and Race*, Berkeley: University of California Press.

Levy, P. (1978) *Queen Village: The Eclipse of Community*. Philadelphia: Institute for the Study of Civic Values.

Ley, D. (1978) "Inner city resurgence and its societal context," paper presented to the Association of American Geographers Annual Conference, New Orleans.

Lipton, S. G. (1977) "Evidence of central city revival," *Journal of the American Institute of Planners* 43, April: 136–147.

Lowry, I. S. (1960) "Filtering and housing costs: a conceptual analysis." *Land Economics* 36: 362–370.

McDonald. J. F. and Bowman, H. W. (1979) "Land value functions: a reevaluation," *Journal of Urban Economics* 6: 25–41.

Mills, E. (1972) *Studies in the Structure of the Urban Economy*, Baltimore: Johns Hopkins University Press.

Muth, R. (1969) *Cities and Housing*, Chicago: University of Chicago Press.

Pitt, J. (1977) *Gentrification in Islington*, London: Barnsbury Peoples Forum.

Smith, N. (1979) (forthcoming) Gentrification and capital: theory, practice and ideology in Society Hill, *Antipode* 11.

Stegman, M. A. (1972) *Housing Investment in the Inner City: The Dynamics of Decline*, Cambridge, Mass.: MIT Press.

Urban Land Institute. (1976) *New Opportunities for Residential Development in Central Cities*, Report No. 25, Washington D.C.: The Institute.

Winters, C. (1978) "Rejuvenation with character," paper presented to the Association of American Geographers Annual Conference, New Orleans.

Wolf, E. (1975) *Philadelphia: Portrait of an American City*, Harrisburg, Pa.: Stackpole Books.

Yeates, M. H. (1965) "Some factors affecting the spatial distribution of Chicago land values, 1910–1960," *Economic Geography* 41, 1: 57–70.

CHAPTER 7

The City as a Growth Machine

John R. Logan and Harvey L. Molotch

Traditional urban research has had little relevance to the day-to-day activities of the place-based elites whose priorities affect patterns of land use, public budgets, and urban social life. It has not even been apparent from much of the scholarship of urban social science that place is a market commodity that can produce wealth and power for its owners, and that this might explain why certain people take a keen interest in the ordering of urban life.

Research on local elites has been preoccupied with the question "Who governs?" (or "Who rules?"). Are the politically active citizens of a city split into diverse and competing interest groups, or are they members of a coordinated oligarchy? Empirical evidence of visible cleavage, such as disputes on a public issue, has been accepted as evidence of pluralistic competition (Banfield, 1961; Dahl, 1961). Signs of cohesion, such as common membership in voluntary and policy groups, have been used to support the alternative view (see Domhoff, 1970).

We believe that the question of who governs or rules has to be asked in conjunction with the equally central question "For what?" With rare exceptions (see Smith and Keller, 1983), one issue consistently generates consensus among local elite groups and separates them from people who use the city principally as a place to live and work: the issue of growth. For those who count, the city is a growth machine, one that can increase aggregate rents and trap related wealth for those in the right position to benefit. The desire for growth creates consensus among a wide range of elite groups, no matter how split they might be on other issues. Thus the disagreement on some or even most public issues does not necessarily indicate any fundamental disunity, nor do changes in the number or variety of actors on the scene (what Clark [1968] calls "decentralization") affect the basic matter. It does not even matter that elites often fail to achieve their growth goal; with virtually all places in the same game, some elites will inevitably lose no matter how great their effort (Lyon et al., 1981; Krannich and Humphrey, 1983).

Although they may differ on which particular strategy will best succeed, elites use their growth consensus to eliminate any alternative vision of the purpose of local government or the meaning of community. The issues that reach public agendas (and are therefore available for pluralists' investigations) do so precisely because they are matters on which elites have, in effect, agreed to disagree (Molotch and Lester, 1974, 1975; see Schattschneider, 1960). Only under rather extraordinary circumstances is this consensus endangered.

For all the pluralism Banfield (1961) uncovered in Chicago, he found no disagreement with the idea that growth was good. Indeed, much of the dissension he did find, for example, on where to put the new convention center, was part of a dispute over how growth should be internally distributed. In his studies of cities on both sides of the southern U.S. border, D'Antonio found that when community "knowledge-ables" were "asked to name the most pressing problems facing their respective cities," they cited finding sufficient water for both farming and urban growth (Form and D'Antonio, 1970: 439). Whitt (1982) found that in formulating positions on California transportation policies, elites carefully coordinated not only the positions they would take but also the amount of money each would give toward winning relevant initiative campaigns. Thus on growth infrastructure, the elites were united.

Similarly, it was on the primacy of such growth and development issues that Hunter found Atlanta's elites to be most unified, both at the time of his first classic study and during its replication twenty years later (Hunter, 1953, 1980). Hunter (1953: 214) reports, "They could speak of nothing else" (cited in Domhoff, 1983: 169). In his historical profiles of Dallas and Fort Worth, Melosi (1983: 175) concludes that "political power in Dallas and Fort Worth has typically been concentrated in the hands of those people most willing and able to sustain growth and expansion." Finally, even the ecologically oriented scholars with a different perspective, Berry and Kasarda (1977: 371), have remarked, "If in the past urbanization has been governed by any conscious public objectives at all, these have been, on the one hand, to encourage growth, apparently for its own sake, and on the other hand, to provide public works and public welfare programs to support piecemeal, spontaneous development impelled primarily by private initiative." And even Hawley (1950:

429) briefly departs from his tight ecological schema to remark that "competition is observable . . . in the struggle for transportation and communication advantages and superior services of all kinds; it also appears in efforts to accelerate rates of population growth."

All of this competition, in addition to its critical influence on what goes on *within* cities, also influences the distribution of populations throughout cities and regions, determining which ones grow and which do not. The incessant lobbying, manipulating, and cajoling can deliver the critical resources from which great cities are made. Although virtually all places are subject to the pervasive rule of growth boosters, places with more active and creative elites may have an edge over other areas. In a comparative study of forty-eight communities, Lyon et al. (1981) indeed found that cities with reputedly more powerful elites tended to have stronger growth rates. This may mean that active elites stimulate growth, or it may mean that strong growth emboldens elites to actively maintain their advantage. Although we suspect that both perspectives are valid, we stress that the activism of entrepreneurs is, and always has been, a critical force in shaping the urban system, including the rise and fall of given places.

[. . .]

THE MODERN-DAY GOOD BUSINESS CLIMATE

The jockeying for canals, railroads, and arsenals of the previous century has given way in this one to more complex and subtle efforts to manipulate space and redistribute rents. The fusing of public duty and private gain has become much less acceptable (both in public opinion and in the criminal courts); the replacing of frontiers by complex cities has given important roles to mass media, urban professionals, and skilled political entrepreneurs. The growth machine is less personalized, with fewer local heroes, and has become instead a multifaceted matrix of important social institutions pressing along complementary lines.

With a transportation and communication grid already in place, modern cities typically seek growth in basic economic functions, particularly job intensive ones. Economic growth sets in motion the migration of labor and a demand for ancillary production services, housing, retailing, and wholesaling ("multiplier effects"). Contemporary places differ in the type of economic base they strive to build (for example, manufacturing, research and development, information processing, or tourism). But any one of the rainbows leads to the same pot of gold: more intense land use and thus higher rent collections, with associated professional fees and locally based profits.

Cities are in a position to affect the "factors of production" that are widely believed to channel the capital investments that drive local growth (Hawley, 1950; Summers et al., 1976). They can, for example, lower access costs of raw materials and markets through the creation of shipping ports and airfields (either by using local subsidies or by facilitating state and federal support). Localities can decrease corporate overhead costs through sympathetic policies on pollution abatement, employee health standards, and taxes. Labor costs can be indirectly lowered by pushing welfare recipients into low-paying jobs and through the use of police to constrain union organizing. Moral laws can be changed; for example, drinking alcohol can be legalized (as in Ann Arbor, Mich., and Evanston, Ill.) or gambling can be promoted (as in Atlantic City, N.J.) to build tourism and convention business. Increased utility costs caused by new development can be borne, as they usually are (see, for an example, Ann Arbor, Michigan, Planning Department, 1972), by the public at large rather than by those

responsible for the "excess" demand they generate. Federally financed programs can be harnessed to provide cheap water supplies; state agencies can be manipulated to subsidize insurance rates; local political units can forgive business property taxes. Government installations of various sorts (universities, military bases) can be used to leverage additional development by guaranteeing the presence of skilled labor, retailing customers, or proximate markets for subcontractors. For some analytical purposes, it doesn't even matter that a number of these factors have little bearing on corporate locational decisions (some certainly do; others are debated); just the *possibility* that they might matter invigorates local growth activism (Swanstrom, 1985) and dominates policy agendas.

Following the lead of St. Petersburg, Florida, the first city to hire a press agent (in 1918) to boost growth (Mormino, 1983: 150), virtually all major urban areas now use experts to attract outside investment. One city, Dixon, Illinois, has gone so far as to systematically contact former residents who might be in a position to help (as many as twenty thousand people) and offer them a finder's fee up to $10,000 for directing corporate investment toward their old home town (*San Francisco Chronicle*, May 10, 1984). More pervasively, each city tries to create a "good business climate." The ingredients are well known in city-building circles and have even been codified and turned into "official" lists for each regional area. The much-used Fantus rankings of business climates are based on factors like taxation, labor legislation, unemployment compensation, scale of government, and public indebtedness (Fantus ranks Texas as number one and New York as number forty-eight). In 1975, the Industrial Development Research Council, made up of corporate executives responsible for site selection decisions, conducted a survey of its members. In that survey, states were rated more simply as "cooperative," "indifferent," or "antigrowth"; the results closely paralleled the Fantus rankings of the same year (Weinstein and Firestine, 1978: 134–44).

Any issue of a major business magazine is replete with advertisements from localities of all types (including whole countries) striving to portray themselves in a manner attractive to business. Consider these claims culled from one issue of *Business Week* (February 12, 1979):

New York City is open for business. No other city in America offers more financial incentives to expand or relocate....

The state of Louisiana advertises

Nature made it perfect. We made it profitable.

On another page we find the claim that "Northern Ireland works" and has a work force with "positive attitudes toward company loyalty, productivity and labor relations." Georgia asserts, "Government should strive to improve business conditions, not hinder them." Atlanta headlines that as "A City Without Limits" it "has ways of getting people like you out of town" and then details its transportation advantages to business. Some places describe attributes that would enhance the life style of executives and professional employees (not a dimension of Fantus rankings); thus a number of cities push an image of artistic refinement. No advertisements in this issue (or in any other, we suspect) show city workers living in nice homes or influencing their working conditions.

While a good opera or ballet company may subtly enhance the growth potential of some cities, other cultural ingredients are crucial for a good business climate. There should be no violent class or ethnic conflict (Agger, Goldrich, and Swanson, 1964: 649; Johnson, 1983: 250–51). Rubin (1972: 123) reports that racial confrontation over school busing was sometimes seen as a threat to urban economic development. Racial violence in South Africa is finally leading to the disinvestment that reformers could not bring about through moral suasion. In the good business climate, the work force should be sufficiently quiescent and healthy to be productive; this was the rationale originally behind many programs in work place relations and public health. Labor must, in other words, be "reproduced," but only under conditions that least interfere with local growth trajectories.

Perhaps most important of all, local publics should favor growth and support the ideology of value-free development. This public attitude reassures investors that the concrete enticements of a locality will be upheld by future politicians. The challenge is to connect civic pride to the growth goal, tying the presumed economic and social benefits of growth in general (Wolfe, 1981) to growth in the local area. Probably only partly aware of this, elites generate and sustain the place patriotism of the masses. According to Boorstin, the competition among cities "helped create the booster spirit" as much as the booster spirit helped create the cities (1965: 123). In the nineteenth-century cities, the great rivalries over canal and railway installations were the political spectacles of the day, with attention devoted to their public, not private, benefits. With the drama of the new railway technology, ordinary people were swept into the competition among places, rooting for their own town to become the new "crossroads" or at least a way station. "The debates over transportation," writes Scheiber (1962: 143), "heightened urban community consciousness and sharpened local pride in many western towns."

The celebration of local growth continues to be a theme in the culture of localities. Schoolchildren are taught to view local history as a series of breakthroughs in the expansion of the economic base of their city and region, celebrating its numerical leadership in one sort of production or another; more generally, increases in population tend to be equated with local progress. Civic organizations sponsor essay contests on the topic of local greatness. They encourage public celebrations and spectacles in which the locality name can be proudly advanced for the benefit of both locals and outsiders. They subsidize soapbox derbies, parade floats, and beauty contests to "spread around" the locality's name in the media and at distant competitive sites.

One case can illustrate the link between growth goals and cultural institutions. In the Los Angeles area, St. Patrick's Day parades are held at four different locales, because the city's Irish leaders can't agree on the venue for a joint celebration. The source of the difficulty (and much acrimony) is that these parades march down the main business streets in each locale, thereby making them a symbol of the life of the city. Business groups associated with each of the strips want to claim the parade as exclusively their own, leading to charges by still a fifth parade organization that the other groups are only out to "make money" (McGarry, 1985: II: 1). The countercharge, vehemently denied, was that the leader of the challenging business street was not even Irish. Thus even an ethnic celebration can receive its special form from the machinations of growth interests and the competitions among them.

The growth machine avidly supports whatever cultural institutions can play a role in building locality. Always ready to oppose cultural and political developments contrary to their interests (for example, black nationalism and communal cults), rentiers and their associates encourage activities that will connect feelings of community ("we feelings" [McKenzie, 1922]) to the goal of local growth. The overall ideological thrust is to deemphasize the connection between growth and exchange values and to reinforce the link between growth goals and better lives for the majority. We do not mean to suggest that the only source of civic pride is the desire to collect rents; certainly the cultural pride of tribal groups predates growth machines. Nevertheless, the growth machine coalition mobilizes these cultural motivations, legitimizes them, and channels them into activites that are consistent with growth goals.

THE ORGANIZATION OF THE GROWTH COALITION

[. . .] The people who use their time and money to participate in local affairs are the ones who—in vast disproportion to their representation in the population—have the most to gain or lose in land-use decisions. Local business people are the major participants in urban politics (Walton, 1970), particularly business people in property investing, development, and real estate financing (Spaulding, 1951; Mumford, 1961). Peterson (1981: 132), who applauds growth boosterism, acknowledges that "such policies are often promulgated through a highly centralized decision-making process involving prestigious businessmen and professionals. Conflict within the city tends to be minimal, decision-making processes tend to be closed." Elected officials, says Stone (1984: 292), find themselves confronted by "a business community that is well-organized, amply supplied with a number of deployable resources, and inclined to act on behalf of tangible and ambitious plans that are mutually beneficial to its own members."

Business people's continuous interaction with public officials (including supporting them through substantial campaign contributions) gives them *systemic* power (Alford and Friedland, 1975; Stone, 1981, 1982). Once organized, they stay organized. They are "mobilized interests" (Fainstein, Fainstein, and Armistead, 1983: 214).

Rentiers need local government in their daily money-making routines, especially when structural speculations are involved. They are assisted by lawyers, syndicators, and property brokers (Bouma, 1962), who prosper as long as they can win decisions favoring their clients. Finally, there are monopolistic business enterprises (such as the local newspaper) whose futures are tied to the growth of the metropolis as a whole, although they are not directly involved in land use. When the local market is saturated with their product, they have few ways to increase profits, beyond expansion of their surrounding area. As in the proverbial Springdale, site of the classic Vidich and Bensman (1960: 216) ethnography of a generation ago, there is a strong tendency in most cities for "the professionals (doctors, teachers, dentists, etc.), the industrial workers, the shack people and the lower middle-class groups [to be] for all intents and purposes disenfranchised except in terms of temporary issues."

Because so much of the growth mobilization effort involves government, local growth elites play a major role in electing local politicians, "watchdogging" their activities, and scrutinizing administrative detail. Whether in generating infrastructural resources, keeping peace on the home front, or using the city mayor as an "ambassador to industry" (Wyner, 1967), local government is primarily concerned with increasing growth. Again, it is not the only function of local government, but it is the key one.

In contrast to our position, urban social scientists have often ignored the politics of growth in their work, even when debates over growth infrastructures were the topic of their analyses (see Banfield, 1961; Dahl, 1961). Williams and Adrian (1963) at least treat growth as an important part of the local political process, but give it no priority over other government issues. There are a number of reasons why growth politics is consistently undervalued. The clue can be found in Edelman's (1964) distinction between two kinds of politics.

The first is the "symbolic" politics of public morality and most of the other "big issues" featured in the headlines and editorials of the daily press: school prayer, wars on crime, standing up to communism, and child pornography, for example. News coverage of these issues may have little to do with any underlying reality, much less a reality in which significant local actors have major stakes. Fishman (1978) shows, for example, that reports of a major crime wave against the elderly in New York City appeared just at a time when most crimes against the elderly were actually on the decline. The public "crime wave" was created by police officials who, in responding to reporters' interest in the topic, provided "juicy" instances that would make good copy. The "crime wave" was sustained by politicians eager to denounce the perpetrators, and these politicians' pronouncements became the basis for still more coverage and expressions of authoritative police concern. Once this symbiotic "dance" (Molotch, 1980) is in motion, the story takes on a life of its own, and fills the pages and airwaves of news media. Such symbolic crusades provide the "easy news" (Gordon, Heath, and leBailly, 1979) needed by reporters pressed for time, just as these crusades satisfy the "news needs" (Molotch and Lester, 1974) of politicians happy to stay away from issues that might offend growth machine interests. The resulting hubbubs often mislead the general public as well as the academic investigator about what the real stuff of community cleavage and political process might be. To the degree that rentier elites keep growth issues on a symbolic level (for example, urban "greatness"), they prevail as the "second face of power" (Bachrach and Baratz, 1962), the face that determines the public agenda (McCombs and Shaw, 1972).

Edelman's second kind of politics, which does not provide easy news, involves the government actions that affect the distribution of important goods and services. Much less visible to publics, often relegated to back rooms or negotiations within insulated authorities and agencies (Caro, 1974; Friedland, Piven, and Alford, 1978), this is the politics that determines who, in material terms, gets what, where, and how (cf. Lasswell, 1936). The media tend to cover it as the dull round of meetings of water and sewer districts, bridge authorities, and industrial development bonding agencies. The media attitude serves to keep interesting issues away from the public and blunt widespread interest in local politics generally. As Vidich and Bensman (1960: 217) remark about Springdale, "business control rests upon a dull but unanimous political facade," at least on certain key issues.

Although there are certainly elite organizational mechanisms to inhibit them (Domhoff, 1971; 1983; Whitt, 1982), cleavages within the growth machine can nevertheless develop, and internal disagreements sometimes break into the open. But even then, because of the hegemony of the growth machine, *its* disagreements are allowable and do not challenge the belief in growth itself. Unacceptable are public attacks on the pursuit of exchange values over citizens' search for use value. An internal quarrel over where a convention center is to be built, Banfield (1961) shows us, becomes the public issue for Chicago; but Banfield didn't notice that there was no question about whether there should be a convention center at all.

When elites come to see, for example, that inadequate public services are repelling capital investment, they can put the issue of raising taxes on the public agenda. Trillin (1976: 154) reports on Rockford, Illinois, a city whose school system was bankrupted by an antitax ideology. Initially, local elites opposed taxes as part of their efforts to lure industry through a low tax rate. As a result, taxes, and therefore tax money for schools, declined. Eventually, the growth coalition saw the educational decline, not the tax rate, as the greatest danger to the "economic vitality of the community." But ironically, elites are not able to change overnight the ideologies they have put in place over decades, even when it is in their best interests to do so.[1] Unfortunately, neither can the potential *opponents* of growth. As the example of Rockford shows, even such issues as public school spending can become subject to the growth maximization needs of locality. The appropriate level of a social service often depends, not on an abstract model of efficiency or on "public demand" (cf. Tiebout, 1956), but on whether the cost of that service fits the local growth strategy (past and present).

By now it should be clear how political structures are mobilized to intensify land uses for private gain of many sorts. Let us look more closely, therefore, at the various local actors, besides those directly involved in generating rents, who participate in the growth machine.

POLITICIANS

The growth machine will sustain only certain persons as politicians. The campaign contributions and public celebrations that build political careers do not ordinarily come about because of a person's desire to save or destroy the environment, to repress or liberate the blacks or other disadvantaged groups, to eliminate civil liberties or enhance them. Given their legislative power, politicians may end up doing any of these things. But the underlying politics that gives rise to such opportunities is a person's participation in the growth consensus. That is why we so often see politicians springing into action to attract new capital and to sustain old investments. Even the pluralist scholar Robert Dahl observed in his New

Haven study that if an employer seriously threatened to leave the community, "political leaders are likely to make frantic attempts to make the local situation more attractive" (quoted in Swanstrom, 1981: 50).

Certainly, politicians differ in a number of ways. Like Mayor Ogden of Chicago, some are trying to create vast fortunes for themselves as they go about their civic duties on behalf of the growth machine. Robert Folson, the mayor of Dallas, has direct interests in over fifty local businesses, many of which have stakes in local growth outcomes. When the annexation of an adjacent town came up for a vote, he had to abstain because he owned 20 percent of it (Fullinwider, 1980). Another Texan, former governor John Connally, has among his holdings more than $50 million in Austin-area real estate, property slated to become its county's largest residential and commercial development ("Austin Boom," *Santa Barbara News Press*, June 24, 1984, p. B-8). According to Robert Caro (1974), Commissioner Robert Moses was able to overcome opposition to his vast highway and bridge building in the New York City area in part because the region's politicians were themselves buying up land adjacent to parkway exits, setting themselves up for huge rent gains. Most of Hawaii's major Democrat politicians, after winning election on a reform platform in 1954, directly profited as developers, lawyers, contractors, and investors through the zoning and related land-use decisions they and their colleagues were to make over the next thirty years of intensive growth and speculation (Daws and Cooper, 1984). Machine politics never insulated candidates from the development process; builders, railroaders, and other growth activists have long played crucial roles in boss politics, both in immigrant wards (Bell, 1961) and in WASP suburbs (Fogelson, 1967: 207). All this is, as George Washington Plunkitt said in 1905, "honest graft" as opposed to "dishonest graft" (quoted in Swanstrom, 1985: 25).[2]

Although a little grease always helps a wheel to turn, a system can run well with no graft at all—unless using campaign contributions to influence elections is considered graft. Virtually all politicians are dependent on private campaign financing (Alexander, 1972, 1980, 1983; Boyarsky and Gillam, 1982; Smith, 1984), and it is the real estate entrepreneurs—particularly the large-scale structural speculators—who are particularly active in supporting candidates (see chapter 6 for additional documentation). The result is that candidates of both parties, of whatever ideological stripe, have to garner the favor of such persons, and this puts them squarely into the hands of growth machine coalitions. Thus many officeholders use their authority, not to enrich themselves, but to benefit the "whole community"—that is, to increase aggregate rents. Again, this does not preclude politicians' direct participation in property dealing on occasion and it certainly does not preclude giving a special hand to particular place entrepreneurs with whom a politician has a special relationship.

Elected officials also vary in their perception of how their authority can best be used to maximize growth. After his thorough study of the Cleveland growth machine, Swanstrom (1985) concluded that there are two types of growth strategists: the "conservative" and the "liberal." The former, paramount during the city's age of steel, favor unbridled exploitation of the city and its labor force, generally following the "free economy" political model. Programs of overt government intervention, for purposes of planning, public education, or employee welfare, are all highly suspect. The liberal growth machine strategy, in contrast, acknowledges that longer-term growth can be facilitated by overt government planning and by programs that pacify, co-opt, and placate oppositions. This is a more modern form of growth ideology. Some politicians, depending on place and time, tend to favor the hard-line "unfettered capitalism" (Wolfe, 1981); others prefer the liberal version, analogous to what is called, in a broader context, "pragmatic state capitalism" (Wolfe, 1981; see also Weinstein, 1968). These positions became more obvious in many regions when urban renewal and other federal programs began penetrating cities in the postwar period. Especially in conservative areas such as Texas (Melosi, 1983: 185), elites long debated among themselves whether or not the newfangled growth schemes would do more harm than good.

On the symbolic issues, politicians may also differ, on both the content of their positions and the degree to which they actually care about the issues. Some are no doubt sincere in pushing their "causes"; others may cynically manipulate them to obscure the distributional consequences of their own actions in other matters. Sometimes the results are positive, for example, when Oklahoma City and Dallas leaders made deliberate efforts to prevent racist elements from scaring off development with "another Little Rock." Liberal growth machine goals may thus help reform reactionary social patterns (Bernard, 1983: 225; Melosi, 1983: 188). But despite these variations, there appears to be a "tilt" to the whole system, regardless of time and place. Growth coalition activists and campaign contributors are not a culturally, racially, or economically diverse cross section of the urban population. They tend to give a reactionary texture to local government, in which the cultural crusades, like the material ones, are chosen for their acceptability to the rentier groups. Politicians adept in both spheres (material and symbolic) are the most valued, and most likely to have successful careers. A skilled politician delivers growth while giving a good circus.

The symbolic political skills are particularly crucial when unforeseen circumstances create use value crises, which can potentially stymie a locality's basic growth strategy. The 1978 Love Canal toxic waste emergency at Niagara Falls, New York, reveals how local officials use their positions to reassure the citizens and mold local agendas to handle disruptive "emotional" issues. In her detailed ethnographic account, Levine (1982: 59) reports that "the city's chief executives, led by the mayor, minimized the Love Canal problem in all public statements for two years no matter how much personal sympathy they felt for the affected people whose health was threatened by the poisons leaking into their homes" (see also Fowlkes and Miller, 1985). Lester (1971) reports a similar stance taken by the Utah civic leadership in response to the escape of nerve gas from the U.S. military's Dugway Proving Grounds in 1969 (see also Hirsch, 1969). The conduct of politicians in the face of accidents like the leakage of poison into schoolyards and homes in Niagara Falls or the sheep deaths in Utah reveal this "backup" function of local leaders (Molotch and Lester, 1974, 1975).

Still another critical use of local politicians is their ability to influence higher-level political actors in their growth distribution decisions. Although capital has direct links to national politicians (particularly in the executive office and Senate, see Domhoff [1967, 1970, 1983]), rentier groups are more parochial in their ties, although they may have contact with congressional representatives. Hence, rentiers need local politicians to lobby national officials. The national politicians, in turn, are responsive because they depend on local political operators (including party figures) for their own power base. The local politicians symbiotically need their national counterparts to generate the goods that keep them viable at home.

The goods that benefit the local leaders and growth interests are not trivial. The development of the Midwest was, as the historical anecdotes make clear, dependent on national decisions affecting canal and railroad lines. The Southwest and most of California could be developed only with federal subsidies and capital investments in water projects. The profound significance of government capital spending can be grasped by considering one statistic: Direct government outlays (at all levels) in 1983 accounted for nearly 27 percent of all construction in the United States (Mollenkopf, 1983: 43). The figure was even higher, of course, during World War II, when federal construction expenditures laid the basis for much of the infrastructural and defense spending that was to follow.

LOCAL MEDIA

One local business takes a broad responsibility for general growth machine goals—the metropolitan newspaper. Most newspapers (small, suburban papers are occasionally an exception) profit primarily from increasing their circulation and therefore have a direct interest in growth.[3] As the metropolis expands, the newspaper can sell a larger number of ad lines (at higher per line cost), on the basis of a rising circulation base; TV and radio stations are in a similar situation. In explaining why his newspaper had supported the urbanization of orchards that used to cover what is now the city of San Jose, the publisher of the *San Jose Mercury News* said, "Trees do not read newspapers" (Downie, 1974: 112, as cited in Domhoff, 1983: 168). Just as newspaper boosterism was important in building the frontier towns (Dagenais, 1967), so today "the hallmark of media content has been peerless boosterism: congratulate growth rather than calculate consequences; compliment development rather than criticize its impact" (Burd, 1977: 129; see also Devereux, 1976; Freidel, 1963). The media "must present a favorable image to outsid-

ers" (Cox and Morgan, 1973: 136),[4] and only "sparingly use their issue-raising capacities" (Peterson, 1981: 124).

American cities tend to be one-newspaper (or one-newspaper company) towns. The newspaper's assets in physical plant, in "good will," and in advertising clients are, for the most part, immobile. The local newspaper thus tends to occupy a unique position: like many other local businesses, it has an interest in growth, but unlike most others, its critical interest is not in the specific spatial pattern of that growth. The paper may occasionally help forge a specific strategy of growth, but ordinarily it makes little difference to a newspaper whether the additional population comes to reside on the north side or the south side, or whether the new business comes through a new convention center or a new olive factory. The newspaper has no ax to grind except the one that holds the community elite together: growth.

This disinterest in the specific form of growth, but avid commitment to development generally, enables the newspaper to achieve a statesmanlike position in the community. It is often deferred to as a neutral party by the special interests. In his pioneering study of the creation of zoning laws in New York City in the 1920s, Makielski (1966: 149) remarks, "While the newspapers in the city are large landholders, the role of the press was not quite like that of any of the other nongovernmental actors. The press was in part one of the referees of the rules of the game, especially the informal rules, calling attention to what it considered violations." The publisher or editor is often the arbiter of internal growth machine bickering, restraining the short-term profiteers in the interest of more stable, long-term, and properly planned growth.

The publishing families are often ensconced as the most important city builders within the town or city; this is the appropriate designation for such prominent families as Otis and Chandler of the *Los Angeles Times* (see Clark, 1983: 271; Halberstam, 1979); Pulliam of the *Arizona Republic* and *Phoenix Sun* (see Luckingham, 1983: 318); and Gaylord of the *Daily Oklahoman* (see Bernard, 1983: 216). Sometimes these publishers are directly active in politics, "kingmaking" behind the scenes by screening candidates for political office, lobbying for federal contracts and grants, and striving to build growth infrastructure in their region (Fainstein, Fainstein, and Armistead, 1983: 217; Judd, 1983: 178). In the booming Contra Costa County suburbs of the San Francisco Bay Area, the president of the countywide organization of builders, real estate investors, and property financiers was the owner of the regional paper. In his home county, as well as in the jurisdictions of his eleven other suburban papers, owner Dean Lesher ("Citizen Lesher") acts as "a cheerleader for development" who simply kills stories damaging to growth interests and reassigns unsympathetic reporters to less controversial beats (Steidtmann, 1985). The local newspaper editor was one of the three "bosses" in Springdale's "invisible government" (Vidich and Bensman, 1960: 217). Sometimes, the publisher is among the largest urban landholders and openly fights for benefits tied to growth in land: The owners of the *Los Angeles Times* fought for the water that developed their vast properties for both urban and agricultural uses. The editorial stance is usually reformist, invoking the common good (and technical planning expertise) as the rationale for the land-use decisions the owners favor. This sustains the legitimacy of the paper itself among all literate sectors of society and helps mask the distributive effects of many growth developments.

The media attempt to attain their goals not only through news articles and editorials but also through informal talks between owners and editors and the local leaders. Because newspaper interests are tied to growth, media executives are sympathetic to business leaders' complaints that a particular journalistic investigation or angle may be bad for the local business climate, and should it nevertheless become necessary, direct threats of advertising cancellation can modify journalistic coverage (Bernard, 1983: 220). This does not mean that newspapers (or advertisers) control the politics of a city or region, but that the media have a special influence simply because they are committed to growth per se, and can play an invaluable role in coordinating strategy and selling growth to the public.

This institutional legitimacy is especially useful in crises. In the controversy surrounding the army's accidental release of nerve gas at the Dugway Proving Grounds, Lester found that the Utah media were far more sympathetic to the military's explanations than were media outside Utah (Lester, 1971). The economic utility of the Dugway Proving Grounds (and related government facilities) was valued by the local establishment. Similarly, insiders report that publicizing toxic waste problems at Love Canal was hindered by an "unwritten law" in the newsroom that "a reporter did not attack or otherwise fluster the Hooker [Chemical Company] executives" (Brown, 1979, cited in Levine, 1982: 190).

As these examples indicate, a newspaper's essential role is not to protect a given firm or industry (an issue more likely to arise in a small city than a large one) but to bolster and maintain the predisposition for general growth. Although newspaper editorialists may express concern for "the ecology," this does not prevent them from supporting growth-inducing investments for their regions. The *New York Times* likes office towers and additional industrial installations in the city even more than it loves "the environment." Even when historically significant districts are threatened, the *Times* editorializes in favor of intensification. Thus the *Times* recently admonished opponents to "get out of the way" of the Times Square renewal, which would replace landmark structures (including its own former headquarters at 1 Times Square) with huge office structures (*New York Times*, May 24, 1984, p. 18). Similarly, the *Los Angeles Times* editorializes against narrow-minded profiteering that increases pollution or aesthetic blight—in other cities. The newspaper featured criticism, for example, of the Times Square renewal plan (Kaplan, 1984: 1), but had enthusiastically supported development of the environmentally devastating supersonic transport (SST) for the jobs it would presumably lure to Southern California. In an unexpected regional parallel, the *Los Angeles Times* fired celebrated architectural critic John Pastier for his incessant criticisms of Los Angeles's downtown renewal projects (Clark, 1983: 298), and the *New York Times* dismissed Pulitzer Prize winner Sydney Schanberg as a columnist apparently because he "opposed civic projects supported by some of New York's most powerful interests, particularly those in the real estate industry" (Rosenstiel, 1985: 21).

Although newspapers may openly support "good planning principles" of a certain sort, the acceptable form of "good planning" does not often extend to limiting growth or authentic conservation in a newspaper's home ground. "Good planning principles" can easily represent the opposite goals.

UTILITIES

Leaders of "independent" public or quasi-public agencies, such as utilities, may play a role similar to that of the newspaper publisher: tied to a single locale, they become growth "statesmen" rather than advocates for a certain type of growth or intralocal distribution of growth.

For example, a water-supplying agency (whether public or private) can expand only by acquiring more users. This causes utilities to penetrate deep into the hin-terlands, inefficiently extending lines to areas that are extremely costly to service (Gaffney, 1961; Walker and Williams, 1982). The same growth goals exist within central cities. Brooklyn Gas was an avid supporter of the movement of young professionals into abandoned areas of Brooklyn, New York, in the 1970s, and even went so far as to help finance housing rehabilitation and sponsor a traveling slide show and open houses displaying the pleasant lifestyles in the area. All utilities seem bent on acquiring more customers to pay off past investments, and on proving they have the good growth prospects that lenders use as a criterion, for financing additional investments. Overall efficiencies are often sacrificed as a result.

Transportation officials, whether of public or private organizations, have a special interest in growth: they tend to favor growth along their specific transit routes. But transportation doesn't just serve growth, it creates it. From the beginning, the laying-out of mass transit lines was a method of stimulating development; indeed, the land speculators and the executives of the transportation firms were often the same people. In part because of the salience of land development, "public service was largely incidental to the operation of the street railways" (Wilcox, quoted in Yago, 1983: 44). Henry Huntington's Pacific Electric, the primary commuting system of Los Angeles, "was built not to provide transportation but to sell real estate" (Clark, 1983: 272; see also Binford, 1985; Fogelson, 1967; Yago, 1983). And because the goal of profitable transportation did not guide the design and routing of the system, it was destined to lose money, leaving Los Angeles without a viable transit system in the end (Fogelson, 1967).

Transit bureaucrats today, although not typically in the land business, function as active development boosters; only in that way can more riders be found to support their systems and help pay off the sometimes enormous debts incurred to construct or expand the systems. On the national level, major airlines develop a strong growth interest in the development of their "hub" city and the network it serves. Eastern Airlines must have growth in Miami, Northwest Airlines needs development in Minneapolis, and American Airlines rises or falls with the fortunes of Dallas-Fort Worth. [. . .]

NOTES

1. Trillin remarks that rejection of high taxes by the citizens of Rockford is "consistent with what the business and industrial leadership of Rockford has traditionally preached. For years, the industrialists were considered to be in complete control of the sort of local government industrialists traditionally favor—a conservative, relatively clean administration committed to the proposition that the highest principle of government is the lowest property tax rate" (Trillin, 1976: 150).

2. Local planning officials also sometimes get in on some of the corruption; they may make real estate investments of their own. Los Angeles Planning Director Calvin Hamilton was pressured to resign after twenty years on the job in part because of revelations that he accepted free rent from developers for a side business and had other conflicts of interest (Clifford, 1985d).

3. Although many suburban newspapers encourage growth, especially of tax-generating businesses, the papers of exclusive suburban towns may instead try to guard the existing land-use patterns and social base of their circulation area. Rudel (1983: 104) describes just this sort of situation in Westport, Connecticut. There are a number of reasons for this occasional deviation from the rule we are proposing. When trying to attract advertising dollars, newspapers prefer a small, rich readership to a larger but poorer one. Maintaining exclusivity is itself occasionally a growth strategy for smaller communities. Opposition to growth in these cases is consistent with the desires of local elites.

4. Cox and Morgan's study of British local newspapers indicates that the booster role of the press is not unique to the United States.

REFERENCES

Agger, Robert, Daniel Goldrich, and Bert E. Swanson, 1964. *The Rulers and the Ruled: Political Power and Impotence in American Communities.* New York: Wiley.

Alexander, Herbert E. 1972. *Money in Politics.* Washington D.C.: Public Affairs Press.

Alexander, Herbert. 1980. *Financing Politics: Money, Elections and Political Reform.* 2d ed. Washington, D.C.: Congressional Quarterly Press.

Alexander, Herbert. 1983. *Financing the 1980 Election.* Lexington, Mass.: D.C. Heath.

Alford, Robert, and Roger Friedland. 1975. "Political Participation and Public Policy." *Annual Review of Sociology* 1: 429–479.

Ann Arbor, Michigan, Planning Department, 1972. *The Ann Arbor Growth Study.* Ann Arbor, Mich.: City Planning Department.

Bachrach, Peter, and Morton Baratz. 1962. "The Two Faces of Power." *American Political Science Review* 56: 947–952.

Banfield, Edward C. 1961. *Political Influence.* New York: Macmillan.

Bell, Daniel. 1961. "Crime as an American Way of Life." Pp. 127–150 in Daniel Bell, *The End of Ideology: On the Exhaustion of Political Ideas in the Fifties.* New York: Collier Books.

Bernard, Richard M. 1983. "Oklahoma City: Booming Schooner." Pp. 213–234 in Richard M. Bernard and Bradley R. Rice (eds.), *Sunbelt Cities: Politics and Growth since World War II.* Austin: University of Texas Press.

Berry, Brian J.L., and John Kasarda. 1977. *Contemporary Urban Ecology.* New York: Macmillan.

Binford, Henry C. 1985. *The First Suburbs: Residential Communities on the Boston Periphery 1815–1860.* Chicago: University of Chicago Press.

Boorstin, Daniel, 1965. *The Americans: The National Experience.* New York: Random House.

Bouma, Donald. 1962. "Analysis of the Social Power Position of a Real Estate Board." *Social Problems* 10(Fall): 121–132.

Boyarsky, Bill, and Jerry Gillam. 1982. "Hard Times Don't Stem Flow of Campaign Gifts." *Los Angeles Times,* April 4, sec. I, pp. 1, 3, 22, 23.

Brown, Mike. 1979. *Laying Waste: The Poisoning of America by Toxic Chemicals.* New York: Pantheon.

Burd, Gene. 1977. "The Selling of the Sunbelt: Civic Boosterism in the Media." Pp. 129–150 in David Perry and Alfred Watkins (eds.), *The Rise of the Sunbelt Cities.* Beverly Hills, Calif.: Sage.

Caro, Robert A. 1974. *The Power Broker: Robert Moses and the Fall of New York.* New York: Knopf.

Clark, David L. 1983. "Improbable Los Angeles." Pp. 268–308 in Richard M. Bernard and Bradley R. Rice (eds.), *Sunbelt Cities: Politics and Growth since World War II.* Austin: University of Texas Press.

Clark, Terry. 1968. "Community Structure, Decision-Making, Budget Expenditures, and Urban

Renewal in Fifty-one American Cities." *American Sociological Review* 33 (August): 576–593.

Clifford, Frank. 1985. "Ouster of City Planner Sought." *Los Angeles Times*, July 15, sec. I, pp. 1, 13.

Cox, Harvey, and David Morgan. 1973. *City Politics and the Press: Journalists and the Governing of Merseyside.* Cambridge: Cambridge University Press.

Dagenais, Julie. 1967. "Newspaper Language as an Active Agent in the Building of a Frontier Town." *American Speech* 42(2): 114–121.

Dahl, Robert Alan. 1961. *Who Governs?* New Haven: Yale University Press.

Daws, Gavan, and George Cooper. 1984. *Land and Power in Hawaii: The Democratic Years.* Honolulu: Benchmark Press.

Devereux, Sean. 1976. "Boosters in the Newsroom: The Jacksonville Case." *Columbia Journalism Review* 14: 38–47.

Domhoff, G. William. 1967. *Who Rules America?* Englewood Cliffs, N.J.: Prentice-Hall.

Domhoff, G. William. 1970. *The Higher Circles: The Governing Class in America.* New York: Random House.

Domhoff, G. William. 1983. *Who Rules America Now? A View for the 80's.* Englewood Cliffs, N.J.: Prentice-Hall.

Downie, Leonard, Jr. 1974. *Mortgage on America.* New York: Praeger.

Edelman, Murray. 1964. *The Symbolic Uses of Politics.* Urbana: University of Illinois Press.

Fainstein, Susan, Norman Fainstein, and P. Jefferson Armistead. 1983. "San Francisco: Urban Transformation and the Local State." Pp. 202–244 in Susan Fainstein (ed.), *Restructuring the City.* New York: Longman.

Fishman, Mark. 1978. "Crime Waves as Ideology." *Social Problems* 25(5): 532–543.

Fogelson, Robert M. 1967. *The Fragmented Metropolis: Los Angeles, 1850–1930.* Cambridge, Mass.: Harvard University Press.

Form, William H., and William V. D'Antonio. 1970. "Integration and Cleavage among Community Influentials in Two Border Cities." Pp. 431–442 in Michael Aiken and Paul E. Mott (eds.), *The Structure of Community Power.* New York: Random House.

Fowlkes, Martha R., and Patricia Miller. 1985. "Toward a Sociology of Unnatural Disaster." Paper presented at the 80th annual meeting of the American Sociological Association, Washington, D.C., August 31.

Freidel, Frank. 1963. "Boosters, Intellectuals and the American City." Pp. 115–120 in Oscar Handlin and John Burchard (eds.), *The Historian and the City.* Cambridge, Mass.: MIT Press.

Friedland, Roger, Frances Piven, and Robert Alford.

1978. "Political Conflict, Urban Structure, and the Fiscal Crisis." Pp. 175–225 in Douglas Ashford (ed.), *Comparing Urban Policies.* Beverly Hills, Calif.: Sage.

Fullinwider, John. 1980. "Dallas: The City with No Limits?" *In These Times* 5(6): 12–13.

Gaffney, M. Mason. 1961. "Land and Rent in Welfare Economics." Pp. 141–167 in *Land Economics Research* (papers presented at a symposium on land economics research, Lincoln, Nebraska, June 16–23). Washington, D.C.: Resources for the Future. Distributed by Johns Hopkins University Press, Baltimore.

Gordon, Margaret T., Linda Heath, and Robert leBailly. 1979. "Some Costs of Easy News: Crime Reports and Fear." Paper presented at the annual meeting of the American Psychological Association, New York.

Halberstam, David. 1979. *The Powers That Be.* New York: Knopf.

Hawley, Amos. 1950. *Human Ecology: A Theory of Community Structure.* New York: Ronald Press.

Hirsch, Seymour. 1969. "On Uncovering the Great Nerve Gas Coverup." *Ramparts* 3(July): 12–18.

Hunter, Floyd. 1953. *Community Power Structure: A Study of Decision Makers.* Chapel Hill: University of North Carolina Press.

Hunter, Floyd. 1980. *Community Power Succession.* Chapel Hill: University of North Carolina Press.

Johnson, David R. 1983. "San Antonio: The Vicissitudes of Boosterism." Pp. 235–254 in Richard M. Bernard and Bradley R. Rice (eds.), *Sunbelt Cities: Politics and Growth since World War II.* Austin: University of Texas Press.

Judd, Dennis. 1983. "From Cowtown to Sunbelt City." Pp. 167–201 in Susan Fainstein (ed.), *Restructuring the City.* New York: Longman.

Kaplan, Sam Hall, 1984. "Will Times Square Plan Destroy It?" *Los Angeles Times*, October 3, sec. I, p. 1.

Krannich, Richard S., and Craig R. Humphrey. 1983. "Local Mobilization and Community Growth: Toward an Assessment of the 'Growth Machine' Hypothesis." *Rural Sociology* 48(1): 60–81.

Lasswell, Harold. 1936. *Politics: Who Gets What, When, How.* New York: McGraw-Hill.

Lester, Marilyn. 1971. "Toward a Sociology of Public Events." Master's thesis, Department of Sociology, University of California, Santa Barbara.

Levine, Adeline Gordon. 1982. *Love Canal: Science, Politics and People.* Lexington, Mass: D. C. Heath.

Luckingham, Bradford. 1983. "Phoenix: The Desert Metropolis." Pp. 309–327 in Richard M. Bernard and Bradley R. Rice (eds.), *Sunbelt Cities: Politics and Growth since World War II.* Austin: University of Texas Press.

Lyon, Larry, Lawrence G. Felice, M. Ray Perryman, and E. Stephen Parker. 1981. "Community Power and Population Increase: An Empirical Test of the Growth Machine Model." *American Journal of Sociology* 86(6): 1387–1400.

McCombs, Maxwell E., and Donald Shaw. 1972. "The Agenda Setting Function of Mass Media." *Public Opinion Quarterly* 36: 176–187.

McGarry, T. W. 1985. "Irish Will March to Four Different Drummers." *Los Angeles Times*, March 14, sec. II, pp. 1, 3.

McKenzie, R. D. 1922. "The Neighborhood: A Study of Local Life in the City of Columbus Ohio—Conclusion." *American Journal of Sociology* 27: 780–799.

Makielski, Stanislaw J. 1966. *The Politics of Zoning: The New York Experience*. New York: Columbia University Press.

Melosi, Martin. 1983. "Dallas-Fort Worth: Marketing the Metroplex." Pp. 162–195 in Richard M. Bernard and Bradley R. Rice (eds.), *Sunbelt Cities: Politics and Growth since World War II*. Austin: University of Texas Press.

Mollenkopf, John. 1983. *The Contested City*. Princeton, N.J.: Princeton University Press.

Molotch, Harvey. 1980. "Media and Movements." Pp. 71–93 in Mayer Zald and John McCarthy (eds.), *The Dynamics of Social Movements*. Cambridge, Mass.: Winthrop.

Molotch, Harvey, and Marilyn Lester. 1974. "News as Purposive Behavior: On the Strategic Use of Routine Events, Accidents, and Scandals." *American Sociological Review* 39(1): 101–113.

Molotch, Harvey, and Marilyn Lester. 1975. "Accidental News: The Great Oil Spill as Local Occurrence and National Event." *American Journal of Sociology* 81(2): 235–260.

Mormino, Gary R. 1983. "Tampa: From Hell Hole to the Good Life." Pp. 138–161 in Richard M. Bernard and Bradley R. Rice (eds.), *Sunbelt Cities: Politics and Growth since World War II*. Austin: University of Texas Press.

Mumford, Lewis. 1961. *The City in History*. New York: Harcourt.

Peterson, Paul E. 1981. *City Limits*. Chicago: University of Chicago Press.

Rosentiel, Thomas B. 1985. "'Killing Fields' Writer Loses N.Y. Times Column, to Be Reassigned." *Los Angeles Times*, August 21, sec. I, p. 21.

Rubin, Lillian B. 1972. *Busing and Backlash: White against White in an Urban School District*. Berkeley and Los Angeles: University of California Press.

Rudel, Thomas K. 1983. "Managing Growth: Local Governments and the Social Control of Land Use." Unpublished ms., Department of Human Ecology, Rutgers University.

San Francisco Chronicle, 1984. "Reagan's Hometown Offers Bounty to Lure More Business to the Area." *San Francisco Chronicle*, May 10, p. 4.

Schattschneider, Elmer Eric. 1960. *The Semisovereign People*. New York: Holt, Rinehart and Winston.

Smith, Michael Peter, and Marlene Keller. 1983. "Managed Growth and the Politics of Uneven Development in New Orleans." Pp. 126–166 in Susan Fainstein (ed.), *Restructuring the City*. New York: Longman.

Smith, Reginald. 1984. "Willie Brown's Big Income Revealed in State Report." *San Francisco Chronicle*, March 7, p. 12.

Spaulding, Charles. 1951. "Occupational Affiliations of Councilmen in Small Cities." *Sociology and Social Research* 35(3): 194–200.

Steidtmann, Nancy. 1985. "Citizen Lesher: Newspaper Publisher." *Bay Area Business Magazine* IV (October 3): 14–18.

Stone, Clarence N. 1981. "Community Power Structure—A Further Look." *Urban Affairs Quarterly* 16(4): 505–515.

Stone, Clarence N. 1982. "Social Stratification, Non-Decision-Making and the Study of Community Power." *American Politics Quarterly* 10(3): 275–302.

Stone, Clarence N. 1984. "City Politics and Economic Development: Political Economy Perspectives." *Journal of Politics* 46(1): 286–299.

Summers, Gene F. et al. 1976. *Industrial Invasion of Nonmetropolitan America: A Quarter Century of Experience*. New York: Praeger.

Swanstrom, Todd. 1981. "The Crisis of Growth Politics: Cleveland, Kucinich, and the Challenge of Urban Populism." Ph.D. dissertation, Princeton University.

Swanstrom, Todd. 1985. *The Crisis of Growth Politics: Cleveland, Kucinich, and the Challenge of Urban Populism*. Philadelphia: Temple University Press.

Tiebout, Charles M. 1956. "A Pure Theory of Local Expenditures." *Journal of Political Economy* 64(October): 416–424.

Trillin, Calvin. 1976. "U.S. Journal: Rockford, Illinois—Schools without Money." *New Yorker* 52(38): 146–154.

Vidich, Arthur J., and Joseph Bensman. 1960. *Small Town in Mass Society: Class, Power and Religion in a Rural Community*. Garden City, N.Y.: Doubleday.

Walker, Richard A., and Matthew J. Williams. 1982. "Water from Power: Water Supply and Regional Growth in the Santa Clara Valley." *Economic Geography* 58(2): 95–119.

Walton, John. 1970. "A Systematic Survey of Community Power Research." Pp. 443–464 in Michael Aiken and Paul Mott (eds.), *The Structure of Community Power*. New York: Random House.

Weinstein, Bernard L., and Robert E. Firestine, 1978. *Regional Growth and Decline in the United States.* New York: Praeger.

Weinstein, James. 1968. *The Corporate Ideal in the Liberal State, 1900–1918.* Boston: Beacon Press.

Whitt, J. Allen. 1982. *Urban Elites and Mass Transportation: The Dialectics of Power.* Princeton, N.J.: Princeton University Press.

Williams, Oliver, and C. R. Adrian. 1963. *Four Cities: A Study of Comparative Policy Making.* Philadelphia: Temple University Press.

Wolfe, Alan. 1981. *America's Impasse: The Rise and Fall of the Politics of Growth.* New York: Pantheon.

Wyner, Allen. 1967. "Governor-Salesman." *National Civic Review* 61 (February): 81–86.

Yago, Glenn. 1983. "Urban Transportation in the Eighties." *Democracy* 3(1): 43–55.

CHAPTER 8

Introduction: Restructuring and Dislocations

David Ley

Late in November 1972, Mrs Edna Shakel received an eviction notice. Mrs Shakel, a widow in her seventies, had lived in a three-room apartment in a converted house in the Fairview district of Vancouver for three years, a house she shared mainly with other elderly women like herself. She suspected that the tenants had not been given adequate notice, but she had no plans to protest, nor indeed did she know the channels for protest: 'At our age, you know, we're not exactly fighters.' None the less, with Christmas and winter at hand, the prospect of a move for an elderly woman in a very tight rental market was extremely unwelcome, particularly as Mrs Shakel wished to remain within easy walking distance of her friends, familiar services, and her church.

In Mrs Shakel's eviction notice we may observe not only a private trouble, but also a public issue, the intersection of a personal biography with a wider historical geography.[1] What are some of the dimensions of that history and geography, the broader contexts which will appear throughout the pages of this study? First, and most visible, was immense pressure on the housing-market in Fairview, Kitsilano, and other neighbourhoods in Vancouver's inner city, where vacancies in private rental units scarcely existed; by 1974 the official vacancy rate for desirable inner-city neighbourhoods like Fairview was zero.[2] Builders were developing a new housing form, the condominium, and recently completed projects formed an advancing wave along Mrs Shakel's street. An agent was attempting to assemble several houses including her own as a site for a 30–40 suite building, but was facing a holdout from at least one property owner. In a hot market, with the prospect of significant profits, the temptation to accelerate the transaction was considerable. A house adjacent to Mrs Shakel's, already purchased, was rented to the Hare Krishna cult on a short lease. The presence of cult members, chanting into the early hours of the morning, brought a discordant presence to a quiet residential street in a conservative district. A neighbouring property owner, unwilling to sell his own house, charged that developers were engaged in blockbusting. Certainly, the transition process was greased, for several houses on the block were speedily emptied of their tenants, including the Hare Krishna group who, after only a few months' residence, relocated four blocks away, again on a short-term lease, as, it was alleged, the blockbusting process was attempted once more. By the summer of 1973, condominiums lined almost the whole block, and were springing up throughout the neighbourhood. By 1976 there were some forty strata-title projects containing 880 self-owned apartments in Fairview, almost all of them built in the previous five years.[3]

An unanticipated inversion was taking place in parts of the inner-city housing-market. Spatial models of the city's social areas showed the innermost districts near the downtown core had for decades been reserved primarily for poorer residents. From the inter-war research of Homer Hoyt in the United States, the conventional wisdom had it that as property aged it filtered down from wealthier to successively poorer households in these old, innermost districts. This wisdom matched the reality marked on land-use maps of Canadian cities into the 1960s. In Toronto, for example, the 1941 map of housing and land use described a zone bluntly labelled as 'fourth-class housing' virtually encircling the downtown area; beyond it was an ageing, hand-me-down ring of affordable rooming houses. So it was that a widow on a fixed pension like Mrs Shakel could afford to live in what had once been a substantial middle-class home. Adjacent to the upper-class Shaughnessy neighbourhood, Fairview had enjoyed a certain reflected glory as a residential area, but by 1970 its middle-class gentility was frayed at the edges; indeed its northern section, the Fairview Slopes, rising above the decaying industrial basin of False Creek, had deteriorated to the extent that it had been red-lined by banks and trust companies, precluding the prospect of commercial loans being secured for home purchase or repair. Nothing seemed likely to disperse the industrial—and chemical—haze around its hippy communes.[4]

But now things were changing. While the transition of the Fairview Slopes was still a decade away, elsewhere in Fairview condominium redevelopment was bringing higher-status groups into the inner city. Mostly they were small households with professional or managerial occupations,

working downtown in business or in the public sector in teaching, health care, or government service. Household heads were either under 35 years of age, at an early stage in their professional and family careers, or else empty-nesters, purchasing with a retirement home in mind.[5] The condominium units that replaced Mrs Shake's house and its neighbours included two company presidents, two business managers, two real-estate agents, an engineer, an accountant, and several technicians. Their desire to live in the inner city and the decision by developers to build for them created a 'value gap' that threatened the existing rental market.[6] Quite simply, land owners received a higher, faster, and more secure economic return from selling apartments than from renting them.

This transition was not of course unique to Vancouver, but began to occur in large cities of other advanced industrial nations at around the same time. In each city, and each nation, there were certain local inflections. In Toronto, Montreal, and the larger cities of central Canada, there was more emphasis on renovation of the existing housing stock, than on demolition and redevelopment, the standard transition process in cities built of wood like Vancouver or Edmonton. Indeed the term 'gentrification' was initially employed in London by Ruth Glass to describe precisely this process, the movement of the 'gentry' into existing lower-income housing which they subsequently rehabilitated and upgraded.[7] Over the past decade, however, many authors, more attentive to changes in housing class than to those in the housing stock in the inner city, have broadened gentrification to include both sides of the middle-class market, the renovation of old properties and the redevelopment of new units, with both conceived as part of a broader restructuring of the city. This book too is concerned with gentrification writ large, the wider processes of economic, social, and political transformation in the downtown and inner city that have both triggered and followed upgrading and reinvestment.

In major cities the consequences of upgrading have been substantial; in central London, the breakup of the private rental market in favour of condominium tenure is estimated to have removed 45 per cent of the purpose-built rental stock between 1966 and 1981.[8] Less firm figures for New York City suggest between 10,000 and 40,000 rental households were being displaced by gentrification *annually* at the end of the 1970s.[9] There are good grounds, then, for seeing gentrification as a major cause of the problems of housing affordability in large Canadian cities since 1970.[10] Simply put, the inner city is losing its historic role as a major reservoir of private, low-cost housing.

In the end, Mrs Shakel was more fortunate than many other displaced households. She was able to find alternative accommodation near her former dwelling, although for it to remain affordable she gave up a self-contained three-room apartment in exchange for a single room with a shared bathroom. This was her home until her death several years later, and soon after it, too, was demolished and replaced by condominiums. The room was close to the church she attended and it was there that I met Edna Shakel and learned of her story, a story that stimulated the lengthy research project which has given rise to this book.

The events that led to the loss of Mrs Shakel's apartment implicated not only residential changes, but also a larger reworking of the *mentalité* of living in a large urban area. A municipal election was held in the City of Vancouver the same month as Edna Shakel was evicted from her apartment. The party in power, the NPA or Non-Partisan Association (a euphemism of the first degree), had ruled City Hall without interruption since its formation as a free-enterprise coalition in 1937. But now it was opposed by two new parties founded in 1968

in the wake of some major land-use controversies in the city concerning urban renewal and freeway development. Dissatisfaction with the one-dimensional thinking of the NPA's pro-growth, pro-development policy mobilized other interest groups. A coalition of liberal middle-class professionals in their mid-twenties to mid-forties formed The Electors' Action Movement (TEAM), while union, tenant, and anti-poverty groups established the left-wing Committee of Progressive Electors (COPE). TEAM offered a complex urban vision of the liveable city, a vision which incorporated growth management, urban aesthetics, and social justice in an uneasy amalgam.[11] If, as Jane Jacobs charged,[12] the modernization of the Canadian city then underway showed no advance upon the modernist visionaries of the 1920s and their dream of the freeway, high-rise city, the urban reformers of the 1970s had a more humanistic view with a complex approach to the quality of urban experience. Theirs would be 'a city people can live in and enjoy',[13] a city of human scale, where the population would find urban government more accessible through participatory programmes, where the ideology of the public household would guide transportation and housing policy, favouring public solutions (transit, social housing) over private ones (the private car, slum housing), and where design guidelines and generous park and landscaping policy would enhance the quality of the built environment. The extent to which all, or even much, of this seemingly progressive agenda was achieved will be a subject for later discussion.[14]

The ideology of the liveable city was supported by a broad public, as a range of participatory planning programmes in the 1970s confirmed.[15] But this is not to state that it was much further removed from a distinctive class interest than the pro-growth coalition which it replaced. The bearers of the liberal ideology were precisely those citizens who saw the benefits of an expanded welfare state. They were educated, middle-class professionals, primarily under 40 years of age, and disproportionately employed in the public or non-profit sectors as teachers, professors, social workers, architects, or lawyers. Such professionals in social and cultural fields have played a distinctive and important part in the reshaping of the inner city. They were not quite the same grouping as had moved into the condominiums on Mrs Shakel's block, underscoring the fact that the professional-managerial category is not a unitary class. While the condominium dwellers were also by and large well-educated, white-collar workers, they were more likely to be private-sector managers, professionals, or salespeople, with interests closer to the private market. The liberals, in contrast, tended to be public- or quasi-public-sector workers who often favoured older properties and saw a broader set of objectives as the responsibility of urban governance. But what both groups shared in common was an orientation to an urbane lifestyle, the cosmopolitan opportunities of central-city living.

TEAM'S ideology was the ideology of the day and the party won the 1972 election in a landslide. It was a local manifestation of a national sentiment. In Toronto and Montreal reform groups sprang up at the same time, with the same opposition to unqualified urban boosterism pursued by a centralized and inaccessible growth coalition at City Hall. A few weeks after TEAM'S electoral success, the reformers in Toronto, 2,000 miles away, were also returned to office in a shaky coalition of liberals, social democrats, and 'red' tories who pressed the conservative vote to the centre or even the centre-left. In Montreal a new civic party made significant gains in the 1974 municipal election, providing the first opposition to Mayor Jean Drapeau's growth machine, but beset by internal rifts between liberals and leftists, the Montreal Citizens

Movement was not elected until 1986. Fainter reverberations were felt in smaller cities. Edmonton, Ottawa, and Halifax also saw middle-class activists elected to city council, pursuing such goals as the defence of neighbourhoods and resistance to extensive redevelopment and freeway construction. In each instance the objective was the turning back of massive urban change, resistance to the wholesale modernization of the city. And in each case the protagonists typically included the same cast of middle-class professionals, frequently employed within the general rubric of the welfare state. A new agenda for urbane, central-city living was being articulated by a newly mobilized cohort of young professional and managerial workers, not only in the housing-market but also in the corridors of power.

The social, spatial, and political reshaping of Canada's major cities was part of a larger national, indeed international, set of events and changing values. The first Liberal administration of Pierre Trudeau was elected in the midst of escalating social movements in advanced societies, including the student uprising of May 1968 in Paris to which Trudeau as a francophone intellectual was particularly attentive. Environmentalism, civil rights, the Vietnam War, the student movement, and the counter-culture all offered a sharp critique of post-war society in the Western nations, societies which had shown an unprecedented level of sustained economic growth. But it was this very success story that received such vehement criticism. If, in the United States, the military-industrial complex was the object of particular excoriation by critics, the broader target was a corporate society whose one-dimensional ideology was alleged to produce a one-dimensional personality.[16] For some thinkers it was *eros* that would liberate an uptight society, and whatever one makes of the sexual revolution that coincided with this period, one emphasis that is noteworthy is the reference to experience, more particularly to the *sensual*, as in some way marking the forward march of freedom. The pursuit of 'joyous festival' by the student rioters in Paris was rapidly domesticated by innovative urban practitioners.[17] So it was that Vancouver residents were offered in 1972 neither lower taxes nor economic growth by aspiring reform politicians, but instead 'a city people can live in and enjoy'.

This was not for a moment intended as an elitist agenda. Trudeau's espousal of an open society, the sense of new beginnings, encouraged social and cultural experimentation in public policy as well as in private life. The politics of inclusion, participatory initiatives offering unprecedented degrees of empowerment to service recipients, represented a real, not a cynical, attempt to expand the public sphere.[18] This expansion (if far from complete) was visible in three areas of the municipal reform movement and its policies. First, a greater range of issues was brought into the public sphere. The unexamined tenets of growth boosterism were interrogated and exposed to scrutiny from such competing objectives as environmental quality, social justice, local empowerment, or 'neighbourliness', a favourite criterion of Ray Spaxman, Vancouver's Director of Planning from 1973 to 1989. The public sphere was occupied no longer by a single, but now by multiple objectives. Second, more voices were admitted to the decision-making process. This was, after all, the period when Canada discovered its multiculturalism and enunciated a formal multicultural policy, a policy which has since evolved in ever more political directions.[19] In the urban arena the terms laid out by federal policy were followed by attempts at local democracy in various participatory programmes, the most sustained being the development of neighbourhood plans with mandated community consultation by municipal planning departments.

Third, the opening up of urban society was inevitably inscribed upon the urban landscape. Concomitant with the expansion of the public sphere has been the enlargement of public space. While the construction of enclosed shopping malls has tended to restrict certain traditional collective rights (such as picketing, or securing signatures for a petition[20]), the action of local government has usually led in the opposite direction. The extension of urban parks, the development of public plazas, and not least the opening up of the waterfront to public use—such as Vancouver's seawall, now accessible to pedestrians and cyclists for more than 12 kilometres around the central city—are all indicative of government action promoting a more accessible and convivial public realm. So too the state has contributed toward the preservation of valued heritage sites, including Montreal's Old Town, the Historic Properties in Halifax, and Vancouver's Gastown. The maintenance of view corridors, *causes célèbres* in Vancouver and Halifax, and downtown height restrictions in Ottawa to secure the skyline of Parliament Hill, are other examples of the state's intervention to maintain a visual resource for public enjoyment.

A ten-minute walk from Mrs Shakel's former apartment is the popular Granville Island, a public space carefully reshaped by the federal government through the Canada Mortgage and Housing Corporation in the 1970s. A mixed-use development, it incorporates a public food-market, theatres, an art college and hotel, and shops and offices cheek by jowl with new and long-established industry, including a cement plant. Formerly the whole island was occupied by manufacturing firms, some of them dating back eighty years to the original creation of this artifical island in the industrial basin of False Creek, on the edge of downtown Vancouver.

On Granville Island an adventure playground was created in the shell of the former Spear & Jackson sawmill, like most of the manufacturing plant an unprepossessing corrugated iron structure, in places rusting, dented, and torn. The playground (as a microcosm of the Island) contained some of the inversions of a contemporary urban aesthetic, an orientation to experience and the sensuous which is so central to the state's intervention in the built environment of the post-industrial city. First, a private space where trespassers would be prosecuted was transformed to a public space where loiterers were welcome. Second, an adult male space was opened up as a space for children, and, predominantly, mothers. Third, through skilful spatial engineering, a site of depreciating value has been revalued, though not yet as a working site for capital accumulation. Fourth, a place of industry became a place of play, a setting for production was turned into a setting for consumption. And yet with postmodern irony, the visual environment was carefully (indeed so carefully, one might think carelessly) retained. The recycling of the whole Island is predicated upon just such an industrial vernacular style, traditional to the site; the new art college looks like an industrial warehouse, the up-market hotel like a factory. What meets the eye is akin to what Sharon Zukin described in New York's SoHo as a 'poetic appreciation of industrial design'.[21] The Island is carefully themed to convey the message of historic continuity. But it is the stability of still life that is on display, for what has occurred is an aestheticization, a taming of a once wild and vigorous industrial landscape. The visual environment now reveals contradiction, complexity, and not a little parody, for beneath rough industrial shells are cultured post-industrial interiors. The only major problem of the Island is its own success, the crowds and congestion drawn to share this experience. Granville Island is a quintessential public space in the post-modern city.

Its retail outlets contain no chain stores, its produce is advertised as direct from regional farms, its goods are personalized by resident artists and craftspeople. The public market in particular is a sensual swirl of colours, sounds, tastes, and fragrances, an aesthetic triumph, joyous festival. Here, amidst the trays of baguettes and oysters, is the epitome of niche marketing for an urbane middle-class population jaded by mass marketing, who seek in shopping and gazing the pleasures of symbolic exchange, the confidence of *savoir-faire*, the delights of consumer distinction.[22] Are such acts of consumer solidarity by the educated middle-class the true harvest of 1968? And are such convivial public spaces the newest incarnation of the welfare state?

THE *EMBOURGEOISEMENT* OF THE INNER CITY

In the questions raised by such vignettes, with their separate but related places and events, we may discern a number of the themes that will be pursued in this book. In a number of districts in a number of large cities, the steady down-filtering of the inner-city housing stock has been abruptly reversed: The *embourgeoisement* of the inner city, accomplished through the twin transition processes of renovation and redevelopment (often to condominiums), is incomplete even in those neighbourhoods where it has been most prominent, but none the less it has contributed to a significant reshaping of the housing-market in cities with expanding downtown employment in advanced services. This qualifier immediately leads to the important recognition that there is a geography to gentrification, that the trends remaking the inner cities of Toronto, San Francisco, or London are not shared by Winnipeg, Detroit, or Liverpool. Nor is every neighbourhood equally susceptible to middle-class settlement. Why did the condominiums arrive in Mrs Shakel's

Fairview in the early 1970s, while avoiding a string of inner-city districts in Vancouver's eastside with permissive zoning, cheaper land prices, and equally close to downtown? And why the 1970s? What combination of enabling and constraining contexts converged on this particular period?

Some provisional answers are suggested by the vignettes. The property industry had detected a new submarket in the central city which it was enthusiastically exploiting. The condominium was a product that solved the developer's problem of decreasing profitability in the rental sector; for contractors the surge in home renovations for the middle class also opened a second profitable niche market. But such development initiatives presupposed the existence of a market worth exploiting, for no entrepreneur supplies a product for which he or she has not already detected potential demand. The existence of that market leads to other contexts, notably to the labour-force of the burgeoning central-city service economy that was replacing the industrial workers of declining manufacturing zones like False Creek and Granville Island. The convergence of rapid economic expansion, the specific growth of white-collar professional jobs, and the maturation of the demographic bulge of the baby boom, all conspired to create a demand surge for housing among the middle class.

But still we have not accounted for the geographic specificity of the inner city as a destination for that population. The suburbs had become the postwar solution to the middle-class housing problem, as developers had perfected the suburban subdivision as the natural nesting area of the young nuclear family. As we will see, the suburbs continued to be the major destination of the middle class in the 1970s and 1980s, but a growing minority bucked the trend. What directed this cohort to the less familiar terrain of the inner city? Was it, as some authors have suggested, the impact of more expensive commuting, as the 1973 oil shock added a substantial economic premium to the social cost of an ever-lengthening journey to work? Or was it a redefinition of the nuclear family itself, as more women sought paid work and professional careers, the birth-rate tumbled, and the single family home in the suburbs became a dwelling form no longer functional to a youthful segment of the middle-class market?

And then there is the historical coincidence with the counter-culture and concomitant urban social movements. The youth ghettos of the 1960s were concentrated in the largest cities, including Toronto's Yorkville and Vancouver's Kitsilano, both districts which gentrified rapidly in the 1970s. What is the relationship between the counter-culture and gentrification? Was the counter-culture simply an unwitting tool of the development industry, like the Hare Krishna cult in Fairview, the urban storm-troopers who established a beach-head for profitable reinvestment? Or should we see a more complex set of interactions, where gentrification is an expression of a critical cultural politics, a rejection of the suburbs and their perceived cultural conformity in favour of the more cosmopolitan and permissive opportunities of the central city? If so, then an inner-city home is much more than a functional convenience; for a particular fragment of the middle class it is an integral part of their identity formation.

Certainly this thesis would fit with the striking historical coincidence between the onset of gentrification in Canadian cities around 1970 and the mobilization of political reform movements, critical of a pre-existing pro-growth regime. Typically, these movements contained at least two, often divisive, elements, a liberal grouping, like TEAM in Vancouver or the supporters of Mayor David Crombie in Toronto, that was primarily contained within the middle class, and a social democratic grouping, like the New Democrats in Toronto, or further to the left, COPE in Vancouver, which comprised an alliance of certain public-sector professionals with union members, some neighbourhood groups, and critical social movements promoting issues such as tenants' rights, feminism, and environmentalism. Both groupings represented a discontinuity with the growth regimes that had monopolized urban politics in the post-war period. Reformers were much more likely to be younger, to be professionals, and to be women, than the old guard at City Hall, a profile which immediately suggests a shared identity with the new middle class in the inner city. The gender complexion of the reformers is of particular interest. In Ottawa, where following the lead of Mayor Marion Dewar there was a continuing representation of professional women on Council, it has been suggested that the gender profile of councillors contributed to policy oriented toward the politics of consumption.[23]

In terms of land use, and the urban tax base, a consumption strategy neatly offset some of the damage exacted by deindustrialization. Most crudely, it served the functional end of political legitimation, in the 1990s as often a strategy of croissants and opera as of bread and circuses. The expansion of a park, the saving of a heritage site, subsidies for the symphony orchestra, the promotion of environmentally friendly policies such as public transportation, were all political winners for citizens endorsing the liveable city. A consumption strategy also laid the base for a new round of economic development predicated upon leisure and tourism, an amenity ethic which might attract (or keep) footloose capital. In this leisure economy, it was the resources of senior levels of government which were able to prime the pump, through investment in such hoped-for multipliers as heritage districts, convention centres, or hallmark events, the round of world's fairs, sporting festivals, and latterly political summit meetings which have been such an abiding feature of Canadian cities since Expo 67 in Montreal.

For municipal councils, hallmark events and urban spectacles provided a third opportunity. Fast-track redevelopment and infrastructure upgrading, often difficult to achieve under normal circumstances, could be more readily rationalized to a local electorate if the outcome was a celebration, for what might be regarded as a land-use transgression in normal times invariably became tolerable. Moreover, the spectacle also provided local government with leverage to apply against higher levels of the state. Funds not forthcoming for rapid transit, or a convention centre, or a new stock of social housing might be (and were) prised loose in the name of a celebration from a senior government which was seemingly more willing to be the donor of party favours. Governments in Canada have been remarkably unwilling to be presented to the electorate as party poopers.

The questions raised above define the subject matter of this book. Of course there are rarely neat solutions where simple lines of cause and effect may be traced. A synthetic interpretation of the changing inner city is a synthesis where the chains of causality are invariably diverted by intervening variables and interaction effects, where the consequences of actions are as often, perhaps more often, unintended as they are intended. Consider, for example, the historical coincidence of gentrification with the maturation of the baby boom, a changing family structure, the counter-culture, urban reform, and the rapid economic growth of the downtown labour-market, disrupted but not ended by the 1973 oil shock. The efficient positivist solution of holding certain variables constant to control for their effects is never available in the complexity of a regional geography. One may demonstrate interdependencies, but rarely causality.

Nor is this account of inner-city transformation a complete one. While the study will range widely in its engagement with economic, political, social and cultural trends—gentrification writ large—there is no claim here to a total history or total geography. The view of the inner city which emerges is a partial one with significant absences. The new middle class is in many respects a group in ascendancy in the inner city, implicating labour-markets, housing-markets, urban politics, and the built environment in the ways I have already outlined. But there are other inner cities I have not mentioned that are also being reshaped, and which will not be prominent in the arguments which follow. The new middle class is the privileged cohort in the post-industrial city, but it does not exist in isolation. In the dual labour-market of a service economy, gentrifiers fall principally in the upper tier. The lower tier of less skilled service workers comprises a workforce with far fewer opportunities, including shop assistants, waitresses, taxi drivers, and bellboys, many of them working near the level of the minimum wage. In New York, Sassen in particular has argued for the interdependence of the two tiers, with the lower circuit serving the middle class in such areas as restaurants and leisure, security, and various forms of personal service.[24] Working in this sector are large numbers of recent immigrants with limited facility in English or French, for, later than some other Western nations, many Canadian metropolitan areas have undergone significant ethnic and racial transformation over the past twenty-five years.

The dual labour-market provides one face of growing social polarization.[25] But even poorly paid, but full-time, service workers are privileged relative to large numbers of part-time and temporarily or permanently unemployed citizens. In extreme cases, as Mike Davis has shown for the asset-stripped inner-city districts of Los Angeles, the informal economy is prevalent, and crime may become the effective face of community economic development.[26] Unlike the achievements of Davis, or Tom Wolfe,[27] who move between the social worlds of high opportunity and deep impoverishment, this book is less ambitious in its scope. Nevertheless, while never losing sight of the place of the new middle class in a broader system of social stratification, a detailed examination of advantaged groups in their own right also adds an important dimension to our understanding of the remaking of the contemporary central city. [...]

NOTES

1. C. Wright Mills (1959), *The Sociological Imagination* (New York: Oxford University Press).
2. Real Estate Board of Vancouver (1977), *Real Estate Trends in Greater Vancouver.*
3. D. Ley (1981), 'Inner City Revitalization in Canada: A Vancouver Case-Study', *Canadian Geographer*, 25: 124–8. A strata-title project involves common ownership of a multiple-unit structure.
4. So pervasive was its counter-cultural ambience that Seventh Avenue, one of the principal residential streets on the Slopes, was known locally as 'Chemical Avenue': C. Mills (1988), 'Life on the Upslope: The Postmodern Landscape of Gentrification', *Society and Space*, 6: 169–90.
5. For a profile of inner city *vis-à-vis* suburban condominium residents in Canadian cities, see A. Skaburskis (1988), 'A Comparison of Suburban and Inner-City Condominium Markets', *Canadian Journal of Regional Science*, 11: 259–85.
6. For further discussion on the value gap and the rent gap, see Chapter 2. While the value gap describes a form of housing transition where a tenant is replaced by an owner in the same (but upgraded) apartment unit, it is a similar logic that demolishes the apartment building and develops condominium units on the site. Indeed both forms of transition often occur in the same district. Certainly to an evicted tenant like Mrs Shakel the nicety that distinguishes the two forms of transition is an academic one. On the supply side, the economic logic of the landlord's decision that leads to a tenancy change in an existing building, described by Hamnett and Randolph (1984), is the same as the rationale for moving from rental apartments to condominium redevelopment included in the 1975 annual report of a leading Vancouver apartment owner, cited in Ley (1981). In

both cases what is involved is 'the existence of a value gap between rented and owner-occupied property and very low rental returns on current capital values compared with those to be obtained by sale and reinvestment elsewhere': C. Hamnett and W. Randolph (1984), 'The Role of Landlord Disinvestment in Housing Market Transformation: An Analysis of the Flat Breakup Market in Central London', *Transactions, Institute of British Geographers*, NS 9: 259–79.

7. R. Glass (1964), 'Introduction', in Centre for Urban Studies (ed.), *London: Aspects of Change* (London: McGibbon and Kee) xiii–xliii.

8. C. Hamnett and B. Randolph (1986), "Tenurial Transformation and the Flat Breakup Market in London: The British Condo Experience', in N. Smith and P. Williams (eds.), *Gentrification of the City* (Boston: Allen and Unwin), 121–52.

9. P. Marcuse (1986), 'Abandonment, Gentrification, and Displacement: The Linkages in New York City', in Smith and Williams (eds.) 153–77.

10. The issue of residential displacement in Canadian cities is discussed in Chapter 2.

11. The contradictions between these elements is considered further in Chapter 8. See also D. Ley (1980), 'Liberal Ideology and the Post-Industrial City', *Annals, Association of American Geographers*, 70: 238–58.

12. J. Jacobs (1971), *City Limits* (Ottawa: National Film Board). In this film Ms Jacobs extended her theses on urban planning to Toronto, following her family's move to the city in 1968.

13. A slogan in TEAM campaign literature for the 1974 civic election.

14. Compare the optimistic scenario of James Lemon's assessment of the political culture of Toronto in 1978 with the more measured tone of 1991: J. Lemon (1978), 'The Urban Community Movement: Moving Toward Public Households', in D. Ley and M. Samuels (eds.), *Humanistic Geography* (Chicago: Maaroufa), 319–37; J. Lemon (1991), 'Toronto', *Cities*, 8: 258–66.

15. Consider for example the outcome of two major participatory planning programs of the 1970s, one in Greater Vancouver, the other in the City, which both ended up by rediscovering the liveable city ideology: Greater Vancouver Regional District (1975), *The Liveable Region 1976–1986* (Vancouver); City of Vancouver (1980), *Goals for Vancouver* (Vancouver: City Planning Commission).

16. H. Marcuse (1964), *One-Dimensional Man* (Boston: Beacon Press).

17. M. Poster (1975), *Existential Marxism in Postwar France* (Princeton: Princeton University Press), 373. For the subsequent managed animation of the Paris streets in the 1970s, see J. DeLacey (1983), 'Cultivating Culture in Paris', *New York Times Magazine*, 22 May.

18. In urban policy, a significant development was the termination of the insensitive and centralized urban renewal programme, and its replacement by a strategy of preservation and enrichment involving substantial public involvement. A parallel development was the winding down of the bureaucratic public housing programme in favour of third-sector partnership schemes, notably community-based co-operatives and non-profit housing societies.

19. A. Kobayashi (1993), 'Multiculturalism: Representing a Canadian Institution', in J. Duncan and D. Ley (eds.). *Place/Culture/Representation* (London: Routledge), 205–31.

20. In the case of the vast West Edmonton Mall, even picture-taking or moving around in large groups is discouraged: J. Hopkins (1991), 'West Edmonton Mall as a Centre for Social Interaction', *Canadian Geographer*, 35: 268–79.

21. S. Zukin (1989), *Loft Living* (New Brunswick, NJ: Rutgers University Press), 174.

22. For the symbolic construction of identity through the selective appropriation of cultural traits, see P. Bourdieu (1984), *Distinction* (Cambridge, Mass.; Harvard University Press). The place of food and other products in the construction of new class identity will be discussed in Chapter 8.

23. C. Andrew (1983), 'Ottawa', in W. Magnusson and A. Sancton (eds.), *City Politics in Canada* (Toronto: University of Toronto Press), 140–65.

24. S. Sassen (1984), 'The New Labour Demand in Global Cities', in M. P. Smith (ed.), *Cities in Transformation* (Beverly Hills, Calif.: Sage), 139–71; S. Sassen (1991), *The Global City: New York, London, Tokyo* (Princeton: Princeton University Press).

25. Amongst others, see Sassen (1991); J. Mollenkopf and M. Castells (1991) (eds.), *Dual City: Restructuring New York* (New York: Russell Sage Foundation); S. Fainstein, I. Gordon, and M. Harloe (1992), *Divided Cities* (Oxford: Blackwell). But consider also the cautions of P. Marcuse (1989), 'Dual City: A Muddy Metaphor for a Quartered City', *International Journal of Urban and Regional Research*, 13: 697–708 and C. Hamnett (1994), 'Social Polarisation in Global Cities: Theory and Evidence', *Urban Studies*, 31: 401–24. For the Canadian situation, see: L. Bourne (1993), 'Close Together and Worlds Apart: An Analysis of the Changes of the Ecology of Income in Canadian Cities', *Urban Studies*, 30: 1293–317.

26. M. Davis (1990), *City of Quartz: Excavating the Future in Los Angeles* (London: Verso).

27. T. Wolfe (1988), *The Bonfire of the Vanities* (London: Picador).

CHAPTER 9

Building the Frontier Myth

Neil Smith

Roland Barthes once proposed that "myth is constituted by the loss of the historical quality of things" (Barthes 1972:129). Richard Slotkin elaborates that in addition to wrenching meaning from its historical context, myth has a reciprocal effect on history: "history becomes a cliché" (Slotkin 1985: 16, 21–32), We should add the corollary that myth is constituted by the loss of the *geographical* quality of things as well. Deterritorialization is equally central to mythmaking, and the more events are wrenched from their constitutive geographies, the more powerful the mythology. Geography too becomes a cliché.

The social meaning of gentrification is increasingly constructed through the vocabulary of the frontier myth, and at first glance this appropriation of language and landscape might seem simply playful, innocent. Newspapers habitually extol the courage of urban "homesteaders," the adventurous spirit and rugged individualism of the new settlers, brave "urban pioneers," presumably going where, in the words of *Star Trek*, no (white) man has ever gone before. "We find a place on the lower [*sic*] East Side," confesses one suburban couple in the genteel pages of the *New Yorker*.

Ludlow Street. No one we know would think of living here. No one we know has ever heard of Ludlow Street. Maybe someday this neighborhood will be the way the Village was before we knew anything about New York. . . . We explain that moving down here is a kind of urban pioneering, and tell [Mother] she should be proud. We liken our crossing Houston Street to pioneers crossing the Rockies.

("Ludlow Street" 1988)

In its real estate section, the *New York Times* (March 27, 1983) announces "The Taming of the Wild Wild West," pursuant to the construction of the "Armory Condominium" two blocks west of Times Square:

The trailblazers have done their work: West 42nd Street has been tamed, domesticated and polished into the most exciting, freshest, most energetic new neighborhood in all of New York . . . for really savvy buyers, there's the rapid escalation of land prices along the western corridor of 42nd Street. (After all, if the real estate people don't know when a neighborhood is about to bust loose, who does?)

As new frontier, the gentrifying city since the 1980s has been oozing with optimism. Hostile landscapes are regenerated, cleansed, reinfused with middle-class sensibility; real estate values soar; yuppies consume; elite gentility is democratized in mass-produced styles of distinction. So what's not to like? The contradictions of the actual frontier are not entirely eradicated in this imagery but they are smoothed into an acceptable groove. As with the Old West, the frontier is idyllic yet also dangerous, romantic but also ruthless. From *Crocodile Dundee* to *Bright Lights, Big City*, there is an entire cinematic genre that makes of urban life a cowboy fable replete with dangerous environment, hostile natives and self-discovery at the margins of civilization. In taming the urban wilderness, the cowboy gets the girl but also finds and tames his inner self for the first time. In the final scene of *Crocodile Dundee*, Paul Hogan accepts New York—and New York him—as he clambers like an Aussie sheepdog over the heads and shoulders of a subway crowd. Michael J. Fox can hardly end his fable by riding off into a reassuring western sunset since in the big city the bright lights are everywhere, but he does see a bright new day rise over the Hudson River and Manhattan's reconstructed financial district. The manifest destiny of the earlier frontier rains a reciprocal Valhalla on the big city.

The frontier myth of the new city is here so clichéd, the geographical and historical quality of things so lost, that we may not even see the blend of myth in the landscape. This merely testifies to the power of the myth, but it was not always so. The analogy between the 1874 Tompkins Square marchers and the Sioux Nation was at best tentative and oblique, the mythology too young to bear the full ideological weight of uniting such obviously disparate worlds. But the real and conceptual distance between New York and the Wild Wild West has been continually eroded; perhaps the most iconoclastic evocation of a frontier in the early city came only a few years after Custer's Black Hills campaign when a stark, elegant but isolated residential building rose in the boonies of Central Park West and was named "The Dakota Apartments."

By contrast, in the condomania that has engulfed Manhattan a century later—an environment in which any social, physical or geographical connection with the earlier frontier is obliterated—the "Montana," "Colorado," "Savannah" and "New West" have been shoehorned into already overbuilt sites with ne'er a comment about any iconographic inconsistency. As history and geography went west, the myth settled east, but it took time for the myth itself to be domesticated into the urban environment.

The new urban frontier motif encodes not only the physical transformation of the built environment and the reinscription of urban space in terms of class and race, but also a larger semiotics. Frontier is a style as much as a place, and the 1980s saw the faddishness of Tex-Mex restaurants, the ubiquity of desert decor, and a rage for cowboy chic, all woven into the same urban landscapes of consumption. A *New York Times* Sunday Magazine clothing advertisement (August 6, 1989) gives the full effect:

> For urban cowboys a little frontier goes a long way. From bandannas to boots, flourishes are what counts. . . . The Western imprint on fashion is now much like a cattle brand—not too striking, but obvious enough to catch the eye. For city dudes, that means accents: a fringed jacket with black leggings; a shearling coat with a pin-stripe suit; a pair of lizard boots with almost anything. When in doubt about the mix stride up to the mirror. If you're inclined to say "Yup," you've gone too far.

New York's upmarket boutiques dispensing fashionable frontier kitsch are concentrated in SoHo, an area of artists' lofts and effete galleries, gentrified in the late 1960s and 1970s, and enjoying an unprecedented boom in the 1980s. SoHo borders the Lower East Side to the west and southwest. Here, "frontier" aspires on occasion to philosophy. Zona, on Greene Street, sells Navajo rugs, "Otomi Indian natural bark notepaper," Santa Fe jewelry, terra-cotta pottery, "Lombak baskets in rich harvest colors," bola ties. Zona oozes authenticity. All the "pieces" are numbered and a catalogue of the "collection" has been produced. On a small, plain, deliberately understated sign, with writing embossed on gold paper, the store offers its "personal" philosophy of craft-friendliness suffused with more than a whiff of New Age spiritualism:

> At a time when the ever expanding presence of electronic tools and high technology is so pervasive the need to balance our lives with products that celebrate the textual and sensorial become essential. We think of our customers as resources and not simply as consumers. We are guided by the belief that information is energy and change is the constant. Thank you for visiting our space.

Americana West, on Wooster Street, strives for a purer desert look. On the sidewalk outside the front door, a patrician Indian chief complete with tomahawk and feathered headgear stands guard. The window display features a bleached buffalo skull for $500 while inside the store are sofas and chairs made from longhorns and cattle skin. A gallery as much as a store, Americana West purveys diverse images of noble savages, desert scenes à la Georgia O'Keeffe, petroglyphs and pictographs, whips and spurs. Cacti and coyotes are everywhere (none real): a neon prickly pear is available for $350. In lettering on the front window, Americana West announces its own theme, a crossover cultural geography between city and desert: "The Evolving Look of the Southwest. Designers Welcome . . . Not for City Slickers Only."

The frontier is not always American nor indeed male. At La Rue des Rêves the theme is jungle eclectic. Leopard coats (faux of course), antelope leather skirts, and chamois blouses seem still alive, slinking off their hangers toward the cash registers. Fashion accessories dangle like lianas from the jungle canopy. A stuffed gorilla and several live parrots round out the ambience. La Rue des Rêves may have been "too, too"—it was a casualty of the late 1980s stock market crash—but the theme has survived in clothing chains as well as boutiques. At the Banana Republic customers have their safari purchases packed in brown paper bags sporting a rhinoceros. On the silver screen, meanwhile, movies such as *Out of Africa* and *Gorillas in the Mist* reinforce the vision of pioneering whites in darkest Africa, but with heroines for heroes. As middle-class white women come to play a significant role in gentrification their prominence on earlier frontiers is rediscovered and reinvented. Thus designer Ralph Lauren began the 1990s with a collection centered on "the Safari woman." He explains thus the romantic and nostalgic ur-environmentalism that drove him to it: "I believe that a lot of wonderful things are disappearing from the present, and we have to take care of them." A mahogany four-poster draped in embroidered mosquito netting, jodhpurs, faux ivory, and a "Zanzibar" bedroom set patterned with Zebra stripes surround Lauren's "Safari Woman," herself presumably an endangered species. Originally Ralph Lifschitz born in the Bronx, but now ensconced on a Colorado ranch half the size of that borough, "Lauren" has never been to Africa—"sometimes it's better if you haven't been there"—but feels well able to represent it in and for our urban fantasies. "I'm trying to evoke a world in which there was this graciousness we could touch. Don't look at yesterday. We can have it. Do you want to make the movie you saw a reality? Here it is" (Brown 1990).

Even as Africa is underdeveloped by international capital, engulfed by famine and wars, it is remarketed in Western consumer fantasies—but as the preserve of privileged and endangered whites. As one reviewer put it, the safari collection "smacks of bwana style, of Rhodesia rather than Zimbabwe" (Brown 1990). Lauren's Africa is a country retreat for and from the gentrified city. It provides the decorative utensils by which the city is reclaimed from wilderness and remapped for white upper-class settlers with global fantasies of again owning the world—recolonizing it from the neighborhood out.

Nature too is rescripted on the urban frontier. The frontier myth—originally engendered as an historicization of nature—is now reapplied as a naturalization of urban history. Even as rapacious economic expansion destroys deserts and rain forests, the new urban frontier is nature-friendly: "All woods used in [Lauren's Safari] collection are grown in the Philippines and are not endangered" (Brown 1990). The Nature Company, a chain store with a branch in South Street Seaport at the south end of the Lower East Side, is the apotheosis of this naturalized urban history, selling maps and globes, whaling anthologies and telescopes, books on dangerous reptiles, and stories of exploration and conquest. The store's unabashed nature idolatry and studied avoidance of anything urban are the perfect disappearing mirror in which contested urban histories are refracted (N. Smith 1996b). In affirming the connection with nature, the new urban frontier erases the social histories, struggles and geographies that made it.

The nineteenth century and its associated ideology were "generated by the social conflicts that attended the 'modernization' of the Western nations," according to Slotkin. They are "founded on the desire to avoid recognition of the perilous consequences of capitalist development in the New World, and they represent a displacement or deflection of social conflict into the world of myth" (Slotkin 1985: 33, 47). The frontier was conveyed in the city as a safety valve for the urban class warfare brewing in such events as the 1863 New York draft riot, the 1877 railway strike, and indeed the Tompkins Square riot of 1874. "Spectacular violence" on the frontier, Slotkin concludes, had a redemptive effect on the city; it was "the alternative to some form of civil class war which, if allowed to break out within the metropolis, would bring about a secular *Götterdämmerung*" (Slotkin 1985: 375). Projected in press accounts as extreme but comparable versions of events in the city, a magnifying mirror to the most ungodly depravity of the urban masses, reportage of the frontier posited eastern cities as a paradigm of social unity and harmony in the face of external threat. Urban social conflict was not so much denied as externalized, and whosoever disrupted this reigning urban harmony committed unnatural acts inviting comparison with the external enemy.

Today the frontier ideology continues to displace social conflict into the realm of myth, and at the same time to reaffirm a set of class-specific and race-specific social norms. As one respected academic has proposed, unwittingly replicating Turner's vision (to not a murmur of dissent), gentrifying neighborhoods should be seen as combining a "civil class" who recognize that "the neighborhood good is enhanced by submitting to social norms," and an "uncivil class" whose behavior and attitudes reflect "no acceptance of norms beyond those imperfectly specified by civil and criminal law." Neighborhoods might then be classified "by the extent to which civil or uncivil behavior dominates" (Clay 1979a: 37–38).

The frontier imagery is neither merely decorative nor innocent, therefore, but carries considerable ideological weight. Insofar as gentrification infects working-class communities, displaces poor households, and converts whole neighborhoods into bourgeois enclaves, the frontier ideology rationalizes social differentiation and exclusion as natural, inevitable. The poor and working class are all too easily defined as "uncivil;" on the wrong side of a heroic dividing line, as savages and communists. The substance and consequence of the frontier imagery is to tame the wild city, to socialize a wholly new and therefore challenging set of processes into safe ideological focus. As such, the frontier ideology justifies monstrous incivility in the heart of the city. [. . .]

REFERENCES

Barthes, R. (1972) *Mythologies*, New York: Hill and Wang.

Brown, P. L. (1990) "Lauren's wink at the wild side," *New York Times* February 8.

Clay, P. (1979) *Neighborhood Renewal*, Lexington, Mass.: D. C. Heath.

Slotkin, R. (1985) *Fatal Environment: The Myth of the Frontier in the Age of Industrialization 1800–1890*, New York: Atheneum.

Smith, N. (1996) "The production of nature," in G. Robertson and M. Mash (eds.) *Future Natural*. London: Routledge.

CHAPTER 10

From Arts Production to Housing Market

Sharon Zukin

A HOUSING SUBSIDY FOR ARTISTS

Until the late 1960s there was no history of funding housing for artists. Just as artists no longer worked exclusively for a particular patron but sold their work on the art market, so they were also expected to buy or rent the housing and studio that they could afford. Although successful artists like Rodin and Picasso, or de Kooning and Calder, could afford to set up comfortable establishments, most artists suffered from a perennial search for cheap but well-lighted space. In New York, the last philanthropist who set up living and work space for artists was nineteenth-century real estate developer James J. Johnson. The Tenth Street Studio, which Johnson built in 1857, had large, loftlike spaces that accommodated studios for portrait sittings (as well as prop rooms for the costumes and accessories that portrait sitters of the day required) and adjacent living areas. After serving as headquarters for the most famous Greenwich Village artists of the 1860s to the 1880s, the Tenth Street Studio was eventually sold on a co-op basis to its artist-tenants. Significantly, the period when it became a co-op—the 1920s—was when gentrification priced most working-class and artist residents out of this part of the Village.[1]

Years later, in the wake of August Heckscher's report on the arts, the Federal Housing Administration (FHA) allocated funds to subsidize artists' rent payments wherever they happened to be living. However, this subsidy turned out to be impractical, or impracticable, for several reasons. On the one hand, artists did not race to apply for funding. They were probably unwilling to submit to the rigid administrative regulations that the FHA imposed, for example, on room sizes and room divisions. On the other hand, the local governments that administered FHA funds were probably reluctant, in the face of greater complaints from ghetto communities, to use the money for a small, unproven arts constituency. Otherwise, the artists who most needed rent subsidies may have had incomes that actually fell below the "moderate" minimum income levels mandated by FHA guidelines for aid recipients. So until the middle of the 1960s, neither individual philanthropy nor national state support had made a significant advance toward subsidized housing for artists.

The breakthrough came in the form of local initiative and institutionalized philanthropy. Again New York was the incubator. Around 1967, George Maciunas had the notion of getting a rich patron of the arts to subsidize his dream of Fluxhouse Number 2. He approached the J. M. Kaplan Fund, a private foundation established and run by members of the Kaplan family, wealthy collectors and amateurs of the arts, and was granted a $20,000 loan to buy three loft buildings in SoHo. Although Maciunas succeeded in setting up only one of three projected co-ops, the Fund eventually "forgave" the loan. But around the same time that they encountered the visionary Fluxist, the Kaplans had also begun to wrestle with the practical problems of artists' housing. An Argentine artist with whom the family had a longstanding patronage relationship needed larger quarters, partly because of his family and partly because of his sculpture, and the Kaplans wanted to help him without overstepping the patron-artist tie. They thought that a low-cost loft co-op might solve all the problems. So the Kaplan Fund bought a loft building on Greenwich Street, in the West Village, and immediately resold it at cost to a group of twelve artists that included the Argentine sculptor.

Evidently encouraged by their success, the Kaplan Fund bought a much larger building in 1969 with the intention of repeating the experience. Westbeth, as the vacant office building beside the West Side Highway at Bethune Street was soon called, was renovated and converted into nearly four hundred large living and work spaces for over a thousand tenants. But the Kaplans' philanthropic intention of making an artists' housing co-op in Westbeth seems to have coincided with certain interests of both national and local political elites. First, the Fund had been encouraged to buy Westbeth by Roger Stevens, who succeeded August Heckscher as President Johnson's special adviser on the arts and then served as chairman of the National Council for the Arts, from 1965 to 1969, and chairman of the National Endowment for the Arts, from 1969 to 1972. Stevens had already made a fortune in the private sector, from the 1930s to the 1960s, as a real estate developer. In addition, the Kaplan Fund's work on Westbeth enjoyed an unusual degree of support from the city, state, and federal governments. Not only were the Kaplans personally well connected in all three capitals, but this was also the period when the New York arts establishment was ably represented by Javits in Washington, D.C., Rockefeller in Albany, and Lindsay at City Hall. Finally, the Kaplans may have been well placed to realize this sort of patronage because they held extensive properties in Manhattan, and the strategic placement of artists' housing could not have damaged their own real estate interests.[2]

Although the impetus for subsidizing artists' housing in loft neighborhoods originated in the upper-class patron-artist connection, the idea became popular because of the active support of a middle-class arts constituency. This constituency played the midwife's role in the curious sequence of events that led up to the birth of the Greenwich Street co-op. Their background is significant to the story. At the end of the fifties and the beginning of the sixties, a number of middle-class families had bought homes among the Federal-style brick and mid-nineteenth-century brownstone townhouses in the West Village around Greenwich Street. The residential properties that these new homeowners so proudly renovated abutted the area's warehouses, printing plants, and garages—the commercial and light industrial facilities which, together with the houses, created the ideal type of mixed-use neighborhood that Jane Jacobs praises in her book *The Death and Life of Great American Cities*. In fact, this was the neighborhood where Jacobs lived at the time. The middle-class families who were her neighbors formed the base of the grass-roots movement for neighborhood preservation that she inspired. It is important to know that the area's residents owed their mobilization to a plan put forward by Mayor Wagner. Sharing the objectives of local business and political elites in many declining cities of the Northeast and

Midwest, Wagner wanted to have the West Village declared a "blighted area" in order to qualify for federal urban redevelopment subsidies. Once the area established an entitlement to Title I funds, the city could use the money to build low-income housing there. Isolated between the unused piers on the Hudson River and the warehouses of Greenwich and Hudson streets, the "projects" would be practically invisible. Nor would they encroach upon potentially revalorized Lower Manhattan land. Needless to say, this plan sparked opposition among the West Village's middle-class homeowners. They saw that if the projects were built next-door to their homes, their modest investments would be eroded by declining property values and their mixed-use neighborhood would be destroyed by blockbusting real estate agents. Organized by Jane Jacobs, the West Village homeowners fought City Hall. When Wagner ran for reelection as a liberal in 1961, he was forced to concede the issue.

This initiation into local politics left two imprints on the West Village. First, the old Jane Jacobs constituency remained mobilized and formed a new, more permanent base in the area's Reform Democratic Club and the community board. Second, the homeowners remained sensitive to issues of neighborhood preservation. When buildings in their purview were put up for sale or vacated, they were vigilant. In 1967 the local city council member started a chain reaction when she heard that a loft building in the neighborhood was going to be auctioned off by the city government for payment of back taxes. The chain ran through the West Village liberal constituency's organizational links and personal connections to the J. M. Kaplan Fund. At the auction, a Fund representative bought the loft building on Greenwich Street with the idea of turning it over to an artists' co-op. Before the Fund announced its intention, however, a Committee for Artists' Housing

from the community board issued a call for artists' housing in the West Village. With great timeliness, the Kaplans were able to respond to this call.

Aside from the developers of Lincoln Center, the West Village homeowners showed a new awareness, at least implicitly, that an arts presence would affect real estate development in the city. The middle-class constituency was most concerned about two issues: the use of space and property values. Fearing disruption by, on the one hand, high-rise new construction and, on the other hand, subdivision of existing units, the homeowners sought a strategy that would counter the spatial consequences of current housing market trends. But as the homeowners' fight against Mayor Wagner had suggested, they also wanted to maintain the emerging middle-class character of the neighborhood without either increasing or decreasing property values. So in this sense, too, the West Villagers wanted strategy to fight market forces. The artists' presence in the neighborhood as both producers and residents seemed to hedge all bets. Because artists wanted to live and work in lofts *the way they were,* they offered the possibility of having a *stabilizing* rather than an *accelerating* effect on a neighborhood in transition. Surely this seemed reasonable at the time.

Initially, the same middle-class dream also dominated the efforts of SoHo's artist-residents to secure the right to their lofts. But SoHo was different from the West Village. In contrast to the narrow strip of land along the Hudson, SoHo took up a sizable chunk of the middle of the island. As a future gateway to a redeveloped Lower Manhattan, the area attracted the interest of big real estate investors and planners. There were also the zoning regulations that prohibited residential use in a manufacturing zone. So in order to assure a housing subsidy in SoHo, artists had to rely on the direct intervention of powerful forces:

the upper-class arts constituency and their patrician politicians. "People with money saved SoHo," an early activist in the SoHo Artists' Tenants' Association says. Another SoHo artist recalls, "We all had 'uptown friends.'" He explains:

> We had gallery owners. Many of us worked in schools and universities. There were wealthy collectors we had sold to. There were some very influential artists in the area—Robert Rauschenberg, Robert Indiana, Julie Judd [wife of Minimalist artist Donald Judd]—who could call on curators and museum board members. Others of us had only an occasional wealthy person who had bought something from us. We all put together the names of who we could talk to and found that between us we had a rather impressive list. It ranged from people who had nothing to do with art, like the chairmen of the boards of banks, to curators and international art dealers. We started to call these people up to let them know, "Hey, there's a unique phenomenon going on right here that nobody knows about, and if we don't do something, it'll be destroyed."[3]

Despite initial misgivings about a common cause, the SoHo artists also allied themselves with the historical preservation constituency in the form of the Friends of Cast Iron Architecture (FCI). An offshoot of the patrician Municipal Arts Society, this organization was formed in 1970, in the midst of the struggle for "saving" SoHo. The group was made up of people with money and power. Several times during the 1960s, these people had suggested that a landmark "Cast Iron District" be declared in SoHo to protect the distinctive loft buildings on Greene Street from being torn down. But the big real estate developers who wanted to redevelop the area had held the historic preservationists to small-scale tactics. Once the artists joined them, the preservationists launched a real offensive. Artists did much of the archival research that buttressed the argument for a landmark district. "We

compounded the developers' difficulties by using historic preservation," an artist-activist says, and when the smoke had cleared over the ruins of the developers' plans, an official landmark district remained.

SoHo artists also learned the value of the print media, beginning with the highly favorable 1970 article in *Life* magazine, "Living Big in a Loft." "Suddenly, following the *Life* story, we were a national phenomenon," an artist says. "We were too big for them to ignore. We became known personally. Then *I* could call up Donald Elliott [the city planning commissioner] and sometimes get through to him. We had a deputy mayor assigned to us." "We learned to use the foreign media," another artist recalls. "Stories about us appeared in newspapers in France or Germany. Our embassies sent them back to the State Department, and the State Department sent them to Mayor Lindsay." Facing a city administration that had visions of presiding over a world capital, the artists realized that these news stories had an effect on City Hall. "We made a policy decision to cooperate with publicity," an activist says. "Many of the group were against it and we agonized over it. We saw what publicity and legalization [of loft living] might lead to. But if we hadn't done it, SoHo wouldn't exist at all today."

Despite their anxiety, the SoHo artists enjoyed certain political advantages in the struggle. "One thing that has never been adequately acknowledged," an early activist says, "is the importance of John Lindsay. We had in the mayor a cultured, sensitive, educated man who understood the value of art in the life of this city. SoHo would not have been established under Wagner and certainly never under Bearne. The Lindsay administration was absolutely vital to our success. Throughout the struggle, we had the support of Lindsay and his personal aides. It was aides to the mayor who told us how to argue our case before the Planning Commission."[4]

Although the artists' original patrician support had been based on elements of cultural patronage, their bid for open political support depended on an economic argument. The advice that Mayor Lindsay's aides gave them was "to show our worth in terms of money. Some of the artists balked," an activist says, "but the rest of us came up with statistics on art employment, tourism, supplies—numbers the commission could understand." In this discussion, Art evidently yielded to the arts economy. "When we worked for the zoning changes we never talked aesthetics," another activist says. "We let *them* talk aesthetics. We took the approach that we were workers who need to work where we live for both economic reasons and the nature of our work. We hit them with vacancy rates and employment figures. We offered to put property back on the tax rolls." A certain amount of organizational confusion also aided their efforts. "We had friends on people's staffs," an early SoHo loft dweller sums up, "especially on the City Planning Commission. . . . We used interagency negotiation and countervailing areas of responsibility to muddle bureaucratic efforts to harass us."

Moreover, by the 1970s, art suggested a new platform to politicians who were tired of dealing with urban poverty. "I'll tell you a nasty little story," an authoritative source on the SoHo artists offers.

> At the final hearing where the Board of Estimate voted to approve SoHo as an artists' district, there were lots of other groups giving testimony on other matters. Poor people from the South Bronx and Bed-Stuy complaining about rats, rent control, and things like that. The board just shelved those matters and moved right along. They didn't know how to proceed. Then they came to us. All the press secretaries were there, and the journalists. The klieg lights went on, and the cameras started to roll. And all these guys started making speeches about the importance of art to New York City. Those same guys who had fought us every inch of the way! It was sickening.*

A PRODUCTION SUBSIDY FOR THE ARTS INFRASTRUCTURE

As the state on both local and national levels intervened more and more in the arts economy, the nature of the loft subsidy changed. It evolved from an indirect subsidy for artists' housing to a direct subsidy for arts production. This was consistent with the reasoning behind the city government's switch to support zoning for artists in SoHo. But it was also consistent with a general support for real estate development. Subsidies for arts production gave artists no claim to a particular place in the city. So they did not interfere with market forces. After the arts presence helped to revalorize a section of the city like SoHo, then the artists could take their subsidies and move to another declining area. Regarded in the short run as a bonanza for creative and performing artists, production subsidies for the arts infrastructure proved, in the long run, to be a cornucopia for housing developers. The use of lofts as performance spaces offers a good example, particularly in the development of the movement known as Loft Jazz.

Beginning in the early seventies, some musicians who played and composed "experimental," or "non-mainstream," jazz gathered to perform in lofts instead of bars or concert halls. To some degree, their work, like that of the artists who formed co-op galleries, was unmarketable. But to some degree, also, these musicians deliberately cut themselves off from the traditional access points to the jazz market. They didn't like the commercialism of hustling for record contracts and concert dates, and as Black Muslims, many of them didn't approve of the boozy atmosphere of jazz clubs. Loft Jazz was more serious, more provocative, and more self-consciously artistic than the jazz scene had been. In 1972, when the annual Newport Jazz Festival moved to New York, several Loft Jazz musicians organized their own "alternative festival," The New York Musicians' Festival. Significantly, their performances were funded by the National Endowment for the Arts and Mayor Lindsay's Parks Department. The following year, the Loft Jazz movement was incorporated into the regular Newport Festival program. Half the performances took place in three jazz lofts: Ornette Coleman's Axtists" House in SoHo, Sam Rivers's nearby Studio Rivbea, and a loft in TriBeCa. Because this part of the festival was billed as a "community" effort, the other concerts were scheduled in community centers in various neighborhoods. But the press conference that announced the festival within the Festival was held at Artists' House. There, the *New York Times* noted, the surroundings were much more comfortable than a smoky little jazz club. Artists' House was a large loft with pillowcovered parquet floors, where the audience could lean back, sipping wine, while they listened to the music.[5]

By the end of the seventies, Loft Jazz had died as a musical movement, but it lived on in the performing of jazz in lofts. Although the entrepreneurialism involved in establishing these performance spaces was no more formal than it had been, the organization of the performances became more institutionalized, thanks largely to new state subsidies on all levels. Generally the new jazz clubs were set up by a new generation of jazz musicians. Young and impoverished, educated, ambitious, these would-be performers lacked a place to operate. Like the artists who had already learned to combine living and work space, the musicians adapted lofts to their needs. Not only did they use part of their loft as a rehearsal studio, but they often rented it out for the same purpose to other impecunious young musicians. Eventually the need for practice space led to a need for performance space, and either for their own sake or in response

to the entreaties of the other musicians, the loft tenants turned their premises into jazz clubs and little theaters. They kept rents and entrance prices low—and usually operated on the fringes of the local laws governing entertainment spots and cabarets—and in time they captured a following. They were known, they were written up in the entertainment guides, and they even got funding from the government. On the one hand, the more serious and avant-garde performance spaces were able to qualify for NEA grants. The more the performers showed college credentials as an indication of their professional training, or in the case of jazz, a degree from the Berklee College of Music or the New England Conservatory, the more qualified they appeared for state support. On the other hand, a variety of local mechanisms was developed to help with operating expenses. In New York City, for example, this sort of aid flows through the Theater Development Fund (TDF). TDF organizes the sale of discount tickets for theaters and other performance spaces that are supposed to be in marginal economic circumstances. Through a system of "TDF vouchers," a theater or a club is reimbursed for every discount admission ticket that it sells. In practice, a performance place makes more money from a TDF voucher than from an ordinary discount ticket, say, for students. TDF is funded by NEA, the New York State Council on the Arts, and corporate and individual donors. As the young owner of a club whose jazz performances are subsidized by both sorts of government grants acknowledges, "This cat named Cy from Brooklyn turned me on. Can you believe it?! Exxon, Ford, and the National Endowment for the Arts are subsidizing my club!"

Unfortunately for such entrepreneurs, state subsidies and public acceptance failed to preserve their lofts as part of the urban arts infrastructure. Like artists in SoHo and the West Village, by their presence they helped to make their loft neighborhoods more visible and more acceptable to the general public. With live-in musical performers as "anchor," their landlords were able to convert their buildings informally to residential use. Performance companies and performance spaces were evicted in favor of residential tenants who could pay a higher rent and, eventually, for complete and legal residential conversions. Ironically, some of the building owners profited from the arts infrastructure in more than one way. In quite a few cases, the people who decided on a residential conversion had inherited or bought their building from the old generation of loft building owners, and these new landlords worked in the arts economy themselves. Many of them even lived in lofts.

But these building owners are only the cutting edge of a larger process of change. In many loft neighborhoods a new type of cottage industry combines with loft living and the arts infrastructure to create a mixed use that remains entirely within the service sector. Generally these loft tenants are graphics or clothing designers—who may farm out the actual production to workers in other areas of the city—and service firms from the low end of the tertiary-sector spectrum, like advertising agencies and architects. Particularly when rents rise in the traditional office market, these sorts of tenants seek cheaper space in marginal areas. Though a corporate headquarters could hardly move to a loft, in their case a loft address is chic. Meanwhile, the loft areas that have been disrupted by a variety of productive uses settle down to a more homogeneous variety of middle-class mixed use.

In this process of social and neighborhood change, a single loft building may represent, in spatial terms, a cross-section. For example, a building in Greenwich Village that was converted "illegally" to co-op lofts shows a mixture of uses on every floor: the ground floor is half residential and half a rehearsal space for a theater company; the second floor is half residential and half a dental equipment business; the third floor is split between two mixed-use lofts, one in which a nurse and an architect live and which the architect uses for his office, and one occupied by a stockbroker and a woman who runs a plant business in the loft; the fourth floor is entirely residential; on the fifth floor, half is a doctor's home, and the other half is a living and working loft for a graphic artist and a fine artist; the sixth floor is half residential, where the original buyer, an architect, sold out to a businessman, and half is for both living and running a catering business owned by a schoolteacher and a man who directs the food department of a hospital (this couple also has a loft in another building which they rent out for parties); on the seventh floor, half was sold by an architect to a doctor for a residence, and half is used by two men who live there and run a mail-order business in the loft; the eighth floor is divided into a living loft for a young widow with children and a living loft for a city planner with work space for her husband, who is a potter; the ninth floor has two living lofts. Such is the physical infrastructure that supports the conversion of an old manufacturing center to a new service-sector capital.

For a while, various sorts of "nonproductive" use can coexist in this infrastructure. The creative disharmony is interesting and sometimes even elegant. But sooner or later, a contradiction develops between the production of art and other, higher-rent uses. At that point, real estate development reasserts its dominance over the arts economy. The development strategy that has been repressed, delayed, or masked by the burgeoning arts infrastructure shows that in the final count, any use of space is expendable. Naturally, the reemergence or the intensification of a development strategy in the loft market arouses resentment and opposition among loft dwellers. The organizations that have been formed over the years to defend the interests of this constituency have had to formulate an increasingly anti-development opposition. But as the market has changed, so has the loft-dwelling constituency. Their stand on real estate development contradicts, to some degree, their own living in lofts. [. . .]

NOTES

*   The Board of Estimate, made up of the highest citywide elected officials, acts as a court of final appeal on land use issues. The South Bronx and Bedford Stuyvesant, in Brooklyn, are racial and ethnic ghettos.

1.   The Tenth Street Studio withstood steadily rising property values until the 1950s. Then it was sold to real estate developers, who demolished it and put up a new apartment house. For its origins, see Mary S. Haverstock, "The Tenth Street Studio," *Art in America*, September 1966, p. 48.

2.   Personal interviews on Fluxus and Greenwich Street, April–June 1980; on Westbeth see Willkie Farr and Gallagher, "Housing for Artists: The New York Experience" (Study prepared for Volunteer Lawyers for the Arts, New York, 1976), pp. 34–35. Eventually Westbeth was developed as artists' rental housing rather than a co-op, and the ensuing problems created or exacerbated certain tensions involving leases and entitlement to space in the building.

3.   Unless otherwise noted, the personal material in this chapter comes from interviews conducted in New York in July and August 1980.

4.   The City Hall–patrician connection contrasts with more distant relations between political officials and social clites in other cities, such as Philadelphia, where artists' access to loft buildings had a much rougher road (see Jim Stratton, *Pioneering in the Urban Wilderness* [New York: Urizen, 1977], p. 87).

5.   *New York Times*, Mar. 19, 1973; also see *Wildflowers: Loft Jazz in New York* (Douglas Records, 1977).

CHAPTER 11

Forging the Link between Culture and Real Estate: Urban Policy and Real Estate Development

Christopher Mele

In the midst of artists' and musicians' self-promotion and hype, the social and built environment of the East Village was further objectified in representations as a backdrop of a flourishing downtown cultural renaissance. In Steven Spielberg's 1987 film *Batteries Not Included*, which was filmed in Loisaida, tiny robotic beings from outer space help a group of distraught residents fight against the demolition of their tenement by developers. The film's happy ending suggests a humane form of urban restructuring in which minorities and Whites, rich and poor, and old-timers and newcomers coexist harmoniously in a pluralist urban landscape. Other media coverage presented experimental cultural forms as an awakening and salvation from the years of neighborhood decline and decay. The blocks between Avenues A and D that had constituted Loisaida became known as "Alphabet City" in the more playful mainstream media representations. The real estate sector brought into the image of decay an image of danger, seediness, and the mystique of "living on the edge," at the same time its investment ventures sought to displace it.[1] In retail, restaurants, and other commercial space, the area's rawness was cleverly packaged as suspense, intrigue, and adventure for those who imagined their visit to the area as an outing to the underworld. Bernard's, a restaurant located on the corner of Avenue C and East Ninth Street, specialized in French organic cuisine and catered to the uptown advertising executive crowd, whose chauffeur-driven limousines were parked out front. The corner of Avenue C and East Ninth Street was also an outdoor drug bazaar where crack cocaine was primarily sold. What went on inside Bernard's and what happened outside were related as patrons consumed a "glamour of poverty" along with their food.

Throughout the mid-1980s, the downtown scene was transformed by media, spectators, and participants from the marginal and rebellious to an urban genre well suited for urban revitalization. Both real estate developers and the city government employed representations of the downtown scene to legitimize neighborhood restructuring practices and policies, to exculpate the social costs of community displacement, and to challenge the validity of resistance efforts mounted by threatened residents. First, the rhetoric of cultural renewal facilitated various development policies that encouraged real estate investment and threatened to wrest control of public space away from low-income residents. Second, symbolic representations positively redefined the image of the East

Village to attract once-skeptical middle-sized real estate developers, brokers, and large lending institutions. Finally, East Village developers employed the allure of downtown to attract mostly White, middle- and upper-income, well-educated people as tenants.

At the height of the city's fiscal crisis, politicians and policy analysts reconceptualized post-World War II urban policies in general and subsidized low-income housing in particular as too economically inefficient and overly generous to the poor. Under the ideological leadership of the Reagan administration, the (few remaining) Great Society urban programs and policies were subject to extensive criticism, disavowal, and ultimately blame for the lack of private growth in the central city. The new urban initiatives and policies developed in the 1980s were shaped and defined by a post-fiscal crisis discourse that emphasized increasing tax revenues through development incentives and the rollback of governmental provision of low-income housing. Political leaders and policymakers drew lessons from the fiscal crisis, which was reconfigured as a crisis of disincentives for urban investment rather than the city's inability to address or contain mounting social problems. City agencies with any degree of authority over private or public land use and development were brought in line with an aggressive entrepreneurial and pro-growth ideology. During the budgetary crisis, for example, the city's planning department was restructured to be less acquiescent to costly neighborhood and community initiatives (roughly, the 1960s democratic planning model) and more amenable to private redevelopment needs (e.g., granting developers exceptions to zoning ordinances).[2] With respect to low-income neighborhoods in particular, the city's position was to encourage and subsidize efforts by the middle-sized and large developers and lending institutions to enter and transform working-class housing

markets for middle- and upper-class consumers.[3]

In the 1980s, the city administration sought to undo most of the programs that had transferred some control over neighborhood space to low- and moderate-income residents. The Koch administration utilized its authority over a large percentage of housing stock to leverage entrepreneurial middle- to upper-class redevelopment of housing in the East Village. The agency ostensibly created to protect low-income neighborhoods from the ravages of disinvestment, the Department of Housing Preservation and Development (HPD), became the institutional strong arm for private revitalization. Many of the city's tenant self-management and ownership programs were severely curtailed, underfinanced, or totally eliminated to promote private redevelopment rather than community empowerment.[4] Throughout the 1980s, HPD demolished city-owned buildings (some occupied by squatters), leaving empty parcels that were more attractive to developers seeking to construct new housing. In addition to undermining the gains of community activists over land use, the city administration devised ways to transfer its control of in rem units to private developers. In 1982, HPD announced its plan to auction part of its stock of TIL (Tenant-Interim Lease) buildings to the highest bidders. Protest by community groups and housing organizations thwarted the auction plan, forcing the city to reinstate a moratorium on sales. In a similar vein, the city's position on the urban garden movement shifted drastically. In the 1970s the city was supportive of gardens, often leasing unkempt lots to residents to grow vegetables and flowers. With the rebound of the housing market, however, the city placed a moratorium on leasing lots to gardeners.[5]

While city officials devised ways to retract the gains of low- and moderate-income residents and their representative housing organizations, they explored new ways to take full advantage of the media attention on the East Village's middle-class cultural settlement. In 1981–82, the Koch administration proposed the Artists Homeownership Program (AHOP) to convert in rem properties into artists' housing. The program called for conversion of abandoned buildings into cooperative housing for artists of moderate incomes ($40,000–$50,000 per year) and was billed as a means to prevent displacement of East Village artists.[6] The city's Department of Housing Preservation and Development chose a site on East Eighth Street between Avenues B and C for the program's first phase. Ten contiguous tenements were to be gutted and rebuilt into small lofts for living and working. The city's Board of Estimate defeated AHOP in 1983, however, after community groups protested the availability of subsidies for middle-income rather than low-income housing development. The Lower East Side Joint Planning Council mobilized against the plan on the basis that its obvious intention was to heighten the neighborhood's allure to investors and private developers.[7] The councilwoman representing Loisaida and the surrounding district referred to the plan as "a front for gentrification."[8] AHOP was a blatant attempt to re-create SoHo-styled development—that is, to harness the downtown culture scene to trigger a domino effect of upscale redevelopment.

Municipal agencies sought to promote their own interests and those of developers through manipulation of certain symbols representative of the East Village art scene and not others. That is, the city's gesture to promote the local arts was not an unequivocal acceptance of downtown subculture but rather of its milder representations conducive to the development agenda. Indeed, the Koch administration's pro-development agenda contained draconian policies to rid the neighborhood of its "unsavory elements," to sanitize its public spaces, and

to rein in the area's free-wheeling, chaotic social environment. City policies, in short, threatened to fundamentally undermine the subcultural basis of the downtown scene that was completely enmeshed in the local drug culture and reputedly derived its creative energy from an environment of despair. In the early 1980s, the police mounted an antidrug effort called Operation Pressure Point, sending over 230 officers and 40 detectives along with numerous vehicles and helicopters to begin what locals described as a military invasion of Loisaida. To drive out the entrenched two-decade-old drug economy, the police occupied streets, corners, empty lots, and parks: within a month 14,285 (!) people were arrested on drug-related charges. Operation Pressure Point was a public relations victory for the Koch administration as sensational scenes of drug busts and police occupation were widely circulated by the media and played well with the image of a neighborhood renaissance. Operation Pressure Point had a less significant effect on the elimination of the local drug economy, pushing transactions farther underground and into apartments and tenement hallways. Under the guise of enforcement, the police also periodically cracked down on ad hoc outdoor flea markets along St. Mark's Place, Second Avenue, and Avenue A, which were a source of income for some residents and many homeless persons. Anti-loitering campaigns along neighborhood streets and corners, ostensibly to curb the drug and prostitution trade, restricted a long Lower East Side tradition of "hanging out," especially among youth. In the mid-1980s, the area's many lots were fenced in, preventing their use as gardens or makeshift junkyards, as well as for nefarious drug transactions. While poor and minority residents felt the brunt of the city's policing and surveillance, the subcultural communities were not left untouched. The downtown scene was, after all, thoroughly steeped in the drug consumption culture. City policies sought to sanitize the area's seamy reputation and to rein in the very same free-wheeling, chaotic social environment that initially gave impetus to the downtown creative scene. Police raided and closed down several of the neighborhood's illegal after-hours clubs, dampening the area's hedonistic atmosphere. The surveillance and regulation of activities within Tompkins Square Park that escalated throughout the 1980s fueled intense neighborhood resistance beginning in 1988, as discussed in chapter 8.

Most of the *public* social and cultural practices of Loisaida emerged within the landscape of wide-scale abandonment and disenfranchisement in the 1970s. As discussed in the preceding chapter, such practices were an assertion of community identity and a collective challenge to the drugs and crimes that plagued the area. All of the city's social control practices in the 1980s were aimed ostensibly at eliminating illicit activities, but no effort was made by the city to stipulate for Latino social and cultural functions that had occurred in these same public spaces. By proclaiming to have improved the "quality of life" for *all* residents through social control of public space, the city also complicated the politics of resistance against neighborhood redevelopment. Operation Pressure Point cleared notorious drug blocks, such as East Second Street, and benefited residents, such as the elderly or couples with children, who felt trapped by the drug trade. Yet the neighborhood's increasing safety also made its housing more attractive to developers and increased the threat of displacement for these same populations. Support for "quality of life" concerns among the area's threatened low-income residents frequently led to their alliances with wealthier newcomers on such issues. City policies shrouded the obvious political economic cleavage and, consequently, diluted political opposition to the intended outcome, redevelopment. "Quality of life" improvements, such as those made to parks, streets, and public buildings, were often used to justify and exculpate the social cost of residential displacement that was the consequence of private redevelopment efforts.

By controlling the use of public space, the city helped construct an identity more inclined toward the middle-class residents that developers ultimately were seeking to attract. Less subtle were city programs that directly encouraged displacement of low-income communities and promoted private upscale residential and commercial initiatives. In the early 1980s, the city capitalized on the burst in economic activity and launched several initiatives to subsidize new business, commercial, and residential construction as well as rehabilitation. Corporations and large developers received extensive tax abatements for the building of office towers, such as AT&T's multimillion-dollar tax break for its new headquarters on Madison Avenue (later sold to the Sony corporation)[9] or the more recent redevelopment of Times Square. The city also subsidized large multiuse development projects, including South Street Seaport and Battery Park City, both in lower Manhattan.[10] Although neither as obvious nor as spectacular, other government intervention policies were geared toward small-scale, piecemeal redevelopment of the city's older neighborhoods. These incentives sought to draw real estate money into low-income and capital-deficient neighborhoods to radically transform their landscapes into middle- and upper-class enclaves. Development programs known as MCI, J-51, and 421-a were the foundation of an ambitious coalition between city agencies and private developers to renew the older housing stock unit by unit, building by building.

The city's pro-development agencies instituted incentives and subsidies for owners to substantially renovate units in their buildings.[11] Because of the design of the incentive programs, they were profitable to landlords only if they could charge substantially higher rents for the renovated units. A program offered by the Division of Housing and Community Renewal (DHCR) called the Major Capital Improvement (MCI) subsidized buildingwide improvements such as new windows, furnaces, and boilers.[12] The program allowed owners to pass on all direct and indirect costs of improvement to tenants by increasing regulated rents gradually and permanently (once the costs were paid, rent hikes remained as profit).[13] Two tax reduction programs, J-51 for old buildings and 421-a for new construction, also promoted neighborhood upgrading. J-51 offered two forms of benefits to owners in return for certain improvements: (1) tax abatements that lowered the amount of property tax for a period ranging from twelve to twenty years, and (2) exemptions from any tax increases that resulted from reassessments based on capital improvements made. The Section 421-a program was part of the State of New York's Real Property Tax Law. For properties constructed under 421-a subsidy, property taxes were phased in incrementally over a ten-year period, including a total exemption during construction and the first two years of operation. Eligible owners agreed to offer rent-stabilized units during the period in which the tax abatement was applied. The construction of Red Square, a massive apartment complex located on Houston Street between Avenue A and First Avenue, was subsidized by the Section 421-a program.

Since these programs fostered significant building renovations or new construction, they directly encouraged the displacement of minority and/ or low-income residents.[14] Significant "loopholes' in rent regulation laws also provided owners a means to quick (re)development. The "substantial

alterations" exemption clause to regulated rents was a popular tool in the East Village. Rent regulation procedures determine the new rent when a unit is vacated, typically a 12 percent increase of the former rent. Landlords circumvented this regulation, however, by substantially altering vacated apartments.[15] In addition to "gut" rehabilitation, developers frequently redesigned interior spaces (e.g., combining two units or converting tenement dumbbell airshafts into elevators[16]). If apartments were altered so that they no longer approximated the size or dimension present when the base (original) rents were first determined, then landlords were eligible to charge much higher "first" rents based on the current free-market value.[17] Significant modifications allowed landlords to escalate rents unit by unit, creating wide discrepancies in rents charged within the same building. When regulated one-bedroom apartments that rented from $90 to $125 per month became vacant, the incentive to renovate was strong. [. . .]

NOTES

1. *Village Voice*, December 14, 1982.
2. Huxtable 1987.
3. Huxtable 1987.
4. Sites 1994: 201.
5. Schmelzkopf 1995: 377.
6. *New York Times*, August 11, 1981.
7. *The Villager*, May 13, 1982: 5.
8. *New York Times*, May 4, 1982.
9. Sleeper 1987: 437.
10. Fainstein 1994: 49.
11. The incentives were typically tax abatements, but certain programs also allowed landlords to pass the costs of renovation on to tenants.
12. Division of Housing and Community Renewal 1987.
13. *Apartment Law Insider*, January 1990: 1.
14. Interviews by author with real estate developers, 1990.
15. The setting of the base rent for rent stabilization was determined not solely by the year the initial lease began but also by the original spatial dimensions of the apartment. The alteration clause in the regulation read that a new first rent

surpassed the original base rent when a unit was substantially altered to the extent that it was not in existence in its present form on the base date. Landlords could charge a new "first" rent only if the outer walls of a regulated apartment had been changed. After renovation, the apartment's outer dimensions were required to be either larger or smaller than before.

16. *New York Times,* January 3, 1988.
17. *Apartment Law Insider,* December 1989: 1.

REFERENCES

Apartment Law Insider, 1989. "Get Free Market Rent for Substantially Altered Apartment." December: 1.

Division of Housing and Community Renewal, 1987. "Major Capital Improvements (MCI)," New York: Division of Housing and Community Renewal.

Fainstein, Susan S. 1994. *The City Builders: Property, Politics, and Planning in London and New York.* Cambridge, Mass.: Blackwell.

Huxtable, Ada Louise, 1987. "Stumbling toward Tomorrow: The Decline and Fall of the New York Vision," *Dissent* 34 (fall): 453–62.

New York Times, 1981. "The Mayor's Lower East Side Story: Tenements into Co-ops for Artists." August 11: 9.

——. 1982. "16 Tenements to Become Artist Units in City Plan." May 4: 6.

——. 1988. "Tenements of 1880s Adapt to 1980s." January 3: Real Estate Section: 1.

Schmelzkopf, Karen. 1995. "Urban Community Gardens as Contested Space." *Geographical Review* 85, no. 3 (July): 364–81.

Sites, William. 1994. "Public Action: New York City Policy and the Gentrification of the Lower East Side." In *From Urban Village to East Village: The Battle for New York's Lower East Side,* Janet L. Abu-Lughod et al. Cambridge, Mass.: Blackwell: 189–212.

Sleeper, Jim. 1987. "Boom and Bust with Ed Koch," *Dissent* 34 (fall): 413–52.

The Villager. 1982. "Artists' Housing Program Meets Resistance from Local Residents Who Fear Displacement," May 13: 5.

Village Voice. 1982. "Space Invaders: Land Grab on the Lower East Side," December 14: 10.

CHAPTER 12

Estate Agents as Interpreters of Economic and Cultural Capital: The Gentrification Premium in the Sydney Housing Market[1]

Gary Bridge

INTRODUCTION

There is renewed vigour to the argument about the causes and character of gentrification (Lees, 1996; Ley, 1996; Lyons, 1996; 1998; Smith, 1996; Butler, 1997; Redfern, 1997a; 1997b; Bondi, 1999). This article pursues the social, economic and cultural consequences of this process and, in particular, how it is maintained. The economic delineations of the market for gentrified housing and the social expression of taste by gentrifiers can be investigated in their dynamic relationships using Bourdieu's concepts of material and cultural capital. The way in which housing taste results in price at the market reveals the boundary marking of gentrification as a form of distinction. Aesthetics are important in consideration of wider issues in gentrification—for instance the degree to which this taste is constituted from within gentrified districts or enforced from without (by 'the market', or class constitution prior to gentrification and outside the gentrified neighbourhood—Bridge, 1994; 1995).

Estate agents are the key intermediaries in the encounter between housing taste and price. This research investigates estate agents' understandings and representations of this relationship in Sydney's inner west. It marks out the aesthetic and social boundaries of gentrification and its economic premium for gentrifiers.

The research was conducted in three districts in Sydney's inner west—Balmain/ Rozelle, Glebe and Newtown. These areas consist of Victorian/Edwardian terraces and detached houses, many with the iron-lace balconies so characteristic of Sydney's gentrification. They are within 1–2 miles of the CBD, with good communications. These are districts which have gentrified over the last 20 years or so. Balmain is the most established and expensive. It is situated on a peninsula and so has no through traffic and plenty of water views. Glebe abuts Sydney University and was initially gentrified by academics and other public professionals. Newtown gentrified most recently and still has a large student population and 'bohemian' atmosphere.

Average capital growth rates of return on residential property in these districts of the inner west from 1987 to 1997 stood at 11.5%, higher than the rate for inner Sydney (11.39%) and considerably higher than in the Sydney metropolitan area as a whole (8.14%) (Residex Pty, 1997). Median house prices ranged from $300,000 in Newtown to $365,000 in Glebe to $500,000 in Balmain. The sociodemographic profile of the incomers is overwhelmingly professional (see Horvath et al., 1989). Typical

134 | GARY BRIDGE

entries for occupation in the book of regis-
tered prospective purchasers (the prospect,
or key book) of an inner-west estate agent
were: corporate communications specialist, director of a real estate company, fund
manager, consultant for Deloitte Touche,
assistant vice president of a bank, senior
civil engineer, executive director of a video
filming company.

ESTATE AGENTS—RELIABLE WITNESSES?

The role of estate agents in gentrification
has received surprisingly little attention in
the literature. Where they have been a part
of the analysis it has normally been in an
institutional context where their activities
have been seen at a general level to encourage gentrification and assist the displacement of working-class tenants and owners
(Williams, 1976; Hamnett and Randolph,
1986) or the niche-marketing of neighbourhoods (Lees, 1996). This is largely an institutional and functional approach. Yet, at
the level of micro-sociology, estate agents
occupy a critical role as both financial and
sociological intermediaries.

One reason for the limited nature of academic research using estate agents is that
they are considered to be unreliable wit-
nesses. Some of their methods involve eva-
siveness at best and duplicity at worst. In
addition, academic research has pointed to
examples of extreme, illegal and deplorable
practices in the real estate industry such
as blockbusting and racial steering and
segregation (Massey and Denton, 1993).
Nevertheless, many individual estate agents
consider that they aim to achieve probity in
their dealings. Indeed, it has been argued
that their reputation as 'slippery customers' is in part an outcome of their role as
intermediaries between vendor and potential purchaser, particularly in the UK and
Australia where they must represent the
interests of the vendor but build up a rela-

tionship with potential purchasers (Clarke
et al., 1994).

In this article I argue that their role as
financial and social intermediaries calls
upon the use of social skills and the ability to 'interpret' and translate between
different tastes and different classes. This
situation is particularly pronounced in a
gentrifying neighbourhood where middle-class purchasers and tastes encounter
working-class vendors and tastes. In this
situation estate agents must also translate
between taste and price. In what ways will
the display of different tastes in the structural and cosmetic appearance of a house
translate into its price on the market (and
in order to set a reserve price for auction in
the Australian case)? This translation work
is implicated in the relationship between
cultural and economic capital: how cultural
capital converts into economic capital;
how taste is reflected in price. Agents must
negotiate the boundaries of class demar-
cation and distinction. These boundaries
are at once fluid (like the edges of flames,
according to Bourdieu, 1984) and rigid. The
fluidity of these boundaries is shown in this
article through the subtleties of the gentrification aesthetic, and rigidities emerge
when that aesthetic is transgressed, in the
examples given, by over-gentrification and
ethnic rehabilitation.

Estate agents must interpret and work on
these social dynamics to succeed at their job
and so their practices and spoken accounts
of these issues is potentially of great value.
Certainly the accounts given to me by
agents in Sydney showed a good degree of
consistency and sociological awareness.

ESTATE AGENTS AS SOCIAL AND FINANCIAL INTERMEDIARIES

As financial intermediaries, estate agents
must first 'make a price'. In the Sydney auction system, this means coming to agreement on a reserve price for the vendor.

This is a highly contested process that can involve dummy bids by the vendor's agents and buyers hiring professional bidders. The property may be withdrawn by the vendor at any time. Agents get commission on sale only and so are keen to make any sale. Vendors must pay the advertising costs whether there is a sale or not. These additional complexities[2] add to the 'interpretative' nature of pricing a property. Unlike other commodities, the price cannot be fixed in advance of sale. Properties are unique (although they have features in common) and the market is essentially local, and so market forces are insufficiently strong to give a clear signal on price. Given these circumstances, valuation 'is based almost entirely on comparability, with gut feeling compensating for those areas where comparison is impossible, and frequently being used as the leading basis for valuation' (Clarke *et al.*, 1994: 76). Valuation is critical in obtaining instructions (the vendor selecting the agent to take on the property) in competition with other estate agencies and as a basis for negotiation of sale. The price is 'not a single figure but a series of meanings affecting the parties involved' (*ibid.*: 75). In the case of gentrification, this price must also reflect the aesthetic mark-up to capture the fact that another class of purchasers value the properties in a different way. As one Sydney agent explains:

> If you get back and look at it as a valuer and I say fine, the land is worth $100,000 and the cost to build the house is $200,000 and the rent is so much, returning that property at 8% or 7% or whatever it is, I can say that property is worth—land and house worth 300, building a little bit of increase for the rent—so it's probably worth 320. That property can sell for $500,000 because it's been restored correctly (WN).

Estate agents are also social intermediaries (House, 1977). When selling in gentrifying neighbourhoods, estate agents must typically move between working-class vendors and middle-class purchasers. The latter group have their own characteristics. As a Sydney agent relates:

> nowadays we have to write ads that appeal to people that are well educated and who are . . . in the upper economic bracket and so they have to be treated from the start (TM).

> if I'm writing an ad for a property, I'll go through the property and I'll look at the character and the Victorian history of the home and write the ad around that, rather than write about how many bedrooms, how many lounge rooms, what it's got. I'll look at the character first. And we're finding the buyers who are buying it are sophisticated, and they're looking for character. They buy it because of the history. They buy it because they're turned off by the modernization of a terrace, so you're looking at a cultural-different type of person who is looking for a home which has character (WG).

Agents show a sensibility to the varying relationship between taste and price. The following statement is almost Bourdieuian in its articulation of the relationship between cultural and economic capital:

> what happens is a lot of the people who live in Glebe, a lot of our clients, whether they be customers, purchasers or owners who have a background or roots in Glebe, they might, they've been to university so they have an academic, more sophisticated background, more cultural background than an average suburb has . . . [they] don't have a lot of money but they have the knowledge, they also have the ability to convert these old homes which were, 20 years ago, turned from beautiful old Victorian homes to just money earning, devoid of character, aluminium-windowed properties and they convert them back into the Victorian home. It's a difference between, it's a different social class, it's a gentrification of it. A lot of the people in Glebe aren't as wealthy as they'd like to be but culturally they're very wealthy so consequently you . . . don't get, well, you don't get, they're not very expensive

homes, a dear home here would be $700,000, $800,000, that's a dear house in Glebe. You get the odd home which is worth over a million but they're spectacular homes and they generally don't change around (WG).

Agents' appraisals of taste provide a contrast in terms of how working-class and middle-class sellers and buyers 'see' value. Looking at the decisions by the children of working-class residents concerning their parents' deceased estates in gentrified neighbourhoods, many of the estate agents interviewed argued that value was constructed differently. This was shown in contrasting reactions to the Victorian terraces.

> when you look at people who are passing away—they are usually in their 70s and 80s, 90s whatever. If the children are in their 50s, 60s—when you look at the age when they were growing up—they were living in small terraces, it was working class, they were considered inferior you know, whatever, and it was always the dream that you have your dream house with a block, your block of land and you go out to the suburbs—and that was the dream you know, that was the thing everyone wanted. So they've all gone out too, they aspired to do it and they have, so the last thing they want to do is to go back to their roots 'cos they still see it as working class (FV).

Another agent put it like this:

> WG: They sell it [deceased estates] . . . I think where they live are cheaper areas and they see the price of a home in Glebe that they can split the money up if it's a family . . . and put it somewhere where they see value, and they don't see value in Glebe.
>
> GB: So they're different . . .
>
> WG: Different group of people, yeah.
>
> GB: It's a different perception of what?
>
> WG: Of what value is.

These observations suggest that in order to understand the class dynamics of neighbourhood change involving working-class

displacement or voluntary departure, the aesthetics of working-class residents must feature more strongly in accounts of gentrification. The relationship between working-class and middle-class tastes and various economic imperatives is especially important.

These contrasts in the class-based judgement of taste must be negotiated by the agent when moving between working-class vendor and middle-class purchaser. This negotiation is put into a public and performative context by the auction system of house sales in Sydney.

CLASS DEMARCATION AS PUBLIC PERFORMANCE: HOUSING AUCTIONS

Auctions in Sydney come in two formats. They can be conducted on the site of the house itself and concern that single property. Alternatively, large numbers of properties can be sold at auctions held by the large estate agencies in various hotels around Sydney. At these auctions each property is introduced by the auctioneer using a slide show and verbal descriptions of the property.

I attended a number of such block auctions in November 1997. The purpose was to compare price with aesthetic 'condition'. In many cases these sales involved working-class vendors and middle-class purchasers present in the auction room. The auctioneers' public presentations thus had to draw the potential middle-class purchasers without offending the working-class vendors. Agents operating as auctioneers used a number of linguistic devices to bridge this taste divide. In some cases, middle-class vendors were selling to middle-class buyers and so the description emphasized the commonalities of taste; 'a home from a bygone era, leaded windows; extremely good taste; it's got apple pie right through it; a lady that appreciates good taste'.

In other cases, the taste line has to be crossed. A range of euphemisms are used to signal acknowledgement of the perception of the property by the middle-class buyers without alienating the working-class vendors (for whom the agents are working after all). These included 'well presented', 'beautifully presented', 'carefully presented home'. In somewhat stronger cases, descriptions include 'full of character but might need a bit of updating'. Describing 'a high pitched-roof cottage' containing reproduction furniture, thick pile carpets and 1970s fittings, the auctioneer recommended that the property 'could be renovated' and then added hastily, 'but don't get me wrong, it's a very well presented property folks' (hotel-based auction, November 1997).

This reveals the class aesthetics of the process. To be successful, estate agents must act as intermediaries between people of different classes who have different tastes in housing, house interiors and furnishings. They must have a sensitive understanding of the subtleties of taste differences. These taste differences are at the heart of what Bourdieu identifies as cultural strategies to maintain distinction.

HOUSING AESTHETICS AND 'DISTINCTION'

In his important article, 'Class definition and the aesthetics of gentrification: Victoriana in Melbourne', Michael Jager started to pull together the links between social class, aesthetics and housing form: 'The gentrifier is caught between a former gentry ethic of social representation being an end in itself, and a more traditional petty bourgeois ethic of economic valorisation' (Jager, 1986: 83).

This points to the tension between economic capital and social representation. It is a tension that is originally thought to arise from the desire for certain sections of the new middle class to achieve social distinction. They have insufficient material capital to do so through obvious displays of wealth (considerable wealth is its own social marker). The new middle class mark themselves out through a cultural strategy that involves displays of discernment and 'good taste'. This cultural strategy relies on the deployment of cultural capital.

Bourdieu's (1979; 1984) arguments are potentially useful in understanding elements of gentrification. Gentrification can be seen as a 'field' in Bourdieu's terms, a terrain where the particular mixtures of economic and cultural capital are deployed by different classes to maintain distinction from each other. These relationships exist both in social space and over time. This again applies to gentrification where the argument in this paper and elsewhere is that economic capital becomes more significant than cultural capital as gentrification proceeds. This, too, captures Bourdieu's idea that economic and cultural capital can, to a certain extent, be exchanged for one another. Bourdieu also offers gentrification researchers the conceptual framework to ask whether this residential strategy is part of a new cultural *habitus* of a putative 'new middle class'. Habitus is both 'the ability to produce classifiable practices and works, and the capacity to differentiate and appreciate those practices and products (taste) [by which] the represented social world, i.e. the spaces of lifestyles, is constructed' (Bourdieu, 1984: 170). Those with social power have a monopoly over ways of seeing and classifying objects according to their criteria of good taste. The ability to create new systems of discernment is class power. Gentrification can be seen as one such reclassification (away from the working-class city and the desirability of the middle-class suburbs) in which inner urban living became once again invested with ideas of status, style and cosmopolitanism. This innovation in taste could be viewed as an act of 'symbolic violence' over others, in this case, the working-class residents of the inner city. This is the aesthetic border that is the equivalent of gentrification-induced displacement in those inner urban neighbourhoods themselves (although this process might be more complex when working-class taste is taken into account, as I have suggested).

Gentrification can be seen as a collection of class strategies involving varying deployments of cultural and economic capital in time and space. Bourdieu (1984) argues that cultural capital is gained through education and family background. The cultural capital of the middle classes contrasts with that of the upper classes. Whereas aesthetic appreciation of the upper classes is innate and intuitive, based on social background, for the middle classes it is learned and self-conscious. This makes the middle-class aesthetic more open to self-conscious discussion and other influences. It makes it more public, more reflexive, less certain. In contrast, the aesthetic sensibilities of the upper class are private, undisputed, invisible.

To adapt Bourdieu's assumptions, what makes the new middle class 'new' is a particular combination of economic and cultural capital that enables them to distinguish themselves from other classes on a number of fronts. Their aesthetic sensibilities are drawn from their education and have to be consciously established and reproduced (most notably as reflexive consumers).

Cultural capital makes up for the shortfall of material capital that would be necessary to have the straightforward distinction of capitalists. The objects and articulations of good taste are varied but are particularly exhibited in spheres of consumption involving food, clothing, the media and certain locations for living and leisure. Of the latter, an inner urban lifestyle is the most characteristic of the new middle class. Writing 20 years ago, Gouldner (1979) prophetically identified the distinctive characteristic of the new class as its 'cosmopolitanism'.

THE CENTRAL CITY AS CULTURAL CAPITAL

The aesthetic redefinition of the central city as desirable is an act of class power. Yet the consumption of inner urban space brings into conflict the cultural strategy of the new middle class and their class relations. An inner urban lifestyle is distinct in two ways. In its location at the historic core of the city, close to the centre, at the heart of things, it is defined against the lack of distinctiveness, the homogeneity and 'anywhereness' of the suburbs (Ley, 1996). This is a separation of the new middle class and the 'middle middle class' who occupy the suburbs. It brings them into direct confrontation with working-class neighbourhoods and working-class history and taste in the central city. The cultural strategy in support of class distinction is direct and uncompromising. It is to transform working-class housing into a display of bourgeois good taste. This involves emphasizing the historical qualities of the house by stripping back to the original. Floorboards are stripped, sash windows reinstalled, fireplaces restored or reinserted in what is familiarly known as the gentrification aesthetic.

One of the features of gentrification has been that the deployment of a cultural aesthetic to provide social distinction has in turn enhanced material capital. The legitimation of this process has been seen in considerable house price rises in the gentrified neighbourhoods of most large western capitalist cities (as noted for Sydney's inner west). In this sense, 'taste' has converted into 'price'. Part of the reason for sustained rises (allowing for general housing market fluctuations) has been the fact that gentrification has increasingly involved wealthier members of the middle class. This is represented by the stage model of gentrification (such as Harrison, 1983) based on earlier ecological neighbourhood lifecycle models (Hoover and Vernon, 1962). In the early days, gentrification is carried out by lower paid professionals (teachers, academics, nurses) and involves modest upgrading of the property. As the process consolidates, higher paid professionals are attracted. The process is also more commodified, involving local builders turning over properties in a gentrified style. When the neighbourhood is fully 'established', large developers might get involved in converting former industrial or commercial properties to inner-city lofts. Larger and larger amounts of capital follow the gentrification aesthetic. At the scale of the city economy, culture attracts capital (Zukin, 1982).

HOUSING RENOVATION, MATERIAL AND CULTURAL CAPITAL

At the level of the personal finances of the gentrifiers in the early and consolidation phases of gentrification, we have a mutually reinforcing relationship between cultural and material capital, or taste and price. In the early stages, cultural capital 'captures' material capital. The relatively small investments by lower-paid professionals in 'risky' inner urban neighbourhoods reap considerable material rewards through large house price gains. However, as gentrification goes on, these social groups have been increasingly excluded and the wealthier professionals have bought into the aesthetic. In this sense, the quotient of material capital required to meet the gentrification aesthetic has risen.

The aesthetic itself also changes in material terms. As Horvath and Engels (1985) noted, in the early days of gentrification, the mark of social distinction was a lick of paint (in a certain pastel shade of course). As the process progresses, more and more is done to the home, from the stripping of floorboards and reinstallation of fireplaces

through to considerable internal structural alterations. Much of this work is changing the historic structure of the Victorian terrace and the question arises as to how much the gentrification aesthetic based on historical qualities of the house can encompass or is in tension with this modernization activity.

Jager (1986) noted the tension between history and modernization in his analysis of press adverts for housing in Melbourne (see also Mills, 1988). '"Victorian with modern additions, "country life" but a well appointed kitchen"' (1986: 82). Jager goes on to argue:

> The combination and 'history' is not conflictual, but rather complementary. For even with renovation, modernisation takes the form of neo-archaism—an attempt to return to a pre-industrial past with handmade bricks, and a refutation of mass products. Victoriana distinguishes itself from an industrialised low culture. In this way the retrieval of history becomes an instance of modernity. This new-romanticism of urban conservation incorporates the most modern functional elements. History is not restored in urban conservation, but recovered in a distorted and partial form (*ibid.*: 88).

AESTHETICS AND THE NEW MIDDLE CLASS

There is an extensive literature on the origins and composition of the 'new middle class' (Carchedi, 1977; Renner, 1978; Ehrenreich and Ehrenreich, 1979; Gouldner, 1979; Goldthorpe, 1982; 1995; Wright, 1985; Resnick and Wolff, 1987). I have applied these debates to the gentrification literature elsewhere (Bridge, 1995). Here we focus on the mix of cultural and economic capital as a key feature of the constitution and characteristics of the new middle class. The changing material cost of the gentrification aesthetic raises the question about the degree to which the gentrification literature has relied on a fairly static view of just what the displays of good taste are that constitute this cultural strategy of the new middle class. Here I argue that the relationship between material and cultural capital (or taste and price) continues to change. The gentrification aesthetic contains a tension over time and space that has implications for our understanding of the relationship between material and cultural capital and the class relations of the new middle class.

The aesthetic sensibilities of the new middle class are publicly discussed. Because of their comparative economic wealth and the self-consciousness of their aesthetic realm, one characteristic of the new middle class is as taste and trend setters. As Jager (1986: 84–5) expresses it:

> Victoriana is a fetish, in Marx's sense, in that the objects of culture are made to bear the burden of a more onerous social significance, and yet retain a distinct material function. This is clearest with internal renovations, where actually the authenticity of the 20th century working-class home was as undesirable as that of the 19th century Victorian home was unrealisable. For the economic investment in Victoriana depended upon thoroughly modern renovations, especially in the kitchen, and the provision of modern appliances. The Victorian aesthetic had its limits; it legitimates but cannot be allowed to compromise economic investment.

Here we have the new middle class as taste-makers. Fashion is part of their class identity. New middle-class gentrifiers recognize the need for a historical marker but also need to be at the edge of taste-making. This balance of symbols of the old and the new is at the heart of the socially differentiating nature of the gentrification aesthetic. This was noted by all the Sydney estate agents interviewed. For example:

> most people here want, they love the exterior, but they just want modern functional style.

> They'll keep the lofty ceilings, the cornices are great . . . the best capital improvement to be made to properties is to include modern, functional kitchens and bathrooms . . . They appreciate Victorian architecture from the outside 'cos the streetscape has to be maintained. That maintains the value of the home. They won't paint it in the wrong colours. They will go to a correct colour chart and do the exterior in a colour that would suit. But internally you will have . . . recessed halogen lighting but fireplaces will be retained, mantelpieces—things like that—but the colour schemes will be very, very contemporary (MT).

> they're giving the Victorian image with the year 2000 amenities and they're really going over the top (JH).

> the majority of them are renovated in fairly similar ways . . . they've got, sure, they've got the floorboards and . . . they modernise them but try to retain the original features. There's not many people that really gut them completely and just completely modernise them and do that; Most people are trying to retain its traditional feel. There are a few exceptions to that rule. Also, because sale-wise they sell better . . . most people are looking for a traditional two-storey terrace that has the ornate ceilings and the fireplace and polished floors and those sorts of things, so people want that so they tend to maintain that. They might change the kitchen and bathrooms, make them modern and open-plan and try to open things up a bit more. But they're fairly standard, just light variations on them (FV).

FV: Not overly tizzy. Very simple straight lines

GB: What do you mean by tizzy?

FV: Like it's not sort of completely sort of flouncy, it's more, you know, like clean colours, clean lines but with the original features intact. So you might have the white walls and the beautiful ceilings and fireplaces, polished floors, simple lines, modern-day kitchen.

This balance of history and modernity can be very fine.

I would just say in my experience most of the good stuff that's been sold has been sombre colours, like in creams and pastels and so on, married up with maybe a rather rich, bold cobalt blue wall or a blood red one or something like that—or maybe a colour that harks back to the olden days which might be a very rich burgundy, which would marry very well above a fireplace with a gilt-edged mirror and things like that—but the rest of the room would be in a very pale colour because you've got to look at the light situation. We can't create light in the classic lounge dining [sic] of a Victorian terrace—you can't do anything about it to put more light in (MT).

Jager explains the fine-tuning of the aesthetic in terms of the size of material capital and the need to match expectations in order to gain a good resale price. As he argues:

The fragility of small domestic capital in relation to other larger economic forces present in the inner city areas ensures that the esthetic disposition will be tightly circumscribed. This also explains the continuance of strictly economic imperatives and determinants embedded in the estheticization of Victoriana. The slightly triumphalist facades of Melbourne Victoriana are matched by more anxiously modelled interiors (1986: 89).

However, the aesthetic can be broken down into elements where a good deal of change is permissible and areas in which stable symbols of good taste must be held in place. In Sydney, behind the traditional facades, considerable internal restructuring was tolerated. As one agent describes it:

What they will even do is in an old style place—let's say, for example, an old place down on 'Dumont' street where you would have a lounge room, dining room, kitchen, bathroom—someone could come in and turn that all around so you have your kitchen there [front of house] because it's the closest place to the noise and normally if you're in the kitchen you're not going to be disturbed by traffic noise because you're going to be

doing something in your kitchen and . . . they will open it up and so rather than having your kitchen and your bathroom at the back . . . and then going past those to your backyard—it's all reversed . . . and lounge and dining is open plan as much as possible and then opening out onto the courtyard (TM).

There are a number of reasons for these alterations. The first is that greater informality in contemporary living means that separate dining and living rooms are unnecessary. Furthermore, the open-plan living space leading into a courtyard or veranda captures most of the sunlight, 'to bring the outdoors in', as one agent put it. Whereas the original design and cultural resonances of Victoriana was privacy, the contemporary gentrification aesthetic in Sydney seeks to capitalize on the natural resource of the Australian sun and open up the house to the light. There has been a move from seclusion to display.

You don't need the kitchen at the back of the house. Why were kitchens at the back of the house? Probably because they were busy working areas and if you're having guests in they didn't come to the kitchen . . . but now kitchens are on display . . . aromas or whatever, it doesn't matter if they fill the house now, that's part of it (TM).

In their original form, status was seclusion in these Victorian terraces, now status means opening up the home to the outside and the appropriation of the outside world within the home. Several agents talked about the importance of skylights to 'open up' the house.

The highest status inclusion of the outside in Sydney is a harbour view. The structure of the Victorian terrace may undergo considerable structural renovation to capture this asset:

this is a two-storey property and the outlook is from upstairs, living is upstairs, kitchen, lounge dining and balcony is all upstairs and it's not a fantastic water view but it's just a city skyline view, maybe the [Sydney Harbour] bridge or something like that, so rather than having that given to one or two bedrooms which are not really going to appreciate it, all the bedrooms are downstairs, there's a bathroom downstairs . . . bedrooms downstairs and your living upstairs 'cos it captures the view—that's what you impress your visitors with, the view. You don't say, yeah, we've got a view, come into my bedroom have a look at that, they go into the lounge (GK). [. . .]

NOTES

1. The research reported here was conducted with the support of a Menzies Bicentennial Fellowship. I am very grateful to Robyn Dowling, Bob Fagan, Richie Howitt, Kevin McCraken and other colleagues at the Department of Geography at Macquarie University who hosted my trip and discussed ideas. Ron Horvath's gentrification tour of Sydney was invaluable. My thanks to Ray Forrest, Suzanne Hodge and Terry Rees who commented on earlier drafts of this piece. The usual disclaimers apply.
2. I am very grateful to one of the anonymous referees for highlighting these contextual issues.

REFERENCES

Bondi, L. (1999) Gender, class and gentrification: enriching the debate. *Environment and Planning D: Society and Space* 17, 261–82.

Bourdieu, P. (1977) *Outline of a theory of practice.* Cambridge University Press, Cambridge.

—— (1984) *Distinction: a social critique of the judgement of taste.* Routledge and Kegan Paul, London.

Bridge, G. (1994) Gentrification, class and residence: a reappraisal. *Environment and Planning D: Society and Space* 12, 31–51.

—— (1995) The space for class: on class analysis in the study of gentrification. *Transactions of the Institute of British Geographers* 20, 236–47.

Butler, T. (1997) *Gentrification and the middle classes.* Ashgate, Aldershot.

Carchedi, G. (1977) *On the economic identification of social classes.* Routledge and Kegan Paul, London.

Clarke, M., D. Smith and M. McConville (1994) *Slippery customers: estate agents, the public and regulation.* Blackstone Press, London.

Ehrenreich, B. and J. Ehrenreich (1979) The professional managerial class. In P. Walker (ed.), *Between capital and labour.* The Harvester Press, Sussex.

Goldthorpe, J. (1982) On the service class, its formation and future. In A. Giddens and G. Mackenzie (eds.), *Social class and the division of labour: essays in honour of Ilya Neustadt.* Cambridge University Press, Cambridge.

—— (1995) The service class revisited. In T. Butler and M. Savage (eds.), *Social change and the middle classes.* UCL Press, London.

Gouldner, A. (1979) *The future of intellectuals and the rise of the new class.* The Seabury Press, New York.

Hamnett, C. and B. Randolph (1986) Tenurial transformation and the flat break-up market in London: the British condo experience. In N. Smith and P. Williams (eds.), *Gentrification of the city.* Allen and Unwin, Boston.

Harrison, G. (1983) Gentrification in Knoxville, Tennesse: a study of the Fourth and Gill neighbourhoods. *Urban Geography* 4, 40–53.

Hoover, E. and R. Vernon (1962) *Anatomy of a metropolis.* Doubleday, New York.

Horvath, R. and B. Engels (1985) The residential restructuring of inner Sydney. In I. Burnley and J. Forrest (eds.), *Living in cities: urbanism and society in metropolitan Australia.* Allen and Unwin, London.

——, G. Harrison and R. Dowling (1989) *Sydney: a social atlas.* Sydney University Press, Sydney.

House, J.D. (1977) *Contemporary entrepreneurs: the sociology of residential real estate agents.* Greenwood Press, Westport, Connecticut.

Jager, M. (1986) Class definition and the esthetics of gentrification: Victoriana in Melbourne. In N. Smith and P. Williams (eds.), *Gentrification of the city.* Allen and Unwin, London.

Lees, L. (1996) In pursuit of difference: representations of gentrification. *Environment and Planning A* 28, 453–70.

Ley, D. (1996) *The new middle class and the remaking of the central city.* Oxford University Press, Oxford.

Lyons, M. (1996) Employment, feminisation, and gentrification in London, 1981–93. *Environment and Planning A* 28, 341–56.

—— (1998) Neither chaos, nor stark simplicity: a comment on 'A new look at gentrification'. *Environment and Planning A* 30, 367–70.

Massey, D. and M. Denton (1993) *American apartheid: segregation and the making of the underclass.* Harvard University Press, Cambridge, MA.

Mills, C. (1988) Life on the upslope: the postmodern landscape of gentrification. *Environment and Planning D: Society and Space* 6, 169–89.

Redfern, P. (1997a) A new look at gentrification: 1. Gentrification and domestic technologies. *Environment and Planning A* 29, 1275–96.

—— (1997b) A new look at gentrification: 2. A model of gentrification. *Environment and Planning A* 29, 1335–54.

Renner, K. (1978) The service class. In T. Bottomore and P. Goode (eds.), *Austro-Marxism*. Clarendon Press, Oxford.

Residex Pty (1997) *Sydney residential property return report*. Residex, Sydney.

Resnick, S. and R. Wolff (1987) *Knowledge and class: a Marxian critique of political economy*. University of Chicago Press, Chicago.

Smith, N. (1996) *The new urban frontier: gentrification and the revanchist city*. Routledge, London.

Williams, P. (1976) The role of institutions in the inner London housing market: the case of Islington. *Transactions of the Institute of British Geographers* New Series 1, 72–82.

Wright, E.O (1985) *Classes*. Verso, London.

Zukin, S. (1982) *Loft living: culture and capital in urban change*. Johns Hopkins University Press, Baltimore.

CHAPTER 13

Tourism Gentrification: The Case of New Orleans' Vieux Carre (French Quarter)

Kevin Fox Gotham

Summary. This paper examines the process of 'tourism gentrification' using a case study of the socio-spatial transformation of New Orleans' Vieux Carre (French Quarter) over the past half-century. Tourism gentrification refers to the transformation of a middle-class neighbourhood into a relatively affluent and exclusive enclave marked by a proliferation of corporate entertainment and tourism venues. Historically, the Vieux Carre has been the home of diverse groups of people. Over the past two decades, however, median incomes and property values have increased, escalating rents have pushed out lower-income people and African Americans, and tourist attractions and large entertainment clubs now dominate much of the neighbourhood. It is argued that the changing flows of capital into the real estate market combined with the growth of tourism enhance the significance of consumption-oriented activities in residential space and encourage gentrification. The paper contests explanations that view gentrification as an expression of consumer demands, individual preferences or market laws of supply and demand. It examines how the growth of securitization, changes in consumption and increasing dominance of large entertainment firms manifest through the development of a tourism industry in New Orleans, giving gentrification its own distinct dynamic and local quality.

INTRODUCTION

Recent years have witnessed the growth of a vast and expanding scholarly literature concerning the novelty, causal dynamics and socioeconomic impact of gentrification (for an overview, see Atkinson, 2003). Since the early 1990s recession, researchers have noted a 'third wave' of gentrification in many cities, including the formation of new alliances between private developers and local government, a 'reinvention' of public institutions, and a 'restructuring' of the gentrification process itself (Wyly and Hammel, 1998, 2004; Wyly, 2002). According to Hackworth (2002), the growth of large corporate developers, real estate investment trusts (REITs) and new networks of mortgage brokers is creating new forms of 'corporatised gentrification'. For Smith (2002), the impulse behind gentrification is no longer restricted to the US or Europe, but is a global and generalised process. As a "global urban strategy", gentrification is now "densely connected into the circuits of global capital and cultural circulation" (Smith, 2002, p. 80). Whatever the differences of emphasis and interpretation, common to analyses of gentrification is a focus on new mechanisms of commercial reinvestment, new public subsidies for private investment and a greater interconnectedness of local and global forces (for an overview, see Brenner and Theodore, 2002). A key feature of recent research on gentrification is the attempt to situate gentrification within larger economic and political processes, including the deregulation of national markets, shifting patterns of global finance and the power of transnational corporations (TNCs) and global production networks (Wyly, 2002; Wyly and Hammel, 1999, 2000). Yet despite much research and debate, few scholars agree on how analysts should conceptualise gentrification, what should be the appropriate levels of analysis for assessing the causes and consequences of gentrification and what data sources researchers should use to measure gentrification empirically. While many scholars contend that gentrification today is different from that of the 1970s and 1980s, they disagree over its form, incidence and impact.

This paper contributes to recent urban scholarship on the causes and consequences of gentrification, using a case study of the transformation of New Orleans's Vieux Carre (French Quarter) since the 1950s. Since at least the 1930s, the Vieux Carre has been a site of intense conflicts over commercial revitalisation, historical preservation and neighbourhood integrity. In 1937, the neighbourhood was designated as a historical district and remained the city's only landmark district until the 1970s. In the 1960s, the local environmentalists and neighbourhood activists joined forces with a burgeoning national anti-expressway movement to halt the planning and construction of an elevated expressway along the Mississippi River (Baumbach and Borah, 1981; Lewis, 1997). Since this time, residents and businesses have teamed with historical preservationists and other activists to protest the growth of fast-food restaurants, mall-like shops and chain-like clothing stores that cater almost exclusively to tourists (Foley,

1999; Foley and Lauria, 2000; 2003). In 1995, the National Trust for Historical Preservation identified the Vieux Carre as one of the 10 most endangered places in the country due to the threat that commercial business growth posed to the residential character of the neighbourhood. In recent years, residents and neighbourhood organisations have lamented the increase of hotels, bed and breakfasts, time-shares, condominiums and large entertainment clubs (Vesey, 1999; Kaufman, 1999). Both median incomes and property values have increased, especially during the 1990s, and escalating rents and conversion of affordable single-family residences to expensive condominiums have pushed out lower-income people and African Americans. As I point out, for most of its history, the Vieux Carre functioned as a residential neighbourhood composed of diverse groups of people. Since the 1960s, however, the area has been transformed into an entertainment destination, marketed vigorously by tourism promoters and redesigned to bring visitors into the city. As a central component of New Orleans' promotion as a tourist and entertainment city, the analysis of gentrification in the Vieux Carre offers a unique case for understanding the connection between global economic process and local actions in the transformation of urban space.

In this paper, I situate the gentrification of the Vieux Carre within the larger transformation of New Orleans into a tourist city. I first specify the conceptual problem and outline a theoretical framework that will guide my analysis. I then provide an overview of residential and commercial change in the Vieux Carre over the past 60 years using data from the US Census Bureau and other government reports. I then focus on the connection between tourism and gentrification. My analysis focuses on the *why* and *how* questions regarding the motivation for using tourism as a strategy of urban regeneration, both of which are central to explaining the process of gentrification. I develop the concept *tourism gentrification* to highlight the role of state policy in encouraging both gentrification and tourism development; and the actions of large corporate entertainment firms in redeveloping the Vieux Carre into a space of entertainment and consumption. I argue that flows of capital in the real estate market combined with the shift to tourism explain gentrification more fully than do alternative accounts that focus narrowly on consumer demand or cultural preferences for upscale neighbourhoods. Tourism is about the production of local difference, local cultures and different local histories that appeal to visitors' tastes for the exotic and unique (Coleman and Crang, 2002; Hoffman *et al.*, 2003; Urry, 2002). At the same time, the tourism industry is one of the largest industries in the world and is increasingly dominated by global hotel firms and entertainment companies—Disney, Universal, Sony, etc.—who have the ability to exploit a wide range of 'brand synergies' to transform locales into spaces for consumption (Hollands and Chatterton, 2003; Fainstein and Judd, 1999; Meethan, 2001). Hannigan's (1998) discussion of the 'maverick' developers of the new entertainment-based 'fantasy city' points to how national or international corporations today dominate urban redevelopment and have the economic and political power to take their investments elsewhere should local officials not prove compliant, a trend observed by Feagin and Parker (1990), Smith (1996) and others. In this light, I view tourism as a globalised process that connects the exogenous forces of multinational corporations and capital flows, with the locally based powers of residents, elites and consumers.

TOURISM GENTRIFICATION

Research on gentrification has exploded over the past two decades. Economists, geographers, sociologists and other urban scholars have studied the causal dynamics, consequence and trajectories of gentrification using diverse sources of data and theoretical orientations (for overviews, see Atkinson, 2003; Brenner and Theodore, 2002: Feagin and Parker, 1990, ch. 5; Gotham, 200lb; Hutchison, 1992; Smith, 1996; Wittberg, 1992; Wyly and Hammel, 2001). In the US, scholars have identified three waves of gentrification (Hackworth, 2002; Smith, 2002). The first wave, beginning in the 1950s and lasting to the 1973 recession, was an outgrowth of the Housing Acts of 1949 and 1954 that provided federal funds for local redevelopment authorities to designate 'blighted' areas, acquire and clear land, and then sell the land to private developers (Gotham, 2000, 2001a). In the process, city governments and federal monies supported private efforts to build new upscale urban housing, thereby allowing a new urban 'gentry' to move into areas previously dominated by the poor and the working class. A second wave followed in the 1970s and 1980s as new public-private 'partnerships' and market-centred subsidies (such as tax abatements and tax increment financing (TIFs)) financed gentrification (Squires, 1989). Two significant features marked this second wave. The first was the integration of gentrification with new 'cultural strategies' of economic redevelopment, including new investments in museums, art galleries and historical preservation (Zukin, 1997, 1995). A second significant feature was the increasing enmeshment of gentrification into global systems of real estate and banking finance. This enmeshment was evident in the creation of new, massive developments including New York City's South Street Seaport, Boston's Faneuil Hall, Baltimore's Inner Harbor and Philadelphia's Society Hill.

In recent years, scholars have argued that inner cities are experiencing a third wave of gentrification and a resurgence of investment but disagree on the sources and causes of this gentrification and reinvestment (for overviews, see Bondi, 1999; Lees, 2000; Ley, 1996; South, 1996). Wyly and Hammel (1999, 2001), for example, maintain that the resurgence of gentrification in many cities emanates from recent transformations in federal regulatory policy and mortgage financing. Specifically, local efforts under the federal HOPE VI programme that decentralises public housing administration and establishes public-private ventures to fund public housing redevelopment have helped spur a new round of gentrification in many cities. In this conception, the federal government's more decentralised and privatised low-income housing policy has altered key facets of the gentrification process itself, opening new markets for low-income and minority borrowers and neighbourhoods, and increasing access to conventional mortgage capital through automation and standardisation (see also Kasarda, 1999; Marcuse, 1999). In a case study of New York City's Lower East Side, Smith, and DeFillippis (1999) argue that the 'economics of gentrification' was transformed in the 1990s as brand-name firms, international developers and multinational banks increasingly supplied the capital to finance corporate-led gentrification. Lees' (2003) study of Brooklyn Heights, New York, suggests that a "new generation of super-rich 'financifiers' fed by the fortunes from global finance and corporate service industries" is the leading edge of "supergentrification" which refers to "the transformation of already gentrified, prosperous and solidly upper-middle class neighbourhoods into much more exclusive and expensive enclaves" (p. 2487). In a comprehensive survey of the literature, Hackworth (2002) argues that four novel changes distinguish the gentrification process in the 1990s and later: corporate developers are now the leading initiators of gentrification, federal and local governments are more

open and assertive in facilitating gentrification; anti-gentrification movements have become more marginalised than in earlier decades; and, gentrification is diffusing to more remote neighbourhoods. Overall, according to Hackworth (2002, p. 839), gentrification now is "more corporate, more state facilitated, and less resisted than ever before".

In this paper, I develop and apply the concept of *tourism gentrification* as a heuristic device to explain the transformation of a middle-class neighbourhood into a relatively affluent and exclusive enclave marked by a proliferation of corporate entertainment and tourism venues. Scholars have noted that gentrification is a "chaotic concept" (Lees, 2003, p. 2491) that lacks theoretical and empirical specificity. In a critique of the empirical literature on gentrification, Wyly and Hammel (1998) observed that "recent criticisms of the coherence of theories of gentrification, ... and methods for assessing its extent and significance have cast doubt on the utility of further research on the subject" (p. 303). Five years later, in a comprehensive review of the literature on gentrification, Atkinson (2003, p. 2343) noted that the "map of gentrification appears to be extending steadily" with dozens of scholars around the world undertaking a variety of case studies, comparisons and statistical analyses of gentrification. A major objective of this paper is to contribute to this burgeoning literature by examining the process of tourism gentrification. Following Wyly and Hammel (1998, p. 302), I argue that research on tourism gentrification is warranted not by the intensity or magnitude of gentrification, "but by the *distinctiveness* of the patterns inscribed by the *process*" (original emphasis). Specifically, I maintain that there are at least two reasons to consider the nature of tourism gentrification.

First, tourism gentrification highlights the twin processes of globalisation and localisation that define modern urbanisation and redevelopment processes. On the one hand, tourism is a 'global' industry dominated by large international hotel chains, tour operators, car rental agencies and financial services companies (American Express, Visa and so on). In addition, tourism sustains many occupations, advertising campaigns, recognisable attractions and diverse forms of financial investment.[1] On the other hand, tourism is a 'local' industry characterised by grassroots cultural production, spatial fixity of the tourism commodity and localised consumption of place. T. C. Chang and colleagues' research on Singapore and Montreal suggests that various public agencies, private firms and tourism interests deploy locally specific images, themes and motifs to stimulate tourist demand to buy and consume local products and services (Chang, 2000a, 2000b; Chang et al., 1996). These points buttress studies by Teo and Lim (2003) and Teo and Yeoh (1996) who find that while tourism may be a 'global' force, it is also a locally based set of activities and organisations involved in the production of local distinctiveness, local cultures and different local histories that appeal to visitors' tastes for the exotic and unique. As I point out below, the nexus of globalisation and localisation is apparent in the Vieux Carre where corporate entertainment firms and retail chains are plugged into global financial circuits to leverage capital to redevelop residential and commercial space. In the process, entertainment and retail firms accentuate the place-theme in their commodities and activities by valorising the milieu where they are located, using place images and symbols that connect the locale with pleasurable experiences. At the same time, the growth of tourism has an 'elective affinity' with widespread cultural and aesthetic changes including the emergence of style as identity, the proliferation of advertising images and media, and development of sophisticated marketing schemes that seek to create demand for gentrified housing (Ley, 1996, 2003).

Secondly, the concept of tourism gentrification presents a challenge to traditional explanations of gentrification that assume demand-side or production-side factors drive the process. During the 1970s and 1980s, scholars developed differing explanations of the etiology, process and consequences of gentrification. Clay (1979, pp. 57–60), Berry (1985; 1999, p. 783) and Kasarda (1999, p. 779) outlined a series of demand-side factors, including demographic and economic factors, and individual preferences and consumer choice for gentrified housing. A second production-side perspective emphasised the importance of state policy and regulation, the role of disinvestment and the actions of powerful actors and organised interests in the gentrification process. This later approach, focused on "capitalist roots of gentrification" (Smith, 1996, p. 41) and viewed gentrification "as part and parcel of the class dynamics of urban transformation associated with capital investment and disinvestment" (Betancur, 2002, p. 781). The example of tourism gentrification provides the conceptual link between production-side and demand-side explanations of gentrification while avoiding one-sided and reductive conceptions. On the production side, for example, tourism is about shifting patterns of capital investment in the sphere of production, new forms of financing real estate development and the creation of spaces of consumption. On the demand side, the socio-physical spaces associated with gentrification are also the "highly visual expression of changing patterns of consumption in cities" (Carpenter and Lees, 1995, p. 288). Analysing tourism gentrification sheds light on the complementary nature of the differing explanations, provides an important opportunity for theoretical development and offers a unique perspective on tourism and urban redevelopment dynamics. While my empirical analysis is specific to New Orleans and the Vieux Carre, I argue that the analysis has broader theoretical generality and applicability to understanding gentrification.[2]

BUILDING A TOURIST CITY

During the immediate post-World War II years, New Orleans city officials and élites began devising strategies to increase tourist travel to enhance the economic prosperity and fiscal status of the central city. In the 1960s, dwindling urban population and burgeoning suburban development raised the spectre of economic stagnation and created the context for city leaders to further the development of tourism in the city. From 1967 to 1977, manufacturing jobs in New Orleans declined in every year except one. By 1977, only 11 per cent of the labour force was employed in manufacturing, a situation that placed the city among the lowest in industrial employment in the nation (Smith and Keller, 1986). In 1974, the Louisiana State legislature passed several statutes that significantly reduced the ability of local governments in the state to raise revenue. These fiscal constraints included: a reduction in the ability of local governments to collect income taxes, thereby increasing their reliance on revenue from sales taxes; a statute that two-thirds of both houses of the state legislature had to approve any increase in an existing local tax; and, an expanded exemption on homeowners' property taxes. The state legislature increased this homestead exemption, from $50 000 of assessed valuation in 1974 to $75 000 in 1982 (Smith and Keller, 1986, pp. 150–154). At the local level, New Orleans' long tradition of elected assessors who owned their assessor databases, and distribution of assessed property values, meant that assessors appraised few homes over $75 000 (Knopp, 1990a; Lauria, 1984). At the federal

level, urban outlays declined from 12.4 per cent of all federal expenditures in 1978 to 7.8 per cent in 1984 (Gaffikin and Warf, 1993, p. 73). In short, reduced federal monies, fiscal constraints imposed on the city by the state government and the suburbanisation of people and businesses caused a significant erosion in the ability of the city to raise revenue to fund basic government operations and provide public services. As a result, by the late1970s, New Orleans was experiencing a fiscal crisis, forced to slash funding for public services while financially pressured to expend greater funds to leverage capital investment and develop new strategies for engineering urban redevelopment.

During the 1980s, New Orleans gained attention as an economically declining city in the prosperous Sunbelt region (Hirsch, 1983). The oil market crash from 1982 to 1987 depressed the local jobs market, causing a dramatic increase in housing foreclosures and the out-migration of thousands of middle-class families from the city and metropolitan area (Lauria and Baxter, 1999). While the suburban areas grew in population, the population of Orleans Parish dropped from a high of 627 525 in 1960 to an all-time low of 484 674 in 2000. The city lost more than 34 000 residents during the 1960s, more than 35 000 during the 1970s, more than 60000 in the 1980s and more than 10 000 from 1990 to 2000 (see Table 13.1). In recent years, local public officials, scholars and journalists have acknowledged the deleterious effects of the racial segregation in area schools and housing, the loss of manufacturing jobs and increasing blight and rising poverty while downtown redevelopment and suburban growth have been taking place (Lauria *et al.*, 1995; Whelan and Young, 1991; Brooks and Young, 1993). As of 1995, more than half the children living in New Orleans, 51.6 per cent, were living below the federal poverty level. In a survey of 216 counties and parishes in the US

Table 13.1 Population and demographic trends for Orleans Parish, Louisiana, 1940–2000

	1940	1950	1960	1970	1980	1990	2000
Total population	494 537	570 445	627 525	593 471	557 515	496 938	484 674
White population (percentage)	69.7	68.0	62.6	54.5	42.5	34.9	26.6
Black population (percentage)	30.1	31.9	37.2	45.0	55.3	61.9	66.6
Other (percentage)	0.1	0.2	0.2	0.5	2.2	3.2	3.7
Median household income ($)	N/A	2 267	3 822	7 445	11 814	12 239	19 453
Median household income, 2000 (S)	N/A	14 914	20 439	31 021	24 715	16 125	19 453
Poverty status							
Families (number)	N/A	N/A	N/A	30 996	29 359	32 616	26 988
Families (percentage)	N/A	N/A	N/A	21.6	21.8	27.3	23.7
Individuals (number)	N/A	N/A	N/A	156 776	143 793	152 042	130 896
Individuals (percentage)	N/A	N/A	N/A	26.8	26.4	31.6	27.9
Median household value ($)	3 033	9 711	16 000	21 000	50 600	69 600	87 300
Median household value, 2000 ($)	N/A	63 888	85 562	87 500	105 858	91 700	87 300
Median rent ($)	15.38	25.18	60.00	67.00	153.00	277.00	378.00
Median rent, 2000 ($)	N/A	165.66	320.86	279.17	320.08	364.95	378.00
Total housing units	137 165	173 608	202 643	208 524	226 452	225 573	215 091
Owner-occupied	31 552	56 091	71 297	73 517	81 970	82 279	87 589
Renter-occupied	101 488	109 962	118 504	117 846	124 465	105 956	100 662
Number vacant	4 125	7 555	12 842	17 161	20 017	37 338	26 840
Percentage vacant	3.0	4.4	6.3	8.2	8.8	16.5	12.5

Source: Census of Population and Housing (1940–2000).

with at least 250 000 residents, the Census Bureau found that the Orleans parish was one of the poorest, ranking fourth, with 25 per cent of its working population living in poverty. Only 5 other counties in the nation had a poverty rate of 25 per cent or greater in 2000. In a study of median household incomes in those 216 counties and parishes, Orleans Parish again ranked among the poorest, third from the bottom at 213, with $27 111 (*New Orleans Times-Picayune*, 2001).

Over the decades, the city of New Orleans has pursued tourism as a strategy to generate urban revitalisation and bolster the tax-base. The various components of this tourism strategy have included the building of a domed stadium, a festival mall, a massive convention centre, new office towers in the central business district, a major theme park and a World War II museum. The city has also staged many mega-events, including the 1984 World's Fair, periodic Super Bowls and (Nokia) Sugar Bowls, the NCAA basket-ball tournaments, the Jazz and Heritage Festival and the Essence Festival. According to data gathered by the New Orleans Convention and Visitors Bureau, there were 8.2 million visitors to New Orleans in 2003, including 485 216 international visitors. Total visitor expenditures amounted to $3.8 billion with $198.34 million in tourism tax revenues.[3] The hotel industry has grown considerably over recent decades as indicated by the skyrocketing number of hotel rooms in the metropolitan area.

In 1960, the city had a total of 4750 rooms. This number increased to 10 686 in 1975, 19 500 in 1985, 25 500 in 1990 and almost 34 000 by 2000. The convention market has also grown from 764 conventions in 1976 to more than 3260 conventions in 1999. Other tourism developments in the 1990s include the legalisation of gaming in Louisiana, the creation of the New Orleans Tourism Marketing Corporation, the establishment of the New Orleans Multicultural Tourism Network, the creation of the Mayor's Office of Tourism and Arts, and the expansion of Convention and Visitor's Bureau efforts to market the region to international tourists (City of New Orleans, 2000).

In sum, the erosion of both federal and state government revenue over the past few decades means that New Orleans is more reliant on sales tax revenue than ever before. This constrained fiscal environment has pressured the city government to intensify partnerships with private capital to promote the growth of a consumption-based tourism infrastructure. Today, the locus of New Orleans' multibillion dollar tourism business is in the downtown and the Vieux Carre. Tourism is a way of importing spending and exporting the tax burden to generate the revenue to facilitate urban redevelopment and gentrification.

DEMOGRAPHIC AND POPULATION CHANGES IN THE VIEUX CARRE

The Vieux Carre, or old French Quarter of New Orleans, is probably one of the most famous historical districts in the US. Established in 1718, the area is bounded by Canal, Rampart and Esplanade Streets, and the Mississippi River. The neighbourhood itself consists of a mix of residential and commercial land uses in a rectangle grid of approximately 120 blocks along the Mississippi River. This area formed the original French colonial town that had been designed by Pierre L Blond de la Tour,

engineer-in-chief of Louisiana, and laid out by his assistant, Adrien de Pauger, in March 1721. The early history of the Vieux Carre was that of a French trading centre and later, after 1762, a Spanish colonial outpost. With the Louisiana Purchase in 1803, the US inherited a thriving commercial centre supported by river trade. During the first half of the 19th century, growth in New Orleans expanded beyond the Vieux Carre, but the neighbourhood continued as a centre of cultural and social life during the century. By the mid 19th century, the city rivalled New York as a commercial and financial hub. The Civil War devastated the city and resulted in a period of protracted economic decline that would last into the 20th century. By the mid 20th century, the Vieux Carre had acquired a reputation as a charming residential neighbourhood with a unique historical background and architectural styles. Today, the Vieux Carre includes all the land within the original French and Spanish city. It functions as a speciality shopping area, an entertainment complex, a centre for arts and crafts, a residential area and a focus of culture and historical preservation of regional and national importance.

Historically, the Vieux Carre has been the home of diverse groups of people. Yet over the past few decades the neighbourhood has become more socially homogeneous. Demographic trends show the social transformation of the Vieux Carre from 1940 to 2000. According to the US Census Bureau, the Vieux Carre consists of census tracts 38, 42 and 47. Between 1940 and 1970, the population of the Vieux Carre plummeted from 11 053 to 4176, a loss of more than 50 per cent of its population. In comparison, the City of New Orleans grew by approximately 26.9 per cent from 1940 to 1960, from 494 537 to 627 525, while losing population over the next four census periods. While the percentage of Whites living in the Vieux Carre increased from 79 per cent in 1940 to 91.9 per cent in 2000; the percentage of Blacks dropped from 19.7 per cent to 4.3 per cent. Interestingly, as the White segment of population has increased in the Vieux Carre, it has declined for the city of New Orleans. In 1960, Whites made up 62.6 per cent of the city's population and Blacks were 37.2 per cent. As of the 2000 census, Blacks made up 67.3 per cent of the city's population and Whites were 28.1 per cent. Today, almost 11 per cent of the population of the Vieux Carre lives below the poverty level, compared with 27.9 per cent for the city of New Orleans.

From 1940 to 2000, the percentage of vacant housing units in the Vieux Carre increased from 9.5 per cent to almost 38 per cent. According to a 1992 University of New Orleans study, the high vacancy rate in 1990 was concentrated in speculative apartments constructed during the 1984 World's Fair (University of New Orleans, College of Urban and Public Affairs, 1992, ch. 2, p. 10). The continuing high rate of vacancy in the 1990s is because the high rental cost of commercial units discourages property owners from maintaining residential apartments above the first floor.

In census tract 38, median housing value in constant 2000 dollars increased more than seven times, from $64 474 in 1950 to $460 000 in 2000. The cost of rent also increased dramatically after 1950, from $193.82 per month in census tract 38 to $549 per month in 2000. Census tracts 42 and 47 show similar trends. As Table A1 shows, median household income, median housing value and median rents are higher in the Vieux Carre than Orleans Parish as a whole. Overall, the census data show a slight decline in median household income (in constant dollars), a loss of population, a decrease in percentage of minority residents and huge increases median household value and cost of rent, from 1940 to 2000—changes associated with gentrifying areas.

Today, only 116 children less than 18 years of age live in the Vieux Carre. This number represents only 2.7 per cent of the total population of the neighbourhood. Of the almost 3000 households in the Vieux Carre, more than 97 per cent do not have children less than 18 years of age. This is in contrast to 64.7 per cent for Orleans Parish, 60.8 per cent for the state of Louisiana and 63.9 per cent for the entire US.[4]

The demographic and population transformation of the Vieux Carre coincides with a dramatic restructuring of the commercial base of the neighbourhood. Vesey (1999), for example, found that from 1950 to 1999, the number of souvenir and t-shirt shops increased from 26 to 110; retail apparel stores increased from 14 to 42; music clubs increased from 7 to 27; hotels increased from 21 to 40; and art galleries increased from 10 to 40. In addition, from 1950 to 1999, the number of groceries decreased from 44 to 4; miscellaneous food stores declined from 44 to 19; hardware stores from 31 to 1; laundry services from 24 to 2. During this time, several 'mom-and-pop' operations that had been stable fixtures in the neighbourhood for decades closed including, LaNasa Hardware, Reuter's Feed and Seed and Puglia's grocery store. Interestingly, the number of warehouses, industrial services, freight distribution and manufacturing services plummeted from 131 to 2. Today, souvenir shops are the most prevalent retail business in the area. Overall, from 1950 to 1999, residential-oriented businesses, such as barbers, department stores, shoe shops, small groceries and laundry services, decreased by more than 15 per cent, while tourist-oriented business, such as t-shirt shops, poster shops, *daiquiri* shops, and commercial tourism information centres expanded by 32 per cent.

The huge increase in median household value and median rent in the Vieux Carre during the 1990s suggests that the neighbourhood may be experiencing a new round of intensified gentrification, or what Lees (2003) calls 'super-gentrification'—for example, the movement of even wealthier residents into a previously gentrified neighbourhood. While the data in Table Al show upward trends in median household income, median household value and median rent, they do not imply that gentrification is a crescive process nor that it has a stable outcome or specific endpoint. Quantitative data do not provide an explanation for the underlying causes of the population, demographic and commercial transformation of the neighbourhood. As I show below, the promotion of tourism has been a major strategy for encouraging commercial development, attracting high-income residents and bolstering gentrification in the Vieux Carre.

THE LOCAL STATE AND THE ROLE OF REAL ESTATE INVESTORS

In the past, reinvestment in the Vieux Carre was associated with the activities of individual gentrifiers, small commercial firms (art galleries, museums and so on) and small property developers (Knopp, 1990a, 1990b; Lauria, 1984). Before the 1980s, federally insured and regulated savings and loans and small banks supplied much of the capital for commercial and residential construction and investment. As a result, only a limited amount of capital funds were available for new construction and renovation. In contrast, the 1980s and 1990s have seen the development of national and global markets for mortgage-backed securities (MBS) and commercial-backed securities (CMBS) that have expanded the investor-base to finance residential and commercial real estate, and have allowed more funds to flow into the mortgage market and commercial real estate sector from broader capital markets. Securitisation implies the transformation of illiquid financial assets into liquid capital market securities and

has been the critical financial innovation that has enabled private and public actors to finance local property development in global markets (Logan, 1993; Sassen, 2001, pp. 71–74). The liquidation of real estate capital through securitisation received added impetus in the 1990s with the growth of real estate investment trusts (REITs), shareholding companies that invest in different types of real estate including shopping centres, office buildings, apartments and hotels. While urban redevelopment involves many small players using local finance mechanisms, they are increasingly operating in a larger context of global capital markets dominated by large investors, a trend documented by Weber (2002), Dymski (1999) and Smith (2002). In this globalising context of local property development, it is the supply and demand for housing and commercial development *funds*, rather than the supply and demand itself that determine the value of local properties. In short, the growth of securitisation and the development of new sources of financing have made it possible for a substantial portion of the commercial real estate industry to invest in entertainment, tourism and leisure-based consumption activities (Hannigan, 1998; Nevarez, 2002; Chatterton and Hollands, 2003; Wyly and Hammel, 2004, pp. 8, 35).

This long-run and complex restructuring of the real estate industry connects with institutional changes on the local level to encourage commercial development and gentrification in the Vieux Carre. Three developments have been important. First, in the 1970s, the city government reorganised the French Market Corporation, one of the oldest public markets in the nation, as a *de facto* private corporation to promote commerce and entertainment in the Vieux Carre. The rationalisation of the leasing structure and tenant mix, the construction of several parking lots and the renovation of buildings focused on restaurants and shops frequented by tourists (Reeves, 2000, pp. 40–43). At this point in the market's history, as the website of the City of New Orleans government mentions, "entertainment and tourism became primary aspects of market life" (www. frenchmarket.org/history.html). While the French Market had been a public—private entity since the 1930s, privatisation in the 1970s and later attempted to reconstitute the organisation as a for-profit organisation under the label of entrepreneurial government. Secondly, the mid to late 1970s saw the building of Canal Place, a high-rise mixed-use retail development on the upriver side of the Vieux Carre. The planning and construction of Canal Place reflected trends towards privatisation and the restructuring of the public sector to promote economic competitiveness, attract investment capital and create a favourable 'business climate' (Brooks and Young, 1993; Lauria *et al.*, 1995). Thirdly, in 1992, city planners rezoned the first two blocks of Decatur Street as a Vieux Carre Entertainment District, a move meant to spur redevelopment of several vacant commercial properties and create an anchor of commercial revitalisation that could have spillover effects into surrounding areas. Large firms such as the House of Blues, Coyote Ugly Bar, Planet Hollywood, Jimmy Buffet's Margaritaville Cafe, Audubon Institute's Aquarium for the Americas and Harrah's Casino have all opened since the early 1990s.

The creation of new real estate financing mechanisms through securitisation combined with local state action to encourage tourism have together promoted the growth of chain-like entertainment venues in the Vieux Carre. Bourbon Street began to experience a new wave of investment with the opening of the Chateau Sonesta Hotel in 1995, Larry Flynt's Hustler Club (225 Bourbon) in 1996, Redfish Grill in 1997 and the Storyville District Jazz Club in 1999. In 1998, Don Kleinhans, a national adult entertainment investor, opened Utopia, a music and dance club at 227 Bourbon, and Opulence, a nightclub a few doors away. Bourbon Street has long been one of New Orleans' most valuable commercial real estate strips (Marks Lewis Torre and Associates, 1977). Nevertheless, space on the street has become more desirable as the tourism industry has expanded since the 1980s. The construction of upscale hotels along Canal Street and in the central business district has increased foot traffic within the Vieux Carre and encouraged investors to renovate properties in the first few blocks of Canal and turn old bars on Bourbon Street into upscale themed music clubs. As a result, rents on the street have risen by at least 50 per cent since the mid 1990s and in some cases have more than doubled. As of 2002, real estate agents were selling space on the street for $175–$250 per square foot.

Real estate agents admit to waging bidding wars with each other to accelerate property turnover and some meet with families who have owned property for generations to see if they would be interested in selling. If so, they go and find national investors who want to invest (*New Orleans Times—Picayune*, 2002). Outside investors and entertainment firms are attracted to the Vieux Carre because of many diverse kinds of tourists that visit the area. Tourism officials note that tourists who come to the Vieux Carre are of varying age levels, have high levels of affluence and exhibit different types of lifestyle. The chance to gain international visibility through the annual Mardi Gras celebration, the ability to do business 7 nights a week and sell drinks 24 hours a day, and the constant flow of tourists allow businesses to achieve quick profits. As large entertainment firms have become the mainstay of capital investment in the area, they have broken down the barriers between residential and commercial use on particular streets—a trend also observed by Chatterton and Hollands

(2002) in their analysis of night-time urban playscapes in the UK. Where there used to be a buffer between the retail commercial zone of Canal Street and the entertainment zone of Bourbon Street, these two streets are now fused together in their use of entertainment and tourism to attract consumers. What is important is that the enmeshment of entertainment and tourism with different land uses and spaces elides the distinction between consumption-based activities and other social activities, opening new contexts and opportunities for powerful actors to market the Vieux Carre for profit and economic gain. Local and national businesses produce and sell Vieux Gras souvenirs and paraphernalia, multinational companies use Vieux Carre and New Orleans imagery and themes to sell their products; and, public—private organisations (tourism marketing corporations and task forces) promote Vieux Carre to support inward investment and economic growth. In the latter case, public and private sectors overlap and place marketers and tourism boosters increasingly emphasise 'synergistic' opportunities for creating commercial value (Hannigan, 1998).

Sharon Zukin (1991) and David Ley (2003, p. 2538) suggest that "learning the field of gentrification is facilitated by a cadre of cultural intermediaries in real estate, travel, cuisine, the arts" who create and reproduce knowledge, transmit images and disseminate information about 'cool' and 'trendy' neighbourhoods. Cultural intermediaries do not exist in a cultural or economic vacuum, but operate through organised networks involving public relations firms, advertising and marketing corporations, festival promoters and city agencies. Thus, organisations like the Arts Council of New Orleans, French Quarter Festivals, Inc., the New Orleans Metropolitan Convention and Visitors Bureau, the New Orleans Tourism Marketing Corporation, the New Orleans Multicultural Tourism Network and the Mayors Office on Art and Tourism produce advertisements, attractive brochure and information packages, provide funding and render services to stimulate consumer demand to travel to or live in the Vieux Carre. For example, tourism websites, vertical banners and billboards that advertise Vieux Carre also promote restaurants, shops and hotels. Streets in the Vieux Carre are laden with historical allusions to a traditional and nostalgic view of the city as a friendly and coherent place, lined with red-brick town houses, cast-iron galleries over public sidewalks and enchanting backyard gardens and slave quarters. Other streets are ornamented with neon signs and punctuated by antique lamp-posts and cajun and zydeco music. These symbols and motifs are selectively incorporated into tourist guides and promotional materials to represent certain visual images of the city. One aim of these advertisements is to conjure up emotionally satisfying themes of past times, to promote an image of nostalgia to attract tourists. Another aim is to remake residential space into commercial space by interlocking visual attractions with profit-making consumption-based opportunities such as eating, drinking and shopping, thereby expanding the repertoire of consumption.

Images and symbols of romance, nostalgia, public sexuality, music, dancing and shopping have long attracted tourists to the Vieux Carre. Before the 1970s, the use of advertising, marketing and other promotional efforts to increase tourism was *ad hoc*, uncoordinated and lacked sophistication compared with the present. Not only was the socioeconomic context different from that of today, but also the intensity and scale of advertising and the organisation of aesthetic production were vastly different. Today, public and private groups such as the New Orleans Tourism Marketing Corporation, the New Orleans Multicultural Tourism Network, the Mayor's Office of

Tourism and Arts and the Convention and Visitor's Bureau 'simulate' the Vieux Carre using sophisticated advertising techniques aimed at promoting desire and fantasy, art and design directed to the production of desirable tourist experiences and other highly refined techniques of image production and distribution. In the process, tourism interests and advertising agencies thematise local traditions, famous buildings and landmarks and other heritage sights to the point that they become' 'hyper-real', with the production of 'illusions' over-riding descriptions of 'reality' (Baudrillard, 1983). The implication is that tourism institutions are not necessarily engaged in promoting and advertising what the city has to offer. They are involved in adapting, reshaping and manipulating images of the place to be desirable to the targeted consumer. Advertising the Vieux Carre as a site of famous architecture, romance, cultural heritage, music and other entertainment activities affects the production and consumption of urban space for tourism. The same symbols, motifs and themes that relate to tourist advertising are equally applicable to people interested in purchasing a gentrified lifestyle.

The growth of tourism in the Vieux Carre has not been without negative consequences and neighbourhood coalitions have opposed the transformation of the neighbourhood into an entertainment destination. The entry of large multinational hotel firms into the Vieux Carre—for example, has sparked much local unrest, leading several neighbourhood groups to launch lawsuits aimed at halting construction. The lure of tourist profits, low labour costs and anti-union sentiment have long attracted large hotels to New Orleans. On the other hand, local preservationists and neighbourhood groups have long fought the intrusion of large hotels in the Vieux Carre. In 1969, the City Council imposed a moratorium on new hotel building to protect the historical district. The City Council enacted the moratorium into law in a comprehensive zoning ordinance in 1976, along with height restrictions. In 1982, the City Council revised the moratorium to allow new hotels on Canal Street and in the Vieux Carre but in existing buildings only. Over the past few years, the City Council has issued permits that allow hotel firms to exceed the height restriction of 70 feet and purchase residential buildings next to hotels and convert them into lodging. Despite vehement opposition from business owners and residents, in August 2004, the New Orleans City Planning Commission voted 6-l to grant a single exception to the 35-year-old prohibition against new or expanded hotels in the Vieux Carre (Eggler, 2004). Local residents and lawyers representing the French Quarter Citizens for the Preservation of Residential Quality and the Vieux Carre Property Owners, Residents, and Associates YCPORA argue that these recent developments essentially nullify the original moratorium, encourage unrestricted development that is not open to public comment and give hotel developers unbridled freedom to build hotels and ignore the historical integrity of the neighbourhood (*City Business*, 23 October 2000, 11 December 2000).

[. . .]

CONCLUSION

In this paper, I have examined the case of tourism gentrification in New Orleans' Vieux Carre. To date, most research on gentrification has focused on issues of spatial differentiation, class transformation of urban neighbourhoods and the displacement of former residents by an incoming gentry. By contrast, tourism gentrification is commercial as well as residential and reflects new institutional connections between the local institutions, the real estate industry and the global economy.

Thus, the phenomenon of tourism gentrification presents a challenge to traditional explanations of gentrification that assume demand-side or production-side factors drive the process. Gentrification is not an outcome of group preferences nor a reflection of market laws of supply and demand. One particular myth is the claim that consumer desires are forces to which capital merely reacts. Consumer taste for gentrified spaces is, instead, created and marketed, and depends on the alternatives offered by powerful capitalists who are primarily interested in producing the built environment from which they can extract the highest profit. As I have shown, the transformation of the Vieux Carre into an entertainment destination enhances the significance of consumption-oriented activities in residential space and encourages gentrification. On the one hand, entertainment and tourism have brought a more upscale and affluent population to the neighbourhood, have increased property values for home-owners, and have attracted national retail chains. On the other hand, entertainment and tourism have priced out working-class residents and have eroded the bohemian character of the Vieux Carre. Finally, the growth of corporate tourism and the increasing penetration of global entertainment firms bespeak a shift in property ownership away from many small groups and individuals towards a more transnational corporate influence in the Vieux Carre. The pretentious and widely promulgated claim that the 'creative class' and 'cultural intermediaries' drive gentrification elides the complex and multidimensional effects of global-level socioeconomic transformations and the powerful role corporate capital plays in the organisation and development of gentrified spaces.

For New Orleans and other US cities, major socioeconomic changes over the past few decades have created a new competitive environment in which cities are increasingly forced to develop new tools and subsidies to attract new investment and, more important, market themselves as tourist destinations. In this new context, more residential and commercial spaces become centres of spectacle and tourist consumption rather than places of material production, a development noted by Lloyd and Clark (2001) in their discussion of the "city as an entertainment machine". Thus, in many urban neighbourhoods there has been a proliferation of varied but similarly themed tourist enclaves including historical districts, cultural districts, redevelopment zones and entertainment destinations (Bures, 2001; Gottdiener, 1997, 2000; Reichl, 1997, 1999; Zukin, 1997). What is important is that local or even national real estate markets cannot generate the huge amounts of capital needed to finance urban revitalisation drives and forms of tourism development. The growth of securitisation in the 1980s and 1990s and the development of new sources of real estate financing have drawn large institutional investors into financing urban entertainment destinations and private residential development. As a result, gentrification and tourism are largely driven by mega-sized financial firms and entertainment corporations who have formed new institutional connections with traditional city boosters (chambers of commerce, city governments, service industries) to market cities and their neighbourhoods. As local elites use tourism as a strategy of economic revitalisation, tourism services and facilities are incorporated into redevelopment zones and gentrifying areas. In this new urban landscape, gentrification and tourism amalgamate with other consumption-oriented activities such as shopping, restaurants, cultural facilities and entertainment venues. That blurring of entertainment, commercial activity and residential space leads to an altered relationship between culture and economics in the production and consumption of urban space.

Finally, this paper is an attempt to widen tourism analysis and move the study of tourism beyond a narrow concern with flows, impacts and forms. It is also an attempt to understand the broader social forces that affect gentrification and to shed light on critical issues such as urban restructuring and socio-cultural change in cities. Thus, according to Smith and DeFilippis (1999, p. 651), "the frontier of gentrification is more than ever co-ordinated with the frontiers of global capital investment" making the newest wave of gentrification in cities "one part of a larger spatial restructuring of urban areas associated with the transformations of production, social reproduction and finance". Following this line of thinking, I believe that tourism analysis can shed light on the causes and consequences of gentrification better than existing accounts that focus on identifying the population and demographic variables responsible for residential and commercial change in cities. Hackworth (2002) has noted that direct displacement no longer seems to have as much meaning in the context of new forms of state action, corporate-led gentrification and larger political-economic shifts. Tourism is about consumption-led growth and the increasing importance of the production of cultural goods, heritage images and other simulacra. Also, tourism development is a dynamic process involving social interactions, relations and conflicts that are global in scale and highly complex in character. As contemporary cities increasingly turn to tourism as a means of economic development, and as gentrification expands in many cities, we need more critical accounts of the nexus of tourism and gentrification. Indeed, tourism studies can contribute much to on-going debates of urban ethnic transformation, globalisation and gentrification. The investigation of the Vieux Carre as a contested landscape takes up this challenge of broadening tourism analyses and in doing so contributes to a more critical urban sociology of gentrification.

NOTES

1. In the past decade or so, tourism has emerged as the dominant sector within the contemporary service economy in the US and around the world. According to US Tourism Industries, tourism's export contributions grew by nearly 250 per cent between 1986 and 1996, from $26 billion to $90 billion (http://tinet.ita.doc.gov/). Despite the recent economic slowdown and September 11, tourism is a $600 billion industry, representing a more than 5 per cent of the nation's GDP and employing over 17 million people. Tourism is also a major services export, producing a $14 billion positive balance of trade in 2000 (US House of Representatives, 2002; for overviews, see Hoffman *et al.*, 2003; Fainstein and Judd, 1999).

2. I employ both primary and secondary data to develop my arguments. The secondary data come from documents and planning reports issued by the New Orleans Metropolitan Convention and Visitors Bureau (NOMCVB) and the New Orleans City Planning Commission, among other agencies. Furthermore, I consulted the New Orleans *Times-Picayune* newspaper annual index, 1972–present, for references to newspaper articles on the Vieux Carre, tourism in New Orleans and other information on the local real estate industry and the role of business élites in redevelopment efforts. I also performed a Lexis–Nexis search of the *Times-Picayune* newspaper for information on the Vieux Carre in the 1990s. The primary data come from 7 years of participant observation (as a resident of New Orleans) and in-depth semi-structured interviews with 36 local residents who have had first-hand knowledge and experience with the socio-spatial transformation of the Vieux Carre. I gathered these interviews through a snowball sample. To protect the confidentiality of interviewees, I use pseudonyms for non-public persons quoted in the paper.

3. Figures come from the New Orleans Metropolitan Convention and Visitors Bureau (NOMCVB) (www.neworleanscvb.com/new_site/visitor/researchfacts.cfm).

4. Source: US Census Bureau, Census 2000 Full-Count Characteristics (SFI). Compilation by the Greater New Orleans Community Data Center (www.gnocdc.org).

REFERENCES

Atkinson, R. (2003) Introduction: misunderstood saviour or vengeful wrecker: the many meanings and problems of gentrification, *Urban Studies*, 40(12), pp. 2343–2350.

Baudrillard, J. (1983) *Simulations*. New York, NY: Semiotext (e).

Baumbach, R. O. and Borah, W. (1981) *The Second Battle of New Orleans: A History of the Vieux Carre Riverfront Expressway Controversy*. Alabama: University of Alabama Press.

Berry, B. J. L. (1985) Islands of renewal in seas of decay, in: P.E. Peterson (Ed.) *The New Urban Reality*, pp. 69–96. Washington, DC: Brookings Institution.

Berry, B. (1999) Comment on E. K. Wyly and D. J. Hammels 'Islands of decay in seas of renewal: housing policy and the resurgence of gentrification—gentrification resurgent?, *Housing Policy Debate*, 10(4), pp. 783–788.

Betancur, J. J. (2002) The politics of gentrification: the case of West Town in Chicago, *Urban Affairs Review*, 37(6), pp. 780–814.

Bondi, L. (1999) Between the woof and the weft: response to Loretta Lees, *Environment and Planning D*, 17, pp. 253–255.

Brenner, N. and Theodore, N. (Eds) (2002) *Spaces of Neoliberalism: Urban Restructuring in North America and Western Europe*. New York: Blackwell.

Brooks, J. S. and Young, A. H. (1993) Revitalizing the central business district in the face of decline, the case of New Orleans, 1973–1993, *Town Planning Review*, 64(3), pp. 251–271.

Bures, R. (2001) Historic preservation, gentrification, and tourism: the transformation of Charleston, South Carolina, in: K. F. Gotham (Ed.) *Critical Perspectives on Urban Redevelopment*, pp. 195–210. New York: Elsevier Press.

Carpenter, J. and Lees, L. (1995) Gentrification in New York, London, and Paris: an international comparison, *International Journal of Urban and Regional Research*, 19(2), pp. 286–303.

Chang, T. C. (2000a) Renaissance revisited: Singapore as a 'Global City for the Arts', *International Journal of Urban and Regional Research*, 24(4), pp. 818–831.

Chang, T. C. (2000b) Singapore's Little India: a tourist attraction as a contested landscape, *Urban Studies*, 37(2), pp. 343–366.

Chang, T. C. Milne, S., Fallon, D. and Pohlman, C. (1996) Urban heritage tourism: the global-local nexus, *Annals of Tourism Research*, 23(2), pp. 284–305.

Chatteron, P. and Hollands, R. (2002) Theorizing urban playscapes: producing, regulating, and consuming youthful nightime spaces, *Urban Studies*, 39(1), pp. 95–116.

Chatterton, P. and Hollands, R. (2003) *Urban Nightscapes: Youth Cultures, Pleasure Spaces, and Corporate Power*. London: Routledge.

City Business (2000) Condo growth irks residents, 12 June.

City Business (2000) Residents, developers trade barbs over hotel, 23 October, 21(17), p. 8.

City Business (2000) Quarter residents to fight hotel, 11 December, 21(24), p. 13.

City of New Orleans (2000) *Master Plan Issues Paper*, December. New Orleans, LA: City of New Orleans.

Clay, P (1979) *Neighborhood Revival: Middle Class Resettlement and Incumbent Upgrading in American Neighborhoods*. Massachusetts: Lexington Books.

Coleman, S. and Crang, M. (Eds) (2002) *Tourism: Between Place and Performance*. London: Berghahn Books.

Dymski, G. A. (1999) *The Bank Merger Wave: The Economic Causes and Social Consequences of Financial Consolidation*. Armonk, NY: M. E. Sharp.

Eggler, B. (2004) Quarter hotel conversion gets panel OK; plan needs waiver of 35-year ban, *New Orleans Times–Picayune*, 11 August.

Fainstein, S. S. and Judd, D. R. (1999) Global forces, local strategies, and urban tourism, in: D. R. Judd and S. S. Fainstein (Eds) *The Tourist City*, pp. 1–20. New Haven, CT: Yale University Press.

Feagin, J. R. and Parker, R. (1990) *Building American Cities: The Urban Real Estate Game*, 2nd edn. Englewood Cliffs, NJ: Prentice Hall.

Foley, J. (1999) *Neighborhood Movements, Identity, and Change: in New Orleans's French Quarter*. Ph.D. Dissertation, College of Urban and Public Affairs, University of New Orleans, New Orleans, LA.

Foley, J. and Lauria, M. (2000) Plans, planning, and tragic choices, *Planning Theory and Practice*, 1(2), pp. 219–233.

Foley, J. and Lauria, M. (2003) Historic preservation in New Orleans' French Quarter: unresolved racial tensions, in: H. Thomas and F. L Piccolo (Eds) *Knights and Castles: Minorities and Urban Regeneration*, pp. 67–89. Burlington, CT: Ashgate Publishing Company.

Gaffikin, F. and Warf, B. (1993) Urban policy and the post-Keynesian state in the United Kingdom and the United States, *International Journal of Urban and Regional Research*, 17(1), pp. 67–84.

Gotham, K. F. (2000) Growth machine up-links: urban renewal and the rise and fall of a pro-growth coalition in a U.S. City, *Critical Sociology*, 26(3), pp. 268–300.

Gotham, K. F. (2001a) A city without slums: urban renewal, public housing, and downtown revitalization in Kansas City, Missouri, *American Journal of Economics and Sociology*, 60(1), pp. 285–316.

Gotham, K. (Ed.) (2001b) *Critical Perspectives on Urban Redevelopment*. New York: Elsevier Press.

Gottdiener, M. (1997) *Theming of America: Dreams, Visions, and Commercial Spaces*. Boulder, CO: Westview Press.

Gottdiener, M. (2000) The consumption of space and the spaces of consumption, in: M. Gottdiener (Ed.) *New Forms of Consumption: Consumers, Culture, and Commodification*, pp. 265–284. Lanham, MD: Rowman and Littlefield Publishers, Inc.

Hackworth, J. (2002) Postrecession gentrification in New York City, *Urban Affairs Review*, 37(6), pp. 815–843.

Hannigan, J. (1998) *Fantasy City: Pleasure and Profit in the Postmodern Metropolis*. New York: Routledge.

Hirsch, A. R. (1983) New Orleans: sunbelt in the swamp, in: R. M. Bernard and B. R. Rice (Eds) *Sunbelt Cities: Politics and Growth Since World War II*, pp. 100–137. Austin, TX: University of Texas Press.

Hoffman, L. K., Fainstein, S. S. and Judd, D. R. (Eds) (2003) *Cities and Visitors: Regulating People, Markets, and City Space*. New York: Blackwell Publishing.

Hollands, R. and Chatterton, P. (2003) Producing night-life in the new urban entertainment economy: corporatization, branding, and market segmentation, *International Journal of Urban and Regional Research*, 27(2), pp. 361–385.

Hutichson, R. (1992) Gentrification and the transformation of urban space, R. Hutchison (Ed.) *Gentrification and Urban Change*, pp. 1–14. New York; JAI Press.

Kasarda, J. D. (1999) Comment on E. K. Wyly and D. J. Hammel's 'Islands of decay in seas of renewal: housing policy and the resurgence of gentrification', *Housing Policy Debate*, 10(4), pp. 773–781.

Kaufman, R. (1999) *The social impacts of condominium conversion in the Vieux Carre neighborhood*. MS thesis, University of New Orleans.

Knopp, L. (1990a) Exploiting the rent gap: the theoretical significance of using illegal appraisal schemes to encourage gentrification in New Orleans, *Urban Geography*, 11(1), pp. 48–64.

Knopp, L. (1990b) Some theoretical implications of gay involvement in an urban land market, *Political Geography Quarterly*, 9(4), pp. 337–352.

Lauria, M. (1984) The implications of Marxian rent theory for community-controlled redevelopment strategies, *Journal of Planning Education and Research*, 4, pp. 16–24.

Lauria, M. and Baxter, V. (1999) Residential mortgage foreclosure and racial transition in New Orleans, *Urban Affairs Review*, 34(6), pp. 757–786.

Lauria, M., Whelan, R. K. and Young, A. H. (1995) Revitalization of New Orleans in: F. W. Wagner, T. E. Joder and A. J. Mumphrey, Jr. (Eds) *Urban Revitalization: Policies and Programs*, pp. 102–127. Thousand Oaks, CA: Sage Publications.

Lees, L. (2000) A re-appraisal of gentrification: towards a geography of gentrification, *Progress in Human Geography*, 24, pp. 389–408.

Lees, L. (2003) Super-gentrification: the case of Brooklyn Heights, New York City, *Urban Studies*, 40(12), pp. 2487–2509.

Lewis, T. (1997) *Divided Highways: Building the Interstate Highways, Transforming American Life*. New York: Viking Press.

Ley, D. (1996) *The New Middle Class and the Remaking of the Central City*. Oxford: Oxford University Press.

Ley, D. (2003) Artists, aestheticization, and the field of gentrification, *Urban Studies*, 40(12), pp. 2527–2544.

Lloyd, R. and Clark, T. N. (2001) The city as an entertainment machine, in: K. F. Gotham (Ed.) *Critical Perspectives on Urban Redevelopment*, pp. 357–378. New York: Elsevier Press.

Logan, J. (1993) Cycles and trends in the globalization of real estate, in: P. L. Knox (Ed.) *The Restless Urban Landscape*, pp. 33–54. Englewood Cliffs, NJ: Prentice Hall.

Marcuse, P. (1999) Comment on Elvin K. Wyly and D. J. Hammel's 'Islands of decay in seas of renewal: housing policy and the resurgence of gentrification', *Housing Policy Debate*, 10(4), pp. 789–797.

Marks Lewis Torre and Associates (1977) *Report on the existing conditions on Bourbon Street*. Marks Lewis Torre and Associates, New Orleans, LA.

Meethan, K. (2001) *Tourism in Global Society: Place, Culture, and Consumption*. New York, NY: Palgrave.

Nevarez, L. (2002) *New Money, Nice Town: How Capital Works in the New Urban Economy*. London: Routledge.

New Orleans Times–Picayune (2001) Most of the city's workers fall into service jobs; Orleans poverty rate among the worst in the U.S., 20 November, p. 1.

New Orleans Times–Picayune (2002) The new Bourbon kings, 10 February, p. F-1.

Reeves, S. K. (2000) Making groceries: public markets and corner stores in old New Orleans, *Gulf South Historical Review*, 16(10), pp. 20–47.

Reichl, A. (1997) Historic preservation and progrowth politics in U.S. cities, *Urban Affairs Review*, 32(4), pp. 513–535.

Reichl, A. (1999) *Reconstructing Times Square: Politics and Culture in Urban Development*. Lawrence, KS: University Press of Kansas.

Sassen, S. (2001) *Global Cities: New York, London, Tokyo*, 2nd edn. Princeton, NJ: Princeton University Press.

Smith, N. (1996) *The New Urban Frontier: Gentrification and the Revanchist City*. New York: Routledge.

Smith, N. (2002) New globalism, new urbanism: gentrification as global urban strategy, in: N. Brenner and N. Theodore (Eds) *Spaces of Neoliberalism: Urban Restructuring in North America and Western Europe*, pp. 80–103. Oxford: Blackwell.

Smith, N. and Defilippis, J. (1999) The reassertion of economics: 1990s gentrification in the Lower East Side, *International Journal of Urban and Regional Research*, 23(4), pp. 638–653.

Smith, M. P. and Keller, M. (1986) 'Managed growth' and the politics of uneven development in New Orleans, in: S. Fainstein et al. (Eds) *Restructuring the City: The Political Economy of Urban Redevelopment*, pp. 126–166. New York: Longman.

Squires, G. D. (1989) Public-partnerships: who gets what and why, in: G. Squires (Ed.) *Unequal Partnerships: The Political Economy of Urban Redevelopment in Postwar America*, pp. 1–11. New Brunswick, NJ: Rutgers University Press.

Teo, P. and Yeoh, B. (1996) Remaking local heritage for tourism, *Annals of Tourism Research*, 21(1), pp. 192–213.

Teo, P. and Lim, H. L. (2003) Global and local interactions in tourism, *Annals of Tourism Research*, 30(2), pp. 287–306.

University of New Orleans. College of Urban and Public Affairs (1992) *Changing Land Use in the Vieux Carre: Managing Growth to Preserve a National Landmark District*. New Orleans, LA: University of New Orleans.

Urry, J. (2002) *Tourist Gaze*, 2nd edn. London: Sage Publications.

Vesey, C. (1999) *Tourism impacts in the Vieux Carre: an analysis of cultural issues, residential perspectives, and sustainable tourism planning*. PhD thesis, University of New Orleans.

Weber, R. (2002) Extracting value from the city: neoliberalism and urban redevelopment, in: N. Brenner and N. Theodore (Eds) *Spaces of Neoliberalism: Urban Restructuring in North America and Western Europe*, pp. 172–193. Malden, MA: Blackwell.

Whelan, R. K. and Young, A. (1991) New Orleans: the ambivalent city, in: H. V. Savitch and J. C. Thomas (Eds) *Big City Politics in Transition*, pp. 132–148. Newbury Park, CA: Sage.

Wittberg, P. (1992) Perspectives on gentrification: a comparative review of the literature, in: R. Hutchinson (Ed.) *Gentrification and Urban Change*, pp. 17–46. New York: JAI Press.

Wyly, E. (2002) Mortgaged metropolis: evolving urban geographies of residential lending, *Urban Geography*, 23(1), pp. 1–29.

Wyly, E. and Hammel, D. J. (1998) Modeling the context and contingency of gentrification, *Journal of Urban Affairs*, 20(3), pp. 303–326.

Wyly, E. and Hammel, D. J. (1999) Islands of decay in seas of renewal: housing policy and the resurgence of gentrification, *Housing Policy Debate*, 10(4), pp. 711–771.

Wyly, E. and Hammel, D. J. (2000) Capital's metropolis: Chicago and the transformation of American housing policy, *Geografiska Annaler*, 82B, pp. 181–206.

Wyly, E. and Hammel, D. J. (2001) Gentrification, housing policy, and the new context of urban redevelopment, in: K. F. Gotham (Ed.) *Critical Perspectives on Urban Redevelopment*, pp. 211–275. New York: Elsevier Press.

Wyly, E. and Hammel, D. J. (2004) *Has mortgaged capital found an inner-city spatial fix.* (unpublished manuscript).

Zukin, S. (1991) *Landscapes of Power: From Detroit to Disneyworld*. Berkeley, CA: University of California Press.

Zukin, S. (1995) *The Cultures of Cities*. Cambridge, MA: Blackwell.

Zukin, S. (1997) Cultural strategies of economic development and the hegemony of vision, in: A. Merrifield and E. Swyngedouw (Eds) *Urbanization of Injustice*, pp. 233–242. New York: New York University Press.

APPENDIX

Table AI. Population and demographic trends for the French Quarter (census tracts 38, 42, 47 and total), 1940–2000

	1940	1950	1960	1970	1980	1990	2000
Census tract 38							
Total population	4 747	3 622	2 889	2 096	2 039	1685	1 726
White population (percentage)	80.6	92.2	92.2	97.7	96.1	95.9	91.9
Black population (percentage)	17.7	6.6	6.1	1.3	2.2	2.3	3.2
Other (percentage)	1.8	1.2	1.8	1.0	1.8	1.8	4.9
Median household income ($)	N/A	2 048	3 917	9 053	12 291	21 923	27 616
Median household income, 2000 ($)	N/A	13 474	20 947	37 721	25 713	28 884	27 616
Poverty status							
Families (number)	N/A	N/A	N/A	32	16	13	N/A
Families (percentage)	N/A	N/A	N/A	9.5	5.0	7.1	N/A
Individuals (number)	N/A	N/A	N/A	320	195	304	182
Individuals (percentage)	N/A	N/A	N/A	15.1	10.1	19.2	11.3
Median household value ($)	2 941	9 800	25 000	44 100	117 500	190 200	460 000
Median household value, 2000 ($)	N/A	64 474	133 690	183 750	245 816	250 593	460 000
Median rent ($)	10.22	29.46	63.00	106.00	228.00	368.00	549.00
Median rent, 2000 ($)	N/A	193.82	336.90	441.67	476.99	484.85	549.00
Total housing units	1 526	1 613	1 709	1 624	1 672	1 692	1 684
Owner-occupied	158	227	208	204	232	234	384
Renter-occupied	1 295	1 208	1 195	1 105	1 133	936	754
Number vacant	73	178	306	315	307	522	546
Percentage vacant	4.8	11.0	17.9	19.4	18.4	30.9	32.4
	1 940	1 950	1 960	1 970	1 980	1 990	2000
Census tract 42							
Total population	5 426	4 734	3 982	2 786	3 049	2 024	2 055
White population (percentage)	77.8	77.7	79.6	90.0	91.7	91.1	92.8
Black population (percentage)	21.1	20.7	18.8	8.3	6.8	6.2	4.1
Other (percentage)	1.0	1.5	1.7	1.7	1.4	2.7	3.1
Median household income ($)	N/A	1 703	4 305	8 196	10 147	23 603	31 903
Median household income, 2000 ($)	N/A	11 204	23 021	34 150	21 228	31 098	31 903
Poverty status							
Families (number)	N/A	N/A	N/A	16	42	47	N/A
Families (percentage)	N/A	N/A	N/A	3.8	10.3	23.0	N/A
Individuals (number)	N/A	N/A	N/A	464	433	382	186
Individuals (percentage)	N/A	N/A	N/A	16.7	14.5	19.3	9.0

	1940	1950	1960	1970	1980	1990	2000
Median household value ($)	3 766	10 000	12 100	37 100	100 000	203 600	353 800
Median household value, 2000 ($)	N/A	65 789	64 706	154 583	209 205	268 248	353 800
Median rent ($)	13.63	38.85	65.00	95.00	202.00	354.00	559.00
Median rent, 2000 ($)	N/A	255.59	347.59	395.83	422.59	466.40	559.00
Total housing units	2 206	2 236	2 790	2 336	2 763	2 512	2 519
Owner-occupied	160	214	191	174	212	211	311
Renter-occupied	1 790	1 780	2 126	1 654	1 865	1 176	1 191
Number vacant	256	242	473	508	686	1 125	1 017
Percentage vacant	11.6	10.8	16.9	22.7	24.8	44.8	40.4
Census tract 47							
Total population	880	1 174	798	375	508	282	395
White population (percentage)	78.0	73.8	67.7	94.9	87.8	91.1	86.8
Black population (percentage)	22.0	25.6	31.1	4.3	11.0	8.9	10.1
Other (percentage)	0.0	0.6	1.3	0.8	1.2	0.0	3.1
Median household income ($)	N/A	1 493	2 610	8 500	11 382	14 830	21 250
Medlan household income, 2000 ($)	N/A	9 822	13 957	35 417	23 812	19 539	21 250
Poverty status							
Families (number)	N/A	N/A	N/A	N/A	19	13	N/A
Families (percentage)	N/A	N/A	N/A	N/A	20.0	26.5	N/A
Individuals (number)	N/A	N/A	N/A	73	139	63	69
Individuals (percentage)	N/A	N/A	N/A	24.2	25.6	22.3	18.3
Median household value ($)	N/A	N/A	N/A	N/A	52	137 500	N/A
Median household value, 2000 ($)	N/A	N/A	N/A	N/A	109 833	181 159	N/A
Median rent ($)	N/A	39.40	38.00	114.00	346.00	395.00	514.00
Median rent, 2000 ($)	N/A	259.21	203.21	475.00	723.85	520.42	514.00
Total housing units	229	376	571	338	430	298	439
Owner-occupied	6	23	23	19	11	12	21
Renter-occupied	175	326	473	243	347	202	247
Number vacant	48	27	75	76	72	84	171
Percentage vacant	20.9	7.2	13.1	22.5	16.7	28.2	38.9
All census tracts							
Total population	11 053	9 530	7 669	5 257	5 596	3	4 176
White population (percentage)	79.0	82.7	83.1	93.4	93.0	93.1	91.9
Black population (percentage)	19.7	16.0	15.3	5.2	5.5	4.8	4.3
Other (percentage)	1.3	1.3	1.7	1.4	1.5	2.1	3.8
Median household income ($)	N/A	N/A	N/A	N/A	N/A	N/A	N/A

	1940	1950	1960	1970	1980	1990	2000
Poverty status							
Families (number)	N/A	N/A	N/A	N/A	77	73	N/A
Individuals (number)	N/A	N/A	N/A	857	767	749	437
Median household value ($)	N/A	N/A	N/A	N/A	N/A	N/A	N/A
Median rent ($)	N/A	N/A	N/A	N/A	N/A	N/A	N/A
Total housing units	3 961	4 225	5 070	4 298	4 865	4 502	4 642
Owner-occupied	324	464	422	397	455	457	716
Renter-occupied	3 260	3 314	3 794	3 002	3 345	2 314	2 192
Number vacant	377	447	854	899	1 065	1 731	1 734
Percentage vacant	9.5	10.6	16.8	20.9	21.9	38.4	37.4

Source: Census of Population and Housing (1940–2000)

PART III

*W*ho Are Gentrifiers and Why do They Engage in Gentrification?

Images of and narratives about gentrifiers are prolific. They can be found in newspaper profiles, such as a *New York Times* article about middle-aged, white restaurateurs opening a French bistro in Brooklyn's Ditmas Park (McNeil 2008). Another article features a thirty-something White woman—a screenwriter who sings in a band—who purchased a house in Los Angeles' Eagle Rock and hopes that a Whole Foods will move to her block (Timberg 2009).

Newspapers are not the only source of images and narratives about gentrifiers. An image dominant in media representations of gentrification is that of the gay male gentrifier, who seeks to restore or beautify property (Brown-Saracino 2009). For instance, in the midst of satirical commentary about gay marriage, Stephen Colbert, the host of the popular Comedy Central program *The Colbert Report*, warned that "the same sex chickens have come home to gentrify their roost" (5/16/09). Likewise, in 2005 the NBC sitcom *Will and Grace* included an episode in which a white, gay attorney purchases a weekend home in an as-yet-ungentrified-village. Locals celebrate the prospect, believing that his presence will ensure property value increases.

These images are not limited to television comedies; they reflect and inform experiences of gentrification (Brown-Saracino 2009). For instance, when I was studying a gentrifying small town in Maine, a group of longtime residents assured me that despite their discomfort with homosexuality they welcomed gay gentrifiers. Referencing one gay couple's elaborate Christmas decorations, they explained that they believed that such men would ensure the town's aesthetic appeal by restoring farmhouses and artfully landscaping grounds.

Embedded in such representations and anecdotes are a number of assumptions worthy of our attention. Most obviously, they paint a portrait of the gentrifier as a person who possesses certain demographic traits. In the first two cases, the gentrifier is depicted as white and creative; as a chef, writer, musician, or some combination of the above. In the next two cases, the gentrifier is presumed to be gay, male, white, highly educated, and affluent. In other instances alternate demographic traits are emphasized. For instance, HBO's *Sex and the City* portrays a white, heterosexual couple—an attorney and a pub owner—who, after the birth of their son, move from Manhattan to Brooklyn and purchase a fixer-upper. Thus, our collective imagination contains more than one image of the gentrifier, but most such images emphasize gentrifiers' affluence, education, and white privilege. When a friend photographed a London billboard that read "Gentrify This!!!" it was easy enough to imagine the artist's intended audience, and for most viewers Stephen Colbert's joke did not require explanation.

Second, such images presume that gentrifiers share a set of cultural orientations and motivations for engaging in gentrification. Note that three of the above examples emphasize gentrifiers' interest in historic preservation or home restoration, attention to property aesthetics, and desire to save or uplift their new place of residence. Most also pay homage to their cultural credentials, such as membership in a band, culinary skills, or sophisticated design tastes. These images suggest that gentrifiers have the ability to recognize the potential of downtrodden places and properties and to direct their transformation.

According to the gentrification literature, the above images are not altogether inaccurate. In fact, some gentrification scholarship, especially work published in the late 1970s and 1980s (e.g., Gale 1979), offers descriptions of gentrifiers that are not wildly divergent from these media representations (with the one important exception that most scholars concur that gay men compose only a minority of gentrifiers). Most scholars agree that gentrifiers tend to be highly educated and residentially mobile, that many are white, and that an ideological justification tends to accompany their movement into previously economically depressed central city neighborhoods (e.g., Smith 1986, Zukin 1987, Spain 1993). Urban and environmental planning scholar Daphne Spain terms this gentrifiers' "frontier and salvation ideology" (1993): gentrifiers' belief that they can move into a downtrodden neighborhood and reinvent or restore it.

However, as with other facets of gentrification, there is debate about precisely who gentrifiers are, as well as about why they engage in gentrification and about the character of their relationship to gentrifying places and the longtime residents who reside there. For instance, is a white, twenty-something undergraduate who supports himself with student loans and a part-time job a "gentrifier" if he rents an apartment in a neighborhood whose residents are predominately Latino and working class? Is he a "gentrifier" if he is deeply self-conscious about his influence on Latino neighbors and avoids patronizing new businesses that seek to attract other young, white "hipsters"? What of a middle-aged software developer who purchases a multi-million dollar home in a neighborhood that has been steadily gentrifying for a decade and that is home to few of the poor and working class individuals who once lived there (see Lees 2003)?

Most gentrification scholars devote at least some attention to such questions, for gentrifiers are quite central to the gentrification process. While, as we have seen, scholars disagree about whether gentrifiers *drive* or *respond to* conditions that enable gentrification, with the exception of those who regard gentrification as driven by commerce or corporations (e.g., Gotham 2005), nearly all agree that gentrifiers are an essential component of gentrification. For this reason a variety of scholars examine the set of questions this section explores. Namely, who are these people (or we, as for some readers the case may be)? Why do they participate in gentrification? What is their relationship to their new place of residence?[1] Embedded in these questions is a set of concerns about the significance and consequences of demographic and ideological differences among gentrifiers, as well as a desire, on the part of most scholars, to offer a precise definition of the gentrifier. The paragraphs below outline each of these questions, as well as the concerns that underline them, and provide a preliminary roadmap of how this section's readings approach and answer them.

Who are gentrifiers? This question has three elements. First, it seeks to map the demographic characteristics of those whom scholars identify as gentrifiers. Second, it asks how we should define the "gentrifier." Third, it calls us to consider how gentrifiers' traits shape their relationship to their place of residence, as well as to gentrification.

Early scholarship emphasized how gentrifiers' demographic traits facilitated their participation in gentrification, which, in the case of home buyers, often entailed willingness to accept financial risk, an ability to invest time and labor in property renovation, and flexibility to reside in places where local amenities and services, such as public schools, are not geared to the middle class (Rose 1984, Berry 1985, Smith 1986, Zukin 1987, Spain 1993). As a result, the prototypical gentrifier is not only imagined to be white and highly educated, but also to work in the central city and to be a part of a childless, dual-income couple (Rose 1984: 62).

However, many of the readings in this section challenge a monolithic view of the gentrifier as a white professional who is affluent and childless. While many gentrifiers fit this bill and such individuals may even compose the bulk of gentrifiers, the readings call us to recognize the participation of other actors, such as African-American professionals (Taylor 2002), single mothers (Rose 1984), and bohemian artists (Lloyd 2005).

What is the importance and consequence of acknowledging the variety of actors who engage in gentrification? Many of those who push for acknowledgement of gentrifiers' diversity do so, in part, because they wish to encourage consideration of how a gentrifier's personal traits shape his or her relationship to gentrification. Specifically, they debate about the precise role different types of gentrifiers play in the gentrification process (see Caulfield 1994, Butler & Robson 2004) and seek to understand the extent to which gentrifiers are "trapped" by their demographic traits. At least implicitly, they seek to determine the extent to which gentrifiers' intentions matter. For instance, are artists, who are often displaced from their rentals as gentrification progresses (Lloyd 2005), perpetrators or victims of gentrification? Does their economic insecurity encourage empathy for longtime residents (ibid.)?

Thus, scholars debate about who gentrifiers are, how to define the term "gentrifier," as well as about how gentrifers' traits shape their relationship to gentrification. In her selection, Damaris Rose rejects the notion that there is a single answer to these questions. She writes, "the terms 'gentrification' and 'gentrifiers,' as commonly used in the literature, are 'chaotic conceptions' which obscure the fact that a multiplicity of processes, rather than a single causal process, produce changes in the occupation of inner-city neighborhoods from lower to higher income residents" (1984: 62). My own research suggests that gentrifiers vary greatly in their attitudes toward gentrification and longtime residents, as well as in their practices, but that this variation cannot be neatly attributed to demographic differences. In contrast, others call for a retreat from this "chaos," urging gentrification scholars to reach agreement about how to identify and define the gentrifier and, in turn, gentrification (e.g., Zukin 1987, Slater 2006).

Why do gentrifiers engage in gentrification? Scholars debate about the possible motivations for gentrifiers' engagement in gentrification. Some point to gentrification's economic benefits, including the affordability of housing in gentrifying areas and the profit gentrifiers may earn from purchasing in revitalizing areas (Smith 1979, Gale 1980, McDonald 1983, Beauregard 1986, Butler 1997). Others argue that central city amenities, such as proximity to work opportunities and cultural amenities, attract gentrifiers (Butler 1997, see also discussion in Zukin 1987). Still others suggest that cultural tastes, such as appreciation for historic homes or urban diversity, draw gentrifiers (e.g., Allen 1980, Zukin 1987, Berrey 2005, Lloyd 2005).

Sharon Zukin's pioneering work, *Loft Living*, a portion of which you will find in this section, complicates the prevailing assumption that gentrifiers' motivations are primarily economic. Zukin accomplishes this by outlining the influence of aesthetic values and the lifestyle attributes of a particular group of middle class urban dwellers on the gentrification process. For instance, she writes that "loft living is part of a larger modern quest for authenticity" (1982: 67) that encourages appreciation for "the size of a house, the layout of the rooms, the passage from one room to another, indicating not only a sense of 'home' but also a sense of the self that is 'at home' there" (ibid.: 66). Without this taste for "authenticity" and a home that compliments a particular sense of self, Zukin argues that "the real estate market in living lofts that has developed over the past ten years could not have begun" (ibid.: 58). Thus, she suggests that it is not enough to say that either individual gentrifiers' or real estate developers' desire for profit drove the loft movement that her book examines.

Tim Butler's London research (1997) finds that some London gentrifiers, like Zukin's New York loft dwellers, move to gentrifying neighborhoods out of a desire to live in a particular type of home. However, Butler argues that this is not the only impetus for gentrifiers' relocation. His essay in this section suggests that some gentrifiers cite a desire to minimize their commute, others suggest that they sought affordable housing or hoped to earn profit by purchasing in a gentrifying neighborhood, while still others express appreciation for a sense of "diversity" that they associate with the central city.

Selections by Richard Lloyd, Monique Taylor and Michael Sibalis argue that gentrifiers engage in gentrification because they wish to reside alongside those who share their traits; to be a part of a community composed of like-minded gentrifiers. For instance, Richard Lloyd captures the desire of artist-gentrifiers, whom he terms "neo-bohemians," of Chicago's Wicker Park to reside alongside other artists and Michael Sibalis demonstrates how Parisian gay men sought to construct a safe haven by investing in the Marais.

A selection from my article, "Social Preservationists and the Search for Authenticity," suggests that, ironically, a subset of gentrifiers whom I identify as "social preservationists" engage in gentrification because they wish to live alongside longtime residents with whom they associate "authentic" community. While at the time that I wrote the article I argued that social preservationists' ideology and practices were so distinct from those of other gentrifiers that they belonged to a separate category, in later work I proposed that the social preservationist is one type of gentrifier (Brown-Saracino 2007, 2009). Building on Damaris Rose, I argue that gentrifiers' motivations for engaging in gentrification, relationship to their neighborhood or town, and daily practices are diverse. Social preservation, I now believe, is one way of "doing" gentrification.

What is the character of gentrifiers' relationships to their neighborhood or town? Threaded throughout the first two questions are concerns about gentrifiers' relationships to their neighborhood or town and how it varies by person and place. Authors debate about the character of gentrifiers' relationships to their place of residence. Some characterize it as uniformly antagonistic (e.g., Smith 1996), while others suggest that sometimes it is quite the opposite (e.g., Caulfield 1994, Butler & Robson 2003, Brown-Saracino 2004, 2007, 2009). Furthermore, those who suggest that gentrifiers vary in their relationship to their neighborhood or town debate about the characteristics of person or place that encourage this variation: that drive one gentrifier's interest in historic preservation and another's enthusiasm for new-build construction.

What are some of the orientations authors identify among gentrifiers? Most apparent in this section's readings is some gentrifers' attachment to local history (Zukin 1982, 1987,

Butler 1997). This is most evident in historic preservation efforts—which range from the restoration of individual homes to efforts to construct historic districts. Some regard this as part and parcel of gentrifiers' effort to "save" their place of residence by returning it to its heyday (Spain 1993). For others, appreciation for a place's past is rooted in taste for a particular architectural style (Zukin 1982, 1987, Butler 1997) or romanticization of a specific dimension of a place's social past or present (Brown-Saracino 2009).

Other readings identify gentrifiers' appreciation for diversity or "social mix" (Butler 1997, Lloyd 2005; see also Berrey 2005). These individuals celebrate an "authenticity" that they associate with places that possess a diverse array of residents—from poor and working class long-timers to more affluent newcomers.

In contrast, others wish to live alongside those who share their social traits. This is true of many of the African-American gentrifiers Monique Taylor interviewed who, after facing years of discrimination in predominately white environs, moved to Harlem to live alongside others who share their racial identity (2002).

Departing from this trend, just over half of the eighty gentrifiers I interviewed for my book, *A Neighborhood That Never Changes*, suggest that their participation in gentrification was motivated by a desire to reside alongside those *unlike* them. Specifically, they sought to live in a neighborhood or town populated by certain longtime residents with whom they associate "authentic" community, such as Portuguese fishermen or Vietnamese merchants (2009).

What explains gentrifiers' distinct orientations? While some scholars debate about whether such diversity exists, many others offer competing explanations for its sources. For instance, many suggest that orientations to gentrification are class-based (Rose 1984, Lloyd 2005): that less affluent gentrifiers have more concern for longtime residents. A related argument suggests that a gentrifier's orientation emerges from the wave of gentrification of which he or she is a part. For instance, Richard Lloyd documents the displacement of the first wave of Wicker Park's gentrifiers, suggesting that it encouraged some to protest the filming of MTV's *The Real World* in the neighborhood (2005: 119; see Clay 1979 on gentrification's stages).

Other traits, such as sexual identity, may also influence one's relationship to gentrification. For instance, Sibalis suggests that after years of seeking a safe place for communion in the city, many gay male gentrifiers of Paris' Marais neighborhood were relatively unselfconscious about their efforts to claim the space as their own (2004). Others counter that gentrifiers' orientations are a product of an interaction between their traits and the characteristics of their place of residence. For instance, Taylor argues that some African-American professionals' concern for preserving Harlem's historical character emerges out of a confluence of their own and the neighborhood's racial identity (2002).

Scholarly debates about whether gentrifiers' demographic traits—such as their class, race, occupation, and sexual identity—shape their orientations to gentrification underline a more pressing question about how to define the gentrifier; a question this section encourages the reader to tackle. Namely, which individuals should we deem "gentrifiers"? Should we identify gentrifiers by their shared economic position, demographic traits, orientation to longtime residents and other gentrifiers, or by their motivations for engaging in gentrification? Do we wish to place the aforementioned college student and software designer in the same category—as gentrifiers—and, if so, what does this suggest about how gentrification works?

DISCUSSION QUESTIONS

1. What is the significance, if any, of gentrifiers' motivations for engaging in gentrification?
2. What roles do gentrifiers play in the gentrification process? Is the gentrifier as central to gentrification as the readings in this section suggest?
3. If, as some of the readings suggest, gentrifiers are demographically and ideologically diverse, what influence might this diversity have on the gentrification process and its outcomes? For instance, what do the readings suggest about how gentrifiers' racial and class identities shape their orientation to gentrification? How might this vary by context?
4. Drawing on this section's readings, draft a definition of the gentrifier. Compare your definition with those of your classmates and consider the roots of the differences, if any, between your definitions.

ACTIVITIES

1. Select a gentrifying neighborhood to study. Interview three to five residents who vary in terms of their length of residence and/or economic position, racial or ethnic identity, or gender. Develop a short set of general questions about their response to the neighborhood's transformation. During the interview, listen carefully for talk of the "gentrifier." If your informants use the term, ask them what they mean by it and to offer a description of a "gentrifier." Determine whether their definitions and descriptions vary. If so, along what lines? What explains this variation? If there is little variation or your informants do not use the term, try to develop an explanation for why this is the case.
2. View the film *Quinceañera*, which is set in a gentrifying Los Angeles neighborhood. In what ways are gentrifiers portrayed? What factors might influence this portrayal?
3. Borrowing from the anecdotes that frame the first paragraphs of this section's introductory essay and the previous excercise, document representations of gentrifiers in newspapers, novels, television shows, movies, or in music. How do the sources you analyze describe and define gentrifiers? To what extent does the sympathy with which gentrifiers are portrayed vary with the economic, demographic, and cultural traits the sources describe them as possessing?
4. Read a first person account of an author's participation in gentrification, such as Kathleen Hirsch's *A Home in the Heart of the City* (1998) about her move to Jamaica Plain in Massachusetts. How does the author understand herself and her relationship to her neighborhood and to gentrification?

NOTE

1. See Lees et al. (2008: 90) for discussion of a similar set of questions.

RESOURCES

Allen, I. 1980. "The Ideology of Dense Neighborhood Redevelopment: Cultural Diversity and Transcendent Community Experience." *Urban Affairs Quarterly* Vol. 15: 409–428.
Anderson, E. 1990. *Streetwise: Race, Class, and Change in an Urban Community.* Chicago: University of Chicago Press.

Barry, J., & Derevlany, J. 1987. *Yuppies Invade My House at Dinnertime: A Tale of Brunch, Bombs, and Gentrification in an American City.* Big River Publishing.

Brown-Saracino, J. 2009. *A Neighborhood That Never Changes: Gentrification, Social Preservation and the Search for Authenticity.* Chicago: University of Chicago Press.

Butler, T., & Robson, G. 2003. *London Calling: The Middle Classes and the Re-making of Inner London.* Oxford: Berg.

Caulfield, J. 1994. *City Form and Everyday Life: Toronto's Gentrification and Critical Social Practice.* Toronto: University of Toronto Press.

Ley, David. 1996. *The New Middle Class and the Remaking of the Central City.* London: Oxford University Press.

Salamon, S. 2003. *Newcomers to Old Towns: Suburbanization of the Heartland.* Chicago: University of Chicago Press.

Spain, D. 1993. "Been-Heres versus Come-Heres: Negotiating Conflicting Community Identities." *Journal of the American Planning Association,* Vol. 59.

CHAPTER 14

The Creation of a "Loft Lifestyle"

Sharon Zukin

Until the 1970s, living in a loft was considered neither chic nor comfortable—if the possibility was considered at all. Making a home in a factory district clearly contradicted the dominant middle-class ideas of "home" and "factory," as well as the separate environments of family and work on which these ideas were based. Since the 1950s, suburbia had so dominated popular images of the American home that it was almost impossible to imagine how anyone could conceive the desire to move downtown into a former sweatshop or printing plant. Yet the real estate market in living lofts that has developed over the past ten years could not have begun without such a desire, at least on the part of a few people. The market could not have grown so fast—in the process, transforming lofts from old factory spaces into hot commodities—if this peculiar desire had not also struck the imagination of more people in cities all over the country. Whether they actually bedded down among the printing presses or merely accepted loft living as a possible residential style, people began to find the notion of living in a loft attractive. This happened because of two changes that occurred in the 1960s: a change in lofts and a change in middle-class patterns of consumption.

On the one hand, the movement of industry and investment out of old manufacturing centers made larger, more impressive lofts available for alternate uses. Until that point, lofts that had been used for living—mostly by artists who were "living poor"—were fairly small, often unheated upper floors of two- and three-story storefronts, and distinctly uncomfortable. On the other hand, an increasing number of middle-class people moved into certain cultural patterns, particularly an active appreciation of "the arts" and historic preservation, which had previously been upper-class domains. Their growing identification with fine arts production and fine old buildings led them first to try to protect space for artists and historic preservation and then to appropriate this space—which was often in loft buildings—for themselves. In this process, art and historic preservation took on a broader meaning. They became both more commercial and less elitist.

The changing appreciation of old loft buildings also reflects a deeper preoccupation with space and time. A sense that the great industrial age has ended creates melancholy over the machines and the factories of the past. Certainly such sentiments are aroused only at the end of an era, or with a loss of function. As a perceptive observer of "eccentric spaces" points out, "We visit the docks in London but not in Rotterdam because commerce is romantic only when it has vanished."[1] Only people who do not know the steam and sweat of a real factory can find industrial space romantic or interesting. But in many ways industrial spaces are more interesting than "post-industrial" offices, apartment houses, and shopping centers. Their structure has both a solidity and a gracefulness that suggest a time when form still identified "place" rather than "function." Their facades are often adorned with archaic emblems and sculpture, apparently showing the equally archaic skills of masons and carvers. Yet this ornamentation is a conceit of nineteenth-century technology. The facades of many loft buildings that were constructed between 1820 and 1880 were cast in standardized iron parts that could be ordered from a catalogue, mounted, and taken apart at will. Ironically, the mass production of an earlier industrial era looks to our eyes like individuality.

During the 1960s a consensus slowly grew that such buildings should not be torn down to make room for new, high-rise construction that bore little relation to the area or the people around it. Though far from the majority view, this line of thought spread from Jane Jacobs's somewhat subversive ideas about neighborhood preservation and urban vitality—which have sold more than a quarter-million copies of her 1961 book—to highly commercial renovations like San Francisco's Ghirardelli Square, Boston's Faneuil Hall, and the New York artists' district of SoHo. An appreciation of "small" and "old," instead of "large" and "new," also appealed to the sixties' liberal social conscience. In America's inner cities, the wholesale destruction of tenements for the sake of urban renewal during the fifties and early sixties gave rise to protest and backlash. Some people blamed the destabilization of low-rent ghetto communities, in part, for the riots of the mid- to late sixties. Several years before, sociologists had called attention to the good social

relations between people who live in such communities, in articles like "Some Sources of Satisfaction in a Residential Slum" and Herbert Gans's elegy on Boston's Italian West End, *The Urban Villagers.* Preserving rather than destroying city neighborhoods took on a broader meaning in the 1970s because of the growing concern with the earth's ecology. Even in the early sixties the impending or real demolition of distinguished old buildings—like Pennsylvania Station in New York City—threatened people with a sense of irreparable loss. Like the recycling of scarce resources, the adaptive re-use of such buildings eventually attracted greater public support.[2]

In this context, loft living is more significant than the relatively small number of SoHos or loft dwellers implies. It marks a different perception of space and time and a new relation between art and industry. In a narrower sense, the market in living lofts that developed after 1970 also sells the social and cultural values of the 1960s to middle-class consumers of the seventies and eighties. But are living lofts really such a radical departure from conventional housing? Although loft living seems to reject suburbia and all it represents, living lofts have some of the same spatial values as a typical suburban home, particularly a preference for lots of air, light, and open space. Certainly lofts are located on busy city streets rather than grassy plots, but inside, a loft has an air of detachment from the city.

This suggests that loft living is appealing, in part, because it is paradoxical. The incongruity of living in a factory does not cease to surprise us. From the outside, of course, a loft building looks like a factory, but inside, we find a home. Although homes are considered private space, the openness of a loft makes it a public space. Lofts are also predominantly homes for non-child-centered households—for single persons and couples without children. Yet the association between loft living and a home-oriented interest in stylish cuisine and décor promotes a new cult of domesticity. Because it represents both home and work, hedonism and domesticity, and public and private space, loft living is paradoxical. Its success in the urban housing market demonstrates that at this time paradox sells.

Discussing the lure of any market is a tricky matter. Consumers' desires are so shaped by the commodities that are available, as well as by image-making and status-seeking, that considering them may be almost irrelevant. The shrinking size of typical new apartments and the mass media's privileged treatment of loft living certainly influenced the market in living lofts. Yet it is a fact that this market did not exist in any significant measure before 1971. Since that time, "living lofts" has become a household word in cities of the United States and Western Europe, and loft living has been elevated to a fashionable residential style. To some degree, deciding to live in a loft may reflect a fairly narrow economic choice. Particularly for artists who want a large space at a cheap rent, renting a loft amid the flotsam and jetsam of urban commerce may be just a question of marginal utility. But many people choose to live in a loft because the space itself appeals to them. On the one hand, they like the giant scale or the "raw," unfinished quality of a loft. On the other hand, they identify with the sense of adventure or the artists' ambiance which still clings to living in a loft neighborhood. To determine why these people want to live in lofts involves more subtle issues than mere supply and demand. Not only have lofts changed over the past thirty years but so have cultural and aesthetic standards.

FROM "LIVING POOR" TO LUXURY

In 1953, New York artist Robert Rauschenberg returned from a trip to Europe and, practically penniless, looked for a place to live. "With his customary good luck," art writer Calvin Tompkins says, Rauschenberg "found a loft on Fulton Street, near the fish market, a big attic space with twenty-foot ceilings but no heat or running water; the rent was fifteen dollars a month, but he talked the landlord into letting him have it for ten. A hose and bucket in the back yard served as his basin, and he bathed at friends' apartments, sometimes surreptitiously, asking to use the bathroom and taking a lightning shower at the same time." Ten years later, when the Jewish Museum on Fifth Avenue organized the first major retrospective exhibition of his work, Rauschenberg was living and working in another loft farther uptown, on the edge of Greenwich Village. Tompkins reports that when he visited Rauschenberg there,

the doors of the freight elevator opened directly into Rauschenberg's loft. . . . Sam, the taciturn black superintendent who operated the lift during the day, had agreed to let Rauschenberg have the key after 6 P.M., so he could get up and down. . . . The loft was about a hundred feet long by thirty wide, A row of supporting columns ran down the middle, but otherwise it was clear, unobstructed space. Tall, grimy windows let in the distinctively white light of downtown New York—also the roar of trucks on Broadway. Near the windows was a big, ramshackle wire cage containing a pair of kinkajous. . . . Beyond the cage stood a group of large objects—a car door, a window frame, a roof ventilator mounted on wheels—components of an unfinished five-part sculpture. . . . Paintings, combines, and sculptures from the recently concluded Jewish Museum retrospective were stacked against the wall farther along. There was a big table in the middle of the room, its surface cluttered with magazines, pictures clipped from magazines, felt pens and pencils, and tubes of paint and other materials. Toward the back of the room, a counter projecting from the end wall formed an alcove for the refrigerator, the electric stove, and the bed—a mattress laid on the floor. All the rest of the loft was work space.[3]

In 1960, Rauschenberg's slightly younger contemporary, artist James Rosenquist, rented a studio for fifty dollars a month. It was not far from Rauschenberg's first loft on the Lower Manhattan waterfront, "in a beautiful area around Coenties Slip. It used to be [abstract painter] Agnes Martin's studio and it was all cracked plaster . . . no decoration . . . very stark." After inventing his new Pop Art style in that studio, Rosenquist was discovered by two art gallery owners. In 1963 he moved to a loft farther uptown, in the area that eventually became known as SoHo.[4]

During the same period, three prominent artists whose standard of living was very different from that of the unknown Rosenquist and the relatively unknown Rauschenberg invited eight hundred members of New York's art community to a social gathering that also "took place in a loft." But this 1961 party amazed art writer Dore Ashton because it was held in "a loft with parquet floors, spotless walls and a majestic colonnade running its length. . . . Pinkerton men were stationed at the door." For Ashton, this loft party symbolized a change from "the comfortable old group" of artists to "the new Artbusiness community." "It was a far cry," she says, "from the days of penniless bohemianism when the lean and hungry artists had themselves resembled thieves."[5]

By the end of the decade, when photographs and descriptions of artists' lofts began to reach a wider public of magazine readers, the journalists declared that loft living had panache. A 1970 article in *Life* magazine, "Living Big in a Loft," could easily inspire either envy or repugnance, and it is impossible to decide which *Life* intended when it wrote about the artists living in SoHo's loft buildings, "Behind these grubby facades lurks an artists' colony. . . . Sixteen-foot ceilings, 45-foot rooms, and community spirit." The large interior photographs show as much air, space, and light as any suburban home could claim. Although

the trapeze that one artist had installed in his loft, or the eight-by-twenty-four-foot painting on which another was working, exceeded the scale of most American houses, the Oriental rug, track lighting, polished wood floors, comfortable sofa and chairs, and bicycle in the background of the most prominent photograph looked reassuring. Indeed, upper-middle-class *Life* readers could probably identify with artists "Bill and Yvonne Tarr [who] still live in Scarsdale, but plan to join Bill's assortment of welded steel and bronze sculptures in the Tarrs' 90-foot-long studio later this year. The kitchen, bath and family rooms will be at ground level, with a living-dining-bedroom combination perched on the elevated platform halfway between the loft's ancient wooden floor and a curved skylight reaching to the 16-foot-high ceiling."[6]

Several months later, the glossy *New York* magazine—the first and most widely copied chronicle of urban "lifestyle"—also focused on SoHo's artists. Although they had come to an industrial area in search of cheap space, these artists evidently knew how to live—which mainly involved combining living and working. "They set up modern kitchens, living rooms, bedrooms and bathrooms along with their studios. When night came they did not go home like everyone else in SoHo, because they *were* home." Home for artist Gerhardt Liebmann, for example, is divided between a studio in the front half of his loft and a fifty-foot length of living space in back, with a rock garden, a skylight, and slate floors.[7]

Over the next few years, magazines praised the versatility and the creativity of loft design. In many lofts, the integration of work space, living areas and art objects was paralleled by a fluid adaptation to structural features (primarily light, floor, and volume) and "incidental" arrangements. Photographed in the professional journal *Progressive Architecture,* for example, "the loft of artist Lowell Nesbitt is divided by eight-foot-high partitions used to display his own work. Various living areas are defined by the semi-open hexagonal spaces created by the partitions, by groupings of plants, and by painted circles on the wooden flooring." Mixed uses and high ceilings continued to invite multilevel design. In a loft that was featured in the Sunday N*ew York Times Magazine* in 1974, architect Hanford Yang built a three-level living area to display his art collection. Artist Gerhardt Liebmann, whose loft had been photographed by *New York* magazine in 1970, turned up again in 1974 with one of "the great bathrooms of New York." By now he "has a flourishing greenhouse in the bathroom of his SoHo loft. 'The bathroom is an ideal place to raise plants if you have the light,'" he says. And SoHo, according to N*ew York* magazine, was now the ideal place to live if you wanted excitement.[8]

A 1976 N*ew York* magazine article on extravagant house plants—"Six City Jungle Habitats"—shows large trees growing in a designer's SoHo loft. Another article, on an architect's elegant 140-foot-long loft, lauds the design detail as "a short course in neo-classical art *trompe l,'oeil*" that evokes "an Italian palazzo." The design of a passage between the loft's columns, or "colonnade," is said to be "loosely derived from a Vicenza building facade by the sixteenth-century architect Andrea Palladio."[9]

By 1978, women's sportwear designer Adri Stecking (known professionally as Adri) was saying to a N*ew York Times* reporter, "I fell in love with SoHo and walked the pavements for months, but I couldn't find the loft I wanted." So she rented a loft—purely for living—near midtown, south of the Flower Market district. "Each floor contained about 4,000 square feet," says the *Times*; "'a quarter of an acre [*sic*]!'" says Adri. "There were big window's facing each point of the compass," and Adri's loft "was high enough to see the roof-tops of buildings on each side and New Jersey to the west, separated by a blue strip of Hudson River. The sun streamed in at all hours." But the focal point of Adri Stecking's spacious new home is even more remarkable. "It's an eight-foot square Jacuzzi whirlpool bath that accommodates ten people, is set into a white tile platform reached by eight steps, and is equipped with a cat board should any [*sic*] of the two resident felines fall into the pool." The *Times* devoted a full page to photos of Adri in her *Jacuzzi* and her kitchen, the floor plan of the loft, and an interview with Adri and her interior designer.[10]*

Although American living lofts generally convey a sense of modern elegance through a spareness of design that is enhanced by the opulence of larger-than-life decoration and industrial appliances, as another *Times* article, also in 1978, showed, the loft style was easily adaptable to an eclectic juxtaposition of seventeenth-century, Art Deco, and "High Tech" design. This time the loft was in Paris, but the language is familiar: "Once upon a time, thermos bottles were manufactured in the lofty space shown above. Then interior designer Andree Putnam moved in on it, connected it to her seventeenth-century Paris apartment and transformed it into elegant quarters for working and entertaining."[11]

By 1980, readers of the *Times* had become so familiar with living lofts that a home furnishings reporter considered a twenty-foot ceiling in the living room matter of factly, as one of several "common design problems." "'The scale was enormous and quite a problem,'" says the designer of a model loft-apartment in a converted factory. "The bare walls . . . were 'too high, too overpowering.'" The reporter recommends his solution as inexpensive and ingenious: "Using nine separate pieces of canvas, the designer created an enormous 12-foot-square hanging that is delineated with adhesive tape into two-foot-square grids. . . . The upper left square sports a black triangle. 'That's the same effect as the . . . window,' he noted, pointing to the skylight on the adjacent wall."[12] Indeed, the high ceilings, exposed brick walls, hanging plants, and open spaces of the loft style have become so well known that they inspire parody. An issue of the satirical *Not the New York Times* that was published during the 1978 New York City newspaper strike featured a bogus interview with Cary Grant and Andy Warhol, who had converted their Upper East side apartments to the "loft look."

With no intention of irony, the overstatement of real estate advertisements reveals what loft living now represents to a sophisticated, affluent public. Directed to "the discriminating buyer"—or at least to someone who can afford the $54,000 to $120,000 purchase price and a monthly maintenance charge between $300 and $600—an ad from the *New York Times* in May 1980 promises "THE ULTIMATE in Loft Living":

> Looking for the ultimate loft apartment? Our large duplexes give you everything that makes loft living so great . . . the expansiveness of OPEN SPACE . . . the spectacularly HIGH CEILINGS (up to 16 ft.) . . . the FREEDOM to create your own living environment . . . PLUS spectacular SKYLINE & RIVER VIEWS!
>
> We've added an elegance you wouldn't expect of the loft lifestyle . . . magnificent lobby, intercom . . . carpeted hallways . . . deluxe appointments & amenities . . . luxurious large new kitchen areas & stylish Oak stripped floors, etc.

An advertisement that was posted, placard style, on a Manhattan lamppost at about the same time plays to both a sense of style and a sense of history.

> These spectacular lofts are for artists, photographers, performing artists and urban pioneers with creative minds. At the corner of Prince Street in the SOHO HISTORIC DISTRICT.
> CO-OP LOFTS:
> — Magnificent gallery spaces
> — Only one loft per floor—5000 sq. ft. . . .
> — Fantastic gallery and performing arts spaces. . . .

Beneath a reproduced drawing of the building as it looked in 1860, the advertisement reads, "The finest business structure and most famous shop of its time . . . the first fireproof building in New York . . . constructed of white marble . . . specially inspected by the Prince of Wales on his visit to the United States. . . ."**

A third ad that ran in the *Times*, in March 1980, appeals to both luxury and practicality. It represents a real estate developer selling co-operative loft-apartments of approximately the same size but "in three neighborhoods, in three distinct price ranges." The first and least expensive loft-apartments are in a converted factory near but not in a gentrifying, brick townhouse neighborhood of Brooklyn. They provide "up to 1400 square feet of open space, enhanced by high ceilings, oversize windows, and beautiful parquet floors." The second option, in a converted office building in TriBeCa, promises "up to 1185 square feet, the space is open, and the feeling is larger than life. . . ." The third and most expensive offering, in a converted warehouse on the fringe of Greenwich Village, marks "the return of The Great New York Apartment. From 1370 to 2850 square feet of the most beautifully laid-out open space in the city. With breathtaking views, terraces, gardens, Manhattan's only glass-walled elevator, and impeccable workmanship." By this point and this price level, lofts have moved "uptown." There is little left to distinguish loft living from luxury housing.

Nevertheless, the advertisements imply that loft living still retains several distinctive characteristics: open space, a relation between art and industry, a sense of history, and a fascination of the middle-class imagination with the artist's studio.

SPACE AND SELF

A home, as French philosopher Gaston Bachelard says in *The Poetics of Space*, can mean many contradictory things to its inhabitants, It evokes an image of both stability and expansiveness, a primal "hut dream" that inspires calm rooms that seethe with inner turbulence. "The house even more than the landscape," Bachelard notes, "is a psychic state."[13] In different periods and different cultures, the size of a house, the layout of the rooms, the passage from one room to another, indicate not only a sense of "home" but also a sense of the self that is "at home" there. In sixteenth-century Europe, for example, people thought that self-expression was possible only in small rooms, yet by the eighteenth century, their descendants preferred large, airy rooms. In the late nineteenth century, tastes changed once again. Mid-Victorian homes were warrens of small, specialized rooms separated by walls, passageways, and closets that "associated each space with a function or activity that assumed cultural, indeed ceremonial meaning."[14]

Needless to say, tastes in housing, like all architectural styles, are constrained by available technology, materials, and costs. Tastes must also change over time. The sixteenth-century preference for small rooms indicates a withdrawal in spatial terms from the corporate identities and large gatherings of medieval society to what we think of as Renaissance individualism. The eighteenth-century room parallels a new conception of the public self, which demanded a more public space even in the privacy of the home. The late-nineteenth-century "specialization of space," as historian Burton Bledstein calls it, symbolizes a retreat into private space to protect the individual from undefined, and therefore dangerous, encounters. All these examples project a middle-class, or even an upper-middle-class, understanding of the relation between space, self, and society. Because the middle class generally neither inherits baronial ancestral halls nor can afford to reconstruct such palaces, the housing that

the middle class builds or buys necessarily reflects new ideas about space, and what it represents, in each time period. In that sense, loft living is part of a larger modern quest for authenticity. Old buildings and old neighborhoods are "authentic" in a way that new construction and new communities are not. They have an identity that comes from years of continuous use, and an individuality that creates a sense of "place" instead of "space." They are "New York" rather than "California," or "San Francisco" rather than "Los Angeles." Such places grow organically, not spasmodically. Because they are here today *and* tomorrow, they provide landmarks for the mind as well as the senses. In a world that changes moment by moment, anchoring the self to old places is a way of coping with the "continuous past." So loft living rejects functionalism, Le Corbusier, and the severe idealism of form that modern architecture represents. As a style, it is respectful of social context. Thus living lofts are a logical continuation of the middle-class movement back to brownstone townhouses that began in the late fifties. Ironically, loft living turns to factories in search of a more human habitat. Living in a loft is an attempt to replace modernism's mass production of the individual with an individualization of mass production.[15]

Living lofts, especially in an on-going manufacturing area, re-create the "mixed use" of earlier urban neighborhoods. To some degree the attraction to artists' living and working lofts—mixed use in the loft itself—represents an attempt to overcome the separation of home and work that some social psychologists find so alienating.[16] If the isolation of middle-class residential suburbs breeds despair, then the mixed use of loft neighborhoods should foster affirmation in the middle-class psyche. Of course, a middle-class preference for strictly residential neighborhoods pre-dates the suburbs by many years. Since the rise of separate middle-class and working-class housing markets in the 1840s, urban houses and neighborhoods have been predominantly either residential or commercial. Most people still prefer purely residential housing and neighborhoods—for either escape or exclusivity. But symbolically, the mixed use in loft living reconciles home and work and recaptures some of the former urban vitality.

In another way, too, living lofts represent an effort to supersede the intense privacy of the detached suburban house with a more public space. The sheer physical layout of most lofts, interrupted by few doors or walls, opens every area and every social function to all comers. This eliminates most rituals *de passage* and creates an impression of informality and equality. In a loft's vastness no single object or person can dominate. Similarly, the absence of architectural barriers between "service" and "entertainment" areas eliminates the hierarchy of functions that is typical of most household arrangements, as well as the hierarchy of persons— either male or female—who perform those functions. Nor does the architectural plan of a loft readily permit the hierarchy of specialized rooms that was so popular in middle-class Victorian homes. Lofts don't have drawing rooms, morning rooms, or dressing rooms. Because loft areas are divided only according to general uses—"living" and "working," for example—they imply an easy transition from one activity to another, a sense of proportion and a purposefulness that may really exceed the loft dweller's. The appropriation of large space in a loft also reverses the sixteenth-century association between small rooms and self-expression. Loft living reflects a self that continually demands "more space" to prove its individuality.

Living in a loft is a little like living in a showcase. Because of the structure of many small industrial buildings, most lofts are entered directly from the elevator. So guests penetrate immediately into the living area.

This contrasts with the gradual transition between, "outside" and "inside," and public and private space, in a typical home. Even in the modest lofts that do have an entrance hall, both guests and hosts feel a mutual obligation to "see" and "show" the whole loft. Of course, the uniqueness of each loft arrangement—due to the absence of standard floor plans and the unexpectedness of architectural detail—makes living lofts a kind of tourist attraction that most houses or apartments cannot be.

But it would be wrong to imagine that lofts use space in a totally new way. Strong elements of continuity connect today's living lofts and older American housing types, beginning with the brick walls, plane surfaces, and exposed structural elements (wooden beams) in early New England houses. Indeed, architectural historian Siegfried Giedion characterized the typical American floor plan that developed between 1850 and 1890 as the most open, the most flexible, and the least subdivided that was possible. Because of both a lack of skilled labor and a colonial dependence on the British Georgian style, American construction throughout the nineteenth century stressed a lack of pretentiousness, a direct approach to building materials, and an attention to comfort. Even the ideal house that Henry David Thoreau imagined before 1850 seems remarkably like a living loft. It would have "only one room . . . where some may live in the fireplace, some in the recess of a window, and some on settees, some at one end of the hall, some at another, and some aloft in the rafters with the sparrows, if they choose."[17]

Thoreau's central image reappears in master-craftsman Gustav Stickley's description of the prototype house that he designed around 1900:

We have from the first planned houses that are based on the big fundamental principles of honesty, simplicity, and usefulness. . . . We have put into practical effect our conviction that a house, whatever its dimensions, should have plenty of free space unencumbered by unnecessary partitions or over-much furniture. . . . It seems to us much more friendly, homelike and comfortable to have one big living room into which one steps directly from the entrance door . . . and to have this living room the place where all the business and pleasure of the common family life may be carried on. And we like it to have pleasant nooks and corners which give a comfortable sense of semi-privacy and yet are not in any way shut off from the larger life of the room. . . .

Equally symbolic is our purpose in making the dining room either almost or wholly a part of the living room: . . . Such an arrangement is a strong and subtle influence in the direction of simpler living because entertainment under such conditions naturally grows less elaborate and more friendly. . . .[18]

Another reason for the decline of formal entertaining, as Stickley also notes, was the increasing number of middle-class households without servants. Unlike the rigid domestic division between "upstairs" and "downstairs," the housewife who did her own cooking did not readily accept an enforced isolation in the kitchen, away from the rest of the family. Early-twentieth-century feminists had demanded that the kitchen be eliminated entirely from individual homes and replaced with nearby communal dining halls. But in the thirties and forties, this radical demand was subdued by the rapidly expanding production of labor-saving, mechanical devices for doing kitchen work and by changes in the physical layout of kitchens. Frank Lloyd Wright's innovative houses opened up the kitchen to the dining room so that the "work-space," as Wright called it, flowed into the living area. Wright also adapted to home kitchens the principle of "streamlining" that had been developed in nineteenth-century railroad travel with the creation of the Pullman dining car. Wright's preference for the open floor plan, along with the home-buying public's desire for ever more open and more flexible living areas, influenced the design of the suburban tract houses that were built in great numbers after World War II. Suburban ranch homes had large efficient kitchens that flowed into multi-purpose "dens" or "family rooms." The open space of this suburban style, as well as the 1960s revival of Early American rural homes and barns, prepared the way for the acceptance of living lofts.[19] [. . .]

NOTES

*   This article caused some dismay because it appeared at a time when the city government's concern over job loss had directed criticism against the residential conversion of loft buildings. The reporter made clear that Adri had bought a co-operative loft that was occupied by an economically viable manufacturer who "was in no hurry to leave." Nonetheless, a commercial tenant has no "statutory right," as some residential tenants in New York do, to remain beyond the expiration of their lease, and Adri "moved in as soon as she was able to."

**   In light of New York City's 1976 zoning resolution on SoHo and NoHo, the adjacent artists' loft districts South and North of Houston Street, respectively, these living lofts seem to have a doubtful legal status. That resolution permits residential conversion of loft buildings in these areas *for artists only,* according to an established certification procedure. Buildings that front on Broadway, as this one does, cannot be converted to joint living and working use *even by artists* if the floor size exceeds *3,600 square feet.* Probably the developers who were selling the floors in this building had applied for a Buildings Department permit for studios with accessory living space, which New York City law did not consider a residential category until recently.

1.   Robert Harbison, *Eccentric Spaces* (New York: Avon, 1980), p. 131. Alternatively, such spaces may be made to appear *as though* they had lost their function (and their human content); hence they become "picturesque." In English art of the late eighteenth and early nineteenth centuries, for example, "the rules of the picturesque allowed the intrusion of steam engines or mills or mines [into landscape paintings] only if they were given an air of decrepitude or made to appear ancient and ruinous, and so harmless" (Francis D. Klingender, *Art and the Industrial Revolution*, ed.

and rev. Arthur Elton [London: Adams and Dart, 1968], p. 74).

2. Jane Jacobs, *The Death and Life of Great American Cities* (New York: Vintage, 1961); Marc Fried and Peggy Gleicher, "Some Sources of Satisfaction in the Residential Slum," *Journal of the American Institute of Planners* 72, no, 4 (1961): 305–15; Herbert Gans, *The Urban Villagers* (New York: Free Press, 1962); Nathan Silver, *Lost New York* (New York: Schocken, 1967); James Biddle, Foreword, in Constance M. Greiff, *Lost America* (Princeton: Pyne Press, 1971).

3. Calvin Tompkins, *Off the Wall: Robert Rauschenberg and the Art World of Our Time* (Garden City: Doubleday, 1980), pp. 83, 211.

4. "Nine Artists/Coenties Slip," Whitney Museum, New York, 1974; Tompkins, *Off the Wall*, pp. 175–76.

5. Dore Ashton, *The New York School* (New York: Viking, 1972), p. 299.

6. "Living Big in a Loft," *Life*, Mar. 27, 1970, pp. 62–63.

7. "SoHo Artists' Bohemia Imperiled," *New York Magazine*, Aug. 24, 1970, p. 46.

8. "A Very Lofty Realm," *Progressive Architecture*, October 1974; Norma Skurka, "Landmark Loft in SoHo," *New York Times Magazine*, Nov. 24, 1974; *New York Magazine*, May 20 and Sept. 30, 1974.

9. *New York Magazine*, Mar. 8 and Oct. 11, 1976.

10. Bernardine Morris, "Built for Healthy Living: A Loft With Splash," *New York Times*, Mar. 9, 1978.

11. Mary Russell, "At Home in a French Factory," *New York Times Magazine*, Dec. 10, 1978.

12. *New York Times*, July 10, 1980.

13. Gaston Bachelard, *The Poetics of Space*, trans. Marie Jolas (New York: Orion Press, 1964), p. 72.

14. Harbison, *Eccentric Spaces*, pp. 22, 33; Burton J. Bledstein, *The Culture of Professionalism* (New York: Norton, 1976), p. 61.

15. See, for example, Orrin E. Klapp, *Collective Search for Identity* (New York: Holt, Rinechart and Winston, 1969), pp. 23–28; Yi-Fu Tuan, *Space and Place: The Perspective of Experience* (Minneapolis: University of Minnesota Press, 1977); Dean McCannell, *The Tourist: A New Theory of the Leisure Class* (New York: Schocken, 1976); Kenneth Frampton, "The Aura of the Past," *Progressive Architecture*, July 1974, pp. 48–79; Ada Louise Huxtable, "The Troubled State of Modern Architecture," *New York Review of Books*, May 1, 1980, pp. 22–29.

16. For example, Philip Slater, *The Pursuit of Loneliness: American Culture at the Breaking Point* (Boston: Beacon Press, 1970).

17. Siegfried Giedion, *Space, Time and Architecture* (Cambridge, Mass.: Harvard University Press, 1941), pt. 5; Thoreau, quoted in August Heckscher, *The Public Happiness* (New York: Atheneum, 1962), pp. 258–59.

18. Gustav Stickley, "Simplicity and Domestic Life" (1909), reprinted in *Roots of Contemporary American Architecture*, ed. Lewis Mumford (New York: Grove Press, 1959), pp. 302–3.

19. Siegfried Giedion, *Mechanization Takes Command* (New York: Norton, 1969), pt. 6; idem, *Space, Time and Architecture*, p. 289; Delores Hayden, *The Grand Domestic Revolution: A History of Feminist Designs for American Homes, Neighborhoods and Cities* (Cambridge, Mass.: M.I.T. Press, 1981); "A Romantic Solution," *Progressive Architecture*, November 1967.

CHAPTER 15

Living Like an Artist

Richard Lloyd

I really love your hairdo, yeah
I'm glad you like mine too
See what looking pretty cool will get you
... But if you dig on vegan food
Well come over to my work
I'll have them cook you something that you'll
    really love
Cause I like you
Yeah I like you
And I'm feelin' so bohemian like you.
                —The Dandy Warhols,
            "Bohemian Like You," 2000

Alan Gugel recalls of his early years in Wicker Park: "When I moved into this neighborhood, that's the one thing they kept saying, 'There's a lot of artists, a lot of artists, move down there.' And when I got there, there were no arts. I couldn't see them." Word of mouth indicated that Wicker Park was a likely site for a penniless young artist to find cheap rents and like-minded individuals, but those who moved in during the 1980s at first found that the local scene was comparatively underdeveloped, lacking public spaces to which newcomers might easily find their way. In the late 1980s, Wicker Park was a neighborhood on the verge, but it required the increasing preponderance of commercial spaces geared toward the needs of the artists and aesthetes moving there for the scene to become recogniz-able to both insiders and outsiders, and for the neighborhood to finally veer onto the path that would differentiate it as Chicago's 1990s bohemia.

Bars, restaurants, and coffee shops were crucial to Wicker Park's emerging neo-bohemian scene, dramatically elevating its visibility to insiders and outsiders alike, They belong to the category of social institution that Ray Oldenberg identifies as ''third places," helping people to make new social contacts and thus extend the local community.[1] Oldenberg is inspired in part by the tradition of café society evident in classic bohemian districts, and indeed sites such as Montmartre, Greenwich Village, North Beach, and the East Village all featured well-known venues—Le Chat Noir, City Lights Books, Cafe Trieste, the Mudd Club, and a host of others—that helped build the bohemian congregation. Such local institutions both drive neighborhood identity and reflect it. Bars and restaurants were hardly unknown to Wicker Park before its neo-bohemian turn, but the character of local venues would change as they increasingly served a new population with distinct social and aesthetic dispositions.

The legacy of the past stages of neighborhood life and demography is not swept away. They form the inheritance of new residents, both in terms of the built environment and the cultural palimpsest. But local businesses that had once catered primarily to members of the Polish or Latino working class would suddenly see a surge in patronage by tattooed young urban hipsters. Local artists—many of whom, like Alan Gugel and Erik Wulkowicz, had advanced carpentry skills—accelerated the rehabilitation process, trading labor for reduced rents or working as local contractors. Michael Warr, the founder and former director of the Guild Complex, points out how the mix of talents contributed to the reproduction of the material landscape, now geared to new styles of culture and commerce:

> When you think of all the performances that have taken place just in Wicker Park alone and all the types of work that go into building stages, you're talking about a lot of skills. Take some of the cafes that have gone up. If you look at Earwax, for instance . . . most of the work that was done in that cafe was done by artists in the neighborhood. One of the things that was great about running the Guild Complex in Wicker Park was that you never had to go far to find what you needed to get things done in terms of design, in terms of printing, in terms of the artists themselves for programming.

The presence of venues like the Guild Complex, a literary nonprofit that has occupied numerous neighborhood locations, increases the attractiveness of the neighborhood for new waves of artists, and the growing number of artists increases the attractiveness of the neighborhood for further investment. Steve Pink tells of the work his theater company did rehabbing space in the Chopin Theater, which shares the building that currently houses the Guild Complex:

> We opened the theater. It was owned by a Polish immigrant named Ziggy, who's still there. We approached him because he had this great space in the Chopin Theater. . . . We

opened that space. We made a good deal with him because our theater company was doing pretty well by that point. So we were like, "OK, you don't charge us that much of anything for the entire space, and we will build out the space, we'll build everything. We'll build out your space entirely, we'll put in a grid, we'll build in the risers, we'll build the stage." He was going to outfit the front for a coffee shop, anyway. "You do all that, you don't charge us rent on the theater, and we will make sure it's sold out. Don't worry." We did *Fear and Loathing in Las Vegas,* that was the first play we did there.

As this shows, artists in Wicker Park help "make the scene" not simply by providing local color, but also with real brow-sweat.

Phyllis' Musical Inn, my own first point of entry into the neighborhood, was among the earliest venues to capitalize on the coalescence of young cultural creators in the neighborhood, and in the 1980s it helped to make the emergent scene visible, thus further magnetizing participation. One future entrepreneur recalls that visiting Phyllis' helped to alert him to the neighborhood as a potential investment location.

> Phyllis' was my introduction to Wicker Park. . . . I had a friend who dragged me down here several times to see bands. That was back when Phyllis' was fundamentally the only thing—we're talking ten years ago [mid-1980s]—Phyllis' and the Gold Star [a bar located across the street on Division] were the only places where non-ethnic white people could go without being in serious jeopardy of their lives.

The grittiness of local bars like Phyllis', which only recently had been propped up by a hardscrabble clientele of grizzled working-class boozers, fit in well with the general construction of neo-bohemian authenticity in the neighborhood, and several such venues were co-opted into the hipster revolution in the manner of Phyllis'. Local performer Shappy Seaholtz recalls of the early 1990s: "There were some bars, but not the kind of bars you want to hang out at except for maybe the brave few that would go to Phyllis' or the Gold Star or the Rainbo. Even then, it was full of hipsters, and I went to a lot of cool art openings and shows." For the most part these venues were not yet widely recognized outside the neighborhood as potential entertainment destinations, and early stalwarts recall them with typical nostalgia:

> Are you familiar with the Borderline? Do you remember what the Borderline looked like in 1989? It used to be you would walk into this place that's literally like a wall, with a bunch of stools on it, with a bunch of cigarettes on one side and a bunch of beer on the other side, and it was covered with this real thick Plexiglas, and it was probably the most dangerous place to be in. About the only places that were relatively fun was Dreamerz and the Rainbo Club. . . . Dreamerz was a total biker bar—that was a rough kind of area to go into. I stayed away from that place on Friday and Saturday nights, I'd go down to Rainbo because that was a little bit more relaxed.

The Rainbo Club, located at Damen Avenue and Division Street on the southern fringe of the neighborhood, became one of the first bars in which local artists and musicians would congregate. A recognizable scene began to take shape, and many musicians whose crossover to national success would help fuel the neighborhood's celebrity were among the regulars, including Phair and the members of the band Urge Overkill (whose cover of Neil Diamond's "[Girl] You'll be a Woman Soon" was featured on the soundtrack of the hipster film sensation *Pulp Fiction*). Jimmy Garbe, a musician who has worked behind the bar at the Rainbo for more than a decade, remembers the scene as not particularly hospitable to outsiders:

> We were kinda pegged as elitist, and I think it's because people would come here, and there would be six or seven different art conversations going on, or possibly music conversations. It was a kind of social (event) for artists to talk about art and music. Some people would come in here, and they'd kind of dig it, but they wouldn't last more than a couple of weeks. They would feel like outsiders, and they wouldn't last, and they would stop coming in. On the other hand, if you were into that scene, it was definitely the place to come because you could walk in and jump in a conversation at a moment's notice if you were into that.

In addition to providing places for hanging out, new spaces in the neighborhood heightened the visibility of local creative efforts. Many new art galleries were opening in the nearby River West area and also in Wicker Park itself. In 1988, the Ricky Renier Gallery opened in what the *Chicago Tribune* still described as "the wilds of Wicker Park,"[2] and quickly switched from displaying European imports to showcasing local talent. In a practice similar to that of the East Village, local bars began to display the work of neighborhood artists, and they still do. Venues showcasing the neighborhood music scene proliferated. On the same block as Phyllis' Musical Inn, live music could be heard at the Czar Bar and the Bop Shop, both venues whose offerings evolved with the changing neighborhood dynamic. As the neighborhood's celebrity increased, the Double Door, a much larger musical performance space, opened. In addition to local acts, it showcased national fare, including such famous rock acts as the Rolling Stones and Smashing Pumpkins.

But even as the neighborhood became more popular and more expensive, the local aesthetic continued to display the image of grit as glamour. This image connoted an authentic bohemianism appealing not only to committed participants but also to sporadic consumers. Michael Warr describes the Hothouse, a performance venue that has since moved from Milwaukee Avenue to the South Loop as having a "real kind of bohemian feel.... That it wasn't just a bright shiny new thing, and when I see bohemia, that's what I see. There's a little bit of the Old World, as close as you can get in the United States. Bohemian isn't just the look, but I do think for me, that kind of grit, I think that is relevant to the picture of bohemia."

Particularly with the popularity of the bare-bones rock 'n' roll styles identified by labels as "grunge," "alternative," and "indie," such venues satisfied the expectations of a range of consumers, and by the 1990s, patrons were drawn from the far reaches of the Chicago area.

In her ethnographic study of "alternative hard rockers" in "Wicker Park, Mimi Schippers illustrates the disdain that many committed scene members expressed when increasing numbers began to invade the gritty venues of the neighborhood:

> We pass the Empty Bottle on our right. The Empty Bottle is a local rock club [on the western fringe of Wicker Park] that serves up strong, cheap drinks and features both local and touring bands for relatively low covers. It is one of the scenes that Maddie and other active participants in the alternative rock scene frequent. However, tonight Veruca Salt, a local band who made it big, is playing to a sold out crowd. Maddie looks at the people waiting outside to get in and grimaces. "What a nightmare. Can you imagine being in there? It's probably packed and full of 708ers...—People from the suburbs. The area code. All those assholes who wouldn't be caught dead in this neighborhood three years ago, but now because Wicker Park is the hip spot, they flock here. Especially for, like, Veruca Salt. Fucking MTV"[3]

The fact that Schippers' informant Maddie was herself a product of the suburbs is a common inconsistency among scene participants, as they make distinctions that place themselves firmly on the cool side of the fence. A species distinction is maintained in noting that these presumptive suburbanites would not have been caught dead in Wicker Park until recently, and

anyway could not have found their way there without a heads up from the agents of the corporate mass media, like MTV or the *New York Times*. In 2001, some locals took the opportunity to protest directly the influence of MTV on the new urban bohemia, attempting to disrupt MTV's staging of its program *The Real World* in a local loft.

The protests against *The Real World* were prefigured by the negative neighborhood reactions to the effects of its showcase arts festival. The ATC was launched in the late 1980s by Jim Happy-Delpeche, a French expatriate art dealer. Its intention was to showcase the work of local artists, with displays in local business venues and in the lofts of artists themselves. Of course, it also had the effect of illuminating the neighborhood's ongoing redevelopment to a wider audience, changing the image of the neighborhood from urban "wilderness" to hip cultural destination.[4] Though the festival clearly abetted the careers of several artists, it also became a center of neighborhood controversy spawning significant opposition and creating strong cleavages within the community.[5]

The controversy over the ATC shows the contradictions that artists face in the convergence of ideological preference and practical considerations, While many members of the arts community had an ideological commitment to maintaining the neighborhood ethos and resisting further gentrification, they also want to sell their work. Thus, few recognized neighborhood artists actually boycotted participation in the festival. However, for many participation was reluctant and surly. Meanwhile, the "Lumpens," the local subgroup behind the leftist neighborhood magazine *Lumpen Times*, were widely believed to be behind (at least spiritually) the defacement of ATC fliers and posters and the dissemination of literature suggesting possible "guerrilla" tactics to disrupt the festival. Despite local opposition, the festival persists and is gaining popularity It has been crucial to the growth of Wicker Park's citywide reputation as an arts center, and to its concomitant redevelopment as an entertainment zone. As it became increasingly established, the ATC enjoyed significant corporate sponsorship and the support of local businesses.[6] [...]

RESIDENTIAL CHANGE

New arrivals in Wicker Park, whether "starving artists" or more affluent young professionals, tend to be well educated. The absolute number of neighborhood residents possessing a bachelor's degree or higher almost tripled from 1990 to 2000. In 1990, Wicker Park, with its high percentage of foreign-born residents, had a much higher than average (for Cook County) percentage of adults lacking a high school degree; in 2000, the percentage of adult residents with undergraduate or graduate degrees significantly exceeded Cook County norms (table 15.1).

Other indicators confirm substantial residential turnover in the decade. The 1990 census indicates that slightly more than half the neighborhood population was Hispanic or Latino (any race); by 2000, that figure had dropped to 28 percent. New residential investment was substantial. In the period between 1993 and 1998, roughly half a

billion dollars in new home purchase loans were issued, with the significant majority of these going to White rather than Latino homeowners (table 15.2); Comparing census data in 1990 and 2000, we can see a staggering increase in median rents, median home values, and median household incomes (table 15.3).

During this period, the total population of the neighborhood remained roughly constant, but the population of children decreased with the displacement of working-class families, and the employed population (people 16 and older) increased from 15,447 to 19,774. Professionals increased from 25 percent of employed neighborhood residents to 51 percent; in absolute terms, this meant an increase from 3,890 local professionals in 1990 to 10,154 in 2000. Despite the loss of children, the median age in 2000 was 31.4, compared to a Cook County median, of 33.6, indicating that the neighborhood was attracting a large number of relatively young adults in professional occupations. Thus, a neighborhood newcomer in 2000 was greeted by a very different local demography than the one encountered by the many artists who broke ground in the late 1980s. Nonetheless, Wicker Park continues to be regarded as an "artist's neighborhood," both by the press and by local residents, and it is distinguished from

Table 15.1 Educational Attainment in Wicker Park, 1990 and 2000 (Percent of Population 25 Years and Over)

	1990			2000	
	Cook County	Wicker Park		Cook County	Wicker Park
Less than 9th grade	12	28		10	11
9th to 12th grade, no diploma	15	16		13	9
High school graduate	26	20		24	12
Some college, no degree	19	12		20	13
Associate degree	5	4		5	4
Bachelor's degree	14	12		17	32
Graduate or professional degree	8	8		11	18
Total	99	100		100	99

Source: US Bureau of the Census (sixteen-tract area).

Table 15.2 Wicker Park Home Purchase Loans for 1993–1998 by Census Tract

Census Tract	Total Loans	% White	% Latino	Total $ Investment	Average Loan
2402	229	86	5.6	48,053,000	209,838
2403	233	66.5	26.1	43,389,000	186,218
2404	215	89.7	1.3	35,358,000	164,455
2405	462	83.3	6	69,918,000	151,337
2412	105	73	19	17,593,000	167,552
2413	143	87.4	4.1	28,538,000	199,566
2414	325	82.7	7.3	65,097,000	200,298
2415	246	80.8	10	43,722,000	177,731
2421	184	76.6	15.2	31,533,000	71,375
2422	220	76.8	18.6	38,083,000	173,104
2423	147	80.9	11.5	40,314,000	274,244
2424	57	78.9	12.2	10,972,000	192,491
	2566			472,570,000	
Average		80.8	10.9		184,166

Source: Home Mortgage Disclosure Act (HMDA), compiled by Gray Data, Inc., analyzed by UIC Voorhes Center.

Note: Excludes Wicker Park tracts 2219, 2220, 2221, 2222.

Table 15.3 Income, House Value, and Rent in Wicker Park (Dollars), 1990 and 2000

	1990		2000	
	Cook County	Wicker Park	Cook County	Wicker Park
Median household income	32,673	23,327	45,922	54,791
Median house value	102,100	109,913	157,700	400,100
Median rent	411	325	648	802

Source: US Bureau of the Census (sixteen-tract area).

lakefront communities like Lincoln Park for its funkier, more offbeat character.

As an Urbus Orbis regular, Borderline employee, and respected local poet, Raul is one of the few individuals to straddle the worlds of the Latino immigrants and the artists in the neighborhood. Raul sees clearly the complicity of the arts community in the transformation of the neighborhood, undermining existing diversity by displacing both the original residents and, over time, many of the pathbreaking artists themselves.

> Those art school kids, what they do is they move into a neighborhood, and they don't care who lives there. They don't give a fuck, and if they do, they still don't give a fuck. Because they're moving in and that's it, that's just their thing, they're going to live there, and they're going to paint there, which is

a great noble idea for an artist. But in time people notice, and start buying up the buildings, and they [decide] "I'm going to rent to these artists, give them a two-year lease, then start making repairs, and before they know it I'm going to start raising the rent." And now you have major developers jumping the gun, seeing what's happening already, and investing. The taxes go up, people can't pay, people move out. The grand migration is what's happening.

Many artists express concern about the displacement of Latino residents when talking about gentrification, although as Raul suggests, these sentiments are bound up with self-interested concerns. Here, the issues are complicated, because young, culturally competent professionals can contribute to the development and maintenance of neo-bohemia, consuming its products and ambiance. The increased visibility of the neighborhood enhances the opportunities for local artists to get their work to a wider audience, and the proliferation of entertainment venues can improve employment opportunities. Nonetheless, the escalation of ground rents generates local contradiction, as it can interfere with the reproduction of a creative labor force in the neighborhood.

The necessary compromise involves young artists being pushed to surrounding neighborhoods like Logan Square, Humboldt Park, and Garfield Park—neighborhoods that resemble 1980s Wicker Park in their composition. These artists continue to avail themselves of the Wicker Park bars, coffee shops, and display venues that have a firmer hold in the neighborhood. Thus Wicker Park remains a central organizing space for new bohemian activity in Chicago even as many artists can no longer afford to live there. Artists hover in orbit, still making the scene as they drop in to work, play, and display. Escalating rents thus drive young artists outside the borders of Wicker Park; they are excluded from living in a neighborhood whose character they continue to influence disproportionately.

The new residents filling more upscale rehabs and condominium developments are the easily spotted culprits in neighborhood change and are blamed by artists for ruining "their" scene. These residents no doubt often earn the enmity of their neighbors by failing to adhere to the same norms of neighborhood diversity, instead forming homeowner associations that resist low-income housing and agitating for increased police presence. But even when the dispositions of new residents mirror those of artists, with whom they share youth and above-average educations, professionals are still lumped onto the other side of the fence in the system of cultural distinctions that remain central to bohemian self-identification.

NEO-BOHEMIA AND THE YOUNG URBAN PROFESSIONAL

In the ideological formulation of neo-bohemia, the yuppie is the imago of the mainstream, playing the role once held by the bourgeois shopkeeper in nineteenth-century Paris or the "organization man" of the Fordist United States. The collective construction of the yuppie, characterized by excessive simplifications, is crucial to the formation of subcultural distinction among artists and their friends in Wicker Park. As Pierre Bourdieu points out, "Nothing classifies somebody more than the way he or she classifies."[7] Though artists in and around Wicker Park are sometimes resistant to labels like "bohemian," they are much less reticent about declaring what they are not, and what they are not are yuppies. In her excellent study of the subcultural construction of the rave scene in England, Sarah Thornton makes a point that also well describes the Wicker Park scene: "Although most clubbers and ravers characterize their own crowd as mixed or difficult to classify they are generally happy to identify a homogeneous crowd to which they don't belong. And while there are many *other* scenes, most clubbers and ravers see themselves as outside and in opposition to the 'mainstream.'"[8]

In Wicker Park, "yuppie" and "mainstream" became practically interchangeable terms. Autumn, a young actress living in the neighborhood during the 1990s, offers an exemplary local take on the figure of the yuppie:

A yuppie would be like, in Lincoln Park or Wrigleyville, the upper middle class, materialistic, out for themselves, not very into community, not very into the arts. Into making themselves secure futures, and that's what's most important. Not that I'm saying there's anything wrong with that, but as an artist you've opened yourself up to the fact that you may not be secure for the rest of your life.

Autumn's broad view illustrates important themes in the species distinction that artists make between themselves and young professionals, including the use of spatial affiliation as a sign of membership. As Autumn indicates, artists live in Wicker Park, or a handful of other gritty neighborhoods like Pilsen, Logan Square, Ukrainian Village, or Uptown, as opposed to the gentrified lakefront communities of Lincoln Park and Wrigleyville.

But by the time that Autumn had arrived in Wicker Park, it was already fast becoming home to a large population of professionals, complicating her spatial distinctions. In some cases these newcomers would be given a pass, so to speak, by their more bohemian neighbors, so long as they performed appropriate respect for the arts. As Tom Lee puts it, "I know several people who were commodities or options or equity traders at the Board of Trade. But they belonged. One of them, even though he trades during the day, he paints through the evenings and supports his wife, who's an opera singer." For Lee, what it comes down to is "priorities—the life of the mind, creativity, is what is valued over the bank account." Few yuppies are considered to have their priorities in order to this degree, however. Most artists concur with Autumn's claim that the yuppie emphasizes security while neglecting community and creativity. This view mirrors the negative image of the organization man and Fordist ideology, even though this is complicated objectively by the changing nature of work in the postindustrial economy, in which even relatively privileged workers endure much higher levels of instability in employment.[9] Against the perception if not the reality of yuppie timidity, the bohemian ethic repudiates security and embraces contingency.

The insecurity and relative deprivation of the artists' lifestyle is often described as an advantage over the staid existence of buttoned-down professionals, and in this way artists signal the superiority of their existence over both the poor and the privileged. Says Shappy, a local performer:

I don't think [yuppies] have any creative gumption. Yes they may take chances on a business deal or an ad campaign or something stupid ... but they don't have the balls to put it in play in their own personal lives. And when they see people *living* I think they're jealous of the artist's lifestyle, wishing they could feel like they could be free and live on macaroni and cheese and not have to worry about these accounts and their bills and their credit cards and their SUVs, and their blah, blah, blah. You know, I think a lot of people want to be more bohemian, but they don't want to take the chance on actually living the life as a bohemian. They're too insecure without their credit cards.

Shappy finds evidence for his theory in the attraction of Wicker Park and its hipster scene for young professionals in the neighborhood, who dabble on the weekends while remaining unwilling to make his level of commitment. Still, he also acknowledges, "I live pretty modestly, and for fuck's sake, I'm 32 years old, and I'm probably still below the poverty level, and it doesn't really bother me, but yeah, it would be nice to have some chump change."

Both the materialism of yuppies and their antipathy toward community have become articles of faith, not just for artists, but also for most academics. According to the ethnographer Gerald Suttles, "The term 'yuppie' most obviously applies to young singles, who are heavily preoccupied with their nightlife, exploring the new reaches of consumerism, and staying abreast of the trends."[10] Gentrification scholar Neil Smith concurs: "Apart from age, upward mobility and an urban domicile, yuppies are supposed to be distinguished by a lifestyle of inveterate consumption."[11]

But the presence of educated professionals in Chicago has been central to the development of neo-bohemia, massively increasing the demand for cultural goods in the city, despite Autumn's stereotypical claim that they are indifferent to the arts.

The omnivorous cultural preferences of the new urban class of postindustrial professionals sit behind the development of "the city as an entertainment machine" generating a range of cultural amenities.[12] Still, while these developments have been critical to the viability of new bohemias, expanding audiences as well as employment opportunities for artists, this has not increased the popularity of young professionals. Distancing themselves from yuppies promotes in-group solidarity for the diverse cast of aspiring artists and hipster hangers-on that populated Urbus Orbis. It also allows them to downplay their own complicity in the gentrification displacing poor Latino residents. Finally, by deriding the soulless search for security, local artists make their own commitment to risk into an expression of comparative virtue. [. . .]

NOTES

1. Ray Oldenberg, *The Great Good Place* (New York: Paragon, (1989).
2. David McCracken, "Reneir Charts New Territory in Wicker Park," *Chicago Tribune*, March 11, 1988, p. CN57.
3. Schippers, *Rockin' Out of the Box*, p. 42.
4. Neil Smith illustrates how the imagery of the frontier wilderness was incorporated into the marketing of the East Village during the 1980s, encouraging affluent residents to identify with the romantic imagery of the Old West pioneer. See Neil Smith, "New City, New Frontier: The Lower East Side as Wild, Wild West," in *Variations on a Theme Park*, ed. Michael Sorkin (New York: Hill and Wang, 1992).
5. Huebner, "Panic in Wicker Park."
6. Lewis Lazare, "The Coyote's Latest Howl," *Chicago Reader*, April 21, 1995.
7. Pierre Bourdieu, *In Other Words* (London: Polity, 1990), p. 132.
8. Sarah Thornton, *Club Cultures: Music, Media, and Subcultural Capital* (Hanover, NH: University Press of New England, (1996), p. 99.
9. M. Brodsky, "Labor Market Flexibility," *Monthly Labor Review* 117, 11 (1994): 53–60; Paul Hirsch and Mark Shanley, "The Rhetoric of

Boundaryless: How the Newly Empowered and Fully Networked Managerial Class of Professionals Bought Into and Self-Managed Its Own Marginalization," in *Boundaryless Careers*, ed. Michael Arthur and Denise Rousseau (Oxford: Oxford University Press, 1996); Katherine Newman, *Falling from Grace: The Experience of Downward Mobility in the American Middle Class* (New York: Vintage, 1988); Vicki Smith, "New Forms of Work Organization," *Annual Review of Sociology* 23 (1997): 315–339.
10. Suttles, *Man-Made City*, p. 97.
11. Smith, *New Urban Frontier*, p. 92.
12. Richard Lloyd and Terry Nichols Clark, "The City as an Entertainment Machine," *Research in Urban Sociology* 6 (2001): 359–380.

REFERENCES

Bourdieu, Pierre. 1990. *In Other Words*. London: Polity.

Brodsky, M. 1994. "Labor Market Flexibility." *Monthly Labor Review* 117, 11: 53–60.

Hirsch, Paul, and Mark Shanley. 1996. "The Rhetoric of Boundaryless: How the Newly Empowered and Fully Networked Managerial Class of Professionals Bought Into and Self-Managed Its Own Marginalization." In *Boundaryless Careers*, ed. Michael Arthur and Denise Rousseau. New York: Oxford University Press.

Huebner, J. 1994. "Panic in Wicker Park: What's Behind the Gentrification Backlash." *Chicago Reader* 23 (August).

Lloyd, Richard, and Terry Nichols Clark. 2001. "The City as an Entertainment Machine." *Critical Perspectives on Urban Redevelopment* 6: 359–380.

Newman, Katherine, 1988. *Falling from Grace: The Experience of Downward Mobility in the American Middle Class*. New York: Vintage.

Oldenburg, Ray. 1989. *The Great Good Place*. New York: Paragon.

Schippers, Mimi. 2002. *Rockin' Out of the Box: Gender Maneuvering in Alternative Hard Rock*. New Brunswick, NJ: Rutgers University Press.

Smith, Neil. 1992. "New City, New Frontier: The Lower East Side as Wild, Wild West." In *Variations on a Theme Park*, ed. Michael Sorkin. New York: Hill and Wang.

———. 1996. *The New Urban Frontier*, New York: Routledge.

Smith, Vicki. 1997. "New Forms of Work Organization." *Annual Review of Sociology* 23: 315–339.

Suttles, Gerald. 1990. *The Man-Made City*. Chicago: University of Chicago Press.

Thornton, Sarah. 1996. *Club Cultures: Music, Media, and Subcultural Capital*. Hanover, NH: University Press of New England.

CHAPTER 16

Rethinking Gentrification: Beyond the Uneven Development of Marxist Urban Theory

D. Rose

IS 'GENTRIFICATION' A CHAOTIC CONCEPT?

[. . .] Both neoclassical and marxist approaches to gentrification have assumed that it is a coherent concept that refers to a single or unitary phenomenon. Despite disagreements about the best term to use (London, 1980; Weston, 1982), everything that is generally subsumed within the concept is usually assumed to be a part of the same phenomenon and assumed to be produced by the same causal process. Whatever the label, it is understood to refer to the replacement of lower income residents of a neighbourhood with inhabitants of a higher income and socioeconomic standing, and different material interests than the incumbent residents, by means of the renovation and 'upgrading' of dwellings. Gentrifying neighbourhoods are those undergoing upward social mobility through this process. The process of change is thought to occur in several stages. In successive stages, waves of in-migration of people with different characteristics from the original residents, and from each other, take place. Properties change hands at least twice; the initial purchaser gets a bargain and then sells at a large capital gain to an individual or company that carries out major renovations, often with a municipal subsidy or tax abatement, Such successive transactions have been documented in a number of cities, including New York (*Village Voice*, 1982), Cape Town (Western, 1981), and Montreal (Dansereau et al., 1983 . . .). For example, in New York City's Lower East Side, the 'first wave' of in-movers consists of young white-collar workers, unemployed but educated young people, economically marginal self-employed young people, middle-class single parents, and so on (*Village Voice*, 1982). The end result, after property values have increased rapidly, is a new equilibrium of socioeconomic and cultural homogeneity (Holcomb and Beauregard, 1981, pages 42–44), As a descriptive model of occupancy change this is reasonable enough. It seems to fit the history of some gentrifying neighbourhoods quite well, However, there are many different routes to the gentrification of a neighbourhood, with different types of actors taking the lead in different contexts (de Giovanni, 1983). If one tries to imbue the simple-stage model with general theoretical significance, it is not only—obviously—teleological, but it may also contain what Sayer (1982) refers to as 'chaotic conceptions':

"In place of a theory of abstract elements of a situation and how they combine to compose concrete phenomena, there is an acceptance of unexamined, largely commonsense definitions of these *empirical* objects, and a generalisation of the features of these 'chaotic conceptions. . . . [T]hese unities of diverse aspects are treated as single objects which can be used as a basis for aggregation or else added up for manipulation in statistical analyses'".

(Sayer, 1982, page 75)

For instance, there is some evidence to suggest that initial in-movers are often "attracted by low prices and tolerance of unconventional lifestyles" (Holcomb and Beauregard, 1981, page 42). The large gay in-migration to certain parts of San Francisco is a good example (Castells and Murphy, 1982). A crucial methodological problem, however, arises here. For in what sense can it be validly said that this is the first stage in *the* gentrification process? What conceptual grounds exist for assuming that these 'first stagers' and the 'end-stage' affluent residents have anything in common other than the fact that their household incomes are higher than those of the original residents? Presumably, some version of the notion of 'housing class' or 'property class' is also implicit in this model. Homeowners (in this instance, first and second waves of gentrifiers) are accordingly viewed as having materially different life-chances than renters (the incumbent residents of the neighbourhood), on account of the wealth-accumulative potential of homeownership in a situation of inflating property values (compare Saunders, 1978; 1979). If this notion is accepted, then there is a firm basis for the assumption that *all* in-moving homeowners have more materially in common with one another than they do with any of the incumbent renters. Yet within this 'all' is also included moderate-income gentrifiers. Among these are people who are buying their first home, choosing the inner-city mainly for reasons of relative cheapness; people whose combined employment and family responsibilities necessitate an inner-city location (see section after next); and the 'reluctant purchasers' or '*les acheteurs non volontaires*' of condominium apartments—who may be long-time residents of a building (L'Ecuyer, 1981). (I shall henceforth refer to all types of moderate-income gentrifiers as 'marginal gentrifiers'—admittedly an unbounded concept, which I use in this paper for heuristic reasons only.) The inclusion of the latter in the 'them' of 'them and us' in the conceptualisation of gentrification/displacement conflicts has important political implications, to which I shall return below.

However, there is good reason to question the validity of such a simply conceptualised material cleavage between homeowners and tenants in gentrifying neighbourhoods in North American cities from the mid-to-late 1970s to the present time. There is mounting evidence in North America to suggest widening gaps within the home-ownership tenure category within the past ten to fifteen years, in terms of initial access to and subsequent material opportunities afforded by homeownership (compare Saunders, 1978; 1979). If this notion is accepted, then there is a firm basis United States of America in the 1970s, housing prices increased faster than median family incomes. This led to substantial capital gains for some of those who were already homeowners at the beginning of this period (Le Gates and Murphy, 1981, page 265). However, this inflation made access to homeownership more difficult for renters wishing to purchase their first home, because, as Rudel (1983b, page 1) points out, with reference to the USA from 1974 to 1978,

"... unlike repurchasers who could apply the equity in their current home toward the purchase of another home, renters usually had to accumulate savings for rapidly increasing downpayments out of incomes which were increasing much less rapidly".

For the young moderate-income household, delaying starting a family and being a two-earner couple became the only way to raise the down payment. Recent evidence from Australia, which had a similar house price inflation, suggests that for such couples the wife's income goes primarily toward the down payment on a house: her income does not lead to a decision to purchase a house that will require two incomes to keep up the payments (Wulff, 1982). In Canada, increasing real rates of interest—in a context where mortgage interest is not tax-deductible, unlike in the USA and Britain—have been more significant than price increases in reducing access to and raising the carrying costs of homeownership for first-time purchasers. It has thus become essential for women to go out to work and put the 'second income' toward sustaining mortgage payments (SPCMT, 1980, pages 117–119). Uncertainty about household incomes in future years, decreased locational mobility, and unpredictable interest rates and loan conditions may create a situation where, for many first-time buyers, the 'wealth-accumulative potential' of homeownership exists only on paper.

One of the most important results of these rapid increases in the real costs of entering the homeownership market has thus been to create widening gaps between long-standing homeowners and first-time buyers (Le Gates and Murphy, 1981, page 265). In the USA, however, this does not appear to have led to a decline in the numbers of people switching from rental housing to homeownership, except in the West, according to a recent analysis of *Annual Housing Survey* data from 1974–1978 (Rudel, 1983b). (Comparable data sets are not available for Canada.) These facts suggest some major problems with the assumption that the category of 'all homeowners', based on a conceptualisation of common wealth-accumulation potential, is a valid one for inferring major cleavages over material life-chances and 'interests', as compared with a category of 'all tenants'.

As Thorns (1981, page 215) points out, not least among these problems is

". . . the range of accumulative potential within owner-occupation itself. When capital gains are examined for specific groups of owner-occupiers it is clear that the rates of gain are highly varied and not assured".

Even within gentrifying neighbourhoods, capital gains are not certain. Houses and apartments renovated from badly deteriorated stock, that was never intended to last a century or so, do literally wear out, as the British experience with 'improvement grants' and the New York City experience of condominium conversions in some districts have shown (Benwell Community Project, 1978, pages 92–108; *The New York Times*, 1983c; 1983d). In such cases the owner may lose money, unless there is tremendous pressure on the location for a 'higher and better use' and governmental structures that enforce on redevelopers large compensation payments in addition to the market value of the house.

Yet it is many of these first-time purchasers of moderate income who are 'putting pressure' on older inner-city neighbourhoods and often displacing poorer tenants. Thus, I would venture to suggest, our understanding of the historical development of this situation, and of the conflicts it is creating, might be enhanced if we made some different types of comparisons than the usual one of incumbent tenant versus incoming home-owning gentrifier, the one the displacee, the other the displacer. Comparing these two is actually rather like comparing apples and oranges, in the sense that their specific circumstances and needs may have been produced by different processes at different times. For example, we might more usefully compare the economic situation of people commonly identified as first-stage gentrifiers with the economic situation of people in the same type of occupation and life-cycle stage a decade or so ago—the latter would probably have been forming their households in suburbia. Compared to existing residents of a working-class neighbourhood, the new people certainly make the neighbourhood upwardly socially mobile, but, compared to their peers of ten years ago, some of these people have been considerably proletarianised, because of the restructuring of white-collar labour processes, rollbacks in public-sector wages, deteriorating working conditions, and reduced job security.

Moreover, we are used to thinking about 'upward mobility' and progression through 'the family life-cycle' in the same breath. As Christopherson (1983, page 24) astutely points out, geographical models of locational preference and change have been imbued with the dual assumptions that a household's residential locational shifts over a period of time are geared to the income of a male head of a nuclear family, that steadily increases as his children grow up and until his retirement. Upward mobility as a condition of years of employment experience and a single head of household who is male are implicitly taken as the norm in such models. Yet, for many so-called 'first-stage' gentrifiers, one or both parts of this assumption may be invalid, as they now are for many other groups in the present phase of advanced capitalism. In the first place, there are often two heads of household whose respective earning capacities may diverge at certain stages in their life-cycles. In the second place, female single parents, even if they hold professional jobs, are most unlikely to have incomes that increase as fast as the male norm, and in any case have major child-care expenses that detract from their incomes. In the third place, divorce, remarriage, complicated custody arrangements, and so on frequently create major disruptions in family life-cycles in relation to incomes and location decisions. Although some recent neoclassical work on residential mobility has endea-voured to take such developments into account, 'induced moves' caused by 'life-cycle changes' or employment changes are still seen, incorrectly, as being analytically separable from 'adjustment moves' based on neoclassical norms of, ceteris paribus, increasing consumer demand for residential space as income increases over time (Clark and Onaka, 1983).

Even more importantly, opportunities for increasing household incomes over time are being severely curtailed, independently of the factors mentioned above, for many people. The present phase of restructuring of industrial and clerical labour processes, and the associated segmentation of labour markets over space—as well as by sex and race—may limit lower income families' chances of upward mobility. This is of course exacerbated for female-headed households (compare Christopherson, 1983). The impacts of new technology on lower level workers' opportunities to move up through the ranks is still hotly disputed. Yet several analysts are arguing that a 'two-tier' work force is being created, with a gap that is very difficult to leap across (*The New York Times*, 1983b).

In addition, many young professionals, though clearly in a much improved material situation, can also no longer assume job security and steadily increasing incomes: college and university teachers, public-sector professionals on fixed-term contracts, and the growing army of professionals turned self-employed because of the recession are examples which spring to mind. All of these people may be excluded from more traditional white-collar housing markets by reason of house prices relative to their incomes. This has to be considered, not only in terms of the increasing real costs of homeownership, but also in terms of the downward social mobility of such groups relative to their parents or their peers of ten years ago. In New York, as previously mentioned, and in Toronto and Montreal, renovation is spreading from the best quality inner-city housing to stock of much lower quality in areas considered less desirable (Dansereau et al, 1981; Weston, 1982). Although evidence about this is piecemeal, it seems that, increasingly, white-collar households of much more modest incomes than the type who gave gentrification its name, predominate among those in renovated properties in such areas.

The changes referred to in this section are clearly among the major reasons for the 'explosion' of condominium conversions in older North American cities since the mid-1970s (Le Gates and Murphy, 1981, pages 267–268) (this is not, however, the only reason for the popularity of condominiums, as will be discussed later). As these writers point out, some of the most bitter gentrification/displacement conflicts that have broken out in the USA in recent years have been around this issue, especially between people in the 'tertiary' work force; young professional and managerial people displacing lower level white-collar workers and essential service workers (Le Gates and Murphy, 1981, pages 266–267). Both of these groups of people have good reasons for wanting an inner-city location. This is partly because of the social and spatial restructuring of employment, which, as previously mentioned, is reducing the mobility of lower level workers and 'marginalised' professionals alike. The continuing controversy over artists' housing in New York City is an interesting case in point. A three-year-long effort by the City's Department of Housing Preservation and Development to establish a scheme for building artists' condominiums out of dilapidated tenements in the Lower East Side, subsidised by federal funds, was defeated at the Board of Estimate in February 1983 (*The New York Times*, 1983e). This Artists' Home Ownership Plan had run into major opposition from neighbourhood groups, and artists themselves became divided over

the issue. The opposition to the plan was due to the fact that it would have drawn upon scarce federal funds designated expressly for low-income groups and that, after three years, artists would have been able to sell their renovated condominiums at market rates, thus making capital gains, reducing the stock of low-income housing, and promoting further gentrification. In April 1983, however, the program was revived; but this time the City proposed to spatially disperse the subsidised housing rather than locate it in an area "already rife with real estate speculation" (*Village Voice*, 1983).

In Montreal, there is also some evidence to suggest that middle level white-collar households (incomes in the range $20000–$25000)[1] are increasingly living in nonprofit rental housing cooperatives—a form of housing originally thought to have appeal only for those on the lowest incomes and/or living in 'unconventional' ways (St Martin, 1982). Funds available for nonprofit housing cooperatives are very limited, and the cooperatives have to become self-financing over time under current Canadian federal and Québec governmental regulations. Thus the proportions in this income category may well increase at the expense of those in lower (but not the very lowest) brackets, which will intensify the bimodal distribution of income categories in cooperatives that now exists, peaking at incomes in the range $7000–$11000 and $20000–$25000 (St Martin, 1982). Furthermore, there is strong pressure from the Canadian federal and Québec governments to 'commodify' housing cooperatives, allowing shares to be sold and capital gains to be made, much as in the New York equity cooperative model (Fincher, 1982). Were this to happen, Canadian housing cooperatives would obviously no longer be outside of the capitalist housing market, as they are at present to a very large extent [see footnote (3)].

BEYOND CHAOTIC CONCEPTIONS

All of these developments mean that a growing number of moderate-income first-time homebuyers are likely to be 'competing' with lower-income tenants for old inner-city housing. Direct competition is of course limited, as separate housing submarkets are controlled by property-owners and developers who carry out the conversion of low-priced rental units into moderately priced owner-occupied units, with the assistance of financial institutions. At the same time, various forms of 'sweat equity' renovation by moderate-income homebuyers (recall that some of this is actually the labour of people working 'informally' who are local renters) seem likely to continue in large cities with a high density of white-collar employment, as long as appropriate and inexpensive old houses and apartments are available and as long as the new purchasers have the necessary resources to do the work[2]. There is no reason to assume that the growth in CBD employment will continue indefinitely and that the prices of properties renovated in the present period will inflate as meteorically as those of recent years. It may well be that many of the current wave of moderate-income buyers are unlikely to accumulate significant real wealth through homeownership.

I am suggesting, then, that the terms 'gentrification' and 'gentrifiers', as commonly used in the literature, are 'chaotic conceptions' which obscure the fact that a multiplicity of processes, rather than a single causal process, produce changes in the occupation of inner-city neighbourhoods from lower to higher income residents. Moreover, the existing concepts are also chaotic in extant marxist usage because they internally combine 'necessary tendencies' with 'contingent conditions' (for example, the law of value combined with a particular housing stock with particular occupants at a particular time). The concepts 'gentrification' and 'gentrifiers' need to be disaggregated so that we may then reconceptualise the processes that produce the changes we observe, and so that we may change, where necessary, our 'ways of seeing' some forms of 'gentrification' and some types of 'gentrifiers'.

In this section, I have gone a little way toward disaggregating 'gentrification'. I have focused on the needs of both of these broad groups (moderate-income 'gentrifiers' and lower income tenants) with respect to considerations of housing costs (relative to income), income prospects, and job security. However, we must also consider the forms of *reproduction* of people and labour-power that are enabled by various types of housing and neighbourhoods through their social and physical design and their locational aspects. These are equally crucial factors because of important changes in modes of reproduction which are historically interrelated to the restructuring of the labour-force (compare Mackenzie, 1983; Mackenzie and Rose, 1983a). These form the subject of the next section.

CHANGING HOUSEHOLD STRUCTURES, 'LIFESTYLES', AND THE REPRODUCTION OF PEOPLE AND LABOUR POWER IN INNER-CITY NEIGHBOURHOODS

Often cited as an additional factor in the condominium conversion phenomenon is the growing number of one- and two-person households who do not conform to the norm of the nuclear family and who have 'nontraditional' or 'alternative' life-styles. They reject, and are repelled from, the North American suburban time-space rhythms of separate spheres of work and daily life and the manner in which the latter is yet dominated by the former. One of the better known examples of this is among the gay population of San Francisco (Castells and Murphy, 1982, pages 254–255). Pilot studies of 'gentrifiers' by urban geography undergraduates at McGill University support these impressions (Ayotte and Cohen, 1983; Chamberland and Hemens, 1983; Lawrence, 1982).

Furthermore, it is now increasingly accepted that women are playing an active and important role in bringing about gentrification (Alonso, 1980; Holcomb, 1981; Ley, 1981; Markusen, 1981; Roistacher and Young, 1981; Wekerle, 1979; 1981). However, as I have argued elsewhere (Rose, 1984), the reasons for this have not yet been adequately conceptualised. In particular, there is a need to explore in detail the changing patterns of female employment and 'career ladders' in white-collar work and how these interact with changing family forms, domestic responsibilities, and life-cycles to produce housing and neighbourhood consumers with specific packages of needs. Moreover, insufficient attention has been paid to differentiating between different groups of women involved in various forms of urban revitalisation, although there is a growing attention to differentiating among single parents (Klodawsky et al, 1983).

Traditional and marxist writings on the so-called nontraditional life-styles of many gentrifiers have both viewed 'life-style' changes as being conceptually separate socioeconomic aspects of restructuring of white-collar employment (for example, see Alonso, 1980; Cox and Mergler, 1982; Le Gates and Murphy, 1981). Attempts at linkage are only made after the various 'elements' have been conceptualised separately (for example, Guterbock, 1980). But as I have suggested earlier in this paper, it is precisely such analytical separations that need to be overcome. I shall now discuss some of the changes in reproduction that appear to be occurring among 'marginal gentrifiers'. Some of the reasons why these changes in reproduction, in interaction with changes in production, may affect the residential location decisions of those concerned will be explored.

Much of what are often referred to as 'alternative life-styles'—reduced to exogenous 'fashions' by neoclassical theorists and viewed pejoratively by some Marxists—in fact symptomise attempts by educated young people, who may be unemployed, underemployed, temporarily employed (or all three simultaneously), to find creative ways of responding to new conditions of paid and unpaid work and worsening economic conditions. For reasons which need further investigation, people in such situations may tend to congregate in certain inner-city neighbourhoods where certain kinds of self-employment—based in people's homes—and 'informal' economic activities are an essential means of 'making-do'. This is frequently combined with unemployment insurance compensation or social assistance. Interestingly, 'under-the-table' private-house-renovation work is an important part of this economic activity (information obtained from Montréal contacts, who will remain confidential for obvious reasons). Such activities have attracted some attention among writers on urban social movements in Europe (Ceccarelli, 1982; Mingione, 1981), but their existence has been largely unexplored in North American contexts. The concept of *chomeur(euse) instruit(e)* (educated unemployed male/female) has been used to describe this group in Québec City (Villeneuve, 1983). They are perhaps 'gentrifiers' in terms of *genre de vie*, but are not able to purchase or even rent units with major renovations. Such developments are worthy of further research which relates them to the specific forms of restructuring taking place in particular cities.

It has been pointed out that gentrification generally results in more living space per gentrifier (Alonso, 1980), but in some cases this may not just be regular living space. Extra space may in particular be sought out by those seeking to work at home—for those on moderate incomes and/or with requirements for a lot of space for their work, this may result in relatively low housing quality. Artists' loft conversions, now famous (or infamous, depending on one's point of view) in New York City (Jackson, 1983; Zukin, 1982), but also found in Montréal and presumably in other places, may be seen as an extreme example of this.

ENVIRONMENTAL DESIGN, HOUSEHOLD ORGANISATION, AND THE PRODUCTION OF GENTRIFIERS WITH 'ALTERNATIVE LIFE-STYLES'

Though many studies have shown that gentrification is not usually a 'return to the city' by former suburbanites, it is now becoming clear that many who become gentrifiers do so substantially because of the difficulties, not only of affording housing, but also of carrying on their particular living arrangements in conventional suburbs (Rose, 1983). The types of household often noted as predominating in the early stages of neighbourhood renovation—single parents, gay couples, unrelated people living together, and so on—have grown rapidly in numbers nationally both in the USA and in Canada in the last intercensal period. Evidence is beginning to surface that single parents are disproportionately represented among the occupants of inner-city condominium conversions in Canada (Dansereau et al, 1981, page 115; *Habitation*, 1982; Klodawsky et al, 1983). These are groups frequently still excluded from suburban communities because they do not meet the norms of the nuclear family still entrenched in zoning regulations (Hayden, 1981; Lees, 1983; Mackenzie and Rose, 1983a; 1983b; Wekerle, 1979)[3]. Exclusionary zoning, by lot size, building regulations, and household types, persists, especially in the USA[4]. In a recent case in a suburban municipality in Denver, for instance, an unmarried couple living together were deemed to be in breach of the law (*Life on Capital Hill*, 1983). Even in inner cities similar norms may prevail over the courts. A recent ruling by the New York State Court of Appeals upheld the provisions of a rental apartment lease in Greenwich Village that prohibited unmarried couples from moving in together (*The New York Times*, 1983a). If this ruling holds it will presumably be a significant 'push' factor from renting an apartment to owning a condominium.

More generally, the design—social and environmental—of even moderately priced suburban residential areas may also be a factor in 'pushing' some of the types of household seen as gentrifiers into the inner-city areas they move to. Recent research on the 'accessory-apartment' phenomenon in a moderate-income Long Island suburb suggests that, where such inexpensive in-house apartments are available, single parents take them up in numbers out of all proportion to their representation in the general population (Rudel, 1983a). Quite possibly, this type of housing is not only attractive in terms of price but also because of the opportunities for informal childcare networks in such demographically mixed neighbourhoods. But the vast majority of suburbs do not allow this type of housing (it may of course exist illegally) or other types of housing and 'social design' appropriate to the needs of single parents (Lees, 1983; SPCMT, 1979).

By contrast, many existing older inner-city neighbourhoods can provide housing with these features; duplex and triplex attached-housing[5] in 'ethnic' areas of Montréal is an example. Such neighbourhoods facilitate access to community services, enable shared use of facilities, provide an efficient and non-isolating environment for reproductive work, and enhance opportunities for women to develop locally based friendship networks and a supportive environment (Holcomb, 1981; Michelson, 1977; Rothblatt et al, 1979; Saegert and Winkel,

1981; Soper, 1981; Stamp, 1981; Women in Planning Steering Committee—Oregon Chapter, no date).

Moreover, a number of studies in the 'residential-satisfaction' literature have concluded that clustered condominium-type housing (whether in new communities, up-zoned suburbs, or older inner-city areas) may have distinct advantages for all women with children, in that they can potentially "provide more efficient and better organised housing environments and a more supportive set of community services" (Rothblatt et al, 1979, page 135; also see Genovese, 1981; Michelson, 1977; Popenoe, 1977). To say this is not to be an environmental determinist, but only—and importantly—to realise that environmental forms may impose real limits on the creation of alternative reproductive forms (Hayden, 1981; Mackenzie and Rose, 1983b). As yet, few new communities have been designed with such goals in mind, and thus existing inner-city neighbourhoods have been the foci of such efforts at developing alternatives[6]. It remains to be seen to what extent redesigning existing suburbs might change the current preferences of the groups discussed here for inner-city living.

REDIRECTING THE QUESTIONS: REDEFINING URBAN REVITALISATION IN PRACTICE

The preceding discussion leads to the conclusion that the 'attractions' of inner-city neighbourhoods for a number of groups of 'gentrifiers' may thus relate to the presence of considerable *need* among such groups and should not therefore be viewed in mere 'life-style' terms. Indeed, the very concept of 'life-style' conjures up scenarios of unbridled choice, influenced only by fashion, in popular parlance. It is not just a matter of simple unrestrained 'preference', given the nature of the available alternatives. This is one of the most important insights to be gained from rethinking the chaotic conceptions of gentrification that have dominated marxist as well as positivist thinking up until now.

Rather than analytically incorporating what I have termed 'marginal gentrifiers' within the same category as wealthy gentrifiers, it would, I believe, be more useful to explore the possibility of such groups having certain needs and desires in common with some of those they now compete with. In some cases they may be able to work together to develop housing alternatives that would provide them with the same 'ontological security' (Saunders, 1982) as homeownership, but without upward redistributions of wealth and compatible with, or even dovetailing with, the needs of low-income tenants[7]. As a caveat to this, I am not suggesting that we naively assume that it would be easy, in a wide range of circumstances, to build such alliances. Yet it does seem important to further explore what the wants and the needs of these 'marginal gentrifiers' are for inner-city housing, above and beyond the limited alternative choices that are currently presented to them. It has been proposed, for instance, to develop 'urban homesteading' programs for New York City artists, in which they would form nonprofit rental housing cooperatives without using any public funds. Although this would not help low-income artists, it would reduce pressure on the low-income housing stock, would remove the units permanently from the speculative housing market, and would integrate artists more into the surrounding neighbourhoods (*Village Voice*, 1983). Explorations of such options should parallel, but interact with, work that focuses on the housing needs of various groups of low-income tenants (compare Klodawsky et al, 1983).

In the process of reshaping the physical fabric and social networks of inner-city neighbourhoods, it may be possible to make them supportive of alternatives to the patriarchal family and conventional divisions and organisation of domestic labour (compare Stamp, 1981). Also, on a very limited scale, such revitalising neighbourhoods may be supportive of alternative ways of making a living for some of those who have been economically marginalised by the present phase of restructuring. There are possibilities of developing collective forms of self-help (Castelis, 1981), rather than the individualistic forms that are an integral part of the ideology of gentrification (Allen, 1980; Beauregard, 1983; Smith, 1983). Self-employment, the informal production of goods and services domestically or within neighbourhoods, producer cooperatives (Blair, 1982; Boyte, 1980; Mingione, 1981; Pahl, 1980; Tabb, 1983), and the democratising potential of new communications (Castells, 1983; Piercy, 1976; Williams, 1981, page 435)—all these are potentially 'prefigurative' forms of social organisation.

Nevertheless, there is no escaping the fact that those groups of people who may be developing alternative forms of reproduction of social life are in many cases displacing poorer residents with far fewer options—including many working-class single parents and minorities. It is easy to forget, for instance, the displacement of low-income single parents while lauding housing arrangements that enable a couple of middle-class single parents to cooperatively manage their multiple roles (Markusen, 1981, page 32).

As I have discussed elsewhere (Rose, 1983), in a sense, gentrification by employed women with children may be a deliberately sought out *environmental solution* to a set of problems that are inherently *social problems*. Becoming a gentrifier makes it easier to have a waged job in addition to doing most of the household work and childcare—in a social context where working hours are fixed, hours of services limited, transportation systems planned

for traditional nuclear families, and traditional gender roles still prevail over the allocation of domestic responsibilities. Sometimes such women may even generate alternatives to the 'double day' and the individualised nature of so much reproductive work—but on a small spatial scale and probably with limited social 'spread effects' to those of lower incomes dealing with the same problems. Yet women with dual roles and low incomes are concentrated in inner-city neighbourhoods, on which they have traditionally relied, not only for cheap housing and transportation, but also for social support systems (Wekerle, 1981, page 197), as are young single women and newly divorced women, who may also be new to the job market as well as the housing market (Roistacher and Young, 1981, page 219). All these are particularly vulnerable to displacement induced by gentrification (Smith and LeFaivre, 1984). Thus the moderate-income woman's environmental solution to the problems created by her dual role exacerbates the problems of the low-income woman who is displaced to other neighbourhoods which are more environmentally restrictive and less socially supportive (Rose, 1983). Holcomb et al (1983) refer to the burden of increased childcare costs incurred by low-income service workers when previous informal social networks in Black neighbourhoods of US cities are disrupted by displacement resulting from gentrification. Goldstein, writing about artists' housing in New York City (*Village Voice*, 1983), makes a related point that is well taken:

"... the needs of artists for cheap housing are ignored by community activists at their peril. Since the poverty of artists is often voluntary, this particular proletariat is infinitely capable of competing with other low income groups".

The restructuring of white-collar work is tending to concentrate low-paid service workers and young unmarried clerical workers in inner-city neighbourhoods at the same time as it promotes gentrification by upper-income professionals and renovation by and for moderate-income white-collar households (Le Gates and Hartman, 1981). Corporate headquarters and financial centres still need the labour of these low-paid workers, and the people who fill these jobs need to live in low-cost housing that is conveniently located in inner-city neighbourhoods. This is likely to remain true even though back-office data processing functions are increasingly transferred to suburban locations (Gad, 1979; 1981; The New York Times, 1983g). The latter article suggests that the gentrification of formerly moderate-income areas is contributing to a shortage of adequately educated part-time clerical workers. Hence restructuring actively contributes to the spatially based housing conflicts between different groups of workers, noted by Le Gates and Murphy (1981) and alluded to above. Moreover, in some US cities, corporate redevelopment and gentrification are proceeding hand in hand amidst extreme poverty and unemployment. This is likely to exacerbate low-income housing problems. A particularly graphic instance of this kind of spatially uneven development is depicted by a recent *New York Times* (1983d) report. Headlined: "In Hartford, It's The Best and Worst of Times", the story focuses on a woman aged forty-four years, unemployed for fifteen months in the inner city, who comments: "The town is flourishing. And I can't find a job, even washing dishes". De Giovanni (1983) reports a wave of speculator-led gentrification since 1977 in the same city. These problems are made more acute by the lack of opportunities for women in clerical and service jobs, in labour markets that are increasingly segregated and spatially differentiated, to increase their income over time (as discussed already).

I do not believe that this conflict between different fractions of labour, and frequently between groups of women, can be seen as matters of housing scarcity and differential access to resources only, although both of these are clearly important. This is a matter for much further research, grounded in the realities of neighbourhood politics as well as in analyses of the forms of restructuring of work processes and their implications (which I have only touched on here). Nor are we looking at a 'simple' class conflict. My perspective here differs from that of Smith and LeFaivre (1984), who appear to see gentrification and displacement in 'pure' class terms, on the basis of the fact (which I do not in principle dispute) that the "effects of this process are sharply delineated along class lines" (1984, page 16). However, the foregoing argument suggests that this conclusion may be conceptually and logically premature, and in some cases perhaps overly pessimistic.

CONCLUDING THOUGHTS

If we are trying to understand how and why gentrification is occurring, with the aim of going beyond sorrow and outrage about displacement and developing some progressive political strategies (Planners Network, 1980), then we need to analyse these processes in terms that go far beyond concepts of undifferentiated 'gentrifiers' and upwardly mobile neighbourhoods. We need, for example, to have a perspective that allows us to understand the situation of this college-educated single parent, who wrote a letter to the *Newsletter of the National Congress of Neighbourhood Women* (1983):

> "I run through the daily obstacle course of taking my daughter to day care, rushing off to work, putting in my 8–9 hour day for my measly $195.00 a week, rushing back to day care to pick my daughter up and home again to our cozy studio apartment tucked in the not-too-nice area of Oakland. I come home, cook, tuck my precious into bed and, and, and. . . . Fall asleep by 9 PM, up at 5 AM and the

race continues. But dammit—I want more!.
. . . I want to get involved in the community and open up new possibilities and options not only for myself but for others living in this neighbourhood".

In conventional parlance, the writer of this letter would be seen as a 'first-stage gentrifier' or a 'pioneer'. But such a conceptualisation does not help us to comprehend her needs, her aspirations, and her relationship to older established residents.

I have argued here that chaotic conceptions of the problems and conflicts around 'gentrification' issues cannot lead us toward solutions. We ought not to assume in advance that all gentrifiers have the same class positions as each other and that they explore to what extent they may comprise different fractions of the labour force. At present, they may have similar locational needs for reasons that may be related to the interrelationships of their roles in social production and changes in reproduction. These relationships are not, however, reducible to structural forces and changes in the economy, and are malleable, potentially, by conscious human agency. It may well be that these groups have some needs and 'interests' in common[8]. Needs for certain types of services, decentralised childcare facilities, and housing that is taken out of the private market come to mind. This is not to paper over the conflicts that also undoubtedly exist, but merely to stress that, if we analytically lump together what I have called marginal gentrifiers with their wealthy namesakes, we are preventing any recognition of the possibility of forming alliances between the former groups and the groups likely to be displaced.

The operation of the private-housing market is the immediate vehicle which pits these two against one another, forcing them into competition or even actual conflict over the displacement issue. However, some of the polarisations between the two

groups, as well as the struggles they share, originate in processes much broader than the operation of the land and housing markets. Yet attempts to overcome such polarisations do not have to be limited to the 'sphere of production'. Indeed, the 'sphere of everyday life' and the reproductive work carried on therein are at least equally crucial and logical starting points of political practice for those socialists who are also feminists (for example, see Luxton, 1980; Rowbotham et al, 1979; Sayer, 1981). For instance, a 'community' newspaper in Denver—clearly a product of the gentrification of the neighbourhood it serves—discusses a local zoning regulation preventing unmarried couples from living together, commenting:

"[This] zoning can be used against persons who are not acceptable in a neighbourhood. That could be the elderly, handicapped and gay. These people have already been discriminated against in many other areas. [Such restrictive] zoning is just one more slightly hidden weapon against those who do not 'fit in'" (*Life on Capital Hill*, 1983, page 11).

Though one might dismiss this as a piece of easily voiced liberalism by the privileged, I do not believe such comments should be so easily discarded. To assess the possibility of developing alliances and organisational forms that could move us a step closer to 'designing a city for all' (Abu-Lughod, 1982) in the smaller scale of a particular inner-city neighbourhood, detailed empirical research is needed. This would explore the interrelationships between the form of restructuring taking place in the city's economy, changes in labour processes, the production of different fractions of labour and changes in their reproduction, and the particular types of gentrification taking place there.

Realistically, we cannot put an end to all gentrification. Moreover, *some* of the changes which are usually subsumed within the concept 'gentrification' can bring into existing neighbourhoods intrusions of alternative ways of living, which would never be tolerated if they were not being introduced by 'middle-class' and 'professional' people in the first instance. Whether or not such alternatives remain limited to versions in the 1980s of bourgeois bohemianism and individualistic self-help, or whether they can diffuse and broaden and consciously and collectively be directed toward 'prefigurative' ways of living and working, is a wide open and contingent question. It is this political (with a small 'p') concern that has motivated the methodological and exploratory discussion pursued in this paper (compare Fincher, 1983).

Thus, rather than being constrained by the 'chaotic concept' of gentrification as it is now generally understood, I believe that it is now an urgent research priority to disaggregate this concept, question some of the existing categories, and start to explore the actual processes through which those groups we now subsume under the category 'gentrifiers' are produced and reproduced. Such work should eventually yield an expanded, and much more adequate, specification of the necessary tendencies and contingent conditions for gentrification (as currently defined) to take place. It is to be hoped that it will also help to generate more subtle and sensitive methods for exploring particular empirical situations where these tendencies may or may not become reality. This may help us clarify what constitute progressive types of intervention and to identify 'oppositional spaces', within the noncommodified sphere of daily life (compare Conway, 1982; Rose, 1980), where such interventions may be tried out.

NOTES

1. Canadian dollars.
2. The literature on gentrification in North America has tended to be dominated by the view that state involvement, in the form of some kind of subsidies to gentrifiers, is essential to the process. This is not necessarily so in all cases of gentrification [a point which Mabin (1983, personal communication) reminded me about]. However, pilot research on renovation by moderate-income gentrifiers in Montréal (Ayotte and Cohen, 1983) does suggest that they might not have carried out the renovation without City grants [which, incidentally, the City will entirely recoup in increased property taxes within eight or nine years, according to an official at the Service de Restauration.

3. An extensive literature now exists on the problems that women, especially those who are both parents and wage earners outside the home, face in conventional suburbs. See Wekerle (1981) for a review of the literature to that date.

4. Exclusionary zoning according to household type was ruled illegal by the Supreme Court of Canada in 1979 (Lees, 1983). In the USA, some relaxations in such zoning have been introduced, but they usually only cover existing residents of the municipality concerned and/or elderly people (Muller, 1981, page 97).

5. 'Plexes' generally comprise two or three *superimposed* dwellings, in which each apartment (or every two apartments) has a private street-related entrance and an individual street address. (Upper-level apartments have an outside staircase to street level.) Since many plexes were originally built for owner occupancy, their structural quality, size and internal arrangement of space are frequently superior to those of purpose-built rental units. These attributes make plex apartments attractive to moderate-income purchasers buying in the copropriété (co-ownership) tenure form, as well as to people who may buy an entire plex building and then convert two of the units into a single dwelling (Wexler, 1984, personal communication).

6. However, there is an interesting review of new projects of Canadian architect-designed suburban housing for mixes of family types and incomes in, significantly, a recent issue of a women's magazine (see Surpin, 1983), and formal shared housing schemes, for reasons of social support for the elderly and for single parents, are being pioneered in the Greater Vancouver area and are now drawing some attention in the USA (*Urban Reader*, 1982b). Small 'grandmother houses' in families' backyards are also beginning to make a reappearance in a few places in the USA, although in most municipalities zoning laws would render them illegal (*Urban Reader*, 1982b).

7. In my view, nonprofit rental housing cooperatives broadly based along the lines of the Québec
model (that is, all members co-own all buildings
comprising the cooperative, but do not own alien-
able shares of the capital value; each member is a
tenant of the cooperative and pays a low to moderate rent for her/his unit; limits are placed on the
income distribution of tenants) are among the
most promising of feasible alternatives, in spite
of the problems they have encountered (Fincher,
1982; St. Martin, 1982).
8. The notion of 'class interests' is a very problematic
one. It is inherently a normative and evaluative
notion, connoting someone's view of what constitutes 'correct' consciousness and/or practice,
and has its origins in the political philosophy of
utilitarianism (Therborn, 1980, pages 100–105).
This is discussed in more detail in Rose (1984,
chapter 5). I am grateful to Mabin (1979, personal
communication) for initially drawing my attention to the difficulties of defining 'interests'.

REFERENCES

Abu-Lughod J, 1982, "Designing a city for all", in *Internal Structure of the City* (second edition) Ed. L. S. Bourne (Oxford University Press, New York) pp. 594–602.

Alonso W, 1980, "The population factor in urban struc-ture" in *Internal Structure of the City* (second edi-tion), Ed. L. S. Bourne (Oxford University Press, New York) pp. 540–551.

Ayotte M, Cohen L, 1983, "A questionnaire on gentrifi-cation in Plateau Mont-Royal (Montréal)" mimeo available from the authors, c/o Department of Geography, McGill University, Montréal, Québec H3A 2K6, Canada.

Benwell Community Project, 1978 *Private Housing and the Working Class* Final Report Series no 3 (Benwell CDP Publications, Newcastle upon Tyne).

Castells M, Murphy K, 1982, "Cultural identity and urban structure: the spatial organisation of San Francisco's gay community" in *Urban Policy under Capitalism* volume 22 of *Urban Affairs Annual Reviews* Eds. N. I. Fainstein, S. S. Fainstein (Sage, Beverly Hills, CA) pp. 237–260.

Ceccarelli P, 1982, "Politics, parties and urban move-ments: Western Europe" in *Urban Policy under Capitalism* volume 22 of *Urban Affairs Annual Reviews* Eds. N. I. Fainstein, S. S. Fainstein (Sage, Beverly Hills, CA) pp. 261–276.

Chamberland D, Hemens B, 1983, "Pilot survey of the McGill Ghetto gentrifiers" mimeo available from the authors, c/o Department of Geography, McGill University, Montréal, Québec H3A 2K6, Canada.

Christopherson S, 1983, "The household and class formation: determinants of residential location in Ciudad Juárez" *Environment and Planning D: Society and Space* 1, pp. 323–338.

Clark W A V, Onaka J L, 1983, "Life cycle and housing adjustment as explanations of residential mobil-ity" *Urban Studies* 20, pp. 47–57.

Conway D, 1982, "Self-help housing, the commodity nature of housing and amelioration of the housing deficit: continuing the Turner—Burgess debate" *Antipode* 14, pp. 40–46.

Cox K R, Mergler G J, 1982, "Gentrification and urban form" RR-27, Center for Real Estate Administration and Research, Ohio State University, Columbus, OH 43210, USA.

Dansereau F, Godbout J, Collin J-P, L'Écuyer D, Lessard M-J, Larouche G, Chabot L, 1981 "La transformation d'immeubles locatifs en copropriété d'occupation" rapport présenté au Gouvernement du Québec, Institut National de la Recherche Scientifique—Urbanisation, Université du Québec, 3465 rue Durocher, Montréal, Québec H2X 2C6, Canada.

De Giovanni F, 1983, "Patterns of housing market activity in revitalizing neighborhoods" *Journal of American Planning Association* 49, pp. 22–39.

Fincher R, 1982, "The commodification of Québec's progressive housing cooperatives" mimeo avail-able from the author, Department of Geography, McMaster University, Hamilton, Ontario LS8 4L8, Canada.

Genovese R G, 1981, "A women's self-help network as a response to service needs in the suburbs" in *Women and the American City* Eds C R Stimpson, E Dixler, M J Nelson, K B Yatrakis (University of Chicago Press, Chicago, IL) pp. 245–253.

Guterbock T M, 1980, "The political economy of urban revitalization: competing theories" *Urban Affairs Quarterly* 15, pp. 429–438.

Habitation 1982 "Pourquoi acheter un condomin-ium?" 4, pp. 5–8.

Hayden D, 1981 *The Grand Domestic Revolution: A History of Feminist Design for American Homes, Neighborhoods and Cities* (MIT Press, Cambridge, MA).

Holcomb B, 1981, "Women's roles in distressing and revitalising cities" *Transition* 11, pp. 1–6.

Holcomb B, Beauregard R A, 1981, "Revitalizing cities" Association of American Geographers Resource Paper, Washington, DC.

Holcomb B, Green P, Page C, 1983, "Blacks and urban revitalization: winners or losers?" paper pre-sented at the Annual Meeting of the Association of American Geographers, Denver, CO, 24–27 April; mimeo available from the authors, Department of Urban Studies, Lucy Stone Hall, Rutgers University, New Brunswick, NJ 08903, USA.

Jackson P, 1983, "Residential loft conversion and neighbourhood change" paper presented at the Annual Meeting of the Association of American Geographers, Denver, CO, 24–27 April; mimeo available from the author, Department of Geography, University College London, London WC1E 6BT, England.

Klodawsky F, Spector A, Hendrix C, 1983, "The housing needs of single parent families in Canada" mimeo available from Ark Research Associates, 165 Hinton Avenue North, Ottawa, Ontario K2Y 0Z9, Canada.

Lawrence J, 1982, "An evaluation of neighbourhood revitalization: Montréal's Shaughnessy Village" mimeo available from the author, c/o Department of Geography, McGill University, Montréal, Québec H3A 2K6, Canada.

L'Écuyer D, 1981, "La conversion: revue de la littérature" rapport intérimaire soumis au Gouvernement du Québec, sous la direction de Jacques Godbout; Institut National de la Rechercher Scientifique—Urbanisation, 3465 rue Durocher, Montréal, Québec H2X 2C6, Canada.

Lees D, 1983, "Suburban dream . . . suburban nightmare?" *Chatelaine* May issue, pp. 49–51, 76, 80, 83–84.

Le Gates R T, Hartman C, 1981, "Displacement" *Clearinghouse Review* 15, pp. 207–249.

Le Gates R T, Murphy K, 1981, "Austerity, shelter and social conflict in the United States" *International Journal of Urban and Regional Research* 5, 255–276.

Ley D, 1981, "Inner-city revitalization in Canada: a Vancouver case study" *Canadian Geographer* XXV, pp. 124–148.

Life on Capitol Hill 1983, "Local zoning struggle affects unmarried couple" by J Carling, volume 9, issue 4, pp. 8 and 11.

London B, 1980, "Gentrification as urban reinvasion" in *Back to the City: Issues in Neighborhood Renovation* Eds S Laska, D Spain (Pergamon Press, New York) pp. 77–92.

Luxton M, 1980, *More than a Labour of Love* (Women's Press, Toronto).

Mackenzie S, 1983, *Gender and Environment: Production and Reproduction in Post-war Brighton* PhD thesis, Graduate Division of Geography, University of Sussex, Falmer, Brighton BN1 9RH, England.

Mackenzie S, Rose D, 1983a, "Industrial change, the domestic economy and home life" in *Redundant Spaces in Cities and Regions? Studies in Industrial Decline and Social Change* Eds J Anderson, S Duncan, R Hudson (Academic Press, London) pp. 155–200.

Mackenzie S, Rose D, 1983b, "Perspectives on urban restructuring: problems for feminist research" paper presented at the Annual Meeting of the Association of American Geographers, Denver, CO, 24–27 April; mimeo available from D Rose.

Markusen A, 1981, "City spatial structure, women's household work and national urban policy" in *Women and the American City* Eds. C R Stimpson, E Dixler, M J Nelson, K B Yatrakis (University of Chicago Press, Chicago IL) pp. 20–41.

Michelson W, 1977 *Environmental Choice, Human Behavior and Residential Satisfaction* (Oxford University Press, New York).

Mingione E, 1981, "Perspectives on the spatial division of labour under the recent productive restructuring and informalisation of the economy" paper presented at the Conference on New Perspectives on the Urban Political Economy, Washington, DC, 22–24 May; mimeo available from the author, University of Messina, Messina, Italy.

Muller P O, 1981 *Contemporary Suburban America* (Prentice-Hall, Englewood Cliffs, NJ).

Planners Network, 1980, "Towards a union of progressive planners" proceedings of the Planners Network Conference, Columbia University, NJ, 10 May; mimeo available from R A Beauregard, Department of Urban Planning, Rutgers University, Lucy Stone Hall, Brunswick, NJ 08903, USA.

Popenoe D, 1977, *The Suburban Environment* (University of Chicago Press, Chicago, IL).

Roistacher E A, Young J, 1981, "Working women and city structure: implications of the subtle revolution" in *Women and the American City* Eds. C R Stimpson, E Dixler, M J Nelson, K B Yatrakis (University of Chicago Press, Chicago, IL) pp. 217–222.

Rose D, 1980, "Toward a re-evaluation of the political significance of home-ownership in Britain" in *Housing, Construction and the State* Conference of Socialist Economists, Political Economy of Housing Workshop (CSE-PEHW, London) pp. 71–76.

Rose D, 1983, "Women and gentrification: some research problems" paper presented at the Third Annual Women in Planning Conference, Rutgers University, New Brunswick, NJ, 22 April; mimeo available from the author.

Rose D, 1984 *Home Ownership, Uneven Development and Industrial Change: The Making of a 'Separate Sphere' in Late Nineteenth Century Britain* D Phil thesis, Graduate Division of Geography, University of Sussex, Falmer, Brighton BNI 9QN, England.

Rothblatt D W, Garr D J, Sprague J, 1979 *The Suburban Environment and Women* (Praeger, New York).

Rowbotham S, Segal L, Wainwright H, 1979 *Beyond the Fragments: Feminism and the Making of Socialism* (Merlin Press, London).

Rudel T K, 1983a, "Household change, accessory apartments and the provision of low-income housing in American suburbs"; mimeo available from the author, Department of Human Ecology, Cook College, Rutgers University, New Brunswick, NJ 08903, USA.

Rudel T K, 1983b, "Inflation and regional change in access to home ownership in the 1970s"; mimeo available from the author, Department of Human Ecology, Cook College, Rutgers University, New Brunswick, NJ 08903, USA.

Saegert S, Winkel G, 1981, "The home: a critical problem for changing sex roles" in *New Space for Women* Eds G Wekerle, R Peterson, D Morley (Westview Press, Boulder, CO) pp. 41–64.

St. Martin I, 1982, "La théorie de l'embourgeoisement et les coopératives d'habitation à Montréal"; mimeo available from the author, c/o Department of Urban Planning, McGill University, Montréal, Québec H3A 2K6, Canada.

Saunders P, 1978, "Domestic property and social class" *International Journal of Urban and Regional Research* 2, pp. 233–251.

Saunders P, 1979, *Urban Politics: A Sociological Interpretation* (Penguin Books, Harmondsworth, Middx).

Saunders P, 1982, "Beyond housing classes: the sociological significance of private property rights in means of consumption" WP-33, Urban and Regional Studies, University of Sussex, Falmer, Brighton BN1 9RH, England.

Sayer A, 1981, "What kind of marxism for feminism?"; mimeo available from the author, School of Social Sciences, University of Sussex, Falmer, Brighton BN1 9QN, England.

Sayer A, 1982, "Explanation in economic geography" *Progress in Human Geography* 6, pp. 68–88.

Smith N, LeFaivre M, 1984, "A class analysis of gentrification" in *Gentrification, Displacement and Neighborhood Revitalization* Eds. B London, J Palen (State University of New York Press, Albany, NY) in press.

Soper M, 1981, "Housing for single-parent families: a women's design" in *New Space for Women* Eds. G Wekerle, R Peterson, D Morley (Westview Press, Boulder, CO) pp. 319–332.

SPCMT, 1980 *Metro's Suburbs in Transition. Part 2: Planning Agenda for the Eighties* Social Planning Council of Metro Toronto, 185 Bloor St East, Toronto Ontario M4W 3J3, Canada.

Stamp J, 1981, "Towards supportive neighborhoods: women's role in changing the segregated city" in *New Space for Women* Eds. G Wekerle, R Peterson, D Morley (Westview Press, Boulder, CO) pp. 189–198.

Surpin M. 1983, "The adaptable environment, part 2: small is beautiful, again" *Homemakers' Magazine* March issue, pp 115–130.

The New York Times, 1983a, "Apartment sharers fret over lease ruling" by G Dullea; 16 May issue.

The New York Times, 1983b, "Computers: worker menace?" by B Nelson; 4 September issue.

The New York Times, 1983c, "Controlling the co-op conversion wave" letter to the Editor from J. Eisland, City Councillor; 13 April issue.

The New York Times, 1983d, "In Hartford, it's the best and worst of times" by S R Freedman; 14 April issue.

The New York Times, 1983e, "A housing plan for artists loses in Board of Estimate"; 11 February issue.

Therborn G, 1980 *The Ideology of Power and the Power of Ideology* (Verso, London).

Thorns D C, 1981, "The implications of differential rates of capital gain from owner-occupation for the formation and development of housing classes" *International Journal of Urban and Regional Research* 5, pp. 205–217.

Urban Reader 1982b, "Three's company" volume 10, issue 3/4, pp 33–34.

Village Voice, 1982a, "Portrait of the artist as a good use" by R Goldstein; 14 December issue, pp. 10, 14, 16, and 50.

Village Voice, 1982b, "Space invaders: land grab on the Lower East Side" by M Gottlieb; 14 December issue, pp. 20 and 22.

Village Voice, 1983, "AHOP vs UHAB: artists' housing, round two" by R Goldstein; 31 May issue, page 21.

Wekerle G, 1979, "A woman's place is in the city" paper prepared for the Lincoln Institute of Land Policy; mimeo available from the author, Faculty of Environmental Studies, York University, Downsview, Ontario M3J 1P3, Canada.

Wekerle G, 1981, "Women in the urban environment: a review essay" in *Women and the American City* Eds. C R Stimpson, E Dixler, M J Nelson, K B Yatrakis (University of Chicago Press, Chicago, IL) pp. 185–211.

Western J, 1981 *Outcast Cape Town* (University of Minnesota Press, Minneapolis, MN).

Weston J, 1982, "Gentrification and displacement: an inner-city dilemma" *Habitat* 25, pp. 10–19.

Women in Planning Steering Committee—Oregon Chapter, no date *Planning with Women in Mind* Region West Research Consultants, 520 SW Sixth, Suite 1107, Portland, OR 97204, USA.

Wulff M G, 1982, "The two-income household: relative contribution of earners to housing costs" *Urban Studies* 19, pp. 343–350.

CHAPTER 17

The Dilemma of Racial Difference

Monique Taylor

"Come on in and don't mind the dust. I'm just here doing Kim's hair". June Wilson, a slight black woman dressed in a bright orange, yellow, and green African-print jumpsuit, welcomes me into the living room of her 145th Street brownstone. The room—a makeshift parlor with cardboard boxes for furniture, and paint-stained sheets draped about—reflects the chaos that entered Wilson's life when she purchased this house and moved to Harlem in the late 1980s.

The room is a wreck—exposed plaster, green paint peeling from the walls, dangling wires, tools everywhere. On one wall, a framed African print—a museum exhibit reproduction—explodes in black, red, and yellow zigzag lines. It hints at a more stylish life prior to this move. In 1988, Wilson moved to Harlem and four years later is still in the midst of the extensive rehabilitation of a nineteenth-century brownstone she hopes to "restore to its original glory." But progress is slow, she explains, "I've had to deal from the ground up, new heating, new heating system, new floors, new roof, new bathrooms, and I still deal with the plumbing."

Kim, a black woman in her early thirties, sits atop a high stool, a towel around her shoulders, a jar of hair cream in one hand, combs in the other. Today is Sunday—hair day, they tell me. Wilson alternately dips her fingers into the jar of hair cream and tugs at strands of Kim's hair. Neatly lined rows of braids take shape around Kim's head as we sip coffee and talk about Wilson's decision to move to Harlem.

Wilson gestures excitedly as she talks about her first years of brownstone living in Harlem. Despite her enthusiasm, it is not immediately apparent why this woman, a magazine editor, would choose to live here. She recites a litany of problems. Banks are not forthcoming with loans. There is no end in sight to living in a shell of a house. Plus there is the crime, the noise of the streets, and the overall negative reputation of the community.

A successful, middle-class professional, Wilson certainly had choices about where to make her home. When her work moved her from the Midwest to New York, why had she not heeded the advice of friends or the prodding by realtors who tried to steer her clear of Harlem when she arrived? For Wilson, living in a black community and working toward its improvement represent a respite from her work in a predominantly white environment:

I know this is not such a positive thing to say, but I worked in an environment where I didn't see many people that looked like me. So it was important for me to set up house in an area where I would be the most comfortable. That meant being around black people who were race-minded.

Seeking "race-minded" people is not new to Wilson. Wilson's racial consciousness and her worldview were shaped by a keen awareness of the color line. This line was solidified in the segregated schools and neighborhoods of her youth. A firm commitment to race was reinforced through black pride at home. Her activist spirit was forged by direct political involvement in the protests and marches of the turbulent 1960s:

> If I see the storm, I usually try to make my way right through the middle of it. My family was very active in the civil rights movement, and we marched with Martin Luther King. So I had, like, several marches under my belt by the time I was eight. And, you know, we had the stuff down. My family was about building little revolutionaries to go out there. So this [the move to Harlem] in my head is easy.

Wilson shrugs off the disarray as a temporary state. Besides, with the racial socialization she gained from family and black institutions, Wilson considers her move to Harlem as putting her racial politics into practice. In fact, Wilson's renovation of the brownstone is meant to convey a larger symbolism, which I detect when she describes her own "revolutionary" role in Harlem:

> It's an easy community to become visible in because there are so many things to be done. And it's an easy community to win over if you have the right words. It's easy because its been hurt so many times. It's like a baby waiting to be nurtured.

Using a language and tone of mothering, Wilson depicts her arrival in terms of race and gender. Her words fall in line with a long tradition of birth and awakening metaphors associated with Harlem. But this is a description much at odds with the images of invasion and conquest that frequently accompany angry rhetoric over gentrification.

Throughout our conversation, Wilson talks about the purchase of her home not as an individual act but as part of a collective restoration and preservation effort. And in a twist, she places herself squarely on the side of those being invaded, though she is among the newcomers:

> I see it as a war, and there are a lot of soldiers here who are ready to do battle. They really are ready to do battle, whether it's working with the community groups, working with the churches, actively purchasing properties here and trying to turn them from diamonds in the rough into something that shines. You know, there are a lot of people who are getting caught up.

A commitment to race and community-building comes through in Wilson's comments. To the extent that she belongs to a broader movement, however, Wilson's account defies conventional wisdom; At a time when political and economic changes seem to obviate such a move,[1] a "return to the city" movement by blacks as gentry in a black community presents a fascinating vantage for examining the nuanced realities of race and class in post-civil rights America.

But new arrivals have at times been greeted with a mix of trepidation, suspicion, and distrust. Vocal opposition to redevelopment depicts a threat to the history and identity of the community. This explains, in part, why some long-term residents, community activists, realtors, and redevelopment officials, heard from in preceding pages, would voice a preference for a *black* middle-class role in revitalizing Harlem.

The arrival of middle-class blacks gives way to other contradictions. Community indecision and a lack of consensus over the years have combined to sustain a long-standing collective worry that "the whites are coming, the whites are coming." Over time, this cry has become one "official reality" defining, in racial terms, a crisis confronting Harlem. Where anti-development rhetoric moves race to a central location, the invasion by gentry is understood as a white-versus-black issue. The community is energized as a collective body when new life is breathed into old enemies—"whites," "outsiders," "the city." Caught in a familiar tangle of "us" and "them," Harlem girds itself against vaguely defined villains.

This community discourse circulates and ends up supporting a view of newly arriving middle-class blacks as Harlem "insiders." Newcomers like Wilson claim a place for themselves in Harlem's redevelopment story through an assumed, and automatic, "insider" status. But while it makes for romantic headlines,[2] the storybook tale of a black "renaissance and revival" is incomplete. By downplaying conflicts embedded in the economic forces that foster neighborhood revitalization, these accounts sidestep the possibility of a not-so-happy ending.

Academic studies of gentrification cast a critical eye at the class inequalities found in such neighborhood changes. From an economic perspective,[3] gentrification is a social process signaled by historical shifts in capital and real-estate markets. Cycles of investment and reinvestment occur in "blighted" and undervalued urban landscapes, pushing aside decades of neglect and decline due to disinvestment. Newly arriving gentry are viewed as class actors whose role in the process prompts questions such as "renaissance and revival for whom?"

In a community, on a block, or at a particular street, real people are actors thrown together to negotiate sometimes shared and often differing views of communities in transition. For an unknown amount of time the process of gentrification throws everything up in the air. The neighborhood, along with its housing stock, its residents, its market value, its reputation, its cherished traditions and shared memories, is pushed onto a stage of history that becomes a maelstrom of markets and money, design and displacement, capital and class struggle. The bottom line, in the end, is that rents tend to rise. Money matters—rising rents, a higher tax base, less desire for affordable or mixed-income housing—make it plain that all do not benefit equally from the urban "renaissance" and "revival" of gentrified communities.

Unfortunately, both of these scenarios—the white takeover and the yuppie makeover—make it difficult to account for Wilson and others like her who claim they are drawn to Harlem as a symbol of racial identity and community. Middle-class blacks are not a neat fit with the 1980s yuppie persona. On the whole, while the 1980s did give us Bill Cosby, in the mainstream of popular culture, middle-class blacks were marginal. But behind the noise produced by yuppie and baby-boomer trends, fads, and accomplishments, middle-class blacks were crying out to be heard. Accounts of (black) middle-class angst in a new cultural landscape by "post-civil rights" and "affirmative action" (black) baby boomers marked a not entirely problem-free coming of age.[4]

By looking at race as a multifaceted reality, we will be attuned to the shifting, fluid, and multiple identities found in the stories of Harlem's black gentry, They reveal identities that fit, and do not fit, within the historical strait-jacket of black and white categories. Along with June Wilson, this chapter introduces eleven other black middle-class newcomers who purchased and settled in brownstones, co-op apartments, or condominiums in Harlem during the late 1970s, 1980s, and early 1990s. Race and racism bind these individuals to a shared narrative of black economic success and a desire to become homeowners in the black community. [...]

HOME AS A REFUGE

Scholars of race and ethnicity explain patterns of migration by looking at push and pull factors, placing history and social structure as a context for movements of human populations. Push and pull are the twin forces that gentrification studies examine as well as they attempt to explain the makeup of gentry and why they end up in the neighborhoods they do. Politics, economy, and culture provide a starting point for narrowing factors that explain the actions of individuals as freely acting agents who are historically and socially situated.

In the case of Harlem, a critical social fact accounting for the presence of a black gentry at this historical moment is the significance of race. Further, the return by middle-class blacks to an inner-city, black community goes against the general trend of suburbanization and decreasing segregation for middle-class blacks on which sociologists have focused since the 1960s. The choice to come "home to Harlem" seems to defy one of the central gains of the civil rights era: the promise of residential integration. In fact, it is what makes Harlem's gentrification a unique case for exploring modern race meaning.

One of the consequences of middle-class black mobility in a post-segregation era is movement into "integrated" work and neighborhood settings that places middle-class blacks at the forefront of racial change in America. In interviews with Harlem's black gentry, I often heard expressed a feeling that they continue to confront a sometimes brutal color line as they integrate neighborhoods and workplaces.

When Reggie Smith, a television journalist, returned with his family from a long-term assignment in Kenya, he wanted to buy a home and to live in the city. He picked

Harlem. Smith had a preference for a black neighborhood, he explained, like the one in Chicago where he had grown up. This preference was reinforced when he experienced what he called "a violent reaction from racism" in Chicago:

> In Chicago we bought a house in a white area that was firebombed before we moved into it. Because I travel so much, I was worried about leaving my wife and kids alone. I made a decision to live in a black community, no matter the ills.

For the Smith family, overt racism accompanied their entry into the white world. The firebombing of one's home, while an extreme case, is a harrowing expression of exclusion from white America. Although Smith's middle-class purchasing power enables him to afford to buy a home in a white neighborhood, his class position does not guarantee the family is welcome. Despite gains from civil rights legislation in the area of fair housing, choices about where to live are nonetheless influenced by racially defined constraints. In this instance, hostility and violent aggression informally replace codified restrictive covenants as a way to keep blacks from buying in white neighborhoods.

The migration of middle-class blacks into Harlem is not only pushed from the outside, though. Networks of people from within and outside of the community support this black in-migration:

> I started to meet people here in Harlem and just felt very much at home, started getting involved in a lot of community-based activities here, so whenever I had a chance, I was here anyway. And I started packing up, spending the night over here. You know, I just had clothes in New Jersey, it got to that point. So finally, a woman that adopted me as a godmother of sorts, she said, well, I think that we just need to have you here. And people started looking out for apartments. And within a year after meeting her, I wound up moving into

her building. So that's how I wound up on Hamilton Terrace and in Harlem.

I do see young professionals like myself moving in here, because I didn't move to Harlem alone, so to speak. I came by way of a network of friends, actually, that I knew from school, from my black-college experience. And then my next-door neighbors I knew from school from Atlanta—they both are professional actors. So I kind of came into a community of people. So I see individuals—musicians like Sherif Ani, people like Barbara Johnson—owning houses here, young professionals wanting to move in because they want to be with their own people, and they want a sense of community that they don't get in other parts of New York.

Malcolm Balderidge, a writer, defines getting "back to the community" as a way to counter the racism he associated with living on Manhattan's Upper West Side:

I wanted to live here because I got tired of living in a very middle-class white community, not because I'm against white folks or anything like that, because I'm not. But I got tired of always having to prove myself.

"I was not willing to change," Balderidge continues, "and become a more proper-looking African American, you know, cut my hair and not be so energetic." He clutches and shakes a strand of his dreadlocks before continuing:

Since I wasn't willing to become a Negro like that, then I decided I would leave. You know, I thought it would be best for my own psychological and mental makeup to live in an African American community where they don't ask me those kinds of questions, where they don't feel threatened.

For Balderidge, the suspicious and often frightened looks of whites in the elevator late at night in his prior residence were part of what he termed "racial harassment" at the hands of his neighbors:

I lived in a luxury building, and getting in the elevator and [having] some white, some little white, snotty-nosed kid coming up to me saying, "What are you doing in the building? Who are you going to see?" You know, the whole kind of trip that I had to go through every day although I lived in there longer than they had. I mean, these were graduate students at Columbia, you know, who were asking me questions like, "Why are you in this building?"

So I got tired of going through that kind of ritual, that ridiculous kind of scenario that you have to go through with middle-class white people who are definitely afraid of their shadow, especially a black shadow. So you get in an elevator when they see you every day and they're afraid. If it's 12:00 at night, they just can't deal with it, you know. So I got tired of that. I got tired of going through that. It wasn't my problem, it was their problem. It was just they weren't willing to change, you know.

Portia Hamilton was born and raised in Scarsdale, a community she describes as "very white, upper, upper-class." After her divorce and a brief period of residence in North Carolina, Hamilton and her two children, Jerry and Shawnee, moved to Harlem in 1986. Hamilton's memories of growing up as one of "a handful of blacks" in Scarsdale point to the more subtle effects that race can have on blacks living in mostly white communities. "As a black female," she told me, "there were very interesting dichotomies. There was the best of both worlds and the worst of both worlds, so to speak":

The white families got to be sure [what black families were there], and they did not offend us in any way, shape, or form. So they made sure we were included. Until we got to high school. And then you can really tell the difference. And I couldn't understand it. What I didn't understand is—it doesn't matter about what goes on when you're in the elementary grades. What makes the difference is when you hit the age where you're sexually active and you think about reproduction. And that's when you can start seeing differences. The parties decrease, the invitations to parties decrease, and that kind of thing. So my friends became more my church friends than my school friends.

While Hamilton notes the acceptance she and her brother experienced in "genteel, old-money" upper-class, white Scarsdale, in her teen years, differences defined along racial lines increased:

> I was just frustrated, and I was sick and tired of being there. And I just wanted to be somewhere else. I think part of it was fear. Most of my friends at the time were white, and I was dating a young man who was white. And we went up and down in that relationship, our mamas and daddies fussing at us. I think it was the fear that motivated me. The fear that I would not have a social life more than anything else.

More and more, Hamilton's childhood friendships and activities with white schoolmates were replaced with a social life centered in the black church she and her family attended.

Hamilton and her brother each reacted in their own way to their social distance from the larger white community. Her brother, she said, became withdrawn and bickered at home more and more. Her strategy was to leave:

> I rebelled against it myself. My brother rebelled against it, too. And we rebelled in very different ways. When I got to eleventh grade, I said, "Listen, I've had it with this white world up here. I've got to do something different." So I did. I convinced my mother to let me go south to live with my aunt. And I thought I'd died and gone to heaven.

Having escaped the alienation of white Scarsdale, Hamilton completed high school living in an all-black community, at an all-black school. Hamilton described the transformation:

It was the best thing that could have happened to me. I was absolutely petrified. I mean kids using profanity and fighting with teachers. I mean, I was not exposed to it. I would sit back like a scared kitten. But my grades improved. I shot up to all A's. And it helped build my self-confidence. What I have since learned as an adult is there were always those subtle messages when we were growing up in Scarsdale that we really weren't quite good enough. And it may not ever have been articulated that way, but you got the message. And so my self-esteem was nil.

Hamilton's move to the South, an experience she likens to having "died and gone to heaven," shaped her later decision as a parent to move with her two children to Harlem.

Hamilton was drawn to Harlem by the press accounts rather than by friends who lived there:

> The kids used to fuss—mommy you have to get married again. And I'm saying, "I'll never get married living in Scarsdale." So I said, let me come to Harlem and be part of this "renaissance" I'm hearing so much about. And I had dreams and visions, and I saw art parties and political conversations going on in homes. And I felt that's where I needed to be. So I came.

Hamilton reasons that her own children, first raised in Scarsdale, then with relatives in a black community in the South, "needed that exposure to a much larger black community."

For Ruth Baxter-Brown, a journalist, the attraction of having a home in Harlem was to provide a balance between two worlds, offering a haven from her job downtown:

> I have real strong feelings—I really wanted to live around black people. I really did. I really got tired of going downtown and having white folks act like I don't belong down there. I get that all day long. I don't want to hear that shit when I get home. When I get home, I want to

have people wave at me when I come up the street. And that's what I get living in Harlem.

Baxter-Brown looks to Harlem as a community that allows her to recreate the world in which she grew up, a black community in the Midwest. In Harlem, she says, community rituals of her neighbors signal that she belongs:

> It feels like home. It's the kind of neighborhood I grew up in. I like being on the street where I know everybody. I like coming up the block and having people stop and say hi. I like knowing who is home from college and who is just out of the hospital.

George Carver also defines the move to Harlem as a way to resolve the tension of straddling two worlds: "I feel that way wherever I live because I'm a black American, African American. We live in two different worlds, different cultures." While he suggests that there may be other strategies that blacks employ to deal with their marginality, the move to Harlem is a statement of the appreciation for black culture among middle-class blacks:

> "Well, I mean, we're talking about blacks being accepted, blacks being comfortable with who they are and what they are, blacks accepting their own culture and their own values. That's what it is. An expression of that may be coming to Harlem. Thinking that I made it is determined by the fact that I have left. That's no longer it.

Carver believes that middle-class blacks, despite having accrued material rewards from their success, are in search of deeper meaning in their lives:

> We used to think having a swimming pool or having that BMW was all that ever mattered, or sending our kids to Harvard was all that matters. Hey, there is a lot more.
>
> Part of the definition is intellectual. It's how you view yourself. And part of the issue about

Harlem is, blacks still think making it is getting the hell out of here, moving to Scarsdale. You know how many people I know who are black who used to live in Harlem, but yet don't read black magazines, but got these nice corporate jobs? They ran away from their culture. Well, they're going to be running back. There's guilt that comes from the reawareness of people saying, "Hey, I ran off and did all of these things, but I'm still the last hired and first fired, I still have less of an economic cushion to fall back on in hard times. I still, after all of this, two cars and all of that, I really when it counts—where it counts—don't really have anything. So, what's been missing is, I've been chasing this dream that really doesn't protect me."

In this comment, Carver argues that the tenuous position of the black middle class, coupled with the lingering racism they experience, fuels this longing for a "return" to something of deeper significance.

But Etta Harrison said a lack of assimilation elsewhere was not a motivation for her own move:

> I don't really give a damn about that. I mean that's why you go home at night. Because this is home. You need to be in an environment where you feel comfortable. Where you don't always have to project a certain kind of image to people. We are here because we feel comfortable to a certain extent. I've chosen to live here in Harlem. That's it. I'm not interested in knowing the white folks who won't talk to me about who I am as a black person. I know who I am. I don't want to discuss it with you, you know. I don't want to be explaining myself. That's why you come home. That's why you're here. Because other people will look at you and know who you are, and they don't have to ask anything about you.

Yolanda Jackson, a city housing official, cited frustrations over racist encounters with her former neighbors as a primary reason for moving to Harlem. Jackson recounted throwing a party for a Senegalese filmmaker in the Upper East Side apartment where she formerly lived. As she and guests enjoyed cocktails on the balcony, neighbors on a balcony overhead began shouting racial slurs. To add to Jackson's embarrassment, another neighbor called the police to register a noise complaint.

Though she laughed as she retold the story, Jackson described that episode as one of a "handful" of unhappy encounters with white neighbors, including the time a neighbor mistook her for a maid when they met up in the building's laundry room. There and at her job, Jackson says, she was always aware of a boundary—made clear through the words of neighbors and coworkers, or simply indifference—that had defined her as an outsider: "It's like always this attitude that you feel and sometimes is articulated in the things people say or how they respond to you [that] you don't belong there." On the one hand, Jackson's job in an integrated setting and her residence on Manhattan's Upper East Side are evidence of the dissolution of a codified color line that once restricted black-white contact. But in those integrated environments, some whites, through words and actions, erect a boundary that to Jackson implies that "you don't belong."

Interviews with Harlem's black gentry revealed, again and again, an emotional tension arising as they crossed once restrictive boundaries:

> When you're out there getting your tail kicked by people who don't care who you are enough to even call you by the right name, or mistake who you are when you walk into a restaurant or a building, even the one you live in, that's important. That's very important, you know. Blacks have to manage a lot of rage. There's a lot of reasons why we suffer from hypertension and other diseases at a disproportionate rate. That happens to be one of them, in my opinion.

Sociologist Orlando Patterson characterized the resurgence of racism in the 1980s as a result of "homeostasis," that is, continuities that accompany change. In any historic era, this homeostatic principle—the maintenance of relatively stable conditions by internal processes that counteract any departure from the norm—is a means of gauging the persistence of certain features of race relations.

"It comes as no surprise," writes Patterson, "that just as the black working and middle classes began to make some headway under the impact of affirmative action laws, there was an upsurge of direct racism, reflected most crudely in the upsurge of KKK and other neofascist groups as well as the increased number of overt racist attacks (including one unambiguous old-style lynching of a randomly selected working-class black southern youth) but more subtly, and far more dangerously, in the powerful cultural signals given by the Reagan presidency that racist intolerance is once again acceptable."[5]

Increased contact with whites gives rise to encounters with racism and heightens, in a way that would seem to defy expectations, racial consciousness among middle-class blacks. As told in stories about work and home, the rituals of segregation that were once used to maintain social distance and establish positions of superiority and inferiority continue to shape contact between whites and blacks. Social scientists argue that "harsh discrimination against blacks . . . leads blacks to form an 'oppositional social identity' and an 'oppositional cultural frame of reference.'"[6] Fordham and Ogbu identify "beliefs and practices that protect black people's sense of personal identity against insults and humiliations of the dominant white group," such as through "unconventional ways of moving, gesturing, talking and thinking that are viewed as irrational and frightening by whites," The push and pull factors that draw middle-class blacks to Harlem indicate the roots of such oppositional practices and identities.[7] [. . .]

NOTES

1. See Massey and Denton, *American Apartheid.*
2. David Sibley, "Outsiders in Society and Space," in *Inventing Places*, ed. Anderson and Gale, 107.
3. Ibid., 120.
4. Ibid., 112.
5. Osofsky, *Harlem*, 90.
6. Ibid., 111.
7. See Osofsky, *Harlem.*

REFERENCES

Anderson, Kay, and Fay Gale, eds. *Inventing Places: Studies in Cultural Geography.* Melbourne, Australia: Longman Cheshire, 1992.

Massey, Douglas M., and Nancy A. Denton, *American Apartheid: Segregation and the Making of the Underclass.* Cambridge, Mass.: Harvard University Press, 1994.

Osofsky, Gilbert. *Harlem: The Making of a Ghetto.* 2d ed. New York: Harper and Row, 1971.

CHAPTER 18

Urban Space and Homosexuality: The Example of the Marais, Paris' Gay Ghetto

Michael Sibalis

INTRODUCTION

During recent decades, 'gay ghettos' have emerged in many large cities in North America and western Europe. The word 'ghetto' originated in 16th-century Venice and initially referred to an area of a city where local authorities forced Jews to reside, American sociologists of the Chicago School appropriated the word in the 1920s to designate urban districts inhabited predominantly by racial, ethnic or social minorities, whether by compulsion or by choice. By the 1970s, sociologists were applying the term 'gay ghetto' to neighbourhoods characterised by the presence of

> gay institutions [like bars, bookstores, restaurants and clothing stores] in number, a conspicuous and locally dominant gay subculture that is socially isolated from the larger community, and a residential population that is substantially gay
>
> (Levine, 1979, p. 364).

such as West Hollywood in Los Angeles and the West Village (part of Greenwich Village) in New York.

The classic (and most studied) gay ghetto is, of course, San Francisco's. A homosexual community first emerged in that city in the 1920s and 1930s, most notably within the bohemian atmosphere of North Beach.

In the early 1960s gay men began moving into Eureka Valley, a working-class Irish-Catholic neighbourhood whose inhabitants were deserting the city's centre for the suburbs, The gay men renovated the dilapidated (and therefore still affordable) Victorian houses, opened new businesses, including gay bars, and created a visibly gay neighbourhood (soon dubbed 'the Castro' after Castro Street) that urban sociologist Manuel Castells has described as "not only a residential space but also a space for social interaction, for business activities of all kinds, for leisure and pleasure, for feasts and politics" (Castells and Murphy, 1982, p. 246; Castells, 1983, pp. 138–170; Duggins, 2002; Stryker, 2002). The pattern apparent in San Francisco has been replicated (with variations) elsewhere, leading to the formation of gay ghettos in many other large North American cities, such as Bay Village in Boston (Patti-son, 1983), the Marigny neighbourhood in New Orleans (Knopp, 1990) and Cabbage-town in Toronto (Bouthtillette, 1994). By constructing their own urban enclaves, gay men have come to "figure prominently" in the "urban renaissance"—which is to say in the redevelopment and gentrification of the inner city (Lauria and Knopp, 1985). An attractive and centrally located but rundown neighbourhood ripe for gentrification draws in gays who are not only responding to economic incentives (low rents and real-estate prices), but also seeking to create a territory which they can inhabit and control and where they can feel at home within a self-contained community set apart from a world perceived as indifferent or even hostile. Their presence encourages the opening of bars and other businesses that cater to a gay clientele. A gay ghetto provides them with a territorial base for the development of a gay movement, which can then become a force in municipal politics.

Great Britain, too, has its gay ghettos, although residential enclaves have been slower to appear there than in North America. In London, the 'gay village' of Soho and especially Old Compton Street ("the gayest 100 yards in Britain") is a commercial and not a residential neighbourhood (Binnie, 1995, pp. 194–198). Newcastle's gay scene is "predominantly non-residential inner-city apart from a large block of housing association flats on Waterloo Street, many residents of which are gay" (Lewis, 1994, p. 90). Manchester's 'gay village', centred on Bloom Street and Canal Street and reputedly the largest in Britain outside London, consists of bars, clubs, businesses and a community centre that serve the city's gay population, but once again it is primarily a social scene rather than a residential district, although single men have been moving into the city centre since the 1990s (Hindle, 1994, pp. 17–22; Quilley, 1997).

France has only one gay ghetto, in the historical Marais quarter of central Paris. This paper is a case study of the Marais. It seeks not only to throw light on the similar processes by which gay ghettos everywhere tend to emerge and grow, but also to examine those features that are unique to the French experience. The gay Marais shares certain characteristics of both the British gay village, which is primarily commercial, and the North American gay ghetto, which is commercial and residential. Like

its British and American counterparts, the Marais came into being largely as a product of impersonal economic forces (the real-estate market) and contemporary social change (the emergence of a significant urban gay population with its own distinctive sub-culture). There are also notable differences, however. Paris' gay ghetto resulted to a large extent from politically motivated decisions made by a few businessmen who intentionally set out in the late 1970s to promote a more open gay lifestyle in France. Another key difference is the hostile reaction provoked by the ghetto in France. While the development of urban gay enclaves has everywhere brought some degree of social and political tensions in their wake, only in France, where the dominant political discourse rejects multiculturalism and minority rights in favour of 'universal' values presumably shared by all citizens, has the existence of the gay ghetto been perceived as a threat to the very foundations of national solidarity and become an issue of broad ideological significance.

This paper begins with a description of the distinctive character of the historical Marais quarter and how it has been shaped by urban development and economic change over many centuries. Gentrification and the proliferation of gay venues constitute only the most recent phase in this neighbourhood's very long history. After examining the relationship between homosexual men and Parisian space during the 20th century, the paper looks at the social and economic factors that fostered the development of the Marais as the site of a gay ghetto in the 1980s and 1990s, and most notably the motives and role of certain gay businessmen who financed the transformation. The paper then turns to the relationship in France between the gay ghetto (territoriality) and the emergent gay community's new sense of identity. It ends with a detailed account of the disputes that have raged around the very existence of the

Marais and the 'ghettoisation' of homosexual life that it purportedly represents, issues that have made the Marais the target of virulent criticism from both outside and inside the gay community.

THE MARAIS

The Marais, situated in central Paris on the Left Bank of the Seine, is the oldest quarter of the city to have survived the centuries relatively intact (Chatelain, 1967), 'Marais' means 'marshland' and most of the Marais was indeed swamp until drained in the 8th century, but in medieval times the word also referred to land used for growing vegetables; the one-time prevalence of market gardening in the area most likely explains its name. The Marais straddles 2 of Paris' 20 *arrondissements* (administrative districts), encompassing most of the 3rd *arrondissement* (everything but those parts west of the Rue Beaubourg or north of the Rue de Turbigo) and about half of the 4th *arrondissement* (excluding what lies west of the Rue du Renard, south of the Seine's Right Bank, or east of the Boulevard Henri-IV). King Philippe-Augustus' fortified wall (built 1190–1215) took in only the southern part of this area and religious orders built convents and monasteries in the fields beyond. Further urban development followed upon the construction of a new wall by Charles V in the mid 14th century, which put the entire Marais within city limits. In the first decade of the 17th century, Henry IV decided to reshape the Marais as a luxurious residential quarter. At its apogee in the mid 17th century, the Marais boasted numerous palaces and town houses inhabited by wealthy aristocrats, high state officials and financiers (Babelon, 1997; Faure, 1997, pp. 7–51; Gady, 2002, pp. 9–21). The result was a

> relatively homogeneous townscape at least as far as age and style are concerned. . . . The *hôtels particuliers* [mansions] of the aristocracy were set among the lesser buildings of their socially-inferior dependents—the whole ensemble an appropriately splendid setting for seventeenth-century life
> (Kain, 1981, p. 209).

The sociale élite began abandoning the Marais after Louis XIV moved the royal court to Versailles in the 1680s. The process continued apace in the 18th and 19th centuries, when aristocrats preferred to live in the new western quarters of Paris: the Faubourg Saint-Germain on the Left Bank and the Faubourg Saint-Honoré on the Right (Le Moël, 1997). Their departure "left room for a new social occupation of the space" by shopkeepers, craftsmen and wage-earners (Prigent, 1980, p. 19). By the late 19th century, the installation of small industry and commerce in the quarter and the sub-division of its mansions into apartments had turned most of the formerly aristocratic Marais into an overcrowded and rundown slum. In 1965, the Marais was still home to 7000 businesses (especially manufacturers and wholesalers in jewellery, optics, leather goods and ready-made clothes) employing 40 000 people (Kain, 1981, p. 213).[1] In 1975, only 17.3 per cent of all Parisian housing dated from before 1871, but the figure was 65.1 per cent in the Marais; 1 in 5 Parisian apartments had been constructed since 1948, but only 1 in 20 in the Marais (Prigent, 1980, p. 32).

> It was perhaps inevitable that the Marais, with its architectural beauty, its calm ambience, and its relatively central location, would one day revert to its original status as a quarter of fashion and wealth
> (Evenson, 1979, p. 320).

This resulted from the Malraux Law of 4 August 1962 (Stungo, 1972). This was "one of the most important and influential pieces of European conservation legislation", which "laid down a 'grand design' for a renaissance of the historical quarters of

French towns" (Kain, 1981, p. 200). The goal was no longer to preserve only individual buildings and monuments, but rather an entire urban site, to maintain a given neighbourhood's traditional character while modernising living conditions within it. In 1964/65, the City of Paris, with the support of the national government, designated 126 hectares of the Marais a "safeguarded sector" for preservation and renovation (Kain, 1981, p. 201).

Gentrification thus began in the 1960s and took off rapidly in the late 1970s and early 1980s. In fact, the Marais had the highest gentrification rate of any neighbourhood in the capital in the period 1975–82 (Winchester and White, 1988, p. 47). The population decline (already evident in the 1950s) accelerated and, as the working class left, the middle class and white-collar workers moved in. The Marais lost about 40 per cent of its inhabitants between the 1960s and the end of the century, as indicated by the population figures for all of the 3rd and 4th *arrondissements:* 1968: 110 281; 1975: 82 172; 1990: 68 903; 1999: 65 979 (Le Clere, 1985, p. 649; INSEE, 2000, p. 75/3). The safeguarded sector accounts for about half this population.[2]

The national and municipal governments promoted the transformation of the Marais by renovating the many public buildings in the sector and by providing owners with grants to improve their properties. Investment by real-estate developers, commercial companies and individual citizens also played an important role (Kain, 1981, p. 214; Carpenter and Lees, 1995). What was once an "uncelebrated area of extreme overcrowding and urban poverty" thus became "a gentrified landscape of consumption" in which, moreover, "consumerism . . . is associated only with the 'best' or most fashionable" (Noin and White, 1997, pp. 212–213), a change that dismayed some people nostalgic for the colourful past of "Algerian workers in the small hotels of the

Rue du Roi-de-Sicile, or Yiddish- or Polish-speaking Jews in and around the Rue des Rosiers" and "the small workshops that cluttered the courtyards of seventeenth-century town houses and palaces" (Cobb, 1985, p. 193). What no one anticipated was that the "aesthetic oasis reserved for the bourgeoisie" created by urban renewal (Prigent, 1980, p. 96) would also draw a flood of gay men and even some lesbians into the quarter. But in fact Parisian gays, like gays elsewhere in the world, had their part in the gentrification process, as one businessman recently recalled with some exaggeration:

> I've seen how in twenty years real estate prices have been multiplied by ten. . . . I knew the Marais when everything was neglected and there were not even mailboxes in the buildings. If the quarter has changed, it's undoubtedly because there has been a municipal effort, but also and above all the investment of gays. The Parisian example resembles other capital cities: gays have always taken over the most decayed, the oldest and at the same time the prettiest quarters
>
> (Garcia, 2002, p. 14).

GAY MEN AND URBAN SPACE IN PARIS

Gay men have a special relationship to urban space. Only in cities are there enough homosexually inclined men to permit the emergence of a self-aware community with its own commercial venues, social and political organisations and distinctive sub-culture (Harry and DeVall, 1978, pp. 134–154). In the words of the Danish sociologist Henning Bech, "being homosexual . . . is . . . a way of *being*, a *form of existence".* Homosexuals belong to one of a number of social worlds (Bech does not identify the others) that are all

> essentially urban: they are largely worlds of strangers and not just of personal

acquaintances; they depend in part upon the non-personal, urban free flow of signs and information, as well as upon the pool of strangers, for recruitment and reproduction; they occupy time-space slices of the city and need urban stages to be enacted on
(Bech, 1997, pp. 153–156).

We know a great deal about the urban spaces used by Parisian homosexuals (generally called 'sodomites' or 'pederasts' before 1900) since the early 1700s, both outdoor ones (parks, gardens, riverbanks, quays and streets) and indoor ones (taverns, bars, clubs and restaurants). In the 18th and 19th centuries, these were spread across the city, but were usually situated on its margins, either literally (on its physical periphery) or figuratively (in poorer and seamier districts) (Sibalis, 2001). Beginning in the 1880s, however, commercial venues catering to homosexuals clustered in the Montmartre quarter of northern Paris, known for bohemianism and illicit sexuality, including female prostitution. In the 1920s and 1930s, other districts, like the Rue de Lappe near the Bastille or Montparnasse in the south, also became important to Paris' homosexual sub-culture. After the Second World War, homosexuals frequented the bars, clubs and cafes of the Left Bank district of Saint-Germain-des-Pres, the centre of post-war intellectual life and non-conformity. In the 1970s, homosexual nightlife migrated across the Seine to the streets between the Palais-Royal and the Opera House and, most famously, to the Rue Sainte-Anne. In marked contrast to Montmartre and Saint-Germain, this was a quiet residential and business neighbourhood, almost deserted after the workday ended; the possibility of going out in relative secrecy is probably what attracted gay customers to its venues (Sibalis, 1999, pp. 26–31).

The popularity of the Rue Sainte-Anne lasted hardly more than a decade. In June 1983, a gay journalist observed that

the homosexual geography of the capital has changed dramatically. Saint-Germain and the Rue Sainte-Anne are out. Les Halles and especially the Marais are in
(Jallier, 1983, p. 35).

Several factors explain the shift. First of all, there was the accessibility of the Marais, which is centrally located and easily reached by public transport. A few hundred metres to the west lies Les Halles, former site of Paris' wholesale food market, which was transferred to the suburbs in 1969. In the 1970s, Les Halles underwent major commercial redevelopment, which included construction of an underground station (opened in December 1977) to link the subway system and the RER (Réseau Express Régional), a network of suburban trains that served 60 per cent of the population of the Paris region (Michel, 1988). The nearby Avenue Victoria, running between City Hall and Châtelet, is also the main terminus for the city's night buses, which operate from 1.30a.m. to 5.30a.m.

Secondly, the renovated Marais had an undoubted aesthetic appeal. In the overblown rhetoric and rather stilted English of a recent bilingual guidebook:

No other area of Paris has such a strong personality in spite of its [architectural] diversity. The same beauty of its dwellings can be seen in every street, the same refinement of the stones, the same warmth of the thoroughfares and everywhere the same poetic poetry [sic]. The Marais . . . has a spirit, a soul, an immaterial existence beyond the mirror of life
(Auffray, 2001, p. 8).

The attractiveness increased in the 1970s and 1980s, when the Marais was turned into an important cultural and artistic quarter. The Pompidou Centre (a new national museum of contemporary art) opened on its western edge in 1977 and the opening or refurbishing of other museums and the proliferation of commercial art galleries soon followed.

But there is a third factor that explains how and why the Marais became the centre of Parisian gay life. Gay businessmen recognised that the Marais, with its low rents and real-estate prices, was ripe for investment. In this respect, the gay Marais, like gay villages and ghettos in Britain and North America, developed spontaneously in response to favourable market conditions. But gay investors in Paris were concerned with more than the balance sheet. They consciously set out to create a new gay quarter as much because of their personal convictions as from their desire to benefit financially from an evident commercial opportunity.

BUSINESSMEN AND THE 'GAY MARAIS'

Joël Leroux launched the first gay bar in the Marais in December 1978. An accountant bored with his job, Leroux decided "to change [his] skin" (as he put it) and bought "for a song" a small cafe on the Rue du Plâtre, which he renamed Le Village after New York City's Greenwich Village and reopened as a gay bar. Le Village was something quite new to Paris. Whereas most gay venues did business only in the late evening and at night, its hours were noon to 2a.m. Le Village also opened directly onto the street, just like any other café in the city, and it charged regular prices for coffee and beer. Gay bars and clubs more usually protected themselves with locked doors guarded by doormen; customers rang for admittance, then paid a cover charge and exorbitant prices for the privilege of entering and consuming. "Starting from the principle that we [gays] had nothing to hide", Leroux has explained, "I wanted people inside to be able to see what was happening outside and vice versa" (*Le Parisien*, 2001). His bar was an immediate success and doubled its turnover within a year: "There was the clientele of the clubs of Saint-Germain mixed in with another clientele that went out less often and with heterosexual clients who stayed or returned" (*Le Parisien*, 2001). In 1980, Leroux sold out (Le Village still survives under another name) and opened a larger gay bar, Le Duplex on the nearby Rue Michel-le-Comte, which he still owns today (Jallier, 1983, p. 36).

Maurice McGrath, a former sailor in the Royal Navy and owner of a Parisian travel agency, soon noticed that "the bar 'Le Village' was starting to do very well and the Marais was promising to become a French 'Greenwich village' " (Le Douce, 1983, p. 40). Eager to embark on a new business venture, he has explained, "I discovered in the Marais, a great many establishments that had been for sale for a long time. These cafes were no longer frequented, because poorly situated, and the quarter's population was changing" (Roland-Henry, 1983). McGrath and eight associates opened a bar on the Rue du Perche in November 1979, but in September 1980 he branched out on his own with the Bar Central, at the intersection of the Rue Vieille-du-Temple and the Rue Sainte-Croix-de-la-Bretonnerie (Le Douce, 1983). Like Leroux, McGrath believed that "It was necessary to change the gay scene in France, . . . The idea of a daytime bar had been launched with Le Village and I took the plunge. . . . One of the goals I set myself in opening Le Central was to make homosexual life part of everyday life" (Roland-Henry, 1983). "My ambition then was to make homosexuality commonplace, to make it visible in broad day" (Chayet, 1996).

For men like Leroux and McGrath, opening a gay venue in the Marais was evidently both a business decision and a political statement. Their bars embodied a new kind of gay culture patterned on the contemporary American scene: militant and self-assertive; the days of clandestinity and internalised shame were definitively over. But militancy did not preclude shrewd business sense and an eye for financial opportunity. As one journalist has put it:

In creating establishments run by and for themselves, gays . . . have grouped together in the same sector interdependent activities, for practical reasons, not without self-interested motives on the part of the businesses: to bring together in the same place offer and demand

(Madesclaire, 1995, p. 48).

Bernard Bousset is today the most successful of this breed of gay entrepreneurs who built up the gay Marais venue by venue. He began his business career in St Tropez in the 1960s and eventually acquired a gay bathhouse in Paris, the IDM, in the 9th *arrondissetment*. In April 1987, he opened Le Quetzal, a gay bar on the Rue de la Verrerie in the Marais, and he soon acquired other businesses in the quarter. In 1990, he founded the SNEG (Syndicat National des Entreprises Gaies, or National Syndicate of Gay Enterprises), a lobby group for gay businessmen that he would lead during the first decade of its existence (Neuville, 1995).

Gradually more and more bars, cafes and restaurants catering to a predominantly gay clientele appeared in the Marais (Martel, 1999, pp. 171–173), while other gay-owned or gay-friendly businesses sprang up to sell books (Les Mots à la Bouche, the city's gay bookstore since 1980, moved to the Marais in 1983), clothing, furniture, art, antiques, home decorations and so on. There has even been a gay pharmacy on the Rue du Temple since the mid 1990s. Its owner has explained, in words that any gay businessman could echo, that

la Pharmacie du Village uses its geographical position, at the heart of the Marais, to target a gay clientele by winning their confidence and establishing a reassuring complicity with its clients

(Laforgerie, 1997, p. 26).

The presence of such establishments inevitably had repercussions for other venues in the quarter as "homosexual visibility indeed spreads into public space but also into nearby businesses" (Bordet, 2001, p. 136). A good example of this spreading out occurred on the Rue des Archives. In 1995, the owners of a traditional café at 17 Rue des Archives, on the corner of the Rue Sainte-Croix-de-la-Bretonnerie, worried by a decline in their regular business, set out to attract the new gay clientele present in the neighbourhood by changing its decor and renaming it the Open Bar, "to show that we are open to everyone: homos, lesbians, heteros, without distinction" (Ulrich, 1996). Bernard Bousset soon bought them out, renovated the place and renamed it the Open Café: "In summer it overflows and on some evenings the Rue des Archives seems to have become the terrace of the Open Café" (Garcia, 2002, p. 11). The year 1995 also saw the opening of the (gay) Café Cox next door at 15 Rue des Archives. Largely because of the proximity of these two gay cafes, four non-gay venues across the street (a Chinese restaurant at No. 16, a pizzeria at No. 12 and two ordinary cafes at Nos 8 and 18) soon found themselves welcoming throngs of gay customers all day and into the early hours of the morning.

The development of the gay Marais coincided with the burgeoning of the 'pink economy' in France—the gay market that business is reportedly eager to tap (Wharton, 1997). By the turn of the century, French gay men had become "a much courted clientele" (Revel, 2001), averaging 25 to 40 years in age, with a purchasing power estimated to be 30 per cent higher than that of the heterosexual consumer (Cornevin, 1996). The Marais has become "a considerable magnet" whose 184 gay or gay-friendly bars, restaurants and shops attract an average 20 000 clients a day. This reportedly generates 1000 jobs directly and another 1500 indirectly, "which makes the gay businesses as a whole the principal employer of the [fourth] *arrondissement*" (Garcia, 2002, p. 10). If one newspaper reporter is to be believed:

From the grocer to the restauranteur, all rub their hands and try to win over this clientele known for its high purchasing power. "They buy without looking at the price" marvels Maryse, saleswoman at the furniture store Maison de Ville

(*Le Parisien*, 2001).

As the above quotations imply, the vast majority of the Marais' gay clientele is male. There are at present no more than three or four lesbian bars in the Marais and, while women can enter most (but not all) of the men's bars, they are rarely made to feel welcome there. Although cafes, restaurants and shops do welcome women, female customers are nonetheless clearly in a minority. Generally speaking, lesbian communities are less territorially based than gay male communities and lesbians socialise far less in bars and clubs than do male homosexuals (Lockard, 1985; Retter, 1997). A study published 15 years ago, and therefore rather outdated by now, suggests that while lesbians are most probably over-represented among the residents of inner Paris, 'lesbian facilities' (bars, restaurants and nightclubs, but also social centres, cinemas and bookshops) are less geographically concentrated than those serving gay men (Winchester and White, 1988).

Even taking into account only homosexual men, however, the expression 'gay Marais' is somewhat misleading. First of all, gays have not taken over the entire Marais. Gay businesses cluster along relatively few streets, principally in the south-western corner of the quarter, like the first 200 metres of the much longer Rue des Archives or the relatively short (300 metres long) Rue Sainte-Croix-de-la-Bretonnerie, which one newspaper has called "gay Paris' display window" (Baverel, 1996). Secondly,

If homosexuals come here to consume and to seduce each other, only an infinitesimal minority have moved into the Marais. The ghetto is primarily commercial

(Chayet, 1996).

Actually, observation and anecdotal evidence suggest that many gay men do in fact live in the Marais, but rising rents and real-estate prices in central Paris make this difficult for all but the relatively well-to-do. As a result, probably more gay men live in adjacent (and somewhat cheaper) districts, like the 11th *arrondissement*, than in Marais itself.[3] Moreover, many gays prefer to put distance between where they live and where they go out to socialise and homosexuals can certainly be found in every neighbourhood of the city (Bordet, 2001, p. 116). Thirdly, the Marais is not the only gay scene in Paris.

The Marais had the pretension to be Castro Street [in San Francisco] or Christopher Street [in New York City]. It has never entirely succeeded. . . . Gay life is spread out and several decades have scattered meeting places to the four corners of the capital

(Vanier, 1991, p. 56).

To take a few of the more obvious examples: Le Palace, which opened in 1978 and became the most fashionable Parisian gay club of the 1980s, was situated on the Rue du Faubourg-Montmartre, well outside the Marais, while Le Queen, opened in 1994 and the most chic gay club of the 1990s, is even further away, on the Champs-Élysées. The Rue Keller, in the 11th *arrondissement* and some 1500 metres east of the gay bars of the Marais, has developed quite independently since the late 1970s into a small but distinct centre of gay bars and clubs; the city's Lesbian and Gay Centre even moved there in the early 1990s.

Emmanuel Redoutey, in studying the geographical distribution of gay and gay-friendly spaces across Paris, has used the image of a cone.

Like the tip of an iceberg, the concentration of establishments in the Marais quarter, where self-identified homosexuals exercise a kind of supremacy over businesses and over the animation of several streets that are also treasured by tourists, plays a central role [in gay life]

(Redoutey, 2002, p. 60).

(By one recent estimate, 40 per cent of Paris' gay or gay-friendly venues are located in the 3rd and 4th *arrondissements*.)[4] About 40 establishments "occupy a broader zone in the heart of Paris" that takes in *arrondissements* adjacent to the Marais. These venues, usually less obvious to pass-ers-by than those located in the Marais, are mainly bathhouses and 'sex bars' with 'back-rooms' or 'dark-rooms' where clients can engage in sexual relations. (There are also nightclubs and discotheques in this zone, which Redoutey neglects to mention.)[5] Finally, the wide base of the cone comprises outdoor spaces (public toilets, streets, quays along the Seine and canals, and public parks) that homosexual men use for pick-ups and anonymous semi-pub-lic sexual relations. This broad base covers the entire city, as well as two vast wooded parks on its outskirts: the Bois de Boulogne to the west and the Bois de Vincennes to the east. For Redoutey, the Marais showcases a socially "acceptable" homosexuality in con-trast to "an underground and disparaged homosexuality [in bathhouses, sex clubs and outdoor cruising-grounds] whose dif-fuse expression occupies the dark corners of the city" (Redoutey, 2002, p. 63). But it is the Marais, precisely because it is more vis-ible and more acceptable, that draws public attention, represents gay life to the straight world and has served as the territorial base for the construction of a gay community.

THE MARAIS AND THE EMERGENCE OF A COMMUNITY

The Marais has thus become a clearly delineated gay space in the heart of Paris, where gay men and lesbians can stroll hand-in-hand or kiss in the street without embarrassment or risk of harassment. In the convoluted jargon of a geographer, such public displays of affection constitute an

appropriation and territorialisation [of a quarter] through the street behaviour of the clientele of gay establishments [who] chal-lenge the hetero-centric character of public spaces and thus give the Marais a conspicu-ous territoriality

(Bordet, 2001, p. 119).

The average homosexual would put it more simply. According to one gay man,

One feels more among family here [in the Marais] than anywhere else in Paris. Perhaps that's what we mean by the [gay] community
(Darne, 1995).

And for another, who recently moved from Lille to Paris, the Marais represents his community's financial clout:

I was glad to see that *les pédés* ['fags' or 'poof-ters'] had money and could open stylish establishments. I was glad to belong to some-thing organized, which represented a certain economic power

(Laforgerie, 1998, p. 20).

Their enthusiastic appreciation of the ghetto is a relatively recent attitude and even today is not shared by all gays and lesbians. As long ago as 1964, the monthly magazine *Arcadie*, organ of France's politi-cally conservative 'homophile' association, the Club Litteraire et Scientifique des Pays Latin (Literary and Scientific Club of the Latin Countries), warned French homosex-uals against copying what was occurring in the US by creating

a little artificial world, enclosed and suffo-cating, where everything would be homosex-ual: not only the bars, restaurants and movie theatres, but also the houses, the streets (in New York several streets are already almost entirely inhabited by homosexuals), the neighbourhoods. . . . A world where one could live one's entire life without seeing anything other than homosexuals, without knowing anything other than homosexuality. In Europe that is called *ghettos*. . . . We hate this false, harmful and grotesque conception of homosexuality

(Daniel, 1964, p. 387).

Radical gay militants of the 1970s had little in common with their homophile elders, but they too denounced gay ghettos—both the 'commercial ghetto', meaning the bars at Saint-Germain-des-Prés or on the Rue Sainte-Anne, and the 'wild ghetto' constituted by the parks, gardens and public urinals where homosexual men hunted for sexual adventure (Martel, 1999, p. 77).

Radicals believed that ghettos encouraged a separatist homosexual identity (J. Girard, 1981, pp. 132–133), whereas they wanted homosexuals to participate in the revolutionary transformation of society as a whole: "Instead of shutting everybody up in their own space, we need to change the world so that we find ourselves all mixed together" (Boyer, 1979/80, p. 74).

Some gay radicals, however, eventually changed their minds and came to recognise the political potential of the gay ghetto. Guy Hocquenghem (1946–88), the emblematic radical militant of the 1970s, told an American interviewer in 1980:

We don't have a gay community in France. That is, we have a gay movement—with several organisations actively working for political rights, as in all the Western countries—but people do not feel part of a *community*, nor do they live together in certain parts of the city, as they do here in New York City or in San Francisco—for example. And this is the most important difference and the most significant aspect of gay life in the U.S.: not only having a 'movement', but having a sense of community—even if it takes the form of 'ghettos'—because it is the basis for anything else

(Blasius, 1980, p. 36).

The relationship evoked here by Hocquenghem—linking territory, collective identity and political activism—is a complex one. Veteran militant Jean Le Bitoux, for instance, has argued that the gay community appeared first and then produced the gay Marais:

The homosexual community that was successfully emerging . . . most likely wanted to complete this social emergence in the 1980s with a space 'for expressing an identity' [*un espace 'idenmaire'*]. An emergent community needed a new geographical anchorage

(Le Bitoux, 1997, p. 49).

Other analyses invert the equation, however, insisting that the Marais created a gay community and not the other way around. For example, Yves Roussel has noted that, whatever their political camp, homosexual activists of the 1950s-1970s rejected the formation of a distinct gay community (conservatives advocating assimilation into society, radicals wanting to overthrow it), but that by the 1990s a new generation had come to embrace 'identity politics'.

Many are the men and women who see themselves as belonging to a minority group, which is the victim of a process of exclusion; this sentiment of exclusion has combined with the intense desire to constitute and to structure a homosexual community

(Roussel, 1995, p. 85).

He has attributed this shift to several factors, including the need to mobilise against the AIDS epidemic, but one particularly significant determinant has been "the emergence of a vast ensemble of gay commercial enterprises [that] have allowed for the constitution of a community of homosexual consumers with characteristic lifestyles" (Roussel, 1995, p. 107). Jan-Willem Duyvendak has similarly concluded that "in the middle of the 1980s, the concentration of gay clubs and bars, such as in the Marais in Paris, provided a certain 'infrastructure' for a community", although he minimises this community's political activism: "the militants took the occasion to go dancing rather than to demonstrate" (Duyvendak, 1993, p. 79).

Gay businessmen share this view that their venues have contributed to the growing sense of community among French gays. In the mid 1980s, the gay entrepreneur David Girard (1959–90) responded to those activists who criticised him for his brazen capitalist spirit by declaring that

> The bar owner who, in the summer, opens an outdoor terrace where dozens of guys . . . meet openly, is at least as militant as they are. . . . I think that I have done more for gays than they ever have
>
> (D. Girard, 1986, p. 164).

He even told his customers: "This gay life that is ever more present and diversified in Paris, . . . it is first of all you who create it by consuming" (D. Girard, 1983). This was precisely the message put out in an advertising campaign by the SNEG in 1996: 'To consume gay is to affirm one's identity" (*"Consommer gay, c'est s'affirmer"*). The campaign's avowed purpose was to promote its members, but "it is equally a communitarian campaign, a way to bring home to people the visibility of gay establishments" (Primo, 1998).

Arguments like these are certainly self-interested on the part of the businessmen who advance them, but that does not mean that they are without merit. As Scott Gunther has recently pointed out,

> The transformed Marais of the 80s provided a space for the development of a gay identity that had not existed before in France. As the community grew, gays themselves gained a reputation as respectable, resourceful, and affluent. . . . Throughout the 80s, the emerging gay identity and geographical space of the Marais became increasingly inseparable and

by the early 90s it seemed impossible to imagine the existence of one without the other. The resulting community, which may initially have been defined by a sexual orientation, became increasingly united by shared tastes, cultural preferences in music and food, and even by a distinct 'Marais look' among the gay male inhabitants

(Gunther, 1999, p. 34).

Not surprisingly, the proliferation and increasing visibility of gay establishments in the Marais and the concomitant development of a self-conscious gay community have re-suited in conflict with some long-time residents who resent the on-going influx of gays and the dramatic changes that they have brought about in the quarter. There is also discord among homosexuals and lesbians themselves, many of whom disapprove of the Marais or feel excluded by its dominant cultural values. [. . .]

NOTES

1. As compared with 22 351 establishments employing 72 374 in 1860 and 9721 establishments employing 44 637 in 1956 (Benedetti, 1960, pp. 9–27).
2. The available figures for the safeguarded sector alone are 1918: 100 000; 1954: 79 000; 1962: 75 000; 1968: 66 000; 1982: 40 000 (Audry and Starkman, 1987).
3. These remarks are based on personal observation and on interviews with officers of several gay associations that draw their membership from across the city. The official census does not categorise the French by religion, race or sexual orientation.
4. In October–December 2001, according to listings in e-m@ale magazine, of 230 gay or gay-friendly establishments in the city, 77 (33.5 per cent) were in the 4th *arrondissement* and 18 (7.8 per cent) in the 3rd (Bordet, 2001, p.64).
5. The SNEG claims that more than half of Paris' gay businesses (252 of 488) are situated in central Paris (the entire 1st, 2nd, 3rd and 4th *arrondissements*, which it misleadingly labels 'the Marais'), including 52 gay bars (of 88 in all Paris), 69 gay restaurants (of 99), 11 gay discotheques (of 17) and 5 bathhouses (of 16) (Laforgerie, 2003, p. 32.)

REFERENCES

Audry, J.-M. and Starkman, N. (1987) L'évolution récente du Marais, in: *Le Marais, mythe et réalité*, pp. 264–269. Paris: Picard.

Auffray, M.-F. (2001) *Le Marais: la légende des pierres, if stones could speak*, trans. by E. Powis. Paris: Hervas.

Babelon, J.-P. (1997) L'urbanisation du Marais, *Cahiers du Centre de Recherches et d'Études sur Paris et l'Île-de-France*, 9, pp. 17–34.

Baverel, P. (1996) Le Drapeau gay flotte rue Sainte-Croix-de-la-Bretonnerie, *Le Monde*, 22 June, p. 11.

Bech, H. (1997) *When Men Meet: Homosexuality and Modernity*, trans. by T. Mesquit and T. Davies. Chicago, IL: University of Chicago Press.

Benedetti, J. (1960) *Préfecture de la Seine: Le Quartier du Marais*. Paris: Imprimerie Municipale.

Binnie, J. (1995) Trading paces: consumption, sexuality and the production of queer space, in: D. Bell and G. Valentine (Eds) *Mapping Desire: Geography of Sexualities*, pp. 182–199. London: Routledge.

Blasius, M. (1980) Interview: Guy Hocquenghem, *Christopher Street*, 4(8), pp. 36–45.

Bordet, G. (2001) *Homosexualité, altérité et territoire: les commerces gais sur le bas des pentes de la Croix-Rousse et dans le Marais*. Unpublished Mémoire de maîtrise de géographie, Université Lumière-Lyon 2.

Bouthillette, A.-M. (1994) Gentrification by gay male communities: a case study of Toronto's Cabbagetown, in: S. Whittle (Ed.) *The Margins of the City: Gay Men's Urban Lives*, pp. 65–83. Aldershot: Arena.

Boyer, J. (1979/80) Quand les homosexuels se lancent à la conquête de l'espace, *Masques*, 3(Winter), pp. 73–74.

Carpenter, J. and Lees, L. (1995) Gentrification in New York, London and Paris: an international comparison, *International Journal of Urban and Regional Research*, 19, pp. 286–303.

Castells, M. (1983) *The City and the Grassroots: A Cross-cultural Theory of Urban Movements*. Berkeley, CA: University of California Press.

Castells, M. and Murphy, K. (1982) Cultural identity and urban structure: the spatial organization of San Francisco's Gay Community, in: N. I. Fainstein and S. S. Fainstein (Eds.) *Urban Policy under Capitalism*, pp. 237–259. Beverly Hills, CA: Sage Publications.

Chatelain, P. (1967) Quartiers historiques et centre ville: l'exemple du quartier du Marais, in: *Urban Core and Inner City: Proceedings of the International Study Week, Amsterdam, 11–17 September 1966*, pp. 340–355. Leiden: E. J. Brill.

Chayet, S. (1996) Marais, le triangle rose, *Le Point*, 1232(27 April), p. 96.

Cobb, R. (1985) *People and Places*. Oxford: Oxford University Press.

Cornevin, C. (1996) 100,000 gays dans la capitale, *Le Figaro*, 25 April, p. 24.

Daniel, M. (1964) Le plus grave danger, *Arcadie*, 11(129), pp. 385–389.

Darne, R (1995) Ghetto? Milieu? Communauté? Un débat ouvert, *Exit, le journal*, 21 July, pp. 8–9.

Duggins, J. (2002) Out in the Castro: creating a gay sub-culture, 1947–1969, in: W. Leyland (Ed.) *Out in the Castro: Desire, Promise, Activism*, pp. 17–28. San Francisco, CA: Leyland Publications.

Duyvendak, J.-W. (1993) Une 'communauté' homo-sexuelle en France et aux Pays-Bas? Blocs, tribus et liens, *Sociétés: Revue des Sciences Humaines et Sociales*, 39, pp. 75–81.

Evenson, N. (1979) *Paris: A Century of Change, 1878–1978*. New Haven, CT: Yale University Press.

Faure, J. (1997) *Le Marais: organisation du cadre bâti*. Paris: L'Harmattan.

Gady, A. (2002) *Le Marais: guide historique et architectural*. Paris: Le Passage.

Garcia, D. (Ed.) (2002) Dossier: le gay Marais, ghetto ou village? *Le Nouvel Observateur: Paris Île-de-France*, 1947 (February–March), pp. 8–16.

Girard, D. (1983) Édito, 5 *sur* 5, 1 (September), p. 1.

Girard, D. (1986) *Cher David: les nuits de citizen gay*. Paris: Ramsey.

Girard, J. (1981) *Le Mouvement homosexuel en France 1945–1980*. Paris: Syros.

Gunther, S. (1999) The indifferent ghetto, *Harvard Gay and Lesbian Review*, 6(1), pp. 34–36.

Harry, J. and DeVall, W. B. (1978) *The Social Organization of Gay Males*. New York: Praeger.

Hindle, P. (1994) Gay communities and gay space in the city, in: S. Whittle (Ed.) *The Margins of the City: Gay Men's Urban Lives*, pp. 7–25. Aldershot: Arena.

INSEE (Institut national de la statistique et des études économiques) (2000) *Populations légales: recensement de la population de 1999: France*. Paris: INSEE.

Jallier, G. (1983) Marais, Halles, le créneau gay, *Samouraï*, 8 (June), pp. 34–38.

Kain, R. (1981) Conservation planning in France: policy and practice in the Marais, Paris, in: R. J. P. Kain (Ed.) *Planning for Conservation*, pp. 199–233. London: Mansell.

Knopp, L. (1990) Some theoretical implications of gay involvement in an urban land market, *Political Geography Quarterly*, 9, pp. 337–352.

Laforgerie, J.-F. (1997) Argent rose, argent roi, *Ex Aequo*, 6(April), pp. 24–29.

Laforgerie, J.-F. (1998) Dehors, dedans: mon ghetto, *Ex Aequo*, 14(January), pp. 16–22.

Laforgerie, J.-F. (2003) Le Marais est-il en crise?, *Illico*, 78(6 June), pp. 30–33.

Lauria, M. and Knopp, L. (1985) Toward an analysis of the role of gay communities in the urban renaissance, *Urban Geography*, 6, pp. 152–169.

Le Bitoux, J. (1997) Marcher dans le gai Marais, *Revue h*, 1(July), pp. 47–51.

Le Clère, M. (Ed.) (1985) *Paris de la préhistoire à nos jours.* Saint-Jean-d' Angély: Éditions Bordessoules.

Le Douce, A. (1983) Maurice McGrath, un patron gay, *Samouraï*, 8(June), pp. 39–41.

Le Moël, M. (1997) Désaffection et dégradation du Marais au XVIIIe et XIXe siècle, *Cahiers du Centre de Recherches et d'Études sur Paris et l'Île-de-France*, 59, pp. 65–78.

Le Parisien (2001) Joël a 'inventé' le Marais en 1978, 18 April, pp. 12–13.

Levine, M. P. (1979) Gay Ghetto, *Journal of Homosexuality* 4(4), pp. 363–377.

Lewis, M. (1994) A sociological pub crawl around gay Newcastle, in: S. Whittle (Ed.) *The Margins of the City: Gay Men's Urban Lives*, pp. 85–100. Aldershot: Arena.

Lockard, D. (1985) The lesbian community: an anthropological approach, *Journal of Homosexuality*, 11, pp. 83–95.

Madesclaire, T. (1995) Le ghetto gay, en être ou pas?, *Illico*, 57(August), p. 48–55.

Martel, F. (1999) *The Pink and the Black: Homosexuals in France since 1968.* Stanford, CA: Stanford University Press.

Michel, C. (1988) *Les Halles: la renaissance d'un quartier 1966–1988.* Paris: Mason.

Neuville, P. (1995) Le Grand Bernard, *Le Frondeur*, 18 December, p. 6.

Noin, D. and White, P. (1997) *Paris.* Chichester: John Wiley & Sons.

Pattison, T. (1983) The stages of gentrification: the case of Bay Village, in: P. L. Clay and R. M. Hollister (Eds) *Neighborhood Policy and Planning*, pp. 77–92. Lexington, MA: Lexington Books.

Prigent, A. (1980) *La réhabilitation du Marais de Paris.* Paris: École des Hautes Études en Sciences Sociales.

Primo, T. (1998) Bernard Bousset: de la mémoire avant toute chose, *e-m@le magazine*, 17(29 January), pp. 18–19.

Quilley, S. (1997) Constructing Manchester's "new urban village": gay space in the entrepreneurial city, in: G. B. Ingram, A.-M. Bouthillier and Y. Retter, (Eds) *Queers in Space: Communities, Public Places, Sites of Resistance*, pp. 275–292. Seattle, WA: Bay Press.

Redoutey, E. (2002) Géographie de l'homosexualité à Paris, 1984–2000, *Revue Urbanisme*, 325(July–August), pp. 59–63.

Retter, Y. (1997) Lesbian spaces in Los Angeles, 1970–90, in G. B. Ingram, A.-M. Bouthillier and Y. Retter (Eds) *Queers in Space: Communities, Public Places, Sites of Resistance*, pp. 325–337. Seattle, WA: Bay Press.

Revel, R. (2001) Une clientèle très courtisée, *L'Express*, 21–27 June, p. 90.

Roland-Henry, O. (1983) Le Central, *5 sur 5*, 4(December), p. 7.

Roussel, Y. (1995) Le mouvement homosexuel français face aux stratégies identitaires, *Les Temps Modernes*, 50(582), pp. 85–108.

Sibalis, M. (1999) Paris, in: D. Higgs (Ed.) *Queer Sites: Gay Urban Histories since 1600*, pp. 10–37. London: Routledge.

Sibalis, M. (2001) Les espaces des homosexuels dans le Paris d'avant Haussmann, in: K. Bowie (Ed.) *La Modernité avant Haussmann, Formes de l'espace urbain à Paris 1801–1853*, pp. 231–241. Paris: Éditions Recherches.

Stryker, S. (2002) How the Castro became San Francisco's gay neighborhood, in: W. Leyland (Ed.) *Out in the Castro: Desire, Promise, Activism*, pp. 29–34. San Francisco, CA: Leyland Publications.

Stungo, A. (1972) The Malraux Act 1962–72, *Journal of the Royal Town Planning Institute*, 58(8), pp. 357–362.

Ulrich, C. (1996) Le Marais, quartier général du lobby homosexual, *L'Événement du jeudi*, 20–26 June, pp. 28–29.

Vanier, L. (1991) Sexe sur Seine, *Gai Pied Hebdo*, 482(21 March), pp. 56–58.

Wharton, S. (1997) Financial (self)-identification: the pink economy in France, in: S. Perry and M. Cross (Eds) *Voices of France: Social, Political and Cultural Identity*, pp. 171–186. London: Pinter.

Winchester, H. P. M. and White, P. E. (1988) The location of marginalised groups in the inner city, *Environment and Planning D*, 6, pp. 37–54.

CHAPTER 19

Consumption and Culture

Tim Butler

STYLE AND ATTRACTIVENESS

If London is to remain at the core of the international service economy, it needs to retain its attractiveness to the highly skilled middle class as a place to work and live. *The Economist*, discussing the future of New York City at the end of the eighties, had this to say about its prospects:

> ... New York has kept its lead in several of the businesses that are destined to grow fastest in the next century: advertising, corporate law, publishing, media (both print and broadcast), management consultancy, accountancy and public relations *(The Economist*, 20 October 1990).

The Economist went on to argue that it is the quality of life in New York City which is threatening to drive these middle-class professionals out:

> There is an increasingly big caveat. The quality of life in New York has fallen below the level that middle-class people are prepared to tolerate. The rich can soar above it all. They send their children to private schools, travel by yellow-cab or stretch-limo, live in apartment blocks guarded by doormen and leave for beach houses in the Hamptons at weekends. But for families living on middle incomes, living in New York is like living in modern Calcutta or medieval London (ibid.).

The importance of ensuring a high quality of life in inner London is now at the top of the agenda of inward investment agencies such as London First. London, despite all of its inner-urban difficulties, remains positively attractive not only to the very rich but also to many 'families living on middle incomes'; in the rest of this chapter I hope to show why. Inner-city gentrification permits a style of life that can still considered positively attractive.

Pahl (1989) has argued persuasively that we need to pay attention not merely to the way that people are defined by structures but also to how they define themselves. In his argument, this is particularly important for 'non-subordinate' social classes—notably the middle class. Thrift (1989) has also argued that service-class culture is' an important starting point for understanding the service class. In his view, consumption and lifestyle are important indicators of self-identity amongst the service class ('You are what you see'). Although this is over-emphasised, he perceptively identifies service-class aspirations with 'traditional values' which are subject to subtle, and not so subtle, manufacture and manipulation by the marketing industry. In particular Thrift identifies 'heritage' and 'the countryside' as pre-eminent bearers of traditional values. These are manifested by appropriate images of country houses and their accoutrements (Barbour jackets; Range Rovers and so on). It is largely irrelevant whether people are buying 'real old country houses', or the carefully-crafted modern imitations heavily larded with 'the vernacular' since both, in their different ways, are seen as statements about how their owners wish to be seen and to what they aspire (Thrift 1987; Hamnett [1973]). Oldness, or images of oldness, are important to a new class that is trying to emphasise its 'place' in the social structure; just as the industrial middle class married and bought its way into the aristocracy in the early nineteenth century so the service class is doing so in the late twentieth century (Wiener 1985; Thrift 1987).

Whilst concentrating on rural images of success and style, Thrift acknowledges that there is another subset of the service class who identify with a set of metropolitan values, associated with urban life and gentrification. What matters most for those gentrifying the inner city is that their houses are moulded from 'real history' and are not pale imitations designed by Barratts, Laings and their ilk (Jager 1986; Wright 1985a, 1985c). To this section of the middle class, modern versions of the old are not acceptable. This is clear in the gentrifying areas of Hackney and particularly in De Beauvoir where considerable store is put on 'historical authenticity'. This however is not simply about housing; it is, as we have seen, also about areas.

In both areas, despite their differences, conservation and preservation struggles have been central to the gentrification process not only physically but also in creating a sense of cohesion amongst the incomers. The struggle to preserve its historical value has, in both areas, served to bring incomers together, at least in the early days of gentrification. In both De Beauvoir and North Defoe there is a sense of history and historical authenticity which newcomers have struggled to save from the 'philistinism' and

narrow self-interest of local authorities, local residents and profit-oriented developers.

The campaign waged by the De Beauvoir Association to save what remained of the 'Old Town' from comprehensive redevelopment in the 1970s was largely successful and resulted in a number of measures to enhance its environmental attractiveness. Many of the busy traffic 'rat runs' were cut off and the social and architectural significance of the area was acknowledged by its designation as a 'conservation area'. Many of the houses were listed as being of architectural importance. The founding of the De Beauvoir Association was therefore a key 'moment' in the gentrification process; style and history were crucial arguments in winning the argument against redevelopment. By the late 1980s, the Association was clearly not the focus it had been which is, in many ways, a tribute to its success.[1]

In North Defoe preservation and conservation struggles have also been part of the process of the area's gentrification but in rather different ways. Two major campaigns in the last decade have been to preserve Abney Park cemetery and to prevent Thames Water filling in the reservoirs—located just to the west of Stoke Newington—for housing development. Both have raised wider planning issues. In the case of the cemetery, the issue has been to maintain it in its present rather wild and overgrown form and to prevent, on the one hand its 'de-naturing' back into a carefully manicured and organized cemetery or, on the other hand, its redevelopment into housing. The attractions of a wild urban green space may be lost on some of the older residents but reflect very clearly the concerns of a newer population to retain the links with the historical past (Daniel Defoe and General William Booth, amongst others, are buried there) but also to encourage urban wilderness areas in order to preserve the flora and fauna.[2] Much the same argument was deployed (less successfully) against the proposal by Thames Water to fill in the reservoirs and build housing on them. In this case the argument also involves one of public access to another 'wild area' but again one with its historical attractions— for example, the spectacular architecture of the Victorian pumping station.

In both areas, conservation/preservation struggles have played an important role in the gentrification process and how the area *should* look. The contrasts are immediate and obvious, in De Beauvoir what is being preserved is an organized townplan, the style of individual dwellings and the architectural integrity of the whole area; in North Defoe it is the 'feel' of the area, its open spaces and what might be termed its communal resources. It is as if in De Beauvoir private spaces are the focus whilst in North Defoe it is public space. There is a danger though that this contrast can be oversimplified, as there is little, if any, green space in De Beauvoir to be preserved and little architectural integrity in North Defoe. The attraction of De Beauvoir is its layout as a 'town', but one that is well provided with large and sunny private gardens. The green spaces are private and off the street. In Stoke Newington by contrast there is—by urban standards—almost a superfluity of green- and open spaces: Clissold Park; Abney Park Cemetery; the reservoirs; Springfield Park and the Lea Valley recreational area. It is therefore perhaps not surprising that there is a different emphasis in attempts to preserve the environment. In De Beauvoir what is being preserved is above all the authenticity of a nineteenth century urban development and architectural style whilst in North Defoe it is a sense of community and a community resource. What is significant is that there *are* preservation issues, since they are the means by which the incoming middle class can impose its meaning on the physical area and impart what Castells (1983) has termed 'urban meaning' as a kind of stamp of cultural ownership.

The preservation struggle is legitimated by continual reference to the significance of the nineteenth century heritage. Suitably sanitized, this history is now a positive attraction for choosing to live in De Beauvoir or North Defoe. Preservation and gentrification thus appear to be inextricably linked (Kasinitz 1988, Cybriwsky 1986, Wright 1985a). The fight to maintain the status quo and an image for the future is therefore firmly rooted in the expropriation of the past. It is also often the means whereby a class of people with this 'cultural capital' can come together to protect 'historical authenticity' and, at the same time, fight for *their* future. In other words, the fight for preservation is a focus for relatively isolated middle-class people to unite together to promote their individual and collective interests. It is an indirect way in which a group of middle-class individuals can identify not only with each other but also with a series of values connected with history and heritage to give themselves and their class a 'place' in the urban social order.

Whilst these have been important issues for respondents and residents in general in the two areas, it may not necessarily account for why they came to these areas, although it is likely to be the case that they wanted to live in an 'old house' in an area with a history (Wright 1985a).

WHY THEY CAME

Respondents were asked why they had moved from their previous residence; Table 19.1 gives their responses.[3] There was no single dominant reason for moving into either of the areas, but strictly labour or housing market induced reasons, such as 'trading up' in the housing market or moving for job-related reasons, were relatively unimportant. The single most important reason was simply that people wanted a bigger house; if they were already owner-occupiers,[4] they were moving in order to get a larger property. In practice, this often meant they wanted to move out of a flat into a house, although in De Beauvoir, where many of the houses were quite small, it often meant moving to a bigger house. If they were not already owner-occupiers, their reasons were a combination of a desire to move into a space they could call their 'own' and a fear that they would be left behind by a property market that seemed (in 1988) to be spiralling upwards out of control.[5] No single reason emerged for why respondents had moved into the area. 'By accident' was a common response, although frequently such people had moved within the area. Olivia is a good example of someone moving out of rented accommodation, who stumbled on Stoke Newington by accident and has now chosen to move again in the area:

> Originally we came here in the late 1970s because we knew we wanted to buy somewhere to live and we had been looking at flats in West London and we began to realise that we might be able to buy houses with tenants on the ground floor; we somehow got the idea that we might be able to buy a house not a flat. A friend who was living in Islington mentioned that there were nice houses in this area and we came here by chance. We walked over one day after we had been at a Rock Against Racism thing at Victoria Park which was about the first time that I had been to the East End; I can't claim any relationship with this area at all, it was like the back of beyond to me and I had never been anywhere near it and we saw this house in H . . . Road and it was three floors and there was nothing wrong with it. We had actually spent about a year looking at houses in Fulham and Wandsworth and they were always terrible—you would always go into a street and the one with stone-cladding was the one that you had the details of, there was always something really terrible about it and this house though it was dilapidated was a fine house, lots of space and it was incredibly cheap. Then it was £13,000—in 1978. So we moved there originally and I think there was always the sense that it was not the greatest area in the world in terms of the upkeep of the buildings, and the streets were really dirty and nobody ever cleaned them but it was quite lively and it never seemed threatening or worrying and it was always nice to be near the park and then Rex got the job [locally] and then it was useful to be in the area and we got more involved in the area and knew more people here.

Table 19.1 Reasons for moving from previous property

Reasons for moving	De Beauvoir %	North Defoe %	All %	All no.
Bigger property	45	42	43	103
Change in household	34	28	31	73
To own 'own home'	31	26	25	62
Get on housing ladder	20	22	21	49
Wanted a garden	20	13	16	39
To trade up	16	13	15	35
To be nearer job	18	11	14	35
Changed financial circumstances	12	10	11	27
Leave shared house	7	9	8	19
To move to area	12	4	8	18
Change in job	8	7	8	18
Wanted freehold	9	4	7	16
Job location changed	10	3	6	15

We had no idea of staying here for long, it was not the idea of 'here I am going to settle and spend my life in'; we were quite young and without much cash and it was the idea that here we could have a nice house and we were just thinking the other day that we could not believe we had been here this long —we have been here ten years. I cannot envisage moving in the next five or six years or ten years.

TB: Were you working at the time?

Olivia: No I was doing my graduate research, so I was on a grant and it was near the station. The main advantage was cheap, economy but at the same time in an urban setting. We had been living in a rented flat in Fulham and part of me thought that living in the inner city was quite interesting but part of me was quite embarrassed about having to explain where it was as nobody knew it. I used to kick myself for hearing myself almost apologising for living here; I would go into a long explanation about that was where I lived and it was really very interesting and full of local colour whereas if you said something like Primrose Hill you wouldn't have to say anything with it. There was the sense that when you were talking to people from the same class or background that you were being somewhat rebellious or strange to be living in Stoke Newington, not just that you were poor.

TB: Might the suburbs have been an alternative?

Olivia: No, never looked, no never thought of it.

TB: Why have you continued to live in the area, what are the attractions?

Olivia: With the boom of prices around here we were able to move from the first house we had. We then had a second stage of looking for houses which was in 1982 and this was still the cheapest area in London. Our house had gone up a lot in value but we still couldn't afford to move out, but we could afford a much better house in the area and when we bought this house, it took several years to get used to the idea of having so much space and that you could live a fairly luxurious lifestyle in. The flats we had been living in before H . . . Road was like one floor of one of these houses and before that when I had been at school I had lived in a flat with my sister in [Chelsea] which was two rooms which fitted into less than this kitchen; so from the age of sixteen for nearly ten years I had been used to really contained small spaces and it seemed really incredible that we had this house. From 1982 we didn't move in until 1983 because it was almost completely shelled by building work. From 1983 until Joseph's birth we put almost all our energies into doing it up. There were other things with our lives and jobs but we put an awful lot into the house, it has eaten up an enormous chunk of our lives almost without our realizing it. We certainly never got the sense of we are all right now and we can have the space to look around and think whether we want to be here. Since Joseph's been born you get all these other types of priorities, about where he has got a nursery, who he is getting to know which school he is likely to go to; I like the idea of him going to Grazebrook, I have got very good friends who live around the corner who I feel are good neighbours. I am used to around here, you can get most of the things that you want. I do get fed up sometimes—I don't like the idea that I would spend my entire life here. I have spent ten years of my life here and I don't want to wake up in thirty years time and be in the same house. Maybe when Joseph has finished at Grazebrook and if we have any more money than we have now, then we might move somewhere else.

TB: Why did you decide that you wanted to move from the original house?

Olivia: I'd always convinced myself that it was nicer than it was; it backed on to some warehouses at the back, it was very dark, it didn't have a garden, it faced north-south rather than east-west so one side of the house tended always to be dark and one wasn't. The kitchen was quite small, things like that which you didn't notice at first since it was so much bigger than what we were used to. We had thought it was the best we could do but when we realized we could do better then we decided to move.

From being here at the time when the only restaurants were unpretentious Turkish kebab houses, when there were hardly any amenities put there specifically to cater to a wealthy clientele, everything seemed very much like living on the edge. Fox's wine bar opened and it made everyone feel terribly reassured that they were living in an up and coming area. Every time you met someone in the park, or the street or somewhere they said 'have you seen there's a wine bar opening'; this ripple went through the entire area, it was almost like a sigh of relief that ' my god, you didn't put all of your money onto a dud and something is happening is changing'. Part of me felt quite resentful, almost a glamour of living somewhere distanced from that kind of world but at the same time it was much more convenient and much easier to pop out and eat something. When we were looking in 1982, we looked at houses in De Beauvoir and it always seemed much more grim and further away from any greenery. There were far more amenities here, Church Street had all the things you needed even before it was done up with the delicatessen, it had the Turkish delicatessen before that, the photography shop, Fox's, different Greek and Indian shops that had quite a good supply of fruit and vegetable whereas in De Beauvoir there wasn't something at the end of the road, you always had to go out in the car if you wanted to shop and you always bumped into people when you went to shop. It was much more a place, I still think that actually Finsbury Park, Stroud Green or down towards the Arsenal which are all a bit more expensive are not such nice places to be living.

Olivia is not atypical of respondents and the complex of reasons she gives for why she and Rex made their series of moves is also not atypical but cannot even be hinted at by survey data.

We saw, in the previous chapter (table 5.5), that 21 per cent of respondents in De Beauvoir and 34 per cent in North Defoe had moved within the area in which they were now living on at least one previous occasion; in both areas about half had previously lived either in Hackney or Islington and three quarters of the residents had moved from within the inner London area. The data suggest that gentrification in Hackney, and especially in North Defoe, is largely by people moving within a fairly tightly defined area of the inner city. Reasons for living in Hackney seemed to be largely social ('friends in the area'), aesthetic ('the style of the architecture'), economic ('the relatively low cost of housing') and often largely accidental. Although travel-to-work and cost reasons were not insignificant, they were rarely the deciding factors. What was clear was that whatever people's initial reasons for moving into the area, many liked living there and had moved again, often more than once. Having made the decision to move, one third of those in De Beauvoir and half in North Defoe decided to look only in those areas. A quarter of those now living in De Beauvoir had decided on the Nl postcode area (as had eight per cent in North Defoe) and, for the most part, ended up where they were now partly because it represented better value for money. Harriet is a 'paradigm case' of someone who moved to De Beauvoir several years ago and has now moved again in the area, even though she and her husband could have afforded to move to a more expensive area:

> Our reason for coming here was very specific, we were living in south-east London and the year after we married my mother died; my father was living in north-west London and we needed to be in-between the two. So we literally took a map of London and stuck a pin in and found ourselves roughly in this neck of the woods and started to look around at houses and found that Islington was just a little bit too expensive and around here was still a bit expensive but better.

TB: So the pin went into Islington?

Harriet: That's right; so that's what brought us here, it wasn't that we knew anything at all about the area before but it was literally the need to be between two lots of families... that's not very romantic... we didn't move to ... first of all. We were in U ... Road to begin with. We had always wanted an old house, having immediately we had married bought a brand new flat. We had always hankered after somewhere old and looking around here we found just the size house we needed at the time, which was a two bedroomed little terraced house with a manageable garden and, at the time we moved in, there were temporary road closures and they were later to become permanent so that was another attraction to the area—the thought that it was all going to become nice and quiet but that didn't come until after the public enquiry...

> We moved into this house in January 1981 ... at that stage we had one child and we had a house where the bathroom was in the basement, it was a rear extension with the bathroom in

the basement and it wasn't wildly convenient especially with a child throwing up in the middle of the night and mother having to run downstairs to the bathroom to clean up, so we were really just looking for somewhere a bit bigger. At that stage we were a little bit richer and we looked in Islington again and we saw houses that were a little bit too expensive and there you were paying for houses that had been done up. Then we happened to hear about this house because we knew the chap who was living here and he had only half done it up and the price reflected that and he was needing to sell.

TB: Did you look at other areas?

Harriet: No, it was either Islington or here and this was, from our point of view, absolutely idyllic—just what we wanted, everyone aspires to a house in ... I suppose. ... we look out at houses that are a long way away, the park, a playground—everything you could possibly want for the kids, no through traffic. The only busy time of the week is Saturday morning when 'The Waste' operates in Kingsland Road and then all the visitors to 'The Waste' park their cars here, but that's all gone by two or three in the afternoon. We've got this wonderful long back garden which is about 120 foot... it couldn't be better. Who needs a house in the country on a day like this!

Both Olivia and Harriet therefore moved into the area for largely accidental reasons, in Harriet's case because of the need to be equidistant between north-west and south-east London and for Olivia because they could buy a house with vacant possession in Stoke Newington whereas the most they could hope for in Fulham would be a flat or part-vacant house. Whilst there were clearly many reasons for why people came to the two areas in the first instance, what is equally clear is that when they might have

Table 19.2 Reasons given for buying present property

Reasons for buying chosen property	De Beauvoir %	North Defoe %	All %	All %
Liked the property	85	77	81	190
Liked the area	45	62	53	125
Price	41	57	49	114
Journey to work	41	39	40	93
Liked the garden	46	25	36	84
Liked the street	28	35	31	73
Friends in area	18	45	31	72
Need to be in area	13	17	15	35
Social mix	8	17	12	28

moved elsewhere they took a very conscious decision to stay largely because of the area.

Not surprisingly, the property itself as well as the area, particularly in the case of houses, was often a major factor in determining where they bought. Table 19.2 indicates the main reasons given by respondents for why they bought their present property:

The property itself was rated rather more important in De Beauvoir than North Defoe. This is not intended to suggest that people elsewhere buy houses they dislike, but rather, given the estate agents' dictum that the prime factors are 'location, location and location', there is an emphasis here on the individual house and its attractiveness—particularly in De Beauvoir. Area and price were the next most quoted factors. The fact that the property, the area and the price were the three most quoted factors for deciding where to buy is unsurprising. The difference between the two areas is however revealing: in De Beauvoir the individual property was quoted more often and price and area were given less importance. Respondents were more concerned about the house they bought, whereas in North Defoe, respondents seemed more interested in the area and in the price.

This impression is reinforced by the relative importance of other factors; in De Beauvoir the garden was given as a factor by 46 per cent compared to 25 per cent in

North Defoe; in part at least this reflects the fact that gardens tended to be large, south facing and therefore sunny as well as the fact that there were few public green spaces. On the other hand, in North Defoe respondents gave greater emphasis to communal factors such as having friends in the area and liking the street. Area factors and social contacts were relatively more important here than in De Beauvoir where the individual dwelling was the determining factor. This was reflected in the stylistic and preservation emphasis on the individual dwelling, whereas in North Defoe the preservation issues were more general to the area and its attractions were its public spaces.

One of the reasons that many people are attracted to inner-city living is that it involves minimal travelling time to work (this is particularly so when both partners are working). Although this reason was not often stated explicitly as a reason for living in Hackney, it was implicitly one of the reasons for living in inner London. Robert and Victoria, for example, had never heard of De Beauvoir when they started to look at houses in London:

We were living in Bristol in 1971 and I passed an examination with my company and was invited to work in London; it was promotion-based and that is really the reason why we are here. Vicky once she learnt that I had been offered work in London, started to look for work in one of the London hospitals and I think at the time you had hopes of working at the London Hospital at Whitechapel. I knew I would be working near St. Paul's so that determined very approximately the part of London that we would start looking for a house in.

Victoria: And we had also made the very basic decision that we would not spend time or money travelling, that was our intention. We thought it would be better both from the point of view of the children as we didn't want to commute . . . you know if you are working 9 to 5 and you have an hour, an hour and a half's travelling on top of that you are out 7.30 to 6.30 and we didn't want to be that far from home with our young kids, neither did we want to be paying that amount of money out so therefore we were thinking if we had to pay a £1000 more on the mortgage was that better than paying a £1000 on travel expenses, the home-help and things like that? We decided 'no', we would pay the bigger mortgage and pay out the money that way. So there was this dual thing about it and, having made this decision that we didn't want to travel, that we were prepared to pay more money for property . . . that was the policy decision we took. As Robert said, at the time we were looking, I had a firm job offer at the London. So quite literally we drew circles in the map centred on the London Hospital and where you knew your office was going to be.

Robert: By St. Paul's, and in fact we connected them by a straight line and bisected the line north and south of the River and said something within a three mile travelling radius.

Victoria: It hit Lambeth, it hit Brixton and we said that's not really on and where do we fancy living?

TB: Why weren't they on?

Robert: I am not really sure that I could echo Vicky's confidence on that one, because we really didn't know much about London at the time.

Victoria: I think the Brixton riots were on . . . having said that I was also brought up in Upper Norwood and therefore knew quite a bit about where *Des Res's* south of the River were and, so that irrespective of where the Brixton riots were, I don't think I would ever have had Brixton as a high priority.

Robert: It was really the house that sold itself to us

Victoria: It was the hall . . . it may sound stupid, but we bought the house for the hall. We realised it needed things doing to it . . . nobody in their right minds would have bought it. . . . if we had rejected this one we would have to have started from scratch.

It is revealing that, in both areas, a relatively low importance is given to the social mix of the area. This may reflect the difference between, on the one hand, a general statement of 'ideal preferences' for living in a heterogeneous neighbourhood (as opposed to a bland single class one) but, on the other hand, a recognition of the actual reality of living in a socially-mixed neighbourhood (Wright 1985a). This is expressed by Harriet, in the following terms:

We like the feeling that it is a mixed neighbourhood but, if we are truthful, we like the feeling that Hackney is a little further away . . . when you have the odd burglars and vandals then you are brought up short and think 'well this is Hackney'. But we do like the feeling that this is a very mixed community and there are people who have lived here for donkeys' years and can talk about what it was like forty or fifty years ago.

David, on the other hand, is very clear that the social mix in Stoke Newington was one of the main reasons why they came to live in Stoke Newington:

> There's a great social mix here, we've got an orthodox Jewish family that side, an English family two doors down who have become great mates. We've got a black family this side who we are very friendly with and an Anglo-French family the other side up there, a New Zealander over there and there's no tension at all in the street. There's a mixture of French, English, Jews, Blacks, Asians and everyone rubs along very happily . . . I don't like to be set in an enclave of all middle class or all anything because I think that as soon as you get all anything the same frictions start, you get the 'one upmanships', the silly, petty 'I have got to be better than the next door.

Suzanne however, is sceptical about the attractions of living in a mixed area and the reasons that are often given for this, although her partner values living in an area where people are 'not dissociated' and where he is not cocooned from deprivation. They were talking about moving to nearer where she works and he objected because he likes living in Stoke Newington and, if they were to move, he would want to find somewhere similar—to which she replied:

> I don't know whether we can find another mildly decaying, vaguely socially mixed area which is not very pleasant to live in. We have other friends who live the other side of the High Street just off Brook Road, and they are no more social activists than we are but they have three kids who go to the local schools and they really are on very good terms with their neighbours, or their kids' neighbours and they genuinely do live a very mixed life

and I am sure it does give them something whereas it doesn't for us. We aren't having our local Indian neighbours to dinner all the time.

There is therefore a gap between sentiment and reality, between the idea of a mixed community and the reality of living in a deprived inner-city area. For some living in such an area is a positive bonus, for others it is a nice idea as long as it does not impinge too closely onto their lives. In practice, the experience of social mix and polarization has not been such a happy one; Patrick Wright (1985a) makes the point that the 'local colour' is fine as long as it is properly in its place and non-threatening. 'Social mix' is a code for 'racially mixed' and this probably underlies the contradiction between fine sentiments and a sense of the vaguely exotic on the one hand (recall how Olivia used to describe Stoke Newington as 'interesting' to her friends) and the real tensions arising out of material deprivation and ethnic diversity on the other.

The differences between the two areas in terms of where one might want to live were the presence of friends in the area in Defoe and the desire to have a garden in De Beauvoir. Both were statistically significant and they neatly summarize the difference in outlook between the two areas and the relative differences in priorities of their residents.

The evidence reviewed so far has pointed to the factors that respondents gave for why they ended up in their current home in the research areas. Often, the original reason for moving to the area was accidental, or else economic ('more house for your money') but many of them became attached to the area and stayed there. Their reasons varied but can be generalised as a liking for their home, the area and their social interactions in the area. Two central questions are left about why respondents chose to live where they do; firstly why they chose to live in inner London at all and secondly how much their decisions about where to live was governed by a desire to make money from their home?

The first question is crucial to the thesis, but is unfortunately one of the most difficult to answer. This is partly because of the survey design which merely asked if they had considered looking outside London and then only prompted for reasons in the case of those who had. The dismissive answers I received to this question reinforce the data—that most had never seriously considered moving out. But for those with children, pondering what to do about their education, many were considering a move out of London, as we shall see later.

Thirteen percent had considered moving out of London when they were planning the move into their present home (15 per cent in De Beauvoir and 11 per cent in North Defoe). Most of those who considered looking outside London, soon ruled it out for a combination of reasons such as a hatred of commuting (26 per cent); both partners having a job in London (28 per cent); a need to be near the job (12 per cent); and, 34 per cent who just wanted to be in London. These figures only relate to those who considered leaving and most of those stressed that it was a combination of factors usually involving all of the above reasons. The overwhelming majority of people (87 per cent) had not considered leaving London, mainly for the above reasons. This comes out clearly in conversation with Harriet:

TB: *You asked who would ever live outside London. Did you ever consider moving out of London altogether?*
Harriet: We hate suburbia . . . it's all the same; we have got for example some relatives who live in Southgate and we get lost every time we go there. We both lived in suburbia for a large chunk of our lives and my husband just wouldn't commute, he would find it intolerable. I think that he finds fifteen minutes driving to work just about all he can cope with. We have toyed with the idea as we have got richer of the possibility of somewhere for the weekends. In fact I think that it was about this time last year that we put in an offer on a place somewhere in Cambridgeshire which I then vetoed because I could see that my husband was just going to take his work there every weekend and I would be packing up the household on Friday night and I think we have really put that idea out of our heads.

Olivia had never considered moving out of London either and stressed the virtues of city living—for her, Stoke Newington was almost rural:

Rex's sister lives in Watford and other people we know live in what you know as the commuter belt around London and that had never appealed to me. I like living in a city and around here seemed like the inner city, in a way, it did seem like the inner city . . . I had always lived for the five or six years previously in the centre of London, big streets, traffic . . . this was our most rural.

This was part of the difficulty, most respondents simply had not considered moving out of London. By virtue of the research design, I was interviewing those who had decided to stay. Many of those with young children were beginning to reconsider the option of moving out of London but, as we shall see below, many of the same reasons for staying in London were still applicable. In the case of families with young children and both parents working, the need to live near work was stronger than ever which mitigated against a move out of London. Respondents lived in London both to be near work and the cultural facilities of London but also, overwhelmingly, because

Table 19.3 Percentage mean gain on current home

Length of residence	House DeB	ND	Flat Db B	ND	All House	Flat
Under a year	15	37	26	26	24	26
1 to 3 years	56	74	60	138	67	99
3 to 5 years	154	159	162	141	156	147
5 to 10 years	186	230	197	—	198	197

they could not envisage living elsewhere: it was where their friends were and where they had lived, for the most part, since leaving university and entering the labour market.

The second issue of capital accumulation is an interesting and complex one. In the quantitative data less than 10 per cent of respondents said that they had looked at their housing moves mainly in terms of capital accumulation; rather more (just under a third) agreed it was a consideration, but the majority view was that they wanted a 'home'. Nevertheless how much their property was worth and how much it had appreciated in capital terms since they bought it, was something they were all very aware of. The rise in property prices had enabled many of them to upgrade their housing and had given them a capital asset far larger than most of them could ever hope to acquire through saving. At the same time many were quite embarrassed about the sums their houses were worth.

Almost everyone stressed their main motivation for moving was because they needed a larger house or wanted to move

from a flat to a house, or felt impelled to get into owner-occupation—very few of them mentioned capital accumulation as an explicit goal. Most of those who did not already own property felt that they had no alternative but to buy. The rise in property prices and the way in which the property market in the UK is skewed towards owner-occupation, left them feeling that they might be condemning themselves to live in a second class property market for ever if they did not make the move into owner-occupation. About 80 per cent of the first-time buyers gave these 'rational' economic reasons and 15 per cent said that they wanted to be able to have more control over their domestic 'space'.

Given the awareness of how property in general in Hackney had risen in price over recent years and the alacrity with which the majority of respondents could tell you what their individual property was worth, I am cautious about accepting at face value the claims that their motivations were strictly, or largely, non-financial. Whatever their expressed views on the subject, most respondents had made considerable

Table 19.4 London and Hackney price rises for all property[6]

Year	London £	index	Hackney £	index
1983	35,860	100	29,888	100
1984	42,629	119	34,049	114
1985	48,880	136	40,465	135
1986	55,999	156	51,357	172
1987	75,501	211	75,055	251
1988	80,827	225	73,175	245

Source: Nationwide Anglia tables supplied to the author.

financial gains from their homes. The percentage gain in table 19.3 was calculated on the basis of what they had paid for the property, taking into account the amounts that had been spent on improving the property, on the basis of the owner's current valuation of it. These figures show that the capital gains which respondents have made from owner-occupation have been substantial, far more than they might have expected from savings out of income. The major discrepancy between the two areas is flats which had been bought between one and three years prior to the survey. During this period flat conversions 'took off' and de facto became the only affordable 'starter housing' and it was this that accounted for their spectacular rise in value. On the whole, such flat conversions were not carried out in De Beauvoir but were more common in North Defoe, which accounts for the rather large gains made in flat values in North Defoe.

The gains are broadly compatible with those reported by the Nationwide Anglia. Table 19.4 indicates price rises from a 1983 base of 100 for London as a whole and for Hackney:

The figures in table 19.4, are not weighted to take into account different mixes of property but give some guide for purposes of comparison. Despite this shortcoming, the increase in prices for Hackney 1983–86 is broadly similar to that enjoyed by the respondents and is slightly greater than the increase for London as a whole. The national increase between 4th quarter 1983 and 4th quarter 1988 would have seen the same index standing at 204 (calculated from Nationwide Anglia 1988). Although there is debate about how these gains should be calculated,[7] there can be little doubt that as a capital asset domestic property in Hackney has shown large increases, which were rather greater than the rise in house prices in the rest of London and the country as a whole.

Owner-occupation and the general long-term rise in property prices meant that, when the survey work was being undertaken in 1988/9, it was largely taken-for-granted that one makes money out of owner-occupation. This was distinguished from making 'super profits' through speculating on areas that might rise faster than property prices in general. Despite what they *said*, my impression is that most respondents expected to end up with a large capital asset and this was seen as one of the not unimportant consequences of buying *and doing up* an old property in an area like Hackney. In the interviews some respondents were quite open about this and it is possible that they were merely stating explicitly a point of view that most of the others held implicitly. Robert and Victoria were very aware of the potential gains to be made in the London housing market and this was a reason for their making the move from Bristol:

We saw the whole move to London as a money-making opportunity . . . it was a promotion but also if we were going to plough money into the house, then we saw that the opportunity of living in London had lots and lots of advantages but one was house prices, that housing was one of the most sensible capital investments that you can make and therefore that we reckoned that we would probably be in London for fifteen to eighteen years but then we would move out. Never having actually saved during that eighteen years we would have the chance for capital accumulation, so again there was that fairly calculating thing when we were looking at house property lists. It had to be convenient, it had to have minimum travelling times, it had to be the right size—we didn't plan to move again. Again from the snotty point of view that this time the company would pay everything and that another time we would have to pay it all so we didn't want to move again, having moved and when we sold we wanted to have had the opportunity for maximum capital asset . . .

TB: *Were you looking therefore for a run-down area that was likely to appreciate faster than average?*

Victoria: No we weren't that clever, no but we certainly looked to buy in at the top of our price range but at the bottom of the range in the area and therefore had the potential to climb. We certainly looked for a house that, if we improved it, would capital appreciate and we rejected a house that we went to look at in Greenwich because the previous owners had done exactly that to it. They had done it badly, that terrible stuff they put on the roof.

Robert: It was quite a clinical operation because my company allowed me so many days to come and find a place, I could have up to a week's special leave, so I took Vicky along to London . . . our search centred around Highbury, this house here and then we had one in Greenwich and one further down south. I know there was a place near Finsbury Park which we just looked at and ran away from . . .

Victoria: We had five or six properties to view of which two were hot favourites, this was one and the one in Greenwich was the other . . . we didn't know De Beauvoir . . . De Beauvoir was a non-existent concept. All I can remember is having a Bristol estate agent saying to me 'Oh, you are not going to 'Flash Hack' are you?' and someone making the comment that Nl put 10 per cent on the house price—Nl was OK and E8 wasn't; no we certainly weren't driven by the gentrification of De Beauvoir or De Beauvoir being a lesser Canonbury.

This was a commonly held view, that one's home was a major asset and that investment of time and money in it was partly justified on these grounds since many respondents when asked if they had any savings, would point around them and say 'apart from the house, no'. What justified it also in their terms was partly that they might have taken a risk (as Olivia expressed it 'put our money on a dud') but more significantly that they had put time and energy into it, thus any capital appreciation was justified ('earned') and not just the result of idle speculation. This was probably reinforced by the fact that they were doing up an old property to be not just how they wanted it but how it 'ought' to be which usually equated with how it 'used' to be. Aesthetic considerations meant that any gain should be contextualised by having made it look 'right'.

'JUST AS WE WANTED IT'

The house was covered in Artex when we bought it and we spent a lot of money doing it up just as we wanted it (*Georgina*).

The desire to live in an old house emerges as a powerful reason for living in the inner city; most of the in-depth interview respondents talked about the significance of 'oldness' (Wright 1985a; Jager 1986). David owns a business which has become increasingly successful over the last few years. He moved into his present house 3 years ago, having previously lived in a modern block of flats in the area. Prior to that he and his wife lived in Dalston for about five years. Despite having enjoyed living in a modern purpose-built flat, he couldn't stand the idea of living in a modern house:

It's too rigid, there's something about houses whose walls which are off key; they are much more human. It's settled, it's been here, things have happened to this house. The people that were before us, had this house for twenty five years; they had a family here and the house reflects that. It was a happy family, I think that's very important. It's all very mystical and hard to prove but I can walk into a house and some houses I have been into on this street and I wouldn't buy. It can be identical but it doesn't feel right. I knew I was taking on various problems here that were going to cost money but it didn't bother me and there is something about the feel of this house that I had an empathy with and that's why I bought it. There's something my lawyer does not understand about me; when we bought this house he did the conveyancing for me and he said 'you've got to sell it, you've got to sell it straight away' because he thought I had got a very good price and he thought I could sell it immediately and make a large profit and buy somewhere nicer. He has known me for fifteen years and he still doesn't understand the way that Ruth and I operate. I have a lot of friends who live in areas like Battersea, De Beauvoir and even Islington and even though there's a slump in property all they talk about is the price of their property and how much it's worth. Round here it doesn't really happen. Property in this street doesn't move very often. We are the newcomers we've been here three and a half years, Richard's been here twenty five, the people two doors up moved in just before us; Nigel and Francois have been here fourteen years, the woman the other side of the road, she's been here just over seventy six years. It's unusual in that respect.

David was at pains to stress how much the social relations of the area meant to him, how important it was that the house had a history and how little he was concerned about making money out of it. Architecture, the layout of the streets and houses, and 'ambience' combine, as it were, to give a sense of meaning both to the locality and to how the individual fits into it.[8] This feeling was strong in both De Beauvoir and North Defoe; what matters is how the area 'feels' and how their house 'looks', and this has some bearing on self-image ('you are what you see'—Thrift 1989) and how 'people like us' live in the inner city doing up an old house (Jager 1986; Wright 1985a; Zukin 1988). Unsurprisingly, respondents were not only keen supporters of conservation and preservation movements in their areas but also had invested considerable amounts of time, thought and money in their homes.

> People like us live in the inner London suburbs really . . . We wanted to live somewhere that was mixed and various and vibrant; full of young middle class people doing places up.

'Doing it up' was therefore a major activity. Sixty four percent of respondents in both areas had undertaken significant improvements.[9] Table 19.5 indicates the main kinds of improvements that had been undertaken. A wide range of improvements have been carried out. What is particularly interesting is that a relatively small proportion were functionally or structurally necessary. Only 19 per cent of respondents had conditions attached to their mortgage offer requiring them to carry out improvements and less than half of these had part of the advance retained until they had carried out the work to the mortgage lender's satisfaction. 'Retentions'[10] were three times as frequent in North Defoe as De Beauvoir (13 per cent against 4 per cent), although this was partly compensated by a larger number in De Beauvoir who were required to make improvements although no money was retained. Three-quarters of those living in houses had undertaken improvements compared to only a third of those living in flats.

Table 19.5 Improvements

Nature of improvement	De Beauvoir %	North Defoe %	Total %	Total no.
Redecoration throughout	43	36	39	95
New kitchen	43	35	39	94
New bathroom	39	37	38	92
Other major improvements	34	37	36	86
Damp & wood treatment	26	36	31	74
Installing central heating	25	34	29	71
New/major repair to roof	30	26	28	68
Major structural work	25	26	25	61
Rewiring	22	25	24	57

On the whole therefore, the houses/flats being bought were in reasonably good structural condition. An 'index of improvement' was constructed on the basis of the number of improvements undertaken by each respondent. Approximately 10 per cent of respondents had almost totally 'gutted' and rebuilt their property, a further third had carried out more than five of the improvements (as itemized in Table 19.5) and about a third had done nothing significant to the property since buying it. Nearly twice as many people in De Beauvoir had completely 'redone' their property compared to North Defoe, although the rate of mortgage retention suggested that property there was in better structural condition. Despite this, considerable sums of money had been expended on improvements.

Sixty four percent of those who had made improvements in De Beauvoir had spent more than £10,000 compared to 38 per cent in North Defoe. Twenty percent in De Beauvoir had spent more than £30,000. The amount spent also varied according to the type of building they lived in, with over 90 per cent of those living in flats having spent less than £10,000 compared to 60 per cent of those living in houses having spent more than £10,000. This is hardly surprising but it does point once more to the large sums being spent by respondents who lived in houses.

Whilst there was clearly a high degree of involvement, time and 'personal capital' invested in doing up the home, relatively few respondents had done much of the work themselves in any real sense. Pahl (1984) has suggested, on the basis of his intensive study of working-class homeowners in the Isle of Sheppey that 'domestic self provisioning' is an important aspect of homeownership. By this he refers to the use of domestic labour to carry out tasks that are otherwise paid for. In particular, he refers to the widespread occurrence of 'DIY' in home improvement. This, in his account, is a major source of capital accumulation and is a point echoed elsewhere by Saunders (1990); "sweat equity" (i.e. the use of one's own labour power) is seen as a route to capital accumulation which would not normally be possible via the capitalist labour market.

Very few respondents used their own 'sweat equity' to increase the capital value of their home. Just over a quarter claimed they had undertaken the work or a large part of it themselves. The figures are somewhat misleading because they include those who basically managed the operation and co-ordinated the work of tradesmen carrying out specific tasks. Of those who claimed to carry out the work themselves, most of these were in North Defoe who were largely driven by economic necessity. This group

Table 19.6 Reasons for doing improvements

Reasons for doing improvements	De Beauvoir %	North Defoe %	All %
Improving the attractiveness	61	47	54
Maintaining the structure	38	49	44
Providing more living space	21	17	19
Fulfilling mortgage requirements	14	17	15
Adding to the capital value	14	9	11

was less than 10 per cent of those undertaking improvements; very few people had done the work themselves either from financial necessity or for the self-satisfaction.

One hundred and forty seven respondents had undertaken improvements but only 41 people had borrowed money to pay for them. In both areas large amounts of money had been spent on improvements, many of which appeared to be paid for without recourse to borrowing. This might suggest this was money that might otherwise have been invested. The key question then is why did they spend so much money and time on carrying out the improvements, especially when not forced to by mortgage lender? When respondents were asked why they had carried out improvements, nearly three quarters said to 'make it generally more habitable'. Their specific responses are given in table 19.6. Aesthetics and a sense of style come through as important reasons for carrying out improvements, particularly in De Beauvoir. Nevertheless we have seen the most frequent kind of work was complete redecoration and the installation of new bathrooms and kitchens, which might be seen both as functional and as having little to do with the house's historical appeal. This apparent contradiction has been noted elsewhere in the gentrification literature; Moore (1982) and Jager (1986) have both noted an emphasis being placed on the 'period' nature of the dwelling from the outside which is often in direct contrast with the modern, and sometimes modernistic, nature of many of the internal improvements. There is though a significance to the changes that are made to the 'functional' areas of the house, notably the kitchen and the bathroom where the style is often modern and functional, which compares with those that are carried out in the 'living areas' where great effort was often expended on re-installing fireplaces, sash windows and elaborate plaster work.

Firstly, respondents valued the labour-saving efficiencies in well-designed modern kitchens as well as appreciating the ergonomics and functionality inherent in much contemporary design. Secondly, it is meant as an indication of their historical and stylistic sensitivity that they can blend the historical and contemporary. Thirdly, it also reflects the contradictory nature of the middle class as a modern (or post-modern) class, but one whose sense of identity is partly drawn from the symbols of the past—they may work in the most modern sectors of the economy yet they seek to give some meaning to their lives through the consumption of symbols of a bygone age (Thrift 1989). The juxtaposition of functionality and style both between the interior and the exterior but also within the interior reflects the contradiction within the middle class between the role they play in the economy and how they might wish to be regarded socially.

This is not to suggest that many of the improvements were not to secure the structural integrity of the property; but all of the respondents quoted so far have stressed that what they were attracted to was the architectural and lifestyle features of old houses and, to some extent, this may resolve the connection between capital accumulation and the attraction of 'oldness'. For Georgina, one of the attractions of De Beauvoir/Islington is the housing style, although she throws an interesting angle on the question of houses both as a source of capital accumulation and as an aesthetic object to be lived in and admired:

> Another interesting thing is why this generation of mine is so fascinated by its original features and doing up old houses; I suppose it's a kind of postmodernism really a kind of rejection of the new. In the culture that I grew up in East London, people were doing it all the time [doing up houses]; you can't restore a house in the suburbs in the sense that we can, like put in a marble fireplace like the one that was here originally but you can do them up. My parents spent the whole of my childhood doing up houses and selling them. Simon's parents even more in the country did up houses, in their case old houses in the country and sold them. And that's how they made their money, they have never been rich but they made far more money from that than they ever made from Simon's father's job. So for our generation, I think we have grown up with this sense that property is a kind of task really and a way to make money just as important as doing a job in a sense. I think there is also an element of fashion, I find it vaguely absurd sometimes all these young people doing up Victorian slums so that they look like the next Victorian slum, with our mahogany loo seats— we are not buying any more because of the rain forests. This kind of obsession in getting your house to look like it should is just so that other people can come and look at it and admire and that I find really weird.

Doing up old houses is perhaps a 'task' but it is one which legitimates both making money and making it comfortable and attractive.

Whilst respondents clearly wished to live in houses that were attractive and comfortable to them, they wished to maximise the capital value of them. As Zukin has demonstrated artistic and cultural values can be a useful smokescreen for more blatant financial motives (Zukin 1988). Whilst housing is clearly the best investment most people are able to make, it has to be seen as a by-product of something that is essentially a use-value (i.e. a place to live). Many of the advantages of property ownership stem from this (for example, tax relief on mortgage payments and exemption from capital gains tax on sale) which is an encouragement to maintain the concept of housing as primarily a use-value. Improvements should be regarded in this light both as something intensely personal but also as a task or duty. Thus if capital appreciation accrues it is something that can be justified both in terms of not only the physical labour but also the conceptual labour that was involved as well as perhaps the risks of putting money into gentrified property. Thus style is the medium by which a class that doesn't like to talk about money in too personal terms is able to justify the capital appreciation it has made.

Once again however, individual accounts point to a more sophisticated understanding of why people like their homes and why they have spent so much time, energy and money on doing them up:

> I would hate to have a [modern] Georgian town-house; I could never see myself living in that sort of thing because it was something that was imposed upon me, there's something

about [a north London terrace] that was here before me. There's something about the way it's laid out and the way it's built that I find empathetic, I don't find empathetic the imposition of Barratt's 'Georgian style' on me. Why can't they just build something new that is designed, why are they harking back? If it's so good, I'll go and get another one. This one was a risk, we originally moved in and it was 'artexed' all over; the original doors had gone off here *(between the front and rear living rooms TB)* and I can't find any to put back on and there's a 'Georgian door' on the front which is a good six inches shorter than it should be and there were certain abominations here but I liked the style of the houses and what I would like to do is put back into it some of what was missing. I know it's silly but there's some horrible bubble glass over the front door, that's coming out tomorrow. Ruth's found a glass engraver around the corner that has just made some plain engraved glass, cut out in the middle with thirty five which is the number; it's very plain, it's not original but it will fit and it will look nicer than what was there. I can't see myself imposing or fitting together with a brand new house in the same way.

Part of the attraction of living in an old house in an old area is that you can restore and improve the property, thus guaranteeing some capital appreciation whilst appearing to be altruistically loyal to a sense of historical and stylistic preservation and conservation. It is perhaps this professed innocence of economic self-interest yet acute awareness of the economic worth of all that one does, which typifies the urban middle class and distinguishes it from the vulgarities of suburban life where the value of everything is written on a brand new price tag.

'PEOPLE LIKE US'

> When you see an old middle-class couple, you know it's someone's parents visiting them *(Olivia)*.

The remarkable homogeneity of respondents as an age group, clustered tightly in their late twenties through to their early forties, is striking. The comment above however also gives an indication of the sense of exclusiveness felt by respondents who, despite the fact they are a minority group and talk (in abstract terms at least) about liking social mix, are largely 'blind' to other social groups. They do not know them, don't interact with them and tend to forget they exist: 'It seems almost over-populated with people with young kids; if you go the Park its almost a nightmare of clonedom. Clissold Park used to consist of all sorts of people from different cultures and communities now it is all people like us'. Of course it isn't; as has been demonstrated, many of the middle class do not have children and many of the non-middle-class majority do still use the Park. Olivia however, tends to see only people like herself, when she has kids others like her have kids and they have a tendency to make themselves highly visible, so she only sees 'clones' of herself when she takes her children to the Park. It's not just that her vision is selective but, as Dickens (1988) points out, the middle classes are remarkably successful in casting 'civil society' in their own image.

This is partly, of course, a result of middle-class spending power and the changes that have taken place in Stoke Newington Church Street are witness to this—the estate agents, restaurants, women's gyms, delicatessens, art shops and so on. It is however more than this, it is about its ability to impose itself and its values on an area. Therefore, whilst Olivia's view of who is having children is clearly coloured by her own situation, it is nevertheless true that she and her kind have largely taken over the Park at certain times of day—lunch time and late afternoon—and one might be forgiven for thinking that this was any middle-class suburb. It is also, as she points out, true that increasingly her friendship circle is comprised of people with children.

As we have seen, it is important to Olivia that it isn't a middle-class suburb but, equally, she is sceptical about those who think they 'live the social mix' -including her partner who worked for many years at a local 'community' venture: 'Rex thought he interacted with others; his organization originally thought it was serving the needs of a mixed population but actually they had to realise that this was not their audience. They did much better when they realised who it was: middle-class people aged between 20 and 40'.

De Beauvoir and, more recently, Stoke Newington have become established as middle-class enclaves and the middle class are an important part of the local structure, not least as consumers. It is precisely because both North Defoe and De Beauvoir have become gentrified areas, where other people like themselves live, that respondents continue to be attracted to living there.

Olivia originally moved into the area for accidental reasons and most of her friends lived elsewhere. Now, as she has said, many of her friends live in the area and if they moved away she would 'be in a bit of a crisis'. Suzanne, on the other hand, has almost no contact with her neighbours and little time for the attractions[11] of living in a socially mixed area:

> Living in comparative opulence next door to people living in comparative poverty, [it] just makes me feel guiltily uncomfortable rather than wonderfully identified. A lot of people that I have, by and large, long term contacts with live within a mile but they are contacts made at university or subsequently.

Most of these people just happened to have moved here and for that reason others of us have arrived.

This reinforces the point made earlier, which is that people often moved into the area by accident in the first place, but they have subsequently stayed and friendships have often been an important reason for staying. Many people, both in the original interviews and the subsequent in-depth interviews, stressed that they preferred to live somewhere where they were on good terms with their neighbours and knew people in the area but at the same time were left alone. For the most part however, their real friends lived in similar areas elsewhere in inner London. David puts it likes this: 'People don't turn a blind eye in this street, but they don't get involved in your day to day business; it's a nice balance'. They want a degree of social closeness without physically being too close; this is the attraction of living in a multi-class area where immediate neighbours are often not likely to be people they will have too much in common with.[12]

Mick was, until relatively recently, heavily involved in local political activity as was his partner. Although he is now more settled into a domestic routine and works from home, their friends still stem largely from their days of political activity and live in other similar inner-city areas:

> If you are interested in political activity there is far more of it in the inner city than elsewhere, than Enfield for example. I don't think there's anything that would have attracted us to moving out of the centre of London except that possibly one might have been able to find somewhere to live more cheaply but there was the whole question of our friends and our social network. You could actually get to see people without making gargantuan journeys and so we wanted to stay within shouting

distance of most of our friends, a lot of whom were Hackney or Islington based and those who weren't who we knew through work or the union, they almost all lived in the inner city in one way or another be it in Wandsworth or wherever, but it was possible to meet them for a drink or whatever without too much difficulty. I think we would have been very much deterred by that aspect of it together with not only the practical feeling that we were cutting ourselves off from our friends but also the feeling that there's a 'living death' out there.

Friends tend not to live in the area but we have a lot of friends we have made who live here, either because they are our neighbours; it's quite a neighbourly area and working at home is a good way to get to know the neighbours because you are always on the street. Or people we know through political activities since we have been here, although neither of us is now as politically active as we have been and through the nurseries. The nurseries generate quite a powerful nexus.

We have got to know a few people from the nursery and those that we have got to know adult to adult is through enjoyment of each other's company but there are more people who we know one way or another because they have their children at the nursery and who we have got to know because they are involved in nursery politics.

In De Beauvoir there is even greater interaction through the children and child-care networks and parents have often got to know each other through the 'nanny network':

We have made masses of friends, though in the last few years since the De Beauvoir Association hasn't really had anything to do we have found that our friendships have changed. We tend to be more involved in people in the area with children who we see whereas in the old days we were more involved with people who were very active in putting through the road closures. This may change again if we have a fight on our hands for more roads.

A lot of the people we now know who have got children came in later than that earlier wave. The people we were friendly with are now quite elderly and one or two have now moved out of London and others have got quite grown up children who we are now using for baby-sitting but I suppose the friends of ours who have got children in the area are not our original contacts.

If we see people at the weekends, it's more seeing the people who are the middle-class professional people, the arty people or whatever you like to call them—the poets and journalists of the neighbourhood.

The interview data therefore suggest that interactions with similar people, 'people like us', who are assumed to live in the inner city is a strong reason for living in De Beauvoir and North Defoe. This is generally supported by the quantitative data on how people spend their leisure time which, given the high level of economic activity, is the only real time that most respondents are in the area.[13] Table 19.7 gives the data for how respondents defined their major leisure activity:

The main problem with this data is that in reality most people undertook a range of activities and this does not appear in the responses. One fifth of respondents in both areas gave their main activity as 'socializing' which reinforces the argument advanced above that a major reason for living in inner London is largely social. It suggests that the existence of other such people with whom they spend significant

Table 19.7 Respondents' major leisure activity

Main leisure activity	De Beauvoir %	North Defoe %	Total %
Home centred	31	27	30
Socialising	19	20	20
Other	20	18	19
Reading	12	17	14
Music	14	6	10
Relaxing	4	12	8

Table 19.8 Frequency of 'going out'

Frequency of going out	De Beauvoir %	North Defoe %	Total %
More than twice a week	37	50	43
Twice a week	29	16	24
Once a week	19	15	17
Less than once a week	15	19	17

Table 19.9 Frequency of 'going out' controlling for children

Frequency of going out 'controlled' by children	Respondents with children %	Respondents without children %
More than twice a week	19	60
Twice a week	20	25
Once a week	26	11
Less than once a week	34	4
Total	100	100

amounts of time, even if they do not live in the immediate area, is important to them, in other words networks are an important fact of life. Respondents were also asked how often they 'went out' i.e. spent time out of their home in non-work time.

In North Defoe half of all respondents went out more than twice a week. The variation in how often people went out is largely accounted for by whether or not they had children.

Table 19.9 illustrates this very clearly and demonstrates how the presence of children had a very significant impact on how 'home-centred' respondents were. There was an area difference here with some evidence for the suggestion that having children has more effect on patterns of socialization in North Defoe than in De Beauvoir. Those without children in North Defoe tended to go out more often and those with children less often than respondents in De Beauvoir. This is possibly accounted for by relative differences in wealth; respondents in De Beauvoir were more likely to have a nanny or to be able to afford to hire a baby-sitter.

The same influence of children in the household can be seen on the kinds of leisure activities undertaken by respondents:

The presence of children in the household appears to have a major impact on the kind of leisure activities; those with children being mainly involved in

Table 19.10 Respondents' major leisure activity

Main leisure activity	Respondents with children %	Respondents without children %
Home centred	42	20
Socialising	10	27
Other	15	22
Reading	18	12
Music	11	10
Relaxing	6	9
Total	100	100
	n = 103	n = 141

home-centred activities, especially if reading is included, whilst those without children are more likely to socialize.

The benefits for the latter group of the inner city are perhaps obvious, the presence of like-minded people and, crucially, places to eat. Most respondents ate out frequently and this appears to have been a major form of socialising. Eating out may appear a somewhat odd indicator of social behaviour, but it is an important focus of social interaction amongst the middle class and is also dependent on the availability of suitable reasonably cheap and convivial eating places. Both Stoke Newington and Islington abound in such restaurants.

Forty five percent of respondents ate out at least once a week; more people tended to eat out in North Defoe than in De Beauvoir and this is partly a function of the area[14] but mainly of whether they had children (table 19.11). The differences between the two groups of respondents are revealing because a third of those with children in De Beauvoir ate out at least once a week compared to only 14 per cent in North Defoe, whilst 30 per cent ate out 'rarely' compared to 52 per cent in North Defoe. This suggests that having children is having more of an effect on respondents in North Defoe, partly perhaps for financial reasons but also because their children tend to be younger, Nevertheless despite the differences, eating out is clearly a significant part of the culture of most respondents, nearly two thirds of all respondents ate out at least once a fortnight.

Respondents were asked how often they made use of central London facilities for film, theatre and art:[15]

A larger number of respondents in De Beauvoir used such facilities, particularly the 'higher' art forms of art galleries and theatre. Even the cinema often meant specialist cinemas such as the National Film Theatre on the South Bank. Roger for

Table 19.11 Frequency of eating out controlling for children

Frequency of eating out 'controlled' for children	Respondents with children %	Respondents without children %
At least weekly	25	59
Fortnightly	16	19
Monthly	18	15
Rarely	40	7
Total	100	100
	n = 104	n-141

Table 19.12 Use of cultural facilities

Facility regularly visited	De Beauvoir %	North Defoe %	All %
Cinema	60	54	55
Theatre	53	31	42
Art gallery	39	26	33

example quoted the easy accessibility of the NFT from their De Beauvoir home as a positive benefit of living there:

> I am a member of the NFT, we go there regularly, we go to the Festival Hall regularly; we have these manic drives, it's about 15 to 20 minutes to the South Bank and we reckon on going to quite a lot of concerts and so on, films and theatre but theatre less so at the moment.

Harriet also talked about the importance of theatre:

> The amenities of London are one of the main attractions *[of living in London]*, theatres are in easy reach. We can go to the Barbican for a concert and be home seven minutes after the end of the show . . . we do regularly, even to the point where one evening my husband was bored in the middle of 'Three Sisters' and came home and did some work and met me at the end of the show. We do make good use of what London has to offer from that point of view and for the children too. For example in the school holidays there's masses on, the Barbican library has activities, there's a Barbican children's cinema club. There are things on at the Geffrye Museum which we take the children to, there's very good leisure centres within easy reach and for adults there's swimming pools around, all those sorts of amenities.

All this is not to suggest that respondents did not feel the strains of living in the inner city; Harriet's comment about how the 'dirt of London rarely got to [her]' is probably the exception to the rule.[16]

For many of the respondents the cultural facilities of the centre were important, for others the ability to socialize with friends was important and a third group were home-centred. It might be argued that the last group gained least benefit from inner-city living but since this was the group that was most likely to have children with both parents at work, the benefits of the inner city have already been discussed. Moreover, as we have seen one of the attractions of inner-city areas is that of buying old housing and restoring it. The data can be misleading since my impression is that most respondents actually divided their leisure time across a range of activities and that the figures quoted here are only for the most salient. Thus, being able to socialize with a wide range of long-standing friends from a similar background and being able to make use of the facilities provided by London were both important concomitants of living in a gentrified area. [. . .]

NOTES

1. The proposals to drive a north London relief road through the Square looked like reviving it.
2. It might also be quite simply that older working-class residents have relatives buried in the cemetery and thus want to see their loved ones remembered in a more dignified and appropriate setting. Very few, if any, of the younger middle-class are or will be in a similar situation.

3. Respondents were not prompted and they could give more than one reason, the figures thus indicate the various reasons cited.
4. Approximately two thirds were existing owner occupiers (see table 5.3).
5. Interestingly, in view of the recent interest in owner occupation, many respondents went out of their way to say that they felt little inherent desire to own property but rather that the consequences of not owning were too awful to contemplate, given the nature of the non-owned property market in the UK. See Saunders (1990) for a discussion of his concept of owner occupation as a 'natural desire'.
6. There was not in fact a decline in prices in 1988 in Hackney. This figure arose form the change in the mix of properties to which the Nationwide Anglia made advances: there was a general increase in advances but particularly of flats and this served to lower the overall average although terraced houses actually increased from 242 in 1987 to 289 in 1988.
7. For a discussion see Saunders (1990).
8. Castells (1983) introduces the concept of 'urban meaning' which relates social and built forms of the urban. Whether there is any basis in reality for the distinctions that are drawn, for example, between liberal North London gentrification and the more yuppie and conservative areas to the South and West, such as Battersea and Fulham, is an unresearched question.
9. 'Improvements' were defined as being more than routine maintenance or small-scale redecoration.
10. This refers to the practice whereby mortgage lenders retain part of the advance until an agreed programme of repairs and renovations has been carried out.
11. 'Just the immediate look makes you think of 1950 and after the war, respectability and ghastly rigid stuffiness, lack of horizons and so on. The people who live there aren't like that at all, but then we turn to who does live there and I feel horribly identified with the joke cliché and I would rather live somewhere that was just much more intensely urban like Clerkenwell . . . not to go for really posh places as that's not really it, somewhere older . . . that has got romance and if I look at the streets I think they are beautiful, if they are not awful, and don't have the leaden respectability bit that the houses here represent even if that's not what's going on.' (Suzanne)
12. This is reminiscent of Richard North's rather sharp characterization in *The Independent* of Stoke Newington being populated by 'Drabbies' who mind everyone's business in theory but 'don't speak to their neighbours'.
13. Most women with children work, so it is only those who work at home who are likely to be around during the weekdays.
14. In North Defoe there are a large number of cheap restaurants on Stoke Newington Church Street within easy walking distance, whereas in De Beauvoir it is necessary to drive to Islington where there is a wide range of restaurants but which tend to be more expensive and require booking. In other words, one can eat out cheaply and on impulse in North Defoe but this is not so easy in De Beauvoir.
15. With hindsight, there should have been a question about live music.
16. Approximately one third of respondents had taken three or more holidays in the previous year. The number of holidays was high and, it might be assumed, was a central 'coping strategy' for dealing with the stresses of inner city living.

REFERENCES

Castells, M. (1983), *The City and the Grassroots*, University of California Press, Berkeley and Los Angeles.
Cybriwsky, R., D. Ley, and J. Western, (1986), The political and social reconstruction of revitalized neighborhoods: Society Hill, Philadelphia, and False Creek, Vancouver, in *Gentrification of the City*, N. Smith, and P. Williams (eds.), pp. 92–120, Allen and Unwin, London.
Dickens, P. (1988), *One Nation*, Pluto, London.
[Hamnett, C. (1973), Improvement grants as an indication of gentrification in inner London, *Area*, vol. 4(4), pp. 252–61.]
Jager, M. (1986), Class definition and the aesthetics of gentrification: Victoriana in Melbourne, in *Gentrification of the City*, N. Smith and P. Williams (eds.), pp. 78–91, Allen and Unwin, London.
Kasinitz, P. (1988), The gentrification of 'Boerum Hill': neighbourhood change and conflicts over definitions, *Qualitative Sociology*, vol. 11, pp. 161–82.
Moore, P. (1982), Gentrification and the residential geography of the new class, unpublished paper available from *Scarborough College, University of Toronto*.
Pahl, R. (1984), *Divisions of Labour*, Blackwell, Oxford.
—— (1989), Is the emperor naked? Some questions on the adequacy of sociological theory in urban and regional research, *International Journal of Urban and Regional Research*, vol. 13, pp. 709–20.
Saunders, P. (1990), *A Nation of Homeowners*, Unwin Hyman, London.
Thrift, N. (1987), Introduction: the geography of late twentieth-century class formation, in *Class and*

Space, N. Thrift and P. Williams (eds.), Routledge and Kegan Paul, London.

—— (1989), Images of social change, in C. Hamnett, L. McDowell and P. Sarre (eds.), Sage, London, pp. 12–42.

Wiener, M. (1985), *English Culture and the Decline of the Industrial Spirit 1850–1980*, Penguin Books, Harmondsworth.

Wright, P. (1985a), *On Living in an Old Country: The National Past in Contemporary Britain*, Verso, London.

—— (1985c), Ideal homes, *New Socialist*, No 31, pp. 16–19.

Zukin, S. (1988), *Loft Living: Culture and Capital in Urban Change*, Radius, London.

CHAPTER 20

Social Preservationists and the Quest for Authentic Community

Japonica Brown-Saracino

There is an ethic and set of practices, unnamed and little noticed, that shape both urban and rural communities. I call this ethic and set of practices *social preservation*; the culturally motivated choice of certain people, who tend to be highly educated and residentially mobile, to live in the central city or small town in order to live in authentic social space, embodied by the sustained presence of "original" residents.[1] Like environmentalists who seek to preserve the natural environment, social preservationists work to preserve the space they have entered. Social preservationists combine the ideology of social preservation—a set of values that demand the presence of old-timers—with practice: they engage in efforts to prevent the displacement of old-timers in their area, despite acknowledging the disruption caused by their own in-migration.[2] This concern for the sustained presence of old-timers is rooted in a combination of altruistic concern for those threatened by displacement and taste for an "authentic" version of community predicated on the struggle of marginalized old-timers.

Sociologists have failed to differentiate social preservation from gentrification, perhaps because both involve participants with similar demographic attributes who move to areas populated by those less educated and affluent. Furthermore, adherence to the ideology of social preservation is fluid—some who practice social preservation become gentrifiers (and vice versa)—and, ironically, the methods of social preservation and their practitioners may serve as (unintentional) conduits for neighborhood reinvestment. Nonetheless, there is an important distinction between the ideologies of gentrification and social preservation: while gentrification is an investment in the social, economic, and cultural *future* of space, social preservation is an investment of economic, political, and cultural resources in the past and present social attributes of a place. Gentrifiers seek to tame the "frontier," while social preservationists work to preserve the wilderness, including its inhabitants, despite their own ability to invest in and benefit from "improvements" or revitalization.

Many people may agree with or express the ideology of social preservation even though they do not relocate to live beside old-timers or fail to put the ideology to practical use. There may be gentrifiers and real estate agents who have a taste for cultural difference, diversity, or "the cultural practices of the categorical 'other'" (Mele, 2000, p. 4). However, there is an important difference between the symbolic consumption of diversity that other authors have noted and social preservation.[3] Social preservationists enact their appreciation and consumption of difference through practices intended to preserve that difference. Such practices are particularly salient given social preservationists' self-reflexive pose: an awareness of their impact on their surroundings, a sophisticated understanding of political economy, and a concern that *symbolic* preservation could cause the *social* displacement of old-timers.

This article, based on a study of four communities where social preservation takes place, two small Massachusetts towns and two Chicago neighborhoods, describes and analyzes the ethic and practice of social preservation.[4] I begin with a review of my research methods, followed by an examination of the literature on gentrification and a discussion of the similarities and differences between gentrification and social preservation.

METHODS

This project began as a comparative study of gentrifying, or gentrified, urban and rural communities. A pilot study of Leyden, Massachusetts,[5] a rural village, indicated subtle but striking discontinuities between the disposition of rural "gentrifiers" and the literature's description of their urban counterparts.[6] To discern between urban and rural gentrification, I selected four research sites, two urban neighborhoods and two small towns, because of demographic changes in them over the past decade that indicated gentrification, such as significant population change, rising property values, and the formation or dissolution of identity groups. I sought communities that were similar in the aforementioned ways, but that remained geographically and demographically distinct from one another.[7] My early findings

demonstrated that the attitudes and behavior of newcomers I identified in my pilot study were not limited to changing rural communities; the patterns I had first noted in Leyden were present in all four sites. I came to call this unexpected orientation "social preservation," an ethic and set of practices that seemed quite different from those of gentrifiers. That is, I came to see that social preservationists are not merely a variant of gentrifiers but an entirely different "species."

The sites do not constitute a random sample, but they do provide valuable sets of variations and comparisons (in terms of population characteristics, political economy, and geographical location). The sites are equally divided between the small town and the urban neighborhood. The sites are as follows.

- Leyden, Massachusetts, a town of approximately 700 residents near the Massachusetts/Vermont border. Over the course of the last half-century, the town changed from a remote dairy farming community to a bedroom village, from which most residents commute to work. Newcomers include organic farmers, artists, and writers, but most are professionals who commute to work in neighboring towns.

- Provincetown, Massachusetts, an isolated beach community on the easternmost tip of Cape Cod. Traditionally a Portuguese fishing village, over the past century Provincetown has become a renowned home and vacation destination for artists and writers, as well as gays and lesbians. The population varies throughout the year from approximately 3,400 (in the winter) to 50,000 (on busy summer day).

- Chicago's Andersonville neighborhood was a stopping point for Swedish immigrants in the 19th and early 20th centuries. In recent decades it has become a popular neighborhood for women, especially lesbians, and is an increasingly trendy place of residence for young and middle-age professionals—both single and coupled heterosexuals and gay men.

- For much of the 20th century, Chicago's Argyle neighborhood, only a few blocks from Andersonville, was home to a large population of Jews and working-class natives of Appalachia. Since the Vietnam War era, many Asian immigrants have established residence in Argyle. Korean, Vietnamese, Chinese, Cambodian, and Laotian establishments dominate the neighborhood's main commercial street. In recent years, young, white professionals have moved to Argyle.[8]

Through a snowball sample, beginning with community leaders and activists, I interviewed 82 individuals: 29 residents of Provincetown, Massachusetts, 20 residents of Leyden, Massachusetts, 17 residents of Chicago's Argyle neighborhood, and 16 of the Andersonville neighborhood. In each site, roughly one-half of the informants are newcomers, and the other half old-timers. Newcomers included both social preservationists and gentrifiers, with the snowball method leading to a greater number of the former category than the latter. The interviews varied in duration from one-half hour to three hours, with most lasting at least one hour. I observed church services, block club meetings, political assemblies, safety meetings, plenary sessions, as well as the daily life of residents on the street, in parks, stores, and other public places. I collected ethnographic data in the Chicago neighborhoods over the course of one and one-half years, in Provincetown for two months with several repeat visits for community events, and in Leyden for a period of six months.[9] In addition, I observed 14 community festivals.

DIFFERENCES BETWEEN GENTRIFICATION AND SOCIAL PRESERVATION

For the past 25 years, sociologists, urban planners, and policy makers have paid much attention to gentrification, the movement of young, affluent professionals into the central city in search of affordable housing in close proximity to employment opportunities. In the last century, gentrification began as baby-boomers sought affordable homes during a housing crunch induced by the sheer size of the generation (Long, 1980, p. 66).[10] At the same time, changes in the national economy after World War II offered both companies and individual professionals greater flexibility in their locations, opening the inner city and small town to industry and an expanding service sector (Spain, 1993, pp. 157–158). Urban "boosters" with an interest in the economic revitalization of the central city, such as businesses, the media, politicians, universities, and cultural institutions, encouraged the return of white professionals to urban areas (Logan and Molotch, 1987, pp. 74, 66–84).

Gentrification often results in neighborhood revitalization, indicated by rising housing costs and infrastructure transformations geared towards gentrifiers. Improvements facilitate the physical displacement of lower- and working-class residents. This displacement is sometimes accidental, while in other instances it is the opposite, as in the case of a Vermont restaurateur who paid the homeless to leave town (Smith, 1996, p. 27).

In addition to physical displacement, old-timers often face social displacement, "the replacement of one group by another, in some relatively bounded geographical area, in terms of prestige and power" (Chernoff, 1980, p. 204), embodied by the replacement of cultural, social, and economic institutions of the poor and working class by those of the gentrifiers, who tend to be racially, educationally, economically, and occupationally distinct from the original inhabitants of the neighborhoods to which they move (Spain, 1980, p. 28). Typically, real estate agents and gentrifiers seek to strip urban space from its "historical association with the poor immigrants" (Smith, 1996, p. 8) who once lived in the central city. Or, in Elijah Anderson's words, "the emerging neighborhood is valued largely to the extent that it is shown to be separate from low-income black communities" (Anderson, 1990, p. 26). Although in some cases gentrifiers preserve aesthetic vestiges of the neighborhood's past, these practices are distinct from social preservationists' as they do not aim to preserve residents.

Urban scholars agree that "economic factors alone [can] not fully account for or explain" (Long and DeAre, 1980, p. 2) the impetus for gentrification. In the 1970s and 1980s, baby-boomers' cultural attributes facilitated gentrification, particularly their predilection for late marriage and child-bearing (Lipton, 1977, p. 146). These lifestyle choices contributed to the differentiation of baby-boomers' housing needs from the previous generation (Long, 1980), as well as from less affluent members of the same generation. At the forefront of such cultural attributes was an ideology that supported gentrification, the "frontier and salvation" mentality. This mentality glamorized personal sacrifice and "sweat equity" as methods for "settling" the untamed central city. Economic boosters and the popular press credited gentrifiers with "infus[ing] moribund communities with new health and an appreciation for cultural activities" (Spain, 1993, p. 158), and with spurring an "urban 'renaissance'" (Zukin, 1987, p. 130).

I have found little evidence that the demographic or cultural attributes of social preservationists are notably distinct from those of the typical gentrifier. Both tend to be highly educated with the cultural, social,

or economic capital that lends itself to residential mobility. In fact, social preservationists and gentrifiers sometimes share neighborhoods or towns. For instance, an Andersonville gentrifier explained why she moved to the neighborhood: "I liked the amount of space I could get for the money . . . and the fact that I could still get downtown very quickly several different ways. . . . You know, I wanted to be near the lake."

Yet, the two groups remain *ideologically distinct*. They diverge in the impetus for their relocation to the central city or small town, as well as in their vision of the future of such space. For instance, the ideology of gentrification often underlines historic and landscape preservation as the cornerstone of revitalization (Zukin, 1987, p. 133), while social preservationists, on the other hand, are more interested in preserving the presence and practices of old-timers. According to a social preservationist who resides near the University of Illinois Chicago campus, historic preservation encourages rising property values and the displacement of original residents and therefore is antithetical to *real* preservation.

> These 7 old buildings . . . they're only saving the shell of the buildings. They're going to completely gut the inside . . . The real big tragedy here is that while I think saving buildings are important, that people are more important than buildings and to have a huge building saved where the people who lived here are all gone is to me not real preservation. What to me real preservation is about—and a lot of even preservationists don't understand this—is preservation of a place, which is the building fabric but it's also the people too, and the culture. And the food, and the signage and the music and the interaction. That's a place, that's culture, and this was a great place and it should've been saved.
>
> (*Eight Forty Eight*, February 28, 2002)

There are moments, however, when the ideologies of gentrification and social preservation seem to confer. For instance, social preservationists and gentrifiers share distaste for homogeneous sub-urbs. Nonetheless, important distinctions remain. For instance, gentrifiers avoid "child-centered" community and seek social diversity (Zukin, 1987, p. 131), while social preservationists seek communi-ties defined by the *presence* of children and the homogeneity of original residents (i.e., residents who are alike, while distinct from social preservationists). The ideol-ogy of gentrification emphasizes a reduc-tion in crime and increased social control. Gentrifiers approach original residents "warily until familiarity with neighbor-hood routine ensures politeness . . . [They] often expect crime to be as prevalent as 'background noise'" (Zukin, 1987, p. 133) and regard this as another threat that they, the "urban cowboys," must contend with (Smith, 1996, p. 13). Social preservationists *embrace* the "background noise" of their neighborhood: crime, an informant said, is necessary to prevent the neighborhood from becoming "too nice." Social preserva-tionists, who tend to be well versed in the language of gentrification (in fact, most are equipped with a sophisticated sociological vocabulary),[11] seek to make acquaintances and friends of original residents.

Figure 20.1 illustrates the key areas of distinction between social preservationists and gentrifiers.

The popular media have recognized the ironic presence of an anti-gentrifica-tion ideology among those who appear to be gentrifiers. An April Fool's Day issue of a San Francisco newspaper "read 'Old Yuppies Decry New Yuppies' and 'Pot Calls Kettle Black'" (Solnit and Schwartzenberg, 2000, p. 122). The satirical newspaper *The Onion* published a facetious article titled, "Resident of Three Years Decries Neighborhood's Recent Gentrification." The article reads:

> A three-year resident of Chicago's Wicker Park neighborhood, lashed out Monday against encroaching gentrification. "See that big Barnes & Noble on the corner? You better believe it wasn't there back in '98," said Smales, 34, a finance manager with Accenture. "This whole place is turning into Yuppieville. You can't throw a rock without hitting a couple in matching Ralph Lauren baseball caps walk-ing a black lab." Smales then took his golden lab for a walk.
>
> *(Onion, 2001)*

While fictional, such satire notes a social trend—young professionals' wariness of gentrification, which has become a power-ful symbol (Smith, 1996, p. 34).

Similarly, a few sociologists have observed urban professionals who actively resist upscale development or who seek relation-ships with the racial or economic "other."

Type of newcomer	Origins	Vision	Attitude toward newcomers	Attitude towards old-timers
Social preservationist	Lifestyle choice and affordable housing for middle class	Wilderness to be preserved and enjoyed; recognition of old-timers' culture	Dilutes the authenticity of space; displaces old-timers	Colorful; "authentic"; desirable
Gentrifier	Lifestyle choice and affordable housing for middle class	Frontier to be tamed and later marketed; embodiments of high culture	Welcome fellow "pioneers"; increased safety; Rising property values	Threatened by; critical of. If preservation occurs it is historic or symbolic

Figure 20.1 Key distinctions between the social preservationist and the gentrifier.

Neil Smith suggests that by the 1980s the anti-gentrification movement induced the Board of Real Estate of New York to print an ad defending the process (Smith, 1996, p. 32). Elijah Anderson describes a movement of white liberals into a neighborhood to establish a racially and economically egalitarian community. "Indeed," Anderson writes, "many found inspiration, if not affirmation, in their relationships with blacks of the Village and the nearby ghetto" (Anderson, 1990, pp. 8, 17). Richard Florida, in his book *The Rise of the Creative Class*, writes: "The creative class is drawn to more organic and indigenous street-level culture,"—specifically a 'cultural community' that is often 'reviving-downscale' (Florida, 2002, pp. 182–183). Like Florida, Richard Lloyd notes an aesthetic appreciation for "urban grit" among neobohemians, artist gentrifiers of Chicago's Wicker Park, who express an appreciation for the neighborhood's "street level diversity, in which even gang activity and homelessness are valued as markers of urban authenticity" (Lloyd, 2002, p. 520). The presence of danger frames the city as distinct from the suburbs, and authenticates urban experience (Lloyd, 2002, p. 528). Still, neobohemians' appreciation for "diversity" is largely aesthetic, and their distaste for newcomers of their own class or culture is more about the disruption of *their* culture than the disruption of old-timers' authentic community (Lloyd, 2002, p. 529). This makes neobohemianism a variant of gentrification, but not a departure therefrom.

In the following sections, I address social preservationists' ideological claims about the social authenticity of the places in which they live, which they formulate by distinguishing between authentic and inauthentic communities. Social preservationists select the arbiters of authentic community by distinguishing old-timers from other residents. They also contrast their community with "inauthentic" communities, most often the suburb and affluent urban

neighborhood. Finally, they distinguish the present state of their neighborhood or town from an imagined, gentrified version of that space. As the empirical evidence demonstrates, for social preservationists, authentic people constitute authentic place, and therefore valuable space.

To uphold these claims of authenticity, social preservationists work to prevent the neighborhood from *becoming* inauthentic by resisting gentrification through political and social *practices*. The practices of social preservation include the symbolic use of festivals, political protest, and participation in political institutions, as well as a set of private practices rooted in their appreciation for the old-timers with whom they live. Before these practices begin, however, social preservationists engage in the construction of the old-timers they later work to preserve.

AUTHENTICITY CLAIMS

The desire to live among those original residents they associate with authentic community is the predominant criterion for social preservationists' residential choice. For social preservationists, community cannot be taken for granted—it arises out of conditions distinct from those that characterize traditional middle-class venues such as the suburb or affluent urban neighborhood. The social preservationist associates community with individuals bound together by shared religion, ethnicity, race, class, and—most importantly—way of life.[12] Specifically, they equate the economic and social struggle of marginalized groups with strong social ties.[13] This notion of community is not unique to social preservation. Common myths of community "emphasize . . . a distinctive 'way of life' that links people in a collective endeavor with otherlike-minded individuals" (Greenhouse et al., 1994, p. 173).[14] What is noteworthy about social preservationists is their relocation in search of community, and their belief that authentic community belongs to a particular group of people—of which they are not a part. For social preservationists the distinction between newcomers and old-timers is the basis for community authenticity. However, they do not deem all original residents (those there before they arrived) to be "old-timers." Rather, they use a complicated and sometimes contradictory set of criteria to define the old-timer, which I discuss below.

REAL PEOPLE: OLD-TIMERS VERSUS OTHERS

Each year, on a Saturday in March, residents of Provincetown gather at their town hall, a white clapboard building at the center of the village, for the "Year Rounders' Festival." The day is complete with informational booths, dinner, a variety show, and a Navy Band. During the variety show in 2002, a middle-aged and amply sized female impersonator, Isadora with More and Moreah, took to the stage. The audience was notably different from Isadora's summer tourist audiences. Children ran between chairs, while grandparents bounced babies on their laps. Neighbors, wearing workshirts and jeans, sat beside each other.

Isadora, wearing a blonde wig and a flowing pink gown, prefaced her perfor-

mance by saying: "This is my seventeenth year in Provincetown," The audience met her announcement with much applause. "Some of us," Isadora said, "come across the bridge [onto Cape Cod] and never leave." The crowd remained quiet. "So... seventeen years," Isadora spoke carefully, "am I a townie yet?" The auditorium resounded with silence. Finally, a few residents replied, "Yes," but a collective, "No," countered their affirmation. "I'm not?" Isadora asked, her tone unsurprised. "Well then, how long do I have to be here to be a townie?" This time the audience agreed, a chorus of "Forever!" rang throughout the hall. "Well you better get used to it," Isadora said before breaking into song, "because I'm going to be."

In all four sites, social preservationists measure the authenticity of their space by the presence of "townies" or "old-timers," whose authenticity is measured against the presence of inauthentic newcomers (Isadora and others of the kind) or original residents outside of the old-timer category.[15] Old-timers' identity is predicated on (1) length of residence, (2) family ties and legacy, (3) economic strata, (4) membership in a geographically rooted social network and the purity of that network, and (5) a configuration of racial, ethnic, and cultural characteristics. As Figure 20.2 indicates, the importance of the above features varies across the research sites.

As is true of many people, particularly those who live in changing communities,

	Leyden	Andersonviile	Argyle	Provincetown
Old-timers' attributes emphasized by social preservationists	1. Length of residence 2. Family ties 3. Membership in geographically rooted network 4. Economic strata, specifically struggling dairy farmers	1. Ethnicity 2. Length of residence 3. Family ties 4. Membership in geographically rooted network	1. Race 2. Economic strata; ownership of a small business catering to Asian clientele	1. Ethnicity 2. Economic strata 3. Religion 4. Family ties 5. Membership in geographically rooted network 6. Length of residence

Figure 20.2 Old timers' attributes emphasized by social preservationists by research site.

social preservationists admire those who have long resided in the locale. Especially in the rural sites, the modal characteristic of old-timers is the *length* of their relationship to place of residence. As a baby born to royal parents is as much a part of the monarchy as her elders, old-timers' status is rooted in relationships to space and particular families that predate the individual old-timer. Therefore, old-timer status largely depends on family ties and legacy. A Leyden preservationist identified old-timers as "families who have been here for generations." Old-timers have blood ties to their place of residence. These ties are inscribed on the landscape: old-timers' family names mark cemetery gravestones, storefronts, and street signs. A Provincetown social preservationist described old-timers as having "40,000 uncles and brothers and kids."[16]

Social preservationists borrow from existing status markers in their appreciation for old-timers. According to rules that old-timers use as much as social preservationists, old-timer status is a birthright seldom transcended by marriage. A woman born and raised in Andersonville teased that her husband is a "newcomer" because he was not born there. In fact, her husband has lived in the neighborhood for 30 years. In an unemotional manner, a Provincetown newcomer said: "I have a lot of friends from all walks of life down here, and I'm very comfortable, but would I ever feel like a townie even though I was married to a townie? No, never. *It's a line you don't cross.*" In this way, social preservationists are not solely responsible for the construction of the old-timer category; they abide by, and often highlight, existing distinctions.

In three of the research sites, social preservationists explicitly identify old-timers by their racial or ethnic identity. In Provincetown, old-timer is synonymous with Portuguese, while in Andersonville it is synonymous with Swedish, and in Argyle with Asian. Although Leyden social preservationists do not mention the race of old-timers, whiteness remains central to their classification schema. At a ceremony on the first anniversary of the September 11, 2001, terrorist attack, an Andersonville minister acknowledged the neighborhood's diversity: "When one walks along [Andersonville's main thoroughfare] you see Pakistanis, Iranians, Koreans, Chinese, and Japanese." Chuckling, he paid homage to the group in whose museum the ceremony took place: "Of course we have our Swedes. We can never forget them!" In fact, the neighborhood does not forget them— when business leaders sought support for a new streetscape on the neighborhood's thoroughfare, residents urged a Swedish theme: "Keep Swedish delis, traditions alive."[17] Indeed, the streetscape has a distinctly Swedish theme: Swedish bells decorate sidewalk cement, and the street banners are the colors of the Swedish flag. Similarly, when the Argyle community planned their own streetscape, many newcomers asked the organizers to emphasize the neighborhood's Asian population: "Please consider capitalizing on the ethnicity of the street. I believe the feel of the renovation should be of the charm of the neighborhood...should be in keeping with the Asian flavor of the neighborhood as it already exists." Thus, social preservationists attach the racial or ethnic identity of old-timers to neighborhood or town identity.

Yet, social preservationists sometimes conflate ethnicity and race with occupation. For example, in Provincetown, involvement with the fishing industry identifies a person as Portuguese, but, as one social preservationist discovered, this is not a fail proof method.

I always thought [this guy] was this old Portuguese fisherman, because he has really brown and leathery skin and he's always lived in P-town . . . but he's not. He's black, I mean, he's African-American . . . Somebody said, "He doesn't want anyone to know he's black." And I'm like, "He's not black, he's *Portuguese.*" And then [the man we were discussing] looked at me like I fell off the turnip truck. I'm like, "Wait, you're black?" He's like, everybody's like, "Look at him! Look at him! How can you not know?" And I'm like, "I just thought he was brown from the sun. I just thought he was old and weathered." And they were like "What?!" Because it's just your assumptions. You don't assume that any African-American person lives in Provincetown or is a *true townie*, because *everybody here is Portuguese.*

In other instances, social preservationists primarily associate old-timers with particular businesses or trades. In Leyden, old-timer is synonymous with "dairy farmer" despite the fact that there are few operating farms in town. In Provincetown, as the population of fishermen diminishes, newcomers identify old-timers by other trades: "The people who do the excavating and the people who are the septic people . . . *you know, the septic people*, it's been in their family for a million years." In the Chicago neighborhoods, newcomers recognize old-timers by their relationship to family-owned ethnic businesses. A newcomer described Argyle old-timers as "struggling new citizens in America, and [they] have their own little ethnic businesses." The discourse that links old-timers to certain businesses or trades is a way of talking about class. When asked what she meant by the term "local," a Provincetown preservationist said: "You don't see them on Commercial Street; they don't eat at all those fancy restaurants . . . They're living in these side streets not a brand new condo . . . A lot of those people spent a lot of time in unemployment." This concern for working-class old-timers is distinct from the typical response of the middle class to those who struggle economically. In fact, social preservationists glamorize old-timers' financial struggle. One reminisced about the "visible poverty" of Provincetown a few decades ago, while another complained that the town is "too nice" and no longer "tacky."

Social preservationists also identify old-timers as members of a geographically rooted social network. A Leyden social preservationist said, old-timers are rich in "friendship [s] that extend back in time." Social preservationists either correlate old-timers with multi-generational residence in their current locale, or with a group displaced from their native land (e.g., Asians on Argyle Street). This stands in contrast to newcomers' geographically dispersed social networks, which some preservationists term "commuter friendships." The "purity" or authenticity of old-timers' networks are preserved through the preclusion of newcomers from them. In the words of a highly educated Leyden social preservationist, deftly using sociological terms to describe old-timers: "They've got an old boy network and an old girl network, and this same sense of a network doesn't exist for newcomers who've moved to town." Deciphering the complex web of old-timers' relationships requires historical, genealogical, and geographic knowledge. The interweaving of individuals and families across time and space distinguishes "real" community members from newcomers. I asked an old-timer the name of another old-timer who stopped to chat during our interview. The man, I discovered, had to be identified through his relationship to other old-timers, beginning with his wife.

Who's Anna? She's of the Steward family, the [famous] sailing ship. Joseph Steward was her dad. He was the first one to do whale watching in pretty much the world. Started the whale watching industry right here in Provincetown. Joseph Steward. Andrew Brown owned the [newspaper]. Andrew's ex-wife is Joan Smith who's the chairman of the board of Selectmen. Anna Steward's his present wife who's on the board of selectmen, who was the president of my high school class. *Those are* real *Provincetown people.*

Similarly, in Andersonville, newcomers and old-timers alike spoke of old-timers in relationship to one another: "Have you interviewed Sven's brother?" Thus, membership in the "old-timer" category is predicated on insider knowledge, as well as relationship to other old-timers.

As obscure as membership rules appear from afar, for residents they are easily understood. One social preservationist recalled her favorite line from a book about Provincetown: "You'll never be a native if you're not." The sentiment resonated with the preservationist's personal observations.

> I meet these old lesbians that [a] re like in their 60s . . . They've lived [here] for years, and years and years and years, but there's always this thing about who's a townie, who's a native, who lives here and who doesn't . . . [They've] lived here for 20 years, they're still not a native.

The line that separates "real" people from newcomers varies within and between the research sites. However, in each locale, old-timer status is not merely a birthright, but also requires a certain "character." For social preservationists, an Ivy League educated Portuguese resident of Provincetown is less "real" than her high school educated counterpart. Similarly, a Vietnamese-American lifelong resident of Argyle Street is more "real" than his African-American counterpart, despite the fact that there are a greater number of African Americans than Asians in the neighborhood (U.S. Census Bureau, 2000). These rules serve social preservationists because they validate the authenticity of old-timers, and hence the authenticity of their place of residence. In each locale, the social preservationist celebrates the racial, ethnic, religious, or cultural *character* of the old-timer; to do this they maintain a composite sketch of what a "real" old-timer is.

The natural landscape so beloved to Leyden newcomers, open fields and care-fully maintained woodlots, is as marked by human hands as Chicago's urban landscape. To preserve Leyden and Provincetown in a natural state, which many newcomers work to do, necessitates constructing what that "natural state" *is*—it is difficult to imagine Leyden newcomers rallying to transform their land to the thick forest that greeted the town's European settlers, or Provincetown to the uninhabitable conditions that encouraged the Pilgrims' move to Plymouth.

The preservation of the social wilderness necessitates the construction of a stage of social development that is no more or less authentic than the preservation of natural landscape. Andersonville's social preservationists devote more attention to the neighborhood's Swedish elements than to its substantial population of Middle-Eastern restaurants and residents, despite the fact that in 2000 Swedes composed less than 4 percent of the neighborhood population (U.S. Census Bureau, 2000). Social preservationists relinquish Argyle's resplendent past as home to one of the first motion picture studios, to a contemporary focus on its Asian population. Similarly, in Leyden they neglect a concentration on white settlers, or even the Native Americans who came before them, for a focus on a moment in the town's history when dairy farms dominated the landscape. Provincetown social preservationists do not highlight the long legacy of WASP whaling captains or the fine houses that compose the historical register. Using preformed notions of authentic community, social preservationists construct the arbiters of that community. In turn, social preservationists rely on old-timers to sketch a picture of authentic community.

REAL PLACES: SOCIALLY PRESERVED LOCALES VERSUS INAUTHENTIC "OTHER" SPACE

In interviews, social preservationists distinguish the authenticity of their town or neighborhood by contrasting it with other places they have lived; the stronger the distinction between the two, the more authentic they consider their current place of residence to be. "Other" places, social preservationists suggest, are characterized by the *absence* of old-timers, and by the *presence* of affluent residents, aesthetic homogeneity, and retail chains. In fact, most social preservationists are equipped with "origin stories": elaborate and rehearsed narratives of how they came to live in a place of authentic community. Origin stories contrast the spiritual, political, or aesthetic qualities of social preservationists' place of residence with the spiritually vacuous, capitalist-driven, aesthetically homogenous place from which they moved. Social preservationists adopt the language of mid- and late-19th-century scholars who worried that with increasing urbanism, "the primary relationships of place and kin give way to rational, individualistic encounters typified by market transactions" (Hunter, 1975, p. 538). The "authentic" community possesses children, extended families, economic diversity, social interaction, ethnic groups, civic involvement, old-timers, their accompanying traditions, and social networks.

Social preservationists measure authentic community by the familiarity or friendship between neighbors. When asked how they evaluate the intimacy of a community, social preservationists repeatedly refer to informal exchanges between neighbors, such as sharing holiday dishes or the simple act of greeting people on the street. A 23-year-old Chicago social preservationist explained why she moved from downtown: "[It's] not *neighborhoody* enough there." Social preservationists seek Geimenschaft: community defined by "binding, primary interactional relationships based on sentiment," which they associate with certain groups living in certain places (Christenson, 1984, p. 160).

The presence of children and their families is important to social preservationists. At a Chicago protest demanding low-income housing, a middle-class speaker said: "We know that gentrification is horrible. It destroys families and communities." Another speaker, a 30-something white homeowner, spoke of his choice to live in a neighborhood adjacent to Argyle: "We wanted to live in a community where families can afford to live... We don't want to lose them." Provincetown social preservationists mourn the fact that in a recent year the town recorded only one birth. In this way, social preservationists often conflate families with those vulnerable to displacement; their demands for low-income housing are synonymous with a desire for community populated by children and their parents. A middle-aged Andersonville social preservationist is nostalgic for his childhood neighborhood, dominated by extended families.

> It is hard as you get older—it is hard the constant transformation and lack of stability . . . It doesn't give you anything to hold on to. This is not an intergenerational community. When I grew up peoples' grandparents were there and parents. When Mrs. _____ yelled at me, I knew it was so and so's cousin. Grandpa was still speaking Hungarian every other word and my other Grandfather, Swedish. . . . All that's gone. There's a total break in continuity.

This nostalgia has transformed into a desire to reside alongside people bound together by Geimenschaft qualities, such as sentiment, intimacy, and blood.

Social preservationists also compare authentic community to the current state of their place of residence—by rallying for turning the clock back to a more "authentic" period in the neighborhood or town, or by preventing further change. Social preservationists express a basic distaste for affluent newcomers, whose presence, like a bulldozer in the natural wilderness, threatens the social wilderness. A Provincetown social preservationist, who is a prominent business owner and civic leader, recounted her memory of the town before newcomers inundated it, positing the past as the site of true community.

> The difference between then and now is that people went out of their way to help you. If you were new in town—like I couldn't find a place to live. [A woman], she got me my first place to live. She went and found it for me. I didn't have to do anything. People, in general, were more friendly, I think. *More community oriented* (emphasis added).

Social preservationists argue that "improvements" displace original residents, especially children. A Provincetown preservationist who works in nonprofit management complained: "Now every house in town has a construction truck in front of it." She expressed sorrow that [t]he fishing community is really gone," and with it the impetus for her relocation.

The social preservationist, whose quest for residence in a socially preserved locale is rooted in the search for authentic community (embodied by the imagined "sameness" of old-timers), *avoids* the formation of community based on the *sameness of newcomers*. An Argyle resident wrote in opposition of proposed improvements to the neighborhood's main commercial strip: "The biggest reason that I like living in this area is the ethnic diversity and the range of incomes and social classes" (Argyle Survey, 2001). Another wrote: "Try to keep Vietnam town a secret. Keep tourists and suburbanites away" (Argyle Survey, 2001). Social preservationists value places that *lack* certain elements associated with wealth. For instance, a Chicago preservationist described the changes she has seen in Andersonville: "It's jogging strollers and Starbucks now, and it makes me sick." A middle-class, lesbian newcomer to

Provincetown juxtaposed herself with more wealthy newcomers: "I sort of have a hatred for . . . the capitalist urge that happens here, or . . . the rich people that move in . . . people who have a million dollars who [think] this is a great gay place to party, and I'm just going to build a huge condo here so I can come here over the summer and party." She expressed concern that wealthy people cannot appreciate the true value of the town as an ethnic enclave and fishing village.

Social preservationists borrow from a discourse about the decline of American community explored by Robert Putnam *in Bowling Alone.* Putnam writes of "the things that have vanished almost unnoticed—neighborhood parties and get-togethers with friends, the unreflective kindness of strangers, the shared pursuit of the public good rather than a solitary quest for private goods" (Putnam, 2000, p. 403). More than anything else, social preservationists search for a community defined by the above qualities. They emphasize neighborhood parties, interactions with strangers, community festivals, and working-class families. In so doing they juxtapose their community against the "socially isolated" suburb or affluent urban neighborhood

The distaste for modern community forms is not a new phenomenon, nor is it unique to social preservationists. In 1887 Toennies suggested that with increasing industrialization and urbanization community would be defined by Gesellschaft, "an interactional system characterized by self-interest, competition, and negotiated accommodation" (Christenson, 1984, p. 160). In 1975, among newcomers to a Rochester neighborhood Albert Hunter noted "a very conscious rejection of suburbia, or rather a conscious rejection of the somewhat stereotyped 'image' of suburbia by residents in the area, and a correspondingly positive assertion of the values of 'urban living'" (Hunter, 1975, p. 546). For Hunter's Rochester informants, as well as for mine in Chicago and Massachusetts, the choice to live in a particular locale is a mode of self-definition: "Community ideology provides a convincing rendering of varied social, moral, and other qualities of communities and their inhabitants, diverse qualities that can be appropriated for self-characterization" (Hummon, 1990, p, 143).

Social preservationists actively construct themselves as distinct from gentrifiers, especially when the lines between the two ideologies blur: At a Chicago protest for affordable housing, a white middle-class man received great cheers when he said: "Our gentrifying friends with their diversity . . . like Lincoln Park Zoo where you can see a polar bear or a penguin. *They* want a neighborhood with 3 African American families, a few gays, a few Spanish speaking people. *Ours* is a community that is as it is today with many people of different backgrounds." Social preservationists derive their identity as much from who they are *not*, or where they do not live, as from who they *are* or where they *do* live. When social preservationists' conflicting values become self-apparent—to live in the central city while simultaneously preserving it, or to maintain the presence of old-timers while simultaneously improving town infrastructure and thereby increasing taxes—they emphasize the hypocrisy of gentrifiers or affluent suburbanites, and engage in practices to prevent gentrification or suburbanization. [. . .]

NOTES

1. The "original" residents that embody the "authentic" community are "original only in the sense that they were there before the social preservationists arrived. This notion does not acknowledge the long history of neighborhood succession. Claims of authenticity discussed in this article are those of informants, not of the author.

2. Social preservationists use the term old-timer, or its equivalent, to differentiate "real" locals or original residents from other inhabitants. Provincetown social preservationists refer to Portuguese lifelong residents as "townies" or locals"; in Argyle they are "the Asians." I use the term old-timer, rather than varying between that term and others, for purposes of ease, as the significance of the term is constant across the research sites. Further discussion of the process by which social preservationists select old-timers from among the pool of original residents is in the section, "The Real People."

3. See Zukin (1995), Anderson (1990), Mele (2000), Grazian (2003), and Lloyd (2002).

4. To give the ethic and practices of social preservation the analysis they warrant, this article primarily uses data on social preservationists, rather than my interviews with old-timers and gentrifiers, and related fieldnotes. Future work will explore other groups' response to social preservationists.

5. This is the real name of the research site, as are the names of the other sites. Real place names, rather than pseudonyms, are used for two reasons. First, Provincetown and the Chicago neighborhoods are easily identifiable, no matter what name they are called. Second, the use of pseudonyms would have required disguising important characteristics of the sites, which would have hindered discussion of the findings. However, all informants are referred to by pseudonym.

6. Much of the data for this research site was collected in 1998 and 1999 by the author (Brown-Saracino, 1999).

7. Examples of other comparative research designs include *Law and Community in Three American Towns* (Greenhouse et al., 1994), *Cultures of Solidarity* (Fantasia, 1988), and *Money, Morals and Manners* (Lamont, 1992).

8. The units of analysis for this study vary across the research sites. Argyle and Andersonville are unofficial neighborhoods within overlapping official Chicago neighborhoods, while Provincetown and Leyden are both incorporated towns.

9. My relationship to the sites studied aided the research. I have either lived in or paid an extended visit to each of the research sites prior to or during the period of observation.

10. Some argue that gentrification began in the mid-19th century, then known as "embourgeoisement" (Smith, 1996, p. 36).

11. For instance, many social preservationists are quick to use terms such as "gentrification," "urban pioneers," and "social networks."

12. In this way, social preservationists regard old-timers as a status group, bounded by "some common characteristic shared by many people," or a style of life that is independent of economic class

(Weber, in Runciman, 1978, p. 48). Indeed, social preservationists give status to those shared characteristics that differentiate "old-timers" from newcomers and make them worthy of preservation. This status is *not* dependent on old-timers' access to economic resources. Rather, "'status' is not necessarily connected with a 'class situation': normally, it stands rather in glaring contradiction to the pretensions of naked property ownership" (Weber, in Runciman, 1978, p. 49).

13. A newcomer described Argyle old-timers as "struggling new citizens in America, and [they] have their own little ethnic businesses." Despite the fact that most of the Asian-American residents of Argyle street have lived in the United States for 30 years or less, social preservationists grant them "old-timer" status. This is indicative of the centrality of "character" to the definition of old-timers—of the extent to which the category is predicated on nontemporal factors such as race, occupation, and class.

14. Some scholars argue that this is not a myth at all. For instance, Amitai Etzioni writes that one of the key principles of community is a "commitment to a set of shared values, norms and meanings, and a shared history and identity—in short, a shared culture" (Etzioni, 1996, p. 5). If this is, in fact, an accurate definition of community, then it is almost impossible for the social preservationist to become a member of a community composed of those whom he or she considers to be "other."

15. "One of the more obvious and unambiguous local social statuses is the number of years lived in a community ... the local distinctions between 'newcomers' and 'old-timers' are very real. It is a social typology that legitimizes and qualifies a person's behavior within a community, signifying investment and commitments to a local area and its citizens" (Hunter, 1974, p. 96).

16. "Scholarship, journalism, and grassroots expressions celebrate white ethnics for their family loyalties and neighborhood ties. In fact, advertising in this period began to exploit 'cute' white ethnic imaginery—the pizza-baking grandmother, the extended family at the laden dinner table—in order to invest frozen and canned foods with the cachet of the gemeinschaft" (di Leonardo, 1998, p. 94).

17. From a survey conducted by an Andersonville streetscape taskforce. Three groups were surveyed: "Customers, operationalized as the attendees of the 1997 Midsommarfest; merchants, surveyed from the fall of 1997, and residents, operationalized as the surrounding block club members, surveyed in the early months of 1998" (Andersonville Streetscape Memo).

REFERENCE

Anderson, E. 1990. *Streetwise: Race, Class, and Change in an Urban Community.* Chicago, IL: University of Chicago Press.

Argyle Streetscape Task Force. 2001. Argyle Streetscape Task Force Over-View & Survey.

Brown-Saracino, J. 1999. *Newcomers v. Old-timers: Symbolic Class Conflict in a Small Massachusetts Town*, unpublished honors thesis. Northampton, MA: Smith College.

Chernoff, M. 1980. "Social displacement in a renovating neighborhood's commercial district: Atlanta," in *Back to the City: Issues in Neighborhood Revitalization*, Laska, S.B., Spain, D., eds. New York: Pergamon: 204–19.

Christenson, J. A. 1984. "Geimenschaft and Gesellschaft: Testing the Spatial and Community Hypotheses," *Social Forces* 63(1), 160–168.

di Leonardo, M. 1998. *Exotics at Home: Anthropologies, Others, American Modernity.* Chicago, IL: University of Chicago Press.

Eight Forty Eight. 2002. *Interview with Maxwell Street Activist.* Available at www.wbez.org.

Etzioni, A. 1996. "The Responsive Community: A Communitarian Perspective," *American Sociological Review* 61(1), 1–11.

Fantasia, R. 1988. *Cultures of Solidarity: Consciousness, Action and Contemporary American Workers.* Berkeley, CA: University of California Press.

Florida, R. L. 2002. *The Rise of the Creative Class: And How It's Transforming Work, Leisure, Community and Everyday Life.* New York: Basic Books.

Grazian, D. 2003. *Blue Chicago: The Search for Authenticity in Chicago Blues Clubs.* Chicago, IL: University of Chicago Press.

Greenhouse, C. J., Yngresson, B., and Engel, D. M. 1994. *Law and Community in Three American Towns.* Ithaca, NY: Cornell University Press.

Hummon, D. M. 1990. *Commonplaces: Community Ideology and Identity in American Culture.* Albany, NY: State University of New York.

Hunter, A. 1974. *Symbolic Communities: The Persistence and Change of Chicago's Local Community.* Chicago, IL: Chicago University Press.

Hunter, A. 1975. "The Loss of Community: An Empirical Test Through Replication," *American Sociological Review* 40(5), 537–552.

Lamont, M. 1992. *Money, Morals and Manners.* Chicago, IL: University of Chicago Press.

Lipton, S. G. 1977. "Evidence of Central City Revival," *Journal of the American Institute of Planners* 43, 136–147.

Lloyd, R. 2002. "Neo-Bohemia: Art and Neighborhood Redevelopment in Chicago," *Journal of Urban Affairs* 24(5), 517–532.

Logan, J. R., and Molotch, H. L. 1987. *Urban Fortunes: The Political Economy of Place*. Berkeley, CA: University of California Press.

Long, L. H. 1980. "Back to the Countryside and Back to the City in the Same Decade," in S. Laska and D. Spain (eds.), *Back to the City: Issues in Neighborhood Renovation*, pp. 61–76. New York: Pergamon Press.

Long, L., and DeAre, D. 1980. *Migration to Metropolitan Areas: Appraising the Trends and Reasons for Moving*. Washington, DC: U.S. Department of Commerce.

Mele, C. 2000. *Selling the Lower East Side: Culture, Real Estate and Resistance in New York City*. Minneapolis, MN: University of Minnesota Press.

Putnam, R. 2000. *Bowling Alone*. New York: Simon & Schuster.

Runciman, W. C. (ed.). 1978. *Weber: Selections in Translation*. Cambridge: Cambridge University Press.

Smith, N. 1996. *The New Urban Frontier: Gentrification and the Revanchist City*. Unpublished.

Solnit, R., and Schwartzenberg, S. 2000. *Hollow City*. New York: Verso.

Spain, D. 1980. "Indicators of Urban Revitalization: Racial and Socioeconomic Changes in Central-City Housing," in S. Laska and D. Spain (eds.), *Back to the City: Issues in Neighborhood Renovation*, 27–41. New York: Pergamon Press.

Spain, D. 1993. "Been-Heres Versus Come-Heres: Negotiating Conflicting Community Identities," *Journal of the American Planning Association* 59(2), 156–171.

The Onion. 2001. "Resident of Three Years Decries Neighborhood's Recent Gentrification" June 20.

U.S. Census Bureau. 2000. *DP-2. Profile of Selected Social Characteristics: 2000*. www.census. gov.

Zukin, S. 1987. "Gentrification: Culture and Capital in the Urban Core," *Annual Review of Sociology* 13, 129–147.

Zukin, S. 1995. *The Cultures of Cities*. Cambridge: Blackwell Publishers.

PART IV

*W*hat are the Outcomes and Consequences of Gentrification?

Many of us have the sense that we know gentrification when we see it (see Jager 1986). For instance, several years ago members of my family visited me in Chicago and, on a sunny spring day, we walked more than two miles north from the Boystown neighborhood—a neighborhood on Chicago's north side that contains many bars, clubs, restaurants, and shops that cater to gay men—to my apartment in Edgewater. As we walked along a single avenue it was apparent that we were coming in and out of pockets of gentrification, or that we were at least walking through neighborhoods that were at different stages of gentrification (Clay 1979).

We left our point of origin—the restaurants, boutiques, condominiums, and gay bars of Boystown—and entered Wrigleyville, where dozens of sports bars and restaurants cluster around Wrigley Field. There was a notable difference in the physical features of the next neighborhood, Uptown, with its dilapidated theaters, discount stores, and Single-Resident-Occupancy buildings. However, even in Uptown we passed the legendary Green Mill Jazz Club and a new sports bar. Had we walked a few blocks east or west we would have seen condominium conversions and newly restored single family homes.

I am not sure if it was spoken, but it is plausible that one of us commented on Boystown's advanced stage of gentrification. As we entered Uptown one of my guests may have asked, "Is this neighborhood gentrifying?"

I raise this to underline the fact that armchair assessment of gentrification tends to rest on visible representations of gentrification's *outcomes*. We look for signs of its "success" or progress, such as commercial establishments geared toward the middle or upper middle class, renovated homes and new condominium buildings, expensively coifed residents pushing baby strollers, or, alternately, young artists and their galleries. We might also determine that a neighborhood is gentrified because of the *absence* of certain features, such as members of the group for which a neighborhood is named (e.g., a Little Italy without Italians, Chicago's Andersonville with few Swedes).

In short, there is much *implicit* agreement—among scholars and others—about how to recognize gentrification. Arguably, this agreement centers on a common set of expectations about gentrification's outcomes and consequences. And, in fact, the gentrification literature suggests that in many cases such assessments are accurate. Depending on the city or neighborhood, visual evidence of gentrification likely includes many of the images I noted on my walk through Chicago: carefully maintained streetscapes, high-end bistros, historically preserved homes, health food stores, and streets marked by expensive vehicles (see Zukin 1987). Behind these signifiers typically rest changes that are less immediately visible: rising housing costs, changing demographic characteristics, shifts in local politics, and tension over norms about the use of public space. Indeed, most scholars concur that, to some degree, displacement, social tension, the privatization of public space, and physical transformation of building stock are part and parcel of gentrification (see Spain 1993).

And yet, despite our implicit attention to these common markers, below the surface there are disagreements—among scholars and laypeople alike—about some fundamental facets of gentrification's consequences and outcomes. For instance, there is debate about the extent to which gentrification produces the displacement of longtime residents, as well as about which population groups are most at risk of displacement. Specifically, many scholars argue that gentrification leads to the widespread displacement of longtime residents (e.g., Sumka 1979, Le Gates & Hartman 1981, 1986, Atkinson 2003), however some counter that the literature overstates displacement rates (e.g., Freeman & Braconi 2004, Freeman 2006; for criticisms see Marcuse 2005, Newman & Wyly 2006). Still others suggest that displacement is widespread, but nonetheless offer caveats. For instance, Derek Hyra (2008) demonstrates that as a result of differences in city politics the magnitude of displacement and the type of individuals displaced varies between two gentrifying neighborhoods: New York's Harlem and Chicago's Bronzeville. Scholars also debate about whether gentrification's outcomes are most pronounced in neighborhood housing stock or commercial establishments, such as transformed shops, restaurants, and other businesses (Gotham 2005, Deener 2007, Hyra 2008, Zukin et al. 2009).

At the center of scholarship on gentrification's outcomes and consequences is debate between those who believe that gentrification is of public benefit and those who argue that such "benefits" are of tremendous cost for longtime residents (on this debate see Smith & Williams 1986, Atkinson 2003, Lees et al. 2008). Those in the first and much smaller camp suggest, often with caveats, that gentrification reversed decades of urban decay by reintroducing crucial economic, cultural, social, and institutional resources to central city neighborhoods (e.g., Florida 2002, Freeman 2006). They suggest that gentrification not only benefits gentrifiers but also many individuals who rely on the institutions that gentrifiers help revitalize, such as schools (Freeman 2006). The second camp counters that gentrification disrupts longtime residents' social and familial networks, severs their ties to important institutions, from health centers to places of worship, and that in many cases it leads to loss of housing and business closure (e.g., Chernoff 1980, Zukin 1987). They suggest that few longtime residents are able to remain in a gentrified neighborhood long enough to benefit from the changes that some scholars celebrate.

That said, it would be an oversimplification to suggest that the two camps are entirely discrete. For instance, Richard Florida proposes strategies for cities to attract members of the "creative class"—"people in science and engineering architecture and design, education, arts, music and entertainment... [and] *creative professionals* in business and finance, law, health care, and related fields" (2002: 8)—to help revitalize urban economies, yet he *also* warns that advanced gentrification can be counterproductive by making neighborhoods unaffordable or unattractive to creative class members (ibid.). Similarly, the book from which the essay in this section by Mary Pattillo was excerpted documents gentrification's daily costs for working class, African-American residents of a Chicago neighborhood, yet acknowledges that in its early stages some longtime residents believed gentrification improved their quality of life.

Likewise, it would be equally simplistic to imagine that within each camp there is uniform agreement about gentrification's precise benefits and costs. For instance, scholars offer competing conclusions about the facet of gentrification that is most harmful to longtime residents. Many of the readings in this section emphasize gentrification's material consequences for longtime residents, such as loss of housing, while Michael Chernoff insists that "social displacement" is equally consequential (1980).

There are three basic questions that scholars within and between both camps ask about gentrification's outcomes and consequences. First, they seek to isolate gentrification's benefits and, second, its consequences. As part and parcel of those questions they ask who benefits from gentrification and who bears its costs. Finally, they seek to isolate and debate the precise factors that produce gentrification's outcomes. The following paragraphs introduce each of these questions and begin to outline the positions of the authors in this section.

What are gentrification's benefits? While Richard Florida's selection is not explicitly about gentrification (he relies instead on language about "revitalization"), it represents the hope that gentrification proponents hold for the return of the middle class to the city. Specifically, they hope it will breed broad transformation by revitalizing economically depressed areas, increasing tax revenues, introducing or rehabilitating cultural and social amenities, and restoring historic properties (Duany 2001, Byrne 2003). In turn, they envision that such changes will lead to job creation (Byrne 2003) and decreased crime rates (McDonald 1986; see discussion in Atkinson 2003, 2004). Indeed, Florida encourages cities to spur an influx of the "creative class" by introducing some changes associated with gentrification with the hope that the creative class will encourage economic growth (see discussion in Atkinson & Easthope 2009).

Others, such as Lance Freeman, attend to gentrification's neighborhood-level benefits. While Freeman acknowledges that class tensions thwart some of gentrification's potential benefits, he nonetheless argues that an influx of residents with high cultural, social, and economic capital heightens collective efficacy that, in turn, improves neighborhood institutions, such as schools, that serve not only gentrifiers, but also longtime residents. In his essay in this section of the book Freeman also proposes that gentrification may benefit some longtime residents by exposing them to gentrifiers' social connections. He writes, "Gentrification certainly brings individuals with more leverageable connections into spatial proximity with indigenous residents" (2006: 147). In addition, he notes that gentrifiers demand, fund, and often receive "better amenities and services" (2006: 152) that benefit an entire neighborhood (see also Henig & Gale 1987). Imagine, for instance, the grocery store that ignores years of complaints only to improve its produce selection in response to gentrifiers' demands, or long neglected sidewalks that the city repairs upon the opening of high-end bistros and clothing boutiques. As Paul Levy and Roman Cybriwsky suggest (1980: 145), the latter is one example of a mechanism by which gentrification may reduce longtime residents' social isolation from the city of which they are a part. Yet, in the same essay, Levy and Cybriwsky caution that many longtime residents, for whom displacement is inevitable, will benefit from this reduced isolation for only a short time.

Who benefits from gentrification? Many contend—particularly in the popular press—that neighborhood gentrification promises to benefit the broader city or town in which it occurs by increasing tax revenues and improving the physical infrastructure of depressed areas (see discussion in Atkinson 2004). As Richard Florida implies, many hope that gentrification will bolster place reputation by cultivating a "'hip' urban lifestyle found in places like San Francisco, Seattle, New York and Chicago" (2002: 285). In addition, some argue that gentrification increases a sense of safety, most assuredly for new residents, as gentrifiers form neighborhood watch committees and call on city police to increase local patrols (McDonald 1986). Most also concur that gentrification benefits gentrifiers by providing them—at least in its early stages—with relatively affordable housing options, lifestyle amenities, proximity to work opportunities, and, in the case of property and business owners, potential financial profit. That said, others, such as Levy and Cybriswky (1980), note that gentrification may displace some early gentrifiers, such as artists and students, suggesting that it is an oversimplification to suggest that gentrification is uniformly beneficial—even for gentrifiers (Clay 1979; Kerstein 1990; Lloyd 2005). And, of course, even some of those who recognize gentrification's benefits for cities or gentrifiers do not believe that it is defensible in light of the process' consequences for long-timers (Peck 2005), particularly for marginalized population groups such as the poor, elderly (Henig 1984), female-headed households (Bondi 1991), and racial minorities (Perez 2005).

Does gentrification benefit longtime residents? Several of the selections in this section suggest in clear terms that it does not, perhaps most notably the essays by Gina Perez and Michael Chernoff. Such authors specify that the achievement of many of gentrification's "benefits," such as an increased sense of safety, harm longtime residents. For instance, several of the selections note that gentrifiers and officials rely, in part, on police harassment of poor and working class residents to achieve a sense of safety. However, others acknowledge that longtime residents nonetheless hope to benefit from gentrification (e.g., Pattillo 2008), and, as mentioned above, a few scholars, such as Lance Freeman, suggest that in some cases this hope is realized. Likewise, while Richard Florida cautions against over-gentrification, he suggests that amenities geared toward the creative class can be shared by all: "amenities—like bike lanes or off-road trails for running, cycling, rollerblading or just walking your dog—benefit a wide swath of the population" (2002: 294).

What are gentrification's consequences? Levy and Cybriwsky remind us that the very measures some use to evaluate gentrification's success, such as rising property values and an influx of affluent professionals, spell "personal disaster" (1980: 139) for others. This disaster often takes the form of physical displacement, which, as several of this section's readings demonstrate, results in the disruption of longstanding ties and, in some cases, homelessness.

However, physical displacement is not gentrification's only consequence. In their selection Levy and Cybriwsky suggest that it is a mistake to measure gentrification's consequences purely in economic or demographic terms, such as by calculating increases in residential and commercial rents and property taxes or the number of individuals displaced. While they wish for us to attend to such factors, they also encourage attention to cultural conflicts that they believe pervade gentrifying places, particularly in gentrification's early and mid stages when longtime and new residents are most likely to comingle (Clay 1979). Likewise, Michael Chernoff points to the practical and psychological consequences of a loss of local power and influence for longtime residents, and, relying on a more contemporary case, Gina Perez argues that this loss of control is heightened when "Gentrification reconfigures a neighborhood's racial and social landscape" (2004: 145). This perspective poses a challenge to those who suggest that longtime residents will benefit from gentrification-induced institutional and municipal transformations (Florida 2002, Freeman 2005).

If gentrification comes with attendant negative consequences, who does it harm? The literature suggests that longtime residents absorb the brunt of gentrification's negative consequences. Although, as mentioned above, some suggest that early stage gentrifiers and their establishments sometimes also suffer consequences, such as displacement, and Levy and Cybriwsky suggest that a broad cross-section of residents experience a "loss of social cohesion" (1980: 145) as they negotiate the economic and cultural divides that permeate gentrifying neighborhoods.

With regards to gentrification's consequences for longtime residents, Derek Hyra's selection (2008) demonstrates that the extent and nature of that harm varies from city to city depending on municipal policies. For instance, the specific segment of longtime residents whom gentrification displaces varies by neighborhood; in Chicago's Bronzeville gentrification displaced many public housing residents, while in Harlem many of those displaced are individuals who earn a moderate income and therefore do not qualify for public housing.

Other authors' work suggests that the harm longtime residents experience varies in accordance with their demographic characteristics, such as their economic position, racial or ethnic identity, gender, and age, as well as in relationship to their personal circumstances, such as whether they own or rent, or whether they share their home with someone else who can help shoulder the burdens of rising costs (Henig 1981, Atkinson 2002, Brown-Saracino 2009). Many scholars argue that the social groups with the fewest resources, such as the elderly, the poor, and racial and ethnic minorities bear the brunt of gentrification's costs (Henig 1981, Atkinson 2002, Vigdor 2002).

What factors are responsible for gentrification's outcomes and consequences? As this book has already demonstrated, there is debate about the precise factors that drive gentrification and this translates into disagreement about the source of gentrification's consequences. This is apparent in this section in, for instance, differences between selections by Gina Perez and Mary Pattillo, each of which profiles the daily harassment poor and working class residents of color face in gentrifying neighborhoods. While Perez attends to the culpability of individual harassers, such as a merchant or police officer who discriminates against Puerto Rican youth, Pattillo emphasizes how formal institutions, such as a university and a neighborhood organization, develop policies that fuel patterns of race- and class-based mistreatment.

Throughout this book, authors have underlined the influence of various factors on gentrification's contours—from the presence and character of corporate interests (Gotham 2005), to a city's relative affluence (Glass 1968), and gentrifiers' characteristics and interests (Taylor 2002, Lloyd 2005, Pattillo 2007). In short, most agree that gentrification varies by place, time, and stage, and, likewise, the authors in this section examine how gentrification's outcomes and consequences vary by context. For instance, they underline the influence of market forces (Pattillo 2008), city policies (Hyra 2008), local institutions (Pattillo 2008, Florida 2002), and a neighborhood's spatial location within a city (Levy & Cybriwsky 1980: 142).

Cumulatively, they suggest that the experience of living in a gentrifying neighborhood varies by place and time, by group, and from individual to individual. Yet, this section reminds us that even those who believe that gentrification benefits neighborhoods and cities acknowledge that gentrification typically produces consequences such as some degree of physical and social displacement, class and cultural conflict, and, in many cases, ethnic and racial tensions and discrimination. They debate the extent to which displacement occurs, as well as about how to measure it (Atkinson 2000), and about the nature and source of neighborhood conflict, but few anticipate a gentrification without such features.

In the opening paragraphs of this essay I argued that gentrification's consequences are often apparent in the physical landscape and that we tend to use visual representations of gentrification's outcomes to define and recognize the process. While the authors in this section might agree with my assessment, they would likely debate about their meaning or significance. Does a new sports bar in Uptown spell hope or doom? Is Boystown an example of an urban revitalization that we should celebrate or of a patterned commercialization of neighborhood culture that we should shun? From whose perspective ought we answer such questions (Lang 1982)? If physical or social displacement occurs, which local population groups are most likely to be displaced? As a result of their different perspectives, the authors' policy recommendations range from methods for enabling gentrification (Florida 2002), to strategies for preventing displacement (Hyra 2008). As you read, you might consider how you would answer the questions and dilemmas that the authors pose.

DISCUSSION QUESTIONS

1. What are the sources of the cultural conflicts that Levy and Cybriswky emphasize and that other authors attend to? How and why do those sources vary by context?
2. What policy recommendations would you offer to address physical displacement? To what extent would your recommendations for addressing "social displacement" (Chernoff 1980: 204) be similar to or different from those for physical displacement?
3. Imagine that you chair a committee of social workers, the directors of city agencies, and nonprofit administrators who share the task of addressing gentrification's costs in your city. Your review of research on gentrification suggests that gentrification's outcomes are context-specific. That is, outcomes vary, within a set of parameters, from neighborhood to neighborhood. How would this acknowledgement influence your committee's recommendations for addressing city-wide physical and social displacement? What neighborhood-level characteristics would you look for to help predict the services required in a given neighborhood?
4. Which population groups are most at risk of displacement or most likely to suffer from gentrification's other negative consequences? Does the level of harm residents experience vary in accordance with the class, cultural, racial, and ethnic characteristics of longtime residents and gentrifiers? If you think that it does vary, what evidence is there in the readings about how and why it does so?

ACTIVITIES

1. Visit a neighborhood that the academic literature or popular press identifies as gentrified or gentrifying. During your visit, walk the neighborhood streets taking careful notes on the neighborhood's aesthetic features (the state and quality of its sidewalks, buildings, cars, green space, etc.), the types of businesses present, and the characteristics of residents as well as of their interactions with one another. Based on your preliminary observations, what outcomes or consequences of gentrification are apparent? Which do you suspect might be present but are not readily apparent?

a. Visit a second neighborhood and repeat the activity. Consider the similarities and differences between the two places. What characteristics of the two neighborhoods or their gentrifications explain any differences that you noted?

RESOURCES

Atkinson, R., 2000. "Measuring Gentrification and Displacement in Greater London." *Urban Studies*, 37, 149–165.

Atkinson, R., & Easthope H., 2009. "The Consequences of the Creative Class: The Pursuit of Creative Strategies in Australia's Cities," *International Journal of Urban and Regional Research*, 33, 1: 64–79.

Hamnett, C., & Williams, P., 1980. "Social Change in London: A Study of Gentrification." *Urban Affairs Quarterly*, 15, 469–487.

Henig, J. R., 1981. Gentrification and Displacement of the Elderly: An Empirical Analysis. *The Gerontologist*, 21, 67–75.

Lee, B., & Hodge, D., 1984. "Social Differentials in Metropolitan Residential Displacement." In J. Palen & B. London, editors, *Gentrification, Displacement and Neighborhood Revitalization*. Albany, NY: State University of New York Press, 140–169.

Marcuse, P., 1986. "Abandonment, Gentrification and Displacement: The Linkages in New York City." In N. Smith, & P. Williams, editors, *Gentrification of the City*. London: Unwin Hyman, 153–177.

CHAPTER 21

The Hidden Dimensions of Culture and Class: Philadelphia

Paul R. Levy and Roman A. Cybriwsky

For more than 20 years reinvestment and resettlement trends have been reshaping residential neighborhoods near downtown Philadelphia. Stimulated initially by urban renewal activity in the 1950s and 1960s, the process of rehabilitation has been proceeding with remarkable speed in that part of the urban core that Philadelphians call Central City. At least 10 neighborhoods already have substantial upper-income populations, while another eight are showing marked reinvestment trends. Nightlife, once virtually nonexistent in central Philadelphia, is booming as well. Fashionable bars, restaurants, nightclubs, discos and cabarets are proliferating in areas where the sidewalks used to roll up after sundown. A recent survey, for example, indicated that no fewer than 150 new restaurants have opened in Center City during the past two years (Thompson, 1979).

Yet from beneath the glitter and enthusiasm, a darker side occasionally surfaces. After months of grumbling about "tourists" parking on their sidewalks, white ethnic residents in one neighborhood recently staged a protest in which they blocked traffic and slashed automobile tires. In a Puerto Rican area, the firebombing of a house by a neighbor undid in one night many months of a new resident's rehabilitation work. And in a black neighborhood, angry protestors attempted to block construction of upper-income townhouses and marched on City Hall demanding an end to "recycling" policies. While these are scattered and unrelated incidents, they are representative of many similar events that point to another side of the reinvestment process: a dimension of cultural and economic conflict that belies the facile optimism of the boosters of "revitalization."

As obvious a lesson as it seems, reinvestors are being reminded almost daily that the inner city is not the open and relatively unpopulated suburban frontier of the 1950s. For despite the grim language of "decline," "disinvestment," "abandonment," and "decay," most older urban neighborhoods hardly ever became devoid of people and supportive social and economic institutions. Instead, the inner city of Philadelphia, like the cores of most other northeastern and north central cities, has been the home for a variety of social groups whose recent experiences and views of the world are markedly different from those of the affluent, enthusiastic and confident professionals who are settling in next door. It is hardly surprising that the "newcomers" are not exactly being welcomed with open arms. Much attention, of course, has been paid to the most dramatic side effects of reinvestment—the phenomenon of displacement. But far too little thought has been devoted to the more subtle and perplexing tensions which are generated simply by mutual coexistence.

Unless planners and policy makers become aware of the nature of these cultural clashes (which involve differing attitudes toward the neighborhood, the home, sex roles, childrearing and work), the next decade of urban resettlement may be characterized by bitter and occasionally vicious conflicts between economic and social groups which have traditionally been segregated in American society. If predictions about population redistribution trends are correct . . ., then we may be involved in nothing less than the complete remaking of the inner residential cores of most older American cities. Put bluntly, we do not have the luxury of doing it badly again.

This chapter focuses on the cultural and class tensions that have emerged in recent years in two reinvestment neighborhoods in central Philadelphia. Yet our context is a much broader overview of the patterns of disinvestment and public urban renewal during the past two decades. For the conflicts generated by private reinvestment have not occurred within a social or historical vacuum. Rather, the perceptions different groups hold of events in the present have been very much influenced by their experiences in the past. Thus, it is important to establish that although the remaking of the commerical and residential downtown has appeared an unquestioned success to some, for others it has been a deeply unsettling experience that has often bordered on personal disaster. [. . .]

CONTRASTING CONCEPTIONS OF THE NEIGHBORHOOD

Perhaps the best way to comprehend the varying interpretations of the term "neighborhood" between new and old residents is to look at the different attitudes toward change in Fairmount and Queen Village. Newcomers chose to reinvest in these areas not only to be close to jobs downtown, but also precisely because these neighborhoods were changing. They saw these areas physically and psychologically as extensions of downtown renewal, and were attracted, in large part, because these were places "on the way up." For them, Fairmount or Queen Village was valued not so much for what it had been, but rather for what it might become.

This generalization might not apply to the few early newcomers who arrived in Fairmount or Queen Village in the 1960s. There were few predictions at that time that these neighborhoods were on the threshold of change, and it is doubtful that many early arrivers knew, or even wanted, the type of transition that would follow. Most of the early migrants came because house prices were low and because they valued socially heterogeneous environments. They decried the "monotony" of suburbia and the "sterility" of Society Hill, and hoped to fit in socially with their new neighbors.

However, by the early 1970s, the type of resettlers began to change. Many were endued with a "pioneer" spirit, and felt that their very presence was pushing back the "wilderness" at the "urban frontier." For them, the prospect of changing a neighborhood was both a challenge and a social responsibility. They undertook major housing renovation projects, which typically employed either ultramodern or "historically authentic" styles, depending on the person and the house. In altering the physical landscape, they contributed to what they defined as urban betterment, and signaled to other young, professional people that the neighborhood might become another Society Hill, a standard against which the extent of reinvestment in other neighborhoods is often compared. As a newcomer to Fairmount said in 1972:

"More and more people like us are moving into neighborhoods like this. The cities are coming around, revitalizing."

For many newcomers the neighborhood was perceived as a means to an end rather than as an end in itself. It was clear by the early 1970s that both neighborhoods were good for investment, and many new residents were drawn partly because they could realize a substantial profit by selling their houses after a short stay. Many saw Fairmount or Queen Village as a way station in their personal life cycles or professional careers. As they advanced economically, or as children were born and approached school age, many newcomers would move to other settings. In this way, residential turnover rates increased greatly in both neighborhoods, because new arrivals started to take the place not only of established residents, but also of earlier newcomers. For a number of reasons that will become obvious shortly, this transience is often deeply resented by the "indigenous" population.

Such attitudes among newcomers contrasted sharply with neighborhood perceptions held by long-term residents. For many adults in Fairmount and Queen Village, their neighborhood is the only one that they have ever lived in. Some have lived in the same house for longer than 50 years, and quite a few can trace their family's presence in the area for three or more generations. Other residents are immigrants from the chaos of post-World War II Europe, and for them Fairmount or Queen Village is the first and only residence they have known in America. Many long-term residents have relatives or lifelong friends in the neighborhood, and until prices escalated recently, it was not unusual for newly married children to buy a house on the same block as their parents. In Fairmount in 1974 after reinvestment had begun, as many as two-fifths of long-term residents had relatives elsewhere in the neighborhood and approximately one-fifth had relatives on the same block.

Community life revolved around the many churches, schools, clubs, and small corner businesses which dot both neighborhoods. Often, these institutions were identified with specific ethnic groups. As Robert Park (1915) noted more than six decades ago, no sooner did European immigrants settle in a place than they attempted to recreate the institutions and folkways of their former village life. As quickly as they moved in and located jobs, they established religious institutions, social clubs and beneficial associations. "The effect of this," wrote Park (1915, pp. 579–580), was

to convert what was first a mere geographic expression into a neighborhood, that is to say, a locality with sentiments, traditions, and a history of its own. Within this neighborhood the continuity of the historical process is somehow maintained. The past imposes itself upon the present, and the life of every locality moves on with a certain momentum of its own, more or less independent of the larger circle of life and the interests about it.

To be sure, ethnicity is now less important in defining social relations than it once was, and old immigrant neighborhoods are not as isolated socially from the surrounding areas as when Park made his observations. But remnants of such patterns persisted into the 1970s both in Fairmount and Queen Village. It is difficult to measure such things precisely, but an indication that ethnicity and propinquity remain important is provided by a survey of marriage patterns in Fairmount. Of 174 marriages which involved at least one neighborhood resident, 43.7 percent involved partners within the same ethnic group. Moreover, in nearly one-half of the cases, husband and wife lived within four blocks of each other prior to marriage.[1] So too, the sentiments and traditions that Park described remain, and have contributed over the years to the neighborhoods' strong sense of identity and cohesion. As Caroline Golab (1977, p. 166) wrote in her study of Philadelphia's immigrant communities, the neighborhood was important to residents in an emotional sense,

> because it was the physical entity embodying their community, their system of social and emotional relationships. Their homes became extensions of themselves and the neighborhood became the physical extension of their homes. The neighborhood was a personalized, almost internalized thing. Any threat to it was a threat to them.

Thus, for long-term residents Fairmount or Queen Village has been "home" in the full meaning of the word. The neighborhood was not just a locale within the city, but also a community of family and friends and the setting for an entire way of life. A social worker in Queen Village explained the conception of neighborhood held by long-term residents as follows: "A neighborhood is more than their house. It's more than the money they can invest or the money they could get. It's a sense of pride, a sense of family. It's a sense of sensitivity. It's a sense of church. It's a sense. It's a sixth or seventh sense that no newcomer can ever have."

USE OF OUTDOOR SPACE

These contrasting conceptions of long-term residents and newcomers manifest themselves in the use of the neighborhood. For example, in good weather, and especially after dinner, sidewalks and streets are crowded with long-term residents of all ages engaged in a social routine that reflects the cohesiveness of the neighborhood. The front steps of houses, which abut sidewalks in these row-house communities, often function as outdoor extensions of living rooms. Inside space is generally reserved for immediate family, but outside, residents sit on their steps or in aluminum folding chairs and greet passing neighbors. Certain doorsteps have become regular congregation points for groups of residents

defined variously by age, kinship, ethnicity and proximity. Children play hopscotch, stickball and street hockey where there are vacant parking spaces or tour the neighborhood on their bicycles, while street corners and playgrounds belong to teenagers who frequently hang out in large groups. During hot summer weather, bar patrons take their drinks outside and form tight clusters at tavern corners. First impressions of such patterns might suggest chaos and crowding in a tightly packed neighborhood, but both areas have a complex territorial order which prescribes a time and place for different people and their activities and thereby reduces conflict.

Newcomers are not part of this way of life. Most are not interested in participating, but even those who came to the neighborhood "to be with the people" generally find that the "people" will have little to do with them. Outdoor life in Fairmount and Queen Village, as it was observed in other urban villages (Gans, 1962; Suttles, 1968), is tightly bonded by social networks, friendships from childhood, common ethnicity and common work experiences. Outsiders cannot possibly share this. Neighboring relations between established residents and newcomers might be cordial, but full integration of the two groups rarely occurs. Only in those specific instances when the two share a common external enemy, such as Queen Village's battle against exit ramps for Interstate 95, have effective bonds been established.

For newcomers, the outdoors is rarely the setting for sustained social interaction. It is used instead for such specific activities as jogging or walking the dog. While new residents might spend some of their free time in restaurants and nightclubs near their homes, they do not consider the immediate neighborhood to be the locus of their social lives. They know fewer of their neighbors, including other newcomers, than do long-term residents, and when they do visit friends in the neighborhood, they visit indoors. In fact, many of the newly rehabilitated or newly constructed houses occupied by newcomers have no front steps at all. Instead, the house presents to the world a locked, iron gateway, or some other system of security.

CULTURE CONFLICT

The transition in Fairmount and Queen Village, has, therefore, brought into contact two groups with contrasting perceptions of neighborhood and with different lifestyles. These contacts have often produced conflict. For example, one source of tension concerns the exterior decor of houses. Many newcomers are interested in the preservation of old housing styles, and have had the facades of their dwellings restored to the "original" appearance. In Queen Village, the older of the two neighborhoods, historic certification of houses is popular among new residents. By contrast, more old-timers prefer simple and functional structures, and have covered their facades with artificial stone and have added aluminum storm and screen doors. Problems arise when well-meaning newcomers suggest to neighbors that they fix up their house "the way it is supposed to be." This is more than an insult about the appearance of a house; it is also indicative of an attitude that consciously promotes neighborhood change. Old residents resist such suggestions because they are well aware that tax reassessments generally follow in the wake of highly visible improvements. Many have thus come to consider renovated exteriors, be they historic or modern, as symbols of unwanted intrusion and unwelcome change.

Similarly, the process of new construction and changing land use patterns can also generate tensions, especially when they interfere with customary lifestyles and routines. For example, in Fairmount an empty industrial property with a large parking lot that children used as a sports field has recently given way to the construction of expensive townhouses. In Queen Village new people have been known to press for the removal of some "obnoxious" non-residential use, only to learn later that they were threatening to eliminate a neighbor's job. So too, there is resentment among long-term residents about the proliferation of trendy boutiques and fashionable restaurants and nightclubs. This is especially the case in Queen Village, which now has 43 restaurants and bars that cater to affluent tastes. Twenty-two of these opened between 1977 and the first half of 1979. In the midst of a recent protest against traffic, trash and late-night noise that results from such establishments, an elderly Queen Village woman contemptuously exclaimed: "Our neighborhood is being used as a playground for the rich!" (Kaufman, 1979).

Indeed, this contrast might be seen as reflective of a major cultural difference between representatives of a declining economy based on the old work ethic and on production, and those employed in expanding service fields oriented toward amenities and the ethic of consumption. In *The Hidden Injuries of Class*, Richard Sennett and Jonathan Cobb (1972) have remarked upon the peculiar ambivalence that blue-collar people show toward those who do not labor with their hands. While they recognize and often resent the superior social status of the white-collar professional, they find it difficult to believe that these people actually work. This is further reinforced by the very different work patterns of the increasing number of artists, professors and self-employed individuals who have recently settled in the two neighborhoods. When new people obviously have the money to afford expensive houses and new cars, or when they frequent new restaurants and bars until all hours of the night, the resentment grows.

Thus, as increasing numbers of new-comers arrived in Fairmount and Queen Village, the basic character of the neighborhoods changed. The tastes of new residents started to dominate the landscape in both areas, and old ways of living started to disappear. Television and air-conditioning have taken their toll as well on old habits of "sitting out." But increasingly with population turnover, old-time residents remarked that "this place isn't like it used to be." Since 1970, a number of immigrant institutions have closed because of suddenly declining patronage, and others are on the verge of closing. As one elderly Ukrainian woman in Fairmount lamented: "Our people keep dying or moving out." So too, many of the small "ma and pa" stores and friendly corner taps are gone, replaced by new business with new owners. An anecdote that is repeatedly told in Queen Village captures well what many old-timers feel is happening in their neighborhood. "You know," one version goes, "it used to be I would go out to the corner store to buy a newspaper and my wife wouldn't expect me back for at least an hour. I'd usually get caught up talking with someone. Now I go out, there's no one on the street, so I'm back in two minutes and my wife asks me what's wrong."

CATACLYSMIC CHANGE

All these conflicts might be considered no more than the intriguing contrasts generated by the diversity of urban life were it not for economic factors which have repeatedly exacerbated tensions. As rehabilitation has proceeded, each neighborhood has been pulled into the orbit of the Center City housing market by powerful economic forces. Very quickly, increasing demand exhausted the supply of vacant properties, and market pressures soon forced the eviction of long-term tenants from apartments and rented houses. Likewise, the price of rehabilitation and new construction soon pushed

housing values and tax assessments sharply upward. For example, the average sales price (adjusted for inflation) in Fairmount rose by more than 400 percent between 1961 and 1976 (Cybriwsky and Meyer, 1977). In parts of Queen Village the increase was even higher.[2] Tax assessments rose in Queen Village by an average of 129 percent between 1970 and 1979,[3] and some properties had increases of between 400 and 500 percent.[4] This compares to an increase of 17 percent in the contiguous First Ward. In sum, the conflicts that we have described involve more than misunderstandings between different cultural groups. Rather, for long-term residents who can no longer afford their neighborhood, an entire way of life is at stake. A community worker in Queen Village summed up her perceptions of the process as follows:

> What you have is a class problem. You have people coming in who have money, who can make repairs. They had very good motives. They were going to upgrade the community and support the ethnic people who were there. They wanted some of the life style, security and safety and knowing neighbors and the friendliness that you don't always get. But what happened is, you had individuals just buying the property and doing repairs or whatever and it caught on. So you had people who could afford $40,000, you know, young married, professionals, some children, moving in. . . . So it became obvious to the community that these were outsiders. You can take one or two, but when you begin to get in the minority. . . .

It ought to be clear from this, though too often it is not, that the "enemies" in reinvestment neighborhoods are neither new people nor old, but a process of change that can only be termed cataclysmic. Our research has indicated that in the initial stages of the process, rehabilitation activity did not seem threatening to a majority of residents. Many were pleased by the arrival of "new blood" and the resulting improvements to deteriorating buildings. But there seems to have been a threshold that was crossed, after which feelings and perceptions radically altered. Some became embittered when a relative or friend suddenly was forced to go. Others became aware of the change only when their recently married children could not afford housing in the area. Many were annoyed by illegal real estate solicitation. Others began to see the consequences of rampant speculation. In Queen Village, the sudden increase in apartments created a dramatic parking problem seemingly overnight. In both neighborhoods, the demolition of old warehouses and businesses to make way for townhouse developments seemed to signal to many that the process had "gotten out of control."

As rehabilitation moved block by block through the neighborhoods, feelings changed from surprise, to helplessness, to rage. Old-timers began to feel that their communities were being bought out from under them. A former resident of Queen Village expressed it this way: "There is an incredible feeling of impotence. I can't do anything about these people. . . . They are coming in and they are liable to do me in. . . . We are at their mercy. They are the big guys coming in. They have the money. I just hope that they don't do us in." The pastor of a black church in Queen Village, whose congregation was rapidly displaced, put it more starkly: ". . .the process looks to me inexorable. Money follows money—and it's just eating the neighborhood alive!"

Indeed, the rate of change has been so intense that newcomers who bought houses not more than five years ago have joined established residents in seeking limits and restrictions on local development. Many in Queen village joke about what is termed the "last-one-in syndrome," but there is serious concern by all residents about parking, apartment density, bars and restaurants, and skyrocketing prices.

THE INNER CITY AT A CROSSROADS

There seems to be no end in sight. Inflation and rising energy costs are increasing the demand for inner-city housing, and within the past two years, reinvestment patterns have surfaced beyond the immediate downtown area. For example, a recent in-house study by the Philadelphia Planning Commission found that in the deteriorating neighborhood of Northern Liberties northeast of Center City, 50 percent of the properties changed hands in 1978 alone. A recent issue of *Philadelphia Magazine* even contained a "handicappers" guide to the next "in" neighborhoods, complete with tips from experts on how to speculate in inner-city real estate (Saline, 1979 and companion articles in the same issue). It appears that several neighborhoods are thus on the verge of replicating the patterns of cataclysmic change which we have observed in Fairmount and Queen Village.

Many observers of the reinvestment process have argued that this is only the inevitable course of neighborhood change. Given the cumulative "snow-balling" effect of market forces, it is often asserted that no other type of transition will be possible. The fact that residential location frequently serves as a symbol for social prestige is one reason why rapid turnover is to be expected. Individuals and groups, it is argued, ultimately prefer to live with those who share their values, their customs and their tastes (Perin, 1977). Indeed, since 59 percent of all the dollars spent on new housing construction and rehabilitation in South Philadelphia were spent in Queen Village alone,[5] there seems to be some evidence for this clustering effect.

Whether this truly reflects individual preference, or is the result of the steering and marketing activities of realtors, developers, speculators, and "fashionable" magazines, remains a question for further research. But let us assume, for the sake of argument, that such "boom town" development will characterize future patterns of urban reinvestment. What then are the consequences for our cities?

One only has to look back at the experience and the literature of urban renewal to become painfully aware of the social and psychological consequences of forced dislocation (Fried, 1963). Similarly, Kai T. Erikson (1976) has analyzed quite sensitively the traumas which result from the loss of the sense of "communality," as all supportive social institutions disintegrated in the wake of the flood in West Virginia's Buffalo Creek in 1972. One does not have to like either the physical appearance or the values of older urban communities to recognize that they created a cohesive moral order that regulated the daily activities of life on the street. As we destroy these social networks and patterns of interaction, we destroy one of the things that has made our cities livable and safe.

But beyond these social costs are obvious economic ones. Just because we have swept the problems of older urban neighborhoods out of the view of the "revived" downtown does not mean that we have solved them. On the contrary, we may actually exacerbate them. Private upper-income rehabilitation decreases the supply of low-cost housing without decreasing the demand. It can thus only impose uprooted people on contiguous neighborhoods, create overcrowding, and further strain already overextended social services. So too, it obviously is impossible to plan adequately or budget appropriately for rapidly changing populations.

Finally, there is the disturbing possibility that if we do not cool off these "hot spots" of reinvestment by moderating the process or dispersing demand, then it is likely that some form of backlash will result. Already in both neighborhoods we have studied, newcomers have been subjected to vandalistic initiations that begin with the arrival of the moving truck. Damage to new people's cars, graffiti painting on their homes, verbal abuse and harassment on the street are not uncommon. Our observations also suggest that such incidents are most heavily concentrated on the blocks which are undergoing the most rapid transition.

Even outside reinvestment areas, there have been significant reverberations. For example, throughout low-income, minority areas of Philadelphia, there is a growing sense of uncertainty about the future. Fears of "recycling" are emerging in some neighborhoods far from downtown where there are no signs of reinvestment activity. In some areas, groups have thus been opposing any public Community Development expenditures out of fear that this will only ignite a wildfire of speculation. Conspiracy theories abound concerning which neighborhoods will be forcibly changed into the "next Society Hill."

It is too early to discern whether reinvestment trends in other neighborhoods will reach the fevered pitch which characterizes Philadelphia's current "hot spots." The public sector may yet be roused to effective action. Differing neighborhood characteristics and land use patterns may moderate the process in other communities, as might mounting resistance from lower-income groups. External influences, such as energy, may take an unexpected twist. Even the fashionableness of the city may prove to be a fad of limited duration. Yet, if trends persist on their present course, it will certainly not be the first time in the history of urban development that short-range, highly profitable gains have been achieved by imposing the costs not only on the poor, but also upon a not so distant future.

NOTES

1. These statistics were obtained from analysis of daily lists of marriage license applicants published in the *Philadelphia Inquirer*, 1968 and 1969. These years were chosen to eliminate

newcomers, who at that time were a small part of the area's population.

2. The data are from the *Philadelphia Real Estate Directory* and are for four representative reinvestment blocks in the neighborhood. We are grateful to Deborah McColloch for doing the tabulations.

3. These statistics are from records of the Philadelphia Tax Assessors Office and were compiled by Lynne Goldman.

4. This information was provided by the Queen Village Neighbors Association from their files on property tax appeals.

5. This figure was made available by the Department of Licenses and Inspections in Philadelphia.

REFERENCES

Cybriwsky, Roman A., and Meyer, James T. 1977. "Geographical Aspects of the Housing Market in a Rejuvenating Neighborhood." *Papers in Geography* 16 (December):

Erikson, Kai T. 1976. *Everything in Its Path.* New York: Simon and Schuster.

Fried, Marc. 1963. "Grieving for a Lost Home." In L. J. Duhl, ed., *The Urban Condition*, pp. 151–171. New York: Basic Books.

Gans, Herbert J. 1962. *The Urban Villagers: Group and Class in the Life of Italian-Americans.* New York: Free Press.

Golab, Caroline. 1977. *Immigrant Destinations.* Philadelphia: Temple University.

Kaufman, Marc. 1979. "Oldtimers Fear They Will Be Forced Out." *Philadelphia Bulletin.* May 13, pp. C1–2.

Park, Robert E. 1915. "The City: Suggestions for the Investigation of Human Behavior in the City Environment." *American Journal of Sociology* 20 (March): pp. 577–612.

Perin, Constance. 1977. *Everything in Its Place: Social Order and Land Use in America.* Princeton, N.J.: Princeton University.

Saline, Carol. 1979. "A New Philadelphia: Get It While It's Hot!" *Philadelphia Magazine* (June): p. 122.

Sennet, Richard, and Cobb, Jonathan. 1972. *The Hidden Injuries of Class.* New York: Knopf.

Suttles, Gerald D. 1968. *The Social Order of the Slum: Ethnicity and Territory in the Inner City.* Chicago: University of Chicago.

Thompson, Bill. 1979. "What's That Boom in Philadelphia?" *Philadelphia Inquirer.* April 29, pp. G1, 4.

CHAPTER 22

Social Displacement in a Renovating Neighborhood's Commercial District: Atlanta

Michael Chernoff

This is a case study of a neighborhood commercial district, Little Five Points (LFP) in Atlanta, which has changed in composition over the past several years. Any city area changes over time, but here the new arrivals share characteristics which distinguish them from the older business people. The newcomers are demographically different and hold different philosophies toward their businesses, and the commercial district as a whole, than do the older merchants. This compositional change and the tension it produces will be discussed within the framework of social displacement, in contrast to physical displacement.

By social displacement I mean the replacement of one group by another, in some relatively bounded geographic area, in terms of prestige and power. This includes the ability to affect decisions and policies in the area, to set goals and priorities, and to be recognized by outsiders as the legitimate spokesmen for the area. Social displacement is then a typical accompanying feature of physical displacement. Yet physical displacement need not always go along with social displacement. In the case considered here, the older group of business people has not been displaced physically, but they have lost a considerable amount of the neighborhood control they once had. This idea provides a guide to understanding the conflict which has arisen in Little Five Points and which may be inevitable in any changing residential or business neighborbood.

Social displacement can manifest itself in several ways. For example, the loss of political control in an area can lead to demoralization, or a sense of one's lifestyle being threatened. At some point, residents or businesses may feel compelled to leave the area; thus physical displacement may stem from social rather than economic pressure. Social displacement might be marked by a gradual withdrawal from neighborhood activities by the displaced. They drop out of local organizations or remove themselves from political activities. Thus, they complete their own displacement by relinquishing attachments to the associations which were formerly the bases of their power. These reactions will be discussed below as regards Little Five Points.

The literature on residential revitalization has documented the demographic features of the new residential inmigrant populations (Black, Chapter 1 in [*Back to the City*], Bradley, 1977, 1978; Fichter, 1977; Gale, Chapter 7 in [*Back to the City*]; Laska and Spain Chapter 8 in [*Back to the City*]; Zeitz, 1976).

In addition, revitalization has sparked interest in the displacement of lower-income groups (U.S. Senate, 1977). Typically the focus is on the physical dislocation of people and the economic impact of this dislocation with an eye toward developing mechanisms to ease the burden of higher rents and property taxes or actual physical displacement (as when a multifamily unit is converted to single-family status). Some small body of research has been concerned with the social problems associated with revitalization, rather than the physical displacement per se (cf. Cybriwsky, 1978; see also Levy and Cybriwsky, Chapter 9 in [*Back to the City*]). Cybriwsky describes the resentment of the new migrants by the old and even some vandalism directed against the property of the new residents. In general, however, relatively little work to date has dealt with the social dynamics which often accompany neighborhood change.

Studies concerned with revitalizing commercial areas have dealt even less with the social than those concerned exclusively with residential areas. Loan availability, the dollar volume in the market area and the mix of goods and services (Goldstein and Davis, 1977; Lemmon, 1978) are examples of types of economic factors which have been examined. While these studies attend to the residential context of the commercial district, they do so mainly in terms of market considerations. Rarely is there mention of the social aspects of the relationship between the two. One can draw a conceptual distinction between a commercial area and its residential context, but in fact the two are typically linked. The former, by offering a particular type of goods and services, may draw a certain population to adjoining neighborhoods. Conversely, the composition of residential neighborhoods can influence the decisions of merchants and proprietors to locate in the area or to modify the nature of their merchandise, hoping to capture a portion of the proximate market. Because of the interrelationships, changes in one can lead to changes in the other.

This chapter focuses on the controversy among the neighborhood and commercial residents over a proposed redevelopment plan for Little Five Points for which $350,000 of federal Community Development Block Grant (CDBG) funds have been allocated. A formal plan exists (City of Atlanta), calling for sidewalk repair, general beautification, and most controversially, the establishment of two small pedestrian malls achieved by an alteration of street patterns in LFP.

The exploration of social displacement in LFP begins in the mid-1960s, with changes in the surrounding residential areas, the spread of change to LFP itself, and the resultant change in the composition of the LFP business community. The dispute over the plan will be examined as it reflects the social displacement problems associated with the compositional changes. [. . .]

THE DEVELOPMENT OF COMMERCIAL CONFLICT

The first clashes among members of the LFP business district occurred in the mid-1960s over transportation. One centered on a state plan to construct two major interstate highways which would have passed close to the center of LFP, one cutting directly through Inman Park. The second involved a plan to widen Moreland Avenue, the main traffic artery through LFP. Part of this latter project was actually completed, running south from the center of LFP; the proposal was to complete the widening through the rest of LFP to the north. In general, the business community at that time was in favor of both projects, believing that they would stimulate business by bringing additional traffic into the area.

This sentiment was not shared by residents of a number of neighborhoods through which the roads were to pass. Although land acquisition and the demolition of housing units had already begun, a coalition of neighborhood groups was formed to fight the highways, an effort that proved to be at least temporarily successful. The Moreland Avenue project likewise fell upon hard times and although not ultimately defeated, it has been halted for the time being. Both these issues represent the first confrontation between the business district and the new migrants to the surrounding residential areas.

While the business community may have been fairly well united in its support for the interstate construction and arterial widening, it did not prevail. The newer residents in surrounding neighborhoods, essentially middle-class, were a political force of growing potency. Coupled with the general awareness across the country of local neighborhood power, whether of the lower- or middle-class variety, the anti-highway victories enhanced the confidence of the neighborhood residents in their ability to affect public plans (cf. Advisory Commission on Intergovernmental Relations, 1972; Cole, 1974; Kansas City Urban Observatory, n.d.; Yin and Yates, 1974; Yin and Lucas, 1973).

The Fight over the Highways

Many members of the LFP business community recognize the controversies over Moreland Avenue and the two freeways as the root of conflict in the area which today is manifested in the dispute over the redevelopment plan to "beautify" LFP. As a plan opponent put it:

> There has been conflict over several things between the business community and the housing restorers, the restoration group. It started a number of years ago when the Stone-Mountain [Interstate 485] Freeway was proposed. . . . And the business community felt it would be the greatest boon to business that had ever come through the neighborhood and the restoration group said no, it would just totally destroy everything they'd been working for. . . . That was the beginning of some conflicts and some disagreements. There have been quite a few other issues.

The conflicts over the highways and street widening are, however, more than just past battles. They continue to provide an explanation for the attitudes people hold toward the LFP redevelopment plan. The plan's proponents are especially sensitive to the situation created by the defeat of the highways. One said:

> The people who have been the most adamant against the plan are people who are major property owners in the area. You go back about ten years. . . . and we were looking to have a freeway through this area and a widened Moreland Avenue and a MARTA [Metropolitan Atlanta Regional Transit Authority] station built right on top of Moreland Avenue down here. So if you were a property owner in Little Five Points, you'd been here 20, 30 years; you'd seen your property values decline and go downhill. You're older; you're thinking about your retirement or where you'd like to live. You'd like to get your money out of your property. You'd like to sell it for a good price. Well, the freeway, the widening, and all this stuff, all of a sudden you see a lot of hope. The property in the area's going to be worth something again. So first of all here come all these neighborhood people and they kill off the freeway. Then they kill off the Moreland Avenue widening. MARTA moves the rapid transit station. . . . So all of a sudden, and then, as if to add insult to injury, now they start coming and talking about closing streets in Little Five Points. It's not hard to see how from some people's point of view, all of a sudden they were going to have this great opportunity to at some point sell their property or redevelop it and do real well and from their point of view all that's been destroyed. And here it's going to be this little neighborhood shopping area where you don't have big companies interested in the land.

Looking back over the same issues, current plan opponents take the view that (1) the widening and the new freeways would have been good for business, (2) the neighborhood people are generally opposed to vehicular traffic for selfish reasons, and (3) opposition to the roads reflects an unrealistic vision of what is necessary in the area. Moreover, several argued that the defeat of these projects involved collusion between area residents and city officials, a "conspiratorial" theory of sorts.

> [Regarding the Moreland Avenue widening] some of the [City] Council people had got some information that the federal government was going to issue some Community Development funds to revitalize some of the older residential-business areas. So they smelt [sic] an opportunity to make a dollar. So they had a meeting that nobody would know anything about and the City voted to turn thumbs down on the widening. . . . Some of this group, friends of the Council group, even one or more Council persons got together and formed a corporation and bought the buildings [in LFP]. . . . They bought that because they were figuring on being able to get this money.

That a "conspiracy" theory should emerge among the minority is not remarkable in and of itself. But the emergence of this explanation of events and the defeat of the roads set the stage for an intensification of such feelings over subsequent issues. The quotation above is a rare expression of "conspiracy" related to the earlier highway issues; it is a more frequent response to the current redevelopment plan. Whereas the controversy over the Interstate and the street widening occurred between the business community and an "outside" agent (i.e., the residential communities), the present conflict illustrates the same attitudinal differences but the range of opinions is now found within the business community itself.

The "Infiltration" of Little Five Points

Although it is impossible to specify the characteristics of a "new" kind of business in LFP, as opposed to the older businesses, observers in the area generally agree that the first "new" businesses began arriving about five years ago. Since that time, many have moved into the area, some of them only briefly. The features of the new businesses which are most pertinent to this discussion are that (1) they are often owned by area residents, often people from Candler Park, (2) the goods and services they offer are more directly aimed at the residents of surrounding neighborhoods, (3) they rely to a large extent on local residents for their business, and, most importantly, (4) they have a view of the kind of business district Little Five Points should be which contrasts with the orientation of some of the older merchants.

These new proprietors, many already active in neighborhood civic associations, began joining the Business Association a few years ago. Now they are the "majority" in LFP. This change is noteworthy because it previews the social displacement experienced by older merchants and property owners in the area. For the first time, the hegemony of the traditional business leaders was challenged. The challenge was, and is, over very real issues, represented today by the redevelopment plan for the use of CDBG funds.

I use the term "infiltration" somewhat facetiously to describe the changing composition of the business district. The new businesses are legitimate rent-paying tenants or property owners. But their arrival represents the spread to LFP and the type of individual who is moving into Inman Park and Candler Park. This development reinforces the link between the two. Whichever is the primary casual direction (the desire by new residents to reform the business area or the lure of new residents to their neighborhoods because of the business district) there is a decreasing distinction between the characteristics of the neighborhoods and those of the majority of merchants in LFP. This difference between the new and old business people will be made clear in an examination of the dispute over the redevelopment plan.

THE CONFLICT OVER THE REDEVELOPMENT PLAN

As mentioned earlier, the redevelopment plan calls for a number of "beautification" projects in and changes in the street patterns within the business district. It is on this latter aspect of the plan that the controversy hinges. The term "street closing" has itself become something of a battle cry for the plan's opponents. Proponents, conversely, use other terms, like "traffic rerouting." Despite the apparent centering of the argument over the effects on business of the new traffic pattern, there appear to be other factors involved and other considerations in the minds of the participants.

Essentially, the conflict over the plan is the first major issue to arise within the reconstituted business district, pitting one portion of the community against another instead of against some outside entity. The framework of social displacement offers insights to the dispute that a consideration of the strictly "economic impact" facets cannot explain. The interviews reveal an awareness by participants of other dimensions. The plan has become a symbolic issue, reflective of control of power over the affairs of the local business community.

The "Conspiracy" Theory

One common thread running through the comments of the plan's opponents is the "closed" and secretive nature of the development of the plan and, indeed, the intentions of its original formulators. Opponents argue that the plan was developed by a small number of local people who had close ties to City Hall and who used those connections to their advantage in getting the plan approved. Also, they believe that the plan is intended to benefit a small number of

business people in LFP, people who established businesses there for the express purpose of taking advantage of the grant money. The conduct of this new group during the development of the plan was believed to be generally secretive and deliberately exclusionary of the older business people. As one of the long-time owners says: "The owners of the [business] and the [business] . . . have some silent partners that have ties to City Hall. Well, I think that some of the people that have stock in those two corporations either work for or hold elected positions in the City of Atlanta." Another, referring to a neighborhood meeting to discuss and vote on the plan: "I hadn't planned to go because I didn't know they were going to have it. That was always the way. Everything was already done and we were not told; we were not supposed to know. They didn't want us to know about it."

Characterization of "the Others"

Along with the lack of trust between the groups over the origin and intent of the plan is a questioning of the character of the "opposition." Some of this uneasiness results from age differences (original business people are older in years than the newer) and the accompanying lifestyle and sociopolitical differences. Older merchants apply such terms as "hippie type" and "radical" to some of the newer proprietors and newer residents in surrounding areas. Beyond this, though, is a tendency to question the legitimacy of some of the newer businesses. Here is a representative statement from an opponent of the plan:

> I don't approve of the type businesses we're getting in here that, to me, have no really visible means of support. And it makes me suspicious really as to how the businesses are being supported. . . . Where's the money coming from? Is somebody else supplying it? Or . . . have we got a marijuana operation on the side

at certain hours? The money has to be coming from someplace and it don't come from the business that walks in the place and buys the merchandise. . . . They're being subsidized or there's something that's not legitimate.

Conversely, plan proponents portray some of the older merchants as "being afraid of change." The older businesses are seen as unwilling or unable to change to take advantage of the new character of the residential neighborhoods. They are carrying goods not desired by those new residents and staying with marketing and display practices that put them at a competitive disadvantage. Plan proponents seem to believe that there is money enough to be made by everyone if only the older business people will face up to the changes which have taken place in the neighborhoods and make the necessary alterations.

These remarks of the plan's friends and foes speak to the replacement of one group by another in the general area which encompasses both the residential and business communities. The proponents of the plan insist that no damage has been done to the older businesses save what they brought upon themselves by not being "smart" in their operations. The opponents of the plan make more personal their attack upon the individuals and business which now form the majority in an area which was once "theirs."

The Prerogatives of Tenure

In the remarks made by some plan opponents concerning the manner in which the plan was developed and "pushed" through the approval process, there is an attitude of having been excluded from that process, even deliberately. In the past, a more homogeneous business community may well have operated in a more informal manner. People were well acquainted with one another, with ties extending back over the

years. These older business people are, after all, people who in the past were dominant in the community and who played a major role in any issue or decision facing LFP. Now, numerically if in no other way, they have been supplanted by individuals they do not know personally. The loss of hegemony, in the Business Association and in community affairs in general, is a critical aspect of the social displacement argument. Several plan proponents seemed sensitive to this issue:

> I think there was a kind of proprietorship, sense of proprietorship, of Little Five Points that maybe it's expected that people would come to them as the people who had been here and ask their advice and ask them what they wanted, and they would be in control.

> They at one time ran the Association, were the Association, and usually had a say. Now they are the minority, and they feel that they have probably been pushed out. And they resent this.

> . . . some people who've been here a very long time, and I'm sure naturally feel they have some prerogative by virtue of how long they've been here. Then me and other people come marching in here with their own ideas of how it ought to be, join the Business Association, and work to support this revitalization plan.

In a straightforward sense, the older business people in LFP have lost their dominant position in the community. It is possible to document the change through the office holding in the Business Association and by votes on community issues. A strictly political transformation has taken place; barring some major reversal, the organizational control of LFP lies in the hands of the newer business people.

Different Visions of the Future

Social displacement is seen not only in the control of the Business Association and the sense of exclusion during the plan development sequence. A different view of the business district has developed among the newer businesses. Or, at least, this "philosophy" is seen by the participants as being distinct. The plan's proponents stress their commitment to a community-oriented, community-controlled business district. They want a strong pedestrian environment as opposed to an automobile oriented "strip." This manifests itself over the Moreland Avenue widening issue. Plan proponents believe older businesses view LFP as a work place only, and their interests in the area are seen to be purely business. Plan opponents, who recognize the plan as an attempt to create this localized, pedestrian shopping center, believe that this thrust is not in the ultimate best interests of business in LFP. The proponents are seen as "illogical" or "dreamers." Moreover they are seen as talking out of both sides of their mouths. On the one hand, say the opponents, they talk "community," but in fact they are interested in making money from the redevelopment plan, and the desire for this profit is what lies behind the formulation of the plan in the first place: "I think that the groups that is [sic] controlling the plan are the ones that expect to benefit from it from a financial standpoint." In contrast to the above, the proponents state:

> I think it has a lot to do with the residential thing, to get back to that—I think it comes down more to community. There are people who feel that this is my community. . . . This is typically of the point of view of people I call new businesses. The old businesses, they don't see it that way. It's a place where they work. Their commitment ends more or less with that.

> They don't live here. They don't have real commitment to this area other than it's where they own a business or own some property. And maybe they were interested in selling off their property or selling off their businesses and moving their business out to where they live. Most of the people that I know that are involved in [business] or any other business

> in this neighborhood . . . live here or nearby. It's not just a place where they work. It's the center of their community.

These distinctions point to the changing dominant philosophy governing decisions affecting LFP. Or at least they indicate a perception of such a difference. And the perception is the more important factor to the people involved.

OBSERVATIONS ON SOCIAL DISPLACEMENT

Social displacement seems to be a good term to describe the process taking place in Little Five Points, wherein one group of individuals is gaining a dominant position at the expense of another. The history of the area in the past 15 years shows, first, a transition in the residential neighborhoods around LFP that evidenced itself in the successful battle against the interstate projects and against the position of the business community. Over time, the effect of the residential transition filtered into the business district directly as the neighborhoods provided a base from which small businesses arose and drew their support. Currently, there is a confrontation between the "old" and "new" interests in LFP over the redevelopment plan.

The plan itself is crucial in highlighting the division which has developed in LFP and in bringing into the open the attitudes and opinions of members of the business community. It is catalytic in its effect. The process of social displacement which has been going on for ten years might have led to a similar division over any such issue. So in some respects, the division over the plan was inevitable; it reflects the changing composition of the residential and business communities. This change, involving people with different characteristics and different viewpoints, has led simultaneously to a transformation in the way the business community views itself, its purpose, and its relationship to the residential neighborhoods.

It is difficult to say whether LFP is more polarized today than a decade ago. Certainly the lack of communication between the two groups contributes to stereotypical thinking. The sterotyping evidences itself in the retrospective construction of reality, wherein past issues, like the highway, are likely to be interpreted in terms of the current division. Moreover, it can be seen in the expectations of the positions individuals will take on upcoming issues, such as the use of the vacant highway right-of-way. These processes play upon one another. Thus, perhaps the reason "conspiracy" is not seen as dominant for the highway conflict is that older-term business people viewed it as an isolated situation. But when the redevelopment plan is added to the picture, the "whole thing is put in perspective."

Policy Implications

Despite the seemingly necessary confrontation, a confrontation found in other studies (Cybriwsky, 1978; see also Chapter 9 in this volume), there are, I believe, steps which could have minimized the severity of the cleavage and "softened" the blow associated with social displacement. The new business people, schooled in neighborhood associations and neighborhood battles, were familiar with the tactics required to manage an issue. They were accustomed to the mechanism of public meetings and the necessity of making sure that one's side is adequately represented at such meetings. Older business people, in fact, make frequent use of the term "packing" to describe the recruitment of support for the plan at public meetings. And they seem aware of the general feeling that they are at a disadvantage in dealing with the government: "I do think that they have advantages that the older taxpayers have paid for and now, as a

result of their being better educated, and in the know about all this stuff, it's being used against us."

One obvious response is that governmental agencies sponsoring plans or projects for changing areas, either residential or commerical, should show a higher level of sensitivity for the older participants and should work harder to make sure they are made aware of and given full opportunity to participate in the development of such projects. The older business people in Little Five Points complain that they were never advised of the redevelopment plan or that they learned about it only after it had been significantly developed. This may well be the case even though announcements of meetings are a matter of public record. But these members of the community may be more accustomed to discussing matters informally with information being passed by word of mouth. They had not been participants in the rise of "community power" and suffered for lack of that participation.

Sensitivity to this problem would not, of course, change the overall course of events in communities like Little Five Points. But it could perhaps reduce the destructiveness of bad relationships in a commercial area which is struggling to revive itself and which can only be hurt by an internal division. Inner-city shopping areas have too many problems to contend with to be able to tolerate "family feuds." In LFP, there is little in the way of personal antagonism except in a few isolated cases. But the general level of mistrust and the absence of communication help explain why the community has found it difficult to reach a compromise on the plan.

The emergence of a common enemy could reunite this area, but it is hardly a development which can be planned or upon which one should base one's hopes. Without assigning blame for the current breakdown in communication, various participants, including the newer merchants and the city itself, could have acted in ways which would have reduced the level of tension. The older business people have a stake in the area and as members of the community should not be overlooked.

REFERENCES

Advisory Commission on Intergovernmental Relations. 1972. *The New Grass Roots? Decentralization and Citizen Participation in Urban Areas.* Washington, D.C.: U.S. Government Printing Office.

Bradley, Donald. 1977. "Neighborhood Transition: Middle-Class Home Buying in an Inner-City, Deteriorating Community." Paper presented at the Annual Meeting of the American Sociological Association, Chicago.

——, 1978. "Back to the City?" *Atlanta Economic Review* 28 (March/April): 15–21.

City of Atlanta. 1976. *Little Five Points Business Revitalization Plan.* Atlanta: Department of Community and Human Development, City of Atlanta.

Cole, R.L. 1974. *Citizen Participation in the Urban Policy Process.* Lexington, Mass.: D.C. Heath.

Cybriwsky, Roman A. 1978. "Social Aspects of Neighborhood Change." *Annals of the Association of American Geographers* 68 (March): 17–33.

Fichter, R. 1977. *Young Professionals and City Neighborhoods.* Boston: Parkman Center for Urban Affairs.

Goldstein, B., and Davis, R. 1977. *Neighborhoods in the Urban Economy.* Lexington, Mass.: Lexington Books.

Kansas City Urban Observatory. n.d. *Citizen Participation Groups: A Report to the National Urban Observatory.* Lawrence, Kansas: Urban Studies Group, University of Kansas.

Lemmon, W. 1978. "Neighborhood Business Districts: Establishing Where the Strength Is . . . and Isn't." Paper presented at the National Conference of the American Institute of Planners, New Orleans.

McWilliams, S. 1975. "Recycling a Declining Community: Middle-Class Migration to Virginia Highland." Master's thesis Georgia State University, Atlanta.

Yin, R.K., and Lucas, W.A. 1973. "Decentralization and Alienation." *Policy Sciences* 4: 327–336.

—— and Yates, D. 1974. "Street-Level Governments: Assessing Decentralization and Urban Services." *Nation's Cities* 12: 34–58.

Zeitz, E. 1976. "The Process of Private Urban Renewal in Three Areas of Washington, District of Columbia." Ph. D. dissertation. American University, Washington, D.C.

CHAPTER 23

The New Urban Renewal, Part 2: Public Housing Reforms

Derek S. Hyra

In the United States, the adverse conditions of inner city, black communities and the history of public housing policies are closely intertwined (Massey and Kanaiaupuni 1993; Plunz 1990). Federal policies, such as the Housing Acts of 1949 and 1954, and local political decisions led to the placement of many public housing developments in black ghettos. Moreover, in the late 1960s and early 1970s, Congress enacted the Brooke Amendments, which set a preference for extremely low-income tenants, further concentrating the poor in African-American neighborhoods.[1]

While much of the past national housing and urban renewal legislation is coupled with the demise of urban black communities, recent public housing reforms are connected with the process of revitalization. In the 1990s federal policymakers passed a series of housing reforms in an attempt to alleviate concentrated neighborhood poverty. In 1992 the U.S. Department of Housing and Urban Development (HUD) began the Housing Opportunities for People Everywhere (HOPE VI) program (Popkin, Levy, Harris, Comey, Cunningham, and Buron 2002).[2] Between 1996 and 2003, this program provided funding for the demolition of nearly 60,000 public housing units nationwide.[3] Then in 1996 Congress ordered public housing authorities to rehabilitate or demolish buildings with excessive code violations or vacancies.[4] Lastly, to make it financially feasible for cities to facilitate the demolition process, the one-for-one replacement requirement for razed units was permanently repealed with the enactment of the Quality Housing and Work Responsibility Act of 1998 (Goetz 2003). Although there is a federal push to demolish the nation's high-rise public housing stock, not every major city follows this directive.

Harlem and Bronzeville are both revitalizing, however, the consequences of development are vastly different for public housing residents in each community. Bronzeville is experiencing massive displacement of public housing tenants; nearly 9,000 public housing units are being demolished and roughly 17,000 people are being removed.[5] While Chicago razes a large percent of its public housing, New York City is rehabilitating their high-rise public housing, especially in Harlem. Some Harlemites claim public housing residents are less likely to be displaced than low-income renters in Harlem's private housing market. Harlem's redevelopment has much less displacement among its most vulnerable population.

Although recent federal housing reforms are important to the revitalization of disadvantaged neighborhoods, they do not completely explain community-level outcomes. Political circumstances in New York City and Chicago, both past and present, are essential to understanding how federal reforms influence Harlem and Bronzeville's redevelopment. As discussed at length in the previous chapter, distinct governance systems in New York City and Chicago yield alternate choices and actions related to the Empowerment Zone implementation. This political difference is critical to the conditions of the public housing stock in these cities: New York City sustains it, while Chicago consistently makes detrimental decisions that deplete their housing stock. The decentralized political environment in New York City results in greater tenant activism and better public housing management, which over time helps explain the city's superior public housing. This situation elucidates why Harlem's redevelopment, compared to Bronzeville's, is associated with significantly less displacement among its low-income residents.

Considerable displacement is connected with the revival of certain inner city areas, but this second round of urban renewal differs from the urban renewal of the 1940s, '50s, and '60s, which was detrimental to urban black America. There is little doubt that whites were the primary beneficiaries of the first round of urban renewal. Institutional racism embedded in federal urban renewal legislation led to increased segregation and isolation for poor urban African Americans and preserved downtown growth in many areas (Hirsch [1983] 1998; Massey and Denton 1993; von Hoffman 2000). Today, however, certain African Americans reap benefits from the second round of urban renewal. Black real estate developers and homeowners are experiencing direct financial gains from the current inner city redevelopment, forcing scholars to reconsider the legacy of institutional racism related to federal development initiatives.

In this chapter I discuss the differences

between Chicago and New York City's public housing and present the Bronzeville and Harlem cases.[6] Both cases illustrate how federal public housing relates to the current redevelopment and how this is important for understanding who is being left out and who is benefiting. I then discuss how past city-level political circumstances surrounding public housing are critical for understanding the present community situations.

PUBLIC HOUSING: CHICAGO AND NEW YORK STYLE

Public housing is often seen as a harbinger of crime, drugs, teen pregnancy, laziness, mismanagement, and corruption, but conditions in public housing vary greatly from city to city. Overall, New York City's and Chicago's public housing are at the extremes of a continuum; the New York City Housing Authority (NYCHA) manages some of the best (Thompson 1999), while the Chicago Housing Authority (CHA) has some of the worst projects in the country (Schill 1997).

The public housing conditions in Bronzeville and Harlem are strikingly different. Most Bronzeville projects are isolated from the rest of the community (see figs. 5.1 and 5.2). For instance, large highways and railroad tracks segregate public housing buildings from the rest of the community. Moreover, the buildings are stepped back from the street and appear as if they were dropped out of the sky onto land more desolate and empty than a ghost town. Few businesses and homes are nearby most of the large-scale projects.

Bronzeville's public housing is extremely dilapidated and controlled by gangs. Entering public housing means stepping into the middle of the drug trade. Gang members monitor the outside of the buildings and sell illicit substances, calling out drug code phrases like "ghost face" and "dog face" from first-floor hallways. The unlawful activity makes public housing quite intimidating and dangerous, especially when turf wars, which often involve gunfire, break out. After negotiating the daily drug activity, residents typically take stairs to their apartments because elevators are often broken. The stairwells are dark, since light fixtures frequently do not work, are covered with graffiti and reek of urine and marijuana. Many apartments suffer from rat and cockroach infestations. Overall, CHA buildings are in a state of disrepair. They are dingy, unsafe and unhealthy environments to raise children.

Harlem's public housing is in better shape and not isolated from the rest of the community. The sixteen to twenty-story buildings abut the street and Harlem's apartment buildings and beautiful brownstones surround some of these high-rises (fig. 5.3). NYCHA projects are not dilapidated, but they are grimy and gritty, like much of New York City. There is significantly less gang presence. Although some drug dealing exists in Harlem's public housing, drug activity usually occurs in nearby abandoned buildings and adjacent streets. Gang violence and shootings occur in and around the projects, but less frequently than in Bronzeville. In New York City public housing floors are cleaner, the elevators usually work and graffiti is much less common. Hallways and stairwells are illuminated and odors are much less potent.

The difference between public housing conditions in Chicago and New York City gives insight into the drastically different results in their federally ordered viability tests. The CHA has the highest proportion of failing housing units in the United States. Barely half of CHA units pass (CHA2000), while nearly all of NYCHA's buildings do (Thompson 1999). Because of the awful condition of Chicago's public housing, the CHA receives a greater portion of urban renewal funds from the federal government. The CHA, under the HOPE VI program, has been awarded thirty-nine grants, totaling $340 million, from the U.S. Department of Housing and Urban Development for public housing demolition and the construction of mixed-income replacement housing.[7] The NYCHA, a much larger public housing system, has received only four HOPE VI grants totaling $90 million. Of the $90 million, only one grant is specifically for the demolition of 102 units, while thirty-one grants are awarded to Chicago for the razing of 12,500 units.[8] As the city of Chicago destroys a vast portion of its subsidized housing stock, New York City puts funds toward rehabilitation, setting the context for public housing resident displacement from Bronzeville and not Harlem.

BRONZEVILLE'S REDEVELOPMENT AND PUBLIC HOUSING REFORMS

The CHA's Plan for Transformation

In 1999 Mayor Richard M. Daley convinced the U.S. Department of Housing and Urban Development (HUD) to return the management of the CHA to the city after a four-year period of HUD receivership.[9] Shortly after, the CHA announced a monumental $1.6 billion "Plan for Transformation." The plan is one of the largest and most ambitious urban redevelopment initiatives to emerge since the 1960s. Chicago proposed to raze nearly all high-rise public housing buildings and redevelop 25,000 units, resulting in a loss of approximately 13,000 apartments (CHA 2000). According to the plan, 6,000 families would be relocated to private housing with Section 8 vouchers.[10] To end their reputation for the worst public housing in the country, Chicago intends to eliminate their dilapidated stock.

In 1999, Bronzeville had the highest concentration of high-rise public housing in the city. Most line the State Street Corridor, a three-mile stretch that runs parallel to the

Dan Ryan Expressway and spans from 22nd Street to 55th Street. Some speculated that this area contained the highest concentration of public housing in the world. South State Street had five major housing projects—Raymond Hilliard Homes, Harold Ickes, Dearborn Homes, Stateway Gardens, and the Robert Taylor Homes. Of these projects, the Robert Taylor Homes, comprising twenty-eight sixteen-story high-rises, was the largest and most daunting. In addition to these housing developments, other large-scale, public housing projects, including the Washington Park Homes, the Ida B. Wells Homes, and the Prairie Court Homes, were scattered throughout Bronzeville. While standing almost anywhere in the community, one cannot escape the sight, or weight, of Chicago's high-rise public housing.

Housing project conditions make the community, at times, unsafe and dangerous. One Bronzeville resident, who worked in public housing during the early 1990s, describes the circumstances at the projects as "frightening": "I remember when I worked in Wells [Ida B. Wells Homes]. We were doing the Wells initiative. At one point I had a girlfriend that lived in Lake Meadows and a girlfriend that lived in Hyde Park. I remember telling this girlfriend who lived in Hyde Park, 'Don't drive down Cottage Grove at night because they're shooting the cars. They were just doing random shooting between Madden Park and Abraham Lincoln Center.' For like four or five years there was gunfire where you couldn't drive down Cottage Grove at night." The harsh reality of gun violence at these developments has inhibited residential investment in the community. However, once the city declared that they were going to demolish all of the community's high-rises, totaling nearly 9,000 units, real estate developers became very interested in Bronzeville.

Bronzeville's economic development is strongly associated with the CHA's plan. A banker employed at a Bronzeville branch of a large commercial bank observes:

> Well, I've been here going on three years working for the bank. What I've seen of course is a tremendous change in housing with the increase in rehabbing. Just improving the stock of the housing, increasing the number of condos, condo conversions . . . And I think losing the public housing is probably having the biggest effect on how the community is changing because incomes are increasing. The low to moderate-income people are leaving, so businesses find this community . . . a lot more attractive because the income is higher, the housing stock is better. So I would say that's the biggest factor [leading to change], it's losing the public housing. . . . When all of the public housing comes down, the impact of losing public housing in this community is going to be tremendous. Property values will skyrocket.

Although Bronzeville's property values were increasing before the CHA's Plan for Transformation, development activity and interest in the area accelerated once demolition began.[11] Large downtown real estate developers, who once overlooked Bronzeville, are now buying tracts of land directly across from lots where high-rise public housing once stood. At the same time, landlords and homeowners are rehabilitating their properties. Moreover, several large apartment complexes that once accepted Section 8 vouchers are being converted to luxury condominiums. As one longtime Bronzeville resident explains, "You are going to see this place go [development] crazy now that they've torn down Stateway and Robert Taylor."

Bronzeville's large public housing projects are being converted into "mixed-income" housing developments. These new developments, which are HOPE VI sites, will have one-third public housing units, one-third market rate rentals, and one-third market rate homeownership.

At the former Stateway Gardens project, now called Park Boulevard, the high-end, marke trate homes are selling for $625,000 (Shashaty 2007).

At the former Robert Taylor Homes, renamed Legends South, prices for single-family homes start at $325,000.[12] The public investment from the federal government, and the city's decision to construct townhomes on and near former public housing lots, helps to increase property values throughout the community.

Local city decisions about where to target federal funding strongly influence Bronzeville's development. While most of Chicago's high-rises, mainly concentrated on the west and south side of the city, are slated for demolition, only certain projects receive HOPE VI funding to build mixed-income replacement housing. Mayor Daley has ensured that Bronzeville receives over half of the city's HOPE VI demolition funds, approximately $45 million. Additionally, nearly $100 million is targeted toward the construction of "mixed-income" housing developments.[13] Other public funds, generated through the use of Tax Increment Districts (TIFs), discussed in chapter 3, are also being used to subsidize the construction of mixed-income replacement housing.[14] According to a local newspaper article, "Mayor Richard Daley has flexed considerable muscle to see this area revitalized."[15]

While Bronzeville develops, an important question becomes: what is going to happen to displaced public housing residents? Theoretically, the demolition process provides an opportunity for public housing residents to find better homes. Sudhir Venkatesh, a sociologist who has done substantial fieldwork at the Robert Taylor Homes, comments, "Outright demolition of the housing developments would enable the integration of tenants into the larger (mainstream) city" (2000, 8).

Studies on public housing resident mobility stemming from the Gautreaux and the Movement to Opportunity (MTO) programs suggest relocating out of public housing and concentrated poverty to more prosperous neighborhoods may be beneficial to households (Orr, Feins, Beecroft, et al. 2003; Rubinowitz and Rosenbaum 2000). However, with Chicago's demolition and relocation most tenants end up in highly segregated, disadvantaged neighborhoods. Beside a 120-day vacate notice, a three-hour "Housing Choice" lecture about housing options, and a three-hour "Good Neighbor" session to learn how to maintain their Section 8 apartments, little guidance is given to tenants. Many of Bronzeville's community leaders are skeptical that two three-hour courses will adequately prepare CHA tenants. One woman, who had worked with residents trying to transition out of public housing before the Plan for Transformation was put in place, asserts that it will take an intensive fourteen-week program to effectively prepare longtime CHA families to move. She calls the Good Neighbor program and the relocation process "a joke."

The Plan for Transformation's relocation strategy is severely under-funded, making it extremely difficult for residents to find decent housing. The CHA budgeted $6 million for relocating residents in its first implementation year, less than 1 percent of its $1.6 billion plan. Successful relocation programs and social service mobility programs have one housing counselor for every 25 to 40 families; the CHA plan has only enough money for one counselor for every 139 families (Synderman and Dailey 2001). Some developments have one relocation counselor for at least 500 families (Sullivan 2003).

Additionally, Chicago's housing market is incapable of accommodating so many Section 8 vouchers holders. A report commissioned by the Metropolitan Planning Council, a citywide civic organization, indicates that the city's private low-income rental market is extremely tight, with a 4 percent vacancy rate (Lenz and Coles 1999). "Very poor African Americans are [being] removed from their homes and given a voucher to find housing that for the most part does not exist" (Ranney 2003, 198).

The public housing demolition in Chicago has relocated neighborhood poverty, not alleviated it. The vast majority of residents are moving to new, segregated and disadvantaged neighborhoods further from the city center. Tom Sullivan, a consultant hired by the CHA to monitor the relocation efforts, claims, "The result has been that the vertical ghettos . . . are being replaced with horizontal ghettos" (2003, 13). As of 2002, 80 percent of those relocating are residing in communities that are over 90 percent black and nearly 70 percent of residents leaving the high-rises with vouchers are going to neighborhoods where the poverty rate is above 23 percent" (Fischer 2003).[16] While this poverty rate is lower than Bronzeville's once was, as more families relocate, poverty rates in communities where former CHA tenants are clustering will likely rise. Additionally, subsequent relocation studies that track the movement of former CHA tenants, such as the one conducted by Venkatesh and colleagues (2004), show that nearly all tenants are ending up in segregated high-poverty areas. These new horizontal ghettos are forming in neighborhoods on the far south and west sides of Chicago and in the inner south suburbs.[17]

The Chicago public housing relocation process may put former tenants in a more vulnerable situation. Many tenants are moving to neighborhoods with less formal and informal social support services and possibly higher crime rates. Low-income residents of inner city Chicago are "closer in proximity to social service providers than poor populations living in suburban areas," where many of the voucher holders are relocating (Allard 2004, 5). Furthermore, Chicago communities with the highest con-

centration of Section 8 vouchers have more crime than some of the locations previously saturated with public housing (Bennett and Reed 1999). Jamie Kalvin, director of the Neighborhood Conservation Corporation (NCC), an organization that advocates for residents of Bronzeville's Stateway Gardens housing project, states, "Individuals and families are being hurt and are being rendered more vulnerable by this [relocation] process. And it's not hard to see, if you actually make yourself available to it."[18] Rather than helping public housing tenants reach mainstream society, the demolition process may be making the situation for many families and children even worse.

Illustration of Displacement

One afternoon, Jamie and I help Tony and his family, who have been squatting at Stateway for almost four years, move to another neighborhood. Tony has worked sporadically at Stateway for ten years as a janitor's assistant. The maintenance staff pays him, under the table, for the work they are supposed to do. Tony and his wife have five- and six-year-old girls. His wife works the night shift at a local fast food restaurant. Even though some reports suggest that 6 to 16 percent of the CHA tenant population is squatting, meaning they are not legal leaseholders and are living in vacant units, the CHA effectively ignores these tenants and provides little relocation support (Venkatesh 2002; Venkatesh, Celimli, Miller, et al. 2004). The NCC has made an effort to help this population at Stateway.[19]

Tony's Stateway apartment is on the fourth floor and we help him move the day before his building is to be razed. Since the elevators are broken, we walk all of Tony's family belongings, including clothing in large plastic bags down the dark stairwells to Jamie's truck. Jamie has connected Tony's family with a housing assistance organization, which has helped Tony get a Section 8 voucher and an apartment. As we help the family leave the building, it is apparent that although Tony's children are excited about the move, Tony is extremely nervous. He has lived at Stateway for almost ten years and he and his wife have not yet visited their new community. His wife tells me that she hopes the apartment is near a grocery store.

Tony's new apartment is in a four story, red brick, horseshoe-shaped building, in an African-American neighborhood south of Bronzeville with a high concentration of Section 8 voucher holders. The apartments have little, rusty metal balconies that overlook a courtyard. The hallways are carpeted and have working light fixtures. This, however, is nobody's dream apartment. The wood floors are old and scuffed up, it needs a new paint job, and bathrooms are grimy. Regardless, this apartment is a marked improvement. Jamie jokingly asked, "So do we want to go back to Stateway?" Tony's wife and children laugh. Tony says nothing and has a look of concern.

I go outside with Tony and we start to bring in his family's belongings. While walking up the stairs, I ask him what he thinks of the new apartment. He tells me bluntly, "I don't like it. I don't know my way around here." He proclaims that he is more concerned about being robbed at this place than Stateway because he knows that people there watch his back. He is apprehensive about the new neighborhood and insists he saw street gangs as we approached his new residence. In addition, he says it will be difficult to get public transportation back to his job at Stateway. Although the new apartment is in better condition than the one they left, there is a strong possibility this neighborhood will become more impoverished as the rest of the CHA buildings come down.

The vast majority of public housing tenants will not benefit from CHA's Plan for Transformation. Possibly, a small percentage may be able to return to the community when the new mixed-income develop-

ments are completed. During the "Housing Choice" sessions, residents are asked if they want the "right of return" to the replacement mixed-income housing. However, most residents know their chances of returning to newly constructed units are slim. Tre, a Stateway Gardens resident, says to me, "Ain't no one gonna come back here. This is prime real estate." A Bronzeville's organizational leader states, "It would be a miracle if a third of [public housing] residents moved back." Many real estate developers are setting very strict guidelines for the readmittance of public housing residents to the new mixed-income projects. This procedure, along with the limited number of available units, makes the promise of a new home an unlikely scenario for former public housing tenants.

Louanna (Lou) Jones, then the Illinois state representative from Bronzeville, explains the difficult situation: "You're between a rock and a hard place. In order to revitalize the area or rebuild the area, and advance the area, you have people getting angry because they [CHA tenants] do not have anywhere [in the community] to go." While massive amounts of low-income residents get displaced, others in Bronzeville benefit from the redevelopment.

Who's Benefiting?

Some claim that Chicago's actions are tantamount to the urban renewal of the past, which was extremely detrimental to African Americans (Bennett and Reed 1999; Popkin, Gwiasda, Olson, et al. 2000; Ranney 2003). Although there are some similarities, the current development in Bronzeville differs. Urban renewal in Chicago between 1940 and 1960 primarily benefited white real estate developers and profit-seeking corporations, while blacks remained segregated and powerless (Hirsch [1983] 1998). Today, however, certain African-American businesses are benefiting.

Although several major white construction firms, architecture companies, and real estate developers have large contracts to demolish, design, and redevelop new mixed-income developments in Bronzeville, politically well-connected, black-owned development, management and construction companies are profiting from Chicago's Plan for Transformation. Black-owned firms such as Elzie Higginbottom's East Lake Management, Allison Davis's Davis Group, Rev. Leon Finney Jr.'s Woodlawn Development Corporation, and Paul King's UBM, Inc hold million-dollar contracts to build and manage new housing developments.[20] In a two-year span, East Lake Management received nearly $30 million to oversee thirteen of the CHA's developments.[21] Smaller black homebuilding companies also receive city funds to construct homes in the community. As Bronzeville's Alderman Dorothy Tillman insists, "We [need] . . . to ensure that African Americans take part in the redevelopment."

Moreover, Mayor Daley nominates respected black leaders willing to support the city's demolition and relocation efforts to high-ranking posts within the CHA. In 1999, when the Plan for Transformation was announced, Mayor Daley appointed Phil Jackson, a former resident of the Robert Taylor Homes, to head the CHA, and Sharon Gilliam as chair of the CHA's Board of Commissioners. Additionally, when Jackson stepped down in 2000, Daley appointed another African American, Terry Peterson, as the executive director of the CHA. These positions are more meaningful than mere tokenism, considering black real estate developers receive substantial CHA contracts.

The public investments in Bronzeville relate to increased property values for a number of black homeowners. Middle- and upper-income families who bought houses in the area in the 1980s and early 1990s are seeing substantial increases in their home equity. Properties worth $100,000 or $200,000 ten years ago are doubling and tripling in value. In other words, the new phase of urban renewal is connected to a certain level of black prosperity.

Although Bronzeville's redevelopment is greatly influenced by new federal legislation, the legacy of Chicago's political machine and its housing management decisions have contributed to the decay and downfall of public housing through a misuse of national housing resources for local political objectives. In short, the political history of Chicago's democratic machine has driven the demolition of Bronzeville public housing. [. . .]

HARLEM'S REDEVELOPMENT AND PUBLIC HOUSING REFORMS

By contrast, public housing in New York City is not being demolished. Instead, the NYCHA is rehabilitating its high-rise housing stock, and displacement among Harlem's low-income residents is less extensive. Many of Harlem's low-income public housing residents will have an opportunity to benefit from the improvement of their neighborhood. This circumstance is connected to the fragmented political structure in New York City, which results in superior public housing management and increased tenant activism. The New York City political system explains why public housing remains in Harlem.

Harlem has a substantial number of sizable public housing projects. The King Towers, St. Nicholas Houses, Rangel Houses, Drew-Hamilton Houses, Frederick Samuel Houses, Taft Houses, Harlem River Houses, and Polo Ground Towers house more than 20,000 Harlem residents (NYCHA 2001). While property values are rising in Harlem, some suggest they would rise faster if public housing was torn down.[22] However, elected officials I speak with insist that razing the projects would "not be politically feasible." The tenants would not tolerate it.

Residents of the NYCHA are more active and connected to their political structure than those in Chicago. Charles Rangel, Harlem's U.S. congressman, considers public housing tenants an essential part of his constituency, and others concur. One high-level NYCHA manager says that New York City public housing residents have a "strong political network" and are important constituents of political leaders—they are politically engaged and force politicians to make public housing concerns top priorities. This level of engagement among the public housing residents with both politicians and NYCHA management at public housing meetings in Harlem has maintained the quality of NYCHA buildings. Tenant advocacy has protected public housing in Harlem from the distress and corruption endemic to public housing in Chicago.

Rehabilitation and Tenant Activism

I attend a monthly meeting of the Manhattan North Council of Presidents, a group of Northern Manhattan Public Housing Projects resident leaders. The meeting is held in the gym of West Harlem's Manhattanville Housing Project, and run by tenant leader Sandra Harper. Attending are tenant representatives, residents, building superintendents, managers, and current contractors for each public housing development. At 6:30 p.m., Ms. Harper, holding a cordless microphone, announces in her deep, gravelly voice, "Alright, let's get this started," as if she was declaring the beginning of a boxing match. She lays out the agenda for the night: NYCHA officials are to update tenants on renovations, and residents are to discuss problems with the buildings.

Ms. Harper gives the microphone to three NYCHA officials who discuss capital improvement funds available for project rehabilitation. The officials hand out an overview of scheduled improvements to be made in Harlem (NYCHA 2002a). In addition to these improvements, the NYCHA has a comprehensive plan for the continual upkeep and long-term preservation of its housing stock.[23]

After the housing officials conclude their talk, Ms. Harper announces the start of the strategy sessions. At each table, residents use easels to write down improvement ideas. I sit next to an older African-American woman from the Frederick Samuel Houses who complains about shoddy tile work recently installed in her building's entrance. I ask her if the contractor who did the work is still around. She says, "Yes, we are still working with them. It don't make no sense. They should just do it right the first time!"

After the strategy session, we socialize over a buffet style dinner. The meal helps ensure friendly negotiations between the factions. After eating, Ms. Harper asks each table to report on their major complaints. The most common concern is the need for more NYCHA inspectors to monitor the contractors working in various buildings. Other complaints include graffiti, broken elevators, and a lack of police presence. After the representatives of each project conclude their presentations, a person from the housing authority collects all written comments. Resident involvement happens not just at these monthly gatherings; it also, and perhaps more importantly, occurs at individual housing projects.

Tenant activism ensures standards are maintained in Harlem's public housing. While working for Assemblyman Keith Wright, I receive a call from one of the resident leaders at the Drew-Hamilton Houses. One building's faulty foundation is causing small cracks in several apartments' walls. The resident leadership convenes an emergency meeting and insists that Assemblyman Wright attend to ensure that NYCHA officials repair the building. During the well-attended meeting, the resident leadership demands that NYCHA officials publicly promise to address the situation. The official agrees that regardless of cost he will have the building's structure monitored and repaired. He and the assemblyman, a member of the state Committee on Housing, agree to find the funding needed to make the building secure and safe. Tenant leadership and action explain why Harlem's public housing stock remains viable.

The viability of Harlem's public housing is critical to understanding the consequences of redevelopment. While displacement occurs among the working poor who are private market renters and those in city-owned buildings, it is not happening to public housing residents. "Public housing is the only thing preventing the total gentrification of Harlem," an individual remarks at a community forum. "Viable public housing ensures that a sizable portion of Harlem's low-income population will have an opportunity to benefit from the community's revitalization.

Displacement in Harlem

Even though public housing residents are not being removed, displacement is still a major concern in Harlem. While not on the scale of displacement from dilapidated CHA buildings in Chicago, low-income residents in Harlem, as well as owners of small businesses are vulnerable. As noted in chapter 3, the city once owned a large percentage of Harlem's housing units. These units, mostly single-family homes and small apartment buildings, were repossessed in the 1970s and 1980s, when landlords failed to pay their property taxes. The city's Department of Housing Preservation and Development (HPD) is now in charge of these properties. At one point in the early 1980s, the HPD housed the homeless in many of these units. In the 1990s the city began selling these properties to nonprofit and for-profit real estate devel-

opers, and giving former tenants Section 8 vouchers. According to Harlem's affordable housing activists most of these Section 8 recipients were unable to find housing in the community and moved to other New York City boroughs, such as Brooklyn and the Bronx, and to parts of Newark, New Jersey.[24]

Many living in private market housing also face the threat of displacement. Some tenants are forced to leave properties when rental brownstones are converted to single-family homes. Further, while working for Assemblyman Wright, I met tenants in rent-controlled apartments who had been offered $10,000 to $20,000 to vacate their units.[25] Some landlords even damaged their buildings to make them temporally unsafe, forcing tenants to vacate.

On an unusually hot April morning, I witness the gentrification pressures in Harlem firsthand. As soon as I arrive in the morning at Keith's office, Mignonne, his executive assistant, tells me I need to head over to 321 St. Nicholas Avenue. She received a call from a resident saying that all the tenants were being evicted.

When I arrive over thirty people are outside the apartment building, crying, screaming, and bewildered. A few feet away from me, a teenage girl hugs her mother and says, as tears run down her face, "Mom, where are we going to go? Are we have to going to become homeless?" Her mother, desperately trying to hold it together, responds calmly, "Baby, we'll probably have to go to a shelter tonight." At this point I am totally confused. I need to know why these families are being evicted. I find Freddy, one of Keith's staff and we find one of the building's tenant leaders who explains that late last night the city determined that the building was "structurally unsound and issued an emergency vacate order. The forty-eight families had to relocate immediately to shelters throughout the city.

The emergency vacate order, according to certain residents, is suspicious. Although sections of the building have been in need of repair, some community leaders and residents believe that there was no need to remove everyone from the building or in such an expeditious manner. The building is in an ideal location, just a block from 125th Street. Buildings in the area, like one just a block north, have recently been rehabilitated and converted to luxury apartments. One tenant of the building claims, "This is criminal . . . They just want us out. This is gentrification."[26] The next day, I overhear on the street two people talking about the building. One declares, "They [the city and developer] are trying to get the people out so they can charge higher rents. They used to burn the roof to get the people out, now they say it's structurally unsound. It's a fraud." Two years after the initial vacate order, the building has not yet been rehabilitated. When the building reopens, it is likely that many of the original tenants will not return, and rental prices will be higher than before the abrupt shutdown.

Several small businesses are also facing the prospects of removal. For instance, small mom and pop businesses along the major streets, such as Adam Clayton Powell Jr. Boulevard, Malcolm X Boulevard, 125th Street, and, more recently, 135th Street are feeling the squeeze as rental prices continue to rise. Small businesses contend not only with rising commercial rents, but with competition from arriving chain stores. A small optometry business on 125th Street was forced out of Harlem when Sterling Optical opened up a franchise in the community.[27] Local coffee shops are also finding it hard to compete with mainstream outlets like Starbucks as landlords seek to increase rents. Donna Lewis, owner of Home Sweet Harlem Cafe, attests, "Landlords are increasingly using legal tactics to push out community businesses all around Harlem in order to make room for investors with deeper pockets."[28] The encroachment of chain stores and increasing commercial rents threaten the viability of indigenous businesses.

Studies conducted in the early 1990s predicted displacement in Harlem (see Smith [1996] 2,000), and others document it vividly (Davila 2004; Taylor 2002); however, a recent study suggests displacement is not as much of a pressing concern in Harlem as it is in other New York City neighborhoods. Using the New York City's Housing and Vacancy Survey Lance Freeman and Frank Braconi demonstrate that displacement rates are lower in gentrifying New York City neighborhoods, such as Harlem than those with more stable real estate markets (2004). Unfortunately they assume only low-income households or those without college degrees face the threat of displacement, and they do not account for the removal of those above the federal poverty line or those with a college degree. While many low-income residents are safe because Harlem s public housing remains, moderate-income renters, whose income likely exceeds the poverty rate, and small businesses remain vulnerable to displacement from the community. Therefore, Freeman and Braconi's study underestimates the percent of displacement in Harlem.[29] While displacement is less visible in Harlem, than Bronzeville, it is occurring and is a major concern.[30] [. . .]

NOTES

1. The Brooke Amendments removed minimum rent requirements and increased the tenant share of rent from 20 to 25 percent (which was subsequently raised to 30 percent) of their income. This policy favored low-income households and unemployed tenants since many working residents could afford private market housing with 25 percent of their income (Popkin, Buron, Levy, and Cunningham 2000). Thus, this policy had the adverse effect of increasing poverty concentration by encouraging working tenants to move out of public housing (Spence 1993; Thompson 1999).

2. The HOPE VI program allocated over $5.5 billion within a ten-year period to demolish distressed

public housing and construct "mixed-income" replacement housing.

3. U.S. Department of Housing and Urban Development's website: http://www.hud.gov/offices/pih/programs/ph/hope6/grants/demolition/.

4. Before the enactment of the HOPE VI program, Congress commissioned a national assessment of the country's distressed public housing infrastructure in 1989 (see National Commission on Severely Distressed Public Housing 1992). The findings set the context for subsequent legislation that would lead to the demolition of the country's distressed public housing stock.

5. In 1996 an estimated 25,413 people lived in Chicago Housing Authority public housing units slated for demolition in Bronzeville. Assuming one-third will return to redeveloped units in the community, approximately 17,000 will be displaced. This is probably a conservative estimate since it does not account for displacement that occurs when private market rental units are converted to condominiums. Chicago does not have strong rent control restrictions and several sizeable Bronzeville rental complexes were converted to condominiums while I conducted my research (see Barry Pearce, "Back to Bronzeville," *New Homes*, August, 2001).

6. Though there are many public housing projects in Bronzeville and Harlem, I chose to focus on Stateway Gardens in Bronzeville and the St. Nicholas Houses in Harlem. Stateway Gardens and the St. Nicholas Houses are large-scale housing developments that are typical of the high-rise housing stock managed, respectively, by the Chicago Housing Authority (CHA) in Bronzeville and the New York City Housing Authority (NYCHA) in Harlem. In addition to the case studies of the two projects, I also visited other housing projects in these communities and attended numerous meetings sponsored by the NYCHA and the CHA.

7. This information is available on the U.S. Department of Housing and Urban Development's website:http://www.hud.gov/offices/pih/programs/ph/hope6/.

8. Of the 60,000 distressed public housing units taken down nationwide, Chicago is responsible for 20 percent.

9. Because of persistent corruption at the Chicago Housing Authority, HUD managed the CHA from 1995 to 1999.

10. The voucher covers expenses beyond 30 percent of household income for a rental of a unit at the 'fair market rate."

11. John Handley, "A New Age for Bronzeville," *Chicago Tribune*, December, 1, 2002.

12. John Handley, "Redeveloping Public Housing," *Chicago Tribune*, August 22, 2004.

13. As of FY 2006, the city of Chicago received $ 340 million in HOPE VI funding for demolition and the construction of "mixed-income" housing, and 43 percent of Chicago's HOPE VI funds were spent in Bronzeville (U.S. Department of Housing and Urban Development's website: http://www.hud.gov/offices/pih/programs/ph/hope6/).

14. Jeanette Almada, "Building to Start in Summer on Stateway Redevelopment," *Chicago Tribune*, February 16, 2003. Also see Shashaty's article "Home Sales Fill Funding Gap for Mixed-Income Redevelopments" in *Affordable Housing Finance* (2007), 47–48, 74.

15. "The Bronzeville Renaissance," *New City*, August 8, 2002.

16. The CHA began its demolition and relocation process before the announcement of the "Plan for Transformation" in 1999. These figures represent residents that relocated from CHA buildings between 1995 and 2002. The data in Paul Fischer's (2003) study were used as evidence in a class action lawsuit against CHA for violating fair housing laws (see Wallace v. CHA 2003).

17. Some of Chicago's inner south suburbs have poverty rates ranging from 30 to 40 percent (Alexander 1998), and the movement of the poor from the inner city in large municipalities like Chicago, New York, Boston, and Washington, D.C., correlates with a rising suburban poverty rate (Puentes and Warren 2006).

18. At Stateway Gardens, I worked with Jamie's organization for six months. The NCC office is a hub for various programs that provide health services, individual and family counseling, employment training, and legal assistance to residents.

19. Estimating the number of squatters in CHA buildings is extremely difficult. The two works cited only document the percent of squatters existing in the Robert Taylor Homes, which may not necessarily be representative of the CHA system.

20. See Keith Robbins, *N'Digo Profiles*, 2003; Angela Rozas, "Revival of an Old Housing Complex," *Chicago Tribune*, December 5, 2003; Jeanette Almada, "Building to Start in Summer on Stateway Redevelopment," *Chicago Tribune*, February 16, 2003; Chinta Strausberg "CHA Panel OK's $10 Mil Contract to King," *Chicago Defender*, December 17, 2002.

21. John Bebow, "The Collector," *Chicago Tribune Magazine*, October 3, 2004.

22. Julia Vitullo-Martin, "Project Vision," *Wall Street Journal*, August 18, 2006.

23. For more on NYCHA's plan to rehabilitate public housing see their 2006 publication, "The Plan to Preserve Public Housing."
24. My analysis of neighborhood poverty between 1990 and 2000 demonstrates that there was an expansion of high-poverty areas (40+ poverty rate) in Brooklyn and in the Bronx, as well as in Newark, NJ. Another study on displacement and relocation in New York City supports this finding (Newman and Wyly 2006).
25. In rent-controlled apartments, if the original tenant moves out landlords can substantially increase the rent.
26. Michael Brick, "Tenants Evacuate Building Deemed Unsafe," *New York Times*, April 17, 2003.
27. Amy Waldman, "Where Green Trumps Black and White," *New York Times*, December 11, 1999.
28. "Assemblyman Keith Wright Holds Press Conference Blasting Happyland Slumlord," *News from Assemblyman Keith L. T. Wright*, March 23, 2006.
29. For a further critique of Freeman and Braconi's (2004) study see Newman and Wyly (2006).
30. Estimating the magnitude of displacement is an extremely difficult task. I do not have data on the level of displacement in Harlem. My point is to merely demonstrate that it is an important community concern.

REFERENCES

Allard, S. W. 2004. *Access to Social Services: The Changing Urban Geography of Poverty and Social Provision*. Washington, D.C.: Brookings Institution.

Bennett, L. and A. Reed. 1999. The New Face of Urban Renewal: The Near North Redevelopment Initiative and the Cabrini-Green Neighborhood. In A. Reed (ed.), *Without Justice for All*, pp. 175–211. Boulder, CO: Westview Press.

Chicago Housing Authority. 2000. *Chicago Housing Authority: Plan for Transformation*. Chicago: Author.

Davila, A. 2004. Empowered Culture? New York City's Empowerment Zone and the Selling of El Barrio. *ANNALS, AAPSS*, 594(1), 49–64.

Fischer, P. 2003. *Where Are the Public Housing Families Going? An Update*. Chicago: Woods Fund of Chicago.

Freeman, L. and F. Braconi, 2004. Gentrification and Displacement. *Journal of American Planning Association*, 70(1), 39–52.

Goetz, E. G. 2003. *Clearing the Way*. Washington, D.C.: Urban Institute Press.

Hirsch, A. R. [1983] 1998. *Making the Second Ghetto: Race and Housing in Chicago 1940–1960*. Chicago: University of Chicago Press.

Lenz, T. J. and J. Coles. 1999. *The Regional Rental Market Analysis*. Chicago: Metropolitan Planning Council.

Massey, D. S. and N. A. Denton. 1993. *American Apartheid*. Cambridge, MA: Harvard University Press.

Massey, D. S. and S. M. Kanaiaupuni. 1993. Public Housing and the Concentration of Poverty. *Social Science Quarterly*, 74(1), 109–22.

New York City Housing Authority (NYCHA). 2001. *Special Tabulation of Tenant Characteristics*. New York: Author.

——. 2002. *Capital Fund Program Presentation: Manhattan North Council of Presidents*. New York: Author.

Orr, L., J. D. Feins, R. Jacob, E. Beecroft, L. Sanbonmatsu, L. F. Katz, J. B. Liebman, and J. Kling. 2003. *Moving to Opportunity for Fair Housing Demonstration Program: Interim Impacts Evaluation*. Washington, D.C.: U.S. Department of Housing and Urban Development.

Plunz, R. 1990. *A History of Housing in New York City*. New York: Columbia University Press.

Popkin, S. J., V. E. Gwiasda, L. M. Olson, D. P. Rosenbaum, and L. Buron. 2000. *The Hidden War*. New Brunswick, NJ: Rutgers University Press.

Popkin, S. J., D. K. Levy, L. E. Harris, J. Comey, M. K. Cunningham, and L. Buron. 2002. *HOPE VI Panel Study: Baseline Report*. Washington, D.C.: Urban Institute.

Ranney, D. 2003. *Global Decisions, Local Collisions*. Philadelphia: Temple University Press.

Rubinowitz, L. S. and J. E. Rosenbaum. 2000. *Crossing the Class and Color Lines: From Public Housing to White Suburbia*. Chicago: University of Chicago Press.

Schill, M. H. 1997. Chicago's Mixed-Income New Communities Strategy: The Future Face of Public Housing? In W. V. Vilet. (ed.), *Affordable Housing and Urban Redevelopment in the United States*, vol. 46, 135–57. Thousand Oaks, CA: Sage Publications.

Shashaty, A. 2007. Home Sales Fill Funding Gap for Mixed-Income Redevelopments. *Affordable Housing Finance*, 15(3), 47–48, 74.

Smith, N. [1996] 2000. *The New Urban Frontier*. New York: Routledge.

Sullivan, T. 2003. *Report 5 of the Independent Monitor*. Document provided by the View from the Ground, www.viewfromtheground.com.

Taylor, M. M. 2002. *Harlem: Between Heaven and Hell*. Minneapolis: University of Minnesota Press.

Thompson, J. P. 1999. Public Housing in New York City.

In M. H. Schill. (ed.), *Housing and Community Development in New York City*, 119–42. Albany: State University of New York Press.

Venkatesh, S. A. 2000. *American Project*. Cambridge, MA: Harvard University Press.

——. 2002. *The Robert Taylor Homes Relocation Study*. Working paper, Center for Urban Research and Policy, Columbia University, New York.

Venkatesh, S. A., I. Celimli, D. Miller, A. Murphy, and B. Turner. 2004. Chicago Public Housing Transformation: A Research Report. Working paper, Center for Urban Research and Policy, Columbia University, New York.

von Hoffman, A. 2000. A Study in Contradictions: The Origins and Legacy of the Housing Act of 1949. *Housing Policy Debate, 11*(2), 299–326.

CHAPTER 24

Gentrification, Intrametropolitan Migration, and the Politics of Place

Gina M. Pérez

As I arrived to teach my G.E.D. class at the Ruiz Belvis Cultural Center one spring afternoon, Eddie Vélez—a seventeen-year-old Puerto Rican/Mexican student—asked if I would switch roles and tell him about my life for a change. "I know you know a lot about me," he said, with a characteristically wry smile. "Now I want to know about you and your family." For months, Eddie and I had been discussing his options for after he passed his G.E.D. Like many of my students, he was considering going into the military. I was encouraging him to go to college, telling him how smart he was, especially in math and science. Eddie admitted that for the first time ever he was actually enjoying school, partly because he realized that he was "good at it". When other students needed help or felt intimidated in math—which was almost daily—Eddie quickly volunteered to explain algebra, fractions, or geometry to them. This, I reminded him, only confirmed that he should continue his studies and become a teacher, the kind of teacher he never had while he was in school, as he said. But on that day Eddie was interested in understanding the roots of our ongoing disagreement about his future, so he asked me pointed questions about my parents, the schools I attended, and where my family lived.

"So when you were my age," he clarified, "your parents were buying a house." I told him that when I was sixteen, my family moved into our own home after years of renting houses and apartments in northern California. Eddie didn't seem interested in hearing about how I had moved frequently when I was younger. Instead, he wanted to compare our lives at his current age of seventeen. At that age, I was living in a house that my parents were buying, attending a good Catholic high school from which I would graduate with high honors, and like him, making post graduation plans. But, unlike Eddie, I *knew* I was headed for college and that I would most likely move away from home to do so. It was just a matter of deciding, based on financial aid packages and scholarships, which one I would attend. This, I believed, was one of the most important differences between us. Eddie had a slightly different analysis.

"See, we come from completely different families," he concluded. "I move around all the time. Every four to five years. Now we have to move again. The landlady came upstairs the other day and started crying because she knows my brother is dealin'. They pass by the house and are whistling for him to come out. She's got kids. And she's scared. So now we have to move again. In our last place, we only lived there a year." Eddie smiled and paused, adding sadly, "Now we have to move again." Even though

I wanted him to go to college rather than enter the military, Eddie explained, I had to consider how different our families and our lives really were. He moved around a lot, while I had lived in a stable household when I was his age. My family was supportive of my decisions, while his father, when he was drunk or high, asked him why he couldn't be more like his brother. Eddie looked at me and smiled. "My brother deals drugs and is in a gang. Why does he want me to be like him?" As the other students returned from break, Eddie concluded, "I just wanted to see how different my background is from your background," and we returned to the classroom to work on the day's math exercises.

Eddie's questions that day underscored my "outsider within" status.[1] As a middle-class Puerto Rican feminist researcher among poor and working-class *puertorriqueños* studying for their G.E.D., my students often reminded me of how class background shaped our understanding and expectations of each other. My role as their teacher accentuated this hierarchical relationship, which was also influenced by education and cultural capital. Eddie's inquiry into my background therefore reveals an important problem with multiculturalist thinking that exhorts ethnic minorities to serve as role models to urban youth. It ignores how one's social location—including class, gender, race, sexuality, and culture—shapes a diversity of outcomes within ethnic groups.[2] This kind of thinking also helps to reproduce the idea of a meritocracy in which those who work hard are justly rewarded. For Eddie, residential mobility is key to understanding one's social location. Living in one's own home provides residential security, freeing one up to pursue goals and dreams that are sidelined when one lives day-to-day, unsure of where one's family might be the next day.

Many poor and working-class Puerto Ricans in Chicago move a lot. Although some of this movement involves return or circular migration to Puerto Rico, most of their mobility entails intrametropolitan migration. Like other economically marginal groups in the city, Chicago Puerto Ricans' housing options are severely limited. Federal cutbacks in community development and subsidized housing construction beginning in the 1970s, as well as municipal failure to maintain low-cost housing, have created a housing crisis for the city's poor and working-class population, which is forced to live in old housing stock, usually in overcrowded conditions. According to the Chicago Urban League, federal funding for low-income housing in Illinois has been cut by 87 percent since the 1980s, and despite state, local, and private efforts to meet the growing need for affordable housing, Chicago's housing crisis has become even more critical in the 1990s.[3]

Poor and working-class residents are also vulnerable to political-economic changes that "revitalize" formerly neglected urban areas, ultimately displacing them. The past decade's prosperity wave, witnessing almost unprecedented growth in middle-income housing construction and rehabilitation of the city's housing stock, has passed by many residents, particularly those shuttling between Chicago and Puerto Rico. In fact, neighborhoods like Humboldt Park, whose residents are largely Latino or African American and poor, have been virtually ignored by affordable housing projects and slated instead for the demolition of buildings, which are usually replaced by high-rent lofts and condominiums.[4] As one *puertorriqueña* remarked to me as we washed clothes at a Laundromat in Humboldt Park, "yuppies" and rehabilitated housing usually result in poor and working-class families getting priced out of their neighborhoods. Comparing her observations in Humboldt Park with the gentrification she witnessed in the Belmont area in the 1980s, she warned us, "Did you see those rehabbed houses on Humboldt Boulevard and Wabansia? When I saw they were rehabbing, I was like, 'Forget about it. We're out of here.'"

In what follows, I focus on the politics of place and the process of place-making in Chicago, another site within a transnational social field linking Puerto Rico to mainland communities. I look at poor and working-class *puertorriqueños'* extremely mobile lives and the factors impelling this intra-metropolitan migration. Evictions, problems resulting from overcrowded living conditions, and domestic disputes contribute to Puerto Ricans' high residential mobility. But like poor whites, blacks, and other Latinos, Puerto Rican residents are also vulnerable to the politics of uneven development targeting their neighborhoods for urban "revival." Low-income residents in gentrifying communities are not only physically displaced by these political-economic processes, but they are also heavily policed by law enforcement officials charged with ensuring a "safe" space for new residents. Grassroots efforts to resist these changes are constructed transnationally, as community organizers strategically deploy cultural symbols to construct a "Puerto Rican space" that preserves neighborhood use value. These efforts to deter displacement through resistance, political mobilization, and coalition-building challenge an image of the underclass that emphasizes pathological behavior, presenting instead a portrait of agency and collective action among poor and working-class Puerto Ricans whose lives are circumscribed by the politics of uneven development that increasingly define the "global city" of Chicago. [...]

THE NEAR NORTHWEST SIDE STORY

Traveling east from Humboldt Park to Wicker Park provides an important glimpse into the geography of gentrification. Just west of Western Avenue on Wabansia Street—the border between Humboldt Park and West Town—lie the elevated El tracks and the Bloomingdale Street viaduct, and below them, a row of old houses badly in need of repair. Next door are new luxury townhomes and lofts. Some of them have been converted from old housing stock, warehouses, and factories, others are new buildings with garages and private yards. Farther east, below the old Canadian railroad tracks, are long cement walls covered with boldly colored murals painted by neighborhood youth participating in the Mayor's Summer Youth Program. One mural features a young man holding a can of spray paint, posed ominously in front of a large shark with the word "CULTURA"—culture—written across it. Against a backdrop of the Puerto Rican flag, the message reads, "This mural is dedicated 2, all the sisters and brothers who hold pride in our culture and defend it. *Boricua, defiende lo tuyo* [Boricua, defend what is yours]."

Still farther east, just before the Ruiz Belvis Cultural Center, are more lofts and new buildings under construction and a sign advertising "an entire block of buildable land, residential or commercial." A billboard in front of elegant new townhouses reads, "Urban Gardens Townhomes. 2–3 bedrooms/2.5–3.5 bath. 5 signature floorplans; 2 car garage; open and luminiferous; private outdoor space; gated security courtyard; formal dining room, family room. From $249,000." More modest lofts ($199,000) lie just to the west on a new, unnamed street. And farther east, as you turn southeast on Milwaukee toward the six corners hub of Wicker Park, are more older buildings, warehouses, and closed factories with signs in their windows saying "For Lease" and "For Sale." The juxtaposition is truly remarkable.

As one stands in front of the Centro—with its brightly painted sign decorated with *vejigantes, maracas,* and *guiros* (Puerto Rican cultural symbols and instruments) above a front window displaying paintings and woodcarvings by local artists—it is clear why developers, the local alderman, real estate agents, and new upwardly mobile professional (and usually white) residents want the Centro to move: It is a risky space frequented by potentially dangerous young men and women who disrupt the new vision of the neighborhood. Since the 1980s, the Centro has resisted myriad attempts to displace them, including arbitrary zoning and building code enforcement; harassment by neighbors complaining about young men "hanging out" in front of the Centro; city fines levied against the Centro for inappropriate licenses; and phone calls, mailings, and periodic visits by private individuals and developers interested in buying the building where the Centro is located. The Centro's board has remained defiant, spending tens of thousands of dollars to remain compliant with shifting city licensing, building, and zoning codes. But like the neighborhood's working-class residents in the early 1980s, the Centro's staff, students, and other patrons are frequently harassed and intimidated by powerful interests, including law enforcement. Their narratives of gentrification's impact on their lives are sobering, and confirm David Harvey's contention that "the perpetual reshaping of the geographic landscape of capitalism is a process of violence and pain."[5]

The young men who study at the Centro and participate in its cultural programs are the most vulnerable to these demographic shifts and the attendant use of state power to protect the neighborhood's newest residents through surveillance and manipulation of young Puerto Ricans' bodies. In her excellent discussion of criminality and the exercise of state power in Brazil, anthropologist Teresa Caldeira provides similar examples of how the body—of both "alleged criminals" and "all categories of people considered in need of special control (including children, women, the poor and the insane)"—becomes the "locus of punishment, justice, and example in Brazil" as well as a legitimate field of interventions and manipulations unprotected by individual civil rights.[6] My male students often arrived in class tired, upset, and frustrated with the ways in which gentrification had transformed their daily routine. Police harassed them, stopped them randomly to question and frisk them, taunted them, and often engaged in unlawful procedures just to humiliate them. One twenty-one-year-old student, Leo Chacón, lived just west of the Centro and complained bitterly about the changes he witnessed in his neighborhood. "The whites," he explained, were moving into the neighborhood, and Latino homeowners were facilitating this process by "selling out," selling their homes to newcomers and then moving to the suburbs. Leo's new neighbors constantly called the police on him and his friends when they were hanging out in front of their own apartments and homes. Now, he explained, the police passed by routinely, and they had stopped Leo and other men frequently enough to know them by name. "Where ya goin', Mr. Chacón? How are ya doin' today, Mr. Chacón?' The cops are always stopping me and trying to pin shit on me. I ain't done nothing. Ever since these white folks moved in, I can't even walk in my own 'hood." Leo was not the only one to complain about how the police treated him. During my three years teaching and volunteering at the Centro, all of the young men with whom I worked had similar stories. As young men of color—most Puerto Rican, others Mexican or Mexican/Puerto Rican—they were clearly marked, embodying a profile targeted by law enforcement officials. During breaks, these young men complained bitterly about how the police treated them, and they were surprised to discover that they were all hassled by the same officers. One day, Leo and Marvin Polanco, an eighteen-year-old Puerto Rican student, described a particular Latino police officer and his white partner, who were known for harassing young men in the neighborhood.

M: It was three guys, right. We were all Puerto Rican. And then . . . these cops . . . they were coming down Evergreen Street [in Humboldt Park]. They were going to stop some gang members, but then when they saw us, they came and stopped us. And we weren't even on the corner. We were like twenty or thirty feet away from the corner, right, and [this Latino cop] comes and stops us. "Hey, you guys" [lowering his voice to sound authoritative], "What 'cha doin'?" He starts checking us out, right, and then this guy, he said his name's Corona, and he comes and hits my friend on the chin. "Oh, why you tryin' to get smart" you know? My friend was like, "No, sir. I'm not tryin' to get smart." You know. And he gave him all the respect. And there was this white guy, right.

L: His white partner, right?

M: Yeah! And he came to me like, "What you ridin' on?" "I'm not ridin' nothin'," you know. He's saying I was gettin' smart with him. He started goin' like [he pokes his finger into his chest], you know? Real hard to me, pointing on my chest real hard. I'm like, "No, why are you doin' this, " you know? He's like, "Shut up." I'm like, "You shut up." And he, the Hispanic one . . . he said, "Why you don't wanna respect us?" And I was like, "I respect everybody who respects me." [Leo huffs knowingly in complete disgust and then puts his hand out to Marvin.] You know what I'm sayin? [taking Leo's hand, and they shake]. So then, um, he hit my friend again. Then we made a report.

When other police officers arrived to take down Marvin's complaint, they asked for a description of the officer. But when Marvin described the officer, the officers dismissed their story, saying that no cops in their district fit that description. Soon after, the original two officers returned and began harassing Marvin again, this time for reporting them.

M: The white guy, he told me, "You want me to take you by the Kings [opposition gang members from another neighborhood] so they could jump you?" I'm like, "Go take me by the Kings. I got an aunt and uncle that live around there. You can do me a favor and drop me off." [Leo laughs.] And then he told me, "Oh, you want me to take you by such and such gang?" I'm like, "Go ahead. I got family there too. You're doin' me a favor." And he's like, "Gettin' smart?" and he pointed in my chest again. And I was like cryin' because it hurt. And I couldn't do nothin' about it.

L: Yes, you could.

M: I mean, 'cuz . . . [pauses] it's your word against a cop's, man. I mean, if you're a cop, man, I don't know. I don't care what anybody says, you understand? They're gonna win. You can't, you can't sue the government, man. I can't sue nobody.

Marvin's feelings were echoed by other men in the class. As I drove another G.E.D. student, Robby León, home one day, he told me similar stories. When I pulled into a grocery store parking lot near our homes, a police officer blocked the way, refusing to let me park in the lot. He just stared at Robby and me in my truck. When I began to roll down my window to say something to the officer, Robby stopped me, "No, just chill. That guy's an asshole. He knows me. That's why he's stopped there." After a few minutes, the officer slowly pulled out of the way, staring hard at Robby. 'I can't believe that guy," I yelled. It was obvious that he was blocking me and I couldn't move. It was the first time I had experienced, albeit in a very minimal way, the mental games and taunting my students consistently described. "That guy [and some other cops] are real assholes. That guy made me pull down my pants in public. Why do you think I wear boxers?" I didn't know Roberto wore boxers, but I did know that like my other male students, he was the target of police harassment. They searched young women too, he explained, but you had to keep calm and know your rights. A woman officer tried to search his girlfriend once, but she refused because she knew that while she was on her porch, the officer needed a warrant, something I did not know. This kind of knowledge, he and my other students assured me, was one of their few defenses against police misconduct. It is also an example of how local knowledge is produced in a context of unequal power relations and subordination.

Law enforcement is a key component in the gentrification process. Like old buildings that are destroyed, gutted, and then rebuilt, gentrification reconfigures a neighborhood's racial and social landscape. In the urban imaginary, young brown and black men are discursively constructed as dangerous, threatening, requiring surveillance and punishment because they transgress norms of dress, class, and ethnicity. As Dwight Conquergood points out, "The discourse of transgression legitimizes official systems of surveillance, reform, enforcement, and demolition."[7] Another example of "legitimate" state surveillance is Chicago's anti-loitering law, which was ruled unconstitutional by the U.S. Supreme Court in 1999. Passed in 1992, the law resulted in more than 42,000 arrests of primarily young black and Latino men, who were charged with unlawfully congregating on the street with "no apparent purpose." In 1995, the Illinois courts suspended enforcement of the law, although police continued to use it to arrest and harass young men. Although

the law's purpose was to fight Chicago's gang problem, it helped to reproduce a kind of racial profiling common in contemporary law enforcement that targets men and women based solely on skin color. Mayor Daley— one of the law's staunchest advocates—lamented the U.S. Supreme Court ruling: "We have to ask ourselves if it is constitutional for gang-bangers and drug dealers to own a corner. . . . [Everybody] knows that they aren't out there cooking hot dogs and studying Sunday-school lessons."[8]

Increased policing of young men of color is one way to sanitize public space. Private businesses engage in similar activities, encouraging patronage from certain clients and discouraging others. This became particularly clear to me one day as I had lunch with Eddie, Nelly, and three other G.E.D. students at a popular diner we all frequented. I had brought my lunch that day but joined my students at their invitation. I entered the restaurant first and sat down at a table near the window, waiting for the others to get their food. Soon we were all sitting together, eating, laughing, and sharing stories, enjoying being together outside of the classroom. As we were getting ready to leave, Frankie, an eighteen-year-old Puerto Rican student, saw us in the restaurant and came in to join us, a Sprite in his hand. As soon as Frankie sat down, an owner whom I had come to know approached him aggressively, asking him what he thought he was doing sitting in his store with a soda he didn't buy there. Frankie had his headphones on, and he looked confused, removed his headphones, and asked the older man to repeat what he had said. By this time, the old man was livid and began screaming, "You get out of my store!" Stunned, Frankie stood up and walked out, mumbling, "This is messed up," and paced in front of the store window while talking to another student, Francisco. The man then turned to a woman who was sitting near us, grabbed her arm, and kicked her out as well. The woman screamed at him to let her go, and she stormed out of the store cursing at him in garbled English.

At this point, my students and I were visibly disturbed. "I'm never coming here again," Nelly said loudly. "He just lost himself a customer doing that." I then suggested to everyone that we should leave and finish our lunch in the Centro. As we walked out the door, I turned to the owner, who recognized me (I stopped at his store almost daily to buy fries), and said very calmly, "You know that student with the Sprite who you kicked out? Well, he's a student of mine and we came here to eat lunch; he was only in here to join me and the rest of the class." Before I could say any more, he started yelling at me in broken English, "You don't know! He comes in here and doesn't eat!" I yelled back that there were others with us who weren't eating food from his store, but he didn't bother to kick us out. He singled Frankie out for no apparent reason. "You get out of here! You are no kind of teacher! My daughter is a teacher, and you are no kind of teacher! You need to learn to control your students!" Control my students? From what? From sitting quietly with me and drinking a Sprite bought from a convenience store?

At this point, Nelly yelled back, "Don't you yell at my teacher! You show her respect!" The man screamed that I was no teacher and to get out of his store. As I left, I turned to him again, "You know, I tried to tell you calmly and I respected you. Why can't you respect me and my students?" He screamed at me again to leave. At this point, Eddie was moving closer to the counter where the man was. I grabbed Eddie's arm and we all left. "I was about to go off on that man," Eddie told me outside. "I was going to push all that stuff from the counter onto the floor. But I thought that wouldn't be a good idea." I agreed with him, congratulating him and the other students for keeping calm as we walked back to the Centro.

When Eddie saw Frankie, he told him breathlessly, "Dog, you missed it. You should have seen what happened." Nelly then explained that we had a fight with the man who kicked him out, and Frankie was really surprised. "Man, I ain't never going there again," Frankie said. "That man's all messed up." For the rest of the afternoon, we discussed what happened. We were all nervous, pumped with adrenaline, thinking of what we should have said to the man. "That was racism, I think," Nelly summed up, and we all agreed. Once we were a bit calmer, Eddie asked me, "Are you going to write this down?" "Of course I am" I answered. And all my students laughed. For me, this was data, a perfect example of how certain people—in this case, young Latino men who dress a particular way—are constructed as dangerous, undesirable, and threatening, and how these discursive practices have very real, material consequences. For my students, this was a common, albeit lamentable, incident reinforcing their marginalization in their own neighborhoods. It was no accident that Frankie was singled out and I was not. Gentrification discursively inscribes who is dangerous and who is a desirable customer, justifying rude treatment of those who appear to pose a threat, namely young, poor people of color.

The consequences of these gentrification processes are extremely gendered. Young women, for example, are less likely than men to be harassed by the police, but they do experience hostility from other city and neighborhood institutions. Many women I knew agonized over their interactions with city bureaucrats and other professionals because they felt marked linguistically, educationally, racially, and in terms of class. They sometimes asked me to accompany them to appointments, to make calls to city agencies for them, and at times, to attend their children's school functions in their place. I usually would do so, but I would also talk with them, explaining that they were perfectly articulate women who didn't have to be intimidated by others.

That was easy for me to say, they told me, since I spoke proper English *and* Spanish. They were poor, sometimes relied on welfare, and barely had a high school education—targets of public derision.

One spring day, for example, Nelly asked me to take her to a lawyer's office in the Loop. Earlier that year, she and her boyfriend had been in a serious car accident, and she had recently been notified that her settlement check was ready for pickup. Nelly was extremely excited, telling me of her plans for the money. Her four-year-old son, Malik, sat between us in my truck and was just as excited as his mom, asking her if she would buy him new toys with the money. We both laughed as she reassured him that he would get new things too. Nelly wanted me to accompany her into the office, but by the time we arrived, Malik was asleep, and Nelly decided she could go in by herself, while I waited in the truck with her son.

When she returned half an hour later, Nelly was visibly upset. After subtracting lawyer's fees, charges for the ambulance, and other hidden costs, it came to less money than she had expected, and when she had tried to talk with someone in the office about this, she was ignored. "I hate going to places like that. I know they're rippin' me off because all they see when they look at me, you know— they think that I don't have any education, or I'm not educated. And they take advantage." As we drove back to her apartment in Logan Square, she fought back tears, telling me that she had been counting on that money to pay her bills. But the worst part of all was the humiliation she had experienced, feeling that she was "looked down on" for who she was.

She expressed similar concerns when looking for a new apartment. After many years of living doubled up with her mother, Nelly had to move. Things were getting tense in the overcrowded apartment they shared, and she needed to find a new place to live.

For a month, Nelly attended class sporadically. When she finally did come to class she explained that she was having a hard time finding an apartment she could afford in her gentrifying neighborhood. Landlords refused to return her calls, were not forthcoming when she tried to make appointments with them, and when she finally was able to see something, they showed her small, dingy apartments with paint peeling from the walls. One apartment didn't even have a back door. "I want to stay in the neighborhood where I am now," she said sadly. But this was looking increasingly more difficult with such high rent. All of this made her very depressed. When she finally did find an apartment, it was in an unfamiliar, largely Polish neighborhood in the western section of Logan Square. Even though it was a nice area, Nelly felt uncomfortable, judged, and at times invisible.

N: If you go to a real nice neighborhood . . . you know, because I'm nappy-headed [she laughs nervously]. You know, they treat you like nothing . . . like they think you steal or like—suppose you buy a pack of cigarettes and they're $2.75, well, they'll count [the money] and assume something like, "Oh, well, this person looks like trouble," you know. This person's Puerto Rican. . . . In their mind, a spic or whatever.

I: How do you know they think that? What do they do that makes you think they think that?

N: Because [she laughs] I could tell because of the way they act. With an attitude, you know. Like . . . they can't even look at you. . . . I don't know how to describe it, but it's a look that I know. It's just—I'm a real nice person. People judge me like—maybe because I'm big . . . I'm like big-boned and I feel like people think that I'm mean. But I'm not. I'm real good. I'm a good person, you know. And I don't like prejudice . . . but . . . sometimes I *do* say something like, "I hate polacks." [She looks embarrassed and laughs nervously. I ask her why.] . . . Because they think of us as like real bad people. They think of Puerto Ricans as like—they don't know our history, you know? You know what I'm saying? They think they're white because they have blonde hair. And being white is no big thing, you know. . . . It's like [we're all] human beings. We all got mouths, eyes, . . . arms, and legs. Not all of us . . . none of us are perfect. You know, there's some people who don't got legs or whatever. But if it's just like they treat you, like we're nothing . . . . I got an example. One day I was with my mom and we went to Walgreens. And my mom, she bought a pack of cigarettes . . . and my mom was like, "Can I have some matches?" And she was a Polish lady. And she looked at my mom and she got a pack of matches and she threw them at my mom. Okay? And . . . I don't know if I overreacted, but I grabbed her arm and I told her, "Don't throw the matches at my mom, because you don't know who I am. You don't know who she is. Just because we're Puerto Rican doesn't . . . mean you have to discriminate." And she was like, "Do you want to talk to my manager?" And I go, "Yeah, I want to speak to your manager." And he was Polish.

I: So what did he say?

N: He was like, "Oh, there was nothing wrong. She didn't mean it. She was probably just in a hurry." I go, "There's nobody in the store barely!" . . . I told him, "I'll never [come] here again. And if I have any friends that come here, I'll never tell them to come here." It was on Belmont [Avenue]. You know, that upsets me. [She pauses.] Like around

here, my neighborhood is 60 percent Polish. So, like, these people—not these people because I don't want to sound like a racist [she laughs]. But I feel like they look at us like nothing. They'll pass right by me. . . . I always say hello to little old men . . . these little old men that pass by. Not that I know them . . . but I always see them and say hi. And sometimes . . . somebody will pass by and I'll just smile and they look at me like, "Why are you even smiling at me? I don't like you." [She pauses.] . . . Lately I don't even smile. I just don't even look at people. I just keep on minding my own business.

Nelly's feeling of being invisible, judged, and uncomfortable in a new neighborhood is one reason why many women resist moving to new areas. In response, Puerto Rican women have come up with new housing options, like doubling up with other family members and close friends, periodically taking in boarders, and squeezing large extended families into smaller apartments in order to remain in neighborhoods where, over the years, they have cultivated rich networks of neighbors, stores, and small businesses that enable them to feed and clothe their families from month to month. Mercedes and her family, for example, could have found a bigger and better apartment farther west in the city, but she would rather stay in Humboldt Park, near her network of friends who provide companionship and financial and emotional help. When she returned to Chicago a year after moving to San Sebastián, she found an apartment around the corner from the neglected and deteriorating apartment where she had lived before. The dangerous but gentrifying neighborhood has an important use value for her that would be difficult to replace, and women like Mercedes have invested great amounts of time and energy in cultivating these relationships and figuring out where to buy basic foodstuffs based on price and quality.

Aida, for example, consistently talked about moving away from the *locura* (craziness) of her gang- and drug-ridden neighborhood, but she recognized the convenience of living in West Town and was proud of her economic strategies, which effectively stretched the household monthly income. "I buy my meat at Lorimar. I get my eggs and milk from Edmar's. And I can walk over to K-Mart, over on Milwaukee [Avenue]. I have everything I need right here." This was often a point of contention between her and her husband, Eli, who wanted to find a larger apartment farther west, away from their troubled neighborhood. But because Aida did not have a driver's license, she didn't want to be far from familiar stores and kin and friendship networks. "One day I'll get my house," she would say. "I'll get my license and my house, but not yet."

These creative strategies for remaining in one's neighborhood are frequently insufficient, however, and Latino families are increasingly forced to move farther west, into new and unfamiliar neighborhoods. According to 2000 census data, Hermosa, Avondale, and Belmont Cragin— the community areas just west of the Near Northwest Side neighborhoods—have indexed a dramatic rise in their Latino population of between 40 and 200 percent.[9] And although these new places may appear to be safer, more spacious, and quieter than their previous communities, women are faced with creating new support networks, learning to navigate unfamiliar surroundings, and becoming more dependent on automobiles—their own and those of friends and family—to get around the city. These changes may seem inconsequential, but they have a profound impact on women both emotionally and materially. The women must invest a lot of time to create relations that are critical for their households in the new neighborhoods. They are often more dependent on others for transportation as well. When *puertorriqueñas* do have their own cars, they rarely own them, instead paying a large portion of their monthly income in order to finance them, an increasingly common strategy among the poor, who rely on what Brett Williams calls the "fringe banking system" in order to get by.[10] Chicago's housing crisis has clearly had a profound impact on the lives of the city's most vulnerable residents.

Residents of the Near Northwest Side often express frustration with the changes occasioned by gentrification. They frequently say they are powerless against the police; against the negative stereotypes that people form about them based on their language, class, education, and phenotype (including skin color, hair, and facial features); and against the economic and political clout newcomers bring with them to their neighborhoods. Indeed, the poor believe they have little power in their lives, and gentrification only heightens their sense of impotence. Of course there are moments of resistance—young men using exceedingly polite language to resist police officers, knowing and claiming one's civil rights to circumvent unlawful police practices, refusing to leave one's neighborhood despite pressures from landlords and newcomers. [. . .]

NOTES

1. Borrowing from Collins's notion of the "outsider within" (1991), Zavella (1993) discusses important ethical questions facing "insider/outsider" feminist researchers navigating the power relations in which they are implicated.
2. Zavella 1991, 314.
3. Dehavenon 1996, xviii; Slayton 1987.
4. See "Humboldt Park residents want buildings salvaged," *Chicago Tribune*, Oct. 20, 1996; "The neighborhood as we know it?" *West Town Tenants Union Newsletter*, fall 1997; "To build or not to build," *Chicago Reader*, Feb. 5, 1999.
5. Harvey 1990, 72. For an excellent analysis of these

dynamics in another Chicago neighborhood involving other ethnic and racial groups, see Conquergood 1992.

6. Calderia 2000, 367–368. See also Roberts 1997 and Aponte-Parés 2001 for analysis of the racialized body and the social construction of place.

7. Conquergood 1992, 135.

8. Quoted in "Chicago expresses annoyance but understanding over decision on loitering," *New York Times*, June 12, 1999 (late edition).

9. Flores-González (2001) documents the following increases from 1990–2000: Hermosa 41.6 percent; Avondale 99.6 percent; and Belmont Cragin 198.1 percent.

10. The American poor's increasing reliance on the fringe banking system includes using pawn shops, check-cashing businesses, and rent-to-own stores to supply themselves with basic necessities, and securing homes and cars with high-interest loans, a strategy that has enriched some of the nation's largest financial institutions while burdening the poor with high-cost debt. Williams 2001, 99. See also Hudson 1996.

REFERENCES

Caldeira, Teresa P. R. 2000. *City of walls: Crime, segregation, and citizenship in Sao Paulo.* Berkeley: University of California Press.

Collins, Patricia Hill. 1991. *Black feminist thought: Knowledge, consciousness, and the politics of empowerment.* New York: Routledge.

Conquergood, Dwight. 1992. Life in Big Red. In *Structuring diversity: Ethnographic perspectives on the new immigration*, edited by Louise Lamphere, 95–144. Chicago: University of Chicago Press.

Dehavenon, Anna Lou. 1996. Doubling up: A strategy of urban reciprocity to avoid homelessness in Detroit. In *There's no place like home: Anthropological perspectives on housing and homelessness in the United States*, 51–66. Westport, Conn.: Bergin and Garvey.

Flores–González, Nilda. 2001. "Paseo Boricua:" Claiming a Puerto Rican Space in Chicago. *Journal of the Center for Puerto Rican Studies* 13 (2): 8–21.

Harvey, David. 1990. *The condition of postmodernity.* Oxford: Basil Blackwell Press.

Hudson, Mike. 1996. *Merchants of Misery.* Monroe, Maine: Common Courage Press.

Slayton, Robert A. 1987. The Reagan approach to housing: An examination of local impact. Chicago: Chicago Urban League.

Williams, Brett. 2001. What's debt got to do with it? In *The new poverty studies: The ethnography of power, politics, and impoverished people in the United States*, edited by Judith Goode and Jeff Maskovsky, 79–102. New York: New York University Press.

Zavella, 1991. *Mujeres* in factories: Race and class perspectives on women, work and family. In *Gender at the crossroads of knowledge: Feminist anthropology in the postmodern era*, edited by Micaela di Leonardo. Berkeley: University of California Press.

——. 1993. Feminist insider dilemmas: Constructing ethnic identity with Chicana informants. *Frontiers* 13 (3): 53–76.

CHAPTER 25

Avenging Violence with Violence

Mary Pattillo

My final example of anticrime activism in North Kenwood-Oakland is the request made to the University of Chicago to extend its police patrols into the neighborhood. The hearty welcome of the University of Chicago police in 2003 was a strong indication of gentrifiers' desire to quell disorder by any means necessary. "There's a new generation now," said Jonathan Kleinbard, former vice president for community affairs at the University of Chicago. He was surprised to hear of the expanded patrol, which would have been unthinkable during his tenure at the university. "I just resisted [expanding the police boundaries] and I thought it would be like declaring war. And it's now happened." Kleinbard's astonishment at the requests for the university's police services by "ministers and home owners" in North Kenwood-Oakland is rooted in the tumultuous historical relationship between the university and its surrounding communities, mostly as a result of its aggressive urban renewal efforts in the 1950s. Given this background, the vision of Kirk Clemons, a middle-class home owner who moved to North Kenwood-Oakland in 1997, is nothing short of amazing: [. . .]

> My grand scheme, what I would have been pushing for from a political point of view, is: You've got three big rental courtyard buildings. I would have loved to have seen the University of Chicago buy one of those, make it a dormitory, forcing integration. Now, that would have immediately added $10,000 to $20,000 in appreciation of property values because [before] you didn't have a mixed income. You also would have had the extra services that would have came with that. The University of Chicago police would have had jurisdiction north of 47th Street. It would have had a higher level of security.

Clemons's vision—illustrative as much for its multilayered attention to racial and class integration, property values, and crime, as for its ahistorical cheerfulness—is now a reality. When the university came to the Conservation Community Council in June 2003 to present its proposal to begin patrols of NKO, the reception was as ebullient as Clemons had imagined it might be. Alderman Preckwinkle presented the proposal as coming at her request. She was not being selfish in taking the credit, but rather making herself liable for the blame if there were a backlash based on the historical suspicion of the university. She repeated her spiel that when people attempt to revitalize a neighborhood, two things are especially important—public safety and good schools. The university had already opened a charter elementary school, and now it was willing to assist with public safety. The latter commitment would cost the university approximately $300,000 a year, plus the cost of installing emergency phones throughout the neighborhood at roughly $10,000 each.

"Why expand into North Kenwood-Oakland?" asked the chief of the University of Chicago police as a set up to his own three-part answer: the neighborhood is getting better, the university feels a greater responsibility for its contiguous neighborhoods, and it's a win-win situation. NKO wins by receiving university police services on top of those of the Chicago Police Department. And the university wins by further "stabilizing" its surroundings, extending the range of neighborhoods in which faculty, staff, and students may choose to live

After the alderman and the police chief concluded their presentations, the meeting was open for questions from CCC members and residents at large. I was the only person to ask a skeptical question: "Have there been any complaints since the university has started patrolling Woodlawn?" I asked. Woodlawn is the community to the south of the university, and is also predominantly black and low-income. "Three that I can remember," answered the chief. "Two were from people who were arrested for selling drugs, and those were unfounded. The third was when two young men were stopped on the way to church, and that one needed to be addressed." I then queried the audience, "Are people in the audience generally supportive or skeptical?" I asked, not wanting to misinterpret the considerable silence. My neighbors looked at me as if I had landed from outer space. For the residents at the meeting, a preponderance of home owners and newcomers, this was a no-brainer. The offer of patrols was unanimously approved. The generations had been replaced in North Kenwood-Oakland, and the young pioneers welcomed any assistance in their increasingly successful efforts to tame the neighborhood.

THE NEXT LEVEL: QUALITY OF LIFE

In his presentation to the community, the chief of the University of Chicago police made explicit the new direction of crime fighting efforts in North Kenwood-Oakland. He told community residents that the university police planned to be helpful not just in fighting major crime incidents, but also in attacking loitering, bottle breaking, and the like. The university specializes in "quality-of-life" policing, he told the audience, ceaselessly observing and investigating nuisances until perpetrators are so bothered that they stop. The steady progression in what behaviors are subject to policing, from violent and property crimes to softer crimes such as loitering and littering, brings us to a turning point beyond which some residents, mostly those who have low incomes and have been in the neighborhood longer, switch from *being part* of the policing effort—complaining about drug dealers, calling 911 when they hear gunshots, taking precautions when walking through the neighborhood for fear of robberies or other assaults—to *being the targets of* policing.

The list of behaviors that evoke the contempt of residents is long, and they are frequent topics of conversation and attention at block clubs meetings, in casual neighborhood conversation, and at the Chicago Alternative Policing Strategy beat meetings. The vignette opening this chapter already raised the issue of where the appropriate place is to barbecue in the summer. Other such concerns include littering and broken glass, loud music, public drinking, fixing cars on the street, "loitering" and other kinds of congregating (which could include standing in front of one's own apartment building), porch sitting, honking horns, double- parking, and unauthorized home repairs. Residents' responses to these activities increase in earnestness from inaction, to making polite pleas to offending neighbors or building management, to making organized efforts through block clubs or approaching offenders as a group, to lodging complaints with or calling the police, to insisting that the police take action. At some point, all of the behaviors in the list above have been raised at beat meetings, and thus all have reached the level of being subject to official policing and official sanction.

The rhetoric around managing neighborhood behaviors is unabashedly normative and charged with the class tensions expected under gentrification. "This again [is] a problem with the CHA," began Robert Blackwell as he explained why he was skeptical about the reconstruction of public housing. "There is very little punishment for bad behavior. And that's what people, I think, are really worried about. I don't think it's the idea of I don't want to live around anybody who doesn't have as much money as we do. It's how are these people going to behave." Blackwell's comments are interesting because he initially denies that his evaluation of appropriate behaviors is based on class considerations while simultaneously setting up his categories based on class, specifically public housing residents versus non-public housing residents. Soon after this comment, he realizes his inconsistency, noting, "So there's a little bit of classism—not a little bit, a lot of classism."

Moreover, his emphasis here is on bad behaviors, like property upkeep, that are not criminal but that, in his view, require sanctions nonetheless. These kinds of behaviors fall into the list of quality-of-life issues that residents often rehearse. Blackwell was quick to add that he has been pleasantly surprised by just how inconspicuous the new public housing and its residents have been. Despite his initial protests, he now sees the mixed-income experiment in

North Kenwood as a success. Part of the reason for this positive evaluation is of course the stringent screening and behavior management to which residents are subjected.

Defining the objectionable behavior more clearly, resident Paul Knight argued about loiterers:

> They don't know what they're doing. And it looks bad. And they're not educating themselves or distinguishing themselves in any way or contributing to the greater good. Hanging out in front of a liquor store makes the neighborhood look bad [even] if it wasn't. I go over on Narragansett [a street on Chicago's predominantly white northwest side], you know, they're inside the liquor store, or sitting in the tavern, or whatever. Bridgeport even [a white and Latino working-class neighborhood] there's nobody hanging out in front of a liquor store.

Soeurette Hector was even more adamant in her dismay over the bad behaviors of fellow residents.

> There are several nuisances, but two I would say would be the top priorities. The first one is the undesirables. You know, either they will have to be taught how to live correctly or they will have to find where they feel comfortable to do whatever they're doing. It's nothing against them, but if they don't know the meaning of community, either they get someone to teach them or they need to go someplace where they can behave, you know, have the same behavior.

Hector illustrates the confidence with which many newer residents assert their vision of proper neighborhood comportment. She went on to give examples of such breaches of residential etiquette, including driving motorcycles at 2 AM, public urination, and drinking in the neighborhood park.

A liberal (or perhaps libertarian) response to Soeurette Hector's protestations can be offered for each of these behaviors: For one thing, not all people are on the same waking and sleeping schedule. Some people work variable shifts, young people have summer vacation, and the self-employed work when they want to. Hence leisure activities at 2 AM including riding motorcycles, do not interrupt the sleep of *everyone,* just those with nine-to-five jobs. As one resident of public housing said, "Sometimes on a hot summer night, I don't blame them [for being in the park after the 10 PM closing time]. Me and my kids don't come in the house at nine o'clock. Yeah, they be woke at eleven. Yup. In the summer what else you got to do with them? You don't want them woke at eight o'clock in the morning." Children playing outdoors at 11 PM is likely to annoy neighbors who must rise early for work. The point of this exercise is not for me to decide the ideological, moral, or legal high ground of different kinds of behaviors, but rather to expose the subjective and prescriptive contours of defining what is "undesirable." Moreover, Hector has relatively more power to actualize her values. Her story about the undesirable young men drinking in the park ends with an action that made her proud. Her ten-year-old son flagged down nearby police officers to report the bad behavior. "I was, like, so thrilled," she recalled. "I remember when I was a little girl, we used to have those things and the police used to be our friends."

Property managers (of private and publicly subsidized buildings) are also subject to the complaints of gentrifiers and are under pressure to keep their tenants in line with the desires of the new neighbors. Tenant screening and selection is just the first step in ensuring a certain kind of resident. Next, building managers see themselves as actively participating in behavior modification. Some of their strategies are structural such as installing barbecue pits behind a building so that residents do not barbecue out front, as one manager told me. Another manager told me she installed individual air conditioning units to cut down on outdoor

socializing in the summer. Many managers make sure that certain rules, such as those prohibiting loud music, are written into their leases and discussed with tenants so that there is no confusion over what infractions could result in eviction. These are relatively routine forms of building management and are appreciated as much by the tenants of the buildings themselves as by their new middle-class neighbors.

Yet sometimes these efforts become more austere and elicit greater resistance from low-income residents. Jenine Harris, manager of a project-based Section 8 building, was very cognizant of, perhaps even stressed out by, the gentrification of the neighborhood. Her awareness was heightened when the apartment building adjacent to the one she managed was converted to condominiums:

> It's been hell because I'm trying to get people to maintain this building in a certain way, but people aren't ready for the change. The tenants aren't ready for the change. They're not ready to live in a certain way that now the new residents of this area are accustomed to, or they expect. Like the condo association next door. You know, they don't hang out in front. But the culture of a lot of the residents in [this] building is they hang out [because] they come from areas or developments that that was the norm. So that was a big change for me to adjust to the hanging out and to not be so aggressive in asking them not to. You know that's been a change. I got a lot of resistance when I first got here because, you know, they gonna buck the system. My approach is a little different from the other management. I don't try to dictate to them, you know, what they should do and how they should live. I just try to incorporate them and show 'em different things and give 'em different things to do. But it's been very, very hard trying to get the residents to understand that there's, you know, no smoking in the hallways, smoke-free environment, drug-free environment, not to hang in front of the area and just some behavioral things.

Harris tried to be a sensitive landlord, but still felt there were certain rules that needed to be enforced, especially given the added scrutiny of the new condo owners next door.

What might have been the response of the tenants in Jenine Harris's building to her gently prodding them away from hanging out? Or the reaction of the young men who were asked by the police to leave the park at the behest of Soeurette Hector's son? "I'll tell you what. When you start paying our taxes, my taxes, then you tell me where to barbeque," was the response of one middle-aged man who had lived in NKO for decades when his new neighbor asked him not to barbecue on his front porch. There was a similar feud about barbecuing on the front porch on Emma McDaniel's block. A new neighbor did not like it, and the old neighbor did not care. McDaniel gave me her interpretation of the whole thing.

> If it had've been me, I'm telling you, honey, they'd have called the police on me. And I said, "You know, what kind of stuff is this?" You know, these are things that they have been doing all these years. And some of our back[yards] aren't like other people. And I can understand if you're out there and you got clowns out there with you and they're acting up and they're cursing and they're all disrespectful. Nobody wants that. Nobody wants that. But, I mean, it's the point that, honey, anything you do in your house or around your house, you don't annoy me. You're not bothering me. I'm not going to bother you, honey, because that is your place to enjoy. To do what you want to do. And I mean, I just said, "What's going on?" You know.

Her frustration with the new rules on her block is palpable. Not surprisingly, she too has a limit. She does not condone cursing, clowns, disrespect, or general "acting up." But the new rules, in her opinion, had gone too far. Her family had personally experienced not only the condescension of her neighbors but, more seriously, the pressure of the police when neighbors complained about her son repairing cars on the street. McDaniel feared for her son, who had spent time in jail and could not risk being on the police radar for even the most minor infraction. Despite her feistiness, she ultimately acquiesced. Emma McDaniel instructed her adult children not to antagonize the new neighbors and to follow the new block rules if confronted. She was already struggling financially and surely did not need any more headaches in the way of complaining neighbors and watchful police officers.

Andrea Wilson took the opposite approach when the management of the apartment building where she, her mother, and her grandmother had all grown up grew progressively more strict. "The management now, I don't particularly care for," she began. "They don't want the kids running around. They can't play in front. They don't want you standing in front of the building. You can't do this, you can't do that. It's like you a prisoner in your own home. Basically, they don't want you to do anything." Wilson was in her twenties and had a young son whom she felt had nowhere to play, even though the U-shaped building enclosed a large grassy courtyard. Her extended family combined the income from her job at a record store and her mother's nursing salary to pay the modest rent. Her grandmother had her own apartment, which she paid for with a Section 8 voucher. But they saw changes coming. Wilson commented on nearby buildings being converted to condos, the new construction, and the remodeling. She appreciated that the vacant lots were being filled, but as a result, she said, "it's getting more expensive to live around here." Furthermore, along with the new housing came new rules, and the landlord began hassling her, her friends, and her family about standing in front of the building. Wilson fought back, and planted herself in front of her apartment building.

Like where I live, my bedroom face the front of the building. So I used to go outside a lot to sit up under my window. [The landlord] didn't want anybody to sit there. My mom felt that if I'm paying rent why can my daughter not sit there. She [was] like, "Well, just go out there and sit anyway. And if he have something to say, tell him to come talk to me." And it was like he'll come, he'll do things like just sit there and watch us to see if his staring'll make us move. We just sit there and not pay any attention to him. And then finally he'd just drive off. I guess he just got tired of it.

Contrary to Emma McDaniel's experience, where she feared police reprisal, Andrea Wilson and her family felt emboldened by their long tenure to defy rules that they perceived to be excessively rigid. Still, the success of Wilson's stoop-sitting protest was short-lived. The landlord got the ultimate revenge, not through the criminal justice system, but through the prerogatives of ownership.

He wanted to raise our security [deposit] from $75 to $900. He wanted to raise our rent to $1,100. We were already paying $875. So by the first of November we had to have $900 rent and a $900 security which is no way. Got to move. So within a month we were packed up and moved in here.

The Wilson family was able to find an apartment that was still near Andrea's grandmother's in a subsidized building a few blocks away. Andrea Wilson's run-in with her landlord, which she sees as connected to the changes in the neighborhood, exemplifies the turning point, where established residents, who initially benefited from change—seeing fewer vacant lots, having more retail options, and so on—start to be hurt by it, either through law enforcement or market forces. [...]

CHAPTER 26

Neighborhood Effects in a Changing Hood

Lance Freeman

SOCIAL TIES

Social ties are another mechanism through which having more affluent neighbors might be an advantage. More specifically, more affluent neighbors might be advantageous for a particular type of social ties. Briggs (1998) distinguishes between two types of social ties, or what he calls social capital. One type of ties refers to those that provide support, or help cope with day-to-day life. These are ties of the type that one might use for a small loan until payday, to watch the kids, and to confide in. We all make of use of such ties, but there some evidence to suggest that the poor are especially reliant on them to substitute for goods and services that the more fortunate among us typically buy. In *American Dream,* journalist Jason Deparle (2004) describes how three women on welfare relied on each other to provide temporary housing to each other's families and supervision for each other's children in addition to emotional support and how this support was necessary for them to survive. [...]

For getting ahead or becoming upwardly mobile, however, these ties were of limited use. To be sure, the women shared with each other information about the superiority of welfare benefits in Milwaukee vis-à-vis Chicago and job information, such as opportunities as nursing assistants.

But while gaining access to higher welfare benefits or a job as a nursing assistant did improve their lives, these improvements were marginal at best and did not put them on a secure trajectory out of poverty. Instead these ties helped them get by but not get ahead. Because the women were themselves poor with limited access to resources, knowing them did not lead to upward mobility.

The second type of ties Briggs describes does just that—help people get ahead. These are ties that can lead not only to a job but a good job, or ties that would help one navigate the wider middle-class world in a way that significantly affects one's life chances. These are where more affluent neighbors are presumably beneficial. Whereas a poor neighbor might provide information on how to qualify for housing assistance or obtain a job at a fast-food outlet, a middle-class neighbor might be able to advise a youth on how to prepare and apply to college or for a stable job with room for upward mobility. Moreover, although some might assume that the notion of social ties implies intimate contacts of the type that I argued were unlikely between the gentry and others, what social scientists refer to as *weak* ties are of import as well (Granovetter 1973). Neighbors and other casual acquaintances are examples of this type. Thus, it would not be necessary for someone to develop intimate relationships with their neighbors; ties of a more casual type will suffice to bring potential benefits. The neighborhood effects thesis therefore suggests that more affluent neighbors might lead to ties that are more leverageable, that is, ties that can lead to upward mobility.

How likely is gentrification to lead to these types of ties? As we saw with the case of peer effects and collective socialization, there is reason to be cautious about expecting neighborhood effects to manifest themselves in the context of gentrification. Relationships between the gentry and indigenous residents appear too fleeting. Is there reason to be cautious when thinking about social ties in the context of gentrification?

Gentrification certainly brings individuals with more leverageable connections into spatial proximity with indigenous residents. Moreover, the type of relationships necessary for leverageable social ties to be beneficial—weak ones—certainly seem plausible in the context of gentrification.

Indeed, my research in Clinton Hill and Harlem did reveal instances where individuals who might be considered part of the gentry played roles that were beneficial to indigenous residents. We were first introduced to Barbara . . . as she related her satisfaction in seeing the value of her home rise. With her suburban upbringing, degree from an Ivy League university, and current enrollment in graduate school, Barbara fits the profile of a pioneer, that is, a middle-class person who serves in the vanguard of gentrification. The neighborhood effects thesis suggests that someone like this living in a neighborhood like Harlem might serve as a role model to others in the community and could potentially serve as a bridge to the wider middle-class world. Below are snippets of some her interactions with the Harlem community that shed some light on these notions.

LANCE: I'll ask you about is community organizations or churches, or religious institutions, have you noticed—I don't know if you are involved or active with them, but have you noticed any changes in those since you've been there?

BARBARA: Well my sorority did a project at Frederick Douglass Academy [a local high school], and we worked with high school girls. We did a project on Saturdays. We worked with the girls. We took them on trips. We had workshops and we mentored them. And a lot of them started coming out. Maybe the first time we had like ten, fifteen. After a while we had like sixty girls coming out. And the principal was very thankful. He said, "Because you do me a favor by being there and having the kids come in to hang out there," because he said that statistics show that between those hours more kids get arrested on a Saturday—because the cops are looking for overtime. And so any little thing can get them. And I thought that was a scary thought, you know. So those type of projects go on unnoticed. You know, we never got an award or a thank you for doing these kind of things.

Barbara also described the process by which her building was converted from a rental to a cooperative. In New York City there are regulations governing this process that are designed to prevent preconversion residents from being displaced. According to Barbara, the landlord was deviating from these guidelines in a way that was disadvantageous to the tenants.

Like, the owners barely advertised to the tenants that that they could purchase a coop. So me and a few owners at the time said, "You need to advertise this place. You need to put a sign up that says it's a coop, in case anybody is interested in buying." There was a time I became very adamant. I was very confrontational with the managing agency who was supposed to be taking these concerns back to the sponsor. Then I found out that the owner of the building has another coop on the Upper West Side. There he was following the rules to a T. And he wasn't getting away with any of the things there. I just found this out, and I went to the state office building and I got lots of information. And I threatened to take him to court and things like that. And they were becoming concerned because they were like, "Uh-oh, she's starting to do her research." And I asked everybody [in the building] to meet in. And I said, "We have to figure out a way to get these apartments. And maybe if we all come together and we ask to purchase, he'll give you a break, because twenty-five percent down is too much. But as a group, collectively, you can go and say to him, 'You know what? We've been here in this building.'"

These examples are instructive in illuminating how even weak ties between the gentry and indigenous residents can nonetheless have important effects. In this case Barbara served as a mentor in a formal capacity through her sorority at a local high school. Her proximity to a local high school no doubt played a role in her getting involved as a mentor, as she frequently mentioned her concern about and desire to assist the people in her community. Certainly her residence in a building with other residents put them in a situation of mutual interest. Her knowing where to turn to obtain information about tenant's rights under a coop conversion as well as her savvy negotiating with the landlord proved to be a valuable resource to her neighbors.

If her mentoring helped persuade a teen to select a college or choose a career or even avoid getting arrested as the principal suggested, her ties to these youths may indeed have helped them get ahead. Choosing a college or a career can be bewildering to any teen; for one who does not personally know adults who have tread in these paths before, the choices may seem not only bewildering but are probably truncated as well. In this way, her mentoring can make

a real difference to some of the residents in the community. Likewise, by informing her neighbors about their rights as tenants and about opportunities to become homeowners, her presence in the neighborhood could make a real difference to at least some of the residents in the community.

From the perspective of some her neighbors, coming into contact with Barbara was potentially very important. Nonetheless, those neighbors who might have benefited from her presence (either through being mentored or being informed of opportunities to become homeowners) did not develop intimate, long-lasting relationships with her. Indeed, when asked to describe her relationships with her neighbors she used the common "hi and bye" refrain described earlier in this chapter. Despite the fleeting nature of these relationships, they still had the potential to connect these residents to important resources.

Barbara's story raises the question of how common are these types of causal but potentially leverageable social ties? To be sure, Barbara is exceptional—most people do not participate in mentoring programs or organize their neighbors. Moreover, active people like this are present in all classes. Nevertheless, Barbara is better situated to navigate the wider middle-class world and provide entry to someone attempting to break into that world. To the extent that gentrification brings into the neighborhood more individuals with access and savvy like her, there is the potential for indigenous residents to benefit.

Casual contact between the gentry and indigenous residents would seem more likely than the type of intimate relationships necessary for collective socialization or peer effects to manifest. But these casual relationships may indeed be important as Barbara's story and the example to follow attests.

Anthony was introduced earlier as a college-educated professional who moved to Clinton Hill four years ago and who grew up in suburban Maryland. As an armchair sociologist, he describes the potential benefits exposure to the gentry could bring to the indigenous residents of his neighborhood:

LANCE: Anything else, um, I guess as far as the neighborhood changing that I haven't touched upon, that, um—

ANTHONY: Not really, and I think it's a general positive because it's maintaining its racial diversity and like I said it's safer, above anything it's safe, the safeness. And I think that there's a certain, I think there's a certain male black crisis. But I think it's good because now you're seeing all types of black folks. You've got your artsy black person in Clinton Hill now, you know the job-like person or whatever it is, and you've got your gay couples, you got your, your suited black person out there, you've got the guys with the baggy pants, whatever, but that shouldn't be all you'll see. 'Cause the media, that's how they portray us in the media, they give you one version and, and you see it on TV, then that's all you see, well that must be all there is. Now you see the dad with the kid, that's a big strong message that these kids never see. On the downside there is some shadiness going on in terms of people trying to raise rent and get people kicked out and stuff, but I think there is a general positive to the people that can stay. But I talk to a lot of black kids from housing projects, lots of kids that never left their block, never even been to Manhattan, you know, never left the Bronx, never left Bed-Stuy, never left East New York, and like well what's out there, they don't really even know. I mean they think the whole world is like what they've seen and the males that they see aren't necessarily the best role models I don't think. And even if you see a white man walking around doing a certain thing, you know, may be he doesn't look just like you, but he's still a man doing something, that's still more positive than not seeing anything at all. So, I think that plays itself out as like a certain positive, I hope some of the kids can come up. Like, for instance, I make it a point to wear, not right now, to wear like suits or like khakis and stuff, not because I'm, I want to be your European, not because I want to simulate, just because I want people to see something different. So, I think that's the biggest positive of gentrification and it's definitely like that in Clinton Hill. And, I'm not saying you have to be white or, you've got to simulate to European ways or American ways, but so at least you know, you can understand, kind of how society works in that, you can, you can have good health care, you can have good food, or you can have good services or like, the police is like another thing, too. But maybe the police is there to serve you, you know. A lot of people are just really scared of the police or they hate the police or all these things, its all stereotypical, I'm not saying the police are the best in New York, you know a lot of them probably are racists, but you know, you are paying taxes and they serve you, you know, and so instead of just being scared of the police, you're saying, a lot of people don't want us calling the police when we see things going wrong in the neighborhood, right, but we have a right to call just like everyone else. So, people need to see that you control the police, they don't control you, you know, so like you demand service in the neighborhood and no you're not going to harass our kids and like, you've got to control the police, you can't just not call them in and but, that people wreak havoc in your neighborhood because you don't want the police to come in.

Anthony articulates in layman's terms the notion that weak social ties can influence the indigenous residents of gentrifying neighborhoods. His theory that the youths of Clinton Hill will be influenced by seeing him and other blacks walking around in suits is speculation and dubious for the reasons described. Without knowing what one does to become a suit, Anthony's mere presence seems unlikely to significantly alter life chances.

Anthony's comments about the police, however, are illustrative of the notion that the gentry can present an alternative way of thinking to indigenous residents. The long-time residents' fears of the police are probably well founded. Nevertheless, Anthony's reasoning that the police should be viewed as servants of the community rather than an occupying force would seem more likely to result in better police protection in the long run. In the larger middle-class world, the notion that the police work for the community is generally accepted, and the police generally act accordingly. In the 'hood, the police behave as an occupying army and are treated that way. But holding the police accountable as servants of the community, rather than ignoring them as appeared to be the inclination of many of the indigenous residents probably holds more promise for getting better police protection. This is not to deny that getting better police protection or any other public service, especially in disadvantaged communities, is an uphill battle. But if Anthony's perspective on how to view the police does rub off on some of his neighbors, they may be more likely to demand and receive better police protection. In this way, the presence of Anthony, who as a gentrifier and a catalyst for demanding and receiving better services, could be beneficial to the indigenous residents. Moreover, better services, whatever their origin, are something that certainly benefit indigenous residents.

Institutional Resources

Anthony's narrative also brings into focus another potential mechanism through which having more affluent neighbors may be beneficial—their impact on institutional resources. As noted before, I use *institutional resources* to refer to those institutions that provide services and amenities to a neighborhood. These institutions might be externally based, such as in the case of the chain stores, police, or public schools; draw their resources from within the community as in the case of community-based organizations like the development corporations; or be some combination of both, as in the case of schools. The neighborhood effects thesis posits that relative to poorer residents, the middle class will bring more institutional resources to the neighborhood for the following reasons: (1) The middle class will be better positioned to create and support community-based organizations. Indeed, when Wilson (1987, p. 56) first wrote about "concentration effects" he described how "economically and stable and secure families" would keep churches, schools, stores, and recreational facilities and other institutions viable even during times of economic deprivation. He reasoned that it was the absence of these families during trying times that would cause these institutions to wither. (2) Because of their greater purchasing power, middle-class residents will be more attractive to commerce and hence stores will follow. (3) More affluent residents, perhaps because of being better connected to the wider society and/or their knowledge of how to manipulate bureaucracy, are able to command better resources for the community. By bringing such middle-class residents to the neighborhood, gentrification would be expected to impact the institutional resources present there. What did my research reveal regarding this thesis?

My conversations with neighborhood residents and observations all strongly suggest that the institutional resources in the form of better amenities and services were improving. Indeed much of chapters 4 and 5 were devoted to describing residents' perceptions of and reactions to these improvements, so I do not reiterate that here. What is less clear, based on my research, is the role the gentry are playing in this improvement. Many of the residents attributed the improvements to the powers that be favoring the gentry and providing them with preferential treatment. Others attributed the changes to the squeaky wheel syndrome—that is, the gentry were more likely to demand and consequently receive better amenities and services. And as was mentioned earlier, some respondents were eager to take credit for the improvements themselves, pointing to their efforts through community-based organizations. As I described in chapter 2, a number of community-based organizations were active in both Clinton Hill and Harlem both before and contemporaneously with the onset of gentrification. Some of their actions, such as building housing and improving storefronts were undeniably having an impact that all could see. In addition, as I noted in several places earlier in this chapter, the gentry sometimes became active in existing institutions, such as the local public school where parents began raising money for supplies or the example where Michael advocated for a new way of dealing with the police. Thus there are several competing and not necessarily exclusive explanations about the role of institutions and how they interacted with the process of gentrification to create better neighborhood conditions.

Given that the research presented in this book did not focus on the evolution of community-based organizations, only how they were perceived by residents, definitively ruling out specific explanations would be premature. It is fair to conclude, however, that the presence of the gentry did attract more commerce to these neighborhoods and that in at least some instances changed the dynamics of institutions serving the neighborhood. Barbara's efforts to organize a coop, Jennifer's experience in the local school where parents raised money, and Michael's attempts to change how his coop board dealt with the police are all such examples. In these instances, gentrification introduced individuals with different outlooks and resources that influenced the type of services residents received and their access to these services.

Thus one could argue that gentrification both strengthened internally based organizations, by bringing people with diverse backgrounds and talents into some groups and changed the way externally based institutions interacted with the neighborhood, encouraging these latter institutions to provide more and better services. Whether the absence of the gentry would cause the internally based institutions to wither as Wilson implies is not clear. When I discussed local community-based organizations with residents these organizations were typically not described in a way that suggested dramatic changes were afoot as a result of gentrification. Thus I have no evidence that gentrification was leading to a widespread increase in community-based organizations that served the neighborhood. Indeed, there were examples of organizations whose raison d'etre was to combat gentrification or the ills associated with it like the West Harlem Tenants Coalition and Harlem Operation Take Back.

The proliferation and maturation of the community development movement should also give one pause before expecting gentrification to substantially increase the number or visibility of indigenous community-based institutions. By the beginning of the twenty-first century when the research that informs this book commenced, an infrastructure of foundations, intermediaries, informal networks, and professional organizations had developed to support local organizations across urban America, and this infrastructure was especially strong in cities like New York with a long tradition of community organizing. It would therefore be surprising if gentrification greatly enriched the community institutions already in place in these neighborhoods. The gentry probably diversified many of these institutions to be sure, but beyond that one should be cautious before inferring much of the changes in amenities and services to them.

The role the gentry seem to have played is not one of creating or supplanting existing institutions. Rather it is one of augmenting these institutions. The narratives cited earlier in this chapter when gentrifiers volunteered at schools, raised funds, or suggested a different way of engaging the police are examples of such. The presence of the gentry could then lead to better services and amenities perhaps because the powers that be are more sympathetic to their needs. It is also perhaps because the gentry are more savvy about demanding better services, as in the story Anthony told about demanding better police service. It could be the gentry have the resources to contribute to improving some services themselves as the story Jennifer related about the local schools earlier in this chapter would seem to suggest. In the case of stores, it could also be that proprietors are attracted to the purchasing power of the gentry and open stores that might be of use to indigenous residents as well. Whatever the mechanism, it seems clear that many residents perceived the arrival of the gentry to be linked to improvements in services and amenities.

Although I would argue that gentrification has the potential to benefit indigenous residents through improving the institutional resources available to them, I would also advise caution in applying this interpretation to different contexts. The narratives I presented in earlier chapters suggested most people were appreciative of the improvements in amenities and services. It is easy to imagine, however, that certain services such as those for the indigent or substance abusers, might decline with gentrification either because the gentry don't want these services around, the service providers cannot afford to stay, or the service provider's clientele base is shrinking. People making use of these services might associate gentrification with a decrease in amenities and services. People fitting this profile were not represented in my conversations (at least no one was obviously a substance abuser), so I cannot rule out the possibility that some residents already hold this sentiment. It should also be kept in mind that Harlem and the section of Clinton Hill that was the subject of this study suffered from a dearth of services and amenities that would be available in most middle-class neighborhoods. Whether residents of a poor or working-class neighborhood that nonetheless had ample services and amenities, such as is common in many immigrant communities, would feel as positively about this aspect of gentrification is open to debate. [. . .]

REFERENCES

Briggs, Xavier. 1998. Brown Kids in White Suburbs: Housing Mobility and the Many Faces of Social Capital. *Housing Policy Debate* 9(4): 177–221.

Deparle, Jason. 2004. *American Dream: Three Women, Ten Kids and a Nation's Drive to End Welfare.* New York: Viking Books.

Granovetter, Mark. 1973. The Strength of Weak Ties. *American Journal of Sociology* 78:1360–80.

Wilson, William J. 1987. *The Truly Disadvantaged.* Chicago: University of Chicago Press.

CHAPTER 27

Building the Creative Community

Richard Florida

How do you build a truly Creative Community—one that can survive and prosper in this emerging age? The key can no longer be found in the usual strategies. Recruiting more companies won't do it; neither will trying to become the next Silicon Valley. The rise of the Creative Economy has altered the rules of the economic development game. Companies were the force behind the old game and cities measured their status by the number of corporate headquarters they were home to. Even today many cities, states and regions continue to use financial incentives—some of them obscenely extravagant—in their efforts to lure companies.

But while companies remain important, they no longer call all the shots. As we have seen, companies increasingly go, and are started, where talented and creative people are. Robert Nunn, the CEO of ADD Semiconductor, told the *Wall Street Journal* the "key element of building a technology business is attracting the right people to the company. It's a combination of experience, skill set, raw intelligence, and energy. The most important thing is to be somewhere where you have a pool of people to draw that."[1]

The bottom line is that cities need a *people climate* even more than they need a business climate. This means supporting creativity across the board—in all of its various facets and dimensions—and building a community that is attractive to creative people, not just to high-tech companies. As former Seattle mayor Paul Schell once said, success lies in "creating a place where the creative experience can flourish."[2] Instead of subsidizing companies, stadiums and retail centers, communities need to be open to diversity and invest in the kinds of lifestyle options and amenities people really want. In fact you cannot be a thriving high-tech center if you don't do this.

BEYOND NERDISTAN

When they are not trying to lure firms, many cities around the country seek to emulate the Silicon Valley model of high-tech economic development. City after city has tried to turn itself into a clone of the Valley by creating R&D parks, office complexes, technology incubators and the like, all on a quintessentially suburban model. Ross DeVol of the Milken Institute has compiled a list of the hundreds of communities that call themselves a "Silicon Somewhere."

This is essentially betting the future on an economic development model from the past. Though successful in its day, this model misunderstands the changing role of creativity in spurring innovation and economic growth. In fact the heyday of the high-tech nerdistan may be ending. Many of these places have fallen victim to serious problems and some may be reaching their limits to sustainable growth. The comfort and security of places like Silicon Valley have gradually given way to sprawl, pollution and paralyzing traffic jams. As we have seen, my focus groups and statistical research tell me that Creative Class people increasingly prefer authenticity to this sort of generica. As a high-technology executive told the *Wall Street Journal* in October 2001, "I really didn't want to live in San Jose. Every time I went up there, the concrete jungle got me down."[3] His company eventually settled on a more urban Southern California location in downtown Pasadena close to the Cal Tech campus.

Places like Phoenix are well aware of the limits of the model and are trying to create concentrated populations and lifestyle amenities in their downtowns. As one of Phoenix's leading business journalists told me, "Our lack of old buildings and authentic urban neighborhoods puts us at a huge disadvantage in attracting top talent." Commenting on the low-wage factory and office jobs that dominate its sprawling suburbs, he added: "We are like Pittsburgh or St. Louis fifty years ago, but without the world-class universities."[4] Joel Kotkin finds that the lack of lifestyle amenities is causing significant problems in attracting top creative people to places like the North Carolina Research Triangle. He quotes a major real estate developer as saying, "We got into the mindset of the 1960s and 1970s. We segregated all our uses and this contributed to the sprawl here." Adds a second, "Ask anyone where a downtown is and nobody can tell you. There's not much of a sense of place here.... The people I am selling space to are screaming about cultural issues." The Research Triangle lacks the "hip" urban lifestyle found in places like San Francisco, Seattle, New York and Chicago, laments a

University of North Carolina researcher: "In Raleigh-Durham, we can always visit the hog farms."[5] Kotkin finds similar problems in Southern California's Orange County. "There isn't that buzz that it's cool and innovative," is the way the Milken Institute's DeVol explains it.[6]

In reality, as Kotkin points out in his book *The New Geography,* there are at least three kinds of high-tech communities. First are the classic nerdistans from Silicon Valley proper and the Research Triangle to northern Virginia. Then there are what David Brooks calls "latte towns" or what Kotkin terms the "valhallas," more rural places with plentiful outdoor amenities, such as Boulder, Colorado. Finally, there are the older urban centers whose rebirth has been fueled in part by a combination of creativity and lifestyle amenities: New York's SoHo, San Francisco's SoMa and Mission districts and Seattle's Pioneer Square, just to name a few.

Leading Creative Centers, however, provide all three options. The San Francisco Bay Area consists of a classic nerdistan (Silicon Valley), several valhallas (from the Napa Valley and Marin County south to Santa Cruz), and a creative urban center. The greater Boston area contains the Route 128 suburban complex, Cambridge, where Harvard and MIT are located, and the Back Bay, Beacon Hill and the North End. Seattle has suburban Bellevue and Redmond, beautiful mountains and country, and a series of revitalized urban neighborhoods. The Denver region combines the university and lifestyle assets of Boulder with abundant skiing and the urban character of its LoDo district. Austin includes traditional nerdistan developments to the north, lifestyle centers for cycling and outdoor activities, and a revitalizing university/downtown community centered on vibrant Sixth Street, the warehouse district and the music scene. In the Creative Age, as we have seen, options are what matter.

BACK TO THE CITY

Virtually all commentators on urban America over the past fifty years had agreed on one thing: Cities had lost much of their historic economic function and were in an irreversible decline. As George Gilder once put it: "Big cities are leftover baggage from the industrial era."[7] Both companies and people were moving away from the city into the new suburban enclaves and what Joel Garreau aptly dubbed "Edge Cities."[8] But urban centers have long been crucibles for innovation and creativity. Now they are coming back. Their turnaround is driven in large measure by the attitudes and location choices of the Creative Class.

During the 1970s and 1980s when I was in college and graduate school, my professors argued that cities' technological and organizational changes had made them irrelevant as economic bases. The rise of large-scale mass production, they said, had brought about a shift in the kinds of spaces required for modern manufacturing. While early manufacturing could be accommodated in multistory buildings of the sort found in many older neighborhoods—such as in New York's SoHo or Flatiron districts— these kinds of buildings and these kinds of neighborhoods were made obsolete by the shift to large-scale factories in greenfield locations. Manufacturing was moving to giant horizontal factories in the suburbs, the Sunbelt or abroad that offered the advantages of mass production and economies of scale. People were following suit, leaving for bigger homes on bigger lots in the suburbs. Government policies helped fuel this shift by encouraging home ownership and constructing extensive freeway systems.

City leaders tried to stanch the trend by buttressing the one economic activity left in cities: building taller and denser central business districts, often increasingly filled with government or nonprofit activities. Others simply decided that some neighbor-

hoods were beyond salvation and bulldozed them in the name of "urban renewal." The replacement of once bustling mixed-use neighborhoods with office buildings created the familiar skyscraper ghost towns— filled with workers by day but empty and dangerous at night, as the middle-class workers climbed into their cars and drove to their lives in the suburbs, leaving only the underclass in the city.

I saw these changes played out vividly in my own life. I was born in 1957 in Newark, New Jersey, the city that became the poster child for urban decay. But Newark in my youth was a wonderland for a little boy, the kind of place Philip Roth has so eloquently written about—a bustling mix of industries with a prosperous downtown and thriving multiethnic neighborhoods. I would sometimes visit my mother in the downtown office building of the *Newark Star Ledger* where she worked. On weekend our extended family would gather at my grandmother's home in the predominantly Italian-American North Newark neighborhood and on warm nights we'd take in the professional bicycle races in Branch Brook Park. During holiday seasons, we shopped in the retail district at department stores like Bamberger's. And among the times I recall most fondly were Saturdays with my father. On some of these, he took me to Newark Public Library, turning me loose in the stacks, where I would eventually devour volume upon volume on urban America.

Then, almost all at once, everything changed. I vividly recall one Saturday drive with my father through downtown Newark in the summer of 1967, when I was ten. The once bustling streets were barricaded, buildings in flames. Everywhere I could see police, National Guardsmen and armored vehicles brought in to quell the riots. My mother's office building in downtown Newark was transformed into a barbed-wire fortress. In subsequent years I witnessed the rise and fall of the once grand factory where my father had worked for many years, Victory Optical, which provided solid livelihoods for ethnic families in Newark and surrounding communities. For many people who grew up as I did, the decline of manufacturing and of America's great urban centers signaled the end of this country's golden age.

But the past decade has seen a dramatic turnaround in the fortunes of urban America. In the face of expert pessimism, cities are back. The 2000 Census documents the dramatic resurgence of cities from New York City to Oakland, California—the latter ranked as one of Forbes magazine's top twenty places for high-tech business in 2000, and among the top twenty on the Milken High-Tech Index as well.[9] Even less established places have bounced back. Jersey City, which ranked sixth on the 2000 Gay Index, grew by 5 percent. My birthplace of Newark at least stopped losing people: It has even seen the rise of a new performing arts center, downtown restaurants and a local arts scene. At the June 2000 meeting of the United States Conference of Mayors, the *New York Times* reported that "The mayors complained about too many high-skilled jobs, and not enough people to fill them; too many well-off people moving back to the city, and not enough houses for all of them, driving up prices for everyone else; and too much demand for parks and serenity, and not enough open space to offer the new city dwellers appalled by sprawl."[10]

Several forces have combined to bring people and economic activity back to urban areas. First, crime is down and cities are safer. In New York City, couples now stroll city blocks where even the hardiest urban dweller once feared to tread. Cities are cleaner. People no longer are subjected to the soot, smoke and garbage of industrial cities of the past. In Pittsburgh, people picnic in urban parks, rollerbladers and cyclists whiz along trails where trains used to roll, and water-skiers jet down the once toxic rivers.

Second, cities have become the prime location for the creative lifestyle and the new amenities that go with it. We have already seen the role that lifestyle amenities play in attracting people and stimulating regional economic growth. In a study for the Fannie Mae Foundation and the Brookings Institution, Rebecca Sohmer and Robert Lang examined the trend of people moving downtown in some twenty-one large American cities.[11] Gary Gates and I compared their back-to-the-city findings to our indicators of creativity and diversity. We found that downtown revitalization is associated with the same lifestyle factors that appeal to the Creative Class. The Gay Index, for instance, is strongly associated with percent change in downtown population; and both the Gay Index and the Bohemian Index correlate with the share of a region's population living downtown. The Composite Diversity Index is the best predictor of both the percent change in downtown population and the percent of a region's population living downtown.[12] We also found that thriving downtowns are associated with vibrant high-tech industries. The Milken High-Tech Index, for instance, is positively correlated with the share of a region's population living downtown.

Third, cities are benefiting from powerful demographic shifts. With fewer people living as married couples and more staying single longer, urban areas serve as lifestyle centers and as mating markets for single people. Cities have also benefited from their historic role as ports of entry. Like most cities, New York lost native-born Americans in the last census, but it more than made up for the loss by adding nearly a million new immigrants. As we have seen, my research documents the striking statistical correlation between ethnic diversity and high-tech industry. Immigrants, seen not long ago as mainly a burden on city services, turn out to be one of the keys to economic growth.

Fourth, cities have reemerged as centers of creativity and incubators of innovation. High-tech companies and other creative endeavors continue to sprout in urban neighborhoods that were once written off, in cities from New York to Chicago and Boston. The 2000 *State of the Cities Report* by the U.S. Department of Housing and Urban Development found that cities have become centers for high-tech job growth. High-tech jobs made up almost 10 percent of all jobs in central cities according to the report, nearly identical to the percentage found in the suburbs. Further high-tech job growth in cities increased by 26.7 percent between1992 and 1997, more than three times their overall increase.[13]

Seattle illustrates the trend. Nearly half of all high-tech jobs in Seattle are located in the city versus 35 percent in the suburbs, according to research by Paul Sommers and Daniel Carlson of the University ofWashington.[14] Almost a third of all high-tech companies and jobs in the region are in the central business district, Pioneer Square and Belltown, even though Microsoft and its tens of thousands of employees are located outside the city in the suburban hamlet of Redmond. Amazon.com put its new headquarters in an abandoned hospital on the outskirts of downtown. Real Networks occupies the waterfront pier where MTV's Real World was filmed. Microsoft founder Paul Allen has acquired and restored whole districts of old industrial buildings for his new "wireless world" complex of enterprises. One of the city's leading real estate firms, Martin Smith Real Estate, has created an "urban technology campus" of buildings in and around downtown. In their study of these shifts, Sommers and Carlson found that many high-tech companies prefer the urban environment for its "vertical character, specialty shops, street life, entertainment and proximity to a great mixture of businesses and cultural activities." This is a great benefit for small companies who do not have to offer the internal amenities like restaurants or health clubs that larger companies do when they are available in the immediate neighborhood. People thrive on the thick labor markets, job opportunities and amenities there. Microsoft even runs a round-the-clock bus to take its employees who live in and around downtown Seattle to its suburban headquarters.

Fifth, the current round of urban revitalization is giving rise to serious tensions between established neighborhood residents and newer, more affluent people moving in. In an increasing number of cities, the scales have tipped from revitalization to rampant gentrification and displacement.[15] Some of these places have become unaffordable for any but the most affluent. In February 2000, the *New York Times* reported that even employed people making $50,000 a year could not find affordable housing in Silicon Valley, where the average housing price was more than $410,000, and the average monthly rent for a two-bedroom apartment was $1,700.[16] More than a third of the estimated 20,000 homeless people in Santa Clara County (the heart of Silicon Valley) had full-time jobs. At the height of the technology boom, the Valley's No.22 bus became known as "the rolling hotel" because a growing number of workers had nowhere else to sleep.[17] In their 2000 book *The Hollow City*, Rebecca Solnit and Susan Schwartzenberg argued that rising rents were undermining San Francisco's unique image as a creative center by driving out artists, musicians, small shopkeepers and people with children. "When the new economy arrived in San Francisco" they write, "it began to lay waste to the city's existing culture".[18]

San Francisco has long been a trend-setting city, and the conflict that emerged there in the summer of 2000 may be a powerful portent of things to come. That summer a powerful anti-high-tech development coalition emerged in the city's SoMa and Mission districts and quickly spread city-wide. The group that brought together artists, club owners and neighborhood residents conducted more than three dozen rallies and protests in the weeks leading up to the November 7th election, including one where a group of demonstrators smashed a computer with a baseball bat outside City Hall. In a protracted battle that ultimately came to be known as the "SoMa Wars," the coalition collected more than 30,000 signatures across the city to successfully place "Proposition L" on the ballot—a measure to ban high-tech development and other forms of gentrification from SoMa, the Mission and other largely residential neighborhoods. The measure was ultimately defeated by less than 1 percent of the vote.[19] While the technology downturn of the last few years relieved some of this pressure on urban housing markets, gentrification in major urban centers continues to threaten the diversity and creativity that have driven these cities' innovation and growth in the first place. As these pressures continue to build, the prospect of a new set of "place wars" threatens to overshadow the development and politics of leading cities across the nation.

Finally, in one of the most ironic twists in recent memory, both sprawling cities and traditional suburbs are seeking to emulate elements of urban life. Cities like Atlanta, Los Angeles, Phoenix and San Jose have all undertaken major efforts to increase density in and around their urban centers, develop downtown housing and redevelop their downtown cores. San Diego has embarked on an ambitious $2.5 billion "City of Villages" initiative to generate more compact, community-oriented development by rebuilding its older neighborhoods as pedestrian-friendly centers, where homes are close to shops, parks and public transit.[20] Under the plan, neighborhoods would get upgraded services and facilities such as parks, libraries and underground utility lines in exchange for higher-density housing development. The San Diego plan also seeks to reduce traffic congestion and sprawl by inducing people to shop and work either a short walk or bus ride from where they live. The reason: The city that ranks third on my Creativity Index wants to continue to attract creative people and is running out of buildable space. Smaller cities like Chapel Hill, North Carolina, have developed urban corridors and street-level amenities and generated thriving music scenes. In the late 1990s, Orange County, California, launched the "Eclectic Orange Festival," a six-week festival of cutting-edge culture, music, art and performance, to counter its staid culturally conservative image.

Furthermore, many formerly buttoned-down suburbs have sought to recreate some of the urban-style amenities that members of the Creative Class desire by developing pedestrian-friendly town centers filled with coffee shops, sidewalk cafes, designer merchants and renovated office lofts. The new urbanist architect Andres Duany has worked with developers to create new suburbs that are denser and more pedestrian-friendly and that have town centers. My friend Don Carter of UDA Architects has worked with cities and suburbs around the country to remake their town centers and neighborhoods into more authentic places, and also with major corporations to transform their surplus industrial land into mixed-use new urbanist communities.

These examples illustrate not only how far the cities have come back, but how truly pervasive the demand for quality of place has become. Now even the suburbs are trying to emulate aspects of the quality of place associated with larger urban centers. And they are doing so for hard-nosed economic reasons—to attract the talented people and thus the companies that power growth in today's economy. [...]

BUILDING A PEOPLE CLIMATE

As I tell city and regional leaders around the country, the key to success today lies in developing a world-class *people climate*. While it certainly remains important to have a solid business climate, having an effective people climate is even more essential. By this I mean a general strategy aimed at attracting and retaining people—especially, but not limited to, creative people. This entails remaining open to diversity and actively working to cultivate it, and investing in the lifestyle amenities that people really want and use often, as opposed to using financial incentives to attract companies, build professional sports stadiums or develop retail complexes. The benefits of this kind of strategy are obvious. Whereas companies—or sports teams for that matter—that get financial incentives can pull up and leave at virtually a moment's notice, investments in amenities like urban parks, for example, last for generations. Other amenities—like bike lanes or off-road trails for running, cycling, rollerblading or just walking your dog—benefit a wide swath of the population.

There is no one-size-fits-all model for a successful people climate. As we have seen, the members of the Creative Class are diverse across the dimensions of age, ethnicity and race, marital status and sexual preference. An effective people climate needs to emphasize openness and diversity, and to help reinforce low barriers to entry. Thus, it cannot be restrictive or monolithic. Truly Creative Communities appeal to many different groups.

I have yet to find an American community whose leaders and citizens have sat down and written out an explicit strategy for building a people climate. Most communities, however, do have a de facto one.

If you ask most community leaders what kinds of people they'd most want to attract, they'd likely say successful married couples in their thirties and forties—people with good middle-to-upper-income jobs and stable family lives. And in fact this is what many communities (particularly suburban ones) actually do by emphasizing services like good school systems, parks, with plenty of amenities for children and strict (read: exclusionary) zoning for single-family housing. I certainly think it is important for cities and communities to be good for children and families, and am fully supportive of better schools and parks. But as we have seen, less than a quarter of all American households consist of traditional nuclear families. Communities that want to be economically competitive need a truly open and inclusive people climate, which can appeal to the diverse groups of people that make up both the Creative Class and American society writ large.

I have already shown the importance of attracting immigrants and bohemians and of being a place that is open to all kinds of diversity including gays ... we saw that openness to immigration is particularly important for smaller cities and regions, while the ability to attract so-called bohemians is key for larger cities and regions. What I would simply add here is that for cities and regions to attract these groups they need to develop the kinds of people climates that appeal to them and meet their needs.

Furthermore, one group that has been neglected by most communities, at least until recently, is young people. Young workers have typically been thought of as transients who contribute little to a city's bottom line. But in the Creative Age, they matter for two reasons. First, they are workhorses. They are able to work longer and harder, and are more prone to take risks, precisely because they are young and childless. In rapidly changing industries, it's often the recent graduates who have the most up-to-date skills. This is why so many leading companies from Microsoft to Goldman Sachs and McKinsey aggressively target them in their recruiting strategies.

Second, people are staying single longer. As we have already seen, the average age of marriage for both men and women has risen some five years over the past generation. College-educated people postpone marriage longer than the national averages. Among this group, one of the fastest-growing categories is the never-been-married. In December 2001, *The Economist* coined the phrase the "Bridget Jones Economy" to reflect the importance of young singles in the resurgence of large cities across the United States and in Europe. To prosper in the Creative Age, regions have to offer a people climate that satisfies this group's social interests and lifestyle needs, as well as addressing those of other groups.

Some commentators have objected to some of my findings, and thus my economic advice, saying that they are overly oriented toward younger Creative Class people, like the Austin-bound student we saw a few chapters back. These people, my critics argue, represent only a small part of the nation's skilled workforce. Of course a spiky-haired college senior would prefer a place like Austin, which has lots of other talented young people and where many of the amenities and nightlife activities are geared to the young. But is making one's city into a playland for single twenty-somethings really a formula for economic success? Does it produce a community that is socially viable in the long run? These critics point to the fact that leading creative cities like San Francisco and Seattle have very few children.[21] And they often ask questions like: Aren't these young, single college grads eventually going to grow up, get married and develop more mature preferences? Doesn't it make more sense for cities to focus on good school systems and safe streets, which appeal to the middle-aged people who hold positions of influence and really make our economy run? I reply that of course it's important to have a people climate that is valued by older people and married couples. A successful city needs a range of options to suit all kinds of people. But an environment attractive to young Creative Class people *must be* part of the mix.

Furthermore, it is clear to me that a people climate oriented to young people is also attractive to the Creative Class more broadly. Creative Class people do not lose their lifestyle preferences as they age. They don't stop bicycling or running, for instance, just because they have children. When they put their children in child seats or jogging strollers, amenities like traffic-free bike paths become more important than ever. They also continue to value diversity and tolerance. The middle-aged and older people I speak with may no longer hang in nightspots until 4 A.M., but they enjoy stimulating, dynamic places with high levels of cultural interplay. And if they have children, that's the kind of environment they want them to grow up in. Some things that benefit young people are even supported by those old enough to be their grandparents. When a colleague of mine spoke to a group of senior citizens in Pittsburgh in the winter of 2000 about the importance of lifestyle amenities like bike paths, he got a fascinating response. The seniors liked the idea a lot, because the bike lanes would keep the cyclists off the sidewalk, where the seniors were sometimes frightened by them and even knocked down.

A woman from Minneapolis that I interviewed put the age issue in perspective. She originally came to Minneapolis as a young single because of the lifestyle it offered. She liked being able to engage in active outdoor recreation with other young singles in the city's fabulous park system and being able to walk from her house to the local nightspots. She never thought it would be a good place to have a family and raise children. But when she got married and had children, she was more than pleasantly surprised to find that many of the same lifestyle amenities she enjoyed while she was single—the parks and walkable neighborhoods—were even more attractive to her as a married person and new parent.

Furthermore, communities that appeal to diverse groups also can be very attractive to traditional middle-income families. Of course many Creative Class people with families are ethnically diverse and many others prefer that their children grow up in diverse environments. But it can go even

deeper. In the summer of 2001, there was a big hubbub in Pittsburgh over a list of America's twenty-five most "child-friendly cities." The commotion was over the fact that Pittsburgh, which has always seen itself as a family town, was ranked thirteenth. Of the twelve cities that ranked above it, all ranked in the top twenty on the Creativity Index—and all but two in the top twenty on the Gay Index.

While some might see this as a contradiction (How can gay cities be family-friendly?), for me the connection is simple. Cities that offer high quality lifestyle amenities to some groups are likely to view quality of place in general as being very important.

Table 27.1 Child-Friendly Cities Are Also leading Creativity and Gay Regions

Rank	Region	Child-Friendly Score	Creativity Index	Gay Index Rank
1	Portland, OR	A+	16	20
2	Seattle	A+	5	8
3	Minneapolis	A	10	31
4	New York	A	9	14
5	San Francisco	A	1	1
6	Boston	A–	3	22
7	Denver	A–	13	18
8	Fort Worth[a]	B+	10	9
9	Houston	B+	7	10
10	San Diego	B+	3	3
11	Silicon Valley[b]	B	1	1
12	Dallas	B	10	9
13	Pittsburgh	B	36	48
14	St. Louis	B	31	45
15	Cleveland	B	30	43
16	Chicago	B	15	26
17	Philadelphia	B	17	33
18	Phoenix	C+	19	16
19	Los Angeles	C	12	4
20	Miami	C	29	2
21	Tampa	C	26	19
22	Washington, D.C.	C	8	13
23	Baltimore[c]	C–	8	13
24	Detroit	C–	39	46
25	Atlanta	C–	13	7

Note: Rankings for Creativity Index and Gay Index are out of forty-nine regions over 1 million in population.

a   Part of region; Dallas region.

b   San Franciscosco region.

c   Washington, D.C., region.

Source: Child-friendly score is from Zero Population Growth.

It's analogous to companies adopting innovative customer-oriented business practices: The best companies tend to get it right across the board. The best cities, like the best companies, do many things well, offering something for everybody. [. . .]

NOTES

1. Peter Loftus, "Location, Location, Location." *Wall Street Journal*, October 15, 2001, p. R14.
2. As quoted in Scott Kitsner, "Seattle Reboots Its Future." *Fast Company*, May 2001, p. 44.
3. Uri Cummings as quoted in Loftus, "Location, Location, Location," p. R14.
4. Personal communication, Fall 2001.
5. Joel Kotkin, "The High-Tech South Part II: Raleigh Durham—The South's Answer to Silicon Valley?" Reis.com, January 10, 2001.
6. Edmund Sanders and P. J. Huffstutter, "Dreams of High-Tech Glory Passing Orange County By." *Los Angles Times*, July 9, 2000; Joel Kotkin, "Orange County" The Fate of a Post-Suburban Paradise." LaJolla, Calif.: LaJolla Institute, October 2000; available at www. lajollainstitute.org.
7. George Gilder, *Microcosm: The Quantum Revolution in Economics and Technology.* New York: Touchstone, 1990.
8. Joel Garreau, *Edge City: Life on the New Frontier.* New York: Doubleday & Company, 1991.
9. On Oakland's turnaround, see Joel Kotkin, "Grass-Roots Business: The City by the Bay? To Them, It's Oakland." *New York Time*, February 18, 2001.
10. Timothy Egan, "Urban Mayors Share the (Not Unwelcome) Burden of Coping with Prosperity," *New York Times*, June 13, 2000.
11. Rebecca R. Sohmer and Robert E. Lang, "Downtown Rebound." Washington, D.C.: Fannie Mae Foundation and Brookings Institution Center on Urban and Metropolitan Policy Center Note, May 2001.
12. The Sohmer and Lang data set covers only a small sample of cities, and Gates and I could only match twenty-one cities to our data. We ran the analyses for two measures of downtown growth: percent change in downtown population and change in percent of the population living downtown. The correlation between the CDI and percent downtown population is 0.52 and for change in downtown share is 0.46. The Gay Index is correlated with percent downtown population at 0.48 and change in downtown share at 0.39. The Bohemian Index is correlated with percent downtown at 0.54 and change in downtown share at 0.35. The Milken High-Tech Index is correlated with percent downtown at 0.50 and downtown share at 0.30. All are statistically significant.
13. *The State of the Cities 2000.* Washington, D.C.: U.S. Department of Housing and Urban Development, June 2000. High-tech jobs made up 9.2 percent of all city jobs compared to 9.3 percent for the suburbs. Suburbs experienced a faster rate of high-tech job growth: 34.7 versus 26.7 percent for cities.
14. Paul Sommers and Daniel Carlson, "The New Society in Metropolitan Seattle: High Tech Firm Location Decisions Within the Metropolitan Landscape." Washington, D.C.: Brookings Institution, May 2000.
15. On gentrification see Neil Smith, *The New Urban Frontier: Gentrification and the Revanchist City.* London: Routledge, 1996.
16. Evelyn Nieves, "Many in Silicon Valley Cannot Afford Housing Even at $50,000 a Year." *New York Times*, February 20, 2000. Also see John Riter, "Priced Out of Silicon Valley." *USA Today*, May 18, 2000; "The California Housing Market: Squeezed Out." *The Economist*, July 22, 2000.
17. Nieves, "Many in Silicon Valley."
18. Rebecca Solnit and Susan Schwartzenberg, *Hollow City: The Siege of San Francisco and the Crisis of American Urbanism.* New York: Verso, 2000. On San Francisco's history, also see Richard Walker, "Landscape and City Life: Four Ecologies of Residence in the San Francisco Bay Area." *Ecumene*, 2(1), 1995, pp. 33–64.
19. See Bill Hayes, "Artists vs. Dotcoms: Fighting San Francisco's Gold Rush." *New York Times*, December 14, 2000. Also see the detailed coverage in the *San Francisco Gate* at www.sfgate.com.
20. See Lori Weisberg and Susan Gembrowski, "Planners Say It Takes Villages to Grow a City." *San Diego Union Tribune*, January 6, 2002.
21. Between 1990 and 2000, San Francisco was the only U.S. city to lose children while adding population. Over this period, the city lost 4,100 children, as the share of the city's population under eighteen years of age dropped from 16.1 percent to 14.5 percent. Nearly a quarter of San Franciscans are between twenty-five and thirty-four, an age group that grew 14 percent during the 1990s.

Conclusion: Why We Debate

Japonica Brown-Saracino

This book has introduced key perspectives and positions on four areas of debate that have colored and structured the gentrification literature for more than four decades. From debate about how to define gentrification and the "gentrifier," to questions about how, when, where, and why gentrification occurs, and arguments about gentrification's outcomes and consequences, our knowledge of gentrification not only produces, but also arises, at least in part, from a series of debates and conversations about the process. In other words, it would be a mistake to regard the debates that this book features as a distraction or nuisance, for they have pushed us to develop and continually reformulate the questions responsible for much of our understanding of gentrification.

That said, I do not wish to suggest that researchers always engage in debate with a goal as lofty as productivity or the development of a vast literature in mind. Why, then, do we debate about gentrification? On the one hand, questions and debates color scholarly literature on *any* topic. Knowledge is refined by authors' conversations about and disagreements over components of their subject. In this sense, the fact that there is debate about gentrification is relatively unremarkable. However, as the reader may have begun to suspect, the gentrification literature is notable in both its breadth and in the intensity of the debates that compose it.

Why is gentrification scholarship particularly contentious? The readings suggest that the literature is far from unruly; there is, in fact, substantial agreement about key facets of gentrification. For instance, scholars debate about the centrality of government policies and culture to gentrification, but few suggest that either facet is without effect. Likewise, some debate the level and nature of harm that gentrification produces for long-timers, but very few argue that it is without negative repercussions for those residents. On the whole, most debates are over apparently small facets or dimensions of gentrification. This invites the question of why scholars fight at all if their debates are not over what seem to be gentrification's central facts.

I believe that there are several reasons why debate is fundamental to the gentrification literature. These include the literature's sheer volume (i.e. debate stimulates yet more debate), the diversity of approaches scholars take to the study of gentrification, the longevity of research on the topic, the speed and breadth by which gentrification emerged and expanded across the globe, and, finally, our collective fascination with the process.

How does each of the above factors lead to debate? The volume of literature on, and the longevity of the study of, gentrification stimulate debate in three ways. First, the centrality of debate about gentrification is a product of the number of academics who study the process, as well as the range of perspectives from which they write. In most cynical terms, much has been written about gentrification, and, as with other topics of study, over time scholars may have, to a degree, engaged in debate to differentiate their work from that of other scholars. Second, and less cynically, researchers have the benefit of decades of scholarship that provides something of a rubric for gentrification and therefore that, somewhat counter-intuitively, can reveal departures from that rubric. For instance, when I began my fieldwork, familiarity with the literature on the role of the "urban pioneer" (e.g., Spain 1993, Smith 1996) helped make departures from that prototype quite glaring. Third, scholars in a variety of fields write about gentrification, and, while there is much within-field variation, the types of questions scholars pose and the arguments they make vary to some degree by their field of study. Thus, in some instances, the literature captures debates between sociologists, anthropologists, political scientists, geographers, planners, and others about not only gentrification, but broader issues, such as the relative import of place, political structures, or historical precedent. This suggests that sometimes we are not just talking about gentrification when we speak of gentrification. As I further explore later in this conclusion, scholars debate gentrification, in part, because it is a potent symbol of broader trends that concern many disciplines.

The magnitude of gentrification itself also contributes to the amount and intensity of debate on the subject. Specifically, the global expanse of the process (Lees et al. 2008: xvii), combined with the small army of scholars who study it (Hamnett 1991), produce diverse accounts of the process. In turn, the diversity of cases challenges any single definition of or explanation for gentrification. For instance, if one scholar suggests that artists are always at the forefront of gentrification, there are a dozen who can provide evidence of gentrifications pioneered by other social groups (e.g., Rothenberg 1995, Pattillo 2007, Hyra 2008, Brown-Saracino 2009). If another proposes that historic preservation is central to gentrification, someone else might present a case of a gentrification dependent on new-build construction (Davidson & Lees 2005).

While editing this book I convened monthly meetings of graduate students from Loyola University Chicago and Northwestern University to read about gentrification and discuss several of this book's central themes and questions. Our collective knowledge of gentrification was quite broad and varied, as most of the participants were conducting their own studies of gentrification. There were moments during our meetings when our spirited discussions quieted and we seemed to reach agreement about one central question or another, such as how to define the gentrifier. However, just as inevitably, after a brief pause one or more of us would report, rather sheepishly, an instance from our fieldwork that challenged the definition on which we had just reached agreement and we were forced yet again to refine our concept. Thus, the sheer number of documented cases of gentrification produces a rich and nuanced understanding of the process, but it also leaves the door open for debate—especially in instances when one seeks to specify gentrification's "rules."

In addition, as I have suggested throughout, many of us have firsthand experience with gentrification. For this reason, many are aware of exceptions to the rules that some scholars propose, and when we pick up a book or article on gentrification we often bring preformed ideas to our reading. Indeed, you may have found this to be the case as you read the essays that compose this book. When you read excerpts on gentrification's consequences, you may have wondered how to explain why political officials in your hometown were more proactive than the literature would predict about preventing long-timers' full-scale displacement. As a result, you might draft a proposal for a policy designed to protect long-timers from gentrification-induced harm. Reading your policy proposal, another might counter that she witnessed the failure of a similar plan in another place, and the questions and debate continue.

In short, at this interval we have the benefit and burden of a wealth of data, both formal and informal, about gentrification. Not only do we know a lot about a few cases of gentrification, such as that which has occurred in New York's Lower East Side or Harlem, we are also aware of gentrification's existence and contours in disparate places and times, as well as of the involvement of a variety of actors. It is difficult to imagine how such conditions could produce anything other than queries and debate.

The fact that gentrification fascinates many of us further exacerbates debate. As anyone who studies gentrification knows, many welcome the opportunity to talk about gentrification. Rarely have I spoken of my research at a dinner party or family gathering without friends or family members jumping into the conversation to volunteer detailed descriptions of gentrifications that they have witnessed, fallen victim to, or perpetuated. Even in instances when those with whom I spoke were unfamiliar with the term "gentrification," recognition always instantly followed my explanation, and, armed with new vocabulary, friends and family typically offer an account of the transformation of their hometown, city neighborhood, or favorite vacation destination. What's more, many seem to take pleasure in discussing the costs and benefits of gentrification. Rarely have I heard an individual speak of gentrification in value-neutral terms (Brown-Saracino 2009). I believe that our value-laden response originates, at least in part, from the fact that gentrification encompasses two conflicts of concern to many: social class conflict, as well as a common internal debate about how to react or respond to change.

Media are also abound with discussion of and debate about gentrification. As one example, cumulatively between 1986 and 2006 nine papers in seven U.S. cities with a population of one million or greater published 4,445 articles on gentrification (Brown-Saracino & Rumpf 2008). Articles that include the term gentrification constituted between .009% and .07% of the papers' material, and in five papers such articles constituted .03% or more of material (ibid.: 8). Furthermore, newspaper coverage of gentrification is not only prolific, but also diverse. Depictions of gentrification change over time, and vary by city and paper (ibid.). Thus, readers are regularly exposed to a variety of representations of gentrification, as, I would surmise, are television and film viewers, and this likely provides fodder for debate.

While, on the one hand, gentrification's place in common parlance and the media may be a product of gentrification's ubiquity, I suspect that it also has something to do with the fact that gentrification has become shorthand for a broad set of transformations. As authors of several selections in the book's first two sections argue, gentrification is symptomatic of a vast social, economic, and geographic realignment that has influenced cities and towns across the globe. To avoid repeating the history of that transformation here, suffice it to say that gentrification arose in many cities with deindustrialization and globalization and a related turn, in many of the world's economic capitals, to an emphasis on the service-sector economy.

As the anecdotes about my conversations about gentrification are meant to illustrate, this change is highly visible and does not go unnoticed. Many cities look nothing like they did even twenty-five years ago; corporate headquarters and elegant condominiums have replaced smokestacks and housing for factory workers and *The New York Times* waxes nostalgic for the grit of Times Square (Ouroussoff 2009: 1) in a city that only a few decades ago many regarded as dangerous and dirty (Greenberg 2008). Those of us who witnessed this transformation, or inherited stories of its costs or benefits—the grandfather forced into early retirement and poverty by the closure of the Portsmouth factory in which he worked, the family friend whose San Francisco apartment quadrupled in value during the dot-com bubble—may find talk of gentrification to be a relatively easy way of broaching discussion of much broader changes. And, as few of us are indifferent to those changes and the personal transformations they have wrought, we welcome the opportunity to explore their implications by debating gentrification. In short, gentrification is a symptom and a symbol of something much broader than itself, and sometimes we use gentrification to debate the vast transformations that shape our lives.

The question of why we debate is accompanied by another and perhaps more important question: what are the implications of the gentrification debates that we inherit (Smith & Williams 1986, Atkinson 2003)? As I suggested at the outset of this conclusion, I believe that debate about gentrification is productive in a variety of ways. First and most directly, it ensures the intellectual rigor of gentrification scholarship by pushing scholars to refine their concepts and develop sophisticated research designs. After all, your research design is likely to be particularly sound if you build on tried and tested concepts and anticipate that others will challenge your thesis. Second, gentrification debate helps fuel the development and evolution of the larger subfields and disciplines of which gentrification scholars are a part. It does so by forcing scholars to engage in conversation with researchers in other disciplines about some of their fields' under-interrogated intellectual foundations.

Finally, the debates are of practical benefit for those who wish to embark on studies of gentrification more than forty years after Ruth Glass first coined the term (1964). Arguably, debate has helped to prevent stasis in the gentrification field and leaves open the door for studies that challenge or expand on existing theses or that explore uncharted territory (and they help us to identify the precise dimensions of gentrification that are uncharted). Over and again I have found that just when I think that we know all that there is to know about gentrification, a new article or book appears that challenges my thinking, or a student comes to my office with a proposal for a novel study of the subject that builds on questions that scholars have tossed back and forth in the literature. In short, the debates have helped to create space for your own inquiries and, by so thoroughly laying out charted territory, help to elucidate that which we have yet to explore.

Specifically, each section of this book contains a variety of models for conducting research on gentrification. The readings illustrate ongoing or emerging debates that one might seek to enter. For instance, you might find the debate about the factors that drive gentrification particularly intriguing. As a result, to test prevailing theories about the variables that propel gentrification you might undertake a study that seeks to understand how the gentrification of some neighborhoods continues or falters during periods of economic recession (Ley 1992).

Just as importantly, the readings provide a set of models of different research designs one might use to conduct a study of gentrification. For instance, if one wishes to isolate the influence of economic recession on gentrification, one might seek to study a neighborhood over time, ideally from the recession's early stages until economic conditions improve (Ley 1992). Alternately, one might, like Derek Hyra (2008) and others, conduct a comparative study of gentrifying neighborhoods. To understand the consequences of recession for gentrification you might select sites in regions of the world differentially influenced by the global recession.

Likewise, the selections outline a number of methods one can rely on to conduct studies of gentrification. Methods range from quantitative measures of changing property values (e.g., Smith 1979), to interview surveys (e.g., Butler 1997, Bridge 2002), and ethnographies of gentrifying neighborhoods (e.g., Taylor 2002, Lloyd 2005, Pattillo 2007, Hyra 2008, Brown-Saracino 2009). Indeed, the selections even vary in terms of the precise employment of these different types of methods. For instance, the selections in the book represent multiple approaches to the ethnographic study of gentrifying places. On the one hand, Derek Hyra conducts a "vertical" ethnography (2008: 179), which prioritizes attention to the influence of national and city policies and politics over daily life in gentrifying Harlem and Bronzeville. On the other, authors such as Richard Lloyd (2005) and Monique Taylor (2002) prioritized observation of gentrifiers and the places in which they congregate, while Mary Pattillo conducted a more holistic ethnography of an entire gentrifying area (2007), frequently observing and speaking with new and longtime residents alike.

The method—and the particular employment of the method that you use—will depend on the research questions you choose to pose. That is, you will select a research design that will allow you to answer your research questions in the most direct and comprehensive manner possible. For instance, Derek Hyra wished to know how city politics influenced the implementation of federal policies, such as those that relate to public housing, and this necessitated that he study neighborhoods that shared several demographic and economic characteristics in two cities with distinct political structures and cultures (2008).

Some readers may find a question lingering behind my suggestions for utilizing this book to conduct further studies of gentrification. In short, you may wonder if we have studied and debated all that there is to study and debate about gentrification. Such concern is not unwarranted, and for that reason the following paragraphs briefly consider this question.

In short, I do not believe that we are done with gentrification, largely because gentrification is not done with us. The process persists in many of the cities in which it was first studied, such as London and New York, and continues to expand to new places, from rural American and European villages to metropolises in nations with less robust economies than those in which it first emerged (Atkinson & Bridge 2005). Furthermore, gentrification still holds a central place in our imagination (see Lees et al. 2008: 243–245). If you begin listening for it, you may note that it is rare to go a day without encountering mention of the process. Recently, I thought I might have, and then, while preparing dinner, I listened to a National Public Radio program that featured discussion of a film that takes the gentrification of a neighborhood as its starting point.

More pressingly, as the selections in this book illustrate, the process itself is continually changing. Gentrification's location, the actors who live in gentrifying spaces, institutional responses to the process, and the interpersonal dynamics that accompany gentrification are in constant flux. Thus, we have a great deal to learn about the new forms that gentrification takes, and much to debate about how limber our definition of and understanding of gentrification's origins and dynamics should be.

For this reason I believe that, whether you wish to write a seminar paper, conduct a thesis, speak to your block club about your neighborhood's gentrification, or, more generally, to become a more informed resident of contemporary cities and towns, this book's selections serve as a resource for posing and answering questions about gentrification. Having outlined gentrification's history, as well as the lineage of scholarship on the topic, the book provides a sense of the direction in which gentrification and the study thereof are moving. As a result, the book equips you to engage in newly emerging conversation and debate about gentrification and to help us better understand the ramifications of the process for cities and towns, as well as for our relations with one another.

The latter is, arguably, the greatest contribution of the gentrification debates. Gentrification does not happen in a vacuum, nor are its discussions limited to academic classrooms or city planning offices. Gentrification has touched—not just influenced, but touched—many of us. As many ethnographers and journalists can attest, gentrification induces private tears and, in some instances, very public shouting matches and heavy silences (Atkinson 2003). I will not soon forget the angry crowd of fishermen who packed a Selectmen's meeting in the town hall in Provincetown, Massachusetts to lobby for the maintenance and preservation of their increasingly tourist-ridden pier. For the most part their voices were subdued, but their head shaking and feet stomping conveyed a quiet rage about the transformation of their home from fishing village to upscale tourist destination. Nor will I forget the community forum at which white, middle class Chicago gentrifiers rose from their seats, shouting, in an effort to silence an affordable housing advocate. Their clamor, as well as the in-kind response of affordable housing advocates, was so great that police officers took to the stage and threatened to disband the meeting. We are rarely privy to the smaller conflicts and moments of unanticipated communion—harsh words between a gentrifier and a long-timer about the early morning noise that emanates from the latter's farm or an elderly long-timers' pleasant discovery that a young gentrifier has shoveled her snowy walk—that shape daily lives in gentrifying places. However, for those who people gentrifying places, these private interactions likely inspire as many questions as do moments of overt, public debate.

Such questions and on-the-ground debates would likely persist with or without the intellectual volleying that this book highlights. However, the book's selections ground the debates that emerge in Provincetown's town hall and a Chicago Community College cafeteria in gentrification's history and in a wealth of empirical data on the process. I do not expect nor wish for this information to resolve the debates I observed in Provincetown and Chicago. However, it is plausible that a reminder of our history will help to shape the direction of future debate about and responses to gentrification as the process and the ways in which we think about it continue to evolve.

DISCUSSION QUESTIONS

1. What directions do you anticipate gentrification will take in the next decade?
2. What topics or aspects of gentrification do you believe scholars will debate over the next decade?
3. Do you agree with the author's argument that gentrification debate is productive? Why so or why not?

ACTIVITIES

1. Review gentrification literature published in the last year. What debates are scholars examining? Is there any evidence of new debates arising?
2. For a week, keep a notebook on hand so that you can record instances in which you hear

talk of gentrification. When people speak of gentrification in the dining hall, at coffee shops, or on television news programs, what debates do they evoke?

3. Develop a research proposal for your own, original study of gentrification. Develop a set of research questions and hypotheses, and select a research site or case and the appropriate method(s). In addition, as you develop your questions and hypotheses, map how they relate to the debates outlined in this book. On which side of the specific debates your research topic relates to do you fall? How does your perspective on the debates influence your questions and hypotheses?

COPYRIGHT ACKNOWLEDGEMENTS

The author thanks the following authors and publishers for generously permitting republication of their work:

Hyra, D. 2008. "The New Urban Renewal, Part 2: Public Housing Reforms," *The New Urban Renewal: The Economic Transformation of Harlem and Bronzeville*. Chicago: University of Chicago Press. Reprinted with permission from the University of Chicago Press.

Pattillo, M. 2008. "Avenging Violence with Violence," *Black on the Block*. Chicago: University of Chicago Press. Reprinted with permission from the University of Chicago Press.

Rose, D. 1984, "Rethinking Gentrification: Beyond the Uneven Development of Marxist Urban Theory," *Environment and Planning D: Society and Space* 2 (1): 47–74. Reprinted with permission from Pion.

Smith, N. 1979. "Toward a Theory of Gentrification: a Back to the City Movement by Capital, not People," *Journal of the American Planning Association*, 45(4): 538–547. Reprinted with permission from Taylor and Francis Ltd., http://www.informaworld.com .

Smith, N. 1998. "A Short History of Gentrification" from Chapter Two, *The New Urban Frontier*. New York: Routledge: 34–40. Reprinted with permission from Taylor and Francis Ltd., http://www.informaworld.com.

Smith, N. 1998. "Building the Frontier Myth," from Introduction to *The New Urban Frontier*. New York: Routledge: 12–18. Reprinted with permission from Taylor and Francis Ltd., http://www.informaworld.com.

Atkinson, R. Y & Bridge, G. 2004. "Introduction," in *Gentrification in a Global Context: The New Urban Colonialism*, Atkinson, R. & Bridge, G., eds. London & New York: Routledge: 1–12. Reprinted with permission from Taylor and Francis Ltd., http://www.informaworld.com.

Ley, D. 2007. *New Middle Class and the Making of the Central City*. Oxford: Oxford University Press. Reprinted with permission from Oxford University Press.

Freeman, L. 2006. "Neighborhood Effects in a Changing Hood," *There Goes the 'Hood: Views of Gentrification from the Ground Up*. Philadelphia: Temple University Press: 144–154. Reprinted with permission from Temple University Press.

Taylor, M. 2002. "The Dilemma of Racial Difference," *Harlem: Between Heaven and Hell*. Minneapolis: University of Minnesota Press: 57–61 and 68–75. Reprinted with permission from University of Minnesota Press.

Mele, C. 2000. "Forging the Link between Culture and Real Estate: Urban Policy and Real Estate Development," in "Developing the East Village," *Selling the Lower East Side: Real Estate, Culture and Resistance in New York City*. Minneapolis: University of Minnesota Press: 236–242. Reprinted with permission from University of Minnesota Press.

Florida, R. 2002, "Building the Creative Community," *The Rise of the Creative Class*. New York City, New York: Basic Books: 283–291 & 293–297. Reprinted by permission of Basic Books, a member of Perseus Books Group:

Levy, P.R. & Cybriwksy, R.A. 1980. "The Hidden Dimensions of Culture and Class: Philadelphia," *Back to the City: Issues in Neighborhood Renovation*, Laska, S.B., & Spain, D., eds. New York: Pergamon Press: 138–139 & 143–153. Reprinted by permission of Daphne Spain and Shirley Laska.

Chernoff, M. 1980. "Social Displacement in a Renovating Neighborhood's Commercial District: Atlanta," *Back to the City: Issues in Neighborhood Renovation*, Laska, S.B., & Spain, D., eds. New York: Pergamon Press: 204–206 & 208–218. Reprinted by permission of Daphne Spain and Shirley Laska.

Lees, L. 2003. "Super-gentrification: The Case of Brooklyn Heights, New York City," *Urban Studies*, 40(12): 2487–2492. Reprinted with permission from Sage Publications.

Gotham, K. F. 2005. "*Tourism Gentrification*: The Case of New Orleans' Vieux Carre (French Quarter)," *Urban Studies*, 42(7): 1099–1111 and 1114–1115. Reprinted with permission from Sage Publications.

Sibalis, M. 2004. "Urban Space and Homosexuality: The Example of the Marais, Paris' Gay Ghetto," *Urban Studies* 41 (9): 1739–1750. Reprinted with permission from Sage Publications.

Zukin, S. 1991. "Gentrification as Market and Place," from "Gentrification and Cuisine" in *Landscapes of Power*. Berkeley: University of California Press: 187–195. Reprinted with permission from the University of California Press.

Logan, J. & Molotch, H. 1987. "The City as Growth Machine," *Urban Fortunes: The Political Economy of Place*. Berkeley: University of California Press: 50–52 and 62–74. Reprinted with permission from the University of California Press.

Perez, G.M. 2004. "Gentrification, Intrametropolitan Migration, and the Politics of Place," *The Near Northwest Side Story: Migration, Displacement, and Puerto Rican Families*. Berkeley: The University of California Press: 127–130 and 142–152. Reprinted with permission from the University of California Press.

Lloyd, R. 2005. "Living Like an Artist," *Neo-Bohemia: Art and Commerce in the Post-Industrial City*. New York: Routledge: 99–106 and 115–122. Reprinted with the permission of Taylor and Francis Ltd., www.informaworld.com

Brown-Saracino, Japonica. 2004. "Social Preservationists and the Quest for Authentic Community," *City and Community* 3(2): June, 2004, p 135–147. Reprinted with the permission of the author.

Butler, T. 1997. "Consumption and Culture," *Gentrification and the Middle Classes*. Aldershot: Ashgate Publishing: 106–136. Reprinted with the permission of the author.

Glass R, 1964, "Introduction", *London, Aspects of Change*. London: Centre for Urban Studies: xiii–xxiii; xxiv–xxvi; xxx–xxxi. Every effort was made to contact the rights holder for this publication. The rights holder is welcome to contact the publisher.

Zukin, S. 1982. "The Creation of a 'Loft Lifestyle'," in *Loft Living: Culture and Capital in Urban Change*. Rutgers University Press: 58–70. © 1982 Sharon Zukin. Reprinted with permission of The Johns Hopkins University.

Zukin, S. 1982. "From Arts Production to Housing Market," in *Loft Living: Culture and Capital in Urban Change*. Rutgers University Press: 112–121. © 1982 Sharon Zukin. Reprinted with permission of The Johns Hopkins University.

Bridge, G. 2001. "Estate Agents as Interpreters of Economic and Cultural Capital: The Gentrification Premium in the Sydney Housing Market," *International Journal of Urban and Regional Research* 25: 87–96. Reprinted with permission of Wiley-Blackwell.

Bibliography

Allen, I. 1980. "The Ideology of Dense Neighborhood Redevelopment: Cultural Diversity and Transcendent Community Experience," *Urban Affairs Quarterly,* 15: 409–428.

Anderson, E. 1990. *Streetwise: Race, Class, and Change in an Urban Community.* Chicago: University of Chicago Press.

Argyle Streetscape Task Force. 2001. Argyle Streetscape Task Force Overview and Survey.

Atkinson, R. 2000. "Measuring Gentrification and Displacement in Greater London," *Urban Studies,* 37, 1: 149–165.

Atkinson, R. 2002. "Does Gentrification Help or Harm Urban Neighbourhoods? An Assessment of the Evidence-Base in the Context of the New Urban Agenda," *ESRC Center for Neighbourhood Research.*

Atkinson, R. 2003. "Introduction: Misunderstood Saviour or Vengeful Wrecker? The Many Meanings and Problems of Gentrification" *Urban Studies,* 40: 2343–2350.

Atkinson, R. 2004. "The Evidence on the Impact of Gentrification: New Lessons for the Urban Renaissance?" *European Journal of Housing Policy,* 4, 1, 2004: 107–131.

Atkinson, R. & Easthope, H. 2009. "The Consequences of the Creative Class: The Pursuit of Creative Strategies in Australia's Cities," *International Journal of Urban and Regional Research,* 33, 1: 64–79.

Atkinson, R. Y. & Bridge, G. 2004. "Introduction," in R. Atkinson & G. Bridge, eds. *Gentrification in a Global Context: The New Urban Colonialism.* London & New York: Routledge: 1–12.

Atkinson, R. Y. & Bridge, G. 2005. *Gentrification in a Global Context: The New Urban Colonialism,* Atkinson, London & New York: Routledge.

Badyina, A. & Golubchikov, O. 2005. "Gentrification in Central Moscow—A Market Process or Deliberate Social Policy? Money, Power and People in Housing Regeneration in Ostozhenka," *Geografiska Annaler: Series, B. Human Geography,* 33, 2: 113–129.

Bailey, N. & Robertson, D. 1997. "Housing Policy, Urban Renewal and Gentrification," *Urban Studies,* 34, 4: 561–578.

Barry, J. & Derevlany, J. 1987. *Yuppies Invade My House at Dinnertime: A Tale of Brunch, Bombs, and Gentrification in an American City.* Winona, MO: Big River Publishing.

Beauregard, R. A. 1986. "Planning Practice," *Urban Geography,* 7: 172–178.

Beauregard, R. A. 1990. "Trajectories of Neighborhood Change: The Case of Gentrification," *Environment and Planning A* 25, 5: 715–732.

Becker, H. 1998. *Tricks of the Trade: How to Think About Your Research While You're Doing it.* Chicago: University of Chicago Press.

Bell, D. 1973. *The Coming of Post-Industrial Society.* New York: Harper Colophon Books.

Berrey, E. C. 2005. "Divided Over Diversity: Political Discourse in a Chicago Neighborhood," *City and Community*, 4, 2, June 2005: 143–170.

Berry, B. 1980. "Inner City Features: An American Dilemma Revisited," *Transactions of the Institute of British Geographers* 5,1: 1–28.

Berry, B. J. L. 1985. "Islands of Renewal in Seas of Decay," in P. E. Peterson, ed., *The New Urban Reality*. Washington, DC: Brookings Inst: 69–96.

Betancur, J. J. 2002. "The Politics of Gentrification: The Case of West Town in Chicago," *Urban Affairs Review*, 37, 6: 780–814.

Bondi, L. 1991. "Gender Divisions and Gentrification: A Critique," *Transactions of the Institute of British Geographers,* 16: 290–298.

Bourne, L. S. 1993. "The Myth and Reality of Gentrification: A Commentary on Emerging Urban Forms," *Urban Studies*, 30, 1: 183–189.

Boyd, M. 2008. *Jim Crow Nostalgia: Reconstructing Race in Bronzeville*. Minneapolis: University of Minnesota Press.

Bridge, G. 2001. "Estate Agents as Interpreters of Economic and Cultural Capital: The Gentrification Premium in the Sydney Housing Market," *International Journal of Urban and Regional Research*, 25: 87–96.

Brown-Saracino, J. 1999. *Newcomers v. Old-timers: Symbolic Class Conflict in a Small Massachusetts Town*, unpublished honors thesis. Northampton, MA: Smith College.

Brown-Saracino, J. 2004. "Social Preservationists and the Quest for Authentic Community," *City and Community* 3, 2: June, 2004: 135–147.

Brown-Saracino, J. 2006. *Social Preservation: The Quest for Authentic People, Place and Community*, dissertation, Northwestern University.

Brown-Saracino, J. 2007. "Virtuous Marginality: Social Preservationists and the Selection of the Old-timer." *Theory and Society*, 36, 5: 437–46.

Brown-Saracino, J. 2009. *A Neighborhood That Never Changes: Gentrification, Social Preservation and the Search for Authenticity*. Chicago: University of Chicago Press.

Brown-Saracino, J. & Rumpf, C. 2008. "Nuanced Imageries of Gentrification: Evidence from Newspaper Coverage in Major U.S. Cities, 1986–2006." Presented at American Sociological Association Meetings, August 2008.

Butler, T. 1997. *Gentrification and the Middle Classes*. London: Ashgate.

Butler, T. & Robson, G. 2001. "Social Capital, Gentrification and Neighbourhood Change in London: A Comparison of Three South London Neighbourhoods," *Urban Studies*, 38, 12: 2145–2162.

Butler, T. & Robson, G. 2003. *London Calling: The Middle Classes and the Re-making of Inner London*. Oxford: Berg.

Byrne, J. P. 2003. "Two Cheers for Gentrification," *Howard Law Journal*, 46: 405.

Caulfield, J. 1994. *City Form and Everyday Life: Toronto's Gentrification and Critical Social Practice*. Toronto: University of Toronto Press.

Chernoff, M. 1980. "Social Displacement in a Renovating Neighborhood's Commercial District: Atlanta," in S. B. Laska & D. Spain, eds., *Back to the City: Issues in Neighborhood Revitalization*. New York: Pergamon: 204–19.

Clark, E. 2005. "The Order and Simplicity of Gentrification: A Political Challenge," in R. Atkinson & G. Bridge, eds., *Gentrification in a Global Context : The New Urban Colonialism*. London: Routledge: 256–264.

Clay, P. 1979. *Neighborhood Renewal: Middle-Class Resettlement and Incumbent Upgrading in American Neighborhoods*. Lexington, MA: D.C. Heath.

Criekingen, M. & Decroly, J. 2003. "Revisiting the Diversity of Gentrification: Neighborhood Referral Processes in Brussels and Montreal," *Urban Economics*, 40, 12.

Davidson, M. & Lees, L. 2005. "New-Build Gentrification and London's Riverside Renaissance," *Environment and Planning A*, 37: 1165–1190.

Deener, A. 2007. "Commerce as the Structure and Symbol of Neighborhood Life: Reshaping the Meaning of Community in Venice, California," *City & Community*, 6, 4: 291–314.

Duany, A. 2001. Three Cheers for Gentrification. *American Enterprise Magazine* April/May: 36–9.

Engels, F. 1975. *The Housing Question*. Moscow: Progress Publishers.

Florida, R. 2002, "Building the Creative Community," *The Rise of the Creative Class*. New York City, New York: Basic Books: 283–291 & 293–297.

Freeman, L. 2006. "Neighborhood Effects in a Changing Hood," *There Goes the 'Hood: Views of Gentrification from the Ground Up*. Philadelphia: Temple University Press: 144–154.

Freeman, L. & Braconi, F. 2002. "Gentrification and Displacement," *The Urban Prospect* 8.1: 1–4.

Freeman, L. & Braconi, F. 2004. "Gentrification and Displacement: New York City in the 1990s," *Journal of the American Planning Association* 70.1: 39–52.

Gaillard, A. 1977. *Paris: La Ville*. Paris: H. Champion.

Gale, D. E. 1979. "Middle Class Resettlement in Older Urban Neighborhoods: The Evidence and the Implications," *Journal of the American Planning Association*, 45: 293–204.

Gale, D. E. 1980. *Neighborhood Revitalization and the Postindustrial City: A Multinational Perspective*. Lexington, MA: Lexington.

Gale, D. E. 1980. "Neighborhood Resettlement: Washington, D.C.," in S. B. Laska & D. Spain, eds., *Back to the City: Issues in Neighborhood Renovation*. New York: Pergamon Press: 95–115.

Glass, R. 1964, "Introduction", *London, Aspects of Change*. London: Centre for Urban Studies: xiii–xxiii; xxiv–xxvi; xxx–xxxi.

Gotham, K. F. 2005. "Tourism Gentrification: The Case of New Orleans' Vieux Carre (French Quarter)," *Urban Studies*, 42, 7: 1099–1111 and 1114–1115.

Greenberg, M. 2008. *Branding New York: How a City in Crisis Was Sold to the World*. New York: Routledge.

Griswold, W. 1986. *Renaissance Revivals: City Comedy and Revenge Tragedy in the London Theatre 1576–1980*. Chicago: University of Chicago Press.

Hackworth, J. 2002. "Post-recession Gentrification in New York City," *Urban Affairs Review*, 37: 815–43.

Hackworth, J. & Smith, N. 2001. "The Changing State of Gentrification," *Tijdschrift voor Economische en Sociale Geografie*, 92, 4: 464–477.

Hamnett, C. 1991. "The Blind Men and the Elephant: The Explanation of Gentrification," *Transactions of the Institute of British Geographers* 16, 2: 173–189.

Hamnett, C. & Williams, P. 1980, "Social Change in London: A Study of Gentrification," *Urban Affairs Quarterly*, 15, 469–487.

Harvey, D. 1985. *The Urbanization of Capital*. Baltimore: Johns Hopkins University Press.

Harvey, D. 1989. "From Managerialism to Entrepreneurialism: The Transformation in Urban Governance in Late Capitalism," *Geografiska Annaler* B 71: 3–17.

Heidkamp, C.P., & Lucas, S. 2006. "Finding the Gentrification Frontier Using Census Data: The Case of Portland, Maine," *Urban Geography*, 27: 101–125.

Henig, J. R. 1984. "Gentrification and Displacement of the Elderly: An Empirical Analysis," in J. Palen & B. London, eds., *Gentrification, Displacement and Neighborhood Revitalization*. Albany, NY: State University of New York Press: 170–84.

Henig, J. R. & Gale, D. E. 1987. "The Political Incorporation of Newcomers to Racially Changing Neighborhoods," *Urban Affairs Quarterly*, 22 3 : 399–419.

Henig, J. R. 1981. "Gentrification and Displacement of the Elderly: An Empirical Analysis" *The Gerontologist*, 21, 1: 67–75.

Hyra, D. 2008. "The New Urban Renewal, Part 2: Public Housing Reforms," in *The New Urban Renewal: The Economic Transformation of Harlem and Bronzeville*. Chicago: University of Chicago Press: 83–96 and 100–105.

Jager, M. 1986. "Class Definition and the Aesthetics of Gentrification: Victoriana in Melbourne," in N. Smith & P. Williams, eds., *Gentrification of the City*. London: Unwin Hyman: 78–91.

Kerstein, R. 1990. "Stage Models of Gentrification". *Urban Affairs Quarterly*, 25, 4: 620–39.

Lang, M. 1982. *Gentrification amid Urban Decline: Strategies for America's Older Cities*. Cambridge, MA: Ballinger.

LeGates, R. & Hartman, C. 1981. "Displacement," *The Clearinghouse Review*, July: 207–49.

LeGates, R. & Hartman, C. 1986. "The Anatomy of Displacement in the United States,"in J. Palen & B. London, eds., *Gentrification, Displacement and Neighborhood Revitalization*. Albany, NY: State University of New York Press: 178–200.

Lee, B. & Hodge, D., 1984. "Social Differentials in Metropolitan Residential Displacement," In J. Palen & B. London, eds., *Gentrification, Displacement and Neighborhood Revitalization*. Albany, NY: State University of New York Press: 140–169.

Lees L. 2000. "A reappraisal of gentrification towards a 'geography of gentrification,'" *Progress in Human Geography*, 24: 389–408.

Lees, L. 2006. "Gentrifying Down the Urban Hierarchy: The Cascade Effect in Portland, Maine," *Small Cities: Urban Experience Beyond the Metropolis*. New York: Routledge.

Lees L. 2007. "Progress in Gentrification Research?" *Environment and Planning A* 39: 228–234.

Lees, L. 2003. "Super-gentrification: The Case of Brooklyn Heights, New York City," *Urban Studies*, 40, 12: 2487–2492.

Lees, L., Slater, T., & Wyly, E. 2008. *Gentrification*. London: Routledge.

Levy, P. R. & Cybriwksy, R. A. 1980. "The Hidden Dimensions of Culture and Class: Philadelphia," in S. B. Laska & D. Spain, eds., *Back to the City: Issues in Neighborhood Renovation*. New York: Pergamon Press: 138–139 & 143–153.

Ley, D., 1986. "Alternative Explanations of Inner-city Gentrification: A Canadian Assessment," *Annals of the Association of American Geographers*, 76, 521–535.

Ley, D., 1993. "Gentrification in Recession: Social Change in Six Canadian Inner Cities, 1981–1986," *Urban Geography*, 13, 230–256.

Ley, David. 1996. "Introduction: Restructuring and Dislocations," in *The New Middle Class and the Remaking of the Central City*. London: Oxford University Press: 1–11.

Ley, David. 1996. *The New Middle Class and the Remaking of the Central City*. London: Oxford University Press.

Ley, D. 2003. "Artists, Aestheticization and the Field of Gentrification," *Urban Studies*, 40, 12: 2527–2544.

Lloyd, R. 2005. "Living Like an Artist," in *Neo-Bohemia: Art and Commerce in the Post-Industrial City*. New York: Routledge: 99–106 and 115–122.

Logan, J. & Molotch, H. 1987. "The City as Growth Machine," in *Urban Fortunes: The Political Economy of Place*. Berkeley: University of California Press: 50–52 and 62–74.

Macgregor, L. 2005. *Habits of the Heartland: Producing Community in a Small Midwestern Town*. Madison: University of Wisconsin Madison, Dissertation.

Marcuse, P., 1986. "Abandonment, Gentrification and Displacement: The Linkages in New York City." in N. Smith, & P. Wiliams, eds., *Gentrification of the City*. London: Unwin Hyman: 153–177.

Marcuse, P. 2005. "On the Presentation of Research about Gentrification," Department of Urban Planning, Columbia University, New York.

Markusen, A. 1981. "City Spatial Structure, Women's Household Work, and National Urban Policy," in C. Stimpson, E. Dixler, M. J. Nelson & K. B. Yatrakis, eds., *Women and the American City*, Chicago: University of Chicago Press: 20–41.

Martin, L. 2007. "Fighting for Control: Political Displacement in Atlanta's Gentrifying Neighborhoods," *Urban Affairs Review*, 42, 5: 603–628.

McDonald, S. C. 1983. *Human and Market Dynamics in the Gentrification of a Boston Neighborhood*. PhD thesis. Harvard University, Cambridge, Mass.

McDonald, S. 1986. "Does Gentrification Affect Crime Rates?," in A. J. Reiss & M. Tonry (eds.) *Communities and Crime*. Chicago: University of Chicago Press.

McNeil, D.G. 2008. "Restless Pioneers, Seeding Brooklyn," *New York Times*, July 9.

Mele, C. 2000. "Forging the Link between Culture and Real Estate: Urban Policy and Real Estate Development," in "Developing the East Village," *Selling the Lower East Side: Real Estate, Culture and Resistance in New York City*. Minneapolis: University of Minnesota Press: 236–242.

Mitchell, D. (2003). *The Right to the City: Social Justice and the Fight for Public Space*. New York: Guilford Press.

Newman, K. & Wyly, E. 2006. "The Right to Stay Put, Revisited: Gentrification and Resistance to Displacement in New York City," *Urban Studies*, 43, 1: 23–57.

Ouroussoff, N. 2009. "Lose the Traffic. Keep that Times Square Grit," *New York Times*, May 25, 2009: 1.

Parsons, D. 1980. *Rural Gentrification: The Influence of Rural Settlement Planning Policies*. Department of Geography Research Paper no. 3, University of Sussex, Brighton.

Pattillo, M. 2007. "Avenging Violence with Violence," in *Black on the Block*. Chicago: University of Chicago Press: 286–294.

Pattison, T. 1983. *Neighborhood Policy and Planning*. Lexington, KY: Lexington Books

Peck, J. 2005 "Struggling with the Creative Class," *International Journal of Urban and Regional Research*, 29, 4, 740–70.

Peck, J. 2006. "Liberating the City: Between New York and New Orleans," *Urban Geography*, 27, 8: 681–713.

Perez, Gina M. 2004. *The Near Northwest Side Story: Migration, Displacement, and Puerto Rican Families*. Berkeley: University of California Press.

Phillips, M. 2004. "Other Geographies of Gentrification," *Progress in Human Geography*, 28, 5: 5–30.

Rofe, M. (2003) "'I Want to be Global': Theorising the Gentrifying Class as an Emergent Elite Global Community," *Urban Studies*, 40: 2511–26.

Rose, D. 1984. "Rethinking Gentrification: Beyond the Uneven Development of Marxist Urban Theory," *Environment and Planning D: Society and Space*, 1: 57–69.

Rose, D. 2004. "Discourses and Experiences of Social Mix in Gentrifying Neighbourhoods: A Montreal Case Study," *Canadian Journal of Urban Research*, 13: 278–316.

Rothenberg, Tamar. 1995. "'And She Told Two Friends...': Lesbians Creating Urban Social Space," in David Bell & Gill Valentine, eds., *Mapping Desire: Geographies of Sexuality*. London: Routledge.

Salamon, S. 2003. *Newcomers to Old Towns: Suburbanization of the Heartland*. Chicago: University of Chicago Press.

Sassen, S. 1998. *Globalization and its Discontents: Essays on the New Mobility of People and Money*. New York: New Press.

Shaw, K. 2005. "Local Limits to Gentrification: Implications for a New Urban Policy," in R. Atkinson & G. Bridge, eds., *Gentrification in a Global Context: The New Urban Colonialism*, London: Routledge.

Sibalis, M. 2004. "Urban Space and Homosexuality: The Example of the Marais, Paris' Gay Ghetto," *Urban Studies*, 41, 9: 1739–1750.

Slater, T., Curran, W., & Lees, L., 2004. "Gentrification Research: New Directions and Critical Scholarship," *Environment and Planning A*, 36: 1141–1150.

Slater, T. 2006. "The Eviction of Critical Perspectives from Gentrification Research," *International Journal of Urban and Regional Research*, 30, 4: 737–757.

Smith, A. 1989. "Gentrification and the Spatial Constitution of the State: The Restructuring of London's Docklands," *Antipode*, 21: 232–60.

Smith, N. & J. DeFilippis. 1999. "The Reassertion of Economics: 1990s Gentrification in the Lower East Side," *International Journal of Urban and Regional Research*, 23: 638–53.

Smith, D. P. & Holt, L. 2005. "'Lesbian Migrants in the Gentrified Valley' and 'Other' Geographies of Rural Gentrification," *Journal of Rural Studies*, 21: 313–322.

Smith, D. P. & D. A. Phillips. 2001. "Socio-cultural Representations of Greentrified Pennine Rurality," *Journal of Rural Studies*, 17: 4: 457–469.

Smith, N. 1986. "Gentrification, the Frontier, and the Restructuring of Urban Space," in N. Smith & P. Williams, eds., *Gentrification of the City*. Boston: Allen & Unwin: 15–34.

Smith, N. 1996. *The New Urban Frontier: Gentrification and the Revanchist City*. London: Routledge.

Smith, N. 1979. "Toward a Theory of Gentrification: A Back to the City Movement by Capital not People," *Journal of the American Planning Association*, 45, 4: 538–547.

Smith, N. 1998a. "A Short History of Gentrification" from Chapter Two, *The New Urban Frontier*. New York: Routledge: 34–40.

Smith, N. 1998b. "Building the Frontier Myth," from Introduction to *The New Urban Frontier*. New York: Routledge: 12–18.

Smith, N. 2002. "New Globalism, New Urbanism: Gentrification as a Global Urban Strategy," *Antipode*, 34, 3: 427–450.

Smith, N., & Williams, P. 1986. *Gentrification of the City*. Boston: Allen & Unwin.

Spain, D. 1993. "Been-Heres versus Come-Heres: Negotiating Conflicting Community Identities," *Journal of the American Planning Association*, 59.

Sumka, H. 1979. "Neighborhood Revitalization and Displacement: A Review of the Evidence." *Journal of the American Planning Association*, 45, 480–7.

Taylor, M. 2002. "The Dilemma of Racial Difference," in *Harlem: Between Heaven and Hell*. Minneapolis: University of Minnesota Press: 57–61 and 68–75.

Timberg, S. 2009. "When the Next Wave Wipes Out," *New York Times*, February 25.

Van Criekengen, M. & Decroly, J. M. 2003. "Revisiting the Diversity of Gentrification: Neighbourhood Renewal Processes in Brussels and Montreal," *Urban Studies*, 40: 2451–2468.

Vigdor, J. 2002. "Does Gentrification Harm the Poor?" *Brookings–Wharton Papers on Urban Affairs*, 134–173.

Warde, A. 1991. "Gentrification as Consumption: Issues of Class and Gender," *Environment and Planning D: Society and Space*, 9: 223–232.

Wyly, E. & Hammel, D. 1999. "Islands of Decay in Seas of Renewal: Housing Policy and the Resurgence of Gentrification," *Housing Policy Debate*, 10, 4: pp. 711–781.

Wyly, E. K. & Hammel, D.J., 2000. "Capital's Metropolis: Chicago and the Transformation of American Housing Policy," *Geografiska Annaler. Series B, Human Geography*, 82, 181–206.

Wyly, E. & Hammel, D. 2004. "Mapping Neoliberal American Urbanism," in R. Atkinson & G. Bridge, eds., *Gentrification in a Global Context: The New Urban Colonialism*. London: Routledge: 18–38.

Zukin, S. 1982. "From Arts Production to Housing Market," in *Loft Living: Culture and Capital in Urban Change*. Baltimore: Johns Hopkins University Press: 112–121.

Zukin, S. 1982. "The Creation of a Loft Lifestyle," in *Loft Living: Culture and Capital in Urban Change*. Baltimore: Johns Hopkins University Press: 58–70.

Zukin, S. 1987. "Gentrification and Capital in the Urban Core," *Annual Review of Sociology*, V. 13: 129–147.

Zukin, S. 1990. "Socio-Spatial Prototypes of a New Organization of Production: The Role of Real Cultural Capital," *Sociology*, 24, 1: 37–56.

Zukin, S. 1991. "Gentrification as Market and Place," from "Gentrification and Cuisine" in *Landscapes of Power: From Detroit to Disney World*. Berkeley: University of California Press: 187–195.

Zukin, S., Trujillo, V., Frase, D., Jackson, T. 2009. "New Retail Capital and Neighborhood Change," *City & Community*, 8, 1: 47–64.

Index